I0801919

COMPENDIUM OF AUTOMATIC MORSE CODE

COMPENDIUM OF AUTOMATIC MORSE CODE

M. Edwin Goss
N3CW

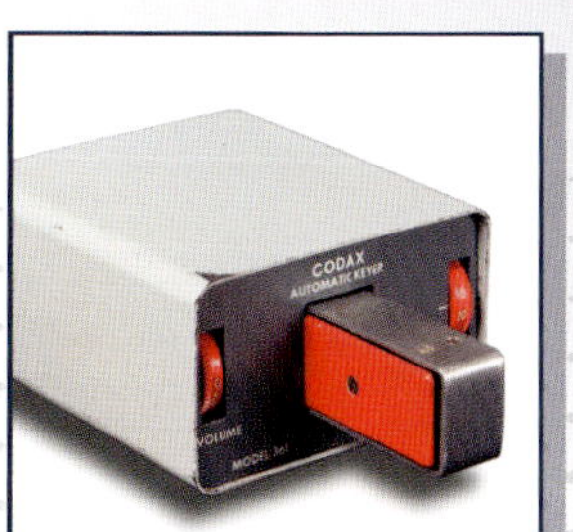

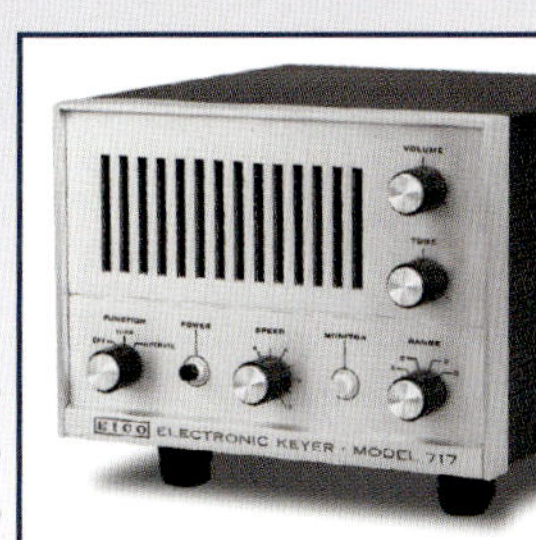

Schiffer Publishing Ltd
4880 Lower Valley Road • Atglen, PA 19310

Library of Congress Control Number: 2016959240

Type set in Agency FB/Times New Roman

ISBN: 978-0-7643-5131-0
Printed in China

Published by Schiffer Publishing, Ltd.
4880 Lower Valley Road
Atglen, PA 19310
Phone: (610) 593-1777; Fax: (610) 593-2002
E-mail: Info@schifferbooks.com
Web: www.schifferbooks.com

*This book is dedicated to my brother Steve,
who was just beginning to study for his
amateur radio license when he lost his battle
with pancreatic cancer in October 2000.*

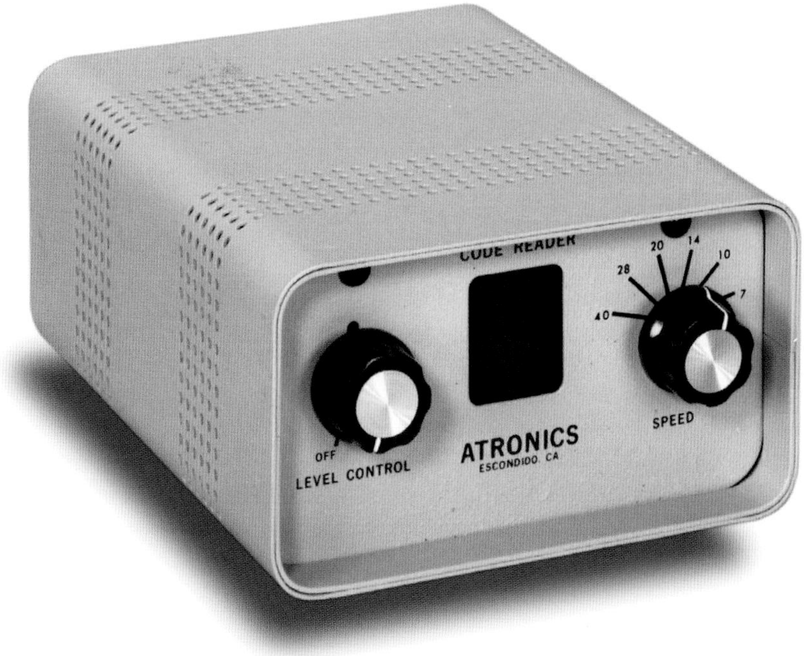

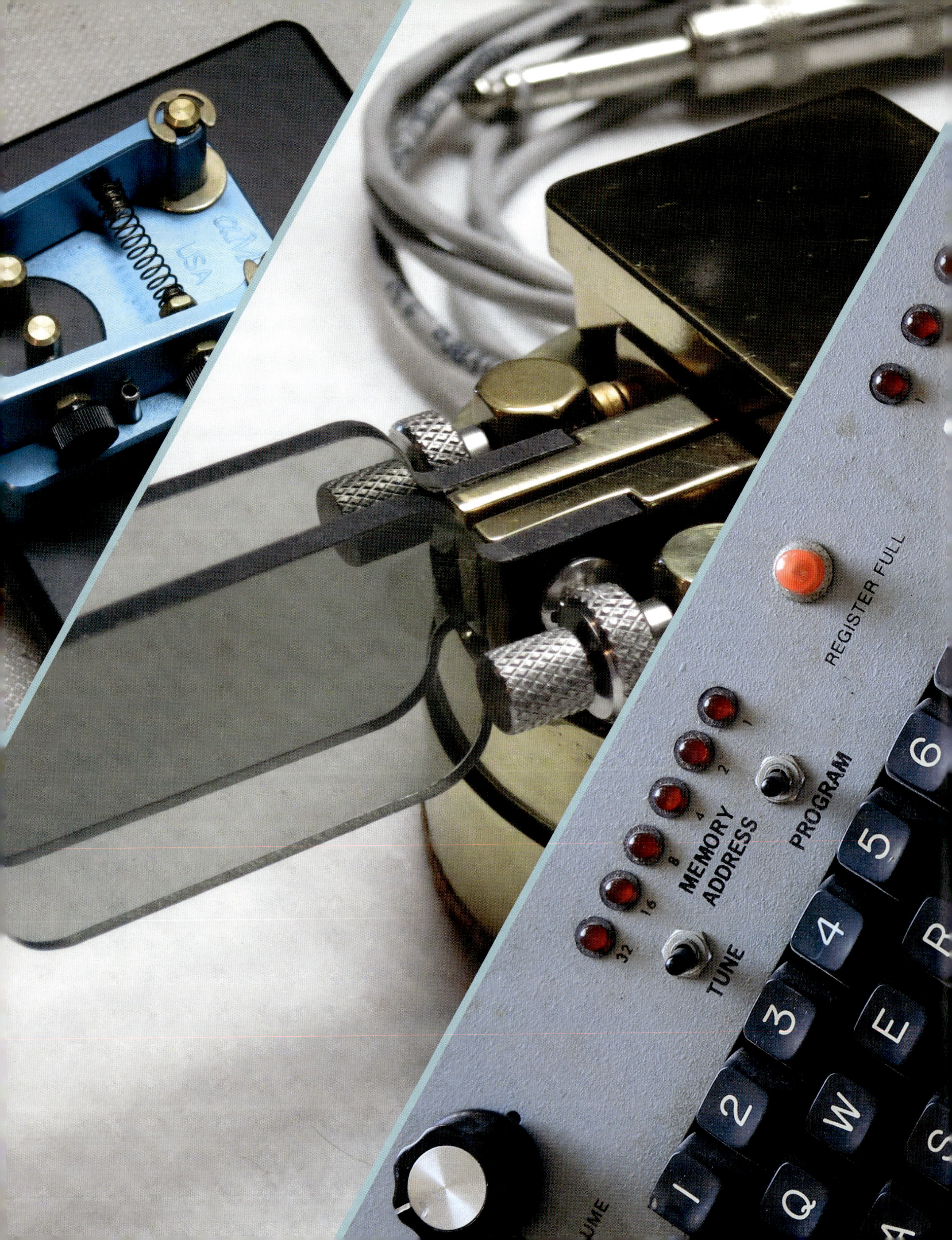
USA
REGISTER FULL
MEMORY ADDRESS
PROGRAM
TUNE
1
2
4
8
16
32

REPEAT
CQ
SK
BACK SPACE
AS
KN
SELECT
MEMORY
O
P
AR
9
O
L
8
I
K
U
J
Y
H
G
F

Contents

Preface

In the world of amateur radio, as of 2016, there are about 740,000 licensed amateur radio operators (hams) in the United States. The International Amateur Radio Union reports about 2.9 million hams worldwide. For several years after February 2007, when the FCC dropped its requirement for Morse code testing, there was a dip in sales and interest of Morse code items like paddles and keys. That trend did not continue, and interest in Morse code operation (CW) has rebounded year-by-year to almost the level it was before the dropped requirement. An analysis of CW logs submitted for contests since 2007 shows an approximately 50% increase in the number of logs after five years (2011), suggesting that interest in CW is growing, regardless of FCC requirements.

Why a specific book on electronic Morse code, keyers, paddles, and keyboards? There have been numerous books and articles on keys in general; most include a paddle or two as a footnote. Electronic keyers are sometimes lumped with articles or books about ham equipment from decades past, but rarely are keyers or paddles the subject of specific focus. Mechanical semi-automatic keys such as those made by Vibroplex have also been the subject of many books. A book dedicated to the history and development of electronic Morse equipment, centered around the keyer and the paddle, was required to illustrate the tremendous range of innovative designs that has gone into these devices. To some extent, the capabilities and features of the electronic keyer have driven design of the paddle, beginning with early integrated paddles. Lightweight arms, special contact materials, use of magnetic repulsion and attraction, and incorporation of exotic materials have become an established part of paddle design. There was a need to illustrate the thought processes that evolved during eighty years of electronic Morse development. If not captured, much of the history of electronic Morse runs the risk of fading—not only becoming harder to find with the passage of time, but open to false assumptions, sloppy research, and conjecture previously published as fact. In addition, the book presents a pictorial celebration of the electronic keyer, paddle, and Morse keyboard so the reader can appreciate the visual impact and diversity of design inherent in these devices.

As an introduction to the keyer and the paddle, the book touches on various historical topics related to telegraphy and Morse code, and includes relevant bits of information on the hand key, sideswiper, and the semi-automatic key (bug). Oscillators, trainers, and code readers will then be presented in more detail. For the most part, the book focuses on commercial devices, although some homebrew models are shown, especially if they are historically significant. A few unknown devices are presented in hopes a reader will identify the device and provide background information. Additional chapters present various types of paddles, keyboards, and accessories, with maintenance and design parameters discussed. A final chapter takes a look at computer interfacing and the Internet, and gives a glimpse at what the future might hold for the Morse enthusiast.

A Chronology

This is not meant to be all-inclusive; rather, it touches on some highlights of keyer and paddle history so the reader can follow the incremental steps of new device development. By looking at new developments in a timeline format the reader can better appreciate the evolution of modern keyers and paddles. The chronology contains some information previously available in other timelines supplemented with additional findings from historical research and information compiled over many years of key and paddle collecting, as well as discussions with other collectors. In some cases, previous timelines propagated incorrect statements or dates, so these statements and dates have been corrected where appropriate.

1823: First electrostatic telegraph.
1832: First electromagnetic telegraph.
1840: Morse and Vail telegraph patent issues (patent #1647).
1842: First commercial electrical telegraph patented by Cooke and Wheatstone (patent #1622).
1844: Alfred Vail's "Lever Correspondent" is the first known key (a straight key design). First telegraph line in operation between Washington and Baltimore.
1850: ABC wheel-type telegraphs first built. First Camelback keys appear around this date.
1861: Beardslee dial-type telegraph invented.
1874: Baudot's "System for Rapid Telegraphy" French patent issues (103,898).
1881: Bunnell's steel lever key patent issues (237,808).
1888 (1904): Bunnell double speed key believed to be the first "sideswiper" paddle. New research by Casale shows the commonly referenced 1888 date to be suspect, and that 1904 is most likely the real year Bunnell's double speed key was invented.
1898: Yetman applies for a patent on the automatic telegraphing machine.
1902: New York inventor Horace G. Martin files for a patent on the first semi-automatic telegraph key, which he began to manufacture as the "Autoplex."
1903: Martin's Autoplex patent issues (732,648).
1904: Horace G. Martin files a patent application for a completely mechanical semi-automatic key he named the "Vibroplex." William Coffe's "Mecograph" appears. Omnigraph is patented by Chinnock. Coffe applies for a patent on a semi-automatic key with vertical pendulum.
1905: First Vibroplex (the Original) is marketed.
1906: John Ghegan's patent issues for the Bunnell double speed key (815,809). Coffe's vertical pendulum telegraph key patent issues (812,183).
1907: H. G. Martin's semi-automatic bug patent issues (842,154).
1908: Mecograph number 2 combination key patent issues (866,755).
1909: First Hulit transmitter patent issues (939,507).
1910: Piersen builds a telegraph machine with mechanical memory.
1912: Second Hulit transmitter patent issues (1,017,054).
1930: Keen-Kode keyboard device is introduced.
1932: Ward Roswell applies for a patent on what appears to be the first electronic keyer.
1933: Roswell keyer patent issues (1,928,967). Traeger Morse typewriter is built.
1937: Bartlett W6OWP begins experimentation with electronic keyers.
1939: Mason *QST* article published on Moto-Key device.
1940: April *QST*, "Electronic Keying" by Harry Beecher, W2ILE. May *QST*, "An Inexpensive Electronic Key," George Grammer, W1DF (uses two tubes). Bernard Breedlove claims to have invented the electronic key. Possibly the first single-lever paddle is built by Beecher (April *QST*). Possibly the first dual-lever paddle is built and described by Grammer (May *QST*).
1941: Lovett Garceau patent for "Key for Communication Systems" issues (2,303,734). Martin's Rotoplex patent issues (2,228,469). Martin's motorized semi-automatic bug patent issues (2,228,470). W1MJU presents an electronic bug and use of a sideswiper as a paddle mechanism in *Radio* magazine.
1942: First commercially produced electronic keyer made by Lovett Garceau, a Harvard professor who founded Electro-Medical Laboratory; Garceau's keyer patent issues (2,303,734). The Equable key is introduced. Breedlove electronic keyer patent (2,302,290) issues.
1944: Two March *QST* articles on keyers discuss code spacing, high speed sending, and keying relays. A July *QST* article presents a single tube 6N7 keyer.
1945: A February *QST* article discusses the W9SOC keyer paddle design eliminating mechanical play; the first modern paddle design. A March *QST* article shows how to add a code monitor oscillator to an existing keyer.
1947: A June *CQ* article describes the "DADIT" keyer, which used a relay and time delay capacitor.
1948: Mon-Key, Electric Eye Equipment Company, is the first commercial electronic paddle/keyer. October *QST*, "Further Advances in Electronic Keyer Design," F. A. Bartlett, W6OWP. March *CQ* magazine presents an article on using a multivibrator circuit for dots; the article also presents paddle construction detail. Bartlett's automatic telegraph key patent issues (2,437,497). Parson's automatic keyer patent issues (2,447,088).
1949: Duomatic AK-7 keyer goes into production made by Electronic Signal Devices. The Bunnell sideswiper in paddle mode may be the first commercial paddle to advertise in *QST*. Harrison Radio advertises the Dash-Bug.
1950: Eldico "Electronic Key" Model EE-1 paddle/keyer. October *CQ* magazine carries an article on a tone-operated keyer. November *QST* presents an article on a tubeless automatic

key. Breedlove's fully automatic keyer patent issues (2,526,001).

1951: February *QST*, "In Search of the Ideal Electronic Key," by Roy Brann, W6DPU. December *QST*, "Compact Automatic Key Design" by F. A. Bartlett (W6OWP), uses a reworked bug.

1953: February *QST*, John Kaye (W6SRY) introduces "The Ultimatic—The Keyer with a Memory," the first in a series of memory keyers.

1955: W6SRY article on tube-type ultimatic keyer appears in April *QST*.

1957: Eldico EE-3 keyer introduced.

1958: OZ7BO conceives single-dot insert method of keying.

1959: W9TO tube-type keyer introduced. ELKEY is introduced by Poucel Electronics; sold until 1963. Guthroel Mill tube keyboard is constructed. A May *QST* article describes a transistor version of the T.O. keyer.

1960: Vibro-Keyer (Vibrokeyer) introduced by Vibroplex, a single-lever paddle using "Original" parts designed by John La Hiff. Autronic, of Newport, California, first offers their single-lever paddle and transistor keyer. Heath green Vibro-Keyer first sold. Transistor version of the T.O. keyer by Old appears in May *QST*. K0MHU article on transistorized version of ultimatic keyer appears in September *QST*.

1961: Auto-Mate K 5/50 keyer begins selling. Hallicrafters HA-4 first transistorized keyer. Tremblay's "Little Monster" patent issues (2,988,597). Lefor describes how to build the Nikey paddle in a July *QST* article.

1962: J. A. Hills' (W8FYO) paddle (rocker on needle posts) introduced at Dayton Hamfest. First dual-lever paddle ad in *QST* by Nikey. Hammarlund HK-1B keyer is introduced. Little Monster keyer first produced. Ricks T.O. keyer patent issues (3,041,397).

1963: Autronic single-lever paddle patented by Jakosky and son (3,098,898). Alkan Ultimatic 200 keyer first sold. Pfieffer (K1KLO) applies for a patent on his magnetic paddle.

1964: Brown Bros. Machine Co., St. Louis, begins offering straight key and paddles using pivot-type mechanism. Waters Codax keyer first appears on the market. The first magnetic paddle is described in a March *QST* article.

1965: Vibroplex bought by John La Hiff. Heathkit HD-10 single-lever paddle keyer (used micro switches). Heath HD-10 was the first keyer kit. W8FYO patent issues (3,166,638), but J. A. Hills has stopped his key making.

1966: Eico Model 717 keyer introduced. Palomar advertises their first electronic keyer (Space Age keyer) using internal Brown Bros. paddle mechanism. K1KLO issued patent (3,293,363) for first magnetic paddle.

1967: Iambimatic (iambic) keying first described by H. G. Gensler (K8OCO). The DA Keyer with integral paddle is first sold by Omega Electronics Company. Pickering K-1 keyer is advertised as the first IC keyer. What appears to be the last FYO paddle is sold in April (possibly from residual Hills personal stock).

1968: Autronic stops making paddle and keyer. John Curtis founds Curtis Electro Devices and produces his first keyer, the EK-38. Samson ETM-2 keyer is introduced. Ten-Tec founded by K4FW and K4JU. WA2YBR (later to be N2DAN) begins experimenting with magnetic paddles; describes possibly the first use of ball bearings in a paddle design.

1970: Ten-Tec paddles and keyers first advertised.

1971: August *QST*, "How to Make a Low-Cost Keying Mechanism," by A. K. Weis (WA5VQC), describes how to convert bug to keyer paddle. Jim Garrett (WB4VVF) builds first Accu-Keyer. HAL Devices 1550 keyer first sold. Curtis EK-402 keyer with programmable memory introduced (reviewed in April 1972 *QST*).

1972: Data Engineering Feather Touch keyer. Nye paddles first offered. William Nye buys Speed-X. MFJ founded by Martin Jue (K4FLU).

1973: August *QST* "The WB4VVF Accu-Keyer," by James Barnett (WB4VVF, also see August 1975 and July 1976) is one of the most built *QST* construction projects; WB4VVF sells more than 20,000 circuit boards. Curtis 8043 keyer chip appears; first "keyer on a chip."

1974: Brown Bros. paddle designs go from pivot to leaf springs. Matric paddles first offered. MFJ CMOS keyer first sold.

1975: Heathkit HD-1410 iambic keyer introduced; uses leaf spring paddles. Ham-Key, St. Louis, dual-lever paddles first sold; keyers and straight keys also offered. Ham-Key sold keys to MFJ, Palomar for resale (Ham-Key, then Ham Radio Center). Ham-Key was first, and possibly only, key with molded plastic frame. HAL licensed W8FYO patent, made dual-lever paddles in 1976. Teletek introduces their FYO-type iambic; design later sold to Bencher. Wm. M. Nye introduces their Master Squeeze Key SSK-1. Ten-Tec brings out the Ultramatic Keyer KR50. An improved version of the Curtis 8043 chip was introduced (8044).

1977: Bencher begins selling paddles based on Teletek design. Palomar IC keyer (second version), Hamkeyer HK5A begins selling.

1978: HAMCO of Eureka, California, bought key production from HAL and added magnets—first commercial magnetic paddle. Peter Garsoe buys Vibroplex and moves company from New York to Maine. Trac-Key by Trac Electronics introduced. J. A. Hills (W8FYO) dies in Phoenix, Arizona, at age 72. Curtis 8044 (then M, B & ABM versions) best-selling keyer chip ever.

1979: Dual-lever paddle introduced by Vibroplex—first new key under Garsoe—used pivoting arms on Original frame. Brown Brothers Machine stops making keys. Accu-Circuits Accu-Memory II keyer appears.

1980: Autronic paddle patent expires.

1981: Heathkit SA-5010 keyer introduced, used capacitive touch paddles and memories; microprocessor-based.

1982: J. A. Hills (W8FYO) key patent expires. Brass Racer by Vibroplex appears (bought from HAMCO based on W8FYO design).

1983: December *QST* "CW on a Chip" by Bob Shriner (WA0UZO) and Paul Pagel (N1FB); Curtis 8044 keyer project, used circuit board design.

1984: Heathkit discontinues the HD-1410, its most popular paddle/keyer. Kansas City keyer introduced; it was one of the first microprocessor-based keyer designs.

1985: Ham-Key stops making keys.
1986: Kent of England introduces twin paddle design (Kent had been making straight keys since 1982).
1987: G4ZPY paddle keys, single and twin; later produces keyers and straight keys.
1988: N2DAN begins production of his Mercury paddles.
1990: Idiom Press K-1 keyer.
1991: Heathkit discontinues SA-5010A, their last keyer (Heath leaves the ham radio market in 1992).
1992: Jones, Surrey, England, paddles/straight keys to 1997, imported by Palomar. Of note for key collectors: N7CFO starts Keyletter. Tom French (W1IMQ) starts *The Vail Correspondent* key collectors' quarterly journal.
1993: MFJ 564 chrome base Bencher-type paddle made in Taiwan. CodeBoy keyer first to use PIC device.
1994: Mitch Mitchell (WA4OSR, now W4OA) buys Vibroplex from Garsoe and moves company to Mobile, Alabama. First readout display keyer, Uncle Albert's, presented in January *QST*; more than 500 kits sold.
1995: Wilderness Radio (NorCal) microprocessor-based KC1 keyer.
1996: Square Racer by Vibroplex, first new key from new owner Mitch Mitchell (W4OA). Mouser discontinues Curtis 8044 "keyer on a chip" produced for eighteen years, partially due to prevalence of HF transceivers with built-in keyers.
1997: NorCal K8FF paddle kit, 1,600 or more sold in two months. Vibroplex comes out with the "double," consisting of paddles and straight key on one base. Steve Nurkiewicz (N2DAN) passes away from liver cancer.
1998: Palomar stops making keyers; had offered many models in thirty-three years, longest run of all manufacturers to date.
2001: First production run of Vibroplex Venus paddle.
2006: First N3ZN paddle sold (ZN-1). FCC drops Morse code requirement for amateur licensing.
2009: Scott Robbins signs agreement to purchase Vibroplex from current owner Felton "Mitch" Mitchell (W4OA).
2011: Vibroplex Vibrocube paddle introduced (followed by chrome version in 2012).
2013: ZN Ultimate paddle introduced by Vibroplex.
2014: G4ZPY passes away.

1 Overview of Telegraphy and Early Key History

The historical and creative significance of electronic Morse devices are often overlooked, especially when the single sideband (SSB) communications capability of today's modern ham equipment offers such popular distraction.

The word "telegraphy" has Greek roots, basically referring to the process used to send and receive text or symbolic messages over long distances. The word "telegraph" can be traced to the 1790s, when French inventor Claude Chappe worked to develop a practical semaphore system using relay towers. Electrochemical and electrostatic telegraph systems were the subject of experiments in the early 1800s. Francis Ronald's 1823 design, considered to be the first working electrostatic telegraph, used wires enclosed in glass tubing, allowing messages to be sent via electrical pulses. Pavel Schilling's 1832 telegraph is said to be the first electromagnetic telegraph; Schilling demonstrated the transmission of signals by positioning two telegraphs of his invention in two different rooms of his apartment and used a rudimentary binary approach (on and off states) to send his messages. In June 1842, Charles Wheatstone and William Cooke received a patent (#1622) for the first commercial electrical telegraph. Their system used a number of needles on a board; the needles moved in response to currents sent through the telegraph wire and pointed to different letters of the alphabet.

In 1846, the Magnetic Telegraph Company installed the first commercial telegraph line between Washington, DC, and New York City; not long after another line was completed between New York City and Boston. Although early telegraph lines were mostly licensed by the owners of Morse patents, other telegraph systems based on technologies that did not use Morse code were being developed (Morse code is just one form of telegraphy): for example, the R. E. House printing telegraph, which printed messages on paper or tape in Roman letters. Other inventions abounded, with various approaches competing with each other and many creations documented in issued patents throughout the period.

Around 1872, Western Union adopted a new method of duplex telegraphy, where two messages were sent simultaneously over the same wire. In 1874, Thomas Edison completed his development of the Quadruplex telegraph, a device that allowed a total of four separate signals to be transmitted and received simultaneously on a single wire. The Quadruplex telegraph used one signal to vary the absolute strength or voltage of the signal and the other signal to vary the phase (polarity) of the line. Soon after Edison sold his patent rights to Western Union. Also in 1874, a French telegraph official named Jean-Maurice Emile Baudot invented a telegraph system that allowed four stations to transmit simultaneously. Baudot's transmitter used five separate keys. The keys could be depressed in different combinations for each letter sent; the Baudot invention received a patent (103,898) in June 1874. Baudot's system achieved speeds of 50 wpm. The Baudot multiplex receiver (below) was a paper tape machine.

In the early 1900s, the International Telegraph Alphabet was becoming standardized around the Baudot code. Soon, commercial printing telegraph equipment called teletype was being developed and usage of this equipment by railroads and news organizations began to accelerate. Throughout the 1920s various new models of code printers were introduced—including paper sheet printers—that helped form the design basis for more advanced teletype equipment to follow. During the early 1900s, Charles Buckingham of New York developed his Machine Telegraph, which was an improvement on the House printing telegraph system in speed and avoidance of the use of paper tape. It printed received messages quickly and very legibly on plain paper or a prepared message blank. Inventions like Buckingham's, and other printing telegraph equipment, encouraged the acceptance and growth of telegraphy—especially printing telegraphy—until an increased focus on radio added wireless telegraphy into the mix.

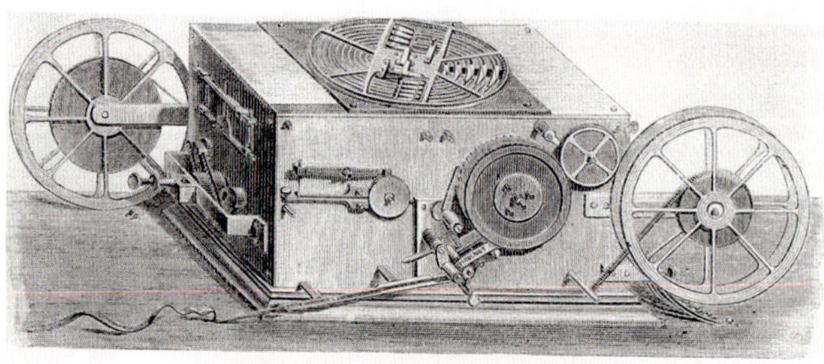

(Courtesy of Smithsonian Institution, Washington, D.C.)
1876 ONE OF THE BAUDOT MULTIPLEX RECEIVERS

The Morse Code

The Morse code was developed so operators had a way to translate the indentations marked on a register's paper tape into actual text messages. In his earliest code, Samuel Morse had planned to transmit numerals only and have operators on the receiving end use a dictionary to decode each number being sent, thereby understanding the corresponding words. Alfred Vail soon modified his code to include letters and special characters. Vail's updated code used "dots" for the shorter tape indentations and "dashes" for the longer indentations. Next, Vail did a bit of ingenious research showing the most commonly used English language letters, so he could assign them shorter sequences of dots and dashes. In 1840, Morse and Vail patented (1647) their new code that used assigned combinations of dots and dashes representing all 26 letters in the alphabet and numbers 1 to 10. It was named Morse code, despite the fact Vail had probably done more to develop it. Many feel Morse improperly assumed credit for the development of the code, and in reality it was Alfred Vail who history has slighted.

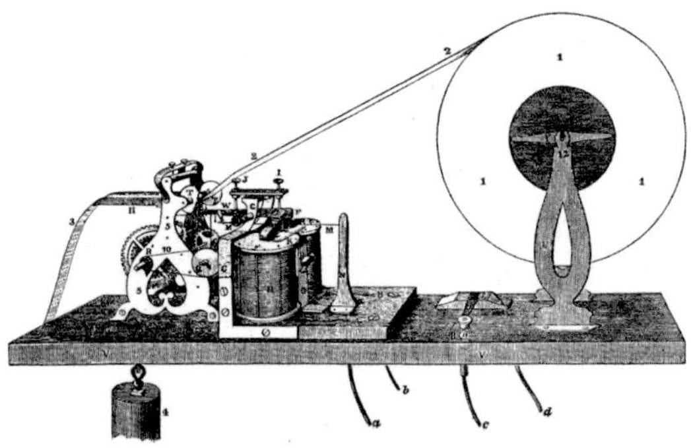

(Courtesy of Smithsonian Institution, Washington, D.C.)
MORSE-VAIL 1845 TELEGRAPH

The first telegram in the United States was sent by Morse on January 11, 1838, across two miles of wire near Morristown, New Jersey. Later, on May 24, 1844, Morse sent his famous message, "What hath God wrought," from Washington, DC, to Baltimore over his newly constructed telegraph line. From that point on, commercial telegraphy grew at a fast pace across the United States, with many new telegraph lines constructed between major cities. In 1851, the Morse telegraph system was adopted as the standard for European telegraphy. By October 1861, the overland telegraph connected the West Coast of the continent to the East Coast, resulting in the end of the Pony Express.

In terms of the Morse code, a significant realization was made around 1850, when operators recognized the clicks of the recording instrument or sounder formed particular sound patterns that they could understand as the dots and dashes being sent. Therefore, the operator could interpret by ear the message being sent and skip over the intermediate step of having a machine decode and print the code; this made the use of paper tape unnecessary. The proficient operator could then add the benefit of increased speed to the Morse telegraphy system. While European systems tended to concentrate on printing telegraphy, American systems focused on sounders and aural copying of the Morse code.

Samuel Morse died in New York City at the age of eighty on April 2, 1872. For more detail on Morse and Vail see George P. Oslin's book *The Story of Telecommunications*. Various sources report Morse was an accomplished painter; a few other sources describe his career as an artist as a failure.

Radio Telegraphy

Prior to about 1920, radio transmitters existed in a basic form that did not allow for transmission of speech. Spark-gap transmitters were used from the late 1880s through about 1917 (a period called the wireless telegraphy era) to send text messages using Morse code. Transmitter emissions were of a continuous-wave type (abbreviated to CW), and communication consisted of turning the CW output on and off with a specialized switch called a hand key, or just simply a key. The key had been developed many years previously for the telegraph industry. In fact, the similarity to landline telegraphy of sending Morse code by radio resulted in the name "radiotelegraphy." The terms "CW" and "radiotelegraphy" became synonymous and were frequently used interchangeably. As radio technology developed over time transmitters would eventually allow voice communications, but for many years radiotelegraphy was the only form of communication available. One of the most well-known usages of Morse telegraphy was during the rescue operations for the RMS *Titanic* in 1912.

The Morse Code Today

Morse code has been in use for more than 175 years—longer than any other electronic encoding system. What we now call Morse code is in reality different from the code originally developed by Vail and Morse. Known today as the International Morse code, or continental code, it was made the norm by the International Telecommunications Union (ITU) in 1865. The code that Morse originally developed became known as the American Morse code, sometimes called the railroad code; it is rarely used today. Since December 2003, Morse code has included the @ symbol. The symbol is a combination of the Morse letters a and c, and is the first change to the Morse code since before WWII.

Morse CW remains a popular form of radio communication, and is still considered one of the most efficient of all ham radio modes. The low bandwidth of the code signal, due in part to low information transmission rate, allows very selective filters to be used in the receiver that block out much of the atmospheric noise that would otherwise reduce intelligibility of the signal. Today, although a knowledge of Morse code is no longer required to obtain a ham license, many amateurs remain devoted CW aficionados. Some of the reasons Morse code remains popular among amateurs include:

Reliability: Morse code will frequently allow a contact to be completed under marginal conditions when other modes will not.

Spectrum Efficiency: Use of IF filters in the 400–500 Hz area allows for several CW contacts in the same amount of bandwidth one SSB contact would require.

Minimal Language Barrier Impacts: Through use of abbreviations and Q codes (standard three-letter codes allowing basic conversation) many language barrier problems can be minimized.

Human factors: The narrow signal bandwidth and ability to apply receiver filtering, combined with the aural selectivity of the human ear and brain, allows one to take advantage of natural aural selectivity to further enhance weak signal readability.

Lower Transmitter Output Power: Frequently, a solid CW contact between amateurs can be accomplished with much less transmitter power than required when using SSB.

Versatility: Morse code is versatile, in that it can be automated to send and be decoded by computer, making its use in emergency situations a valuable option. Airline pilots are usually familiar with Morse code, as it is used with various navigational aids. Morse code can also be understood without decoding devices, adding to its versatility.

Less Complexity: Because Morse transmissions employ a basic on-and-off type keying of the transmitted signal, CW requires less complex transmission equipment than other modes of radio communication. CW requires less signal bandwidth than the typical voice transmission (usually 100–150 Hz), as compared to the approximately 2400 Hz used by a typical SSB voice transmission. Morse code transmissions are easier to copy than SSB voice when noise and interference from other stations are present. In addition, CW allows the use of narrow filtering that can help reduce or eliminate splatter and loud adjacent transmissions. The efficiency of a CW transmission compared to a voice transmission of equal power makes CW an ideal choice for reliable low-power (QRP) use.

Until 2003, code proficiency was a requirement of the amateur radio licensing procedure worldwide; this requirement was mandated by the ITU. However, the World Radiocommunication Conference of 2003 made the Morse code requirement for amateur radio licensing optional, and many countries subsequently removed the Morse requirement from their license requirements.

Morse Key (Straight Key) Development

The telegraph key was invented in 1844 by Samuel Morse's associate, Alfred Vail, and was called the "Vail Correspondent," or by some the "Lever Correspondent."

W1TP's reproduction of the Vail Correspondent made by Kent of England.

The Vail Correspondent was basically a switch with a knob mounted on a spring-loaded lever. As key design evolved, various attempts were made to consider operator comfort. One of the first keys to address ease of use was the camelback, which appeared around 1850.

An 1850s European Camelback key.

The camelback key's design continued to evolve until the modern design was developed and patented by Jesse Bunnell. In 1878, Bunnell created J. H. Bunnell and Company, and on February 15, 1881, Bunnell received a patent for his steel lever key (237,808). Historian John Casale (W2NI) reports the 1881 key is sometimes erroneously called the Triumph key, which did not appear until some twenty-five years later.

J. H. Bunnell's steel lever solid trunnion key.

Physical Limitations of the Hand Key

Tapping a Morse key forces your hand into a tight, bunched-up position that can start hurting if you tap for too long and do not relax your hand. If an operator continues sending for long periods of time, the pain would likely become very severe and result in a more permanent condition. Today this type of condition is known as a repetitive strain injury (RSI), but in earlier times it was known as telegraphist's cramp or glass arm, and it was a serious problem for operators and their employers, who took steps to resolve the issue. For example, a book published by the Postal Telegraphic Clerks Association advised members to follow safe practices when sending the code.

In addition to the liniment discussed in the advertisement, some thought was given to prevention through more efficient use of the key. Variations on Morse key design were intended to force operators to adopt specific and better hand posture when using the key. Fred Catlin, a prominent telegrapher for Western Union and a winner of various telegraph tournaments, became well known for his Catlin grip, a standard method of handling a telegraph key. Many operators felt the Catlin grip allowed them to maximize sending speed while minimizing fatigue.

Other key add-ons, such as Seward's Correct Key Attachment, were pitched to operators as solutions to operator paralysis; Seward's device sold for $2.

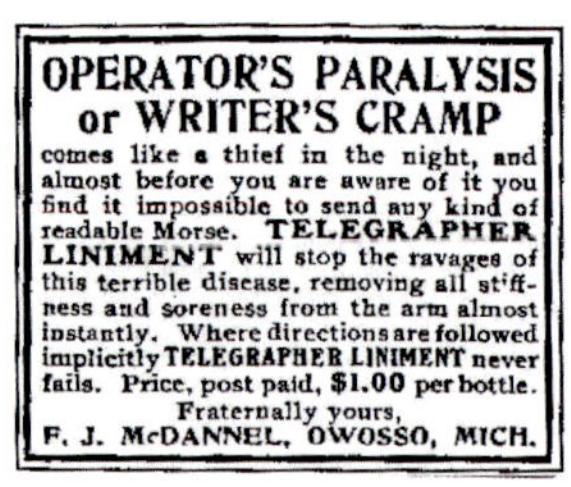
OPERATOR'S PARALYSIS or WRITER'S CRAMP comes like a thief in the night, and almost before you are aware of it you find it impossible to send any kind of readable Morse. TELEGRAPHER LINIMENT will stop the ravages of this terrible disease, removing all stiffness and soreness from the arm almost instantly. Where directions are followed implicitly TELEGRAPHER LINIMENT never fails. Price, post paid, $1.00 per bottle.
Fraternally yours,
F. J. McDANNEL, OWOSSO, MICH.

IT'S SOMETHING NEW
SEWARD'S Correct Key Attachment
R. SEWARD.
Connersville, Indiana
Patent applied for.

The Sideswiper, or Cootie Key

As one approach to help avoid operator cramping, Bunnell introduced his double speed key, also known as the sideswiper; Bunnell sold this model until the 1920s. It had two fixed left and right contacts; sending required the operator to use a horizontal motion that moved a paddle arm between the two contacts. While sending, the operator's wrist used a side-to-side rocking movement with the thumb and first two fingers held in a relaxed and slightly open position. The rocking movement was continuously repeated as the dot and dash elements of the code were sent. The Cootie key seems to produce its best code at speeds less than about 22 words per minute; adequate contact-to-swiper arm spacing is an important concern at top speeds. Compared to the semi-automatic bug that can be used to send up to 60 wpm, the Cootie key requires a wide gap, firm tension, and longer swiper arm travel. The bug does best with a narrow gap, lighter tension, and shorter swinging arm travel.

The Bunnell sideswiper is considered the first horizontally operating manual key. The original Bunnell keys were not portable, and were typically screwed to the operating desk to prevent key movement. Although thought of as a precursor to the semi-automatic bug, the sideswiper has recently been the focus of a detailed study by John Casale (W2NI). Casale's research indicates the Bunnell sideswiper was actually patented after 1900, not in 1888 as many timelines indicate. As Casale points out, the oldest examples of this key do not really have the appearance of a key that was manufactured during the 1880s.

Included in Casale's list of evidence supporting the later date is the very first ad found for the double speed key in the *Journal of the Telegraph* from November 20, 1904. Casale's conclusion was J. H. Bunnell & Co. introduced the double speed key in late 1904 (not in 1888), at the same time the semi-automatic key was emerging. In addition, Casale gives credit for introducing all three double speed keys to John Ghegan, who was president and head of manufacturing at J. H. Bunnell & Company. Some additional research reveals John Ghegan was issued a patent on March 20, 1906, (815,809) for a "Telegraphic Key," most probably the Bunnell double speed key. Bunnell could have easily introduced the double speed key just before filing for the patent in 1905.

The photo above shows the Bunnell radio sideswiper, also known by the more generic double speed key or Cootie key. This sideswiper had no circuit closer, and utilized heavy contacts for early spark radio work. This key is assembled on a piece of rectangular Bakelite mounted on a cast iron lower base. The markings on the Bakelite indicate "patented, J.H. Bunnell & Co. Inc., New York USA." Key dates to the mid-1920s.

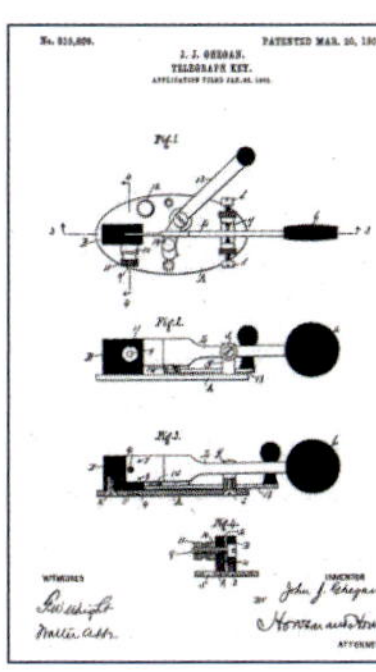

John Ghegan's telegraph key from the March 1906 issued patent.

A 1906 Bunnell double speed key.

Origins of the Semi-Automatic Key, or "Bug"

Bug operation was based on forming the code characters using a sideways movement of the hand and fingers. Hand key operation utilized the more traditional up-and-down vertical motion of the key lever/knob. The bug was immediately favored by operators because it allowed sending Morse code with less repetitive motion, and using the bug was less fatiguing than using a hand key for longer periods. Less fatigue meant the operator could send more code, and in turn the operator earned more money, since most telegraphers were paid by the word.

There are several possible sources for the term bug as it relates to the semi-automatic key. The first semi-automatic keys appearing around 1904 and 1905 were often called transmitters. Among the first to adapt and become proficient at using the new transmitters were the first class telegraphers, who were some of the fastest senders of the day. Another group of transmitter users—a group not quite as skilled—became known for their sending errors due to inexperience and lack of proper adjustment of the transmitters. The truncated dots and sometimes sloppy sending often sounded like telegraphy circuit problems, or what was then called a bug on the circuit. Around 1908, telegraphers started calling the semi-automatic keys by the nickname bug because of the association with circuit problems. Others think the term bug came from the Vibroplex trademark bug that appeared on many of their labels and key bases. In the early 1920s, Vibroplex Company President James Albright designed a new metal name plate that included the Vibroplex bug trademark. Having the bug logo on the key labels most likely made the names Vibroplex and bug synonymous from that point on.

In 1902, New York inventor Horace G. Martin filed for a patent on the first semi-automatic telegraph key, which he began to manufacture as the Autoplex. The patent issued on June 30, 1903 (732,648). Martin used a battery and coil similar to coils used in the electric bell, allowing the Autoplex to make endless strings of dots when the operator pushed a lever in one direction. Dashes had to be made manually by pushing the lever in the opposite direction. Since only the dots were made automatically, the Autoplex was called a semi-automatic key. Unfortunately, the Autoplex required a separate battery and was considered rather expensive for the time. According to the first Vibroplex ad shown below, orders for the Autoplex were taxing the manufacturer's facilities.

On May 7, 1904, Martin filed a patent application for a new type of semi-automatic key, a completely mechanical device he called the Vibroplex. Martin's patent (767,303) issued on August 9, 1904. This new key incorporated a design using a lever with an integrated vertical pivot; the pivot allowed the lever to rotate from right to left with almost no friction. When the operator pushed a paddle mounted on one end of the lever to the right a spring-mounted contact on the other end of the lever would vibrate against a stationary contact, resulting in a string of dots. Dashes were made manually by pushing the lever to the left, with the operator holding the paddle to determine the length of the dash.

Two years after starting production of the Vibroplex in New York Martin moved to Georgia. He produced a few keys in Norcross under the name United Electrical Manufacturing

Horace G. Martin's Autoplex key.

A Mecograph right-angle bug with horizontal pendulum from 1908.

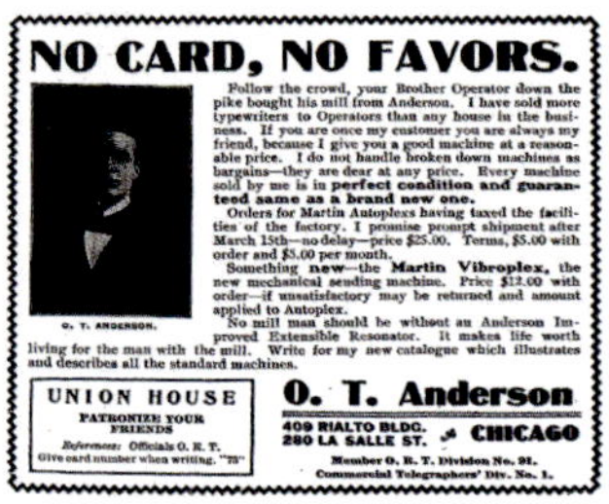

NO CARD, NO FAVORS.

Follow the crowd, your Brother Operator down the pike bought his mill from Anderson. I have sold more typewriters to Operators than any house in the business. If you are once my customer you are always my friend, because I give you a good machine at a reasonable price. I do not handle broken down machines as bargains—they are dear at any price. Every machine sold by me is in **perfect condition and guaranteed same as a brand new one.**

Orders for Martin Autoplexs having taxed the facilities of the factory. I promise prompt shipment after March 15th—no delay—price $25.00. Terms, $5.00 with order and $5.00 per month.

Something **new**—the **Martin Vibroplex,** the new mechanical sending machine. Price $12.00 with order—if unsatisfactory may be returned and amount applied to Autoplex.

No mill man should be without an Anderson Improved Extensible Resonator. It makes life worth living for the man with the mill. Write for my new catalogue which illustrates and describes all the standard machines.

O. T. ANDERSON.

UNION HOUSE
PATRONIZE YOUR FRIENDS
References: Officials O. R. T.
Give card number when writing. "75"

O. T. Anderson
409 RIALTO BLDG.
280 LA SALLE ST. CHICAGO
Member O. R. T. Division No. 91.
Commercial Telegraphers' Div. No. 1.

According to Tom French, the earliest ad offering the Vibroplex for sale was in the March 1905 issue of *The Railroad Telegrapher*.

Company, then produced a few more in Atlanta under Martin Manufacturing Company. Martin met with some success selling his devices, but did little if any advertising. He did not have the marketing skills to help his business grow; instead, he preferred to design the keys. Around 1911, Martin partnered with J. E. Albright, an entrepreneur who had been selling typewriters since 1890. Albright seized the task of manufacturing and selling the Vibroplex products, and with Albright's guidance business greatly improved. Albright and his brother William formed the Vibroplex Company, Inc. in 1915, with Martin remaining as an employee.

Another inventor, William O. Coffe of Cleveland, applied for a patent on a mechanical semi-automatic key with a vertical pendulum on January 11, 1904 (812,183), so Martin should not be considered the sole inventor of the semi-automatic key.

A G3YUH reproduction of Coffe's 1904 semi-automatic vertical pendulum design.

It is suspected Coffe did not sell many of his Mecograph semi-automatic keys with the vertical pendulum because only one is known to exist today, but there were various other versions of Mecographs that used horizontal pendulums; these were bought in higher numbers.

The Mecograph Company was owned by Benjamin Bellows. J. E. Albright, who owned Vibroplex at the time, entered a patent infringement lawsuit with Bellows. The lawsuit did not prevent either litigant from continuing to manufacture or market their semi-automatic keys. Marketplace results gave the edge to Vibroplex, possibly because of their aggressive marketing. Upon the sudden death of Benjamin Bellows, Albright bought Mecograph from Bellows' widow, Nellie. Mecograph keys essentially disappeared from the market after the company was absorbed by Vibroplex. It is thought by some collectors that for a brief time Vibroplex made a few keys using Mecograph parts, including the very rare Premier model (shown below).

In 1920, Horace G. Martin sold his interest in Vibroplex to J. E. Albright. Albright continued at the helm of Vibroplex for more than forty years, although many of them were spent in court defending his products. Martin did not lose interest in designing and manufacturing keys; after Vibroplex patents expired on their original models in the late 1930s, Martin completed designs for his own versions of many of the Vibroplex original models. In 1938, two of Horace G. Martin's sons, J. W. Martin and R. W. Martin, joined with three investors to form the Martin Research and Manufacturing Company (MR&M) at 233 Broadway, New York, New York; very little is known about

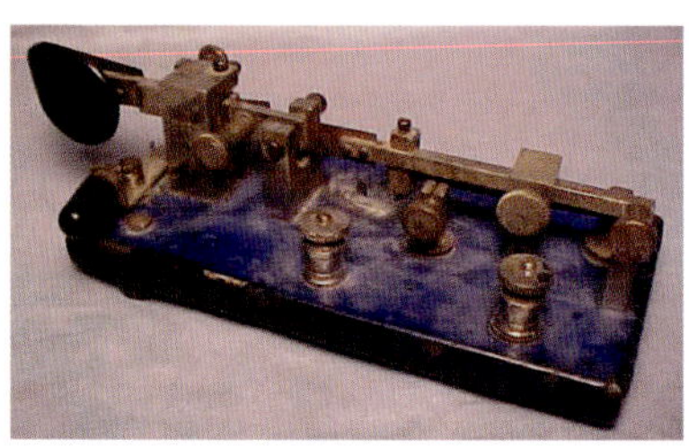

A Vibroplex Premier dating to about 1914.

A Vibroplex Original dating to 1918.

the company. Bill Holly's book on Vibroplex history describes an agreement between Vibroplex and MR&M, whereby MR&M would develop and manufacture bugs and Vibroplex would sell them. Holly reports this agreement was apparently never completed, or was short-lived. Martin Research and Manufacturing made four models, three of which were patterned after the Vibroplex #1 (Original), #4 (Blue Racer), and #6 (Lightning Bug). These keys were called the #1, #4, and #6 Martin Flash Key. The fourth was an inexpensive model unlike any other Vibroplex, although it had a mechanism similar to the Midget; Martin's sons sold these as "Martin Flash Keys." Apparently less than 2,000 of the Martin versions were produced.

One unique Martin Jr. design called the Rotoplex was developed in the early 1940s, and is still sought after by collectors today. The Rotoplex was the last production key Martin designed; it incorporated a rotary pivot mechanism, or central bearing, making it a visually striking key. Some other Rotoplex features included use of a flat rubber sheet under the base instead of feet, thumbpiece and fingerpiece molded in a single unit, and an integral cord eliminating binding posts for the connection to the transmitter. In 1941, Martin was issued patent 2,228,469 for his Rotoplex design. The Rotoplex was manufactured by the James Clark Jr. Electric Co. in Louisville, Kentucky.

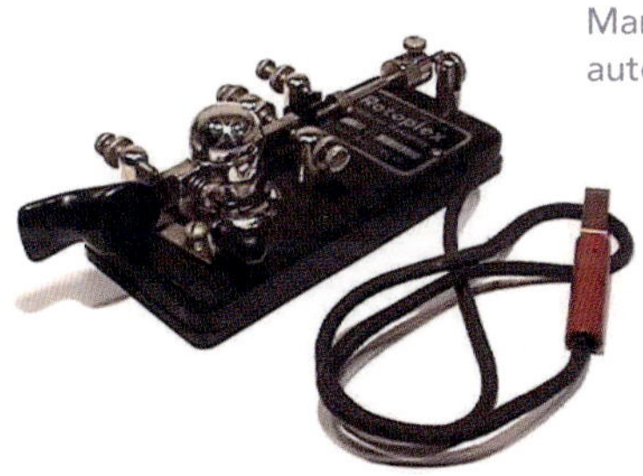

Martin's Rotoplex semi-automatic key.

Several other manufacturers made clones and copies of Vibroplex models, some legal and some illegal. One of the most well known clones was made by the A To Z Manufacturing Company; its bugs carried the ATOZ label.

The Vibroplex Company continued to be owned by Albright and his family until about 1965, when it was sold to John La Hiff, a mechanical engineer and long-time Vibroplex employee. La Hiff also happened to be the designer of many popular Vibroplex models, including the Lightning Bug, Zephyr, and the Champion—many believe the Presentation model as well. Later, La Hiff would also design the popular Vibro-Keyer paddle. La Hiff's sons sold the company to Peter Garsoe in 1979; Garsoe then moved Vibroplex to Portland, Maine. In 1994, Garsoe sold

"Mitch" Mitchell (W4OA) symbolically turns over the Vibroplex Company to Scott Robbins (W4PA).

the company to Felton "Mitch" Mitchell (W4OA), and shortly thereafter it was moved to Mobile, Alabama. In December 2009, Mitchell sold Vibroplex to Scott Robbins (W4PA, formerly of Ten-Tec); Robbins moved the company's operations to Knoxville, Tennessee. Vibroplex remains the oldest key production company and is still in business today.

The Automatic Keyer and the Paddle

Some of the earliest electronic keyer concepts date from the 1930s. With the advancement of tube designs, fully automatic keyers that generated dots and dashes were documented in many *QST* magazine articles beginning in the 1940s. Since then, considerable developments have been made in Morse keyer technology. Simple RC (resistor-capacitor) circuitry soon was replaced by flip-flop based designs. Tube circuits were redesigned to use transistors while saving power and keeping all previous keyer features. Discrete transistors were replaced with integrated circuits, either TTL (transistor-transistor logic) or the Curtis keyer-on-a-chip approach. The revolution continued with the use of microprocessors and microcontrollers in keyers. Each step in the process seemed to add new and exciting features, such as beacon modes, serial number generation, and message memory. Advanced keyer designs of the 2000s were able to interface with personal computers or utilize built-in microprocessors, offering many new conveniences, including automatic logging.

The original paddles used for homebrew keyers began serious development and refinement in the 1960s. From dual-lever devices with adjustable contacts and tension, paddle design and innovation progressed steadily into the 2000s. Use of magnetic tensioning, refinement of contact material, introduction of low-mass arms, and understanding of arm moment of inertia all became important elements of modern paddle design.

Even the best of operators could not reliably send accurate code at speeds much above fifty words per minute. Although considered a departure from traditional telegraphy, Morse keyboard use would grow in popularity in the 1960s and 1970s. In retrospect, Morse keyboards unintentionally provided the skills needed for operators to easily transition to computers and software for Morse sending.

The Morse Keyboard

As the name implies, sending Morse code using a keyboard is done by typing on a standard computer keyboard or a special Morse keyboard. The computer keyboard may be connected to a dedicated keyer that accommodates a keyboard input, or it may be connected to a personal computer, where the Morse is generated by software, such as Fldigi, CW Type, and others. Morse keyboards are self-contained units that include the keyboard and the keyer electronics to generate the Morse code elements. QRQ (high speed) CW operators can use their keyboards to transmit 60 to over 100 words per minute.

As personal computers developed and became widely incorporated in ham shacks, sound card technology was employed to not only send Morse code, but to decipher it. Although many of the hardware/software Morse code readers are not able to copy as well as the human mind under conditions where interference levels are very high, they are nevertheless able to provide good copy under many conditions.

Morse keyboards can be very useful when generating long Morse transmissions. While many hams think Morse keyboards are recent innovations, they were actually conceived as far back as 1898 (not the widely used 1893), when Charles Yetman applied for a patent on his telegraphic transmitter. The Yetman machine consisted of a typewriter keyboard that converted key depressions into Morse characters. Unfortunately, the need for a Morse typewriter had not yet materialized. In addition, Yetman's transmitter was large and expensive, discouraging potential buyers (much more on keyboards can be found in Chapter 14).

Some Definitions

There is much confusion—even among die-hard CW radio amateurs—regarding proper usage of terms, such as keyer, key, bug, fingerpiece, and paddle (refer to chapter 12 for more detail on the various parts and adjustments for a typical paddle).

Bug: Historically referred to the Martin semiautomatic key introduced in 1906 as the "Auto," and later as the Vibroplex. Bug is now a generic term for semi-automatic keys that are typically non-electronic and usually only produce automatic dots. There are some exceptions, such as the 1920s Australian Automorse bug that had a third lever and independent mechanism allowing for automatic mechanical dash generation. Richard Meiss (WB9LPU) has produced several mechanical bugs that also accomplish automatic dash generation. Those and some other fully automatic keys are covered in chapter 10.

Code Reader: A Morse decoding device designed to read incoming Morse code and display the decoded message for reading by an operator.

Dah: Used synonymously for the "dash" part of a Morse code element.

Dit: Used synonymously for the "dot" part of a Morse code element.

Dual (inaccurately often called Iambic) or Double-Lever Paddle: Has dual actuating arms and a mechanism allowing simultaneous closure of dot and dash contacts. The Bencher paddle is a good example. Dual or double-lever paddles are frequently used with iambic keyers; the terms are used interchangeably throughout this book.

Fingerpiece: The part of the actuating arm on a paddle the operator manipulates with his hand/fingers to actuate the paddle mechanism according to the Morse code letter being sent. Fingerpieces can be plastic, wood, carbon fiber, aluminum, or other material selected to minimize sending flex. In most cases fingerpieces are an important aesthetic design element of the paddle, and shape and color add to the overall impact of the paddle design.

Key: Often refers to a hand key or a "straight" key, as it is sometimes called. A key is the basic switch used to turn a transmitter on and off in the proper sequence corresponding to the Morse code letter being sent. A bug or a paddle can also be called a key.

Keyboard Keyer: A keyboard keyer typically looks much like a computer keyboard, but contains circuitry for electronic keying that allows for output switch closure based on the letter or symbol typed in by the operator. Keyboard keyers can also be standalone devices that operate by plugging in an external computer keyboard.

Keyer: Refers to a device, usually electronic, to send Morse code via automatic dot and dash generation. The keyer will typically produce perfectly timed Morse code elements and spacings. Keyers are usually controlled by the operator using a paddle. Keyers may incorporate electronic buffers and memories, allowing convenience and operator options for sending groups of letters and even complete messages. Keyers may offer several different types of operation, including iambic keying. Iambic keying allows the operator to squeeze the fingerpieces on a dual-lever paddle, resulting in a keyer output of alternating dits and dahs. Bugs, paddles, and hand keys are not keyers.

Lever, Arm, and Lever Arm: Used interchangeably, they all refer to the moving part of the paddle mechanism, usually with contacts on one end and fingerpieces on the other end; the arm can use springs or magnets for return to neutral.

Oscillator, or CPO (code practice oscillator): Frequently used for an electrical, electronic, or electromechanical device allowing the attachment of a Morse code key for code practice. Technical correctness means a CPO is an electronic device, but in actuality the term is sometimes used for any code practice device. Oscillators are not keyers.

Paddle: The actuating device for an electronic keyer; usually the paddle is a mechanical switch of various design, although there are variations in how the switching is implemented. Paddles can incorporate many different approaches allowing for the switching function, including single and dual actuation levers and magnetic or spring actuating arm return. Context is important when the word "paddle" is used, as the entire key is sometimes called a paddle. Some operators refer to the fingerpieces as paddles, possibly because fingerpieces vaguely resemble ping-pong paddles. Either usage is appropriate, hence the recommendation to consider context.

Semi-automatic: A term first used by Horace Martin in his 1904 patent, it refers to a key or keyer mode where dots are automatically generated and dashes are manually generated.

Sideswiper (Cootie) Key: Sometimes called a double speed key. The paddle of its key lever closed the circuit whether moved right or left. Its sidewise movement offered relief to operators suffering from glass arm.

Single-Lever: A paddle with one actuating arm, usually moved side-to-side to produce dot and dash switch closures. Both closures cannot be made simultaneously, so the single-lever paddle would not be a good choice for an iambic keyer. A well known example would be the Vibroplex Vibrokeyer paddle.

Words Per Minute: Morse code transmitting speed is measured in words per minute (wpm). The word "Paris" is used as the standard length of a word. If an operator were to transmit the word "Paris" five times, requiring 50 units of time, the operator's sending speed would be 5 words per minute (5 wpm).

2 Code Readers, Oscillators, and Morse Trainers

The devices comprising the three categories presented in this chapter represent a mix of technologies and span the time period of Morse telegraphy. A complete history of these devices, while beyond the scope of this book, is actually not necessary to appreciate the conceptual thought and innovation that have continued to drive the design of modern Morse equipment.

Morse code practice oscillators, Morse trainers, and Morse code readers all share a common feature: they are designed to help proficiency at sending and copying Morse code. The first electromechanical paper tape code readers were intended to help users who did not know the code. Later, Morse practice sets, followed by code oscillators, can be considered the earliest Morse learning devices and the forerunners of today's more sophisticated training devices. A few of the later practice oscillators also had built-in paddles. Although some early code learning units had an almost toy-like appearance, many hams got their start with Morse code from "toys" such as the ones shown in this chapter. Some of the more modern devices, in addition to having beacon and trainer modes, also functioned as Morse keyers. If the trainer also featured a keyer mode you will find it in chapter 3; otherwise, it is shown in this chapter.

There is a varied mix of items presented in this chapter, including so-called toys, military training units, paper tape machines, oscillators, code readers, and other related devices. Some of the oldest devices are electromechanical; it is hoped their inclusion will add to the appreciation of all the learning and display devices that followed. By showing representative samples of some diverse and popular devices, the reader can begin to understand the progression of design from electromechanical and electromagnetic devices through tubes and transistors and on to ICs, and the more sophisticated microprocessor-based code readers. Strictly software approaches (CW Skimmer and MRP40 are two Morse reader/decoder programs that are highly rated) are not included.

Some Early Code Registers

The first Morse code register (reader) dates to 1845, when Alfred Vail designed a code register that used electromagnets and pens to emboss received code elements (dots and dashes) on paper tape. The paper tape was drawn through the register by a mechanical clockwork. Vail's design was fabricated by Mr. John Stokell, a New York City clock maker, in 1844. On May 24, 1844, a register was set up at the B&O railroad's Mount Clare Station in Baltimore. From the Supreme Court chamber in the basement of the US Capitol building in Washington, DC, Morse used the newly completed Washington to Baltimore telegraph line to send his famous "What hath God wrought" message to Vail's register in Baltimore.

A Cornell-furnished image showing one of two original Vail registers at Cornell University. The second register is unaccounted for.

Many competing electro-mechanical printers were marketed in conjunction with keyboard telegraphy sending machines (chapter 14). Standalone code registers and printers continued to be developed and used as telegraphy grew and became more established in the mid- and late-1800s. Some of the earliest tape reader designs used inkless embossing of paper tape to indicate the letters being sent; the long and short impressions on the tape were then read by eye and transcribed into letters.

The Caton Machine—a device made in the 1850s by the Caton Instrument Company—is an example of an embossing reader. It was powered by a weight and used a stylus that made indentations on the paper tape (no ink was used) to indicate Morse elements being sent.

As code readers evolved ink printing replaced the embossing technique, but machines still remained centered on the use of spooled paper tape. Although copying the code by ear was possible, many operators, especially in Europe, preferred paper tape, because it was a permanent record of the code transmission. Several of these devices are shown.

The above photo shows the Gurlt writing apparatus, also called a remote printer or write telegraph. The mechanical parts are brass, and are affixed to a wooden base. The drawer in the base provides storage for the paper tape roll. The tape is fed through a spring-wound motor and two electromagnets move the write wheel. This machine dates to 1894.

A German strip chart recorder.

A Swedish paper tape register made by L. M. Ericsson.

C. F. Lewert's brass device on a mahogany base made in Berlin, Germany, around 1880. This device includes a drawer for storage of the paper roll.

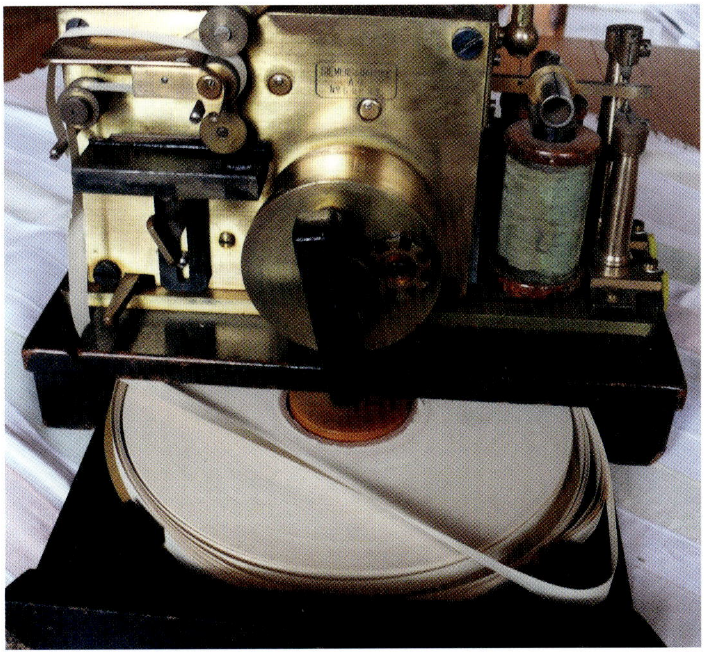

A Siemens and Halske machine circa 1868.

A Siemens Brothers reader.

Code Sounders/Resonators

The telegraph sounder is very similar to a relay. The sounder is designed to make an audible click sound when actuated by a current flowing in a telegraph circuit. When the current stops flowing, the part of a sounder called an armature is released and a weight pulls the armature back up to its resting position, making a clack noise. As the telegraph key on the sending end of a telegraph circuit is manipulated to send code elements the sounder follows the sending, making noises corresponding to the long and short elements being sent by the key. The resonator is merely a wooden box that helps direct the sounds toward the operator, aiding the copying effort.

Note the use of the Prince Albert can in the adjustable-arm sounder shown below. The can was typically wedged between the sounder and the resonator box. Operators could fine tune the sound they heard by opening and closing the can and varying its position on the sounder. Many operators thought the can seemed to amplify the sound.

As an emphasis on authenticity, some collectors of antique sounders and resonators also collect old Prince Albert cans.

A typical vertically mounted sounder with wooden resonator box.

Syphon Recorders

The syphon (or siphon) recorder was invented in 1858 by William Thompson. The siphon recorder automatically recorded a telegraph message as it was being received. The recording showed the message as an oscillating line on a paper strip. Because actual letters were not printed—an ink line followed along with the code being sent—reading the message required a trained telegrapher to translate the recorded lines into letters. Siphon recorders were very sensitive instruments. They were developed for use on trans-oceanic telegraph systems, where weak signals were often unable to actuate traditional sounder devices.

Two Muirhead Syphon Recorder designs.

Syphon recorders were still being marketed into the 1930s. This is a Visasig ad from the August 1936 *QST*.

Code Trainers and Sending Machines

Teleplex Company of New York City first started advertising in *QST* magazine in 1927. Their ads proclaimed "The Easy Way to Learn the Code Cuts Learning Time in Half. The famous Teleplex for self-instruction at home. The quickest, easiest and most economical way of learning Morse or Continental. Faithfully reproduces actual sending of expert operators." The company provided a code instruction manual and personal help and advice via correspondence.

The early Teleplex machines were spring-motor driven, but later used an electric motor drive for the recording tape. The machines were also capable of sending code using pre-recorded paper tape. The Teleplex Company later introduced a mechanical keyer using an inked paper tape; this keyer was marketed for several years. It used a pen with a conducting ink—possibly made from a silver compound—and was soon followed by a similar mechanical design using a chemically treated paper tape. A user could record from a receiver or make his own tapes using a key. When the tape was played back, a pair of spring-loaded fingers made contact with the conducting ink on the paper tape, completing the sending circuit. Teleplex would later improve the design so conducting ink was no longer required; they used a photocell to detect the presence of the inked line and then actuated the sending circuit via the photocell output. The 1942 and some later Teleplex machines were interesting, using a

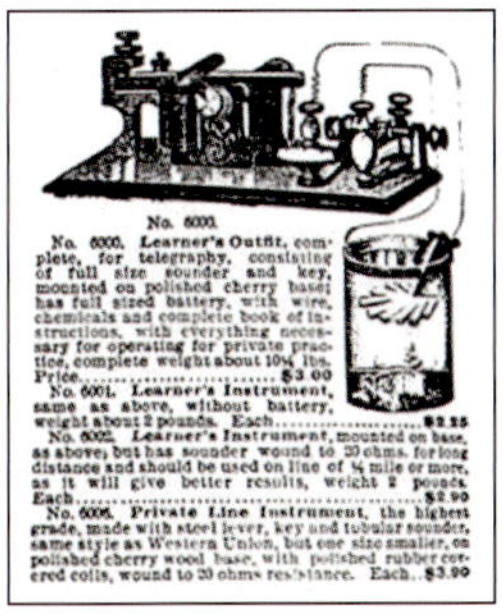

An 1897 Sears catalog ad for a Morse trainer learning outfit. Note the device came with its own battery and chemicals; pictured are a glass jar, zinc electrodes, and chemicals are included. The device was typical of many sold during the late 1880s as code practice aids.

A French code practice set.

An early German Siemens practice machine. Siemens designs were licensed to many other manufacturers.

A Teleplex code sending and practice machine.

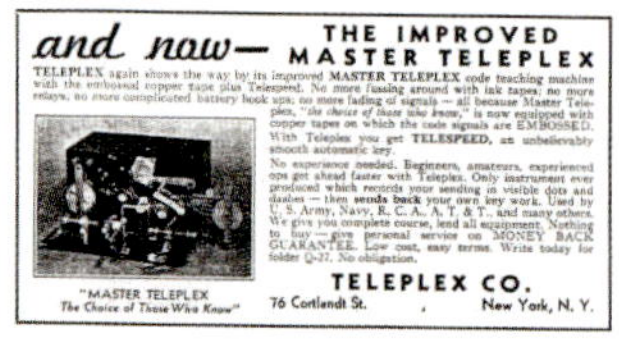

March 1935 *QST* advertisement for the Master Teleplex.

copper tape to record the operator's sending and sending it back for further listening and learning improvement. In 1956, Teleplex machines reverted to using punched tape, and in 1959, their machines evolved to something resembling the Omnigraph. Teleplex never published their prices in ads, but these types of automatic sending devices were usually far beyond the average ham's budget.

Another of the many paper tape code sending systems was the Gardiner-Levering Automatic Code Sender marketed in the mid-1930s. Some of their ads called the unit a "Robot Radio Key." Gardiner-Levering was based in New Jersey. This tiny unit (3" × 4" × 4") punches holes in a paper tape using two telegraph key-like levers: one moves the tape forward and the other punches the holes. The tape may then be sent at a later time. The paper tape sending machines seemed to be more popular for code practice and teaching, rather than on-the-air use, even though some ads appealed to the automatic keying aspects of the devices. Gardiner-Levering later became Gardiner and Company, and sold Morse paper tape machines into the early 1950s, until electronic devices became the best choice.

The remainder of this chapter presents a closer pictorial look at many of the code readers, trainers, and oscillators of interest to hams today.

T. R. McElroy produced several code keying and recording units as seen in this October 1941 *Radio* advertisement.

A Gardiner-Levering Automatic Code Sender and periodical advertisement dating to the mid-1930s.

A. C. Gilbert Tele-Set

Alfred Carlton Gilbert's Tele-Set sold in the 1920s and 1930s. The set included some Western Union message blanks and two key/buzzer units, along with a spool of wire.

Gilbert was a Princeton and Yale scholar. He received a medical degree from Yale and focused his creative abilities on the interests and curiosities of boys, mostly ages 6–16. In 1913, he introduced the Erector set. Three years later, Gilbert founded the A. C. Gilbert Company. Gilbert had a strong interest in creating toys that would instill in boys a desire to learn science and technology. Gilbert's company also produced American Flyer toy trains, microscopes, chemistry sets, building blocks, and other educational toys. Through his skillful marketing Gilbert became known as the "man who saved Christmas." More recently, a made-for-TV movie detailed this aspect of Gilbert's life.

Advanced Electronic Applications (AEA) BT-1 Trainer

The BT-1 Basic Trainer was designed for the person just beginning to learn the Morse code. The BT-1 could send Morse as individual code characters or as a sequence of characters with adjustable character group spacing. Features include an on-off-volume control, speaker, earphone jack, and the keypad. The BT-1 also functioned as a code practice oscillator for improving one's sending. This trainer was also available as the BP-1P, offering a rechargeable internal NiCad battery pack. The BT-1 dates to 1982.

AEA MBA-RO Reader

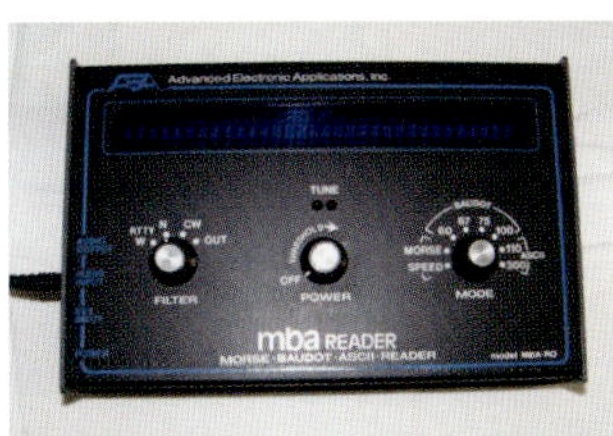

The AEA MBA-RO is a Morse code reader from 1982. The MBA-RO can copy Morse code from 3 to 99 wpm, as well as copy Baudot radioteletype up to 100 wpm and ASCII at 110 baud. Decoded text is presented on a 32-character alphanumeric vacuum fluorescent display. This device requires 12 volt DC external power and receiver audio to operate. The MBA-RO also features an internal 100 kHz filter centered on 800 kHz.

Allied/Knight Oscillators

The Allied/Knight S-239 is a one transistor device available starting in 1956 as a Knight-Kit. Power was supplied by an internal 1.5 volt battery. Front panel jacks were provided for headphones.

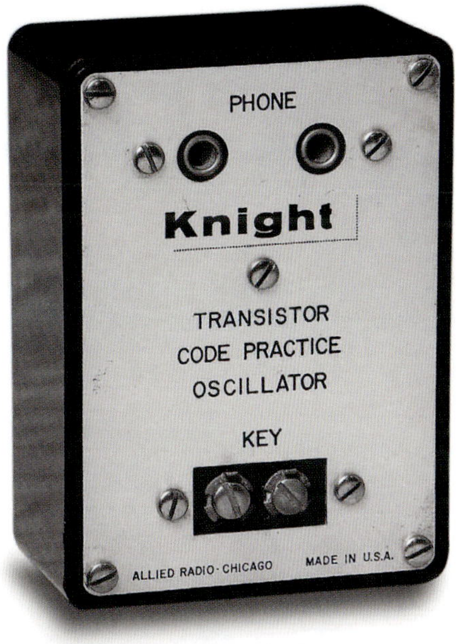

The Allied/Knight LC-1 allowed the user to select either a light or use of the internal sidetone with a speaker or headphones.

Ameco Model CPS Oscillator

The American Electronics Company (AMECO) CPS uses a 35W4 rectifier and a 50C5 audio amplifier tube; it runs on AC or DC current. At least two different configurations carried the "CPS" model number: the earlier CPS (front and rear) is shown. The two-tube design was typical of the time and was used in other oscillators, such as the Bud Codemaster. This AMECO device was first available in 1955 as a kit or factory-wired by AMECO. The front panel featured a tone control and could also be used as a CW monitor. Early AMECO oscillators had a shock hazard on the key jack, where B+ voltage is present. When a key is connected B+ voltage is also present on the key; this hazard was corrected in later AMECO production versions.

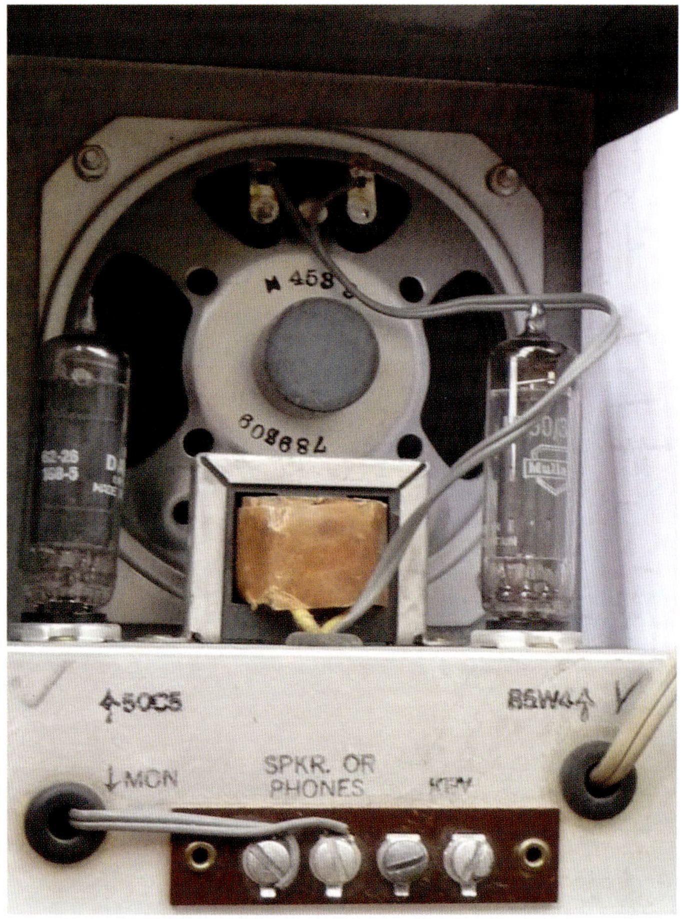

A front panel view of the later AMECO Model CPS with obvious cosmetic changes from its predecessor.

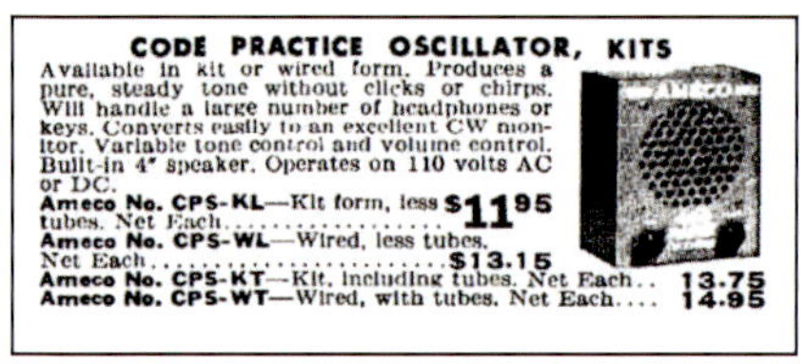

Ameco Model OCM Oscillators

The AMECO OCM was a one-transistor unit powered by AA batteries featuring an internal speaker. The OCM models, when used with grid-block keying transmitters, could also be used as CW monitors. The OCM devices date back to 1965.

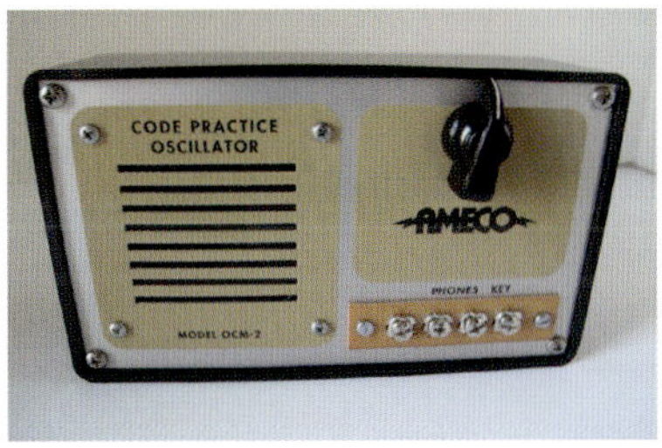

AOR Radio Telegraph Terminal

The AOR AR-501 offers three main functions: a Morse decoder, a Morse code trainer, and an electronic keyer. The decoder is specified to copy CW at speeds of 5 to 30 wpm. The CW trainer will generate random five character code groups from 5 to 30 wpm, and the keyer function supports speeds of 5 to 30 wpm. Also offered are a sidetone oscillator and speaker. Connections are provided for either a standard or dual-lever paddle, a straight key, and headphones. This device runs on 12 volt DC. An interesting note on the name "AOR" is found on the company website. The founder and president of AOR, Ltd., Shigeru Takano, received the amateur radio call sign JA1AOR, and this is the origin of the name "AOR" (Authority On Radio communications).

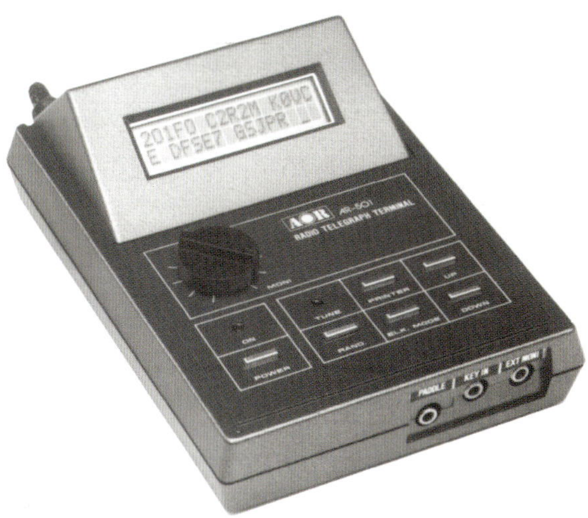

ARRL Morse Code Oscillator Kit

The American Radio Relay League presents this oscillator as a great beginner's electronics kit. The kit is recommended as ideal for ARRL members, amateur radio newcomers, clubs, instructors, and teachers seeking a classroom kit building experience. Circuitry is based on the NE555 timer chip and includes an adjustable pitch control and a small PC board mounted speaker. The kit uses a 9 volt battery.

Atko Model 10A Mini-Keyer

Atko was the Automatic Telegraph Keyer Corporation; they made the Model 10A around the early 1960s. Atko was based in New York City and manufactured a variety of Morse code instruction equipment for the military and various FCC field offices. Two additional capstans can be seen; these capstans were interchanged with one on the unit to control Morse sending speed. The Model 10A featured an internal power supply and a Hartley oscillator for code monitoring. There was no take-up reel; Atko suggested in their manual that users set up the keyer to allow for tape to unwind into a clean box on the floor. The selling price was approximately $50.

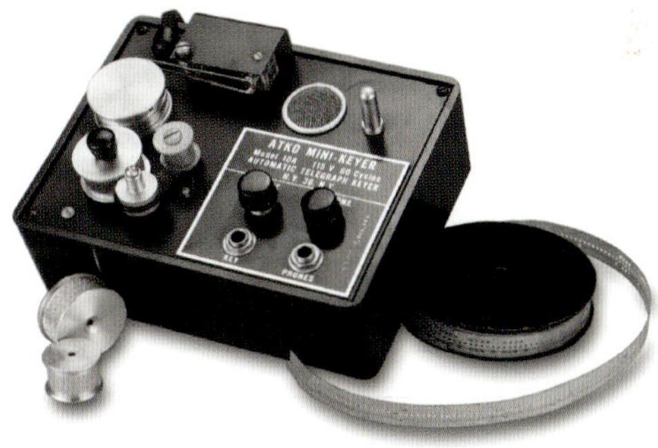

Atronics CR-101 Code Reader

The Atronics Model CR-101 was simply connected to a receiver's speaker and used the audio to decode and display Morse letters, numbers, and punctuation marks at speeds up to 50 wpm. RTTY signals could be displayed if an optional interface was purchased. The CR-101 started selling in 1976.

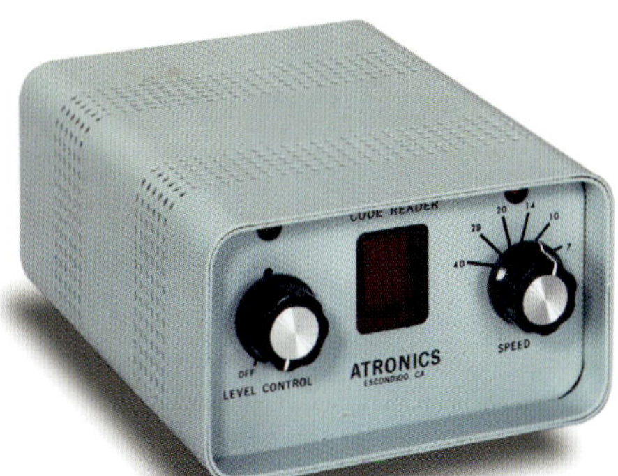

Autokey Morse Code Beginner II

The Morse Code Beginner II is a new Chinese version of a Morse training device. It will accept paddle, bug, or straight key inputs. Random individual letters or code groups can be generated. Monitoring is done via an external headset. Power required is 7 to 28 volts DC.

Boehme Automatic Keying Head

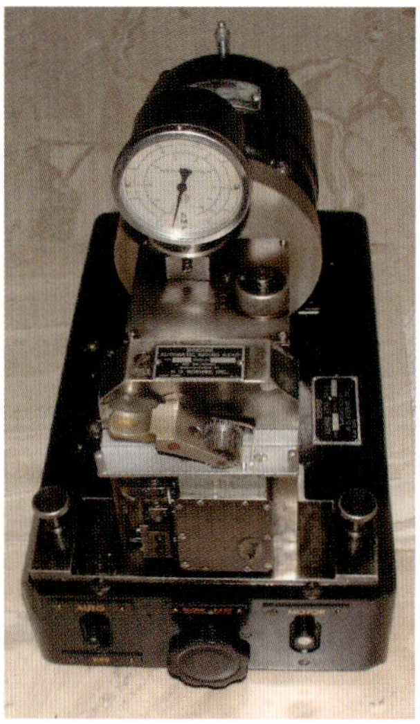

H. O. Boehme, Inc. manufactured a series of paper tape readers and motorized tape drive keying heads for the military. The Boehme system allowed high-speed transmission of Morse code that was then recorded on paper tape at the receiving station and transcribed by an operator at a slower, more readable speed. Some of the Boehme machines claimed code transmission speeds of 400 wpm; 100 wpm was a more typical usage.

Boy Scout Twin Signal Set

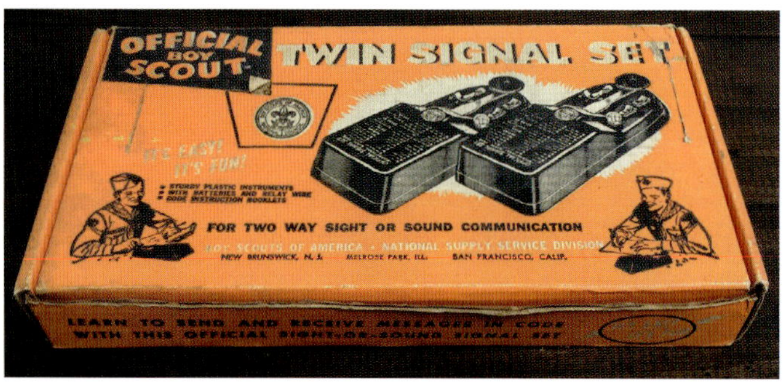

Issued by Boy Scouts of America, New Brunswick, New Jersey. The box included four D-cell batteries and hookup wire. This set dates to about 1948.

Brumberger Codemaster Telegraph Signal Set

The Brumberger set shows another way many learned the Morse code in the 1940s. The device allows the user to select a buzzer, light, or a clicking mechanism to send code. The example shown included a Morse code learning record. Ideal Toy also put out a version of the Brumberger set (shown in the blue box).

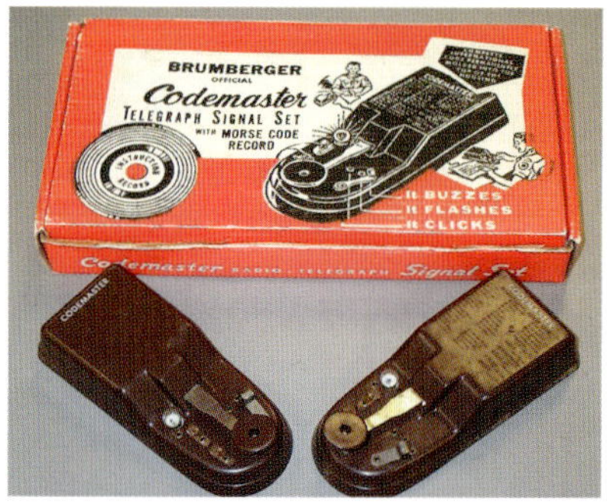

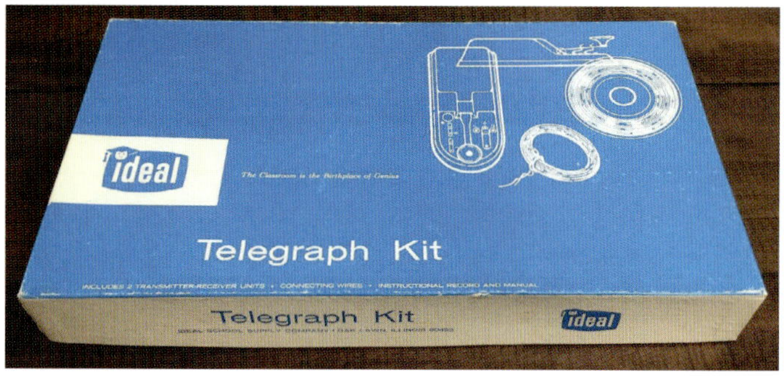

BUD Code Practice Oscillators

These BUD 128-A & 128-B Codemaster oscillators use the common two-tube oscillator design typical of the 1950s. They feature an internal speaker and have the ability to switch between being a code practice oscillator or a CW monitor. The unit on the right is a newer model and has the B+ design change to eliminate shock hazard where B+ voltage is found on the key. Note the use of rivets to hold the speaker in place on the newer unit with the white lettering.

The BUD 155-T used a single transistor and internal penlight cells and had no speaker. Screw terminals were provided for a headphone connection. This device was first offered in 1957.

An early BUD audio oscillator from the K2TQN collection. BUD also produced a similar model without the internal speaker.

Buzza Code Practice Keys

The Buzza devices were made in Australia and included a small buzzer on the base of the code key. The image below shows a somewhat crude early version that dates to the 1930s; the image at right shows how the key was improved visually for sale in the 1940s.

Calrad Practice Buzzer Set

This vintage Calrad code practice set was made in Japan and dates to the 1960s; it was sold by the Burstein-Applebee Co. of Kansas City, Missouri. This practice set uses one battery and includes a buzzer for sound. Instructions included a recommendation to adjust the buzzer magnet and diaphragm for maximum sound output. A note on Burstein-Applebee: many catalogs that include radios, televisions, and other electronics were issued until the end of the 1960s. Their advertising offered "Everything in Electronics." Burstein-Appleby had twenty-nine stores at their peak.

Calrad Code Oscillators

The Calrad Model 70-376 is a fairly rare code practice oscillator. Features included selectable tone, light, or both. Pitch of the oscillator tone was variable with a front panel control. Inside was a simple one-transistor circuit, speaker, and battery holder.

Many brands produced a code oscillator using the one-transistor design and had similar front panel layouts; here (right) is the Calrad version, which was labeled the C. O. 5. Features included adjustable pitch, switchable tone/light modes, headphone jack, and a rudimentary key for sending.

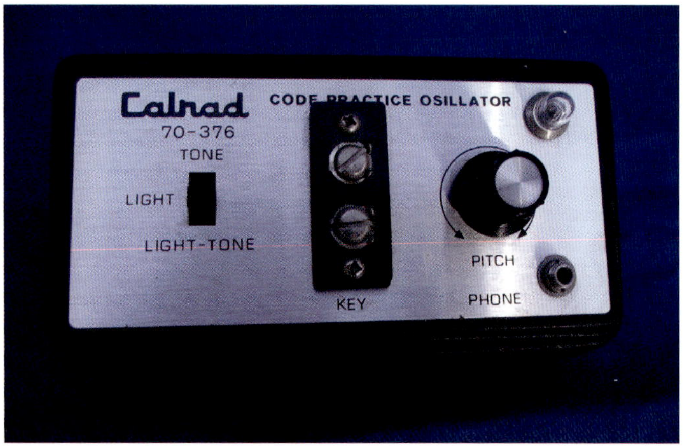

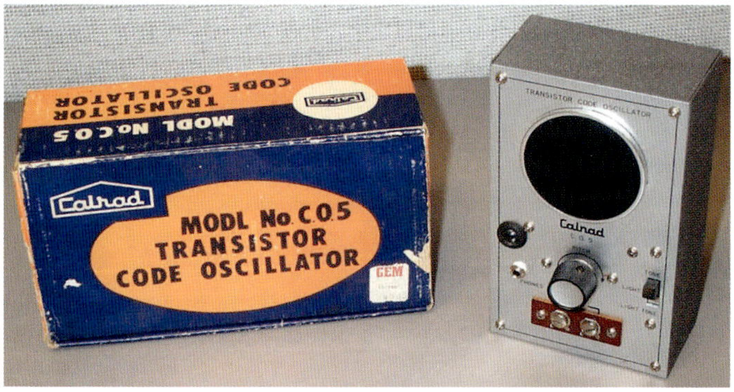

Calrad's T.C.O. was a self-contained code practice oscillator in a small plastic case. Batteries, speaker, and volume control were all inside.

Claricon 85-120 Code Oscillator

The Claricon 85-120 is another of many similar oscillator designs using a one-transistor circuit, switchable light/tone mode, internal speaker, and adjustable tone control. The Claricon is a lesser known brand; many hams were more familiar with the Lafayette or Ameco branded oscillators. Claricon literature states this unit was especially designed for Boy Scouts and novice radio amateurs. This unit uses two internal C-cell batteries.

Code Master Model K Practice Set

The Code Master Model K is built in a wooden box with a hinged cover. This oscillator uses a large, pushbutton type switch as the key, although an external key can be connected using the front panel terminal strip. The circuit uses one tube and is powered by 115 volts AC.

CODOME Morse Code Trainer

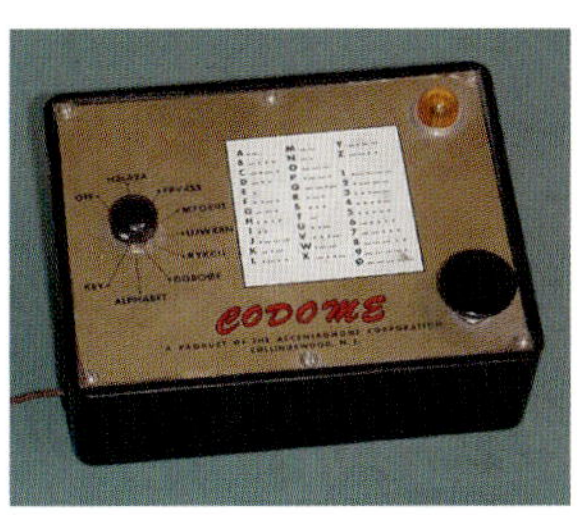

Pictured above is a vintage Morse code trainer called a CODOME made by the Accentronome Corporation of Collingswood, New Jersey. A knob on the front panel allows selection of different code groups or alphabet letters. When turned to "KEY," the large black button allows practice sending. The CODOME used a rotating disc inside the box with preset code sequences to send six 6-letter code groups.

CQ ham radio (Japan) Magazine Trainer

The *CQ ham radio* Morse trainer was sold at the Japanese Ham Fair in 2012, as a promotion of the publisher. Its major features include speed and volume controls and selectable fully automatic or bug mode operation. An internal speaker is provided. There is a memory for about 250 characters. Power is obtained from three external AA batteries.

Cumbria Designs Morse Code Reader

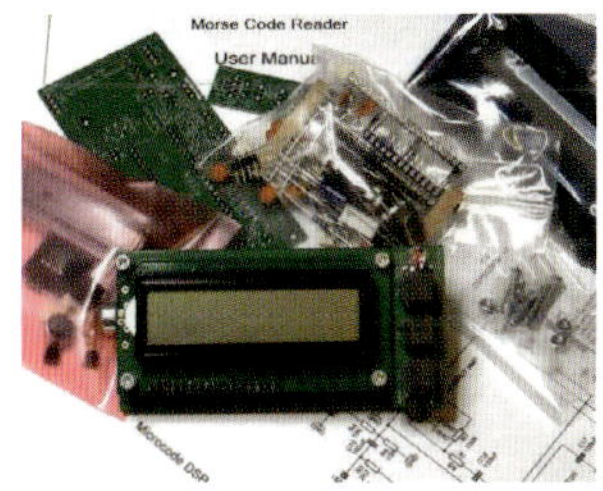

Cumbria Designs was formed in 2003, in the United Kingdom. They produce this Microcode DSP kit that can be assembled into a handy Morse code reader. This Microcode reader is capable of decoding and displaying audio Morse code signals from a few words per minute to over 50 wpm. Cumbria states the design uses a sensitive integral microphone and a bank of narrow finite impulse response (FIR) bandpass filters to decode effectively when placed near a receiver's loudspeaker. Alternatively, a line input allows direct connection to the audio output from a receiver. The decoder also includes an LED signal detection indicator and offers selectable functions using front panel pushbuttons with an on-screen menu system; menu settings are stored in memory.

Curtis IK-440 Instructokeyer

The IK-440 is an early Morse code instruction aid; the keyer portion of the IK-440 uses a design similar to the Curtis EK-430 keyer. The Instructokeyer included a random character generator that was very useful for code practice. This unit could be isolated from the transmitter's keyed line for off-the-air code practice using a front panel switch. The Instructokeyer sold in the mid-1970s.

Datong Model D70 Morse Tutor

Datong was a British corporation in Leeds, England. The Morse Tutor was an eleven integrated circuit device designed to send continuous Morse code in five character, non-repeating groups. The Model D70 also offered variable speed and variable delay between characters: letters only, numbers only, or mixed. The unit included a built-in tone oscillator for sending practice when the user connected a key. A headphone jack was provided.

Dewsbury Electronics (G4CLX) Supa-Tuta

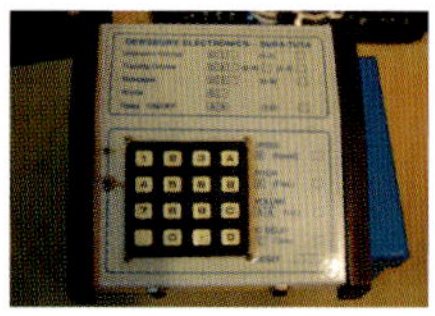

The Dewsbury Supa-Tuta is an innovative Morse tutor device with a vocabulary of no less than 4,260 words and characters offering speeds of between 10 and 100 wpm. Also available to the student are random letters, random numbers, random callsigns with over 3,000 stored, and 150 practice QSOs stored for playback and practice. In addition, the Supa-Tuta provides Morse tests, punctuation, abbreviations, and Q-Codes.

DGM Electronics MVD-1000 Morse Video Display

DGM Electronics was in Beloit, Wisconsin; they manufactured the MVD-1000 Morse video display device in the late 1970s. Using a receiver's audio output, it copied and decoded the CW for display on a TV set. One useful design feature was the inclusion of active filtering and digital sampling to reduce effects of noise interference. Other features included automatic speed tracking from 6–60 wpm and manual tracking adjustment.

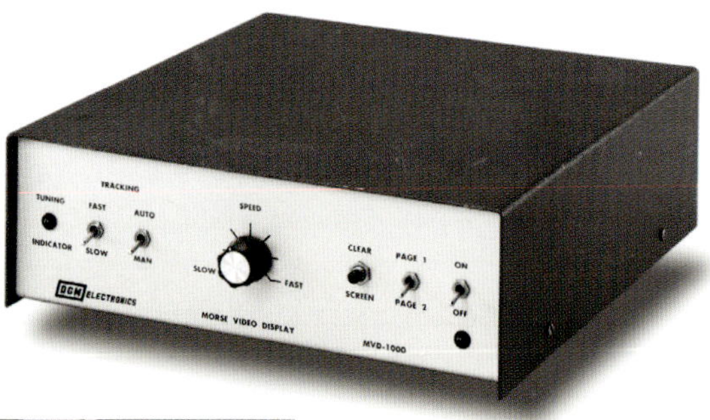

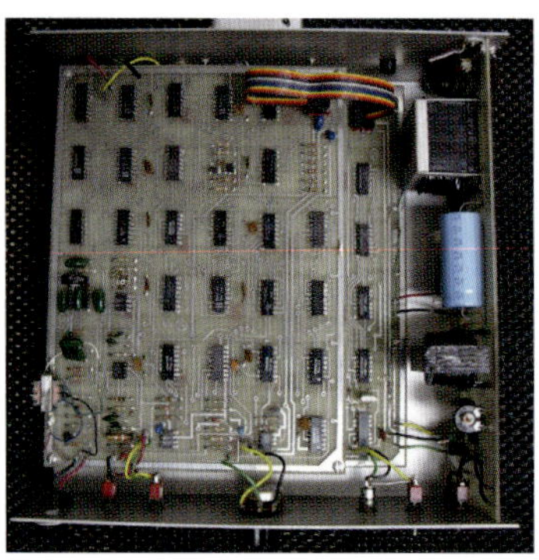

DRAE Morse Tutor

The DRAE Morse Tutor was designed and manufactured by Davtrend Ltd. of Portsmouth, United Kingdom, circa 1980. It features variable speed rate and individual random character generation. Other options include the ability to generate groups of five random characters and numbers.

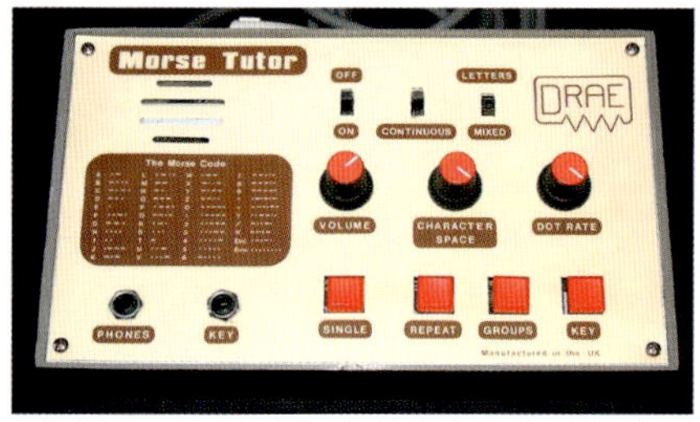

Eico Model 706 Code Oscillator

The Eico 706 is another of the common code practice oscillator design. Features similar to the Calrad device include adjustable pitch, switchable tone/light modes, and a headphone jack. The Eico did not include the metal strip for keying as seen on the Calrad oscillator. This oscillator uses internal batteries.

ERA Microreader

Enterprise Radio Applications (ERA) of Warrington, United Kingdom, manufactured the Microreader using a design based on a microprocessor and ICs. The front panel was available in at least two colors. The Microreader used receiver audio and required 12 volts DC for operation. The main display was a

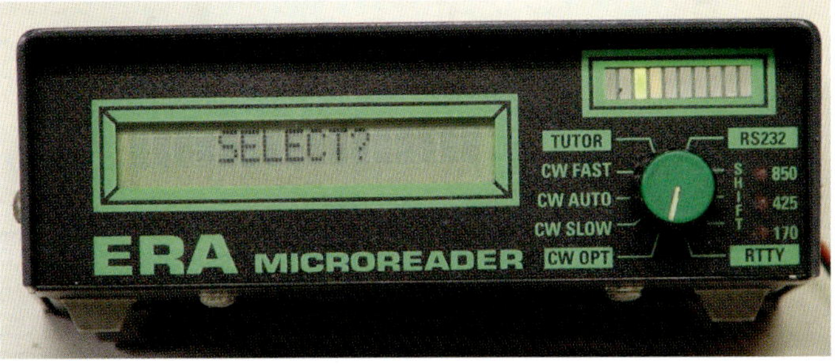

16-character LCD, and the smaller indicator was a 10-element three-color tuning bargraph. This device could copy Morse up to 80 wpm, as well as RTTY. The Morse tutor function of the Microreader sent letters, figures, letters and figures, or code groups of five characters per session. The rear panel gave the user an RS-232 output. The top photo shows the Microreader with ERA's BP34 external filter.

Etas GMZ Morse Code Generator

The GMZ provides an example of a military Morse code generator/trainer. It was made in 1983 by a Yugoslavian firm named Etas. The design allows generation of 44 randomly produced Morse code characters. Code generation can also be set up as individual lessons. The unit features a tone oscillator and 1 watt audio amplifier, and allows for teaching in small, improvised classrooms.

Fleron Signaler

The Fleron Signaler was the official Boy Scout Morse code learning device; two different configurations are shown. The Fleron signaler was sold by M. M. Fleron and Son, Trenton, New Jersey, and has the Boy Scout National Council insignia on the box. The case is Bakelite. Fleron Signalers used two D-cell batteries for the buzzer and lamp; devices date to about 1935.

Fleron was not a manufacturer, but a family-owned retailer. The company was founded by Louis Fleron, who emigrated from Fleron, Belgium, in the 1880s. The company's name comes from Fleron's wife, combining her initials with the Fleron hometown. The company also sold insulators and antenna accessories.

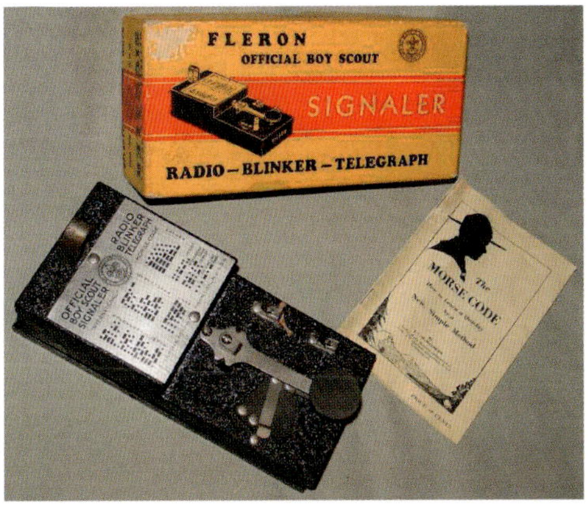

Geobra Telegraph Morse Key Set

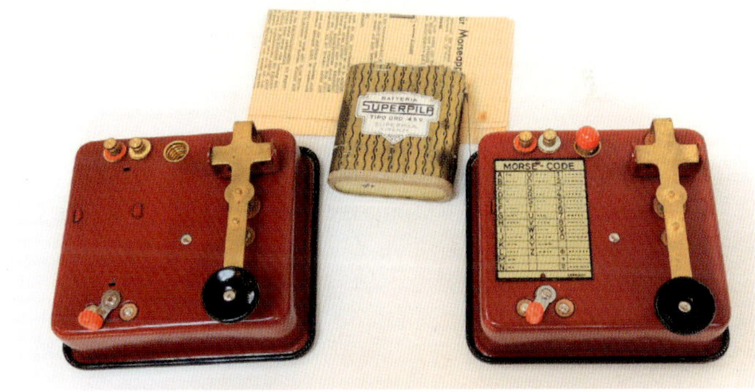

The Geobra was a German Morse practice set made in the late 1930s. A switch allows selection of the internal buzzer or light.

GHD GR-301A Morse Training Unit

The GR-301A Morse Training Unit is a combination code practice oscillator and an iambic keyer with 600 character message memory. There is also an option to select "E-bug" mode, where the paddle can be used as if it were a semi-automatic bug. Speed range of the keyer is 7–50 wpm. This unit runs on two internal AAA batteries. GHD devices are made by Toshihiko Ujiie (JA7GHD) in Sendai City; the company takes its name from his callsign.

Guthman U-35 Keytoner

This U-35 code practice oscillator was made by the Edwin I. Guthman Company of Chicago, Illinois.

HAL Telereaders

The Hal CWR-6700 receives Morse code using receiver audio with a speed range of 4–50 wpm. It also decodes regular Baudot radio teletype at 45, 50, 57, and 75 baud, and ASCII at 110 and 300 baud. Video output is to a composite video monitor (not included). The design is centered on the HD 46802 CPU and has two EPROMs: one contains the firmware, the other contains the video character set. The output of the Telereader is standard composite video (75 ohms).

The Hal CWR-6850 receives Morse code from 4–50 wpm and decodes regular Baudot radioteletype at 45, 50, 57, and 75 baud, as well as ASCII at 110 and 300 baud. Unlike the CWR-6750, the CWR-6850 features a transmit keyboard, allowing the user to transmit Morse, Baudot, and ASCII through an amateur transmitter or transceiver. The CWR-6850 also features a built-in 25 line CRT monitor. The unit requires 13.8 VDC at 1.6 amps.

Hallicrafters HA-18 Code Oscillator

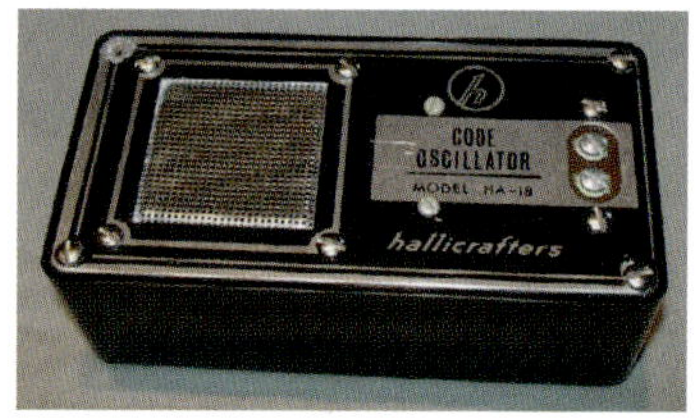

The Hallicrafters HA-18 is a very basic practice oscillator. Front panel terminal-type connections are provided for a key connection and internal batteries are used for power. No other controls were included, although the HA-18A that followed added a pitch control. The HA-18 dates to the 1960s.

Hamcrafters (K1EL) Oscillators and Code Reader

The K1EL code practice oscillator can be used with almost any keyer, and provides a true sine wave output with adjustable frequency and volume. The kit includes a built-in speaker with a provision to drive an external speaker or headphones. RCA phono outputs with external power and a speaker/headphone connector are provided on the rear panel.

The K40CW Board has been designed as an accessory board for the K40 CW Keyboard Keyer. The board allows for decoding and display of received Morse CW; the reader accepts receiver audio and decodes CW into digital serial data that is fed into the K40 for display. Power for the interface is obtained from the K40 PCB.

Heath Code Oscillators

The HD-16 code practice oscillator kit was available 1967–1975. It used a one-transistor circuit powered by two nine–volt batteries and one C-cell. Oscillator output was either tone or visual by a light mounted on top of the case. The kit also included a straight key.

The Heath HD-1416 code oscillator was produced as a kit 1975–1989. This oscillator uses a three-transistor circuit with components—including a small speaker—mounted on an internal circuit board.

The Heath CO-1 code oscillator was produced as a kit. In later production models, Heath changed the transistor to a 2N407 and added a .1 uF capacitor from transistor base to ground; these changes were meant to reduce key clicks. There was no associated change in the model number.

Hi-Mound Code Practice Oscillators

Hi-Mound has been in business since just after WWII, and their keys, paddles, and bugs have a reputation for quality and reliability. The High Mound name comes from the closest English translation of the founder and president's name—the late Mr. Takatsuka. Models COK-1 and COK-2 are shown, one with and one without internal speaker. There may have been a business relation between Hi-Mound and Skillman, a producer that sent many key models to catalog sellers like Lafayette and Allied.

HH Smith Code Practice Devices

Herman H. Smith, Inc. (more commonly known as HH Smith) was founded in 1946, and conducted business from Brooklyn, New York. The top photo shows one of their code practice keys with buzzer imported from Japan. There were literally dozens of nearly identical buzzer/key sets made in Japan, then rebranded and sold under names including Herald, Calrad, Philmore, and Lafayette. Bottom photo shows HH Smith's code practice oscillator, which is very similar to units from Bud and AMECO.

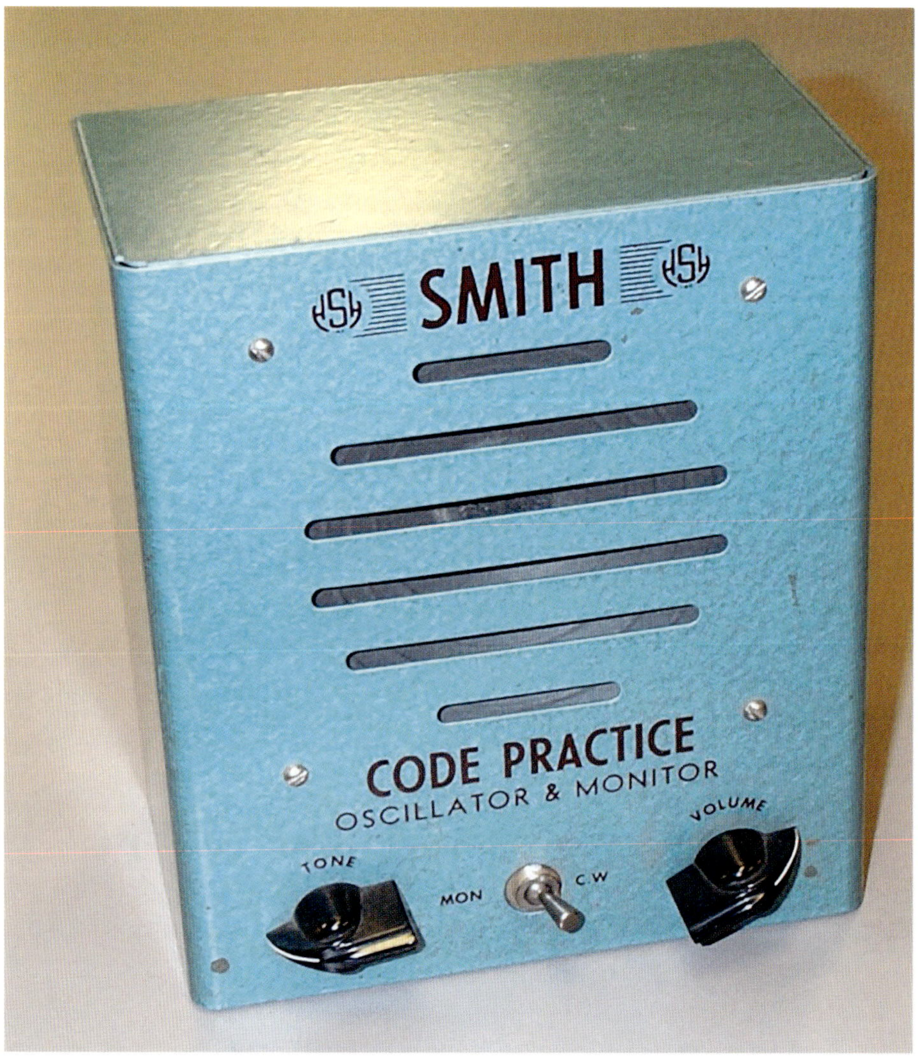

ICA Signa-Tone Oscillator

The ICA Signa-Tone used a two-tube design. Versions were available with and without internal speaker. Front panel controls were for oscillator tone (three positions) and volume. Key and headphones were plugged in the front of the units. Some variations of the internal speaker model had louvers punched in the front panel for the speaker instead of the perforated speaker cover shown.

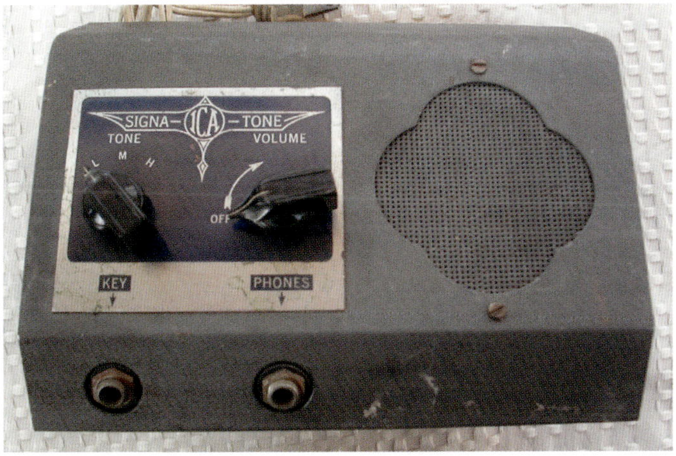

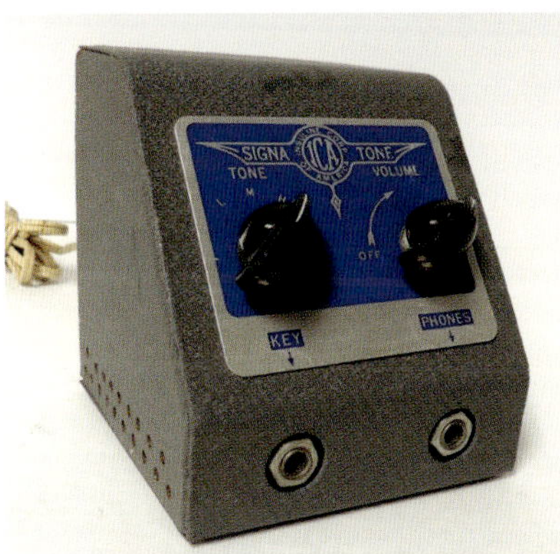

IK1OJM Register

For those who think paper tape recording registers are antique devices, here is a modern one made by IK1OJM. The felt-tip pen records the dots and dashes being received almost like the old days.

A modern-day code register.

Paper-tape recording of received Morse code.

Instructograph Code Trainer

The Instructograph was a Morse code sending machine manufactured in Chicago from about 1920 through 1983. The machines were billed as "the scientific, easy and quick way to learn the code." Instructograph machines used paper tape that was punched to correspond with the code being sent. The punched holes were detected and used to actuate a set of contacts that keyed an audio oscillator or a light bulb. The original 1920 version used a hand-wound spring-driven motor. The long production life of this training device is a bit unusual; the last version marketed was the Model 500 (bottom picture), which included a solid state oscillator, and the last advertisements were seen in the 1970 *ARRL Handbook*.

A note on early Morse code instruction machines: manufacturers included Ayers, whose ads imply some involvement with Ted McElroy, Instructograph, Teleplex, Gardiner-Levering, Gardiner, Perfectograph, Necograph, Nacrometer, and Natrometer, among others. One model of the Omnigraph training machine appeared in the 1902 Sears catalog.

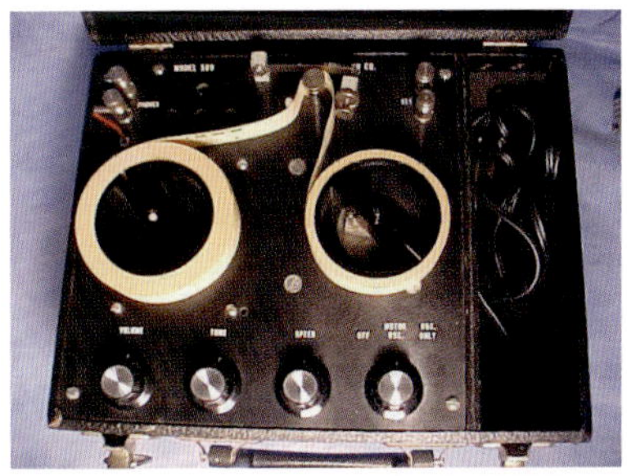

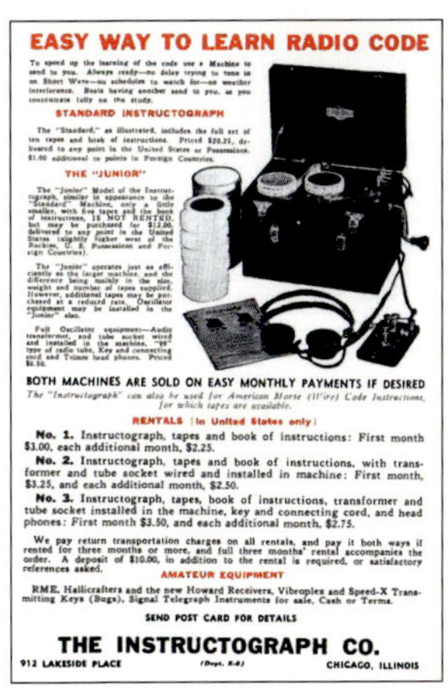

A 1938 *Radio Handbook* Instructograph advertisement.

Irwin Desman Morse Key Trainer

The Irwin Desman Morse Key Trainer is a British military device. The unit uses two internal 9 volt "PP3" batteries and features a built-in sounder with external speaker jack. Controls on the front are for volume and tone adjustments.

Japanese Type 99 CW Trainer

The Japanese Type 99 from Army Radio Sales was a WWII vintage vacuum tube unit that used either AC or DC input to power the circuitry. The unit featured a selectable tone output, and the front panel had terminals for a key connection, as well as a volume control knob.

Kantronics Code Practice Oscillator

Kantronics produced this small code practice oscillator as part of their amateur product line. This oscillator is not commonly seen. Kantronics was founded in 1971; they also made a series of small, low-power HF transceivers that sold during the 1970s and '80s.

Kantronics Mini-Reader

The Kantronics Mini-Reader sold around the 1980s and was designed to copy Morse, RTTY, and ASCII signals. The display was a 10-character blue fluorescent type, allowing for ease of reading at greater distances than other displays. The Mini-Reader also displayed Morse code speed and time of day. Although this small reader is no longer in production, Kantronics continues to make modems, TNCs, and data controllers.

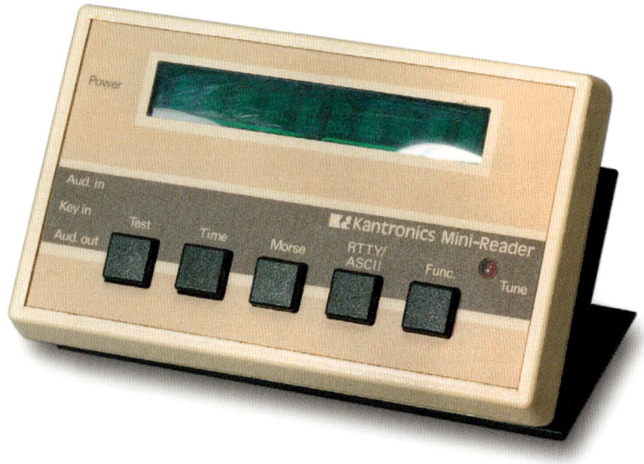

Katsumi EKM-1 Code Monitors

Two very early and basic Katsumi code monitor devices: the EKM-1 and the EKM-1A. The president of Katsumi Electric Company passed away in March 2011, and it appears the family has no interest in keeping the company going. Apparently, they have been unable to find someone to take it over. Katsumi produced excellent products that were a part of the communications scene in Japan and their products will be missed.

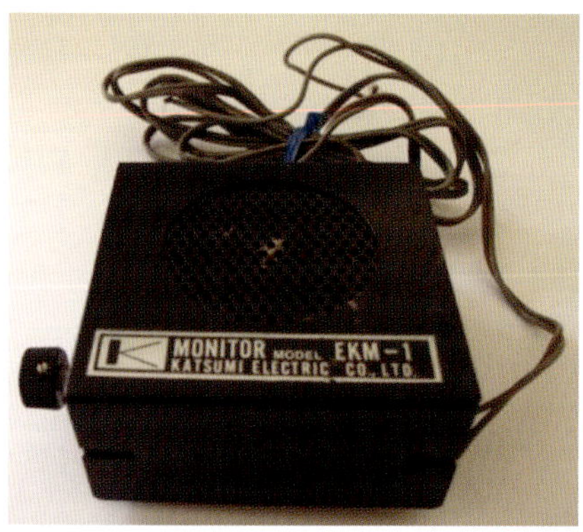

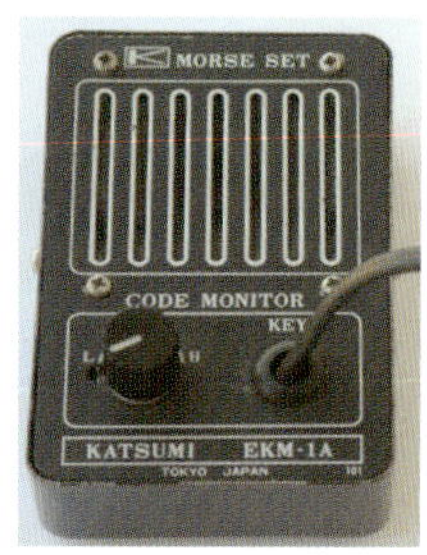

Katsumi EKM-2B Code Monitor

Katsumi's EKM-2B Code Monitor has developed a reputation for having a great sound that users claim allows for many hours of comfortable listening. Features include an on/off switch, green LED power light, adjustable sliding controls for pitch (600–1800 Hz) and volume, a headphone jack, and a jack labeled "record" that provides line-level audio for tape recorders and other recording devices.

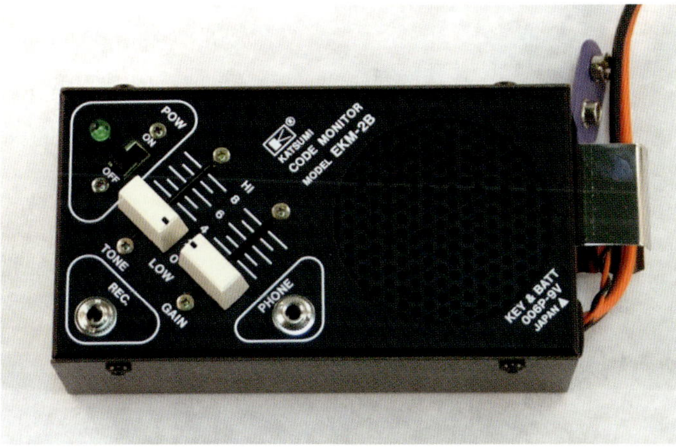

Kent Morse Trainer

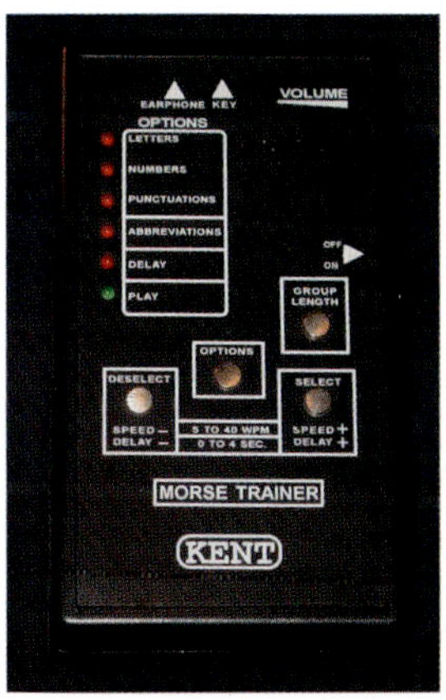

The Kent Morse Trainer generates random Morse in groups of 5, or random length groups of 1 to 8 characters. Speed range is 5–40 wpm. Letters, numbers, and punctuations can be played individually or in any combination, while the abbreviations option plays the most commonly used abbreviations at random. There is also a selectable independent delay of up to four seconds available for insertion between characters. This feature allows for listening to characters at higher speed with up to four seconds between characters, giving the student time to correctly "hear" the sent character. The Kent Trainer has a built-in loudspeaker; an earphone jack is also provided. Another useful feature allows the student to practice sending via an internal oscillator; a jack is provided for key connection. The unit runs on four internal AAA batteries.

Kent Morse Practice Oscillator

The Kent Morse practice oscillator offers an easy, portable way to learn Morse code. The device is based on a CMOS 4047 multivibrator and runs on an internal 9–volt battery. Tone pitch is adjustable from 500 Hz to 3 kHz; amplified output is approximately 0.25 watt.

R. A. Kent Engineering was founded in 1965 by the late Robert A. Kent. The present owner is his son, Robert S. Kent, who joined the firm in 1971, and took over the management of the firm in 1988. The company was originally based in Banks, Southport, but moved to Tarleton, Preston, in 1982. The family run company originally provided engineering services, starting the design and production of Morse code keys in 1983. Over the following five years, the Morse key manufacture virtually took over the business and today Morse related products constitute the majority of the business.

KEY-municator Telegraph Set

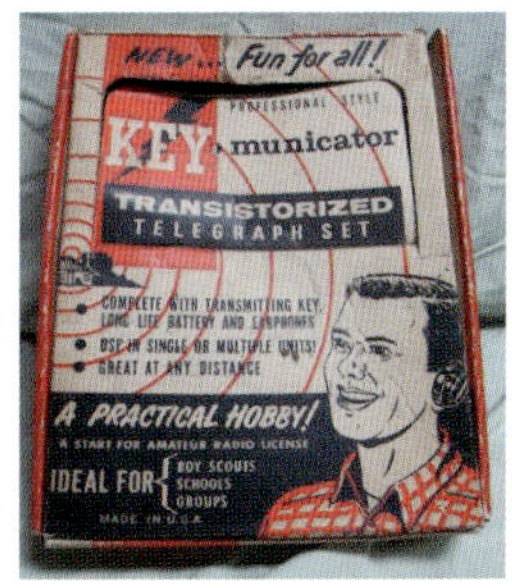

The Key-municator telegraph set is another example of a Morse telegraph based device aimed at Boy Scouts, school groups, or others of a younger age who might be interested in learning Morse code as a hobby, or as a start toward obtaining an amateur radio license.

Lafayette Code Practice Telegraphic Set

The Lafayette practice set was a small battery powered training device with a buzzer mounted underneath the base.

Lafayette Code Oscillators

The Lafayette 99-2560 Code Oscillator is another of the oscillator "cousins" that have similar circuitry and features. The device is nearly identical to the Ameco OCM, Calrad C. O. 5, Claricon 85-120, Eico 706, Midland 18-273, and the Realistic 20-007. All of these oscillators are presented in this chapter because they were so prevalent during the 1950s and 1960s, and many hams first learned Morse using them, so each slightly different front panel configuration has the capability of bringing back many memories.

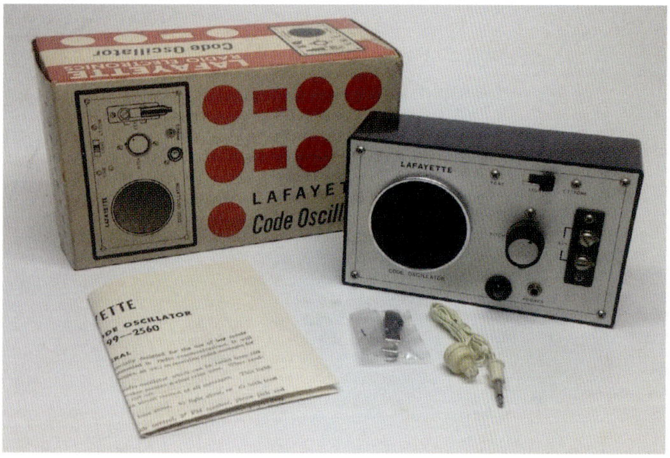

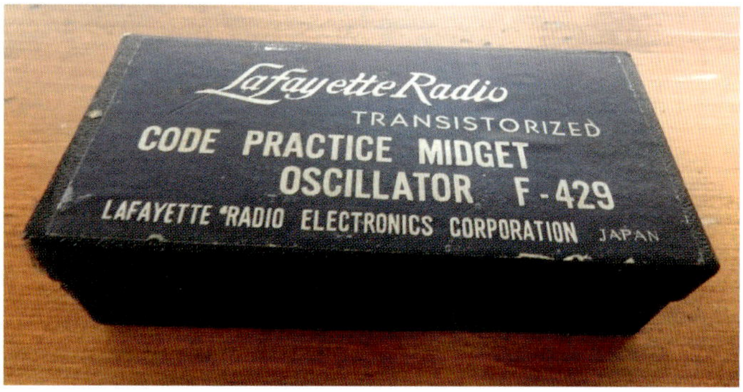

Lafayette's Model F-429 was a midget battery powered oscillator with leads provided for key hookup. An earphone was used for listening. On some units the brand name Swallow appears on the molded case of the F-429 oscillator.

Mars Code Practice Oscillator

The Mars practice oscillator was another product of the Mars amateur radio division of the Japanese Paulsan Company. In addition to the sidetone allowing for Morse practice, the unit could pick up RF and trigger the sidetone feature, providing a "monitor" for transmitted signals. This unit was powered by a 9–volt battery accessible through a compartment on the bottom of the case. Mars equipment was designed in the USA but built in Japan for the American ham market.

McElroy (TAC) Code Practice Oscillators

The Model 700 McElroy code practice oscillator was enclosed in a cast iron box. Fahnestock clip terminals were marked for headphones and a key connection. Research suggests this is a very rare unit, with only a couple known to exist. There are no volume or tone adjustments as part of this particular design and may be partly why it was never marketed for very long. The one tube used, an 117L7GT, has its number cast into the front panel. This unit dates to about the 1940s. TAC was John McElroy's Telegraph Apparatus Corporation.

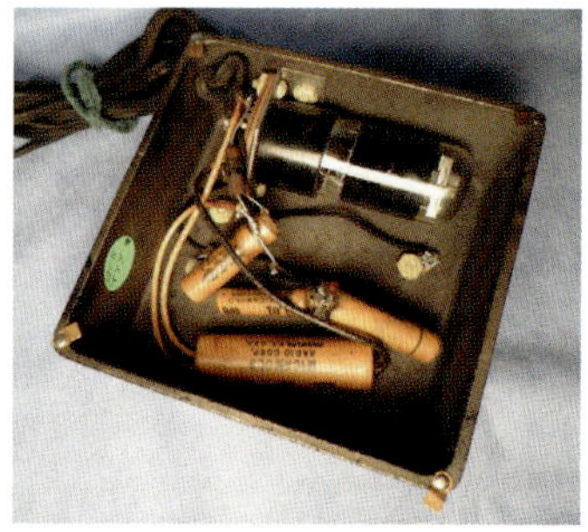

Shown below is a rare code practice oscillator from the early 1940s. The on-off switch, volume/tone controls, and screw terminals for a key connection are on the rear panel. As with the cast iron unit, this oscillator uses one 117N7GT tube. The owner of this particular device notes the speaker is unusual, having the coil mounted to the side of the cone and connected to the cone by a lever.

Some versions of the early 1940s TAC oscillators featured a key mounted inside the cabinet. The key became known as the TAC cut-off key; it protruded out of an opening in the front of the case.

One of only two known McElroy S-710 practice sets. The set consists of a cast iron base, upon which is mounted an S-700 Oscillatone oscillator—also sold separately—and an S-100 polystyrene plastic key. The S-700 oscillator has switches to set volume and tone, with a third switch to turn the unit on or off. This set appeared in a McElroy advertisement in the October 1941 *Radio* magazine, and it appeared as Model S-895 in a catalog of that era. Shortly thereafter the S-700 Oscillatone was discontinued.

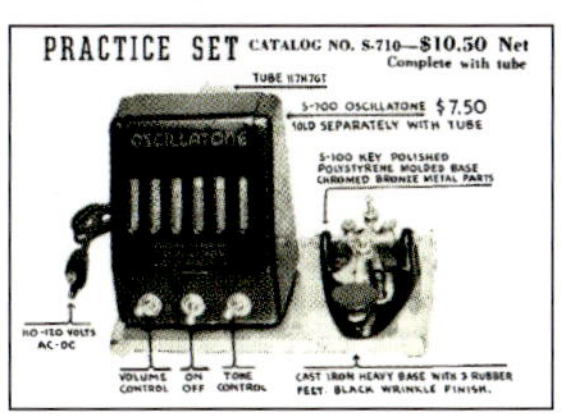

It's easy to see the effects of internal tube heating on the S-100 Oscillatone's plastic case.

Theodore R. McElroy was born in 1901, and became famous for his ability to copy Morse code at high speeds. He could copy code at 77 wpm and type at 150 wpm, giving McElroy legendary status in the telegraphy community. In 1934, McElroy began manufacturing telegraph equipment, including the famous MAC-KEY and the Streamkey. McElroy and several friends formed a partnership based in Chicago (TAC, the Telegraph Apparatus Company) to produce equipment for the commercial market. McElroy's Massachusetts company made equipment for the Signal Corps and continued production after the war, with accessories and other key models with unique variations. The Littleton, Massachusetts, operation ceased production in 1955 when the company was sold.

MFJ CPO-555 Code Oscillator

The MFJ CPO-555 code practice oscillator, as the model number hints, centered around an NE-555 timer chip. This device was first sold in 1981. Circuitry was powered by an internal 9–volt battery and included an internal speaker. The unit featured the standard volume and tone controls, as well as key and headphone jacks.

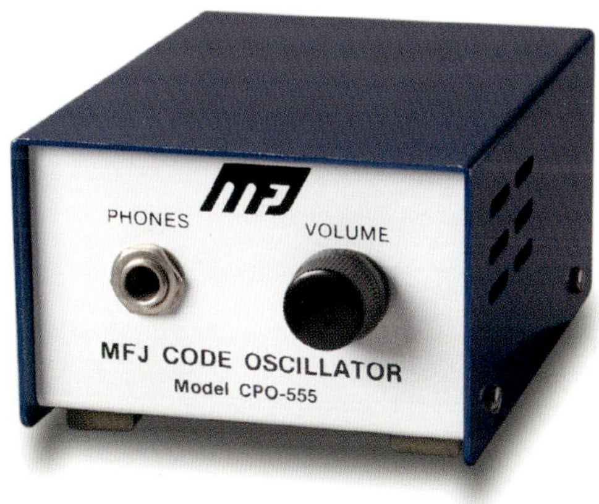

MFJ-414 Classroom Morse Tutor

The MFJ-414 is aimed at classroom Morse code instruction, but is also a full-featured memory keyer. It is capable of delivering a maximum of approximately 1.2 watts into an 8-ohm load. The amplifier circuitry is designed to produce a true sinewave sidetone with no harsh keyclicks. A serial port allows uploading and downloading of custom practice groups from a computer. Storage

is provided for 16 FCC exams—an attractive bonus for volunteer examiners. Morse test answers can be printed via the rear panel printer port and a tape output is provided for recording devices. The memory keyer offers 1,000 character memory. The MFJ-414 requires either 115 VAC or 12 volt DC for operation.

MFJ-464 CW Keyer/Reader

The MFJ-464 is a combination Morse code reader with built-in keyer. The scrolling LCD display allows the operator to see text messages and received Morse. The design includes a type-ahead buffer, message memories, and adjustments for speed and volume. This unit uses a standard AT computer keyboard.

MFJ-557 Practice Oscillator

The MFJ-557 Deluxe Morse Code Practice Oscillator features a Morse code straight key on a non-skid heavy steel base. Included are volume control, tone control, and an earphone jack for private listening. Although a built-in speaker is included, a jack for an external speaker is also provided. The MFJ-557 is powered by a 9–volt battery or 110 VAC.

MFJ-418 Pocket Morse Tutor

The MFJ Pocket Morse Tutor is a small, convenient training device able to help the student learn Morse code almost anywhere. It allows for generation of fixed sets of characters, with previously learned sets combined with new sets to reinforce earlier learning. Morse used for practice can be replayed to verify copy by using the 2-line LCD display. This device also offers a word recognition mode that sends hundreds of commonly used words in ham radio, allowing for practice of word reception. The user can select letters, numbers, punctuation, prosigns, FCC character sets, random call signs, random words, QSOs, or combination sets for practice. Also selectable is normal or Farnsworth spacing. Speed is adjustable from 10–60 wpm. This MFJ tutor uses a

sinewave oscillator that gives a more pleasant tone than some other timer generated square-wave oscillators. The user can select earphones or a built-in speaker, and it is powered by an internal 9–volt battery.

Microcraft Morse-A-Word

The Microcraft Morse-A-Word code reader decoded CW using audio output from the receiver. Decoded Morse was displayed on an eight-character scrolling display. It featured a speed range of 5–35 wpm. A smaller four-character model was also available. The Microcraft Corporation was in Thiensville, Wisconsin; they produced this code reader beginning in 1979.

Microcraft also made this smaller code scanner that could decode Morse, Baudot, and ASCII. The scanner offered a Morse training feature that displayed the sent code as the user practiced.

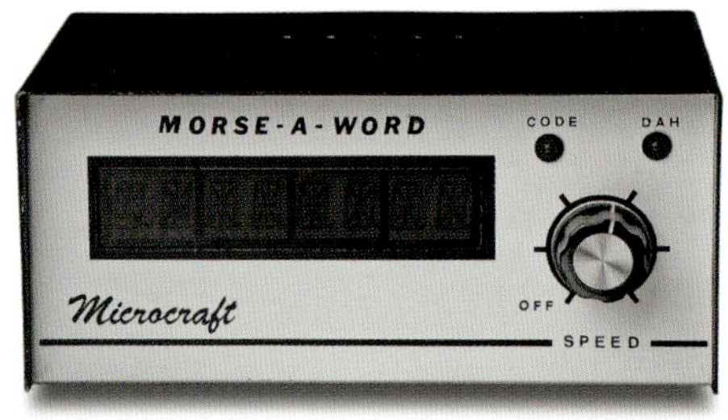

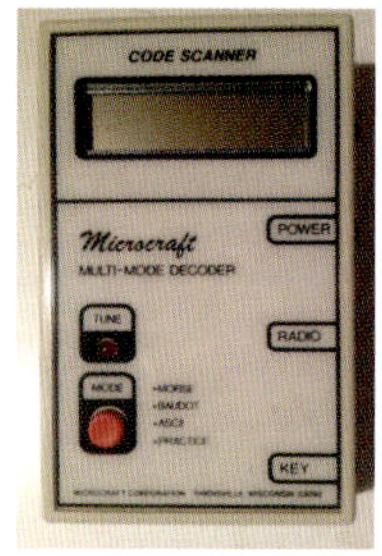

Microwave Modules Morse Talker MMS 1

The MMS 1 is a Morse tutor that utilizes a microprocessor based speech synthesis feature. Different combinations of letters and numbers can be selected for Morse training, and speeds are variable (2–20 wpm). Although an internal speaker is included, there is a headphone jack on the rear panel. The MMS 1 is ideal for Morse practice while using the built-in sidetone. Additional EPROM memory can be added, allowing the operator to increase speed range up to 48 wpm. This device operates on 12 volts DC.

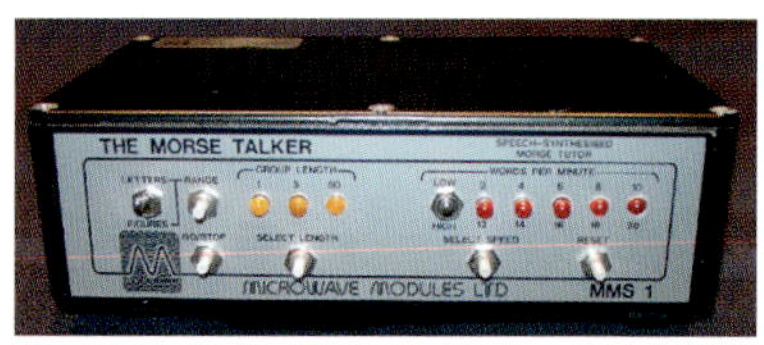

Microwave Modules Advanced Morse Trainer MMS 2

Like its MMS 1 sibling, the MMS 2 is also a speaking Morse tutor that uses synthesized speech as part of the training approach. The MMS 2 offers random code practice and adds features to improve the user's sending skills. The MMS 2 can copy what the user has sent and let the user know immediately whether the code was sent correctly. Improperly sent code triggers a loud 80 Hz tone. Both MMS units were sold around 1984.

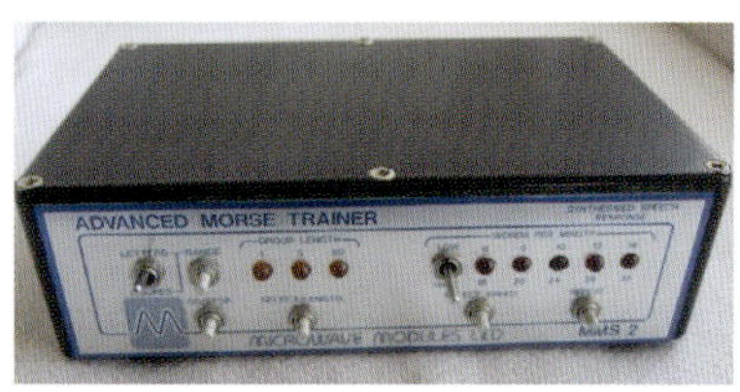

Midland 18-273 Oscillator

The Midland 18-273 Code Oscillator is another similar commercial code practice oscillator. Like the others, such as the AMECO and Eico, this unit offered variable tone (pitch) control and selectable light or tone output. Key and headphone connections were provided.

Morse Code Trainer

The Morse Code Trainer is a good example of the many lab kits aimed at the younger generation. This trainer was a 9–volt battery powered lab kit aimed at those interested in not only learning Morse code, but in basic electronics assembly. The design used a single transistor and provided a place to connect an external key.

N4YG Precision Sidetone/Code Practice Oscillator

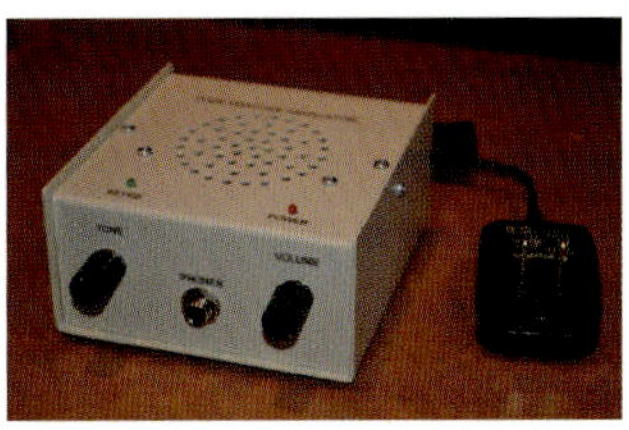

N4YG states a nice sounding sidetone requires a good sine wave and proper shaping of the leading and trailing edges of the keyed waveform. He described his approach to me as follows:

While analog techniques can provide a good sidetone, direct digital synthesis (DDS) has been found to provide a superior sound. While it may seem difficult and overkill for audio applications, the implementation at audio frequencies is much simpler than with RF. The only active component, other than a 5 volt regulator, is a single 18-pin 16F88. The hardware is not only simple but inexpensive, yet it provides a predictable, repeatable and stable sidetone. The frequency determining components normally seen in analog sidetone circuits are absent in the DDS circuit. The internal 8 MHz oscillator in the 16F88 provides the timing for the entire operation. The leading and trailing edges are digitally shaped so that popping and thumping is eliminated to the extent not possible in analog circuits. The entire circuit is contained on a PC board measuring 1.2 by 3.0 inches. It is specifically designed for older Ten-Tec rigs and interfaces with the audio and keying circuits with 4 connections through which the board receives power and keying and output the sidetone to the audio amplifier in the transceiver. Output level and tone are adjustable with trim pots on the board. The printed circuit board has been designed so that it can also be used as a code practice oscillator. An audio amplifier is provided which gives ample sound even for demonstrations. Some components positions are left unfilled in either the sidetone or code practice application with only the components required installed.

Nacometer Automatic Code Transmitter

The Nacometer Automatic Code Transmitter was made in the 1920s for the National Radio Institute of Washington, DC. The Nacometer is a spring-wound device with a removable hand crank that uses paper tape wound on wooden spools. The user was instructed to connect a battery and a sounder to the terminals and the paper tape acted like a set of contacts to close the circuit. An adjustable lever on top allows the user to set speed. Housing is red cloth-covered fiberboard with metal fittings and includes a leather handle. Peerless made a similar set called the Signagraph Code Tracker for the Radio Institute of America.

For some years NRI aimed their ads at those interested in becoming a ship radio operator. At least one ad for NRI in the January 1928 *Popular Mechanics* mentioned NRI code courses included the Natrometer code machine, a mechanical metal code wheel device made by the Natrometer Corporation of Washington, DC. An NRI ad appearing in *Popular Mechanics* in October 1929 is visually very similar, except now the included code machine is a Nacometer, which is the paper tape machine shown. It is understandable that the names of these two machines could become interchangeable over time, especially given their connection to NRI.

NUE-PSK Digital Modem

The NUE-PSK Digital Modem is a fairly new device that dates to around 2008; it was designed for PSK31, RTTY, and CW field use by W8NUE without the need for a computer interface. The NUE-PSK is a standalone, battery-operated digital modem using a dsPIC33F microcontroller. The NUE-PSK uses a single graphic display showing transmit and receive text data, band spectrum, and tuning indication. When coupled with an SSB-capable transceiver and a standard PS2 keyboard, the NUE-PSK Digital Modem forms an effective, compact, and portable station for working the digital modes on the amateur bands. This device has the ability to copy low, nearly inaudible signals and is ideally suited for low power QRP enthusiasts. Version 4 software gives the operator CW mode capability, offering a combined CW reader and Morse keyboard. Transmit speed is 1–50 wpm. Additionally, version 5 software adds a CW direct mode, allowing the user to connect directly to a CW rig for digital mode (CW) QSOs by connecting the modem's push-to-talk (PTT) line to the transceiver's key in line or PTT.

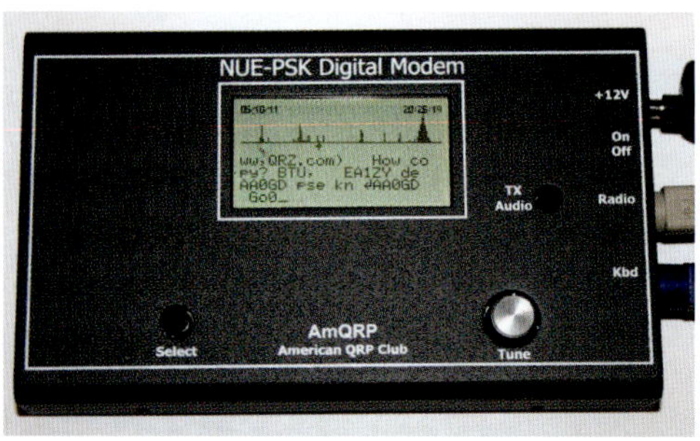

Omnigraph Trainers

An Omnigraph transmitter (date unknown) from an ad appearing in the MESCO (Manhattan Electrical Supply Company) catalog. As described, the device allowed the user to select a Morse code letter and a speed, and then automatically send the letter. This device apparently is the first of many in a series of trainers called Omnigraphs; several other models are shown.

"OMNIGRAPH" TRANSMITTER.

LIST No. 177.

To be used in circuit with Learner's telegraph set, or local sounder.

The very best way to learn to read by sound is in a telegraph office with the aid of an expert operator. But it is not always convenient or possible to have this advantage.

The "OMNIGRAPH" will bring that telegraph office to you, including the expert operator. The Transmitter allows you to tick off a message containing every letter in the Morse alphabet absolutely correct and at any speed you desire. The dots, dashes and spaces can be seen as well as heard; it makes learning easy as well as interesting.

Messages 5 x 5 x 2 inches. Weight 1 lb. with book, "How to Become an Expert Operator." Guaranteed to work perfectly with any instrument or on any line.

Fourteen extra dials, each containing a message, the set constituting a comprehensive dispatch of three hundred words, all the letters, numerals, punctuation marks, etc. The dials can be changed about, making new messages without limit, and you cannot anticipate more than in ordinary commercial practice.

List No.		Price.
177	"OMNIGRAPH" Transmitter with one dial, A to Z	$3.80
174	Extra Dials	.20

These various Omnigraph trainer models generated Morse code by using indented metal discs turned by a hand-wound clockwork motor. A stylus was set up against the metal indentations, completing a circuit contact corresponding to the Morse code desired to be sent. These machines were frequently distributed as part of mail order Morse code courses.

The Omnigraph first came out in 1901; it was made by the Omnigraph Manufacturing Co. of New York City. In 1918, the Electro Importing Co. of New York advertised them starting at $16 for a five disk machine and $23 for a fifteen disk model. Additional disks were available at five for $1. Different Omnigraph models used different stylus arrangements, interchangeable metal disks, methods of controlling speed, and hand crank vs. electric clock motor power. In the unit shown, the motor drove a stacked assembly of thin interchangeable metal disks bearing the code characters. A metal arm/follower device rode along the disc edge and performed the keying according to indentations on the disc. From 5 to 10 discs could be stacked together, and by adjusting the arm/follower up or down, different character group sequences could be sent. The machine offered a speed range of about 5 to over 60 wpm. Speed was adjustable by moving a brake lever that regulated a flyball governor on the motor.

The Omnigraphs were frequently used for administering code tests, as well as for basic learning, but once paper tape code machines began to appear, the metal disc designs became obsolete.

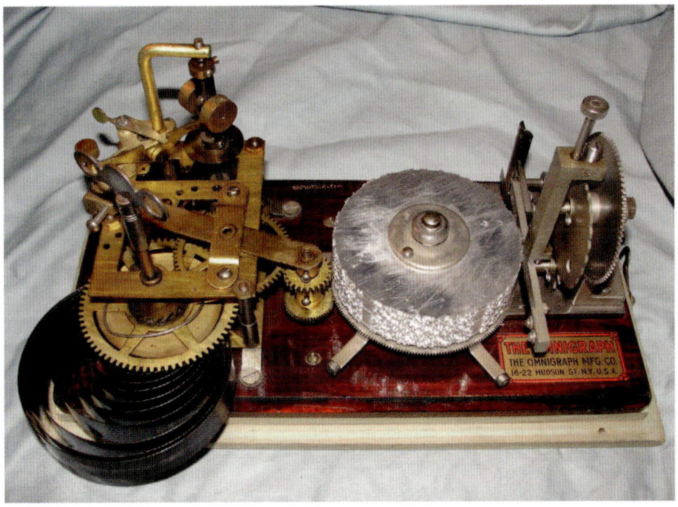

Palm Radio Tone Tube

Palm Radio developed the Tone Tube in response to inquiries about a small oscillator that would work with Palm mini keys and paddles. The Tone Tube contains a speaker mounted in a resonator, and is designed to mount to Palm keys. The device will work with other external keys or paddles. The sidetone produced is adjustable in frequency and volume, and a jack for headphones is provided. The Tone Tube is powered by an integral CR2032 battery that should last 100–200 hours. A built-in LED gives optical indication of keying.

Perry Radio Blinker Signal Set

The Perry Radio Blinker Set was made by Frank B. Perry of Newton Center, Massachusetts (see label), and patented in 1917 (1,238,937). This set was a WWI military training device made under contract for the US Army Air Service. It used an internal battery housed in a wooden box with a buzzer and code key on top. A metal lever allowed the user to select buzzer or light; the user could then practice sending Morse code. Two of these units could be connected together for sending to each other. The buzzer included a screw that allowed for some adjustment in tone. Two different models are shown.

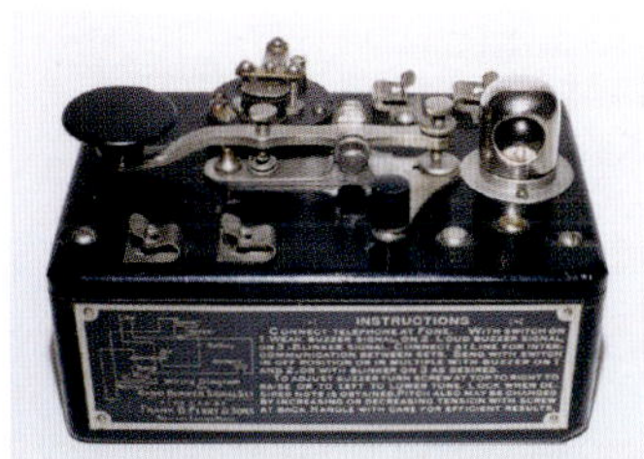

Philmore Telegraph Code Practice Set

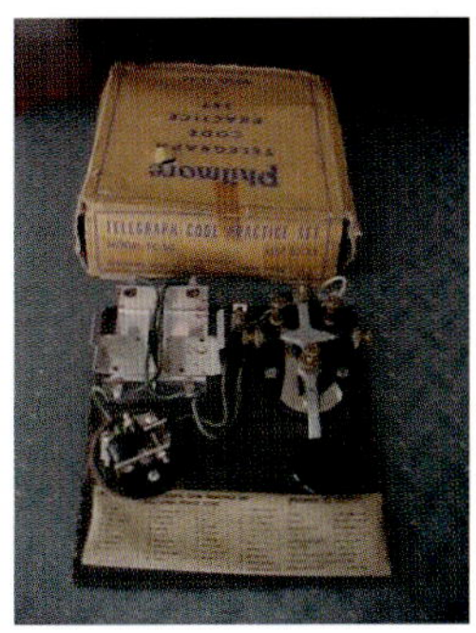

This code practice set was made by the Philmore Manufacturing Company of New York; it is powered by two batteries installed in the metal holder. The user practices Morse code sending using the attached hand key and buzzer. Philmore made several different models of code buzzer practice sets, some made in Japan. The Model TC 50 pictured used a Lionel J-38 key and dates to WWII.

Poly Electronic Decoders

Poly Electronic was a Swiss company that produced several models of decoders in the 1980s. Most of the Pocom models (as they were known) were used for RTTY, although several offered CW decode capability, including the AFR-1000, AFR-2010, and AFR-8000. The Pocom Model AFR-2000 was identical to the AFR-2010, except it did not offer the CW decode module. Pocom decoders typically featured Baudot, ASCII, and AMTOR decoding, automatic speed and shift recognition, and display capability using an external monitor. In 1985, the developer of the Pocom decoders, Mr. Christian Kesselring, formed the Wavecom Company in Hohentengen, Germany. Wavecom produces the Model W 4010 decoder, as well as other high reliability decoding and surveillance gear.

Postal Telegraph De Luxe Set

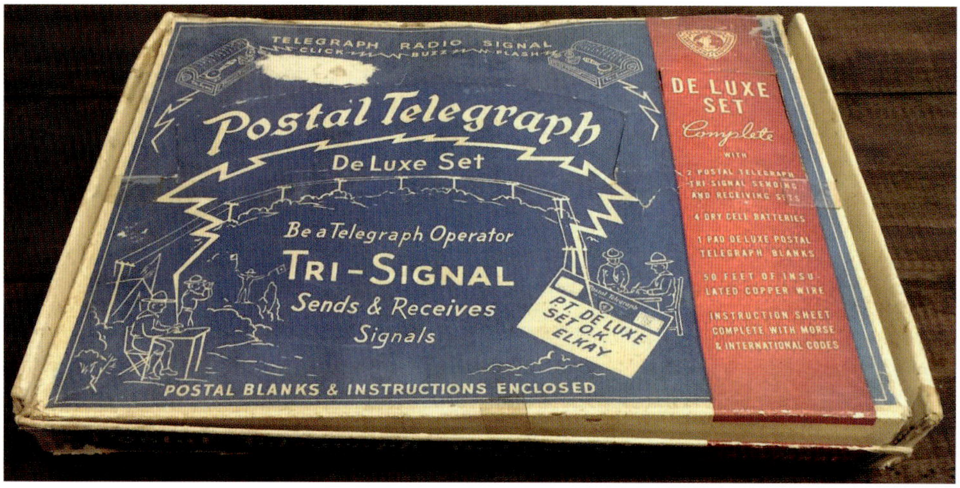

The Postal Telegraph set dates to the 1940s and 1950s, and was aimed at getting boys interested in Morse telegraphy as a career. A similar set was also sold under the Western Union name.

Realistic Code Practice Oscillators

This 20-005 version of the Radio Shack (Realistic) code practice oscillator is meant to be a portable device. This oscillator uses essentially the same circuit as the one-transistor version (opposite), with similar features. The Realistic manual states this unit was designed for Boy Scouts, novice radio amateurs, and groups interested in radio communication. The two terminals seen on top of this unit allow two of these oscillators to be connected together for 2-way communication.

The Realistic 20-007 Code Oscillator is yet another variation of similar commercial code practice oscillators. This unit also offered variable tone (pitch) control and selectable light or tone output; one cosmetic deviation is the use of a square speaker grille. Key and headphone connections were provided for the user.

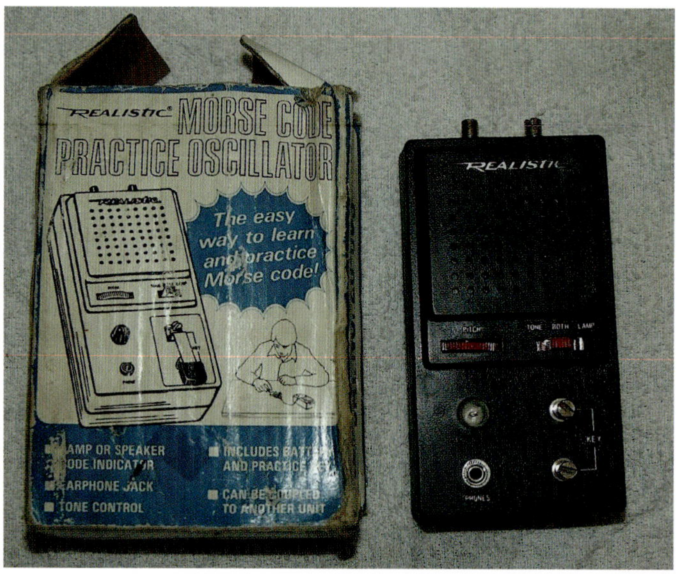

Russian Morse Code Training Set

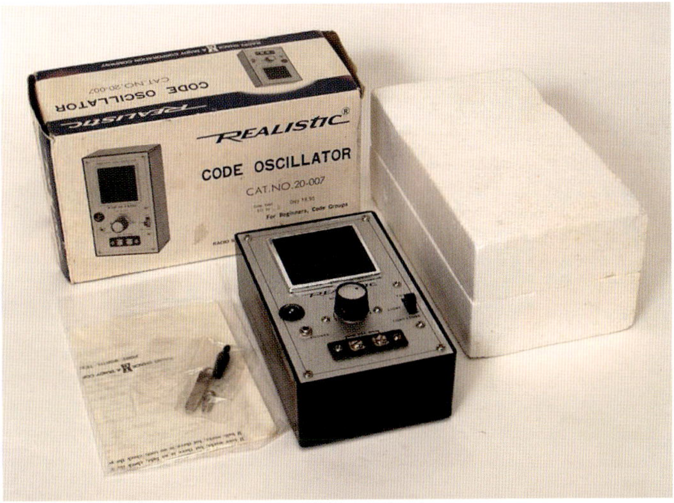

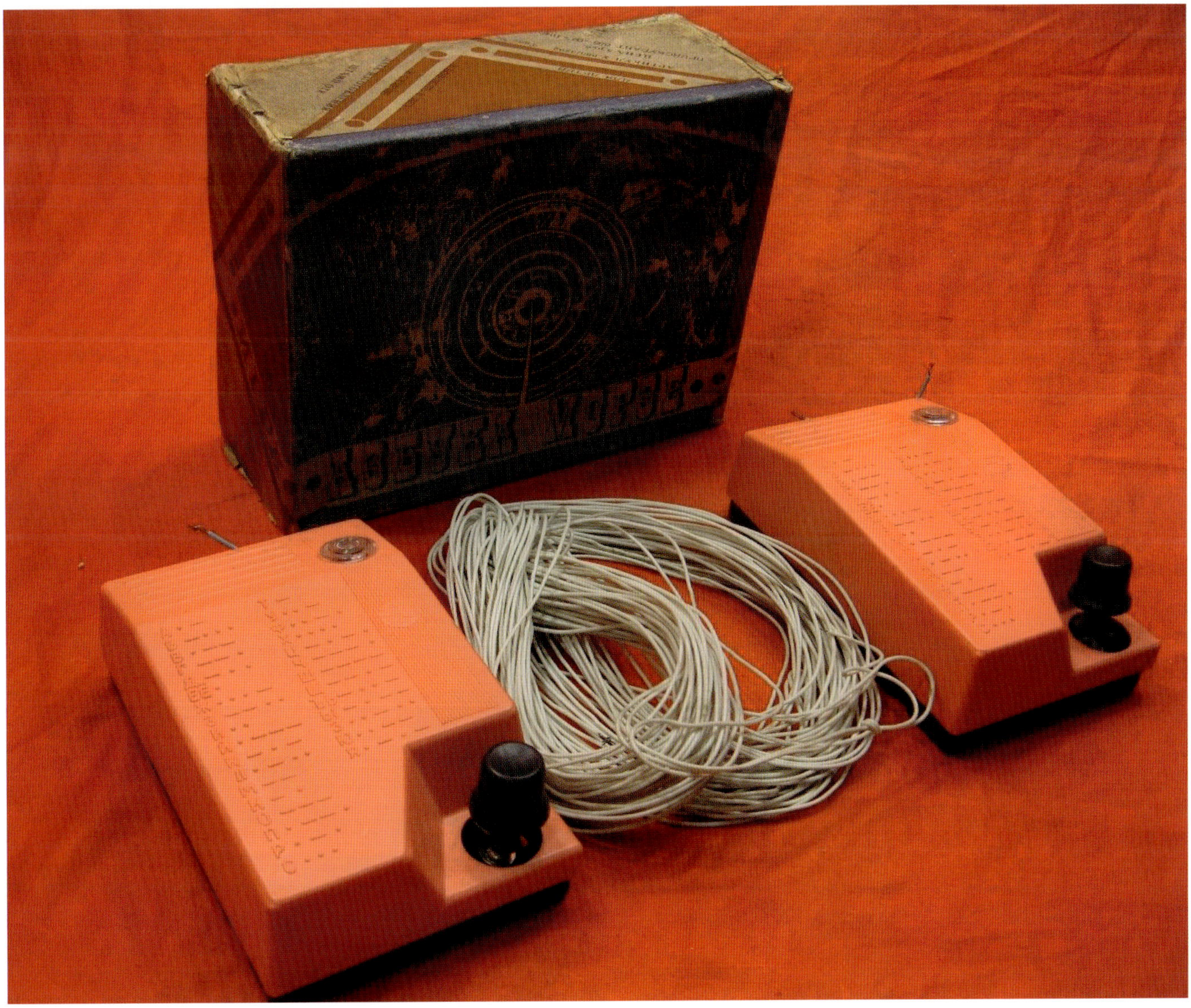

A Russian Morse code training outfit; little else is known about this set, but it appears to date to the 1950s.

Signal Corps Keyer Trainers

These Signal Corps Morse trainers are very similar in design and share a common operating manual. Morse code is generated using marked paper tape and a photocell detector. Units use two tubes and have an internal speaker. The left photo shows the KY-127/GG, while the other two photos show the TG-34-A trainer. The Army technical manual tells us the units differ, as the TG-34-A has auxiliary photoelectric cell control and provisions for adjusting the exciter lamp.

The KY-127/GG Trainer.

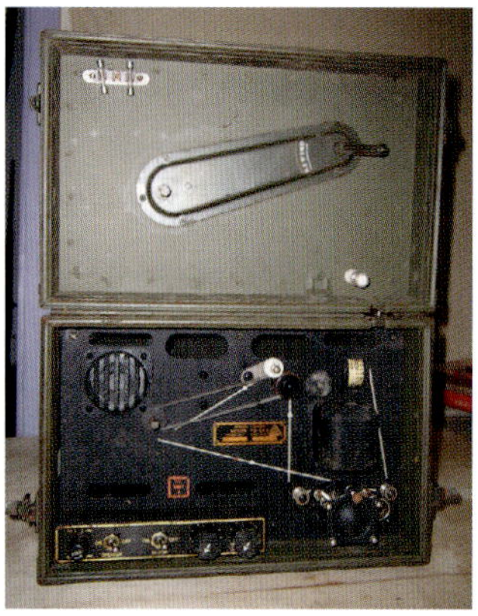

The TG-34-A Trainer.

Signal Electric Practice Set

The Signal Electric Company of Menominee, Michigan, manufactured this R-68 Morse practice set using a high-quality hand key and buzzer. Some units show the manufacturer as Menominee Manufacturing Company (right). They also made the Signal Jr. (above right).

Manufacturers frequently advertised their buzzers as having pleasing tones or tones that sounded like commercial radio station emissions. Many buzzers included a control to vary the pitch of the tone, in an attempt to make the sound less annoying. At least one proclaimed the adjustment let the user instantly vary the pitch to a soft, low hum to rest the ear.

Space Station Morse Code Signaling Set

The Space Station Morse code generating set makes a great example of the many Morse related "toys" available in the 1940s and 1950s. These sets encouraged learning of Morse code and provided a gateway for many to enter commercial radio, ham radio, or even technical careers.

Speed-X Practice Set

Many manufacturers had a version of the hand key / buzzer Morse practice set. This is the one Speed-X sold, their Model 450.

Swallow Model DTO-2 CPO

The Swallow DTO-2 was typical of many of the small, transistorized code practice oscillators coming out of Japan in the 1960s. This model featured a built-in speaker and tone adjustment. Swallow was a Dentsu-Seiki brand; they also produced a black plastic-based semi-automatic key.

Triplex Radio and Telegraph Code Practice Set

The Tri-Signal was made by the Insuline Corporation of America, in New York City. ICA also made Morse code oscillators: one in a metal case called a "table model," as well as several models of broadcast receivers. Later, in the 1930s, Insuline made several models of mechanical televisions. Insuline also worked with the US Naval Training School to present a Morse code training course consisting of ten lessons on double-sided gramophone records.

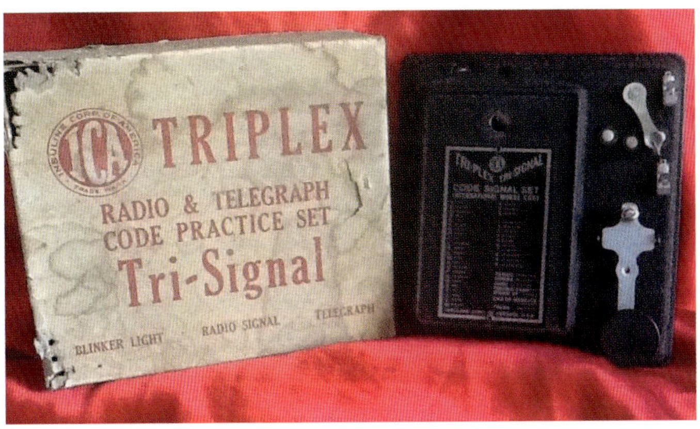

Triplex Signal Set for Boys

The Triplex set for boys was manufactured by the Connecticut Telephone and Electric Corporation of Meriden, Connecticut. CTE also made industrial wall-mount intercoms and other telephone models, as well as audio amplifiers, radio receiver parts, and an early airplane transmitter.

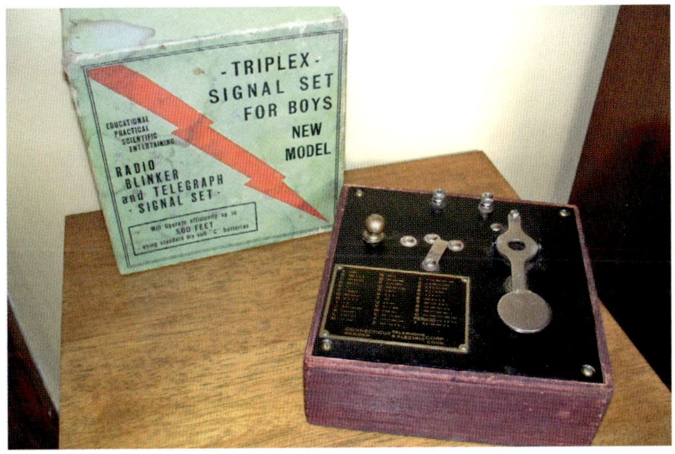

Vibroplex Code Practice Oscillator Kit

Vibroplex code practice oscillators (CPOs) are available in two models and are ideal for Boy Scout or radio club classes. Either unit is an inexpensive solution for Morse code practice, or as a basic electronic construction project. Included in the kit are the circuit board and speaker; the user must add a code key and a 9–volt battery. The circuit design produces a 700 Hz tone from an LM386 audio chip with 350 mW audio output. Their CPO Plus model includes a two-wire cable for your key connection.

Wavecom W 4010 Decoder

The Wavecom Company was founded in 1965 by Christian Kesseling in Hohentengen, Germany. Wavecom's W 4010 is known as a very high quality and versatile CW and teletype decoder. The decoder uses the line out signal from any receiver, and provides connections for an external video monitor to display decoded text. Other outputs are included for a Centronics compatible printer or serial RS232. The Wavecom's front panel features a power-on button and function keys for various optional modules. A Print button switches on the printer port. Other indicators are for Baudot and RTTY modes. The two knobs are used to adjust the bandwidth of the audio filter and for signal level for CW decoding. Power required is 12–14 volts DC.

Western Union Radio Telegraph Signal Set

A Western Union Radio Signal Set made by the S. B. Manufacturing Company of Brooklyn, New York.

3 The Electronic Keyer

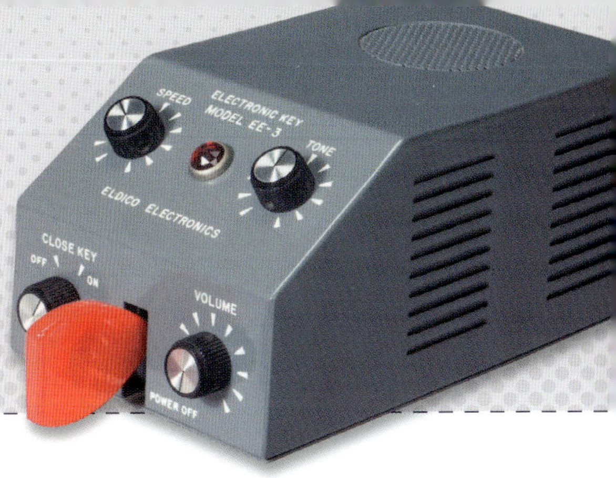

Most early electronic keyer designs resulted from homebrewers' efforts and were documented in patents or amateur radio journal articles. The first keyers were electro-mechanical or used tubes; the 1960s saw transition to solid state devices such as the transistor, and then to integrated circuits. Keyer designs continued to evolve in the 1970s and 1980s, moving to smaller sizes permitted by the use of specialty keyer chips and (into the 1990s and 2000s) microprocessors and microcontrollers.

The importance of the electronic keyer to Morse code transmitting capability cannot be overstated. The keyer was mostly responsible for higher Morse code sending speeds and corresponding receiving ability, less repetitive motion injuries from semi-automatic bugs, and new integral features for keyers, such as sidetone and memory. A careful read of some early automatic keyer patents and related journal articles shows a large part of the motivation behind initial development was to eliminate repetitive motion. Operators were taken with the automatic dots that semi-automatic bugs like the Vibroplex provided, but they wanted automatic dashes too, as well as the extra speed. Designs for many of the early tube-type keyers and paddles that appeared in journal articles in the early and mid-1940s can be credited to homebrewers, as can many of the advancements of the 1950s, such as memory and fully electronic circuitry.

The first "memory" keyers used that term to indicate the keyer had dot and dash memory. As electronic keyer design progressed, iambic keyers were introduced and message memory was added as a feature. New circuit designs using microprocessors and microcontrollers allowed for the addition of even more new keyer features, such as beacon modes, serial number generation, and QSO simulators. Advancements in keyer chips allowed for size reduction and led to built-in keyers inside transmitters or transceivers.

Some of the first homebrew and even commercial electronic keyers—such as the Mon-Key and the Eldico—included a paddle as an integral part of the keyer design; this was mostly because separate paddles were not readily available. The majority of hams who wanted a separate paddle either made their own or modified existing bugs. The limitations of basic integral paddles or modified bugs quickly became apparent. The electronic keyer then drove the innovation behind paddle development; the T.O. keyer (1959) should get a lot of credit for this. New paddle designs like the Vibro-Keyer in 1960 were followed by dual-lever devices such as the Nikey. Soon paddles with new approaches were introduced, such as the FYO with its needle bearings. Later paddles using magnets in place of springs (like the N2DAN) became popular. What history shows is that this parallel evolution of paddles and keyers actually worked together, alternating step by step to redefine the state-of-the-art and help create better CW.

The two paddles described in the 1940 *QST* articles on Beecher and Grammer keyers were pre-leading edge; they appeared years ahead of their commercial paddle relatives. Because they are very much a part of the keyer history that is presented, and to preserve continuity of thought, I have chosen to include some information on these unique paddles in this keyer chapter; more detail on them is provided in the paddle chapters. Many of the early keyers presented here were likely one-of-a-kind, and few if any photos still exist. I have chosen to use what is available, even though photo or scan quality is poor. My assumption is the reader would prefer to see even a marginal quality image of these valuable historical items rather than no image at all.

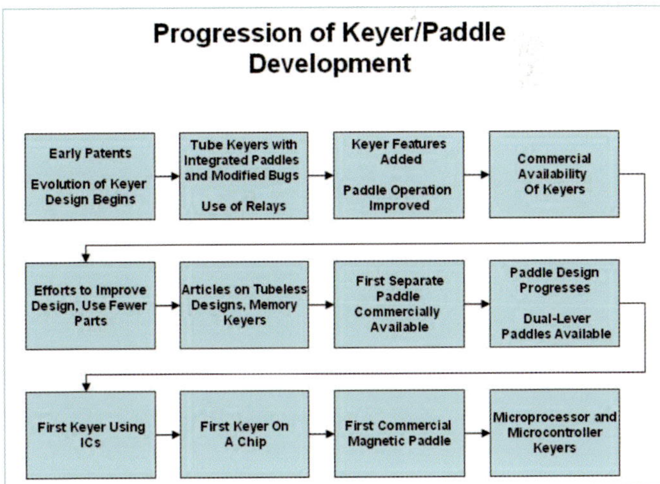

The First Ten Years, 1932–1942

Some of the earliest electronic keyer ideas were documented in patents or journal articles—mostly in *QST*. Almost all sources reviewed by the author cite Harry Beecher (W2ILE) as having written the first article on electronic Morse code manipulation.

Beecher's first article appeared in the April 1940 *QST*. Over time, the 1940 date of that article has been widely assumed to be the birth date of the electronic keyer. It is important to realize an article publication date is not necessarily where one should affix a starting point. There are several other claims, articles, and patents that, when examined, can help determine when the historical beginnings of the electronic keyer took place. For this reason, a more focused look at some electronic keyer articles and patents 1932–1942 is important.

It is my belief that the first conceptual presentation of the electronic keyer occurred in December 1932, with the submission of the Ward Roswell patent application for an electronic keying device. Therefore, the electronic keyer is much older than existing literature assumes. Roswell's patent (1,928,967) was issued in October 1933, and covered "improvements in keying devices for code sending." Roswell's intention was to minimize the number of hand movements required to send code, thereby reducing operator strain and fatigue. The concept also presented a way to control time intervals in code sending while automatically generating dots and dashes. Roswell's invention used a relay in combination with charge and discharge of a capacitor through a resistance, with the rate of charge and discharge adjustable to produce dots and dashes. Roswell claims use of a "special side action key" that obviously refers to a paddle device used to actuate the keyer. The patent states: "a special side action key is associated with the relay circuit in such manner that a succession of dots will automatically be transmitted so long as the key is held to one side of its neutral position; similarly a succession of dashes will be transmitted while the key is deflected to the opposite side of neutral. In the neutral position the relay is stalled and no signals sent."

In 1932, Roswell had envisioned a device to automatically send dots and dashes, and the special key required to actuate the device. Apparently, Roswell was not an amateur radio operator, and he does not appear to have followed up on any commercialization of his device. In 1937, F. A. Bartlett (W6OWP) began experimenting with ways to automate sending. His first keyer prototype used a relay and a series capacitance timing circuit; the approach sounds very similar to the Roswell concept. It is not unlikely that Bartlett picked up Roswell's idea and began efforts to develop it further, although no evidence was found to support this hypothesis. Bartlett's prototype keyer is shown; the drawing is by Dale Martin (W7LOG) from the *N7CFO Keyletter*.

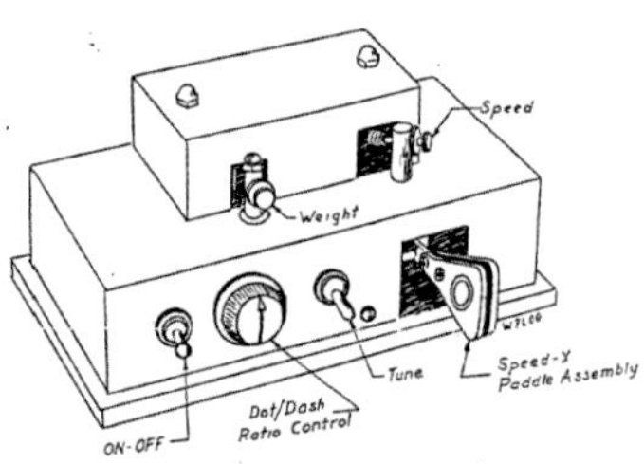

The early Bartlett design was the vbasis for the commercial Duomatic AK-7 keyer offered in the 1940s. Bartlett applied for a patent in May 1944 that was issued in March 1948 (2,437,497). This patent claimed several refinements for the automatic telegraph key. Soon Bartlett built a second keyer prototype using a dual-purpose 117L7 tube and a modified Speed-X bug for the keying mechanism. After further development this model was sold commercially as the AK-7. Bartlett later produced the Duomatic Auto-Key (model AKS-7), featuring integral paddles and the tube design. Bartlett was first licensed in the 1930s. In addition to the electronic keyer designs he worked on, Bartlett was also involved with ham radio radioteletype (RTTY) operating. Bartlett died on July 3, 2006, at 92.

QST ad for the Duomatic AK-7.

Several other inventors were also at work experimenting with electronic keyers. Howard F. Mason, licensed as 7BK in 1917, designed and built the Moto-Key at his home in Seattle, Washington. The Moto-Key was described in an April 1939 *QST* article on new apparatus.

The Moto-Key was not an electronic keyer per se, but was functionally the same; the Moto-Key could be more accurately called an electrical/mechanical keyer. Dashes and dots were formed automatically by the Moto-Key. The 1939 *QST* review describes the Moto-Key's operation:

The Moto-Key with cover installed.

Inside view of the Moto-Key.

> The mechanism includes a 110–volt AC induction motor, which is geared through suitable speed-changing cones to a spindle carrying two pairs of friction discs. Associated with these discs or clutches are two cams, one for sending dots and spaces and one for sending dashes and spaces. One or the other of these cams is released to revolve by pressing the operating lever to the left or to the right. Either cam will continue to revolve and repeat its proper-length dots or dashes and spaces so long as the lever is held over and will continue to revolve to complete its cycle after the lever has been released. An interlock prevents one cam from releasing until the other has finished its cycle. It is not necessary to hold the lever over for the entire duration of a dot or dash; an instantaneous contact will release either. The human element enters only in spacing. While it is impossible to run characters together by cutting spaces too short, the space length in other respects must be controlled by the operator.

Speed is at an enforced even rate adjustable from approximately 18 to 40 words per minute.

N7CFO reports three Moto-Keys were manufactured. The first was sold to a radio operator in Bremerton, Washington, who used it at the Navy station; its whereabouts are unknown. The second was scrapped by Howard Mason to fix the third one, which was sold on August 31, 1992, to N7CFO. The Moto-Keys were not serially numbered or otherwise marked.

Bernard Breedlove (N4BKR) is famous among key collectors for his Codetrol semi-automatic bugs. Not as well known is that Breedlove claims to have invented the electronic keyer. Breedlove applied for a patent on his keyer idea in February 1940, and it was issued in November 1942 (2,302,290). The Breedlove patent cited presented his concept of a telegraph key and associated circuitry to form automatic dots and dashes. The Codetrol keyer entry in this chapter shows what is believed to be an early Breedlove keyer and a Codetrol paddle.

The April 1940 edition of *QST* carried the frequently referenced Harry Beecher W2ILE article on electronic keying. The circuit is based on a triode Type 885 tube and offers speeds of 15–40 wpm. Extensive explanations of circuit function are given, as well as construction details. Details were included for construction of a key for optional use with the keyer, although Beecher recommended a modified bug be used as the actuating mechanism for the keyer. This article may very well present the first instance of a non-integrated electronic keyer paddle. Two views of Beecher's keyer and the optional single-lever paddle using jack switches are shown; the top photo shows a modified bug as the keying mechanism.

Two views of the April 1940 Harry Beecher W2ILE electronic keyer with and without the ventilated cover.

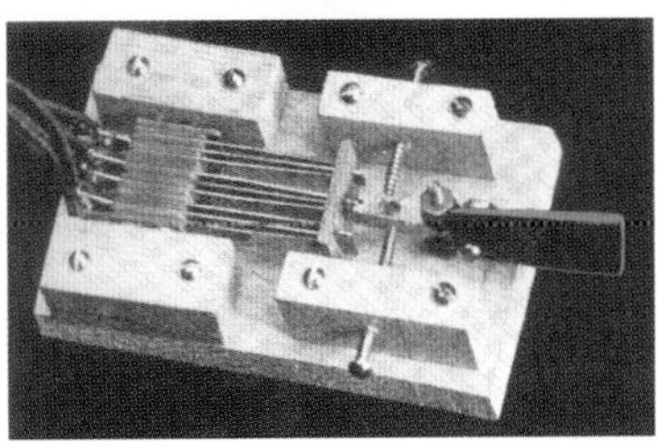

The first single-lever paddle, April 1940.

George Grammer (W1DF) followed up with an article in the May 1940 *QST* describing an improved W2ILE design with cost and size reduction as goals. Essentially, Grammer presented an economy version of the Beecher keyer. The Grammer device pictured did not have a built-in power supply.

The 1940 George Grammer (W1DF) keyer.

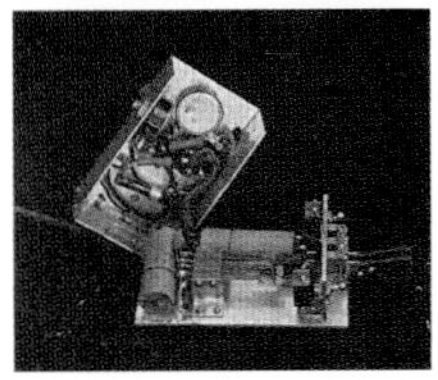

Inside view of the May 1940 Grammer keyer showing the built-in double-lever paddle.

The Grammer article also included detail on a new double-lever keyer paddle designed to overcome the deficiencies of the one presented a month earlier in the Beecher article. The Grammer paddle used one lever for dots and one for dashes. The base of the paddle was made of quarter-inch thick brass plate cut with a hacksaw. The paddle used two levers with spring adjustments; the springs were taken from the insides of a tire valve. Advantages of the two-lever design over the single-lever were listed, including fewer problems with centering the mechanism. Here we have what is essentially the first dual-lever paddle years before any commercial competition. Grammer's approach was improved upon by H. B. Savage (W4GRB) in a March 1942 *QST* article; Savage used a more bug-like design, eliminating the use of jack-switches in the paddle.

Discrete version of the first double-lever keyer paddle, May 1940.

In the late 1930s, Lovett Garceau, a professor at Harvard University, formed the Electro-Medical Laboratory in Holliston, Massachusetts. Garceau was an early proponent of using electronic methods to assist medical research. He built the first cathode ray oscillograph while at Harvard and built the first EEG machine for Hallowell Davis. In April 1941, Garceau applied for a patent on an automatic keyer with electronic dot and dash features; the patent (2,303,734) was issued in December 1942. Garceau's keyer used a jackswitch-type paddle.

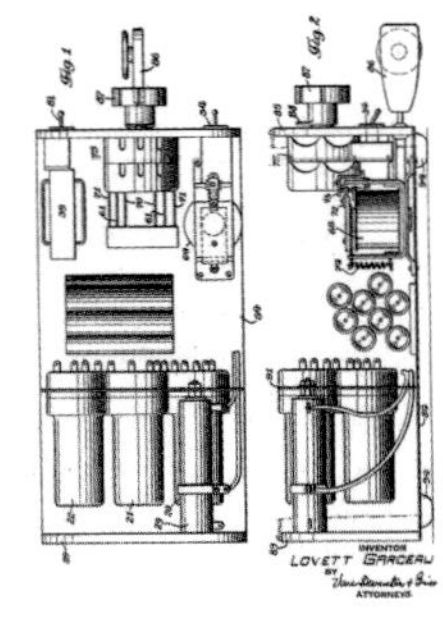

Garceau's electronic keyer as shown in the 1942 patent.

In the October 1941 issue of *Radio*, D. L. Clark (W1MJU) presented his design for an inexpensive electronic bug (see p 60). Clark's circuit utilized three tubes (two 6F6 and one 6N7) and was a multivibrator-type design, but required the adjustment of two knobs to set the keyer's speed. Clark admitted he had not yet mastered the art of sending on his device. Although Clark recommended a modified bug be used for the keying mechanism, he discussed use of a

The Lovett Garceau keyer, circa 1942.

sideswiper-based paddle. The paddle arm had no centering feature and would need further development. Although the Clark paddle concept comes after the 1940 Beecher paddle, it is still significant, as it establishes another data point in the development timeline for keyer paddles.

The 1941 W1MJU electronic bug.

The January 1942 issue of *Radio* included plans for an electronic keyer by J. W. Stuerhoff (W6UMZ). The keyer featured automatic dots and dashes and offered a selectable bug mode, allowing for manual dashes. This keyer used a one tube design (an 117L7GT) and was powered from 115 volts AC.

J. W. Stuerhoff (W6UMZ) keyer.

Another fully automatic key called the Equable Key was described in a March 1942 *QST* article. The key was developed and produced commercially by W. R. Starkens of Rochester, New York. Although some collectors call this a motorized bug, it should be more accurately called a motorized keyer. The device was capable of sending automatic dots and dashes at speeds up to 45 wpm. The mechanism used a motor, reducing gears, and two keying wheels—one for dots and one for dashes; the entire mechanism weighed over ten pounds. The wheels were controlled by an integral double-lever paddle. The designer of this key recommended the thumb be used to send dashes and the forefinger to send dots, which is just the opposite of convention.

It is interesting to note the dates on some of the motorized keyers. Howard Mason's Moto-Key was reviewed in *QST* in April 1939. The Starkens Equable motorized key was described in a March 1942 *QST* article. The reason these dates are intriguing and offer a subject for further research is that on May 11, 1940, Horace Martin Jr. filed for a patent on a motorized semi-automatic key that exhibited a number of similarities to the Mason and Starkens keys. The patent issued on January 14, 1941 (2,228,470), and appears to be Martin's last patent. Clearly there was some developmental focus on motorized devices in 1939–1942. Questions are raised regarding who may have conceived which features first, but more importantly to key collectors, did Martin ever build the semi-automatic device described in his 1941 patent? Although Martin's 1941 motorized key was described as a semi-automatic, text in the patent says: "My [Martin's] improved instrument may be constructed for transmitting only dots, or only dashes, or both." Indeed, the drawing seems to show the device as being capable of fully automatic operation.

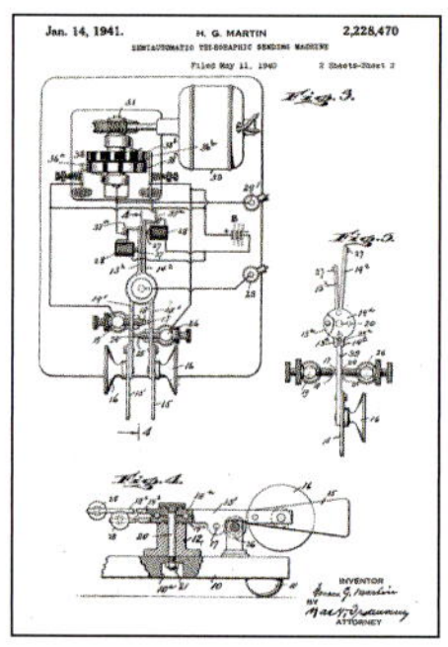

Detail from Martin's 1941 key patent (2,228,470) showing the motorized continuously running dot and dash wheels.

The invention also included a way to inhibit transmission of partial code elements; this Martin key essentially had self-completing dots and dashes.

The Advancement of Tube Keyers 1943–1947

WWII saw a variety of *QST* articles on electronic keyers; most covered modified designs offering some improvement in physical size, ease of construction, or use of more readily available parts. In March 1944, a *QST* article by William L. Gardner described a simplified version of the W2ILE device, offering a solution to the spacing problems he blamed on the use of gas triode tubes. In the same *QST* issue Chester Page (W3IKI) described a multivibrator keyer offering improved spacing and timing.

The July 1944 *QST* presented an article by Lawrence Wiley (ex-W9YDA) on a simplified electronic key. One of Wiley's design goals was to end up with a keyer he could place on the operating desk and still have room for the receiver. The Wiley device used a single 6N7 tube and included a built-in keyer paddle Wiley called the "control lever." The article gave paddle construction details for the design, which was meant to minimize the number of mechanical parts and the physical size compared to paddle units in previous keyers. It is noted the paddle design used by Wiley had similarities to the Vibro-Keyer (eventually called the Vibrokeyer) paddle that came about twenty-five years later.

Two views of the Lawrence Wiley (ex-W9YDA) keyer.

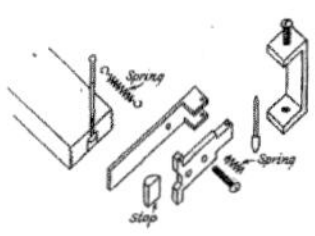

Wiley's paddle design with arm and pivot similarities to the Vibrokeyer.

Norman Snyder (W3HRD) discussed his updated version of the Wiley keyer in a March 1945 *QST* article. The Snyder keyer included a monitor oscillator that could be used alone for code practice, or as a monitor to aid the operator while transmitting. This version used two tubes (6N7 and 117L7) mounted externally on the rear of the keyer to keep heat away from other circuit components. Snyder offered the use of external tubes eliminated the need for a pilot light, as the operator could easily see when the keyer was turned on by observing tube filaments. Five front panel knobs controlled speed, length of dots and dashes, tone, and volume. The paddle mechanism was a modified Vibroplex Champion bug.

Norman Snyder (W3HRD) keyer.

Harry Beecher (W2ILE) wrote about his better electronic keyer in an August 1945 *QST* article. Beecher was responding to critics that his original 1940 design was too complicated for most amateurs to build. The new design, based on a multivibrator neon tube oscillator, was more reliable and easier to use. The keying mechanism was a modified bug that Beecher added an extra contact to, giving contacts for dots, dashes, and spaces.

Harry Beecher's better electronic keyer.

The April 1946 issue of *QST* presented a brief "Hints and Kinks" article on an electrostatic keyer. The article, by Harris Adams, described a very simple device that did not use tubes, instead working by capacitive discharge through two relays: one for dots and one for dashes. Adams claimed a top speed of 35–40 wpm for his design. Just two months later, in June 1946, Donald Parson applied for a patent on an automatic keyer using a very similar approach; that patent issued in August 1948 (2,447,088). It is not known if the Parson device was ever built.

Wilbur De Hart (W9DED) talked about his deluxe "electronic bug" in a September 1946 *QST* article. De Hart combined many features from earlier keyer designs and added some of his own, resulting in a device that used a keying tube in place of a relay and added a sidetone monitor. The keying mechanism was made from brass and steel, with the design based on existing mechanical bugs. De Hart's keyer existed in two boxes: one for the keying unit and a larger one for the power supply, monitor, speaker, and keying tube.

Two views of Wilbur De Hart's deluxe "electronic bug."

C. F. Bane (W6WB) wrote an article that appeared in the June 1947 *CQ*. Bane's article presented the DADIT keyer, a device that attached to the side of an existing semi-automatic bug and allowed the operator to make automatic dashes. The circuit that produced the dashes used a relay and time-delay capacitor. The DADIT device included a built-in keying monitor, but the device was never produced commercially.

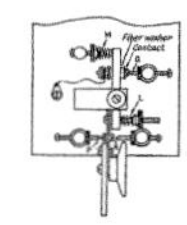

De Hart's keying mechanism was made from brass and steel, with the design based on existing mechanical bugs.

The Refinement of Tube Keyers 1948–1959

In the late 1940s, there was a minor focus on break-in keying, and advancements of existing electronic keyer designs had slowed somewhat from the fast pace of the early 1940s. There were a couple journal articles of note. The March 1948 edition of *CQ* carried an article by Richard Talpey (W2PUD) on keyer and paddle design. An October 1948 *QST* article by F. A. Bartlett (W6OWP) discussed advances in electronic keyer design, including a better approach for proper timing between dots and dashes and more consistent speed adjustment. Bartlett again used a modified bug for the control lever. The keyer's size was reduced to where it takes up no more table space than a traditional bug.

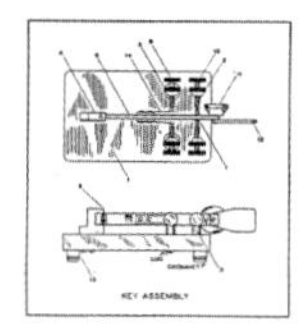

Talpey paddle design from the March 1948 CQ.

The reduced size of W6OWP's advanced keyer.

The late 1940s also saw the appearance of the commercial electronic keyer: the Mon-Key, manufactured by Electric Eye Equipment Co. The Mon-Key sold until about 1953. It was the first keyer that sold well, and it began a long period of commercial keyer and paddle design with an accompanying drop in bug sales. The Mon-Key ad (p 62) is from February 1948 *QST*.

Internal view of the 1948 W6OWP advanced keyer.

F. A. Bartlett (W6OWP) used his early keyer designs to go into production with the Duomatic AK-7, as advertised in the February 1949 issue of *CQ* and other journals. This device was followed by the AKS-7 model, of which up to 300 units were sold. Bartlett

used paddle mechanisms made by the Les Logan Speed-X Company in his AKS-7.

A November 1949 *QST* ad for Harrison Radio announced the Dash-Bug, an electronic keyer with self-completing dots and dashes. A user-furnished external paddle mechanism was required. According to the ad this device was made by Electronic Workshop, and was only available through Harrison Radio. Not much else is known about the Dash-Bug (Harrison Radio was formed by Bill Harrison, W2AVA).

In 1950, the Eldico Electronic Key Company started selling their Model EE1. The ad seen at left first appeared in April 1950 *QST*. The EE-2 used the same circuitry, but included a keying monitor and speaker.

Eldico would later come out with the EE-3 in 1957. The EE-3 featured an internal power supply, built-in paddle, and featured self-completing characters.

A couple of interesting keyer-related articles were published in *CQ* in the last part of 1950. October *CQ* contained an article on an updated version of the code wheel written by M. E. Heihle of Culver City, California. He used a notched aluminum wheel that actuated microswitches; it appears the device was used to call "CQ," or for other repetitive code uses. There was also a W2ZDE article in the November issue of *CQ* on the topic of low cost vacuum keyers.

G. Franklin Montgomery (W3FQB) presented the "Corkey" tubeless automatic keyer in the November 1950 issue of *QST*. It offered a single speed control, self-completing dots and dashes, and a dedicated, easy-to-construct keyer paddle called the key lever in the article.

The G. Franklin Montgomery (W3FQB) "Corkey" tubeless automatic keyer.

Roy Brann (W6DPU) described the search for the ideal keyer in a February 1951 *QST* article. One of the keyer deficiencies pointed out by Brann was the tendency for keyers to miss sending a trailing dot if the operator was too fast on the key. Brann uses the letter "G" as an example, where an operator who is sending too fast will find the keyer sending the letter "M" because the keyer circuitry did not register the last dit the operator thought was sent. Brann cautioned operators to be aware of this tendency and hold the dash lever until that element was finished sending. The John Kaye keyer of 1953 would address this issue.

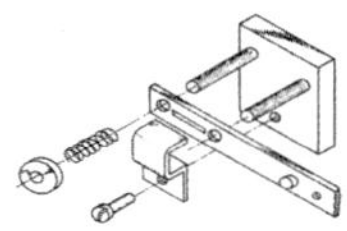
The Montgomery key lever mechanism was made of brass, then nickel-plated.

Another W6OWP keyer article on compact auto key design appeared in December 1951 *QST*. Bartlett was continuing with his work on keyer refinements. Features included equalized spacing between dots and dashes, correct dot-dash ratio at all speeds, no interaction between speed and spacing controls, quiet operation, and mechanically stable lever control.

Possibly the first electronic memory keyer is discussed in a John Kaye (W6SRY) *QST* article in the February 1953 edition. The keyer was described as something "as close to being an electronic brain as you are likely to encounter in amateur radio." The keyer used four tubes, and had the ability to hold a dot or dash and send it at the proper time. The keyer used a free-running time base with marking pulses to effect proper sequencing.

The December 1951 W6OWP keyer. The two views show the front panel with cover on and a rear view with cover off.

The 1951 W6OWP paddle mechanism.

W6SRY's ultimatic keyer, 1953 version.

Another significant keyer of note was John Kaye's (W6SRY) tube-type ultimatic keyer. This device was described in an April 1955 *QST* article. The term "ultimatic" originated in 1953 in a John Kaye February *QST* article and was essentially a contraction for "ultimate automatic." W6SRY suggested this name may have been a bit premature, as his new all-electronic keyer was further advancing automatic spacing and marking character storage features. W6SRY also introduced the sending technique of squeezing the paddle to create letters. The built in dual-lever paddle used a rubber band spring for arm return.

According to European sources, Brondum Bo Nielsen (OZ7BO) invented the iambic keyer in 1958. After some investigation, it appears Nielsen's invention is a variation of the true iambic system that would first be described in 1967 by K8OCO. Nielsen's keyers used a "single-dot insert" method of keying, allowing the operator to insert a dot into a stream of dashes as the dashes were being sent. This approach was used in OZ7BO's MSK-5 keyer and the Tempo DKT keyer.

The W6SRY ultimatic keyer, 1955.

The T.O. keyer (model HA-1) should also be noted as the first of its kind: an electronic keyer that precisely generated code digitally based on a single timebase. The T.O. keyer was introduced by Hallicrafters in 1959 and was a very popular keyer, as much due to its aesthetics as performance. The HA-1 was reviewed in the November 1960 *QST*.

A March 1960 *QST* ad for the T.O. keyer.

Some Early Transistor/Integrated Circuit Keyers 1959–1967

Although tube-type keyers continued to be popular in the early 1960s, it was becoming clear the future would be focused on solid state devices. Even though some new tube-type keyers were coming to market, such as the Auto-Mate K 5/50, the onslaught of transistorized and integrated circuit keyers was beginning.

The May 1959 issue of *QST* carried an article by Marland M. Old (W5LAN) who presented a transistorized version of the W9TO keyer. Old documented construction of the keyer, which included a 22.5 volt battery to power the transistor circuitry. Also included were a keying relay and a sidetone speaker. Old constructed his key lever from some relay contact assemblies and made fingerpieces from Plexiglas sheet. The Old article is the first mention in *QST* of the W9TO keyer.

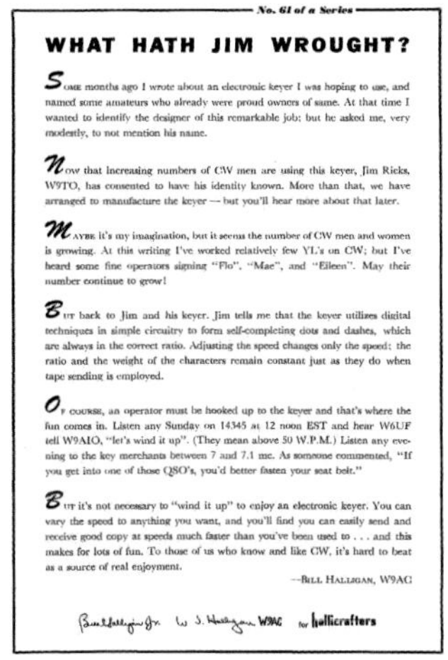

Bill Halligan composed this ad in the January 1960 *QST*, discussing his thoughts on the W9TO keyer and its designer. Many credit the T.O. keyer for an upsurge in CW interest.

A March 1960 *QST* article documented the "Magkee" keyer, a device using a magnetic core shift registers and all transistor circuitry. The article, written by Joseph Thornwall (W4FGM), presented ways to use magnetic cores to perform many of the keyer functions while offering the advantage of low power consumption, reliability, and small size.

In September 1960, a *QST* article by Alvin Kanda (K0MHU) presented an updated version of the W6SRY ultimatic keyer. The K0MHU device featured an all-transistor circuit. Kanda stated his keyer did everything the original did, but more efficiently. This keyer used an internal dual-lever paddle fabricated using parts from two straight keys.

Two views of the 1959 Marland Old W5LAN transistor keyer.

Once again, it would appear amateur homebrewers led development of devices that would soon be commercialized. Some of the earliest commercial transistor keyers included the Autronic keyer, a ten transistor device that came out in 1961; and the Hallicrafters T. T. O. Model HA-4 keyer, which used eight transistors and also came out in 1961.

The September 1963 issue of *QST* presented an article by Gilbert Boelke (W2EUP) titled "The Bugless Bug." Boelke claimed to have investigated why so many earlier keyer designs gave erratic operation; his conclusion was poor performance was due to unreliable paddle contact closure. Boelke's transistorized keyer design centered on his improved keying mechanism.

A 1966 article in the July issue of *73* magazine presented a follow-on device to the Bugless Bug called the Kindly Keyer.

External view of the K0MHU ultimatic transistor keyer.

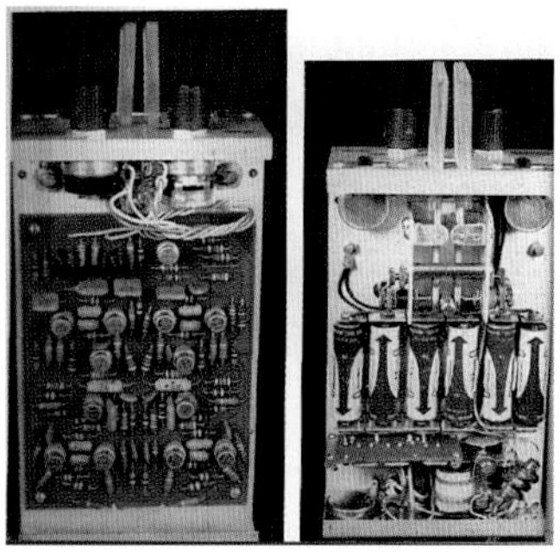

The K0MHU ultimatic transistor keyer, 1960.

The article, by George Daughters (WB6AIG), discussed a keyer circuit based on Boelke's techniques. Daughters' design used a mix of transistors and some early Fairchild ICs, but appeared to completely ignore the keying mechanism. In fact, Daughters' only mention of the paddle was to state that if one had a machinist friend make it total keyer cost can be kept to under $30. What exactly is to be made is unclear. One is left to wonder if a poorly designed mechanical paddle with erratic contacts would affect the WB6AIG keyer design as the Boelke article suggested.

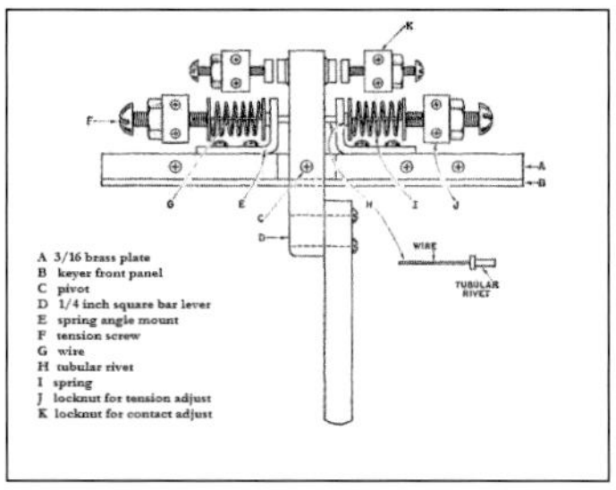

The W2EUP keying mechanism, 1963. The lever used a 4-40 screw for the pivot.

The Pickering Micro-Ultimatic keyer was described by Thomas A. Pickering (W1CFW) in a *73* article in June 1966. Pickering claimed to have produced the first IC keyer; this keyer was first advertised in 1967. Meanwhile, Palomar was also manufacturing integrated circuit keyers and sold their first one (the first version Space Age IC keyer) in 1966.

The "iambimatic" keyer concept was first presented by Harry Gensler (K8OCO) in a January 1967 *QST* article. Gensler built what was likely the first iambic keyer. Gensler discussed his approach of giving alternating dots and dashes when a dual-lever paddle's fingerpieces were squeezed together. The concept, according to K8OCO, could be applied to almost any keyer; the article documented three scenarios: a modified W9TO keyer, a homebrew iambimatic keyer, and a universal iambimatic modification. Gensler's homebrew device was transistorized and used two 9 volt batteries. The dual-lever paddle was also homemade, using saw blades with foam rubber for spacing and mitigation of contact bounce.

K8OCO's homebrew iambimatic keyer, 1967.

The July 1967 issue of *QST* included an article by Jimmy Moss (W5GRJ) that described the W0EPV squeeze keyer. The significance of this keyer was it incorporated the single-dot insert method of keying with dash override. A patent on this keying approach would be issued to Edward Brown (W0EPV) in February 1968 (3,369,230). Moss presented the keyer as having the potential to change the whole concept of keying code. The keyer circuitry was a mix of tubes, transistors, and diodes, but was simple enough to lend itself to homebrewing.

The W0EPV squeeze keyer, July 1967.

In the August 1967 issue of *QST*, Chet Opal (K3CUW) presented the Micro T.O. keyer, a solid-state version of the popular W9TO keyer. This project described an integrated circuit version of the original T.O. keyer using vacuum tubes. The Micro T.O. keyer was designed to use small Fairchild IC devices fabricated with RTL (resistor-transistor logic). The Fairchild ICs looked much like small signal transistors, with the exception of their 8-lead construction and epoxy cases.

The Chet Opal (K3CUW) micro T.O. keyer, August 1967.

Microcontroller/Microprocessor Keyers

Soon the microprocessor revolution and the Curtis keyer chip would forever impact the electronic keyer. Chet Opal (K3CUW) wrote several articles in *QST* about his keyer designs in the early '70s. The term "memory keyer" first meant a keyer with dot and maybe dash memories, not message memories, which came later on as memory chip technology matured.

Some of the first microprocessor keyers used microprocessor ICs with external program and data memory, like the Intel 8080, Zilog Z-80, or National 8051. The Curtis keyer chips soon changed almost everything in the electronic keyer world; they were used by many manufacturers and essentially put a stop to the use of microprocessors in keyers just before new microprocessor designs could become established.

Various keyers in this chapter are described as being microcontroller-based, and some are described as utilizing a full microprocessor, which needs external program memory, RAM, and I/O support chips. In actuality, very few keyers were made with microprocessors, with many of the AEA devices being successful exceptions.

What is the difference between a microprocessor and a microcontroller? A typical microprocessor is an integrated circuit that has only the central processing unit (CPU) inside. The microprocessor IC does not have any peripheral devices—like RAM or ROM—on the IC chip; the peripheral devices need to be added externally to make the microprocessor functional. With a microcontroller, all of the necessary system components—the CPU, a fixed amount of RAM and ROM, I/O ports, and other peripherals—are all included on a single chip. Microcontrollers are designed to perform specific tasks where the input and output are defined. A main advantage to using microcontrollers is reduced size and cost of circuitry. In comparison, microprocessors are often used where tasks are unspecific and the relationship between input and output is undefined. Typically the application requires high amounts of resources, such as RAM, ROM, and I/O ports. The clock speed of the microprocessor is high compared to the microcontroller. A microcontroller may operate from a few MHz to 30–50 MHz, but a modern microprocessor typically operates above 1 GHz. It is usually a safe assumption that a system utilizing a microprocessor would be more costly than a similar microcontroller-based system.

There are a couple of microcontroller devices that are becoming very popular among experimenters and builders, and they have found their way into some recent keyer designs. The "Peripheral (or Programmable) Interface Controller" (PIC) is part of a family of microcontrollers made by Microchip Technology derived from the PIC1650 originally developed by General Instrument's Microelectronics Division. PICs are popular due to their low cost, wide availability, large user base, extensive collection of application notes, availability of low cost or free development tools, and serial programming and re-programming with flash memory capability. PIC microcontrollers can be bought as pre-built circuits or as kits that can be assembled by the user. The CodeBoy keyer was the first keyer to use a PIC device.

Another microcontroller called the Arduino consists of a hardware board designed around an 8-bit or 32-bit Atmel microcontroller. An Arduino board typically features a USB interface, 6 analog input pins, and 14 digital I/O pins that allow the user to attach various extension boards. Introduced in 2005, the Arduino platform was designed to provide an inexpensive and easy way for hobbyists, students, and professionals to create devices that interact with their environment using sensors and actuators. The platform comes with a simple integrated development environment (IDE) that runs on a personal computer. Users can write programs for Arduino using C or C++. The open source code allows for full customization to fit the user's particular needs. As an example, a circuit board and parts kit called the nanoKeyer is available from Oscar (DJ0MY); this keyer is designed to use the K3NG Arduino keyer open-source firmware.

Arduino and Raspberry Pi devices have resulted in some confusion for beginners regarding what these two devices actually do. Although they are roughly the same size and look similar, they are actually very different. The Raspberry Pi is a mini-computer running a Linux operating system loaded on an SD card. It also has audio out, HDMI, and RCA video output and an Ethernet port. The Arduino is a microcontroller, without the typical operating system you may expect, and is more appropriate for basic keyer applications.

USB/Computer-Interfaced Keyers

USB and other dedicated computer-interfaced keyers are presented in chapter 15, but there are a few devices shown in this chapter that in addition to standalone functionality also offer connectivity for USB interface to computer; if that is the case they are mentioned in the keyer description.

Some Important Keyer Characteristics

Self-completing dots and dashes. Most any keyer of modern design is capable of producing dots and dashes of the correct length independent of the amount of time the paddle lever is held. The keyer must also be able to properly space between elements, and the spacing must not be affected by early key closure. Early closure happens to be a requirement for smooth sending, allowing for the keyer circuitry to determine the length of the element spaces. Some keyers also allow for automatic character and/or automatic word spacing.

Dot and dash memories: Dot memory allows the operator to hit the dot key early and have the keyer remember it. Keyers without dot memory will only send the letter "T" when the operator is trying to send a fast letter "N." Dash memory is somewhat like the inverse of dot memory, where the keyer must remember a momentary closure of the dash paddle, even if it comes quickly after a dot. Both memories are required for true iambic keyer operation.

Weight control: Keyer weighting refers to the code element space ratio; the standard baseline for this is a 1:1 dot-space and a 3:1 dash-space ratio. These spacings are felt to provide efficiency in sending and maximum readability. A weight control allows the operator to vary the keyer element weight from the standard baseline. At slow sending speeds, many feel lengthening the dots and dashes with respect to the spaces sounds somewhat better. Somewhere around 15 wpm added weight seems to make code reception more difficult. Adjustment of keyer weighting was frequently a hot topic of discussion among CW operators in the '70s and '80s. The issue was of more importance in that era, given that some transmitters did not do a good job following the keyer output, and as a result the actual transmitted signal required a weighting adjustment on the keyer to compensate.

The Echo Effect: Somewhere around 1974, Chet Opal first described what he called the echo effect, where different keyers feel different to different operators. The echo effect is admittedly subjective, but nevertheless a big factor in whether a keyer is used or sits on the shelf. Related, or perhaps part of, the echo effect is the perceived difference between iambic Modes A and B. The result is some very proficient CW operators cannot send on an iambic keyer and must use something like an ultimatic keyer, or vice versa. Some operators have mitigated the echo effect by careful choice of a paddle. Other operators have eliminated it by using a keyboard.

Keyer mode: An electronic keyer will typically advertise the operating modes it has available, such as semi-automatic, automatic, ultimatic, or iambic Mode A and Mode B. A single-paddle basic keyer will generate continuous dots and dashes depending on which way the operator moves the paddle fingerpiece, but the keyer has no ability to accept a dual-lever paddle or allow squeeze (iambic) keying. Iambic keying creates alternating dots and dashes when a dual-lever paddle's fingerpieces are squeezed together. Iambic keyers usually function in one of two modes. Mode A, known as the original iambic mode, is where alternate dots and dashes are produced when both fingerpieces are squeezed together. When the fingerpieces are released the keying stops with the last dot or dash that was sent while the paddles were depressed. According to John Curtis, Mode B resulted from a logic error in an early design by an unnamed company. With Mode B, dots and dashes are produced as long as both fingerpieces are squeezed together. When the fingerpieces are released, the keying continues with the sending of one more element: a dot is sent if the fingerpieces are released during a dash, or a dash is sent if the fingerpieces are released during a dot. Individual operators usually prefer the mode they learned on, and it is with difficulty that they try sending on a keyer using a different mode (see appendix A).

The remainder of this chapter focuses on some of the wide variety of keyers that have appeared over the past decades. Many of these devices remain in daily use and are still available for purchase. Some are now considered historical pieces. Assuredly, all have been used at some point in time to converse with fellow hams.

2Bears Enterprises Model 2B2 Keyer

The 2Bears Model 2B2 was not a well known device, and no evidence could be found that more than a few were ever made. This keyer featured a built-in sidetone with front panel controls for speed, volume, and tone. Other front panel switches indicate that keyer Mode A or B was selectable, as was keyed line polarity. Scotty (KG4YGS) reports you could buy this keyer in several versions, both kit or assembled, and with or without the keyer chip.

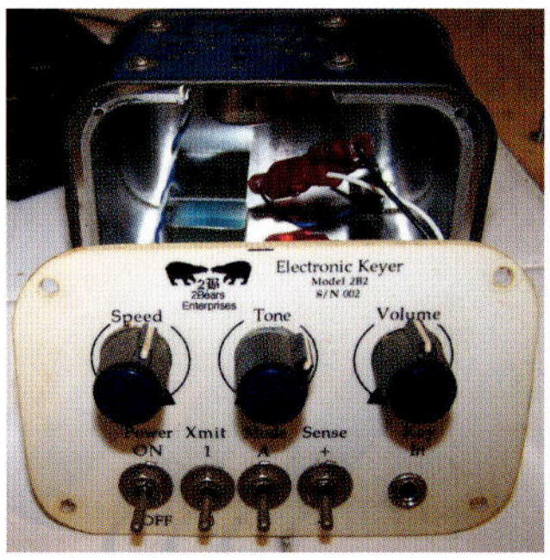

AA0ZZ EZKeyer

The EZKeyer was a keyer kit offering from the Four State QRP Group. The keyer was PIC based and included three memories. The PICs were programmed by Craig Johnson (AA0ZZ). The keyer featured twelve direct-entry commands, non-volatile memory, and a speed range of 5–55 wpm. Also featured were iambic Modes A and B operation, a tune and beacon mode, operating voltage of 3–5 volts, a sidetone, character autospacing, and long battery life. Although designed to mount in an Altoids tin, it could be enclosed in other small cases.

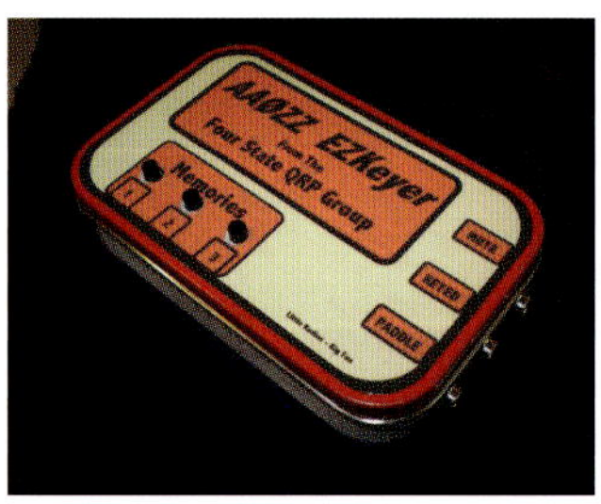

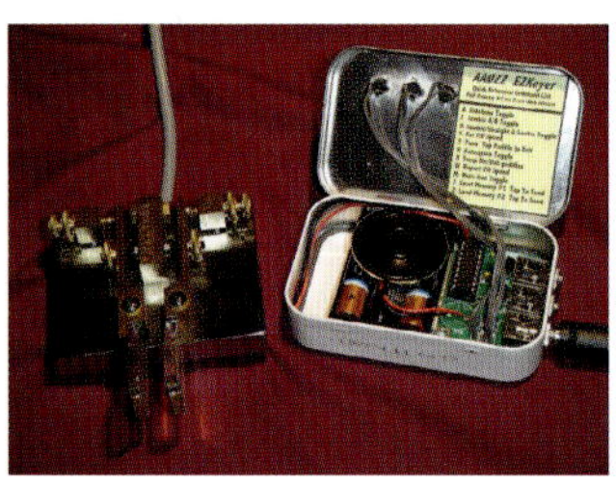

Ace Systems Keyers

Ace Systems was based in Pennsylvania. The Ace Systems Opto Keyer is a very competent solid state keyer, offering the user a variable sidetone pitch, volume, and speed controls. This unit uses an internal 9–volt battery or wall wart supply.

Accu-Circuits Accu-Memory II Keyer

An enhanced version of the Jim Garrett design was commercially produced and marketed partially due to the success of the WB4VVF Accu-Keyer and Accu-Memory designs. The unit shown featured eight 512 bit message banks, 24-hour clock, and a digital speed readout. Speed range of the iambic keyer was 6–50 wpm. This Accu-Circuits keyer had an internal 117 VAC power supply; unit dates to 1979.

AEA (ADVANCED ELECTRONIC APPLICATIONS, INC.) KEYERS

AEA, Inc. of Lynwood, Washington, produced amateur radio products up until 1996. Their data products line was sold to Timewave Technology of Saint Paul, Minnesota, and the antenna products line was sold to Tempo Research of Vista, California.

AEA CK-1, KT-1, MT-1 Morse Memory Keyer/Trainers

The AEA CK-1, KT-1, and MT-1 Morse Memory Keyer/Trainers all looked similar and shared the same manual.

The AEA CK-2 Contester

The AEA CK-2 Contester is an electronic memory keyer dating to 1982. The keyer has a speed range of 2–99 wpm and features 500 character memory capacity. The CK-2 offers similar features as the MM-2, but does not have trainer or beacon capability. The CK-2 can store up to 10 programmable messages and has an automatic serial number generator. This unit also features a repeat mode and selectable speed, tone, dot-dash ratios, and auto/semi-auto capability. It uses a keypad to set up the functions; unit requires 9–16 volts DC for operation.

The AEA KT-2

The AEA KT-2 was a "computer trainer" keyer. Two basic modes were available: a CW trainer or a keyer. The keyer offered selectable speed, tone, dot-dash ratios, and full or semi-automatic operation.

The AEA KT-3

The KT-3 was a memory keyer and Morse trainer combination. This unit had an internal speaker and jacks for headphones, key, and keyer output. The keyer's speed was 5–90 wpm. The KT-3 was often part of Morse learning programs thanks to the built-in Morse teaching features, but many used it only as a keyer.

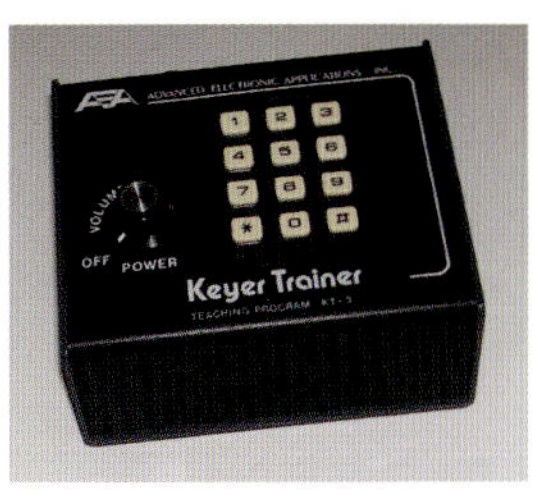

The AEA MM-1

The MM-1 was the first in a line of "Morse-Matic" devices, combining features such as a beacon message keyer and a Morse training device with a full-featured memory keyer.

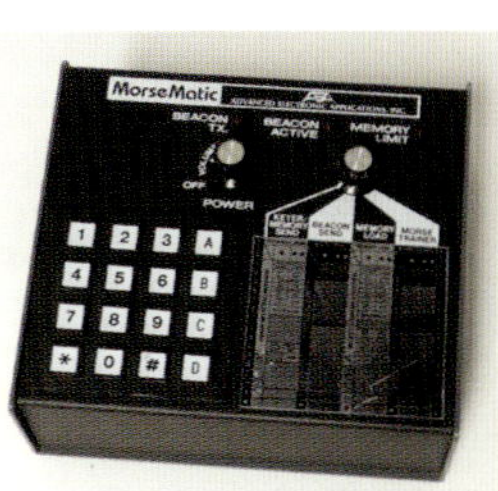

The AEA MM-2

The next AEA device in the Morse-Matic line was the MM-2, an iambic keyer that featured selectable dot/dash memories and customizable dot/ dash weighting and bug mode; memory capacity was 500 characters. Also included were contest-oriented features, such as auto serial number generation. The MM-2 allowed for positive and negative keying. This unit also featured a beacon mode, a CW trainer with random practice modes and Farnsworth spacing option, and memory modes with ten memories provided. The MM-2 keyer could be set for speeds from 2–99 wpm. This device requires 9–16 volts DC.

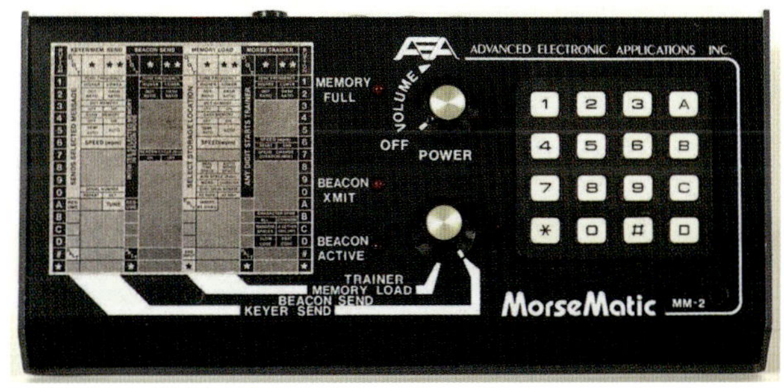

The AEA MM-3

Like its predecessors, the MM-3 Morse Machine is a combination memory keyer, Morse trainer, and CW beacon. The Morse keyer can be set from 2–99 wpm and features an 8,000 character memory capacity that can be stored in 20 memories. The Morse code proficiency trainer allows random code group practice with steadily increasing speed. A random word generator generates four-letter words for a more realistic practice session. A built in QSO simulator allows you to call other stations, answer a CQ, or just sit back and listen to realistic QSOs. The MM-3 can be programmed as an automatic beacon to repeat a Morse message at an interval from 1–999 seconds. Another unique feature offers the ability to listen in on simulated QSOs as the Morse Machine carries out two-way QSOs with itself. The user can also choose to participate in the machine-generated QSO by using an external paddle. The rear panel has an RS232 I/O port. This device requires 12 volts DC. The MM-3 can be controlled via a computer; RS232 interface is provided for serial port communication. The MM-3 also has upgradeable firmware and memory (up to 128k) options, allowing for up to 36,500 characters.

AEA product description for the MM-3 Morse Machine.

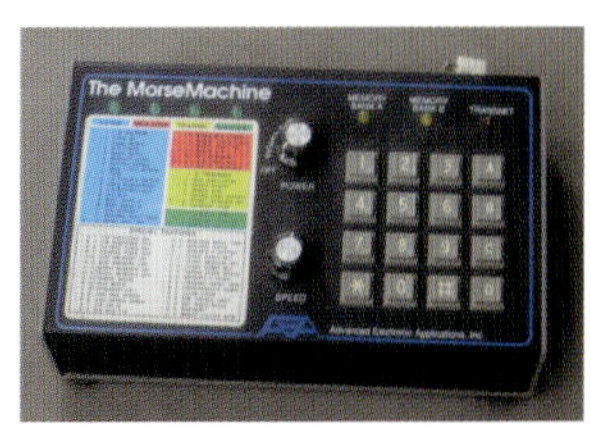

Alkan Products

The Alkan Ultimatic 200, made by Alkan Products of Minneapolis, Minnesota, was an Ultimatic solid state keyer with dot and dash memories and a front panel selectable "bug" mode. Another unique feature was the coarse and fine concentric knob adjustments for keyer speed. This keyer's predecessor was a tube version documented in 1953 and 1955 *QST* articles by John Kaye (W6SRY). Later (see the September 1960 *QST* article by Alvin Kanda, K0MHU) a solid state adaptation of the design appeared and was the basis for the 1963 introduction of the Alkan Ultimatic 200.

Amtron UK-850 Electronic Keyer

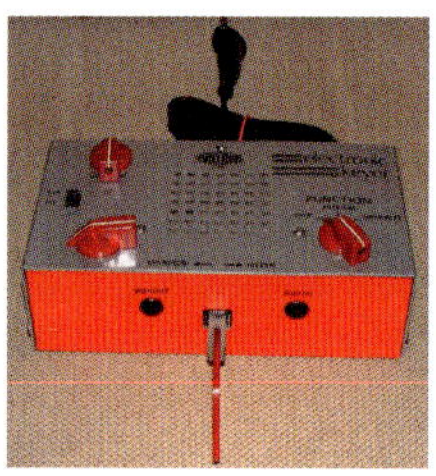

The UK-850 was made around the 1970s in Milan, Italy. The rear panel has keyer output and tone adjustment. Top panel controls are for volume, tone, and function; the keyer allows for either full automatic or semi-automatic (bug) operation. The keyer's circuitry uses six transistors and is powered from 220 VAC. The adjustments on either side of the paddles are for weight and ratio. The paddle mechanism is a single-lever design. The manufacturer (Gian Bruto Castelfranchi, or GBC) was the first Italian corporation to fabricate and sell transistor radios; they used the Amtron trademark on their electronic kits.

Autek Research MK-1 Message Memory CMOS Keyer

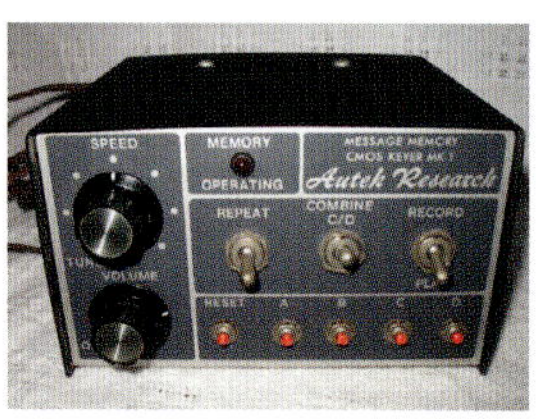

The Autek MK-1 is a CMOS memory keyer dating to the 1970s. There are four message slots available; the MK-1 has a large 1024 bit total memory that stores about 100 characters. Each of the four message slots hold about 25 characters, depending on character length and pauses. The C and D message slots could be combined to program a longer message. An expansion memory option was available, allowing 16 messages to be programmed. This keyer also features self-completing dots and dashes, and has two transistor outputs for negative and positive keying. Front panel controls for volume and speed are included, and an internal adjustment for tone is provided. Wiring options allow selectable 120 VAC or battery power.

Auto-Mate K 5/50 Keyer

This keyer is a tube and relay device designed by Ben Woodruff (W9UE) in collaboration with W9TO in Chicago. Two color schemes were available, either gray or green front panels. Although both versions carry the same model number (K5/50), the gray version includes a built-in speaker and speaker cutouts on the front panel, and has some different front panel wording. The two versions also used different knobs. When W9TO sold his rights to Hallicrafters for the well-known W9TO keyer, W9UE began to manufacture the Auto-Mate in assembled and kit form. In the early- to mid-1960s, Woodruff was threatened with legal action by Hallicrafters and Auto-Mate production ceased.

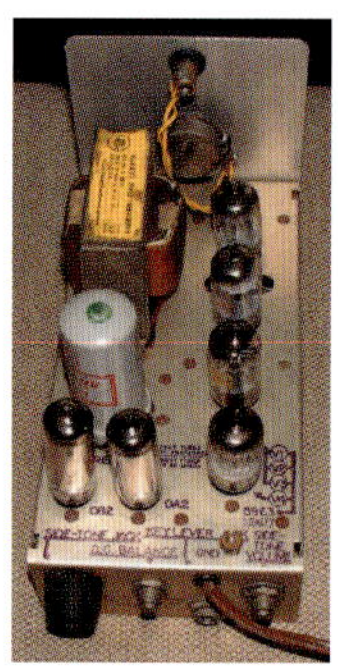

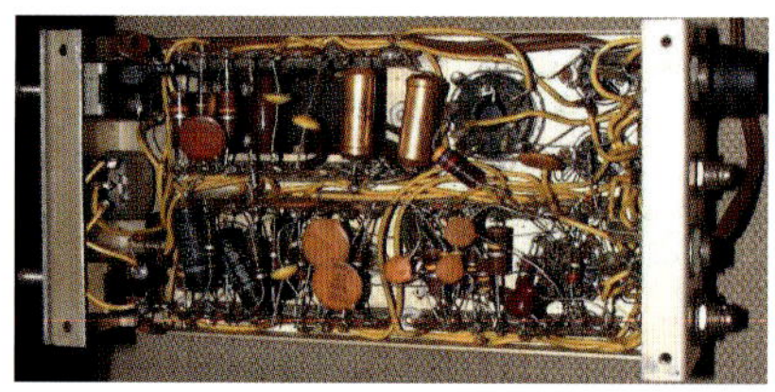

Autronic Keyer

In addition to the well-known Autronic paddle, the Electrophysics Corporation of Newport Beach, California, also produced the Autronic keyer. It was advertised as being fully transistorized, with a built-in speaker, and having separate weight and speed controls. The Autronic keyer used an etched copper circuit board with 10 transistors and 10 diodes, and the unit could be mounted either vertically or horizontally; that is why the knob lettering is rotated from center. This model was designed for grid-block

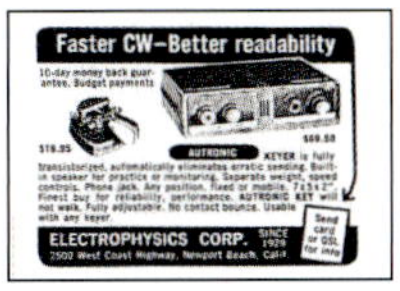

keying and had a transistor-switched output. Note the volume control is ganged with the weight adjustment control; weighting is adjusted using a screwdriver on the slotted center portion of the knob. The user can select fully automatic code or a mode that simulates a semi-automatic bug. This keyer used a built-in power supply and was powered from 115 AC line voltage. It was introduced in July 1960 and sold through the mid-1960s; it was reviewed in the October 1961 issue of *QST*.

B&W Codax Keyer

The B&W Model 361 Codax keyer was first marketed in 1964 under the "Waters" name; early 361s have the Waters name silkscreened above the "Model 361" on the front panel. The 361 is a non-iambic keyer, all solid state, and was powered by internal AA batteries. The circuitry used a reed relay for transmitter keying, and front panel controls are for speed and sidetone volume. The keyer's built-in paddles used a beryllium copper spring plate that could be individually adjusted for gap and tension (pressure).

Begali CW Machine

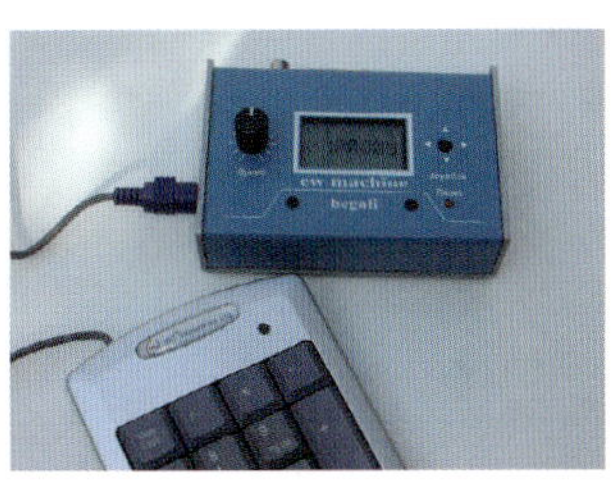

The Begali CW Machine was designed by Ulrich Steinberg (N2DE) and is based on an AVR Butterfly microprocessor board. The CW Machine is a unique software-defined keying device combining the functions of an advanced iambic memory keyer and a keyboard keyer with the functions normally performed by a logging program. The CW Machine will collect the information for a log record from the signal that you are sending out and store up to 12,000 log records. The firmware in the device can be updated; this update capability also lets you load the optional CW Trainer, a combination of Windows software and firmware that runs on the CW Machine device. Also offered is a CW-over-IP function that lets you connect to another CW Trainer over the Internet to practice QSOs off the air.

Ulrich's product description describes the CW Machine features as follows:

An electronic keyer with iambic A/B modes and analogue / digital speed control. In addition a bug mode and straight key hook up are supported.

A memory keyer with 30 variable length messages with a combined total of up to 12,800 characters—more than most memory keyers and more than enough for typical recorded messages. Messages can be chained and they can be interrupted and resumed at any point.

A real time clock and calendar.

A semi-automatic logger that keeps the usual information for up to 12,000 QSOs in non-volatile memory. This logger can also be used for SSB QSOs.

An instant search of the log for a previous QSO when you start a contact. Even with thousands of QSOs in the log that search will typically take about half a second and will barely interrupt your normal pace.

Two "personalities" that can be switched instantly. Each personality has a set of messages, a call, and a name associated with it. The second personality could also be used for /P operations where the operator might have different messages, or for that second ham in your family.

Intelligent messages that automatically insert calls, names, or the QTH of the other station, in addition to all the usual functions like delayed repeat, serial numbering, local speed-up etc. Since the keyer "knows" if a previous QSO with a station is in the log, it can modify messages if that is the case.

A user friendly configuration and information system using an LCD display and a joystick for navigation.

An optional Windows program, the CW Machine Manager, that turns the CW Machine into a full featured keyboard keyer with an unlimited type-ahead buffer, message templates that can be inserted with F-keys, and much more. In addition it manages all configuration aspects of the keyer and allows the bi-directional exchange of QSO information with all logging programs that support the ADIF format. It can also download and install software updates for the keyer and the Windows program itself from the Internet.

Brown and Simpson MK-75

Brown and Simpson Engineering was in Ontario, Canada; they produced this MK-75 memory keyer that was reviewed in the August 1976 issue of *QST*. Front panel controls were for speed and weight, with switches for the memory functions. This keyer was described as a cross between the Accu-Keyer and the T.O. keyer. Other features included iambic operation, self-completing dots and dashes, and automatic letter and word spacing. Also included was a built-in oscillator with tone and volume controls. The programmable memory included an insert feature popular with contesters. The MK-75 sold for approximately $350.

Brown Brothers Prototype Keyers

The Brown Brothers keyer never completed development and was never marketed. There are two known variations of Brown Brothers prototype keyers, with some unverified reports of a third. The top photo shows one version, while the next two photos show a second version with a different base and control configuration; both are from my collection. The fourth photo shows an internal view of components and wiring as seen in the second version keyer, with definite use of prototype construction techniques. Both versions exhibit similar construction techniques; the second version has some adhesive residue on the base, suggesting a label was once applied. It is known Brown Brothers experimented with many different designs of

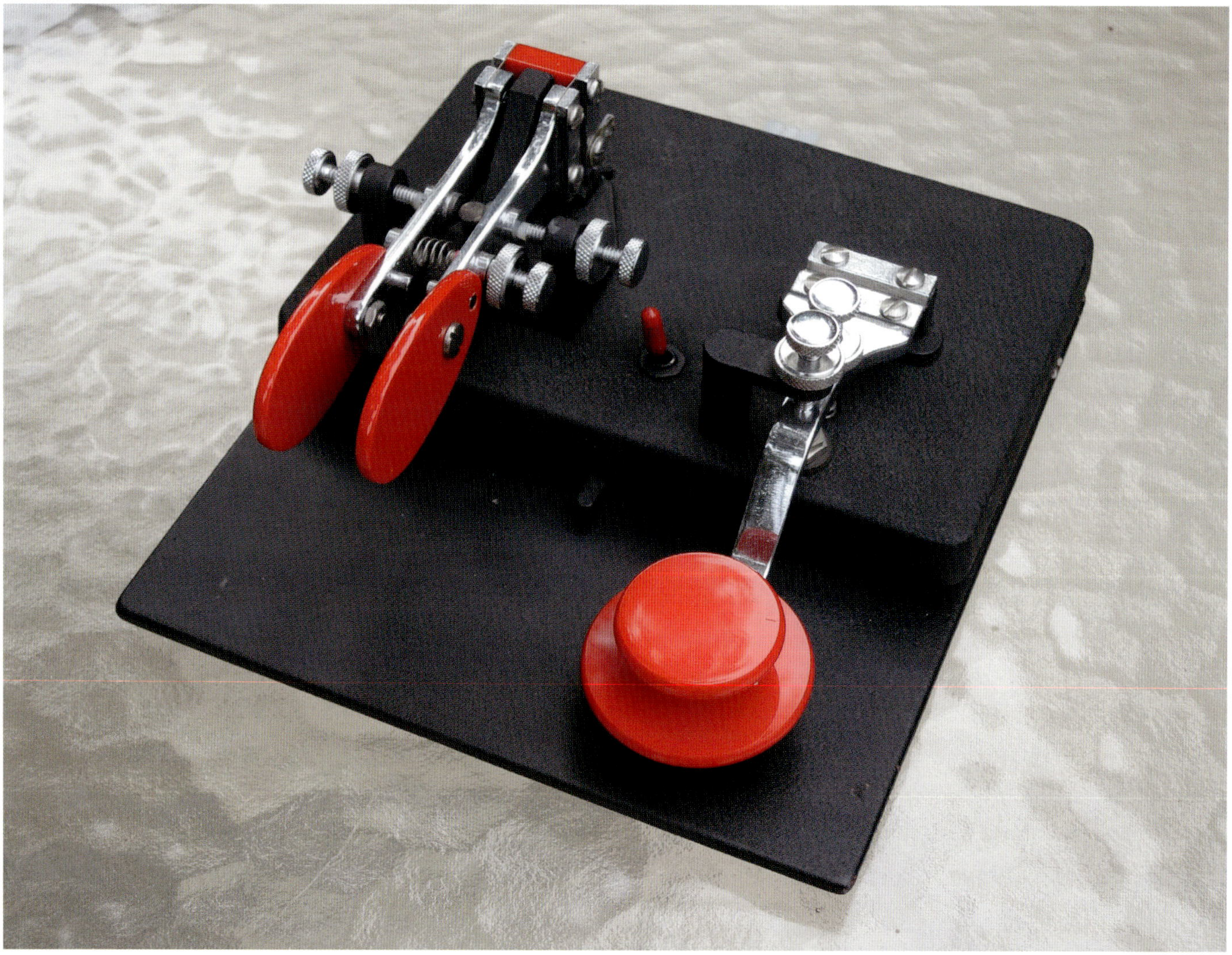

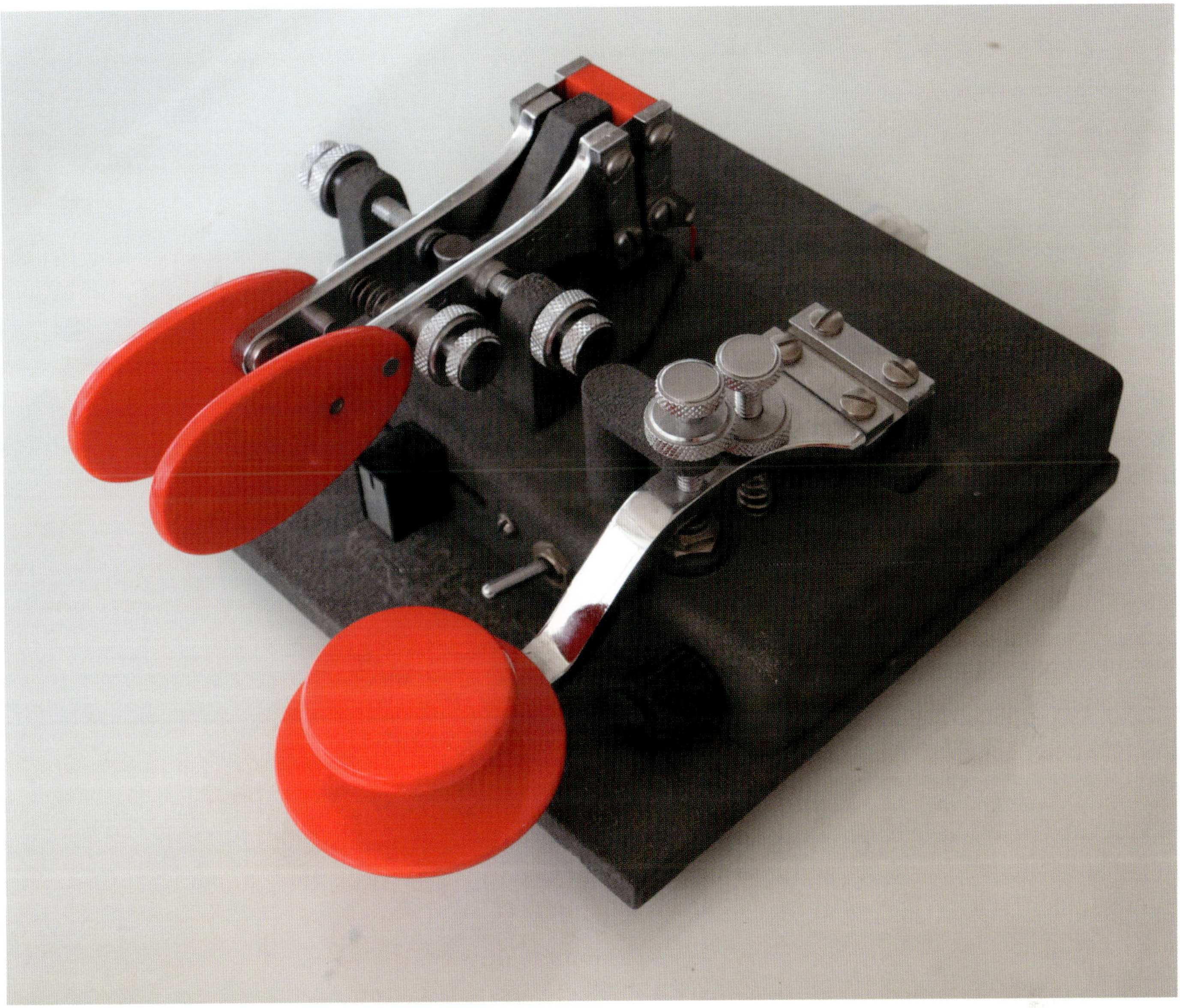

B10KΩ
7400N

paddles and keys, including a single-lever paddle and a magnetic dual-lever paddle, but not many are aware of these Brown Brothers keyers.

Bulgarian Memory Keyer

This is a Bulgarian-designed memory keyer. Front panel controls include keyer speed and memory start/stop buttons. This keyer is identified by the "club 73" on the front panel.

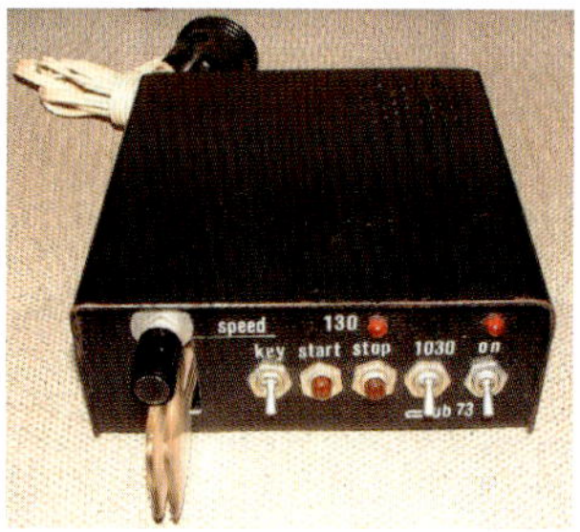

CAL-AV LABS Advanced Mobile Keyer

California Avionics Laboratories was established as a sole proprietorship in Palo Alto, California, in 1959. It was incorporated in 1968. The name was later shortened to CAL-AV LABS, Inc. Its primary business has been the manufacture of electronic instruments, primarily for the research community. In 1997, the company moved to its present location in Tucson, Arizona.

The Advanced Mobile Keyer incorporated a paddle unit from the Spirit key (see chapter 5). The paddle unit was split, and its left side moved forward and bent right to form an ergonomic fit for a right-hand thumb and index finger. The modified paddle unit was then incorporated into an enclosure aimed at automobile or aeromobile use. The resulting keyer was based around a super CMOS 2 circuit board, with the design creating a vibration-proof keyer. Ken (K6HPX) reports this advanced brassboard has been in mobile use for many years but was never produced commercially. Note this may be the only electronic keyer designed primarily as a mobile device.

Cleaver Model 33A Keyer

The Cleaver Model 33A is an obscure device made by the Cleaver Company of Dallas, Texas. The 33A keyer uses an internal 115 VAC supply and provides sidetone and keyer outputs on a rear panel terminal strip.

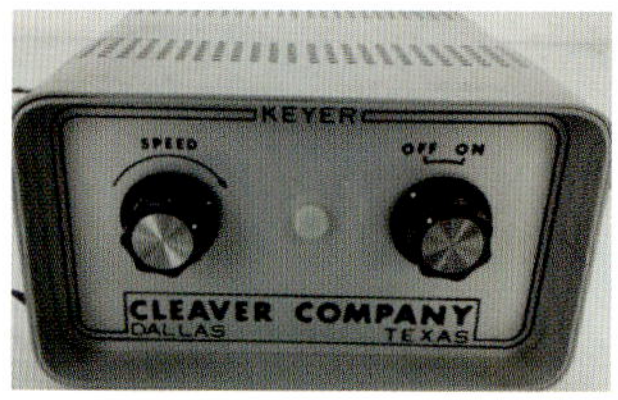

Cleng Electronic Bugg Keyer

The fairly scarce Cleng Electronic Bugg keyer utilized a basic design, and included a built-in power supply. In addition to the keyer, Cleng manufactured the TWB-1 paddle (see chapter 5).

CodeBoy Model A1 Electronic Keyer

CodeBoy Model A1 as shown on the Morse Express website (morsex.com).

Radio Adventures is a small engineering company in Franklin, Pennsylvania. The company specializes in the design and manufacturing of ham radio equipment components, kits, and accessories for the amateur radio and commercial communications markets. The CodeBoy Iambic Keyer Model A1 offers many advanced features in a very small package. Speed range is 10–40 wpm, and iambic A or B operation can be selected by the operator. The keyer also has dot and dash memory, space and weight compensation, paddle or straight key/bug input, selective autospace on straight key/bug, debouncing of all inputs, MOSFET keying transistor output, and a built-in long life battery. An accessory interface is available to operate grid-block keyed rigs. The CodeBoy was the first keyer to use a PIC device in its design.

Codetrol Keyer

Bernard Breedlove of Atlanta, Georgia, claims to have invented the electronic keyer in 1940 (patent 2,302,290). The paddle for Breedlove's keyer is described by Breedlove as "double circuit, side action, manually operable control key for the manual transmission of the radio code to the relay box." The device was part of Breedlove's approach for learning Morse code that he called the "Aural and Visual System of Teaching the Morse Radio Code." This keyer is not known to have ever been in production, but based on the "Patents App'd For" notation on the front of the keyer, this unit would date to between 1940 and 1942.

Breedlove was the consummate tinkerer, and always tried to find a better way of doing things. It is believed many of his approximately 240 Codetrol semi-automatic keys were made from parts and pieces he bought from surplus McElroy inventory. Unfortunately for Codetrol sales, Breedlove was competing against the growing popularity of electronic keyers. Breedlove also patented a fully automatic key similar to the Melehan Valiant device (2,526,001 issued in October 1950), but he only made less than five (see chapter 10).

Collins Version HD-1410 Keyer

This keyer is essentially a Heath HD-1410 cosmetically modified to look like a vintage Collins S-Line accessory. The Collins HD-1410 was sold for a brief period on the Michael March paddle website.

Cosmatic Mark IV Keyer

The Cosmatic Mark IV is a limited production keyer most likely from Canada, with little information found to document it. Paul (WA9PWP) reports the callsigns of two VE3 hams were etched on the PC board. The paddles use wire arms embedded in a molded block.

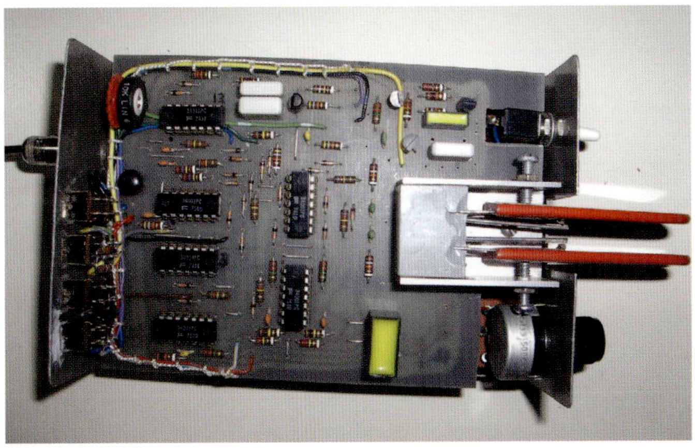

CURTIS ELECTRO DEVICES
KEYER AND KEYER ICS

Curtis Electro Devices was founded in 1968 by John G. Curtis (K6KU). Curtis was born in Bradford, Pennsylvania, in 1930. The company's name comes from an early product ad that was rejected by a ham radio journal. The name selected at the time was "Curtis Electronic Devices," and this was apparently too long for the ad; Curtis shortened it by removing some letters, and the company forever became "Curtis Electro Devices."

The company was started by Curtis as a hobby; he began manufacturing with his first keyer, the EK-38 "Electronic Fist." The EK-39 followed in 1970, adding a weight control, as well as dash memory. Curtis designed and produced a variety of electronic keyers, Morse keyboards, and a line of PROM and EPROM programmers. In 1973, Curtis introduced the 8043 keyer chip. The 8043 had dot memory only and sold for $7.95 in 1973. It was the first integrated circuit designed specifically to perform the electronic Morse keyer function. Production of the Curtis chip benefitted from John's industry contacts at Signetics. The chip included debouncing circuitry for the key paddles, a clock oscillator, the divider and logic to produce dashes and iambic mode (alternating dots and dashes when both paddles are closed), a sidetone oscillator, weighting circuitry to lengthen dots or dashes at the expense of the intervening spaces, and an output stage capable of driving an NPN keying transistor. Curtis followed by introducing several keyers incorporating his new full-featured ICs: the first was the EK-430, which used the 8043 chip. The 8044 chip was introduced in 1975, and added dash memory; it sold for $24.95. The 8044 was fabricated by International Microcircuits; the chip was used to test their gate array manufacturing technology. The 8044 sold for $24.95 in 1975.

Some popular Curtis keyer chips.

Popular keyers at the time offered Mode B keying, which many hams preferred. With Mode B, keyer circuitry added an extra dot or dash at the point the operator stopped sending according to which code element was sent last. The Curtis keyers up to that point did not do that, so the Mode B feature was added, resulting in the 8044B. The 8044B was used in many commercial keyers, including some from Ten-Tec, Heath, and Nye Viking. In 1980, the "M" versions of the 8044s were created, adding a speed indicating function to the circuit. In 1981, Curtis also introduced a fully integrated keyboard chip called the 8045. In early 1986, the last Curtis keyer chip was announced—the 8044ABM; it featured both A and B modes, and an output for speed indication. This was considered a top-of-the-line chip and became an industry standard. There are some who believe the Curtis ASIC 8044-based keyers actually impeded market acceptance for 1980s keyers based on the popular microprocessors of that era, including the Intel 8085, Zilog Z80, and Motorola 6800. With further development of keyers based on microcontrollers and their growing popularity, interest in the Curtis chips declined to the point Curtis stopped selling them. The 8044 series was acquired by MFJ; several MFJ keyers now feature Curtis chips in their design. Curtis Electro Devices officially ended operations on April 1, 2000.

Curtis Model EK-38

The Curtis EK-38 "Electronic Fist" is an iambic keyer with speed adjustable from 8–50 wpm. This keyer has controls for sidetone volume, speed, and a tune switch for transmitter tune-up. The rear panel includes jacks for a paddle, keyed line, and straight key input. The design also offers switchable relay/transistor output keying. This unit runs on 115 VAC and dates to around 1969. The particular keyer shown is finished in the scarce Heath green color. The "38" in the Model number comes from John Curtis' age when he built the first one.

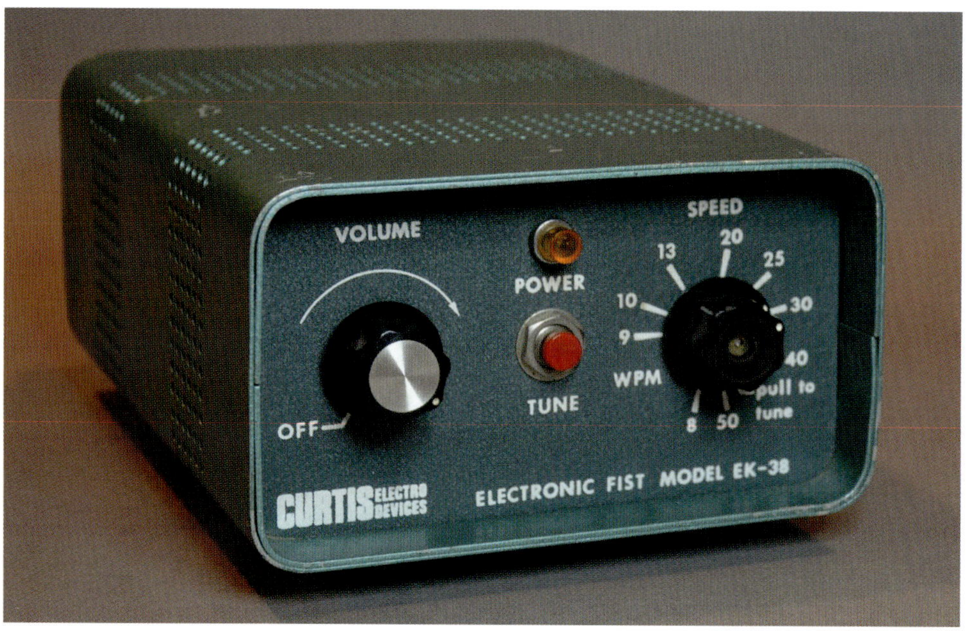

Curtis Model EK-39

The EK-39 was the next update of the "Electronic Fist" model of Curtis iambic keyers. Circuit design offered self-completing dots and dashes, as well as the features of the earlier EK-38. The EK-39 also added weight control. The EK-39 could be ordered in several different color schemes, including a Collins gray cabinet, a black cabinet to match Drake and others, and a blue/green combination to match Heath SB-series gear. A message memory version of this keyer was offered as an "M" version; it used a Curtis-programmed ROM IC. This keyer first sold in 1971.

Curtis Model EK-402

The Curtis EK-402 keyer offered 64-bit programmable memory with selectable memory banks. Programmable messages offered the user a delay and repeat function. The EK-402 keyer was powered by 115 VAC using an internal power supply; a 9 volt battery was used to retain programming when the keyer was disconnected from AC line input. The EK-402 first sold in 1971 for $289.95.

Curtis Model EK-404 Deluxe Keyer

The Model EK-404 was introduced in June 1972. It was functionally similar to the Curtis EK-402, but it lacked a programmable memory. This keyer could be powered using an internal 115 VAC supply or a 12 volt DC input. It is reported that if the EK-404 case is opened, use of either an early Curtis IC (8043, 8044) or discrete components for the keyer functions can be determined. The EK-404 first sold for approximately $125. Product reviews for the EK-404 were published in the January 1972 issue of *CQ* and the March 1972 issue of *QST*.

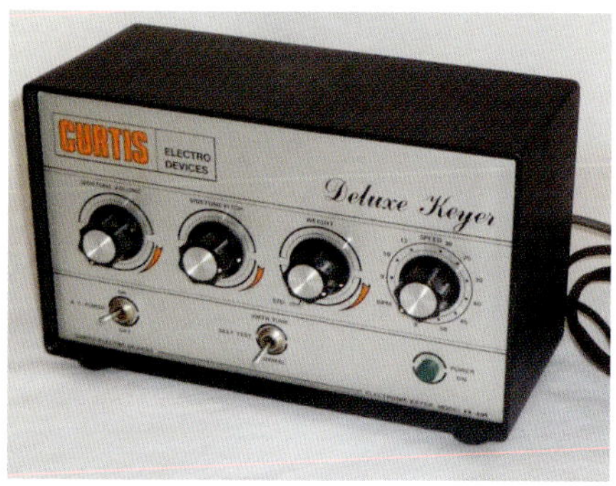

Curtis Model EK-420A

The EK-420A was billed as a "deluxe" keyer, and indeed offered some new features along with convenient front panel controls. The design incorporated transistors and ICs, and included measures to eliminate faulty keying due to contact bounce. Also, this keyer used filtering to reduce susceptibility to RFI. Transmitter keying was via a relay. The EK-420A dates to 1973.

The KM-420 was an additional accessory that allowed the user several configurable banks of memory. Programming was via an external paddle, and a repeat function was offered for memory playback.

Curtis Model EK-430 CMOS Keyer

The EK-430 came out in 1976. This keyer used the Curtis custom designed 8044 CMOS keyer chip and operated from either the 115 VAC line using an internal power supply (factory model only) or from a 9 volt battery. The Curtis EK-430 was reviewed in the February 1976 *QST* and sold for $125.

Curtis Model EK-480 CMOS Keyer

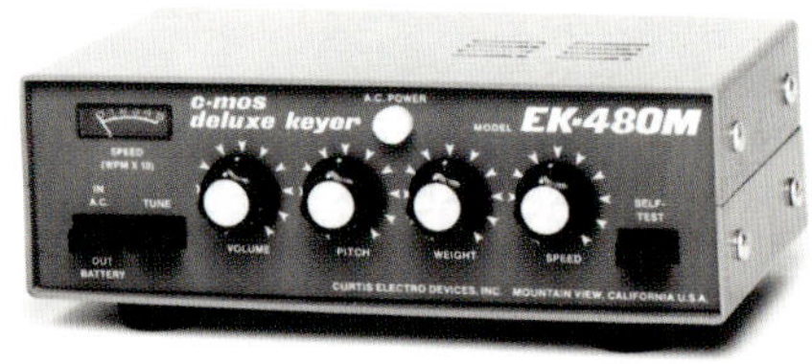

The EK-480M version included a speed meter.

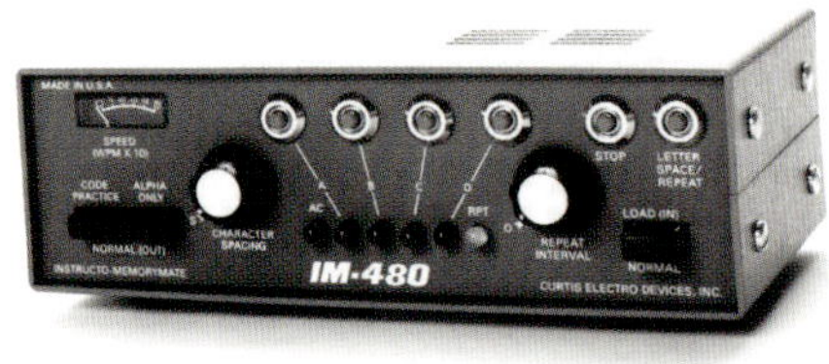

The EK-480 was reviewed in the June 1980 *QST*. The EK-480 design will key plus or minus 300 volt, 100 mA transmitter circuits with polarity selectable. Power is obtained using an internal 115 volt AC supply or internal battery. The keyer includes a self-test switch that removes the keyer from the transmitter line for code practice purposes. Code speed is 6–50 wpm, and a sidetone oscillator is included. The EK-480 sold for $150.

Curtis also produced an add-on accessory called the Instructo-Memorymate (model number IM-480). The IM-480 gave the user random code practice capability (6–50 wpm), and provided message storage for the EK-480 series keyers. The message memory function included four messages of 32 characters each with a repeat function. Messages were programmed using the paddle. The IM-480 attached to the EK-480 keyer using 14-conductor ribbon cable with DIP plugs.

The Curtis EK-480 CMOS deluxe keyer.

Curtis Lil' Bugger Keyer

The small size of the K5 "Lil' Bugger" keyer attracted lots of attention when it first appeared in June 1982. This keyer was available as the K5 (using the 8044 chip) or the K5B (using the 8044B chip). The K5 was the last keyer produced by Curtis Electro Devices.

CW Sendin' Machine Model 2048

The CW Sendin' Machine was an iambic keyer with dot and dash memories and eight 256-bit message memories. The keyer (model 2048) was designed by H. Alan Harp (K4PB) in the late 1970s. The keyer manual, with hand-drawn schematics and illustrations, recommended an external battery backup—using a provided circuit—to keep the memory alive in case of power loss. Two key jacks were included: one for positive keying and one for grid-block keying.

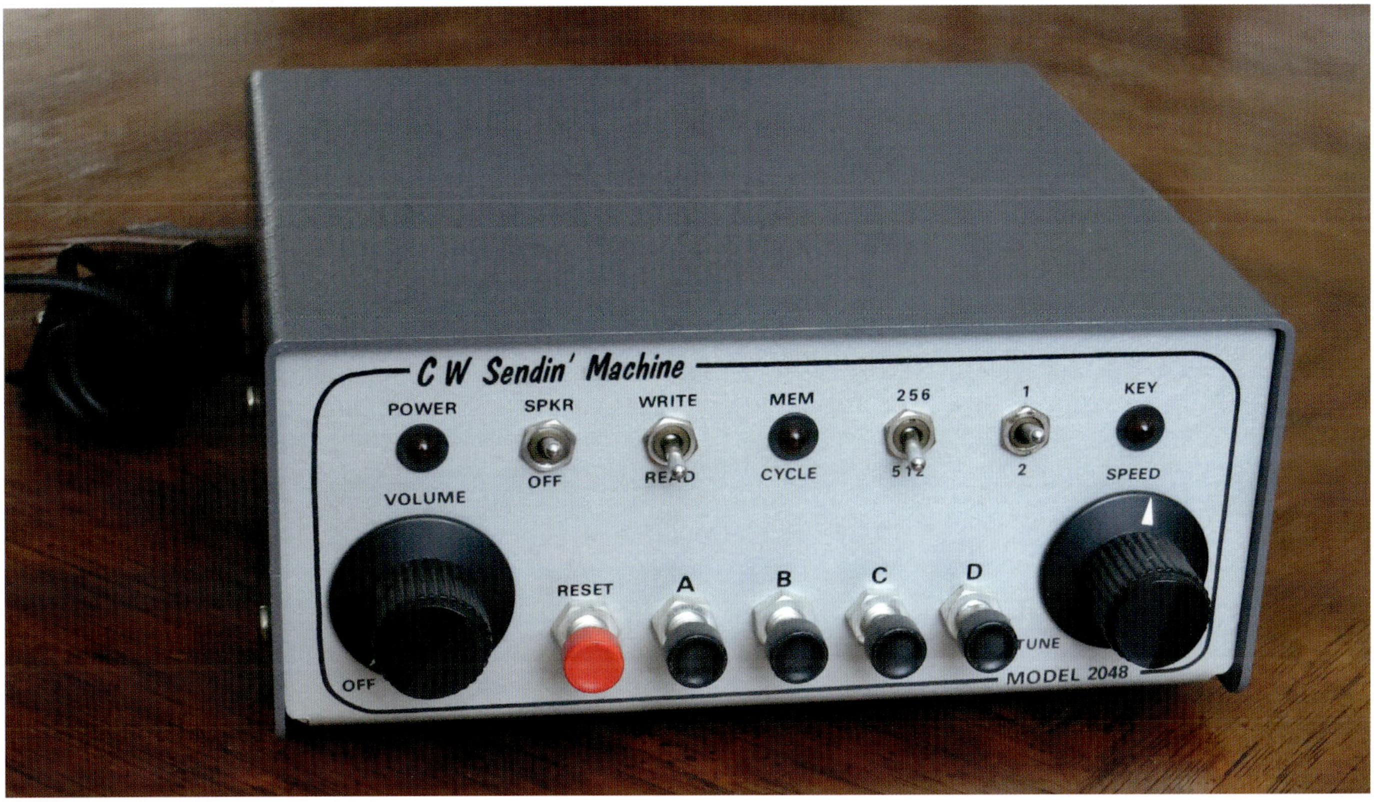

CW Touch Keyer Model P-1

The CW Touch Keyer is produced by Sumner (WA1JOS); this keyer is also sold by West Mountain Radio under their name. The device uses gold-plated paddles to sense finger touch. Three outputs are provided: one for the keyer, one for the paddles only, and one for an external speaker. An internal sidetone speaker is included. The unit will key only positive voltage lines of 13.8 volts or less. The keyer features a callsign memory and an optional 40 character programmable memory. Model P-1 weighs 15 ounces and measures 4.5 × 3 × 2 in.

Daiwa DK-210 Keyer

The DK-210 is a full-featured iambic keyer offering convenient front panel controls. It can be powered by an internal 9 volt battery or through an external 13.8 volt supply. Speed is adjustable from 10–50 wpm; weight (dash/dot/space ratio), sidetone, and monitor volume are also adjustable. The DK-210 includes a front panel 5-segment LED bargraph indicator for speed. The keyer can be set for semi or fully automatic operation, and a tune position gives continuous key-down for transmitter tuning purposes.

DATA ENGINEERING MORSE KEYERS

Data Engineering, Incorporated, of Springfield, Virginia, made electronic keyers and other accessories.

Memory-Matic 8000

Shown is a Memory-Matic 8000 product ad from the December 1972 edition of *73*. The Memory-Matic 8000 was Data Engineering's most advanced keyer and sold for $398.50.

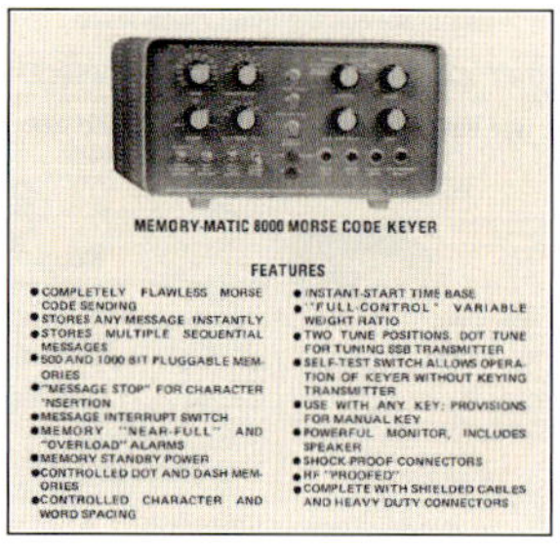

MEMORY-MATIC 8000 MORSE CODE KEYER

FEATURES

- COMPLETELY FLAWLESS MORSE CODE SENDING
- STORES ANY MESSAGE INSTANTLY
- STORES MULTIPLE SEQUENTIAL MESSAGES
- 500 AND 1000 BIT PLUGGABLE MEMORIES
- "MESSAGE STOP" FOR CHARACTER 'NSERTION
- MESSAGE INTERRUPT SWITCH
- MEMORY "NEAR-FULL" AND "OVERLOAD" ALARMS
- MEMORY STANDRY POWER
- CONTROLLED DOT AND DASH MEMORIES
- CONTROLLED CHARACTER AND WORD SPACING
- INSTANT-START TIME BASE
- "FULL-CONTROL" VARIABLE WEIGHT RATIO
- TWO TUNE POSITIONS. DOT TUNE FOR TUNING SSB TRANSMITTER
- SELF-TEST SWITCH ALLOWS OPERATION OF KEYER WITHOUT KEYING TRANSMITTER
- USE WITH ANY KEY: PROVISIONS FOR MANUAL KEY
- POWERFUL MONITOR, INCLUDES SPEAKER
- SHOCK-PROOF CONNECTORS
- RF "PROOFED"
- COMPLETE WITH SHIELDED CABLES AND HEAVY DUTY CONNECTORS

Memory-Matic 500-B

The Memory-Matic 500-B with a relatively busy rear panel is shown. It is suspected some of the rear panel controls may not be original.

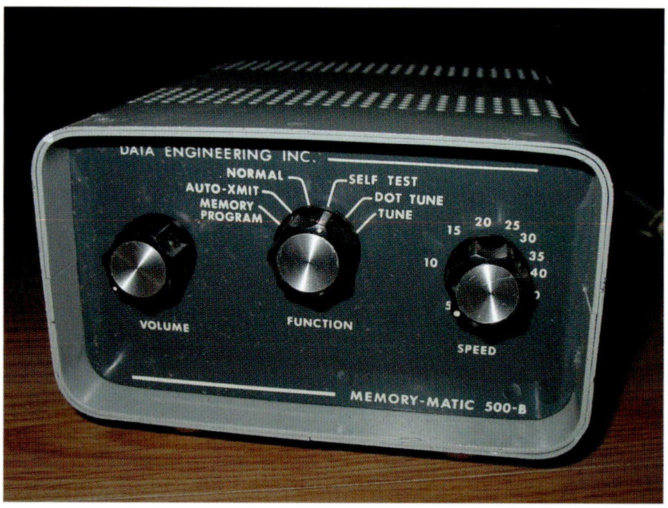

Cricket 1

The Cricket 1 was first sold in 1973. It was an all-IC keyer with internal AC power supply, and offered built-in paddles and a sidetone monitor. Rear panel adjustments included weight and a semi-automatic mode.

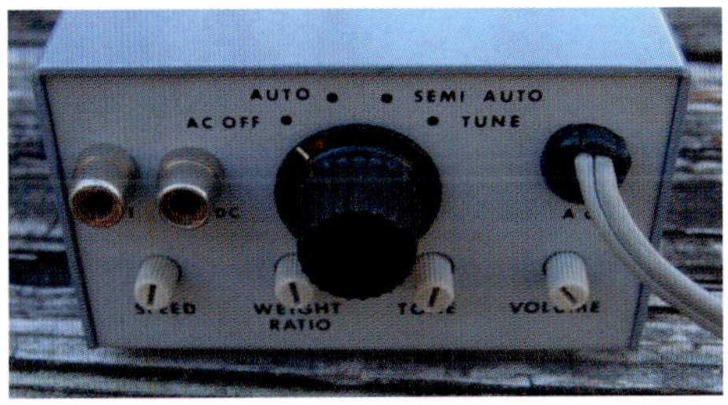

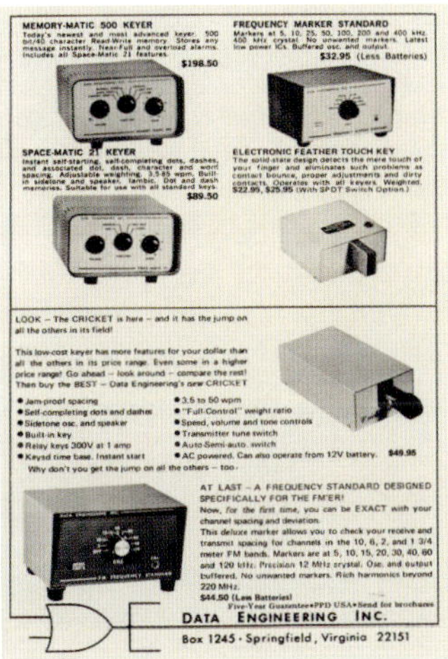

A Data Engineering advertisement from the June 1972 issue of *73*.

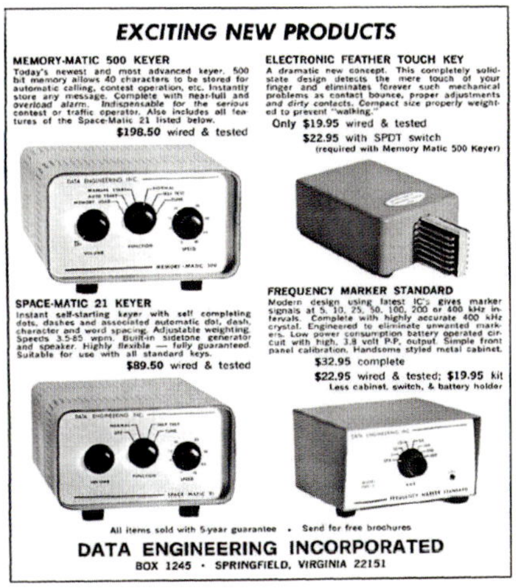

A Data Engineering ad from the October 1971 *Ham Radio*.

Electronic Feather-Touch Key

Data Engineering also produced the Electronic Feather Touch Key, an all solid-state device introduced in 1972. This may be the first device to offer a touch-sensitive paddle design with no paddle movement, dot/dash contacts, or spacing adjustments. The keyer was actuated by sensing the contact of the operator's fingers on the fingerpieces. This keyer used a transistor output arrangement, and so did not work with older grid-block keyed transmitters. A selectable option allowed this device to function as a single or dual-lever key. The product advertisement (below) apparently shows an earlier version of the Feather Touch key, without the selection buttons and with a different mechanical fingerpiece arrangement.

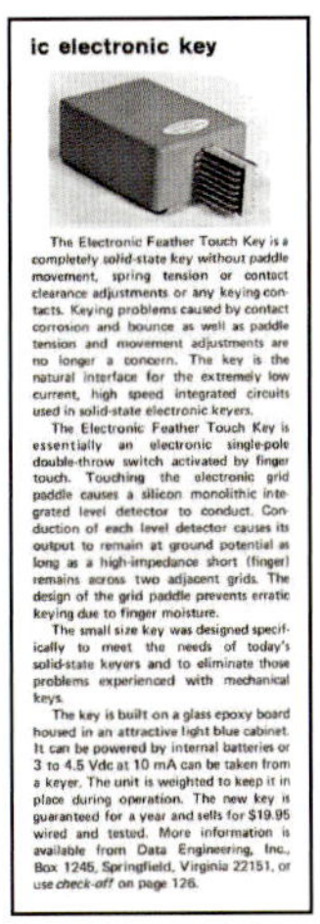

ic electronic key

The Electronic Feather Touch Key is a completely solid-state key without paddle movement, spring tension or contact clearance adjustments or any keying contacts. Keying problems caused by contact corrosion and bounce as well as paddle tension and movement adjustments are no longer a concern. The key is the natural interface for the extremely low current, high speed integrated circuits used in solid-state electronic keyers.

The Electronic Feather Touch Key is essentially an electronic single-pole double-throw switch activated by finger touch. Touching the electronic grid paddle causes a silicon monolithic integrated level detector to conduct. Conduction of each level detector causes its output to remain at ground potential as long as a high-impedance short (finger) remains across two adjacent grids. The design of the grid paddle prevents erratic keying due to finger moisture.

The small size key was designed specifically to meet the needs of today's solid-state keyers and to eliminate those problems experienced with mechanical keys.

The key is built on a glass epoxy board housed in an attractive light blue cabinet. It can be powered by internal batteries or 3 to 4.5 Vdc at 10 mA can be taken from a keyer. The unit is weighted to keep it in place during operation. The new key is guaranteed for a year and sells for $19.95 wired and tested. More information is available from Data Engineering, Inc., Box 1245, Springfield, Virginia 22151, or use *check-off* on page 126.

A product review for Data Engineering's Feather Touch key from the May 1972 *Ham Radio*.

Space-Matic 21-B

Data Engineering's Space-Matic 21-B keyer featured a "dot tune" mode that sent a string of dots, allowing transmitter tune-up with less stress on the finals. Also offered were selectable modes emulating eight popular keyers. This keyer dates to around 1973.

Data Signal Mighty MOS Keyer

The Mighty MOS keyer was made by Data Signal Incorporated of Albany, Georgia. Circuitry includes four CMOS logic gates. This device was manufactured in the mid-1970s. The keyer has adjustable controls for weight, speed, volume, and pitch. The Mighty MOS requires 6–12 volts DC for a power source.

Dentsu Seiki Model DA-1 Keyer

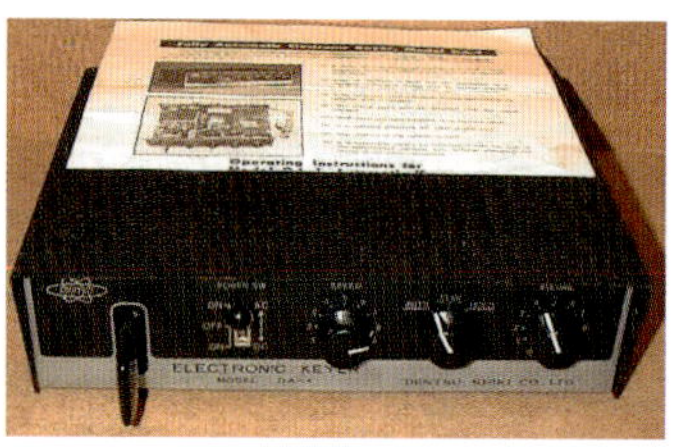

The Dentsu Seiki DA-1 was a user-selectable fully automatic or selectable semi-automatic keyer. It operated either on AC or 12 volt DC power. A built-in single-lever paddle was included. Controls were provided for speed and sidetone volume, and a selectable semi-automatic mode was offered. This keyer dates to the mid-1960s.

DEWSBURY ELECTRONICS STAR-MASTERKEY DEVICES

Dewsbury Electronics was started by G4CLX in Stourbridge, England. The company produced a line of several very competent automatic keyers and a memory keyer with various versions of the name "Star-Masterkey."

Star-Masterkey

Star-Masterkey Mk II

The Star-Masterkey and Star-Masterkey Mk II offered either full automatic or semi-automatic modes. Front panel controls for speed, weight, sidetone level, and tone were provided. Rear panels included a socket for external power and two phono sockets for the transmitter keyed line.

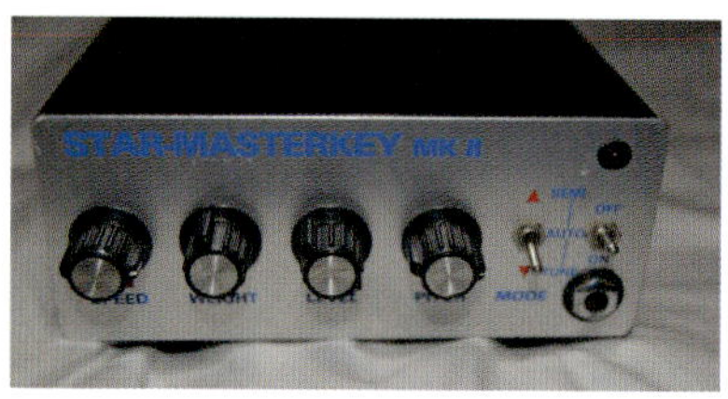

Star-Masterkey CMOS Memory Keyer

The Star-Masterkey CMOS Memory Keyer has 8 memory banks, 2 of which can be set for beacon/repeat CQ mode; the keyer uses four internal AA cells for power. Speed range is 7–42 wpm. This keyer also offers a tune position for transmitter tune-up, a headphone jack, keyer output compatible with grid-block keyed transmitters, and adjustable sidetone.

Dick Smith Morse Keyer

The Dick Smith device is an Australian keyer dating to the 1970s. Dick Smith was an Australian ham who at one time owned a chain of Woolworth stores. Many of these keyers were used with the New Zealand Galbraith paddles. The keyer also has a tone input that allowed it to be keyed from a tape recorder audio signal.

Digi-Key IC Keyer

Digi-Key Corporation was founded by Dr. Ronald Stordahl in 1972; the company is the fourth largest electronic component distributor in North America and the fifth largest electronic component distributor in the world. It was Stordahl's interest in ham radio that is credited for providing the incentive to form Digi-Key. The name "Digi-Key" comes from an electronic keyer kit (the Digi-Key IC keyer kit) that Stordahl developed while he was in college and sold to the amateur radio community. The original kit consisted of an IC keyer chip, a small PC board, and miscellaneous parts; it sold for about $15. The Digi-Key IC keyer is no longer produced.

"The *FACE THAT LAUNCHED A THOUSAND FISTS*"!

DIGI-KEY IC KEYER

FEATURES:

- all solid state
- linear speed control 5-50 wpm
- exact weight and ratio for perfect code
- self-completing
- transistor output for most grid block rigs —100 V. at 35 MA. maximum. Optional relay available for cathode keying.
- completely wired and guaranteed with full instructions.—Furnished less power supply, chassis, and paddle.

PRICE: $16.50 POSTPAID WORLDWIDE **RELAY: $3.00**

Digi-Key ad from the December 1969 issue of *QST*.

Note: There was also a keyer project called the "Digi-Key" published in the October 1989 issue of *Ham Radio*. The article by Ronald King detailed the construction of a basic TTL 7400-based keyer with dot/dash memory.

Digi-Yama ME-II Keyer

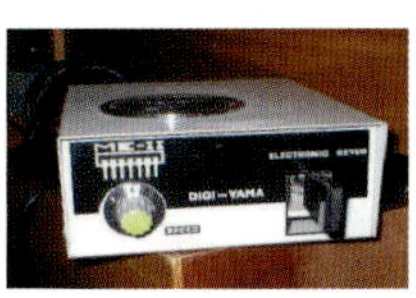

The ME-II is a seldom seen 1980s vintage Japanese keyer. Rear panel connections are for 220 volt AC input and a keyed line output for the transmitter. The built-in single-lever paddle is a simple piece of bar stock with stiffness adjustable via a sliding damper; contact spacing is set using screw adjustments and locking thumbwheels. This keyer includes a sidetone monitor but no memories.

Drake, R. L. CW75 Keyer

The Drake CW75 Electronic Keyer was developed as a matching accessory for the TR5 and TR7 series of Drake equipment. It can be used with straight keys, paddles, or squeeze paddles for iambic operation. The keyer will provide keying for transmitters using cathode keying, grid-block keying, or solid state transmitters. CW75 speed range is 5–50 wpm. This keyer features an internal speaker with an adjustable sidetone from 700–1000 Hz. Terminals are provided on the rear panel for 12 volt DC input, keyed line, and a hand key or paddle. Alternative DC power can be obtained by mounting an internal 9 volt battery.

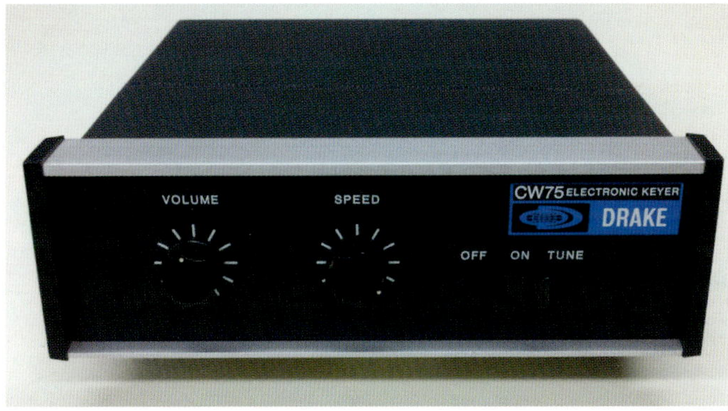

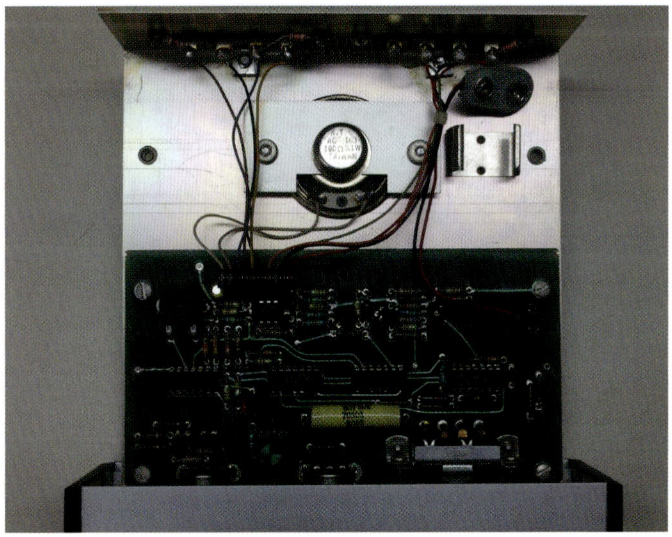

Duomatic Auto-Key Model AKS-7

The Duomatic AKS-7 was manufactured by Electronic Signal Devices of San Carlos, California. This early electronic keyer featured internal relays for keying and used two 50B5 tubes. Speed range was variable (12–50 wpm), with dots and dashes self-completing. An adjustment on the rear panel allowed for setting the dot/dash ratio. There was also a front panel switch

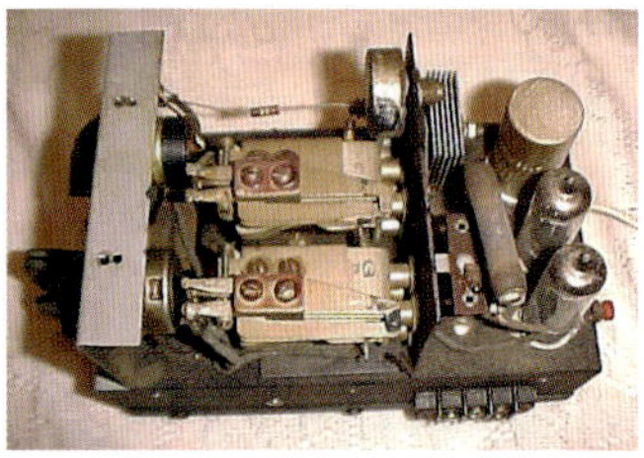

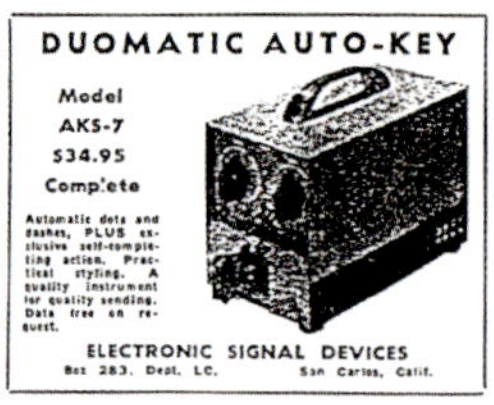

for keyed line closure to aid transmitter tune-up. Flyers for this keyer noted the controls were recessed to not interfere with operator sending. This device dates to the late 1940s.

Dynamic Electronics DE-130 Keyer

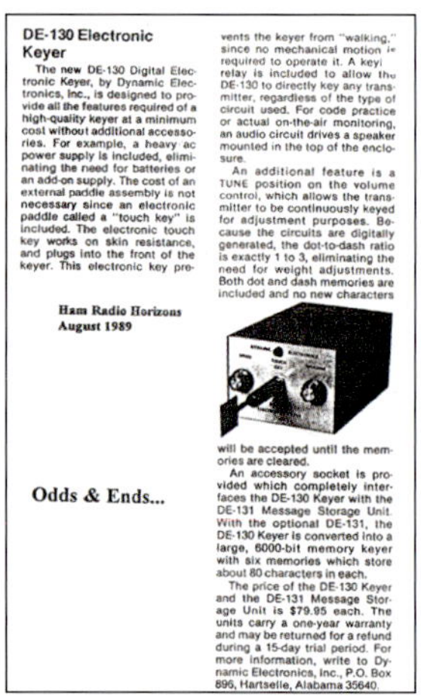

DE-130 Electronic Keyer

The new DE-130 Digital Electronic Keyer, by Dynamic Electronics, Inc., is designed to provide all the features required of a high-quality keyer at a minimum cost without additional accessories. For example, a heavy ac power supply is included, eliminating the need for batteries or an add-on supply. The cost of an external paddle assembly is not necessary since an electronic paddle called a "touch key" is included. The electronic touch key works on skin resistance, and plugs into the front of the keyer. This electronic key prevents the keyer from "walking," since no mechanical motion is required to operate it. A keyi relay is included to allow the DE-130 to directly key any transmitter, regardless of the type of circuit used. For code practice or actual on-the-air monitoring, an audio circuit drives a speaker mounted in the top of the enclosure.

An additional feature is a TUNE position on the volume control, which allows the transmitter to be continuously keyed for adjustment purposes. Because the circuits are digitally generated, the dot-to-dash ratio is exactly 1 to 3, eliminating the need for weight adjustments. Both dot and dash memories are included and no new characters will be accepted until the memories are cleared.

An accessory socket is provided which completely interfaces the DE-130 Keyer with the DE-131 Message Storage Unit. With the optional DE-131, the DE-130 Keyer is converted into a large, 6000-bit memory keyer with six memories which store about 80 characters in each.

The price of the DE-130 Keyer and the DE-131 Message Storage Unit is $79.95 each. The units carry a one-year warranty and may be returned for a refund during a 15-day trial period. For more information, write to Dynamic Electronics, Inc., P.O. Box 896, Hartselle, Alabama 35640.

Ham Radio Horizons
August 1989

Odds & Ends...

A product review from *Ham Radio Horizons*, August 1989.

A DE-131 message storage unit advertisement from the January 1979 *QST*.

East German Elektronische Morsetaste

Shown is an Elektronische Morsetaste keyer. This is an East German (GDR) single-lever keyer dating to 1968 from the DL3HRT collection. The circuit is transistorized and uses 26 germanium transistors. The model number is EMT 567 of GDR production.

Eico Model 717 Keyer

The Eico Model 717 was a very popular kit sold in the mid- to late-1960s. The Model 717 featured a speaker and internal AC power supply. The keyer has design similarities to the T.O. keyer, with one major difference being the Eico used a reed relay/field coil for transmitter keying, as opposed to the T.O.'s mercury-wetted relay. This keyer also featured variable pitch for the sidetone and selectable speed ranges. The keyer was reviewed in the July 1967 *QST*.

ELDICO KEYERS

Eldico was owned by Donald J. Merton (W2UOL/K2AAA); he was also the CEO. Merton was sometimes called Mr. Eldico. Merton was born in 1916 and passed away in 1996, after he retired and relocated to Port St. Lucie, Florida. In the 1940s, Merton chose Queens, New York, as his company location. Eldico employed many locals and area hams. At one point Eldico had a large military contract that proved good for business and allowed Eldico to advertise more extensively in *QST*.

The Eldico EE1

Eldico introduced the EE1 tube keyer to the ham market around 1950 called the "Electronic Bug." This keyer featured a built-in paddle, and had controls for speed and weight. The EE1 also featured self-completing characters, and was available as a kit or factory wired. Eldico ads listed a "jewel-mounted keying mechanism" as a feature.

The Eldico EE-2

The EE1 was soon followed by Eldico's EE-2, which included a keying monitor and built-in speaker. The EE-2 (Eldico had started using hyphens in the model designation) used four 6C4 triode tubes. Keyer speed range was 8–50 wpm. The EE-2 sold for $39.95 wired and tested in 1950.

It is interesting to see how one of the old tube keyers fit into the whole of an early boat anchor station. The equipment belonged to Robert Singer (K2LEM) and his daughter, Margie Wenski (K2UTS). Margie furnished this wonderful old photo, which seems to be centered on the Eldico EE-2 keyer. Although some remember the mechanical noise of the paddle and the clacking relays, Margie had much fonder memories of the EE-2. "I loved using that Eldico keyer and could really send code like the devil. That keyer with the red paddle was so cool. It was the best part of our station and I truly loved using it. I did not operate phone, I was strictly a CW gal all the way."

The Eldico EE-3

The EE-3 electronic keyer used some creative mechanical design to fit in all the components required for the tube circuits. It had an internal 117 VAC supply and a built-in paddle, and featured self-completing characters. Speed range of the EE-3 was 5–50 wpm. The EE-3 had the ability to mute the station receiver while routing keyer sidetone through the station headphones or to its own internal speaker. The EE-3 dates to 1957; the advertisement is from the March 1957 *QST*.

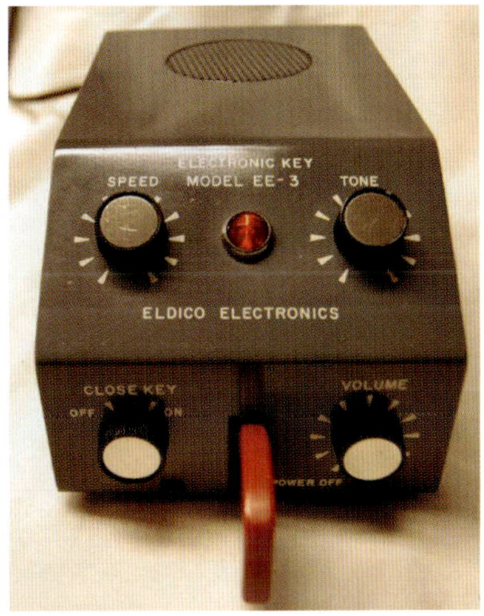

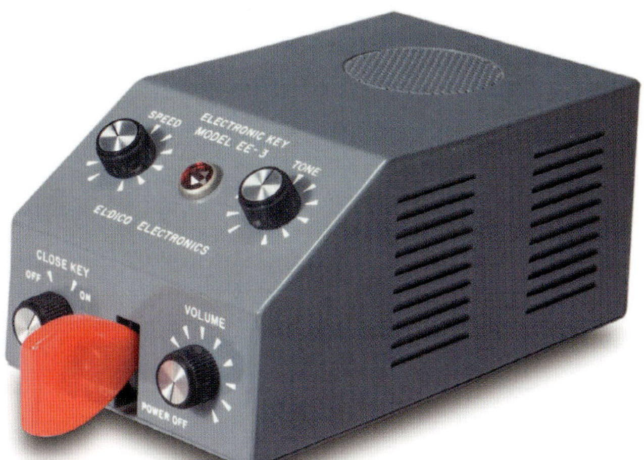

Elektor Ultimatic Keyer Kit

Elektor is an independent, international electronics magazine in circulation since 1974. *Elektor* has developed their ultimatic keyer kit with PCB and 16F688 PIC device; they also provide the software. The keyer features standard and ultimatic operating modes and 5–100 wpm adjustable speed. The circuit is designed to give automatic character and word spacing, and there is a sidetone monitor. Output keying is via a transistor or reed relay. Power can be from 110 VAC or 13.8 volts DC.

Embedded Research Super TiCK Keyers

The TiCK-4 is the fourth generation of the Tiny CMOS keyer chip from Embedded Research of Rochester, New York. The device was designed in the late 1990s, and sold very well due to its performance and low price (approximately $15). The TiCK-4 is a great example of RISC-based microcontroller technology. Users built the keyer and installed it in the case of their choice, or in the rig itself. The TiCK-4 was pin-for-pin compatible with earlier TiCK chips, so a user could simply

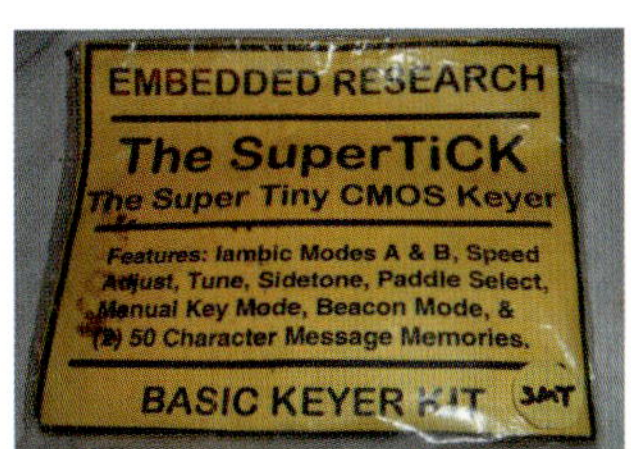

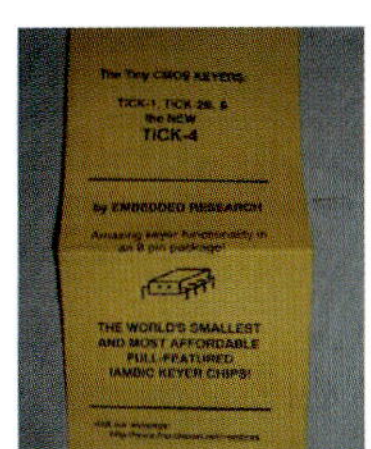

replace the older IC with a new TiCK-4 and have all the new features. This device featured iambic A and B modes, adjustable speed control, tune mode, paddle select, sidetone on/off, and straight key mode. Two 50-character message memories were offered, as was a beacon mode. The TiCK-4 requires 3–5 volts DC. Embedded Research also offered a deluxe kit including the chip, all parts and PC board, and case.

Note: Brad Mitchell, founder of Embedded Research and the TiCK keyer, agrees that N6KR's Wilderness Radio keyer predates his first PIC-based Atomic Keyer—introduced in Dayton in 1996—but says his later TiCK models were the first use of an 8-pin PIC as a keyer.

FISCHER KEYERS

Fischer keyers are made by Dirk Fischer (DK2FD); he marketed a series of iambic and memory keyers known for their aluminum cases and very solid internal paddle construction. At least one model used a paddle made by Schurr. The company also sells microwave and RF products worldwide.

DFM-1

The DFM-1 is an iambic keyer offering both A and B modes in an attractive aluminum case; speed range is 8–80 wpm. Front panel controls are for weight and keyer speed. There is a transmitter tune button on top of the case. The rear panel includes a coding switch, allowing the user to disable the dot or dash memory, disable the 800 Hz sidetone, choose reverse paddles, do a keyer reset, or turn off the internal battery supply; a jack for an external paddle is also provided. After five minutes the keyer electronics enter a "sleep" mode to conserve power. Battery life of the three internal AA batteries is projected to be around 1,000 hours. Transmitter keying is isolated via optocouplers.

DFM-2

The DFM-2 is a memory version of the Fischer iambic keyer with four memories provided. Three different versions of the DFM-2 are shown: one without internal paddles, one with the standard mechanical internal paddle, and one with the optional Schurr-made internal paddle.

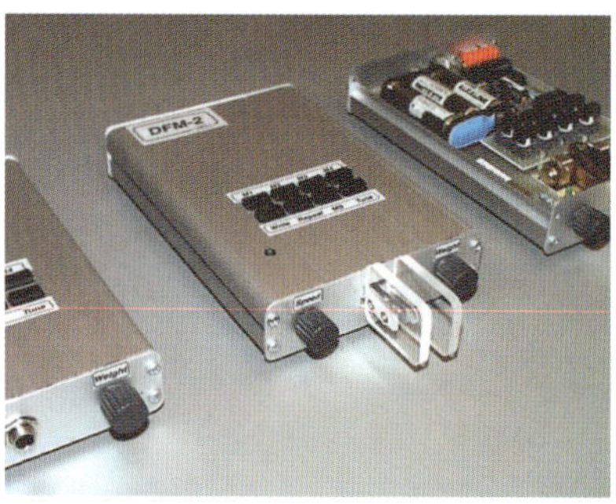

DFM-3 and DFM-4

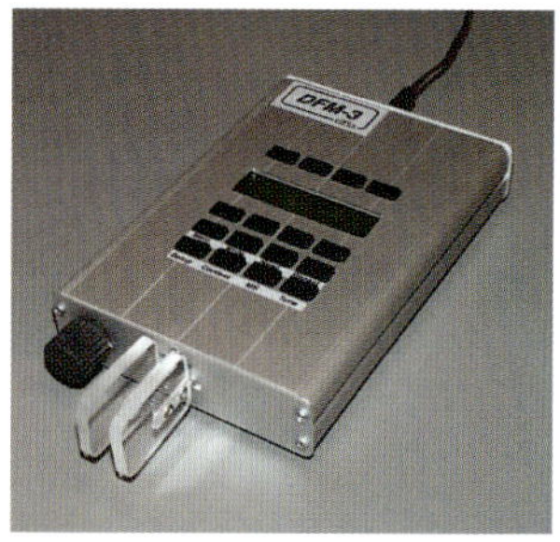

The DFM-3.

DFM keyers are also available in -3 and -4 versions, giving expanded memory capabilities and digital readout for menu display and memory programming.

Fist Fighter Keyer

The Fist Fighter keyer was produced by the Blacksburg Group of Blacksburg, Virginia, and was available in kit and assembled form; selling price for the assembled version was $79.95. Product literature states this keyer was designed for easy transition by

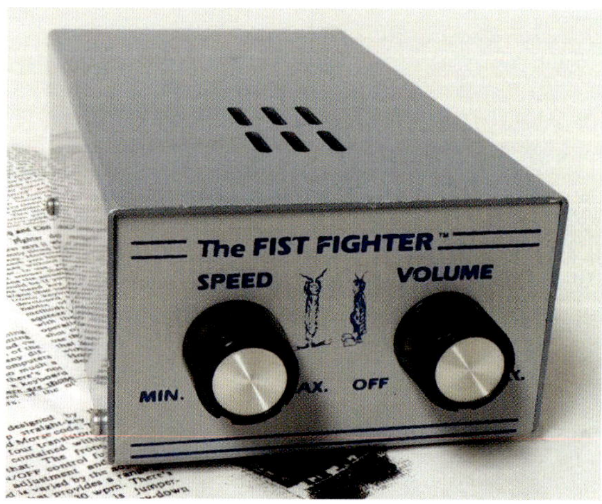

straight key users. Speed was advertised as 3–30 wpm. The keyer also featured a built-in sidetone and internal speaker. CMOS circuitry was employed, and the design allowed for keying grid-block and solid-state transmitters.

Frankford Radio Club (FRC) Keyer

The FRC keyer was designed by N3RD; the device pioneered the use of memory keyers among contesters before commercial units were available. According to the FRC website, this keyer became a standard part of the contester's arsenal in the 1970s. The FRC provided bare boards and a schematic; it was up to the user to populate the board and find a suitable power supply and enclosure. Many continued to use this keyer for decades. Hundreds of circuit boards were distributed by FRC; the keyer was never commercialized or advertised, and exists in many form factors due to homebrewing of the enclosures.

G3KHZ Keyers

G3KHZ is the callsign of Derek Cox, who built a number of electronic keyers and dual lever squeeze keyers in the early 1970s. The two arm elements of this single-lever paddle move independently from one another. This paddle also uses silver-plated contacts, and is known for its light action when sending.

The base measures approximately 4 inches square and houses the electronic keyer and internal 9 volt battery. The keyer design allowed for dot and dash memory; the dot "store" feature could be delayed via a jumper setting. G3KHZ produced these devices for almost twenty years.

G4ZPY Keyers

The G4ZPY TiCK combination features one of Gordon's miniature paddles mounted on top of an enclosure housing a TiCK keyer. The keyer was also available as a separate item.

Gordon (G4ZPY) built and marketed an entire line of Morse keys and paddles. The combination devices included a keyer that formed part of the base. The product's description states this unit has been designed with speed control of 8–60 wpm, power switch/key down switch, automatic inter-character spacing, and a loud/off/soft sidetone switch. Also, a stereo socket is underneath the paddles so the iambic keyer may be used with another key. The keyer is powered externally with a 9 volt DC supply or battery.

GHD KEYERS

GHD keyers are made by Toshihiko Ujiie (JA7GHD) in Sendai City, Japan. GHD is known for being innovative, and also for the high level of quality in their devices. The GHD website proclaims GHD keys as "the telegraph key of the world."

The GHD GK607A Super Memory Keyer

The GK607A is an iambic keyer with memory built in the base of a dual lever paddle; no sidetone monitor is included. The keyer allows the user to select between full or semi-automatic modes. Six memory banks are available. The device offers a paddle reversing switch for left hand operation. Power is obtained from two internal AAA batteries. A translation of the GK607A Japanese manual provides a wonderful prediction: "By using this machine, ham life becomes fun."

The GHD GD263 Switchable Bug/Keyer

The GHD GD263 Super Autobug keyer is a somewhat rare device; apparently GHD did not sell too many when it was in production. It was a combination "e-bug" and electronic keyer, with a switch provided to select between the two. In the bug setting, the device became an electronic semiautomatic bug key. The GD263 was able to record CW messages with whatever "bug spacing" or rhythm the operator used. Standard ⅛ in. phone jacks were provided on the rear of the key for external key or

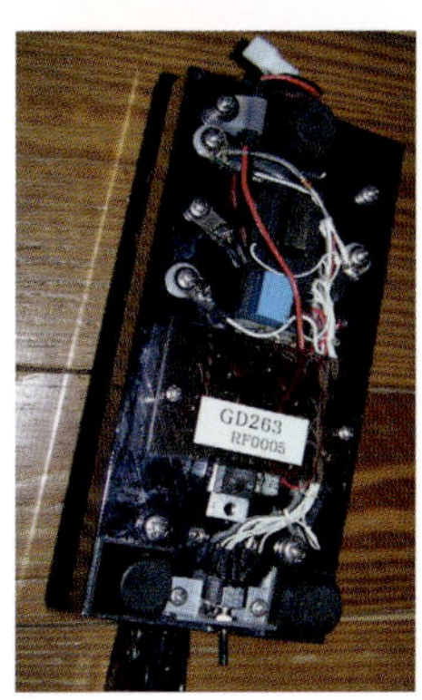

paddle, and for keyed line to the transmitter. The keyer was fully shielded by a metal enclosure. The GD263 was powered by internal batteries and offered low current consumption.

The GHD GK509 and GK509A Memory Keyers

GK509 and GK509A memory keyers are feature packed, small keyers designed to mount on top of GHD paddles, although the keyers can be used standalone. The GK509A adds message memory from the basic 509, giving eight message memories with a 6,000 character capacity and a built-in speaker for sidetone; power is supplied from internal batteries. Each keyer can switch up to 60 volts DC at 200 mA. Also offered is a bug mode for semi-automatic sending.

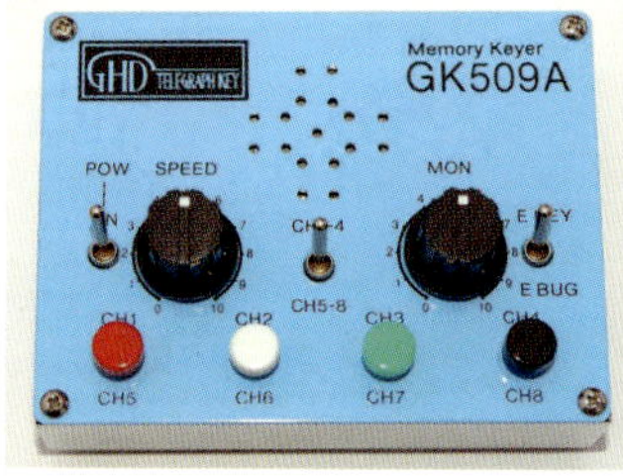

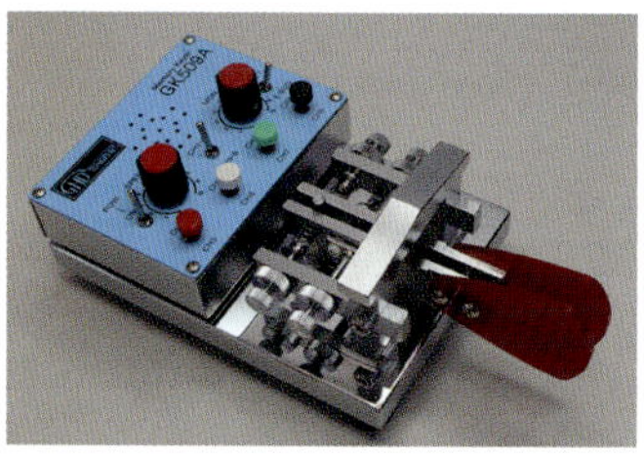

GI4CFQ Keyer

The GI4CFQ keyer combines a Brown Brothers paddle with an 8044 Curtis chip (Mode A). The keyer output uses a reed relay, and provisions are made for key and paddle input, as well as sidetone on/off. Power is from an internal 9 volt battery.

Globalman EK-108D Keyer

The Globalman EK-108D is apparently the same device as the Katsumi EK-108D, but is a version imported by the Global Import Company (W6PHA) sold under the Globalman name.

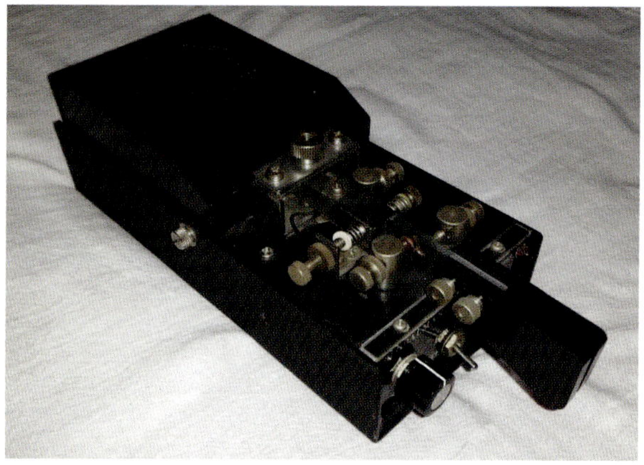

NEW!
GLOBALMAN™
IC KEYER
EK-108D
with built in monitor
$64.95 ppd.
W6PHA — GLOBAL IMPORT CO.

A March 1974 *QST* advertisement for the EK-108D.

This keyer was advertised in the March 1974 *QST*. Speed range was 5–50 wpm, with self-completing dots and dashes and a dot memory feature. This device uses two internal D-cell batteries. Controls are included for tone and sidetone volume. The Globalman EK-108D can key a transmitter of nearly any type with permitted voltage to 250 volts and up to 2 amperes current. The keyer also included a built-in speaker and offered an earphone jack.

Greek KK Series Keyers

The KK-4 (above) was also available in a black finish. The KK series of keyers was designed by Kostas Kambakis. The KK-4 offers selectable auto or semi-automatic modes, and an adjustment for weighting. Power is supplied by internal batteries or can be provided from an external source.

The KK-5 is a basic keyer with a switchable 110/220 volt internal power supply. Front panel controls are provided for keyer speed and tone. An internal speaker and a relay for the keyed line are part of the design. The rear panel includes the power on switch and a jack for keyed output to the transmitter.

Greek Lycos Keyer

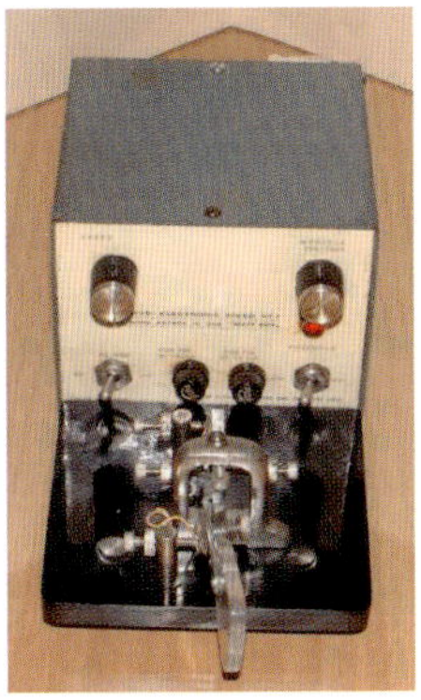

This "Electronic Speed Key" features an integral mechanical paddle with similarities to the Vibroplex Vibrokeyer. Keyer design includes an internal AC power supply and front panel fuses with controls for keyer speed and sidetone volume, and a combination of transistors and tubes.

Close-up of the keyer's integrated paddle mechanism.

HA5IW Memory Keyer

Simon (HA5IW) runs a small amateur radio product business in Hungary that designs and sells antennas, tuners, amplifiers, and other RF-related products. The memory keyer shown features adjustable speed, internal sidetone generator with speaker, character spacing, and LED display. A dual memory is included, and output is via keying relay. Power is obtained from an internal 9 volt battery, or externally with a 7–20 volt DC power source. The circuit is based on a 16F84 PIC device.

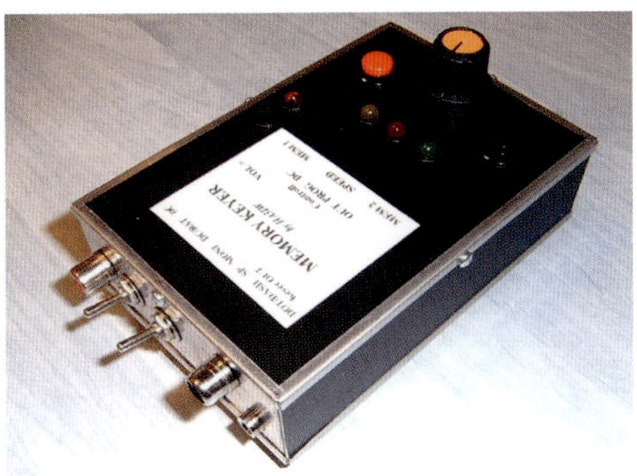

HAL Communications Corporation Keyers

HAL Devices started as a partnership in 1966, but not long after that (1972) became HAL Communications Corporation. They are based in Illinois, producing modems and communications related software products. In 2012, HAL was bought by Barrett Communications of Australia. Bill Henry (K9GWT), HAL's retired president, says the name "HAL" was chosen because it was one letter ahead of IBM. The first HAL keyers were models 111, 211, and 311, followed by the 1550 and the 2550.

One of HAL's earliest keyers was the Model 311.

The HAL 1550 was reviewed in the December 1972 *QST*.

The HAL 2550 keyer.

The HAL 2550 as shown in one of their product advertisements.

Hallicrafters (W9TO) Keyers

Southern Illinois native and Purdue University graduate Jim Ricks (W9TO) developed the famous W9TO keyer, a 6-tube device licensed for production by Hallicrafters. On June 26, 1962, Ricks received a patent for his invention, called the Telegraphic Keyer (3,041,397). Beginning in May 1959, Hallicrafters marketed the device as the HA-1 T.O. keyer; it was reviewed in the November 1960 issue of *QST*. The T.O. keyer uses a mercury-wetted relay for keying the transmitter. The T.O. keyer was the first to precisely generate dots and dashes digitally based on a single timebase. Compared to modern keyers,

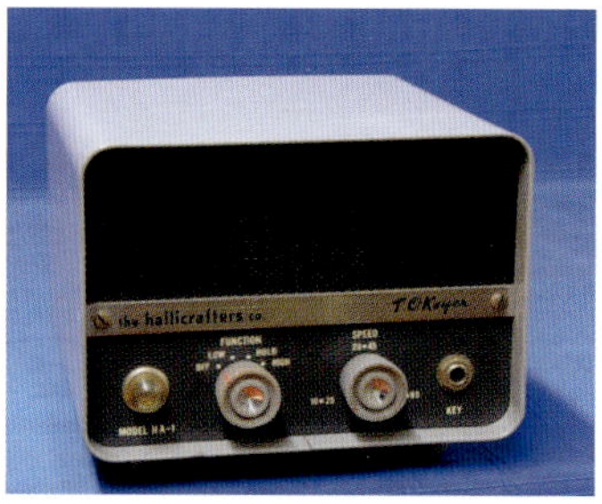

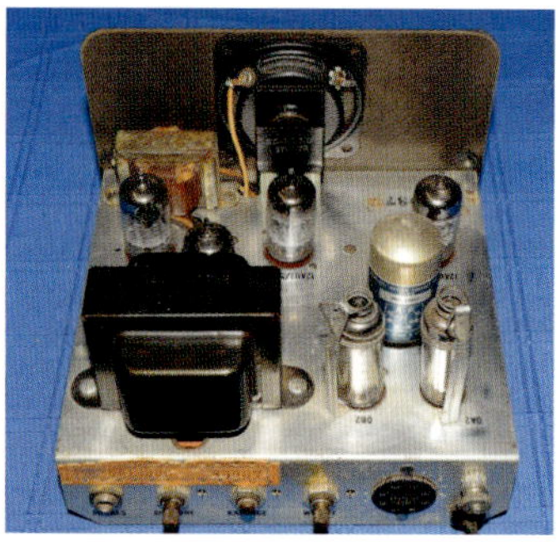

Jim Ricks (W9TO).

the T.O. keyer had some minor flaws. Because the keyer did not have a dot or dash memory, the operator could easily send too far ahead of the keyer, the result being an extra character was sent, or a character was inhibited and did not get sent. The T.O. keyer required the operator be aware of input timing, but this was a skill that most easily mastered, and it did not seem to affect the T.O. keyer's popularity at the time.

In 1961, Hallicrafters introduced their transistorized version of the T.O. keyer and called it the T.T.O. keyer. Known more formally as Model HA-4, it sold for $60. The Hallicrafters HA-4

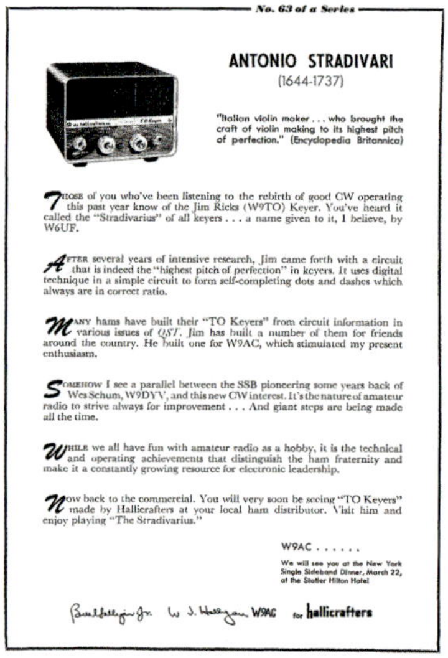

No. 63 of a Series

ANTONIO STRADIVARI
(1644-1737)

"Italian violin maker . . . who brought the craft of violin making to its highest pitch of perfection." (Encyclopedia Britannica)

THOSE of you who've been listening to the rebirth of good CW operating this past year know of the Jim Ricks (W9TO) Keyer. You've heard it called the "Stradivarius" of all keyers . . . a name given to it, I believe, by W6UF.

AFTER several years of intensive research, Jim came forth with a circuit that is indeed the "highest pitch of perfection" in keyers. It uses digital technique in a simple circuit to form self-completing dots and dashes which always are in correct ratio.

MANY hams have built their "TO Keyers" from circuit information in various issues of *QST*. Jim has built a number of them for friends around the country. He built one for W9AC, which stimulated my present enthusiasm.

SOMEHOW I see a parallel between the SSB pioneering some years back of Wes Schum, W9DYV, and this new CW interest. It's the nature of amateur radio to strive always for improvement . . . And giant steps are being made all the time.

WHILE we all have fun with amateur radio as a hobby, it is the technical and operating achievements that distinguish the ham fraternity and make it a constantly growing resource for electronic leadership.

NOW back to the commercial. You will very soon be seeing "TO Keyers" made by Hallicrafters at your local ham distributor. Visit him and enjoy playing "The Stradivarius."

W9AC . . . . . .

We will see you at the New York Single Sideband Dinner, March 22, at the Statler Hilton Hotel

W9AC for **hallicrafters**

This Bill Halligan (W9AC) essay from the March 1960 *QST* was clearly meant to generate interest in the W9TO keyer, but it also does so for CW in general. Hams were excited about this keyer and the Vibroplex Vibro-Keyer that came out almost at the same time. The keyer and the paddle were sometimes referred to as a matched pair.

Front panel and inside view of the Hallicrafters HA-4.

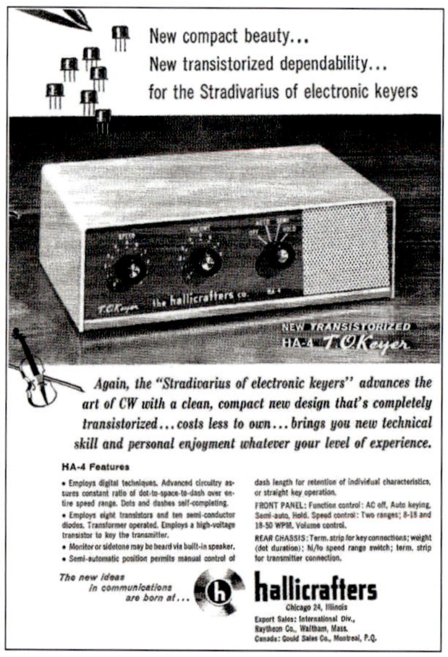

An HA-4 T.O. keyer ad from the June 1961 *QST*. Very early keyers such as the one shown in the ad have "T.O. Keyer" on the front panel; soon this was changed to "T.T.O." for Transistor T.O. keyer.

employs solid state circuitry to form perfect code characters and dot-space ratios; speed range is 8–50 wpm. The HA-4 design uses 8 transistors and 10 diodes. Some of the features of the keyer include a sidetone signal generator with built-in speaker and volume control. The front panel features a speed control knob, volume control knob, and a four position rotary control knob (with power on/off, auto, semi, and hold positions).

The rear panel has one 3-terminal strip used to connect the keyer to the transmitter and a second 3-terminal strip for the CW paddle connection. Two other controls are provided for weighting and high/low speed. The keyer requires a power source of 125 volts AC.

Hamcrafters (K1EL) Keyers

Steven Elliott (K1EL), who sold products as K1EL Systems, is now known as Hamcrafters. The K8, an 8-pin mini DIP, was K1EL's first keyer I.C. back in 1997, followed by the K10, K12, K14, WK1, WK2, K42, and now the WinKeyer version 3 is available (see chapter 15). K1EL is noted for compiling a list of "please add this" requests, as well as things that no other keyer chip offers. K1EL has been selling keyer ICs for more than 18 years.

The K16 is Hamcrafters' latest keyer kit. K1EL notes Microchip continues to offer higher functionality in their PIC microcontrollers, allowing him to offer better and better keyer ICs. The K16 has non-volatile EEPROM memory; when power is removed the chip retains messages and settings. Twelve memory slots are provided, along with many new embedded commands. You can buy just the I.C., or choose between two K16 kits. Speed range is 5–59 wpm.

HamGadgets Keyers

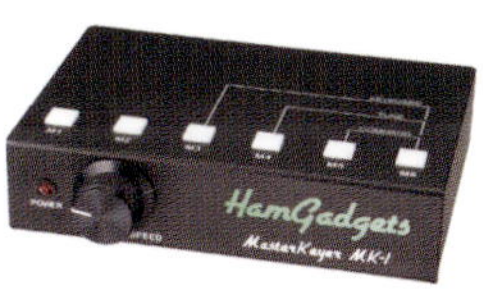

HamGadgets is the creation of Dale Botkin (N0XAS). The HamGadgets website and all associated with the company is run by Dale; it was established in 2003 in response to interest in the PicoKeyer. Some of Dale's family members often help with assembly of HamHadget devices, such as the MasterKeyer MK-1.

The MasterKeyer MK-1 is a microcontroller-based keyer offering five banks of six memories per bank (30 total) for over 7,500 characters. Memory selection uses one of the six LED-lighted pushbuttons on top of the keyer. The color of the pushbutton changes according to whether the operator is recording or playing a message. A large front panel knob allows for speed adjustment. The MK-1 includes sidetone, and lets the operator decide on program options by using a paddle or via computer using a text-based interface. The MK-1 can be updated by installing new firmware available periodically from HamGadgets. The MK-1 also has built-in USB capability; the USB host connector can be used to load updates directly from a USB flash drive. All operating parameters and memory contents can be saved to a flash drive; different operators can simply plug in their flash drive and load their unique keyer parameters into the keyer, making the MK-1 versatile.

The HamGadgets PicoKeyer Plus is an improved version of the original PicoKeyer. The new Version 4 firmware adds a number of new features, including the ability to set the speed control upper and lower limits, auto-resume for pauses in stored messages, instant access to messages 2, 3, and 4, and more. The on-board lithium coin cell battery will last at least a couple years of normal use. The PicoKeyer Plus includes a small on-board speaker and works with single or dual lever paddles and straight keys, and the device can be used as a code practice oscillator. FLASH memory updates are offered periodically. Iambic Modes A and B and an ultimatic mode are offered, as is QSO serial number generation. There is a beacon mode and four memories available. Even the tune-up mode has been thought through: it can be set to give "dits" for a 50% duty cycle. The keyer operates on 2.5–5.25 volts DC. No battery power is required for memory retention; the device uses FLASH and EEPROM memory to store all settings and message memory. Keyer output is through dual MOSFETs and will handle transmitters using positive or negative keying up to 60 volts.

Hamco Carson with EK-1 Keyer

HAMCO bought the key business from HAL in 1978, and was the first production company to use magnetic tensioning in their designs. The Carson base consisted of a hand-polished brass plate mounted on a wooden bottom section. The bottom enclosed the EK-1 keyer using a Curtis 8044 keyer chip. The speed control is visible in the indented area of the wooden base. Vibroplex eventually bought HAMCO in 1982, and used the design to

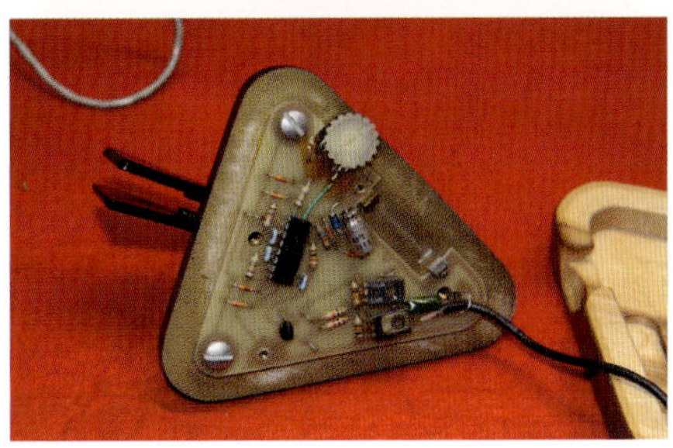

The Carson with an EK-1 keyer, which used a Curtis 8044 chip.

produce the Brass Racer. The HAMCO version of the design incorporated updates to the original FYO approach, helping keep all the mechanical parts from accidentally coming loose. The Carson with EK-1 keyer was produced 1978–1982 and sold for $129.95. HAMCO devices are considered scarce by collectors.

Hamkeyer HK5A

The HK5A is a house brand keyer offered by Ham Radio Center in St. Louis, Missouri. The keyer is based on the Curtis 8044 chip and offers Mode A keying. This is a good basic electronic keyer for those who prefer Mode A keying. Rear panel jacks are provided for paddle/key connection, as well as for transmitter keyed line, for either grid-block, cathode, or solid state keyed transmitters. The HK5A uses internal C-cell batteries. Some users have reported RFI problems, possibly exacerbated by the plastic case of the HK5A.

Hammarlund HK-1B Keyer

The Hammarlund HK-1B is a transistor keyer that can be used in automatic, semi-automatic (bug), or straight key mode. Hammarlund advertised this device as the "personal touch" keyer. Controls are provided for sidetone volume, keyer speed, weighting, and mode selection. The HK-1B was first sold in 1966 for $39. Hammarlund Manufacturing Company takes its name from founder Oscar Hammarlund, who arrived in the US from Sweden in 1882.

Hamshop CW Keyer

Hamshop is a Czechoslovakian company; they make this iambic memory keyer with integrated touch paddles. Ondra (OK1CDJ) is responsible for developing this device.

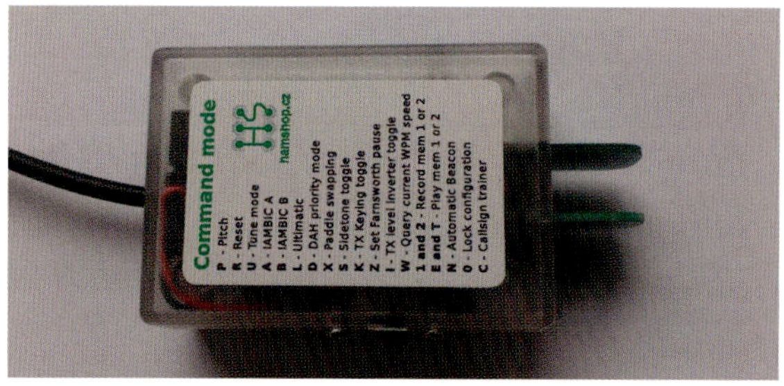

Heathkit Keyers

The HD-10 was Heathkit's first electronic keyer. It was non-iambic, and used an internal single-lever paddle design that actuated two microswitches for dots and dashes. Circuitry was all transistor, with components mounted on one large circuit board; power was 115 volts AC using an internal supply, although provisions were made for external battery power. Other controls included standard speed and sidetone volume, and a screwdriver-adjustable pot—concentric with the speed control—was provided for setting weight. A "hold" switch on the top panel was used for transmitter tune-up. Two speed ranges were offered to the builder (10–20 wpm or 15–60 wpm); the range desired was selected during the kit build. This keyer design only accommodated grid-block keyed transmitters. The HD-10 was sold 1965–1974; it was reviewed in the January 1967 issue of *QST*.

The Model HD-1410 (circa 1975) keyer unit has a nice appearance with the traditional Heathkit two-tone paint scheme. Front panel controls were for keyer speed, sidetone volume, and a volume knob pull switch for keyed line "hold," allowing convenient transmitter tune-up. The circuit design included a highly rated dot/dash weighting scheme. The paddle mechanism used aluminum arms with brass shim stock elements providing the arm return force. Adjustments were coarse, and it was not always easy to open up the unit to make additional tweaks. Once set, mechanical operation of the internal paddles tended to loosen up over time. Many HD-1410s were modified to allow use of external paddles. The HD-1410 was susceptible to RF, sometimes leading to erratic code. Over time reliability issues crept up for many owners due to IC/socket intermittents.

The Heathkit Model SA-5010 uMatic keyer is a 3870 microprocessor-controlled iambic device with speeds of 1–99 wpm. All operating parameters are controlled by the keypad. One unique feature of this keyer is the use of removable touch-sensitive dual-lever paddles. Ten CMOS memories are available for up to 240 character storage. The SA-5010 can insert incremental serial numbers as well as other command strings. Four levels of random code generation allow for 6,400 different practice sessions. A rear panel jack is included that permits use of an external mechanical paddle. The CMOS memory has a battery backup and the keyer includes a built-in sidetone oscillator and speaker. Two alternative keying outputs (positive and negative for grid-block keying or for an RS232 port) are provided on the rear panel. This keyer can be powered by batteries or 115 volts AC. The basic and the -A versions were produced for ten years beginning in 1981.

HFB Keyer

The HFB keyer was designed by Howard F. Batie (W7BBX) and carries the model number PMK-1. This keyer was produced by HFB Enterprises of Herndon, Virginia, in the mid-1970s. Batie specifically designed this keyer for the contest operator, including features such as high memory capacity and nonvolatile, nondestructive memory readout. The design centers on an Intel P2102, a 1024 bit static-programmable random access memory (PRAM) in a 16-pin package. Circuitry includes 26 ICs, 8 transistors, and 16 diodes. Programming is done directly from the paddle. The keyer offers speeds of 10–60 wpm with iambic operation. Included is a built-in AC supply, as well as a set of four AA NiCad batteries. An optional accessory (PMK-1R) allowed for remote control of the four memories.

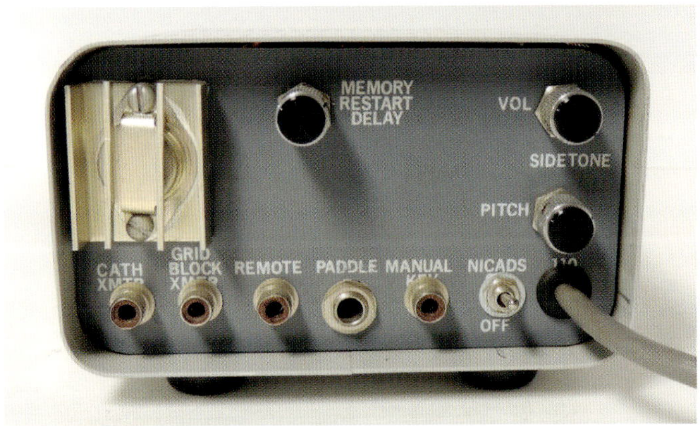

Hi-Mound Keyers

The EK-100 features internal or AC power and an internal sidetone monitor with volume control. The unit is housed in a horizontally oriented plastic case with a single paddle extending from the front.

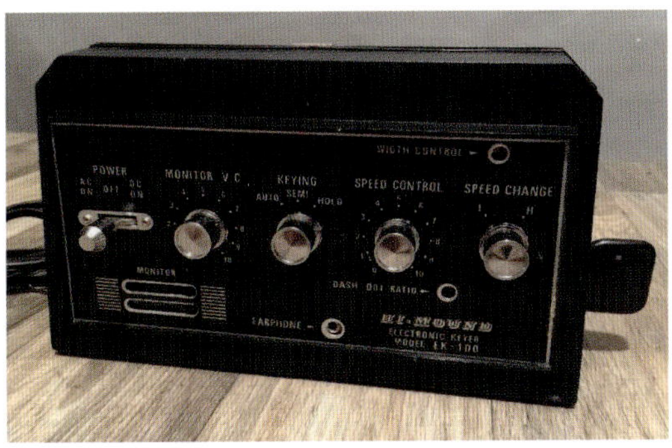

The Hi-Mound EK-101 CW electronic keyer. This rare keyer offers a straight key on the top panel in the form of a large black push button. The front of the keyer incorporates an internal single-lever paddle. The EK-101 was able to interface with the optional AA-101 Adaptor (a keying relay accessory covered in chapter 13).

The Hi-Mound Electronic Keyer DA-1. The DA-1 appears to be the same device as the Dentsu Seiki DA-1, which was the earlier keyer sold before Hi-Mound marketed their brand.

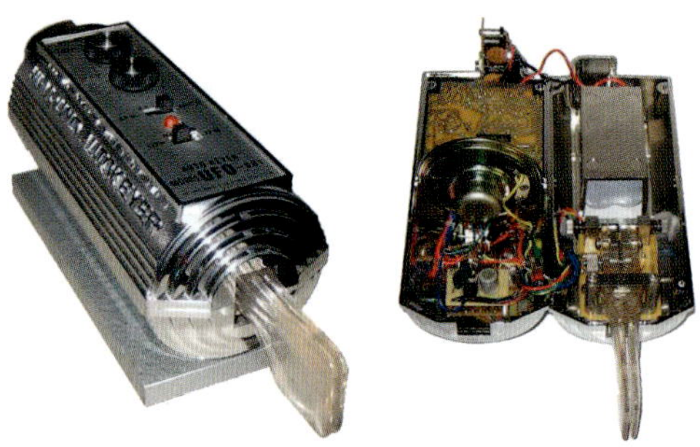

The Hi-Mound UFO-001 (above) is a dual-lever, non-iambic keyer famous for its art deco design. This keyer uses internal NiCad batteries for power with a floating charge system, and also has a built-in speaker for the sidetone monitor. Basic keyer functions, such as selectable full automatic or semi-automatic modes, are offered. The rear extension includes jacks for an external paddle and keyed line.

The EK-103 keyer (below) features built-in sidetone, selectable power source, selectable speed range, and a large button functioning as a manual key. Mechanical dual-lever paddles are also built in. This keyer runs on external AC power or 12 volt DC power. The rear panel includes a keyed line output and jack for an earphone.

Idiom Press Keyers

Idiom Press was formed in 1982 by Bob Locher (W9KNI). The name comes from a derivative of the phrase "I Did It On My Own." The Logikey K-1 came out around 1990, and was the first in a series of increasingly sophisticated CMOS microprocessor memory keyers; the K-5 is the latest version. The K-1 is a multifunction keyer that uses commands sent to the keyer in Morse from a paddle; there is also a group of four memory/function buttons on the top of the unit. Some of the features include iambic keying with dot-dash memories, ability to store multiple messages, generation of contest serial numbers 0001 to 9999, speeds from 6–60 wpm, built in sidetone, adjustable weight, and a tune function. The K-1 is powered from an internal 9 volt battery.

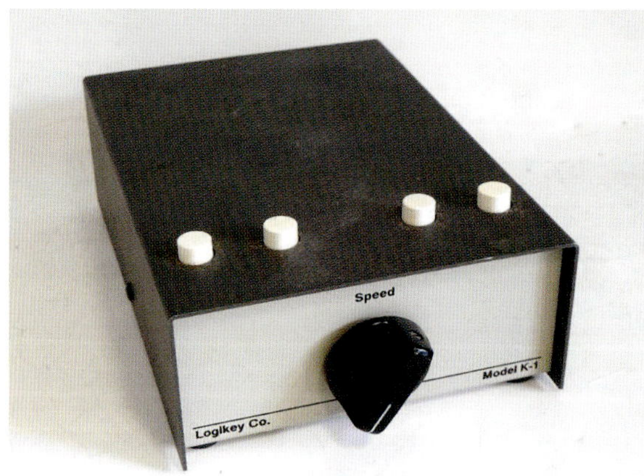

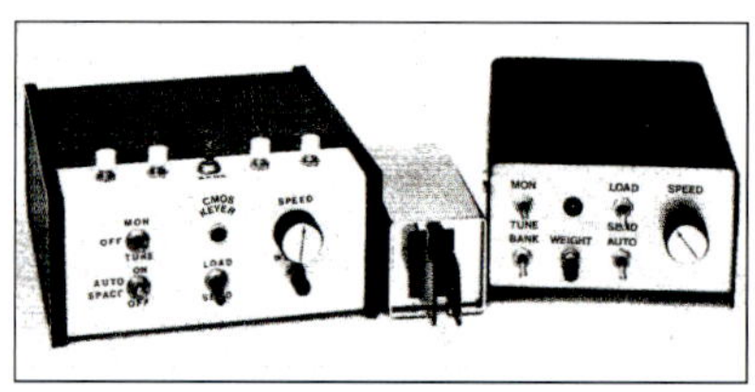

The original Russell/Southard 1981 CMOS Super Keyer.

A LogiKit CMOS-4 keyer with heritage based on the 1981 and 1990 designs.

Idiom Press also puts out a corresponding series of CMOS keyer kits called "LogiKits." The first, the LogiKit CMOS Super Keyer II, came out in the early 1990s. The November 1990 *QST* carries a more complete description of the CMOS Super II keyer. The article, by Jeff Russell (KC0Q) and Bud Southard (N0II), also offered a kit of parts and a PCB. The successful Logikey series of keyers followed this introduction. Idiom Press used a powerful and well integrated Motorola chip called the 68HC705C8 that had built-in program storage, RAM, and sufficient I/O, including an ADC for the speed port. The original CMOS Super Keyer used twelve ICs; it was described in an October 1981 *QST* article by Russell and Southard. The Super CMOS II keyers marked a quantum jump in keyer technology, with one chip offering numerous features, several memories, and very low power consumption.

Note the Super CMOS II keyer represents the first commercial use of a single chip microcontroller in a keyer application. This predates the PIC by five full years and this product line had a full and respected life. The Curtis 8043 and 8044 series predated this product, but the Curtis chips were "hard-wired" ASIC chips that did not involve code and lacked the inherent power and flexibility of the microcontroller used by the Idiom Press developers.

IK1OJM "Psychedelic" Keyer

This unique IK1OJM unit has colored lights that flash in coordination with the message being sent. A YouTube video at one time showed this keyer in action. With the exception of the colored lights this keyer is a fairly straightforward device. While it will definitely serve the purpose of a keyer, it may also give operators incentive to call *CQ* more frequently.

IK5XCT DXKEY Keyer

The DXKEY is described as an "interactive" CW keyer. This keyer was designed by IK5XCT around a PIC device and is also available as a kit. The front panel offers simplicity in the form of two controls for keyer power and keyer speed (variable 5–60 wpm). Iambic Modes A or B are selectable, and means to adjust weighting and program messages are offered; four programmable message slots are available, and sequential serial number generation is part of the design. A beacon mode is available, as are incremental serial numbers for contesting. Keyer programming is done via the paddle in CW. A remote, two-button keypad is also included, allowing easy access to keyer features.

Italian KK58 Electronic Keyer

This Italian device may appear to be homebrew, but the fact it has a model number may mean it was a limited production device. It is a dual-lever keyer—probably iambic—and has at least one memory function. It can be seen on the home page of Domenico (I6HWD).

Jackson Harbor Press Keyers

The Jackson Harbor Press series of keyer kits and keyer chips are designed and produced by Chuck Olson (WB9KZY). The Jackson Harbor keyers require few external parts and can easily be built on a small perforated board, then enclosed in a metal tin or within a transceiver. Alternatively, some kits come with a PCB. The chip designs are very popular with portable and QRP operators.

The PK-Basic chip was a simpler, inexpensive device offering pot or paddle speed control, 16 character memory, a beacon mode, speed readout, and iambic Mode A and B keying. The chip required very little power to operate. Speed range was 5–39 wpm.

Jackson Harbor continued to improve the PK series with PK-2 and PK-3 models being offered. The PK-2 keyer kit was a PIC-based keyer; among its features were pot or paddle speed control, two 52 character RAM-based memories, embedded pause, iambic Modes A and B, 10 character callsign memory, and 2N7000 MOSFET output transistor. Speed range was 5–39 wpm. The PK-2 kit price was $18. The PK-3 dates to around 2003, and was an 8-pin PIC-based keyer that was an exact drop-in match for the TiCK. This device also offered pot or paddle speed control and an auto character space feature. The PK-3 featured pot or paddle speed control and a speed range of 5–39 wpm. Other features included one 57 and one 52 character memory, a callsign memory, Mode A or B iambic keying, beacon mode, variable delay up to 60 seconds, one touch CQ using callsign memory, speed readout via the sidetone, and low standby power. The PK-3 sold for $8.

The PK-4 is the most recent Jackson Harbor keyer chip and features two separate 80 character memories, plus an 80 character callsign memory. The callsign memory can be split into two 40 character segments, resulting in three programmable message memories plus callsign; message and callsign memories are non-volatile. An option for a solid-state relay (SSR) offers nearly universal keying; any rig with a key line carrying less than +/- 400V at 120mA can be keyed if the SSR option is installed. The PK-4 has a variable pitch sidetone oscillator and pot-controlled or programmable speeds from 5–50 wpm. Also featured are program selectable ultimatic or iambic Mode A or B keying, automatic CQ, beacon send mode, non-volatile settings, and programmable pause. The programmable features of this keyer are available with a single-lever paddle. The PK-4 is pin compatible with previous PK keyers, as well as the TiCK and K8 keyer chips with the addition of a 10k ohm pullup resistor between pin 1 and 4 of the keyer chip socket, adding more features and flexibility—especially pot speed control—at a lower price. In a typical configuration the user supplies a pot, two jacks, a push-button switch, piezo speaker, and a battery holder. The PK-4 is designed to key modern transistor rigs with a low positive key-line voltage (without the SSR option).

The Island II Keyer kit from Jackson Harbor Press sold for $32 in 2003. The kit included a MOSFET keying transistor and two onboard tone and weight adjustment pots. The buyer supplied the cabinet, speed control, knob, all input/output jacks, and a power source. This keyer offered a 5–70 wpm speed range, 56 non-volatile memories, ultimatic mode, and iambic Modes A and B.

JEM Electronics JK-1E Keyer

The JK-1E was produced by JEM Electronics of Maumee, Ohio, most likely in the early 1980s. It uses an internal Ham-Key paddle, and the basic circuit utilizes several ICs on a single circuit board. Power is from an internal 9 volt battery.

JFE Keyer

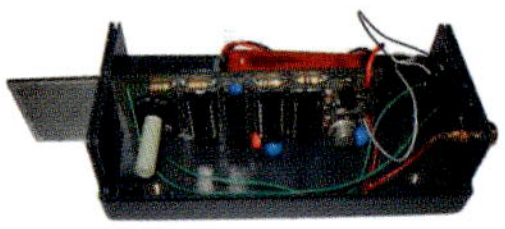

JFE is based in Munich, Germany, and is the manufacturer of this CMOS squeeze Morse key.

K3NG Keyer

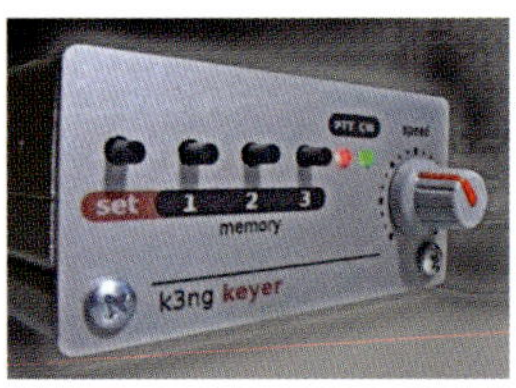

This is the K3NG-branded version of the nanoKeyer, an Arduino-based CW contest memory keyer (refer to the nanoKeyer entry in this chapter for more information).

K7SRA Keyer

Don (K7SRA) built this keyer/paddle combination in the early 1990s. It is machined from brass and mounted on a wood base, with a CMOS Super Keyer II in the base. The memory keyer is similar to the Logikey CMOS keyers and works the same way. The red wheel adjusts keyer speed. The Plexiglas bottom cover allows viewing the keyer parts. AA batteries can be seen around the perimeter. This paddle was reviewed in the December 1992 issue of *73*.

Kanga Products "The Oner" Keyer

This kit is an inexpensive single IC Morse code keyer/processor based on the K14 IC developed by Steve Elliot (K1EL). Although the original "Oner" keyer (PIC-based) is no longer supported by Kanga, they do support their K14 and K16 designs.

Kansas City Keyer KC-1

The Kansas City Keyer Model KC-1 was produced by Lance Johnson Engineering; this keyer is a compact, feature-rich memory keyer with 1,500 characters of memory. The keyer was introduced in 1984 at the Dayton Hamvention and was sold until 1989. The KC-1 was one of the first microprocessor-based CW keyers ever sold; most keyer designs that followed would use microcontrollers (AEA being a successful exception).

The KC-1 used the Rockwell/Motorola 6502 8-bit microprocessor—which the first Apples were based on—and became very popular among CW contesters. Lance Johnson Engineering offered three different remote memory accessories (RM-1, MM-1, and BR-1) to enhance the keyer's memory functions. The KC-1 featured analog and digital speed controls and a flexible serial number generator. Basic keyer functions were controlled by a 16-position keypad and external paddle. The KC-1 was reviewed in an October 1985 *CQ* article written by Bob Locher (W9KNI) of Idiom Press fame.

Katsumi Keyers

Katsumi Electric Co. began making commercial keyers in the 1960s; their equipment has a reputation for high quality and reliability. Katsumi equipment can be found in many markets in Japan, including amateur radio, commercial, and military. There has been little family interest in keeping the business running and Katsumi manufacturing has apparently ceased.

EK-9X top and inside view. Note the simple single-lever aluminum bar and the nut/bolt contact adjustments.

The EK-26 and an inside view.

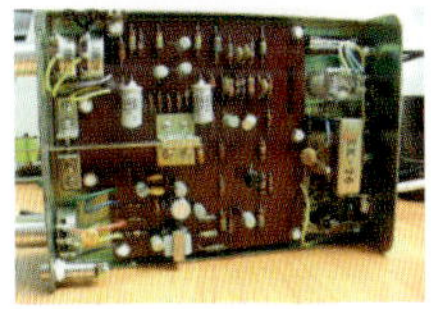

As with the earlier EK-9X, mechanical design of the EK-26 internal paddle is very basic. Note the thin flexible arm on the single-lever paddle; contacts are mechanically adjustable.

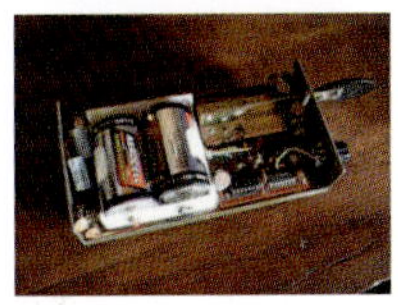

The EK-105D's built-in paddle has adjustable machined spacing and uses two internal D-cell batteries for power. Optionally, 3–6 volts DC can be provided externally by hooking up to a power jack on the rear panel. Controls include variable speed adjustment and a momentary pushbutton allowing transmitter tune-up.

The Katsumi Ele-Key EK-127 (below). This keyer uses an internal 115 VAC supply. The rear panel contains a terminal board for keyed line and the fuseholder. The EK-127 has a built-in sidetone and selectable full or semi-automatic modes.

The EK-130 Deluxe Electronic Keyer is a commercial grade electronic keyer; it is claimed to be the keyer used for Japanese Morse code examinations. The front panel contains the most frequently used keyer controls, including a switch to select full or semi-automatic mode. A unique feature is the speed meter, which displays the operating speed in words per minute, characters per minute, and Japanese commercial radio class test speeds. Rear panel terminals are provided for connecting an external paddle, bug, or straight key.

Katsumi's EK-150 offers adjustable keying paddles, a sidetone monitor with adjustable volume, speed control, and selectable transistor or relay output. This keyer does not include any memory functions.

The mechanical paddle arrangement of the EK-150, typical of many Katsumi keyers.

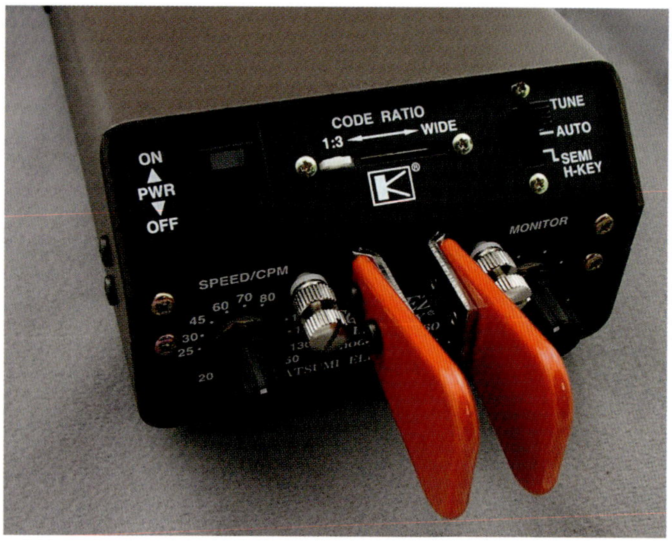

The EK-160 electronic keyer/paddle combination provides a step up in packaging aesthetics. It is a commercial grade device with a precision dual paddle built in. Terminals are provided for connecting a paddle and/or bug or straight key, and the keyer offers a selectable auto or bug mode. Speed is adjusted by using a front panel control labeled in characters per minute (5 characters per minute is approximately equal to 1 wpm). The fingerpieces can be removed and switched for left-handed operators. One added feature not usually seen with built-in paddles is the front panel adjustments for contact spacing. Full dot and dash memories are available in the iambic keying mode. Weighting (called "code ratio" on the front panel) can be adjusted from 1:3 to about 1:4 using the sliding control. The EK-160 includes a code monitor with volume control on the front panel and pitch control on the back. The rear panel also includes a jack for headphone connection. A high-speed reed relay is part of the circuit design, allowing the keyer to support negative-keyed rigs with up to 280 volts DC and 2A on the key line, or JFET keying for transistor-keyed positive voltage rigs can be selected.

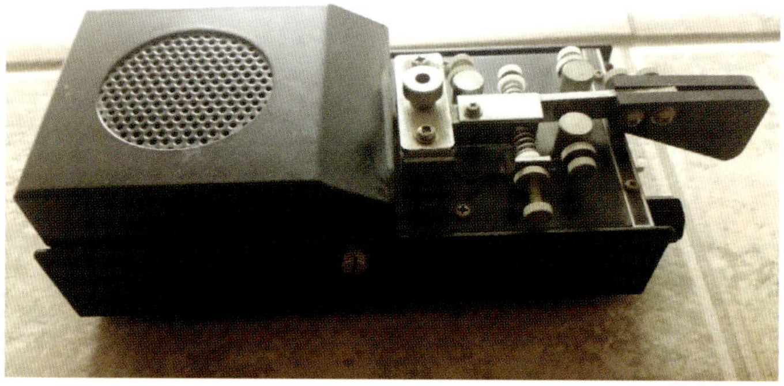

The Katsumi EK-108D is functionally and visually nearly the same device as the Globalman EK-108D, except the Katsumi name is on the front panel. Both devices offer a speed range of 5–50 wpm, with self-completing dots and dashes and a dot memory feature. Power is supplied from two internal D-cell batteries. Controls are included for tone and sidetone volume. The EK-108D can key a transmitter of nearly any type with permitted voltage to 250 volts and up to 2 amperes current. The keyer also includes a built-in speaker and an earphone jack.

The EK-121 keyer is one of many keyer designs marketed by Katsumi; this one carries the name "Katsumi Globalman." Katsumi also calls this model the "Ele-Key/Trans-Key." It is not an iambic keyer and uses a single lever to generate dots and dashes. This keyer will operate in a semi-automatic mode, simulating a bug. Speed adjustment is made by a sliding control,

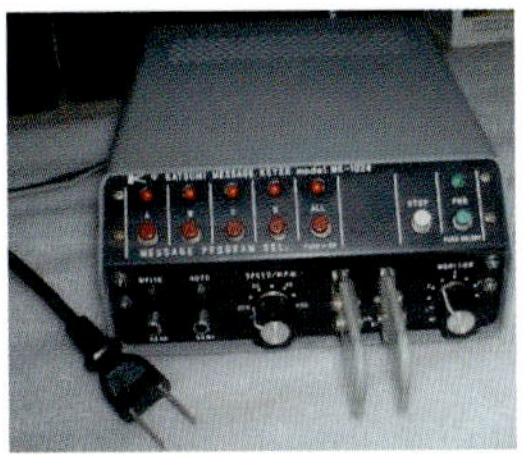

not calibrated in wpm, but in a linear scale 1–5. Two fingerpieces are mounted on a single-lever paddle.

The Katsumi MK-1024 is a dual-lever programmable memory keyer. The keyer features four memory locations that can be combined by pressing the "ALL" button. This device uses power from either the 115 volt AC line or externally supplied DC. The MK-1024 also has selectable relay or transistor output keying. Circuitry used ICs mounted on two plug-in circuit boards and a built-in speaker is included.

KC9ON Keyer

KC9ON calls this model the 3CPO. The unit combines the keyer, a twin-T oscillator, and the transmitter keying circuits into a single device. The keyer itself also includes a memory based on the DK3LJ memory keyer IC. It offers an iambic training mode and a QRS button to slow down speed. The twin-T oscillator is advertised as having wave shaping, providing a near-sine wave signal properly shaped for CW. The output keying circuit can key rigs using positive and negative grid keying. Protection against reverse polarity input voltage is provided.

KEA Keyer

A very limited number of keyers combining the Galbraith paddle with a circuit based on the Curtis 8044ABM keyer chip were produced in 1997 by a club in Christchurch, New Zealand. Although most of the devices were kits, a small number of pre-assembled units were sold. The keyer was described in an article by K. P. Barnsdale (ZL3KB). This Brass Pounder club project was the result of a desire to combine the Galbraith paddle with an iambic electronic keyer circuit. The Curtis 8044ABM keyer chip was selected for this project.

All components were fitted to a PCB to minimize the amount of wiring; all that was required were the three wires to connect the paddle contacts and the two wires for the battery clip. Two key jack outputs were provided so a straight key can be connected in parallel for tune up or code practice.

K.E. Electronics Keyers

The KE-1X was an engineering model keyer built in 1976 while K.E. Electronics of Santa Ana, California, was designing their SQ keyer. Dual paddles were included, with tension and spacing adjustable from the front of the keyer. The only other front panel control was for keyer speed.

The K.E. Memo 4096 memory keyer provided the operator with four 1024-bit message locations; two of these could be combined for a longer message. This keyer's design also included a "loop" switch, allowing the user to continuously repeat the selected message. The Memo 4096 had a built-in squeeze paddle with tension adjustment from the front. The basic keyer design of the Memo 4096 was similar to other K.E. keyers, but the Memo 4096 added memory capacity and some associated features.

Although a bit puzzling, K.E. offered the Memo-512 in two different configurations, each with the same model number. Both units were essentially the same keyer, but one had a built-in squeeze paddle. Front panel layouts of the two keyers were quite different. Both Memo-512 keyers had two 256-bit message memories. The Memo-512 version without the built-in paddle had a rear panel input jack for an external paddle. Both devices offered iambic operation and dot and dash memories; both also used internal AC power supplies and included an internal speaker and adjustable sidetone.

Two different K. E. devices were called the SQ-Auto; photos show both versions (with and without internal squeeze paddles) These iambic keyers had dot and dash memories, as well as an AC power supply. The keyers were available with either reed-relay or transistor output keying and were first sold in 1977.

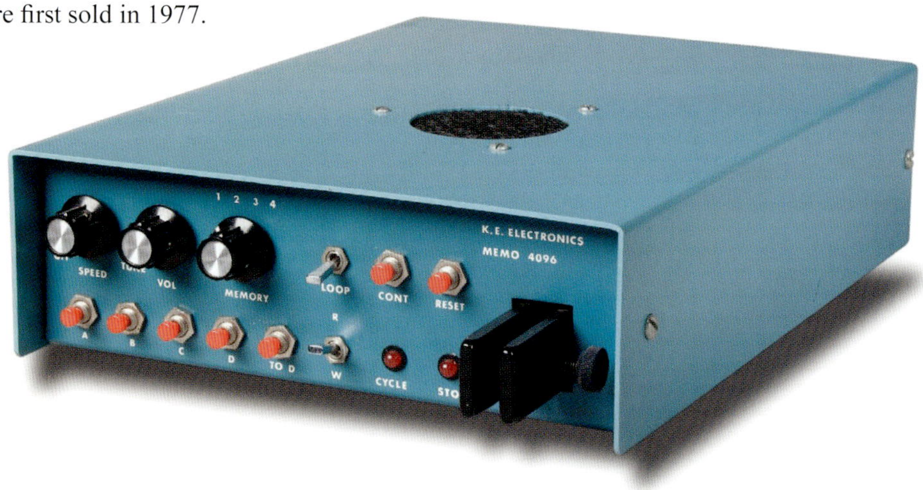

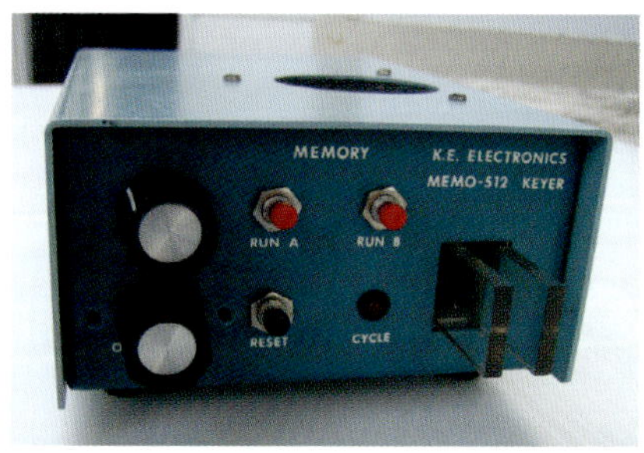

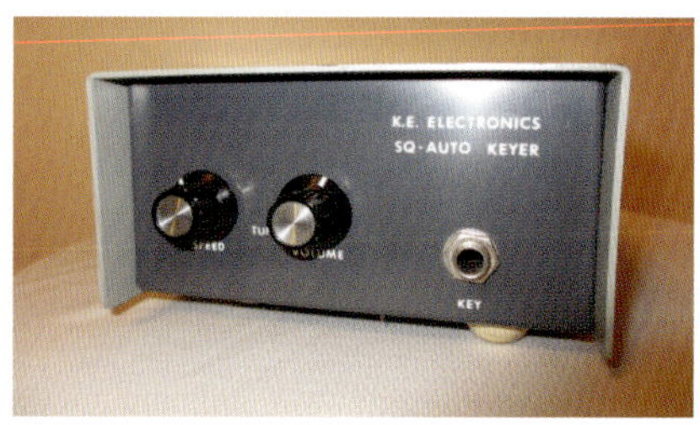

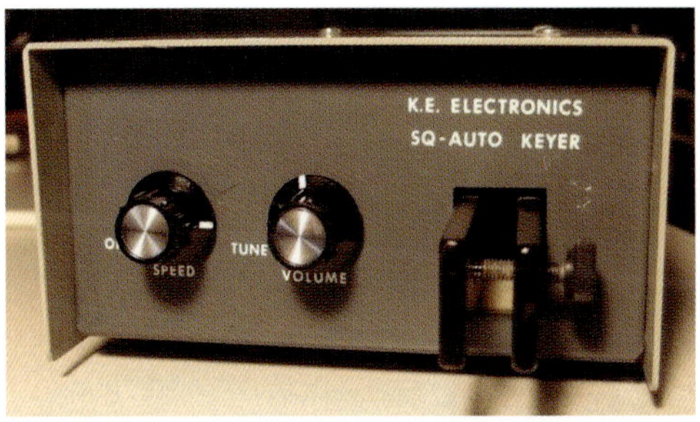

There was also a gray version of the SQ-Auto Keyer (the one with the built-in paddle).

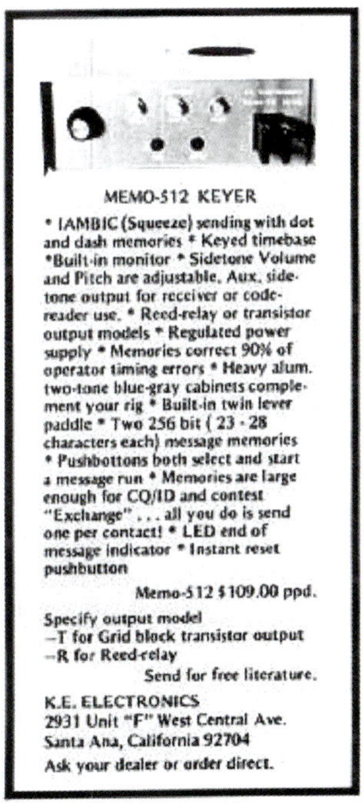

A K.E. Electronics Memo-512 keyer ad from the June 1977 *Ham Radio*.

Kenpro Keyer

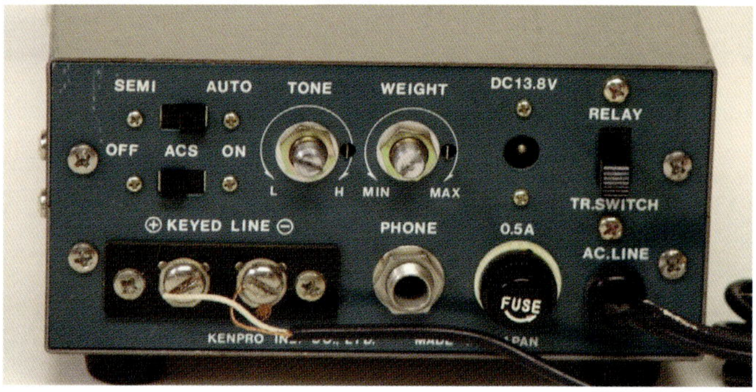

The Kenpro Model KP-100 is a basic iambic keyer with built-in paddles and front panel controls for keyer speed and sidetone volume. Integral switches are used with each of the two controls for transmitter tune and power on/off functions. Eight CMOS integrated circuits and associated components, as well as the AC power supply, are contained on one large circuit board. The internal paddles offer spring tension and contact spacing adjustments. The rear panel has a terminal strip for the keyed line and controls for tone and weight. Also on the rear panel are switches for relay or transistor keying and auto or semi-auto operation. A headphone jack is provided. The KP-100 was sold in the late 1990s.

The Kenpro KP-200 was a solidly built memory keyer with internal dual paddles and two banks of four 512 bit programmable memories that could be combined for a long message. Internal memory backup power was provided. Transmitter keying was done using selectable relay or transistor output. A monitor speaker was included, as was an internal AC power supply; the unit could also run on external 12 volt DC power. The design offered self-completing dots and dashes. The rear panel included controls for tone and weight.

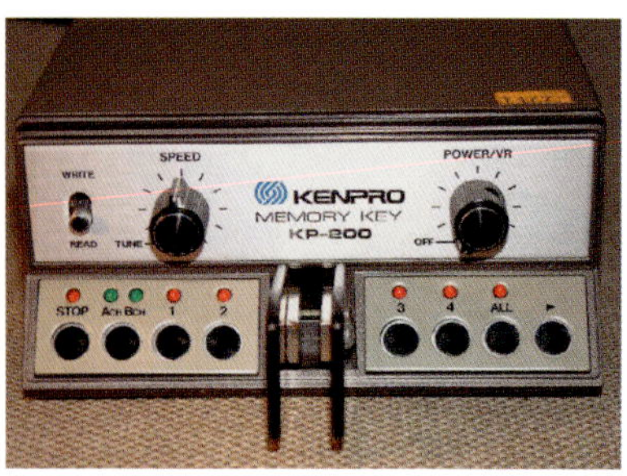

Kent Keyers

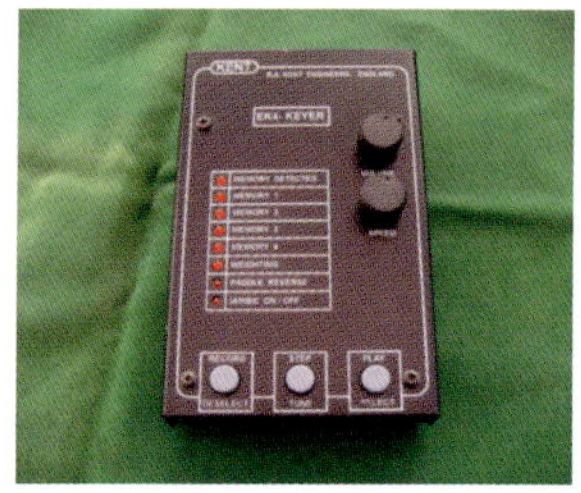

The EK4 is an attractive CW keyer made in England by R. A. Kent Engineers. The EK4 requires an external 9–12 volt DC power source. This keyer has four memories that can be programmed using the paddle. Memory playback can be looped, with variable time delay an associated feature. Paddle operation can be reversed for left-handed operators. Front panel controls include keyer speed and sidetone volume; a status indication is provided by a bank of eight LEDs. The EK4 keyer is available as the memory keyer (above), or as a basic keyer that can be upgraded to the memory device. Other keyer features include adjustable weighting, switchable dot and dash memories, and sidetone with variable volume and pitch.

At right is a generic Kent (because no model number is marked on the front or back of the unit) electronic keyer. Robert Kent said this model was referred to as the "Kent Electronic Keyer," and indeed it had no model number. It was made between 1988 and 1993. The keyer was designed by Lancaster University in the UK. Basic controls on the front panel are for speed, pitch, sidetone volume, and a pushbutton to allow for transmitter tune-up. Eight ICs are used in the design, with parts mounted on one large circuit board; there is an internal speaker included. The rear has a terminal board for the keyed line and an external DC power jack.

The Kent touch keyer is a twin touch paddle key and electronic keyer combined. The key is all electronic, with no moving parts, and the keyer is based on the Kent iambic keyer kit. The key and keyer kit, although small, is advertised as being within the building capabilities of a novice constructor using only a few basic hand tools and a small soldering iron. Kent states the unit's compact size and light weight make it the ideal portable unit, while the relatively low cost makes a perfect introduction to electronic keying. The key/keyer is only supplied by Kent in kit form, and includes a good quality PCB together with the two paddle PCBs. All components are supplied, as is a hardware pack and keyer base.

Kentronics Memory Keyer

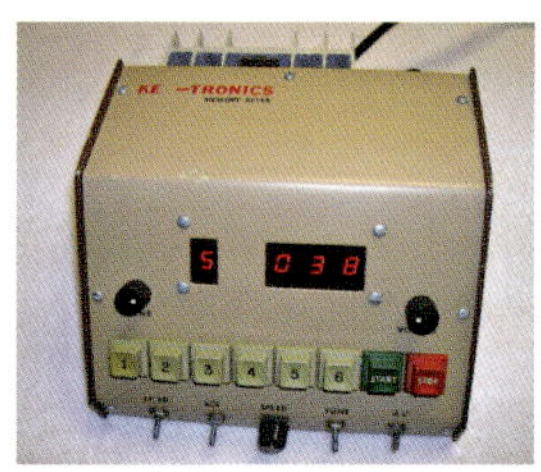

Not much is known about the manufacturer of this Kentronics keyer, but it is estimated to have been made around the mid-1970s. Power is provided by an internal AC supply. The six memory buttons give a clue as to number of memory banks and the switches provide power and tune functions. This unit also has a built-in sidetone.

Korean Hi-Speed Keyer

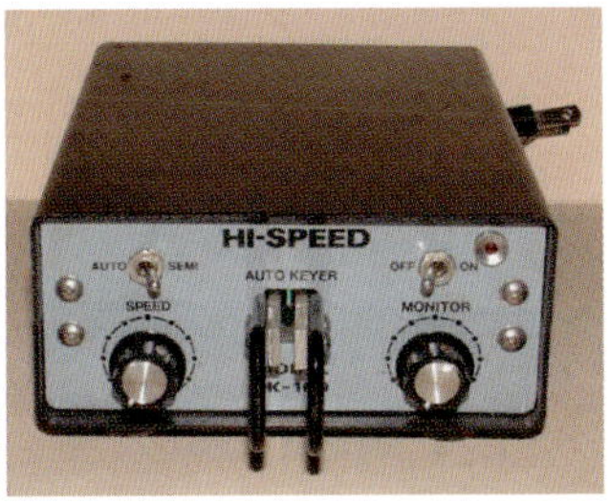

This small Korean-made device carries the model number EK-100, which is similar to the numbers Katsumi keyers use. The keyer is solidly built; the design uses ICs mounted on a single circuit board. The rear panel includes a terminal strip with connections for keyed line. Also on the rear panel is the adjustment for monitor tone, a selector switch for relay or transistor keying, a headphone jack, and DC power input jack. Typical power for this device comes from the 115 volt AC line.

Lance Johnson Engineering Cadet-CMOS Keyer

Lance Johnson Engineering, in addition to producing the Kansas City keyer, built this more basic CMOS keyer, the Model CC-1.

Little Monster Auto-Key

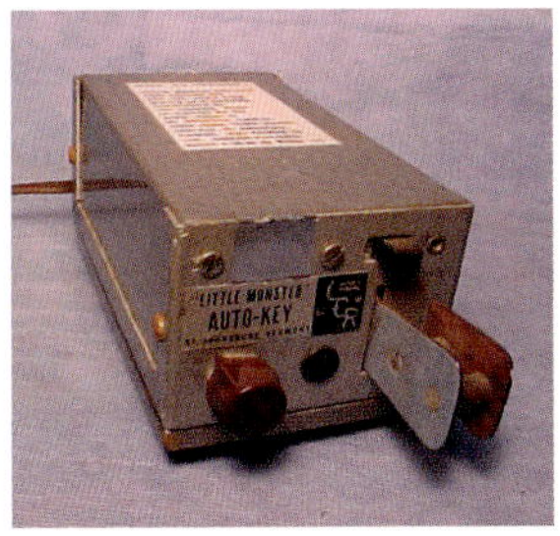

This small electronic key with unique 4-ball bearing pivot mechanism was manufactured by Alex Trembley (W1GQJ). The label on top reads: "Little Monster Auto-Key, St. Johnsbury, Vermont. Pats Pending by LCR." This device dates to about 1960. The idea for this keyer was patented (2,988,597) by Alexander Tremblay in June 1961, so the label must predate that. The circuit uses no transistors or tubes; it operates using R-C timing networks and relays.

June 1962 *QST* advertisement for the Little Monster.

M&M Electronics Dah-Ditter Model EK-1 Keyer

Dah-Ditter keyer ad from the February 1968 *QST*.

The Dah-Ditter (models EK-1 and EK-1A) was a solid state keyer made by M&M Electronics of Atlanta, Georgia. These keyers sold for a couple years starting in 1968, but apparently were not very popular. They were built in a plastic box with connections made using a screw-type terminal board mounted on top of the box. There was a top panel tune/operate switch and a control for keyer speed. The terminal board provides for paddle hookup and a relay output for transmitter keying.

Mars EK-75 Keyer

The Mars EK-75 was produced by the Amateur Division of the Paulsan Company of San Rafael, California. It was a five transistor device with relay output to key the transmitter. Features

included self-completing dots and dashes, as well as automatic spacing. An internal power supply was included, as was a tone generator for monitoring. Weighting was adjustable using a control on the rear panel. Controls for speed and sidetone volume were on the front panel. Mars also made the EK-20 transistorized keyer that was advertised in the June 1963 edition of *73*.

Matric Model 10A Keyer

Very little information is available about the Matric 10A keyer, other than what is in their ads. The Model 11A paddle appears to have been an optional accessory. Matric was in Franklin, Pennsylvania; one ad for the Matric keyer and paddle appeared in the March 1974 *QST* and mentioned use of internal penlight cells and a reed relay.

MFJ KEYERS

The Martin F. Jue (MFJ) Company was formed in 1972 and manufactured many electronic keyers and ham-related devices. Jue holds the callsign K5FLU. MFJ's first offering was a CW filter. MFJ bought Curtis' product line and used the 8044 and 8045ABM chips in quite a few of their keyer models.

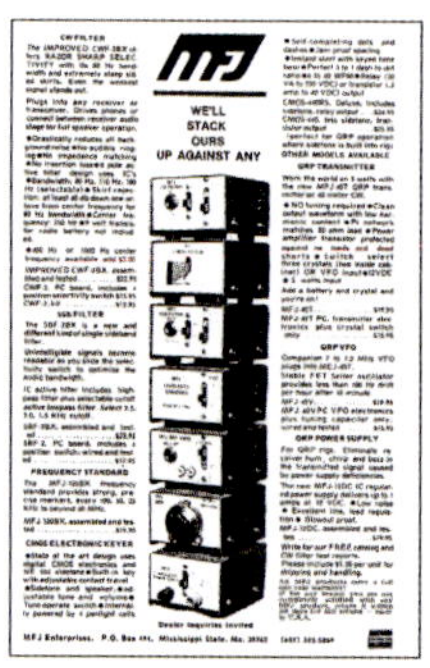

An MFJ product ad from the December 1974 QST. One of the products shown is the early version of their CMOS keyer.

MFJ-402 Econo Keyer

The MFJ-402 Econo Keyer was based on the Curtis 8044 IC and included a built-in, adjustable single-lever paddle. If the operator desired iambic operation an external squeeze key could be connected. Speed range was 8–50 wpm. There was no sidetone monitor included. The MFJ-402 first sold in 1978.

MFJ-422 Electronic Keyer Paddle

The MFJ-422 (the 422D version is below) is a Curtis chip-based device designed to mount on top of the MFJ or Bencher dual-lever paddle. The fully shielded layout presents the user with top mounted switches for power and auto/semi-auto operation; volume and speed adjustments of 5–65 wpm are on the left side, where the typical right-handed sender could reach them easily with his left hand. The keyer also has built in dot-dash memories, speaker, and sidetone. The rear panel has keyer output and power jacks, as well as access to the screwdriver adjustable tone and weight controls. The MFJ-422 keys solid state or tube transmitters and uses an internal 9 volt battery or 110 VAC with a wall wart adapter.

MFJ-408 Deluxe Electronic Keyer

The MFJ-408 Deluxe Electronic Keyer II is based on the Curtis 8044 chip. This keyer makes use of the chip's speed readout function to drive a front panel meter calibrated in wpm code speed. The MFJ-408 is able to accommodate code speeds up to 50 wpm. A semi-automatic "bug" mode is offered, and the keyer will function well with either single or dual-lever paddles. Keyer dates to 1980.

MFJ-482 Grandmaster Keyer

The MFJ-482 Grandmaster keyer was a popular memory keyer that first sold in 1978. It had 1024 bits of memory in four 25-character banks, and banks could be combined for one 50-character message and two 25-character messages. Typical controls were included, such as weight and tone, and a built-in speaker allowed keyer monitoring.

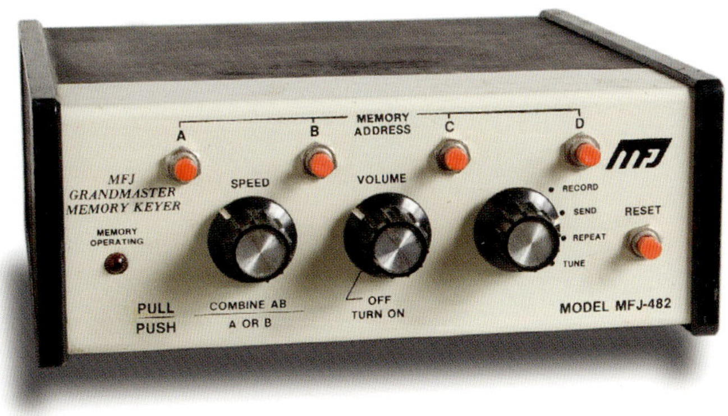

MFJ CMOS Keyers

The CMOS-440 was one of the first MFJ products and was offered in 1974; it carries the same name as the device shown below, which does not have the CMOS-440 model number on the front panel. It was a basic keyer with operating controls on the rear panel. Output was via a keying relay. Power was obtained from internal batteries.

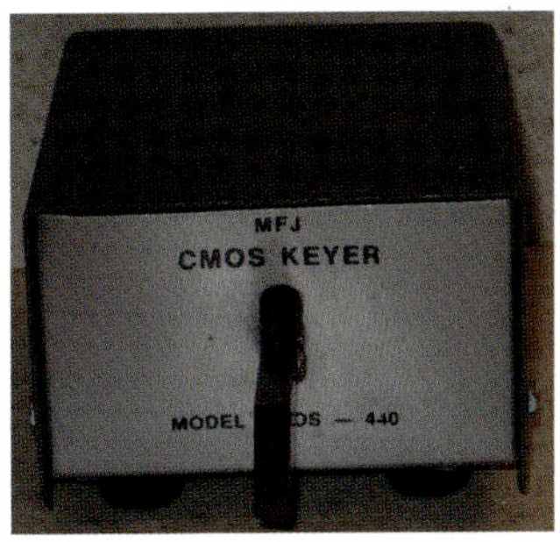

The MFJ CMOS keyer version used a Curtis 8043 chip, and is thought to be an update of the earlier CMOS-440. The keyer featured a built-in paddle and speaker. Speed range of this device was 8–50 wpm. This keyer was capable of operating in iambic mode if the user connected an external squeeze key. This version of the CMOS keyer first sold in 1977.

MFJ-403 Pocket CW Keyer

The MFJ-403 Pocket CW Keyer is sometimes referred to as the "Travel Iambic." Although small in size, this keyer offers many features and appeals to the QRP and backpacking crowd. It offers self-completing dots and dashes and dot-dash memory, and speed adjustment using a thumbwheel control on the front panel. Speed range is 3–65 wpm. The MFJ-403 has adjustable weighting and sidetone, with Iambic Modes A and B available. The enclosure is RF shielded. Keyer output is positive keying through a FET device. The 403 is powered with an internal 9 volt battery.

MILAG YD 2000

The MILAG YD 2000 is a very basic electronic keyer of Italian manufacture with built-in paddles. This device does not appear to be very well known outside Europe.

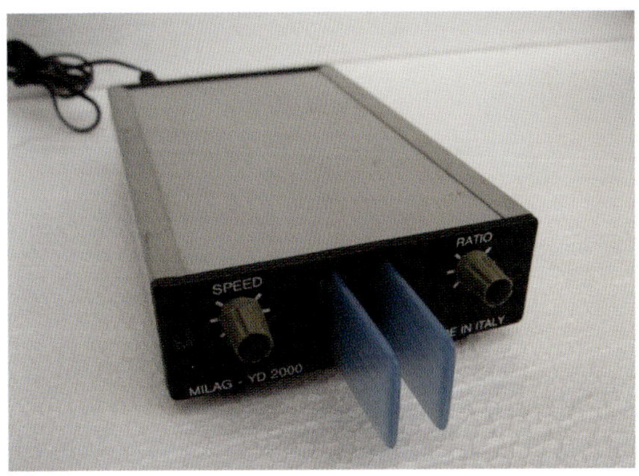

Minix MCS-1K

The Minix MCS-1K is a memory keyer made in Germany around 1980. The device uses eleven integrated circuits and two transistors, with power supplied from internal batteries or external DC. This keyer measures approximately 4 × 4 × 1.5 inches. The rear panel includes a terminal strip for the keyed line and a key jack. No sidetone output is provided.

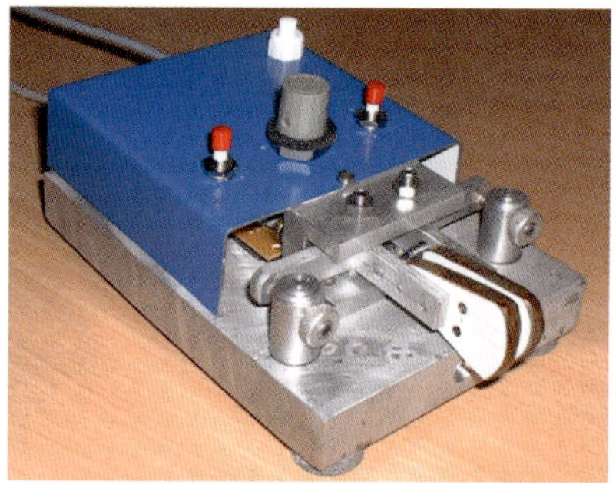

A DM2AF homebrew keyer with integral dual-lever paddles and aluminum base.

Early unknown, likely European, and dating to the 1950s.

Miscellaneous Keyers

This section is somewhat of a catch-all for some unknown keyers and homebrew devices that show a high level of build quality or are aesthetically interesting, but about which not much is known. In all cases they represent the range of thought that went into the device, and show attention to design and an appreciation for electronic Morse CW. In some instances not much at all is known about the device presented; perhaps an alert reader can send along some notes to me so that future editions can be updated.

This keyer was built around 1958, in the German Democratic Republic; not much else is known about it. It is a tube design with built-in power supply and single-lever keying with what appears to be a relay output for the keyed line.

DK4MX version of his WinKeyer device, 2007.

This device dates to the early 1950s, and may also have been built in East Germany (GDR). The builder clearly put some thought into layout and fitting all the parts into this cabinet. The keyer includes a built-in hand key and a single-lever paddle.

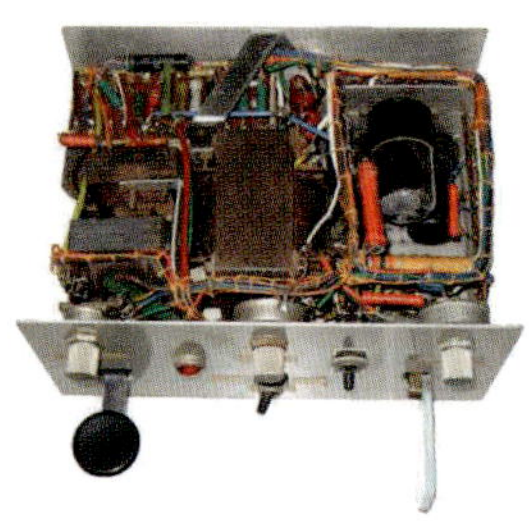

Front panel controls include speed and weighting. There is an audio output for headphones and relay output to key a transmitter. The circuit uses two tubes: a 6C5 and a 6SN7.

Although this keyer had a notation on it dating it to 1968, it looks much older. Characteristics of the paddle design and the enclosure appear to date this keyer to the 1950s or early 1960s. Little else is known about the design, except DL6TR was mentioned in the notation.

John (K2TQN) reports this mystery keyer is very well made and appears to be a commercial unit, but there are no marks anywhere to give a clue. The cabinet color looks like the old Western Union or WU Teletype color (green). Lynn (N7CFO) believes this keyer may be an F. A. Bartlett (W6OWP) design; Lynn sees similarities with Bartlett's Duomatic AKS-7 model. John reports the keyer schematic has been found thanks to Bruce Conner (WB8OGK), who spotted it in the 1963 *Handbook*, but the keyer's builder remains unidentified.

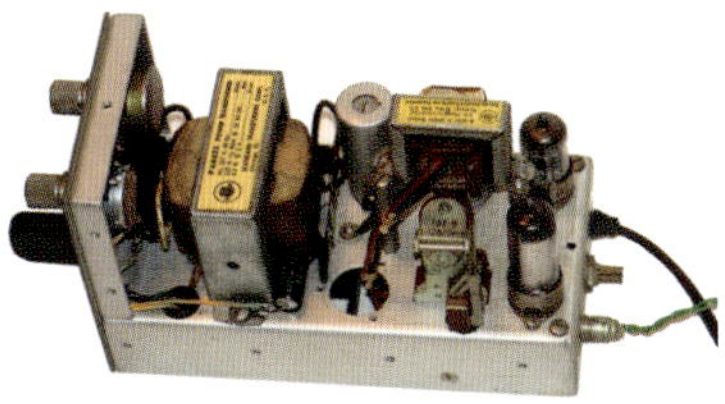

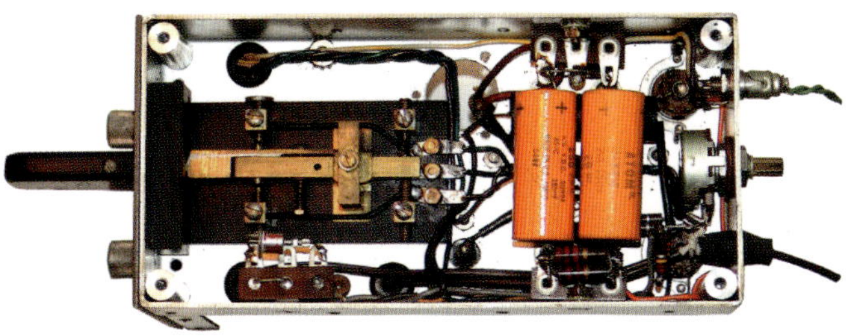

This keyer (below) was identified as coming from India, although one source mentioned it as being of Russian design. No other information has been found on it, although it is believed to have been used aboard a commercial shipping vessel. The keyer appears to be of 1960s vintage.

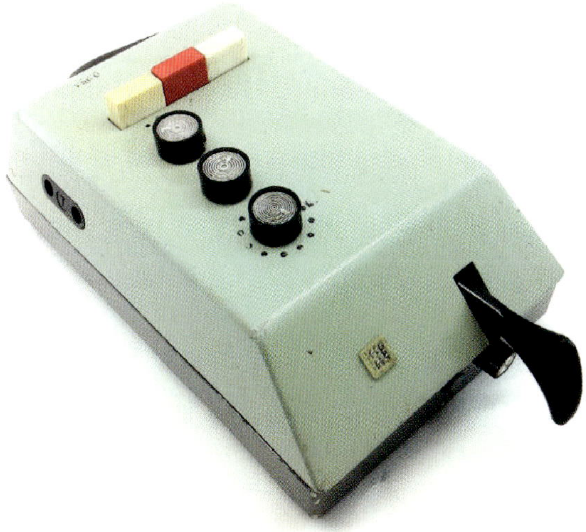

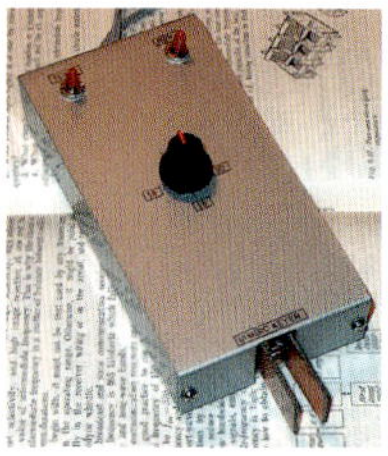

This PA2OHH keyer appears to be a basic iambic-type device with controls for speed and a built-in dual-lever paddle, possibly with touch-type sensing.

The following pictures present a selection of various Russian keyers that appear to be commercial devices. Operating details and circuit parameters are not known.

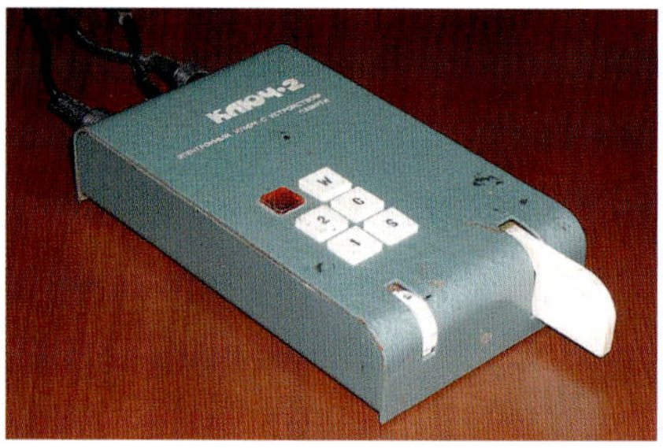

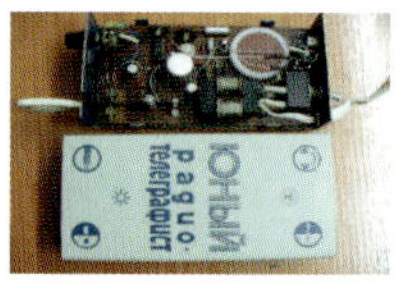

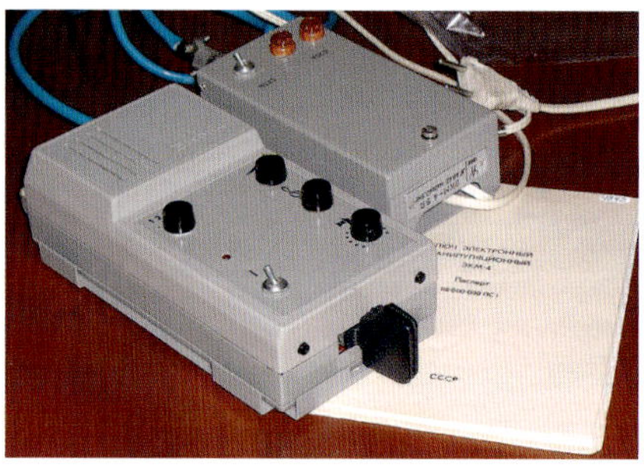

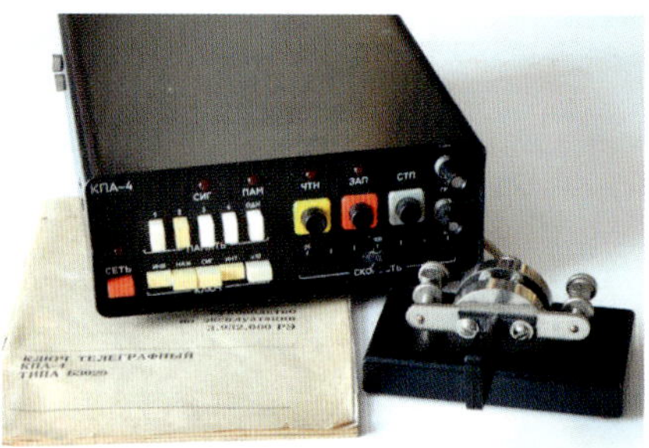

Mizuho CK-1D Keyer

Mizuho is a Japanese company owned by Mr. Takada (JA1AMH). The company's name means "beautiful riceplant." Mizuho produces small QRP transceivers, amplifiers, antenna tuners, and other amateur gear. Their CK-1D keyer is based on the Curtis keyer chip; front panel controls are for keyer speed and sidetone volume.

Mon-Key Electronic Keyer

The Mon-Key was the first electronic keyer manufactured and sold commercially. The Mon-Key was invented by Wiley D. Wenger while working at Electric Eye Equipment Company in Danville, Illinois. The Mon-Key was being manufactured and sold by spring 1948. It was popular at the time and used a standard tube lineup, including 12AU7 (two) and 35W4. The base of the Mon-Key is Bakelite and the cover is aluminum. There was no power transformer; the 110 VAC was applied directly to the keyer paddle and definitely presented a safety hazard. Speed range was 10–42 wpm. Note the Electric Eye Equipment Company became Hurletron, Inc. around 1960; Hurletron made graphic arts related items. Apparently the Mon-Key stopped production around 1959; while it sold the price was $29.95.

Several Mon-Key keyers with the paddle and keyer covers removed.

Morse-O-Matic Keyer

Morse-O-Matic's Model 60 keyer is based on a vacuum tube circuit design and was made in Denmark by Larsen and Company. Features include an integrated single-lever paddle, sidetone, and built-in power supply. Also included is a shorting switch for transmitter tune-up. It is estimated this keyer was manufactured in the late 1950s or early 1960s.

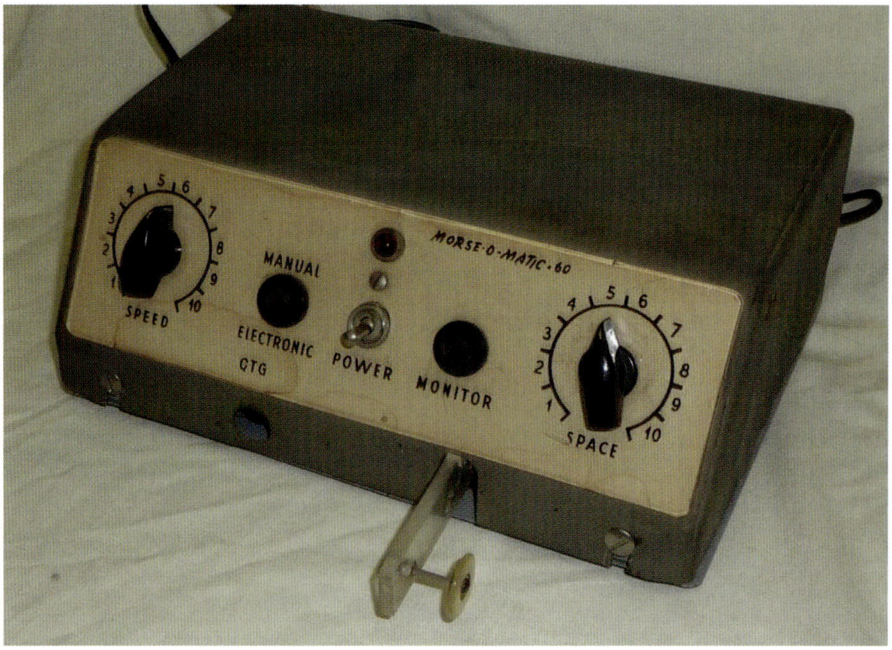

MSC (Modular Systems) SMART Keyer

The SMART Keyer series was designed by Joe Lunsford (N4YG) and offered for sale during the 1980s and 1990s. The basic SMART Keyer circuit design was based on an Intel 8749 microcontroller. Non-volatile memory was used to preserve messages and keyer setup parameters. There were three different versions of this keyer in the series, with the latest version offering an RS232 port, ability to load messages via software on a PC, selection of positive or negative keying, message status lights, and improved software. Some of the functions available and the status lights are shown from a SMART Keyer III.

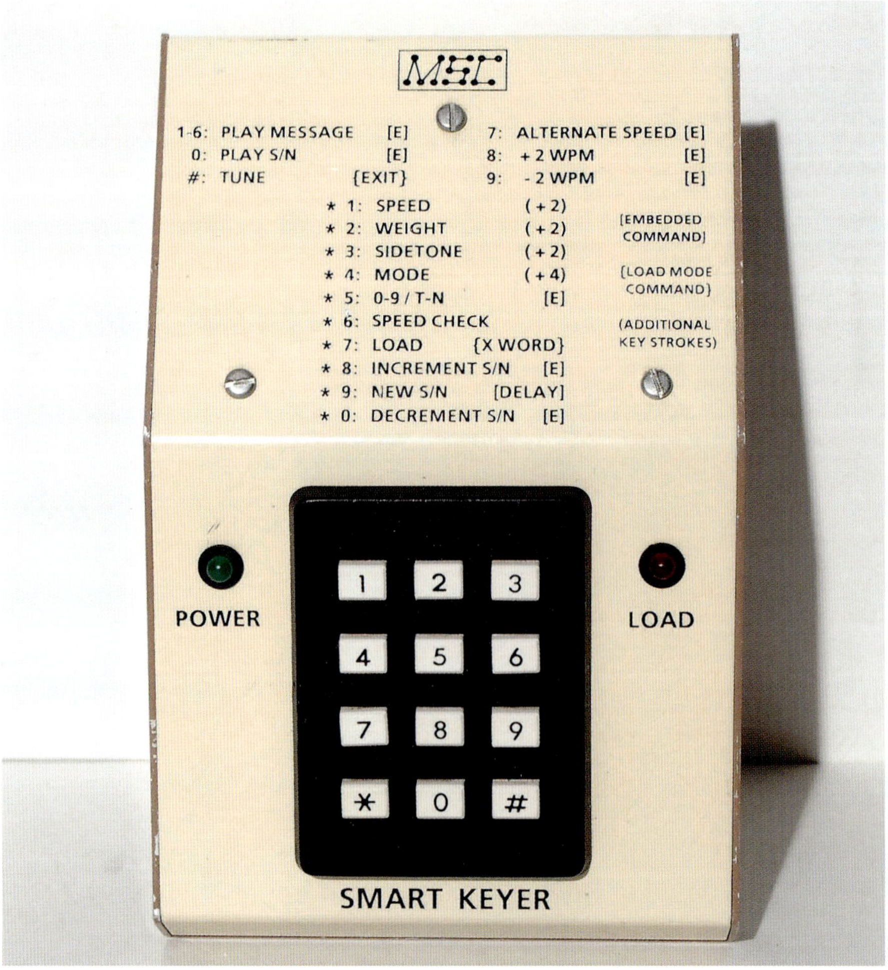

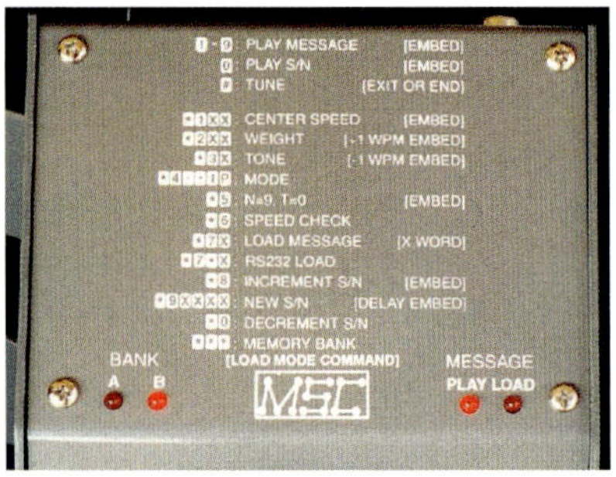

MSK-5 Squeeze Key

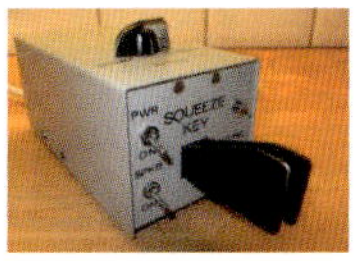

The MSK-5 was sold by XB-Electro of Reading, United Kingdom (run by Stan Cook, G5XB), and imported for sale in the US by N4SU. It is reported some of these keyers are marked with the word "Denmark" on top of the case. The MSK-5s were designed by OZ7BO and sold around the late 1960–early 1970s; this keyer was more popular in Europe than the US, although only a few hundred units were sold. The MSK-5 used a keying method called the "single-dot insert" method—it was a different system than ultimatic or iambic. With single-dot insert, the operator can squeeze the dot lever in the middle of a string of dashes and the keyer will insert the dot. Supposedly all the code letters can be formed by this method of squeeze keying, with the exception of the letter "X." The MSK-5 appears to be the model for the Tempo DKT keyer, which looks nearly identical and also features single-dot insert keying.

On September 18, 1956, Gus Fallgren (who was W1OGU) used two small Raytheon germanium transistors to transmit a signal across the Atlantic to Brondum Bo Nielsen (OZ7BO). This was the first documented transatlantic contact using ham radio and transistor technology.

nanoKeyer

The nanoKeyer is an Arduino nano keyer offered by Oscar (DJ0MY). The Arduino nano is a small microcontroller based on the ATmega328 (Arduino nano 3.x) or ATmega168 (Arduino nano 2.x). Included with the keyer is a hardware kit featuring three memory buttons, a speed potentiometer, a PS2 keyboard connector, and optically isolated keying and PTT lines. The Arduino nano module that mates with the nanoKeyer supports the K3NG keyer code command line interface and K1EL Winkey emulation via the built-in USB port. The Arduino nano is programmed via a typical Windows, Mac, or Linux machine with free software.

This kit offers commercial / contest quality performance and features an open source package that can easily be assembled by beginners or customized by advanced experimenters.

The nanoKeyer kit offers commercial and contest quality performance and features in an open source package that can easily be assembled

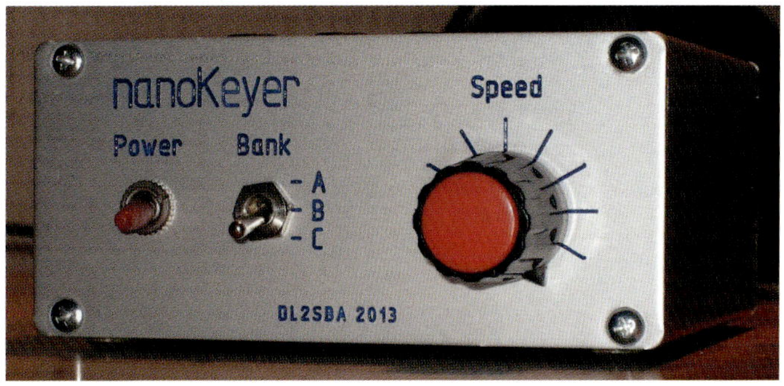

Two different versions of the Arduino nano-based CW keyer.

by beginners or customized by advanced experimenters. This keyer was designed specifically for use with the K3NG Arduino keyer open source firmware. Some operating features include adjustable speed from 1–999 wpm, K1EL WinKeyer interface protocol emulation, support for major logging applications, setup using the paddle, 12 memories, and ultimatic plus iambic Modes A and B, with auto word spacing. The nanoKeyer is suitable as a standalone keyer, or for keying the radio via the USB port by using the K1EL WinKeyer protocol from a connected computer and most contest logging software packages. Use of the K3NG firmware allows this keyer to be used as a computerless keyboard keyer by attaching a PS2 keyboard. The keyer uses open source code and open hardware so it can be customized to fit the user's needs. Note: RemoteQTH.com also offers hardware that runs the K3NG code.

Nye Viking Keyers

The Nye Viking Company is now William M. Nye Co., Inc.; as of May 1995, they are based in Priest River, Idaho. Early devices show them previously in Bellevue, Washington. The company was founded in 1972 by William Nye (W7DZ) as a retirement undertaking after Nye sold his business machine company. Nye bought the rights for the Speed-X series of keys and continued key and keyer manufacturing and assembly on site with newly bought tooling.

The Nye Viking ESK-001 keyer is a somewhat scarce device. Those still in use are appreciated by owners of some

older boatanchor transmitters, as the ESK-001 is capable of positive and negative keying at greater than 300 volts via a switched transistor output. Few other transistor keyers can handle cathode keying and grid-block keying at higher voltages.

The Nye Viking SKM-1 is an iambic memory keyer. Four memory buttons can be seen on top of the keyer; LED status lights indicate the message is playing or recording. The keyer operates from a 9 volt battery or the included AC power supply. There is a monitor speaker on the rear panel.

The SSK-1-K is an iambic keyer without the memory feature. This keyer operates from a 9 volt battery or the included AC power supply. There is a monitor speaker on the rear panel.

The SKM-016 is another in the line of Nye Viking keyers; it is an iambic keyer with a 16,000 bit memory in eight 2,000 bit channels. The SKM-016 operates from a 9 volt battery or the included AC power supply. There is a monitor speaker on the rear panel.

Omega Electronics Digital Electronic Keyer

Omega Electronics was a small corporation in San Diego, California. Their DA (digital automatic) keyer was an iambic device with integral paddles using integrated circuits and transistors. It can be operated from a variety of power sources, including internal batteries. Speed range is 6–60 wpm, and the keyer output uses a reed relay. The rear panel has controls for tone and volume, and a terminal strip for external power. Jacks are provided for paddle, key, and keyed line connections. The DA keyer was sold in the late 1960s, and was reviewed in the March 1968 issue of *73*.

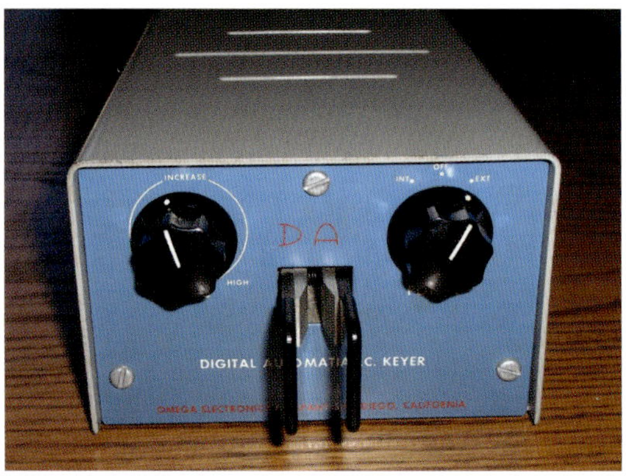

Paddlette Company KP Model Keyers

The Paddlette Company of Edmonds, Washington, produced several very small keyers with integrated paddles in the late 1990s. The KP-3 keyer circuitry is based on the TiCK-3 keyer and the KP-4 is based on the TiCK-4. The KP-3 and KP-4 models are shown. These keyers offer memory storage, a small speaker on top, and a pushbutton switch for sending messages in memory. The keyers use an internal battery for power. The paddles are adjustable, and there is a small jack on the rear of the keyer for keyed line connection to the transmitter.

Palm Radio Code Cube

Palm Radio is a German company specializing in CW related amateur products. Their Code Cube device is a small (1 × 1 × 1.25 in.) full featured electronic memory keyer that plugs into any Palm mini paddle. Photos show the Code Cube before and after integration with the paddle. The Code Cube is also available as a standalone version. It utilizes a custom version of the Jackson Harbor Press PK4 chip. The device is powered by a CR2032 3V lithium cell. Keying speed is adjustable from 5–39 wpm via a thumbwheel and a sidetone oscillator is included. The Code Cube has over 100 characters of message memory allocated as either two or three messages and features storage of your callsign for automatic CQ generation. The Code Cube can be linked to the transmitter using Palm Radio's IR link accessories, giving the operator wireless keying.

Palomar Keyers

Palomar Engineers was formed in 1965. As the Palomar folks explain, the name comes from several local influences. Palomar is the Spanish word for "dove cote" (*la Paloma* means "the dove"). The mourning dove is a common bird in Southern California. A major feature of San Diego County is 6,000 ft. tall Palomar Mountain. Some of Palomar's early keyers are shown; note Palomar had three different keyers they called the "IC Keyer," with an additional one being called the IC Keyer Mark V.

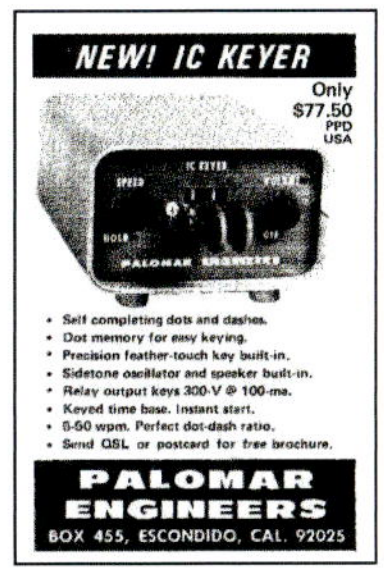

An ad from *QST*, August 1971. It is not known why a keyer that had been advertised and sold since 1966 was now being called "new," but the price had gone up by $10 and the device was renamed. The ad discrepancy points out the difficulty of trying to draw conclusions about product introduction dates using only advertising material.

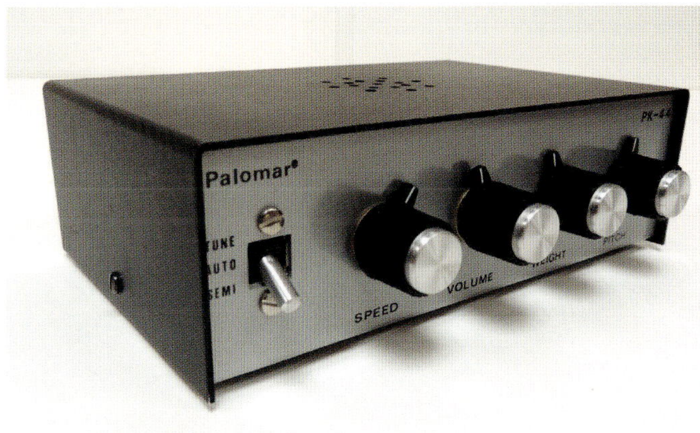

Palomar's "Space Age" IC keyer (above) appears to be a fairly scarce item. A *QST* ad for this keyer in August 1971 proclaimed it was a new device, although ads going back as far as 1966 have been found. This design used an internal Brown Brothers Model UTL paddle mechanism and an all-IC circuit for reliability. The advertisements do not mention the Brown Brothers UTL paddle, but the use of that paddle is a big part of what makes this particular keyer quite collectible today.

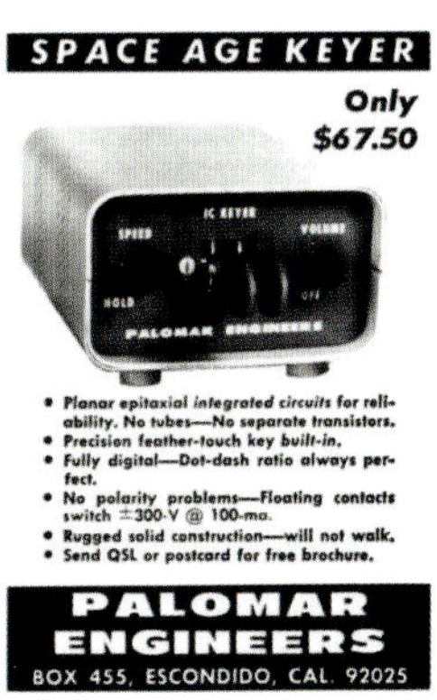

An ad from the December 1966 issue of *73*.

The Palomar PK-44 is an attractive, basic keyer with front panel adjustments for speed, volume, weight, and sidetone pitch. The PK-44 circuit design includes dot and dash memories. A switch is provided for easy transmitter tune-up, and for selecting auto or semi-auto operation. Relay output is provided for transmitter keying, with contacts rated at 1 amp. An internal monitor speaker is included. This keyer requires a DC power source, either from a rear panel mounted 9 volt battery or an external supply. Palomar also produced a PK-50 keyer that had message memories (more information is available on the Palomar Engineers website).

A Palomar IC Keyer ad from the June 1982 *CQ*. This particular keyer appears to have been introduced around March 1976.

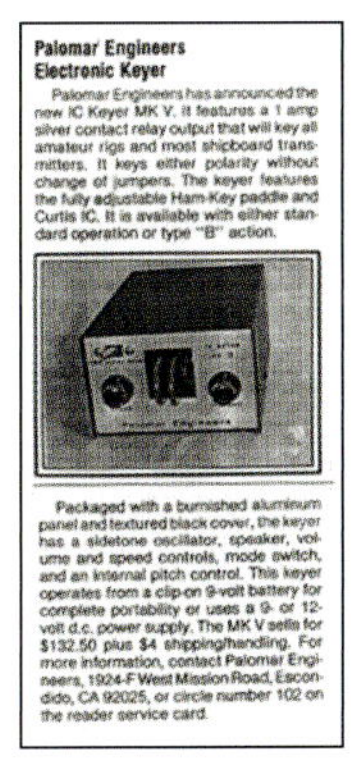

A Palomar product announcement for the new IC Keyer Mark V.

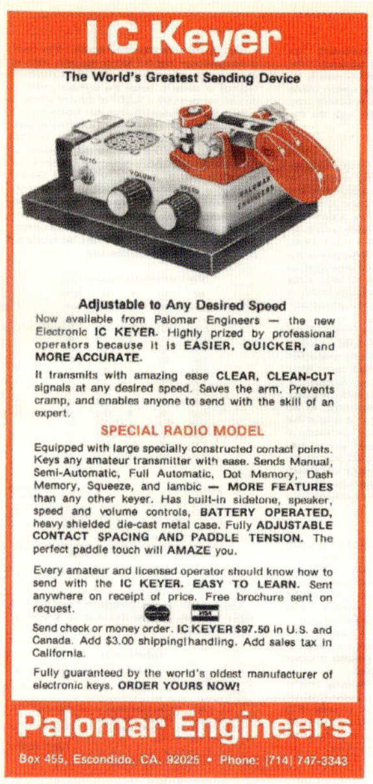

This version of Palomar Engineer's IC Keyer in this advertisement was a very popular IC device that used an integral HamKey paddle mechanism. The IC Keyer offered dot and dash memory and iambic operation, and was powered by an externally mounted 9 volt battery. The outboard mounting of the paddle mechanism allowed for easy adjustment of spacing and tension. This keyer dates to the late 1970s.

Palstar CW50A Keyer

The Palstar CW50A is a microprocessor-based electronic keyer advertised to work with any transmitter or transceiver. Front panel controls are provided for speed, monitor volume, and pitch. Speed range of the CW50A is 10–40 wpm. The keyer will operate using iambic Mode A or Mode B, and separate rear panel outputs for grid-block or cathode keying are available. Other keyer features include adjustable spacing and weighting, and it is programmable to allow full or semi break-in when used with a separate transmitter/receiver combination. The CW50A requires power from either a 9 volt battery or an AC adapter. The Palstar keyer actually uses a C1S PIC chip that Codeboy sold for OEMs to use in their own keyers.

Pickering K-1 micro-ultimatic Keyer

The Pickering K-1 micro-ultimatic offered a 10–60 wpm speed range, and could operate in either standard or iambic modes. A built-in code monitor was included, and the K-1 could key most transmitters using either a relay or transistor output. Pickering was headed by Thomas A. Pickering (W1CFW) and was in Portsmouth, Rhode Island. This device was first sold in 1967; it was reviewed in the August 1969 *QST*.

The K-1 used seven ICs and six transistors. It has been referenced as the first IC keyer, but the claim is arguable, because the circuitry is not totally based on ICs. There were two versions of this keyer available: the K-1R used a reed keying relay at the output, and the K-1G used a high–voltage transistor with grid-block keyed transmitters. The K-1 sold for $85.

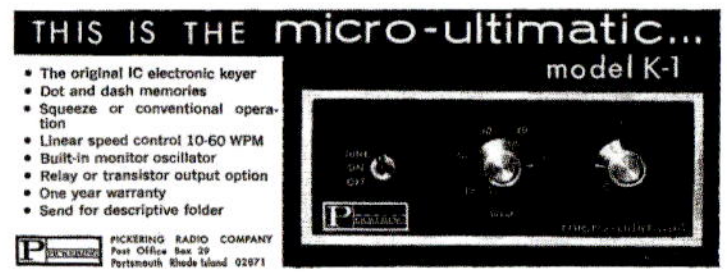

Pickering K-1 ad from the January 1968 *QST*.

Rainbow Kits APC-1 Keyer

Rainbow Kits advertised this keyer as the "Perfect Code" Keyer. It was aimed at the beginning keyer, although ads also mentioned old timers would like it. This keyer offered the basic adjustments, including speed and sidetone volume control. There were built-in paddles, or the user could plug in their own. The APC-1 operated from internal AA cells.

Ramsey Electronics CW700

The Ramsey CW Morse code electronic memory keyer Model CW700 was available as a kit or factory assembled. Power source was either an internal 9 volt battery or an AC/DC adapter. The CW700 featured built-in paddles, with rear panel connections for an external paddle if desired. The CW700 offered four message memories and originally sold for $125.00.

Redi-Kilowatt Electronic Memory Keyers

Redi-Kilowatt International of Holland, Pennsylvania, manufactured the Model 406. It was an early design with two banks of memory; shown is the unit used in the W2MFT hamshack. The rear panel included outputs for either grid or cathode keying and a jack for the key. A speaker for keyer sidetone was included, as well as an internal AC power supply.

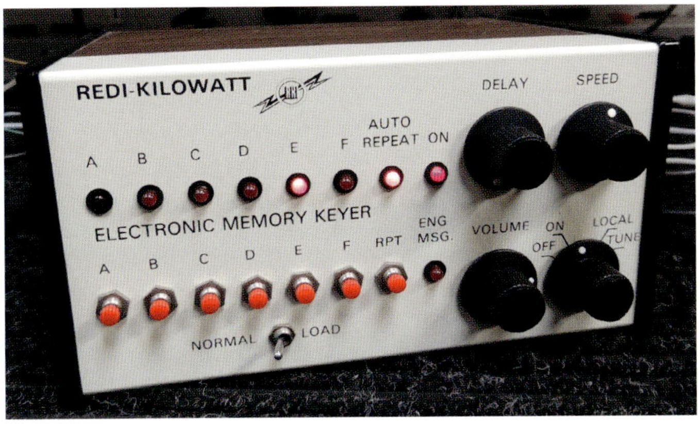

Redi-Kilowatt's Model 401 memory keyer represented the next iteration of the company's memory keyer. Although not well known, the keyer offered six message memories in an attractive package. As with the Model 406, the rear panel included outputs for either grid or cathode keying.

Russian KEY-8/ARE-90/SB-90

The KEY-8 and its other named cousins are paddles with an integrated keyer and an interesting history. In the early 1990s, this device was known as the Novosibirisk paddle, imported by Yuri Sushkin. Advertisements (*CQ*, April 1993) show it as the ARE-90 model, claiming it is the first Russian amateur product for sale in America. Amateur Radio Engineering was a small company that apparently obtained some of these keys from Yuri and had some business relationship with Yuri's company. In 1993, this model was included in the Advanced Electronic Applications (AEA) listings as the SB-90; supposedly less than thirty-five were sold. A few others may have been brought into the US from Europe by collectors, as the above paddle was. Updated versions of this model are now called the "KEY-8" and are imported from ElectroInstrument in Voronezh, Russia. ElectroInstrument apparently also makes components for Soviet missiles. The KEY-8 device uses solid silver contacts and a needle bearing/pivot design with separate tension and travel adjustments for each arm. The KEY-8 has an integrated non-iambic keyer in the four-inch diameter paddle base; the same keyer was distributed in Poland, known as the "Telegraph Electronic Key." There is a unique 5-pin connector on the rear

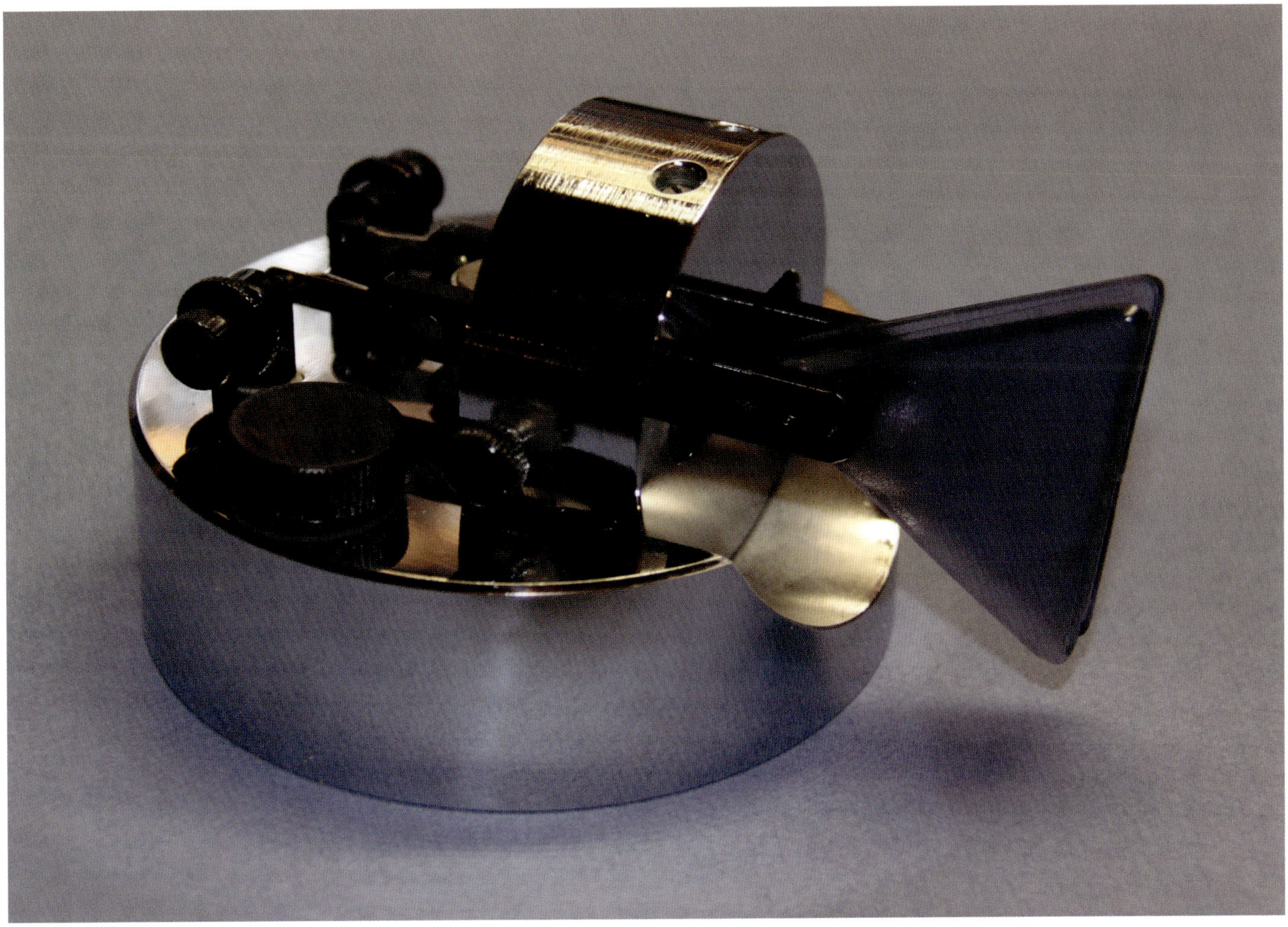

of the paddle base for 12 volts, paddle out, tone out, and relay-keyed line. Speed (5–50 wpm) is adjustable by using the small black control on top of the base, and device weight is about three and one-half pounds. The keyer requires +6 to 15 volts DC. A sidetone oscillator is included.

An ARE-90 ad from the April 1993 CQ.

SAMSON ETM SERIES KEYERS

The ETM (Electronic Transistor Morse) series of keyers were German built by Herman Samson (DJ2BW). Earlier models (1967 to the early 1970s) used transistors, while later models used CMOS ICs. Gerhard Schurr (DH2SAA) made the Einbau Wabbler ("built in" paddle) for some of the ETM models.

ETM-1C

The ETM-1C dates to 1968. This model used four 1.5 volt batteries to power the nine transistor circuit. It did not include an internal speaker; the keyer was meant to be used with headphones or an amp.

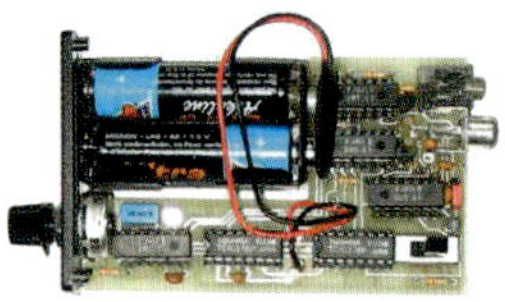

ETM-2 and ETM-2b

The ETM-2 and -2b model keyers added an internal single-lever paddle and a control for adjusting dot-dash ratio. Rear panel connectors were provided for sidetone output and keying output. The -2 model used 10 transistors and the -2b model used an 11-transistor design on one circuit board; they were powered by four internal AA cells.

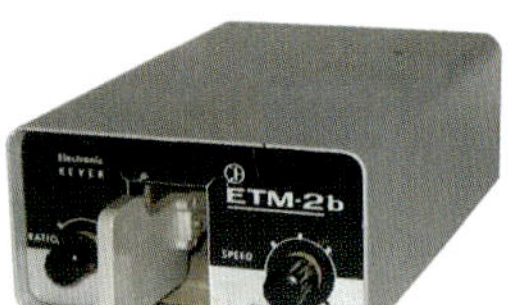

ETM-3 and ETM-3b

The ETM-3 and -3b models were available 1984–1987. They used a metal case and did not utilize an internal speaker, but did have a rear panel sidetone output. The design progression now used nine transistors and four ICs. The keyers featured dual lever paddles and squeeze keying. Power was obtained from the 115 volt AC line.

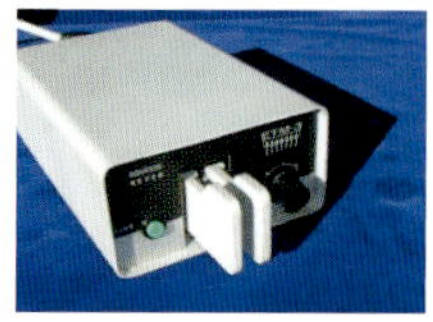

ETM-4C

The ETM-4C model was a CMOS memory keyer designed around 14 integrated circuits. Transmitter keying was via a relay output. Three user memories were provided.

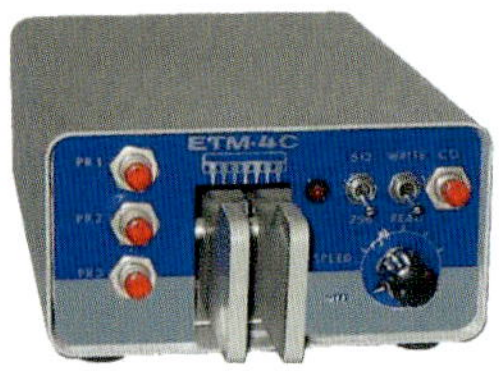

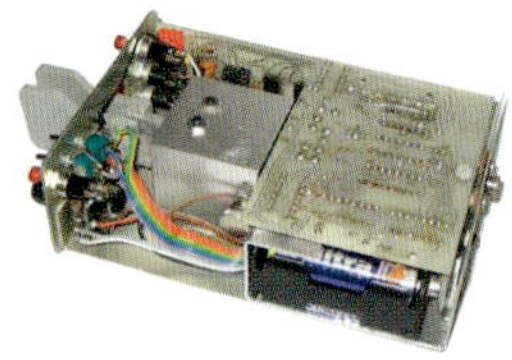

ETM-5C

The ETM-5C was a CMOS keyer first built in 1983. It used a six IC design, and appeared to be an effort to get total parts count down while retaining the features of earlier iambic keyers. A transmitter tune button was added to the top of the case.

ETM-8C

The ETM-8C and -8C extended version were CMOS iambic keyers. Samson added additional memory accessible by the top-mounted pushbuttons; eight 512 bit memories were offered. The built-in dot and dash memory could be disabled by a slide switch. Speed range was 8–50 wpm. Transmitter keyed line output was either via relay or transistor.

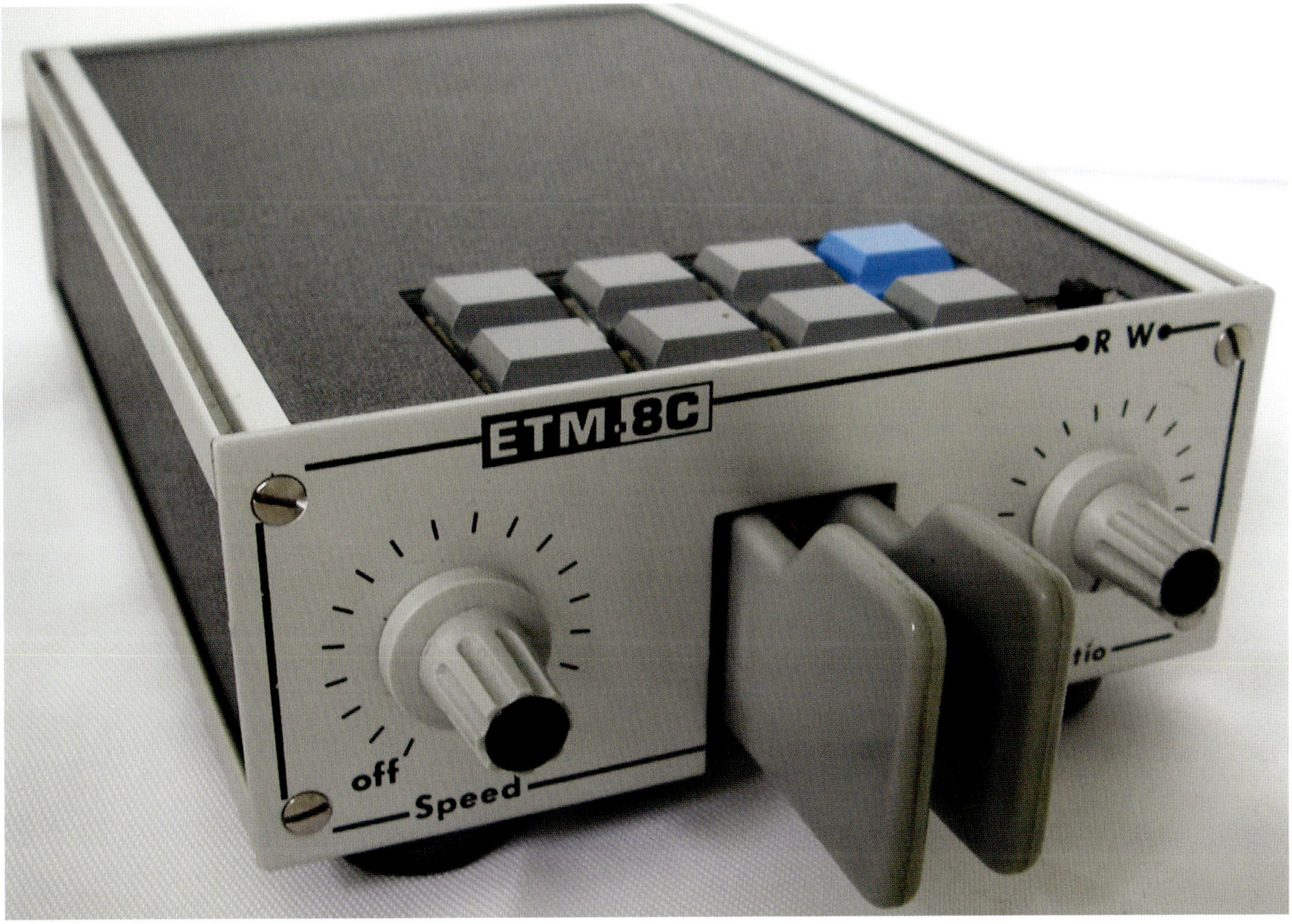

ETM-9C and ETM-9C-X3

The ETM-9C was the last in the series of ETM keyers that started with the original ETM-1 in 1967. The ETM-9C's firmware was produced by Jeffrey Russell (KC0Q) and Bud Southard (N0II) of CMOS Super Keyer fame. Details of the CMOS Super Keyer were covered in an October 1981 *QST* article. When Russell and Southard released the Super CMOS Keyer III, the ETM-9C was updated and called the ETM-9C-X3. Gerhard Schurr (DH2SAA) furnished the Einbau Wabbler paddle, which was specifically designed for inclusion within certain models of the ETM series keyers.

One very useful feature of this keyer is the ability to control all the functions by sending commands in Morse code using the keyer paddles. The keyer includes six memory buttons, a speed control, and an on/off switch. Keyer control is exerted through several menu structures. Function commands are used to configure the keyer. Inquiry commands are used by the operator to determine the keyer's current configuration. Embedded functions are used to implement commands held in memory. Various button functions are also available for menu items. Other features include a contest number generator and various message related functions, such as loop and pause.

ETM9COG-X3

The ETM9COG-X3 is visually quite different from earlier ETM series keyers. It is an excellent iambic keyer based on the CMOS Super Keyer III. The device has dot and dash memories, and offers four message memories of 220 total characters with message loop capability. It also features automatic serial number generation, adjustable weighting, sidetone monitor, and transmitter tone function. A major feature is that commands can be sent using the CW paddle.

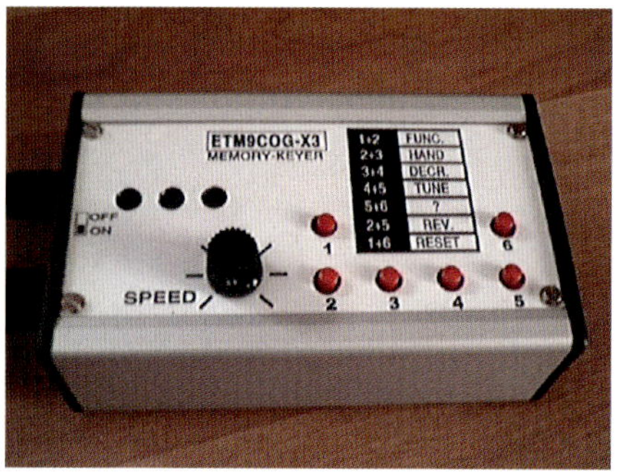

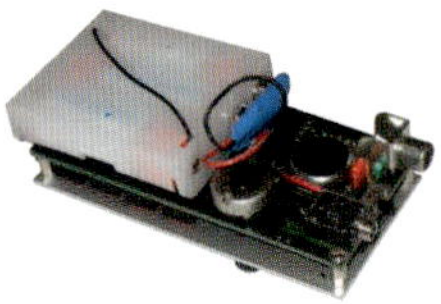

Satatuuli Osk KBX 101A Keyer

The KBX 101A is a Finnish device from Satatuuli Osk; his paddle is shown equipped with an additional keyer. This keyer has a top speed of 50 wpm and has two memories of 50 characters each, as well as dot and dash memory that will help additional high speed keying. The housing can be bought separately and can be fitted to a user's unique electronics, or equipped with the full featured electronic keyer as pictured. This keyer will work for many years with a single lithium battery and has its own piezo buzzer built in. Operation is accomplished by using the two pushbuttons on the front of the keyer. Keying is done using an open collector that works with most modern transceivers.

Schurr Einbau-Wabbler with Keyer

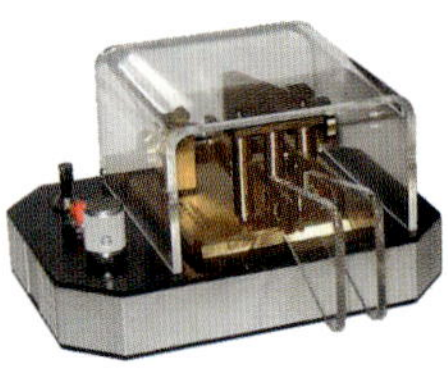

The Schurr Einbau-Wabbler integrated with electronic keyer in the base dates to about 1985.

S. E. M. Iambic Keyer

S. E. M. is an Isle of Man company; they made keyers and other amateur radio related devices, such as a QRM eliminator. The S. E. M. devices shown are iambic keyers, and the two versions are packaged quite differently. Both of these devices use the Curtis 8044 keyer chip.

Slovenian Elektronski Taster ET4C

The Slovenian "Elektronski Taster" (Electronic Keyer) is a single-lever, solid state design with built-in sidetone speaker and selectable positive or negative keying. A front panel control for speed can be seen. At least two versions using different white and black color schemes were available.

Special Devices Model 100A Keyer

The Model 100A is a tube-based keyer using a 6AL5 dual diode, a 6J6 dual triode, and an OB2 regulator; it was made by Special Devices of Barron, Wisconsin. Output keying is via a relay. In addition to the compact size of this keyer, the construction and feel of the dual-lever paddle assembly is notable. The fact it is a dual-lever design, when other integrated keyer mechanisms of the time were single-lever or converted bugs, makes the Model 100A stand out. Dual-lever paddles started gaining widespread acceptance with the Nikey paddle around 1960, and when early transistor ultimatic keyers became popular. The Model 100A mechanism features elongated aluminum fingerpieces, eliminating the need for separate paddle arms. For those familiar with the W9WBL paddles, there is a vague similarity to the Model 100A paddle as seen in the WBL's use of square brass bar stock and Bakelite-type blocks for the paddle's frame. There are two embedded pivot bearings in each fingerpiece; the top and bottom adjustment screws are hollow at the ends, allowing the operator to set bearing feel. Two pairs of contacts are used, with contact points provided on fingerpiece standoffs and on the ends of the contact adjustment screws. Locking nuts are included for all adjustments. Paddle return to center is via spring tension, which is also adjustable. Despite the age of this integrated paddle, it is velvety smooth and consistent in operation. The low moving mass of the mechanism is far ahead of its time.

Using the limited information available, it is estimated the Model 100A may have been produced at some point during 1958–1961. The estimate is based on introduction of the OB2 tube in 1957, beginning widespread usage of commercial dual-lever paddles around 1961, and increasing availability of transistorized keying devices starting approximately 1960. Despite much research, little has been found in the way of product advertising or background information on Special Devices.

Suntronix Keyer

Automatic Electronic Keyer. All solid state construction. Reliable reed relay switching. Complete with paddles. Sidetone generator. Precise Dot-Dash space timing. Self completing Dots and Dashes. Dot memory. Speed adjustable from front panel. Weighted to stay put. Needs only +5 v.d.c. at 150 m.a. $39.95. **Suntronix Company,** 360 Merrimack Street, Lawrence, MA 01843.

Product announcement for the Suntronix keyer, CQ, December 1976. This device was all solid-state, with self-completing dots and dashes and dot memory, as well as internal paddles.

Tempo Model DKT Keyer

The Tempo DKT has built-in paddles, an internal speaker, and runs on external AC or batteries. The front panel contains the power switch, speaker on/off switch, and a tune/cw switch. The rear panel includes the transmitter output connector, mark/space adjustment control, a 5-pin female connector, and is labeled 9v, relay contacts, and ext. monitor. The speed adjustment is found on the top of the keyer case. The Tempo DKT appears almost identical to the MSK-5 Squeeze Key.

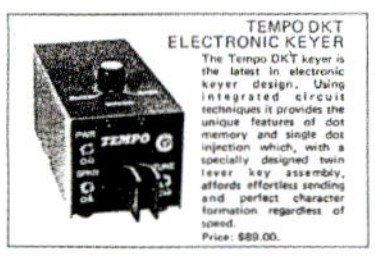
TEMPO DKT
ELECTRONIC KEYER
The Tempo DKT keyer is the latest in electronic keyer design. Using integrated circuit techniques it provides the unique features of dot memory and single dot injection which, with a specially designed twin lever key assembly, affords effortless sending and perfect character formation regardless of speed.
Price: $89.00.

Tempo DKT keyer ad from *73*, May 1972.

Ten-Tec Keyers

The Model 670 Ten-Tec keyer (top right) was designed specifically for use with the Ten-Tec Century/21 transceiver, but would also work with Ten-Tec's single band QRP transceivers. The keyer included wired-in cables with RCA phono plug connectors that Ten-Tec claimed could be used with adapters to match any rig's connector requirements. Low voltage positive transistor switching is incorporated to interface with the transceiver keying circuit. The Model 670 features self-completing dots and dashes, preset weighting in the most used speed range, and speed control with a 6–50 wpm range. Power for the keyer is obtained from the Century/21 or a similar transceiver's power supply, so no separate on-off switch is included for the keyer.

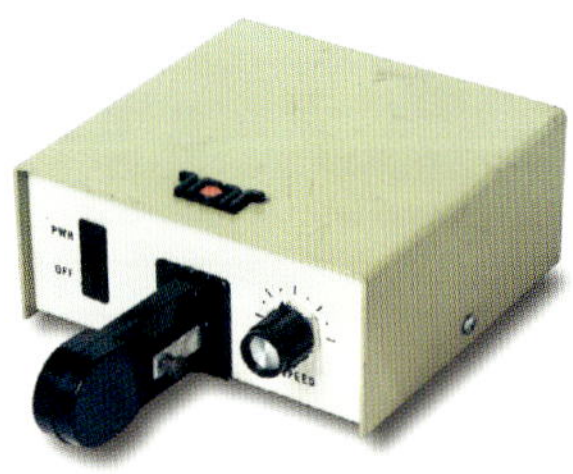
This is the Ten-Tec KR-5 single-lever keyer; this device was reviewed in the December 1973 QST. It uses solid-state circuitry with a reed relay for keying output.

The Ten-Tec KR-5A is a single-lever integrated circuit keyer with reed relay keying output. Speed range is 6–50 wpm.

Note: In addition to the Model 670, several other Ten-Tec keyers (such as the Model 645) were designed to work with Ten-Tec transceivers. These keyers obtained operating power from the transceiver itself.

Here (right) is the Model KR-20A keyer. The built-in paddle has its actuation force adjusted at the factory but offers contact adjustment from the front panel. The keyer's weighting factor is factory set for optimum smoothness and articulation. There is a button on top Ten-Tec calls the over-ride "straight key" that allows for QRS sending or transmitter tune-up. The KR-20A uses a reed relay output with 15 volt-amp contacts (400 v max), and includes a sidetone generator with adjustable level. Keyer circuitry gives self-completing characters and uses a plug-in circuit board with one IC and nine transistors. Power is provided by 117 VAC or 6-14 VDC. The advertised speed range is 6–50 wpm.

The Ten-Tec KR-50 Ultramatic keyer (bottom) offers a built-in AC supply and internal sidetone generator. This keyer also features dot and dash memory and an automatic weighting capability. Despite the similarity in names, this is an iambic or conventional mode keyer and does not offer the ultimatic mode.

This is the Ten-Tec KR-40 iambic keyer, a dual-lever magnetic return device. Paddle tension is adjustable from the front panel. The KR-40 was reviewed in the December 1973 QST.

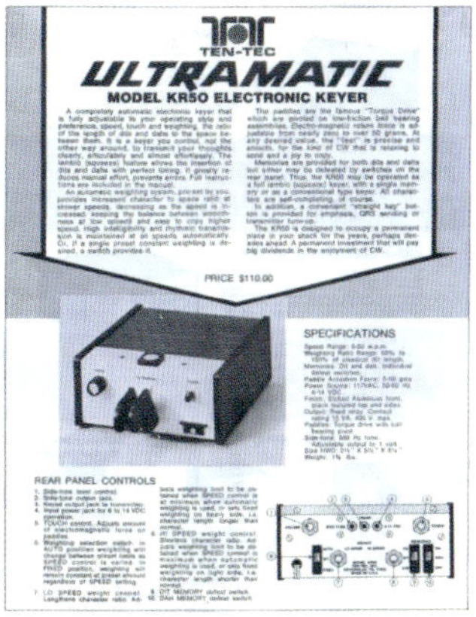

Specification sheet for the Ten-Tec KR-50 keyer.

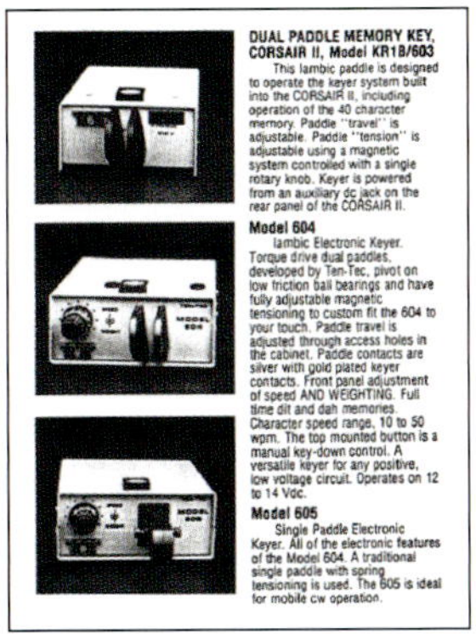

Advertisement for several popular early model Ten-Tec keyers.

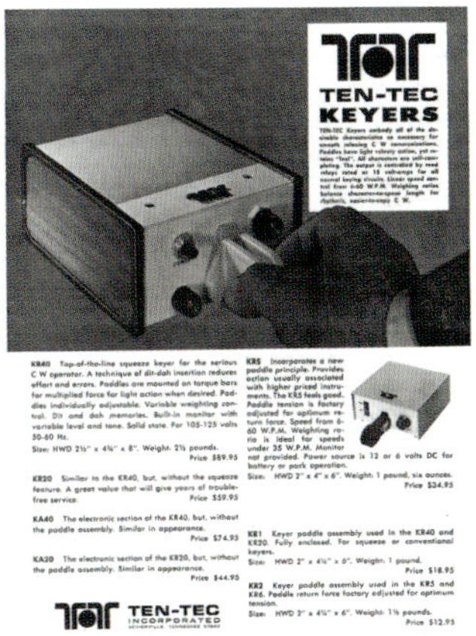

Early 1970s Ten-Tec keyer flyer. Note some of the models were available as electronics only, with no internal paddle. Ten-Tec was founded in 1968 by Al Kahn (K4FW) and Jack Burchfield (K4JU).

Trac Keyers

Trac Electronics, Inc. was in Buffalo, New York. They made a dual-lever CW paddle and a series of six different keyers during the early 1970s through the 1980s. L. B. Cebik (W4RNL) of antenna design fame briefly did some design work for Trac. Cebik wrote about the Trac designs:

> In the era before the single chip keyer and the present encoded CPU keyers, the Trac used an interesting technique of ensuring a full length first dot—they used a basic oscillator that ran at several times the actual baud rate for the code produced and divided down with flip-flops. Hence, only a fraction of the first dot was lost. I had one to use while designing a speed readout for them that would fit in the case with a cut-out for a couple LED digits. The higher-speed oscillator made the time constants shortened, allowing virtually instantaneous speed read, even though it used the old standard speed pot. Unfortunately, they [Trac] ceased operations before implementing it, and technology has long passed the board full of chips keyer. However, it produced very reliable and clean CW.

The Trac TE122 used a combination of CMOS ICs and transistors all mounted on one circuit board. Rear panel jacks were provided for connection to a paddle and keyed line to the transmitter. An internal 9 volt battery provided power to the TE122. Some very early versions of Trac CMOS keyers did not include a model number on the front panel.

The Trac TE133 CMOS keyer (middle) was an updated version of the TE122, and included rear panel switches for transmitter tune-up and selection of positive or negative keying. One additional IC was added to the circuit design.

Trac's TE144 (bottom) was also all CMOS and offered selectable auto or semi-auto operation and dot/dash memory. The TE144 added front panel controls for weight and sidetone pitch. Speed range was 5–50 wpm. Power was supplied by an internal 9 volt battery. This keyer was designed to key either positive or negative voltage transmitters.

This early 1970s Trac ad ran in several different ham radio journals.

Trac made three different memory keyers: the basic Message Memory Keyer TE201, the Deluxe Message Memory Keyer TE284, and the Champion Message Memory Keyer TE292.

Uncle Albert's Unique Keyer

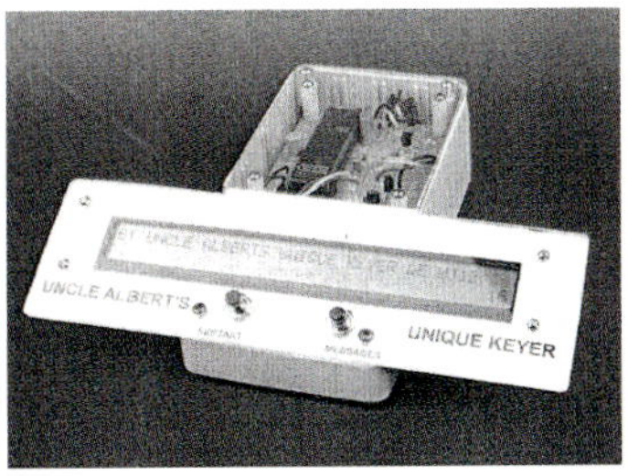

Uncle Albert's Unique Keyer was a project described by N4UAU in the January 1994 issue of *QST*. The device was the first readout display keyer; over 500 kits were sold as a result of the *QST* article. The Unique keyer provided four main functions: it was an 8–40 wpm iambic keyer with a 47 character memory, it could calculate code speed, it was a CW reader that could display the text of sent code, and it was a random character generator that displayed what it sent. The keyer was based on an 87C51 microcontroller and used a two-row liquid-crystal display (LCD) for the readout features.

Unified Microsystems Keyers

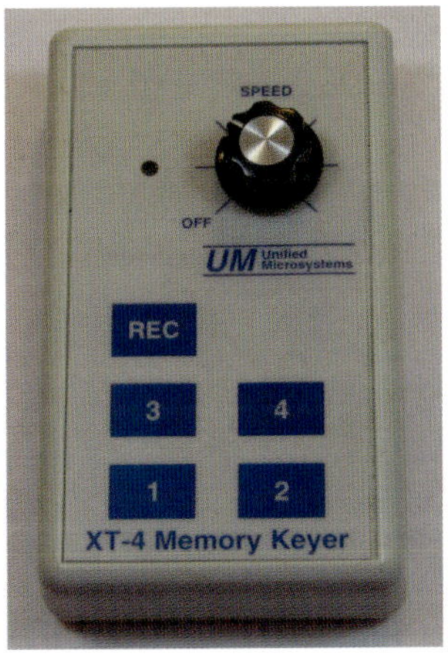

The XT-4 Memory Keyer is fully iambic with self-completing characters. There are four memories available; each can hold approximately 110 Morse characters. Memory locations are non-volatile, so programmed information is saved even when power is removed. The XT-4 is powered by a 9 volt alkaline battery, allowing for several hundred hours of heavy use. A paddle reverse function lets the user swap the dot and dash keys without rewiring the cable. The XT-4 will key solid state rigs with positive keying. Speed range is 8–45 wpm.

The Unified Microsystems VK-64 is a combination voice keyer and CW memory keyer that can be operated by either front panel controls, or by using a PC or personal computer. The voice keyer has four 15-second messages. Messages are stored in non-volatile memory, remaining stored until recorded over with a new message. The CW keyer is iambic and has memory with four programmable messages, each one capable of storing over 300 Morse characters. A front panel knob adjusts speed from 8–45 wpm. Selectable keyer configurations include Mode A or B, adjustable weighting, adjustable sidetone, selectable paddle configuration, and a transmitter tune function.

Unimor K2216 Electronic Key

The K2216 is a Polish keyer. This keyer uses an internal paddle with dual arms; adjustments are made via springs and utilize

locking contact spacing. The K2216 has controls for keyer speed and sidetone volume, and automatic or semi-auto modes are selectable by the user. In addition to the white color shown a black finish is also available.

Vectronics Keyer

The Vectronics CK200 features a Curtis 8044ABM keyer chip with adjustable weight and tone, volume and speed controls (6–50 wpm), and dot-dash memories. Volume and pitch are controlled from the outside panel controls, while weighting is adjustable internally. The CK200 offers iambic Mode A or B keying and works with all tube and solid state rigs. The CK200 is powered by either a 9 volt battery or an AC adapter. The type of keying required—either negative grid-block, solid state, or relay—is selectable by using a front panel rotary switch. There is also a front panel "tune" control and a built-in speaker for the pure sine-wave sidetone.

Vibroplex Brass Racer EK-1

The Vibroplex Brass Racer with EK-1 built-in keyer's major paddle parts are solid brass and the base is oiled hardwood. The device was first sold around 1982, after Vibroplex bought the designs from HAMCO and applied the "Brass Racer" name. The keyer was iambic with dot and dash memory and used a Curtis 8044 chip mounted in the base. The speed adjustment control is visible in the indented area in the base. Power is obtained from an internal MN-175 battery. Note the earlier HAMCO versions had locking screws on the top of the paddle yoke; the Vibroplex versions did not have these.

An October 1984 *CQ* article by Albert Jackson (VE3QQ) described how to modify the EK-1 to take advantage of several

Curtis 8044 chip functions not used in the original circuit. New keyer features included a sidetone, weight control, and a transmitter tune switch. Jackson also presented a capacitive touch control modification for the EK-1 in a January 1986 *CQ* article. The touch control feature allowed the user to operate the EK-1 keyer using just a fingertip touch on the paddle arms, which were replaced with stationary versions after the modification was performed.

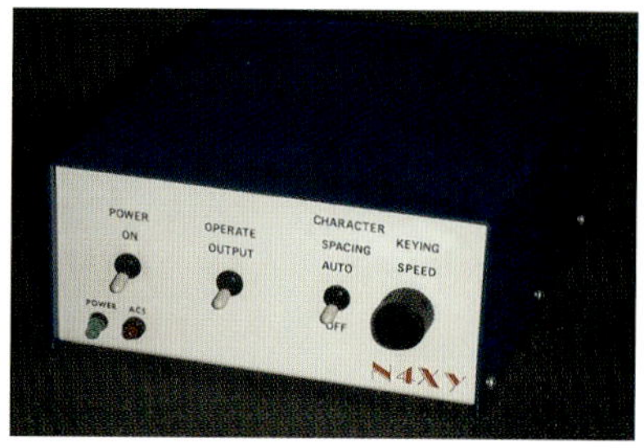

WB4VVF Accu-Keyer

The Accu-Keyer was designed by James Garrett (WB4VVF), and was one of the first TTL iambic keyers developed in the 1970s. The Accu-Keyer project was described in a 1973 *QST* article and in the 1975 *ARRL Handbook*; many units were built by amateurs all over the world. The original circuit was based on 7400 TTL technology, but was later updated to use CMOS devices. The design provides for self-completing dots and dashes, iambic operation, and automatic character spacing. One option provided for programmable 256 or 512 bit memory. One of the main goals was low cost; the designer estimated this keyer could be built for less than $15. The original design was intended to key a vacuum tube transmitter with grid-block keying. It is reported that some 20,000 Accu-Keyer kits were sold by Garrett, but very few remain, making this unit rare and collectible. Because this keyer basically consisted of a parts kit, many different physical versions of the device were conceived; several different builders' versions of completed Accu-Keyers are shown.

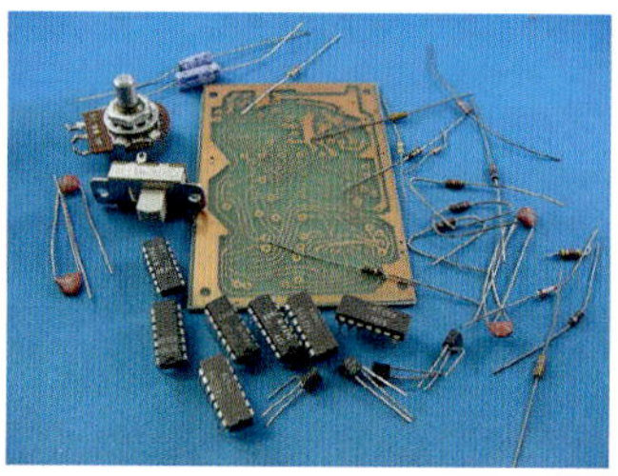

A Bryan Levin (ex-N2HI) Accu-Keyer.

WB9LPU Integrated Keyer

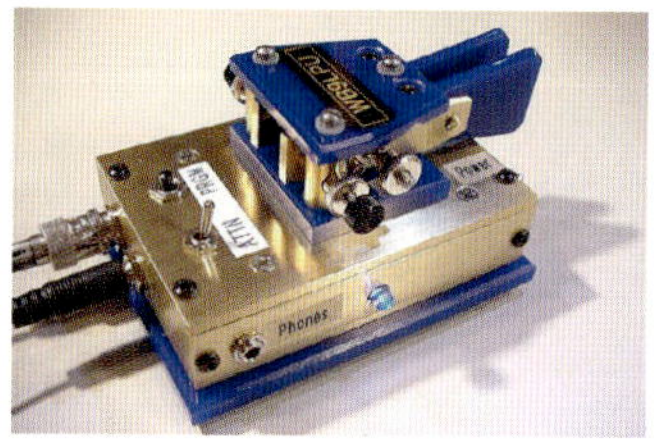

Richard Meiss (WB9LPU) is famous among key collectors for his innovative designs and machining skills. Shown is a Rock-Mite QRP rig with a PicoKeyer iambic keyer built into a base made from flat brass stock integrated with a Parkwood paddle. This Rock-Mite runs 500 mW on 40 meters.

Watson W-CRIOK Memory Keyer

The Watson W-CRIOK electronic memory keyer is shown with an LTA double-lever paddle. LTA is Llaves Telegraphicas Artisanas ("Telegraph Key Craftsmen"), from the Balearic Islands of Spain. LTA paddles were hand assembled; this one used a Spanish oak base with teak fingerpieces. The iambic keyer is programmable and has storage for up to 50 characters; it is based on a PIC device. Speed range is 5–50 wpm. The keyer offers two separate outputs for rigs requiring positive or negative keying, and the circuit is powered by an internal 9 volt battery. The keyer's circuits and controls are contained within a polished wooden base.

West Mountain Radio TOUCHkeyer

The TOUCHkeyer has no moving parts, no mechanical adjustments, and no clicking sounds; the operator merely has to touch the paddles to send code. The keyer's speed is adjustable from 5–50 wpm, and there is a built in sidetone for listening or practice. The TOUCHkeyer also gives the user an output for an external speaker and a direct paddle output for use with other keyers. The paddles are gold-plated and will not tarnish. The keyer weight is 2 lb. and is designed to stay in place during use. It can be programmed for 32 functions and has two 80 character memories for CW messages.

Wilderness Radio KC1 Keyer

Wilderness Radio designed the KC1 to be incorporated within a QRP transceiver, but it can easily be adapted for use as a standalone keyer. The KC1 can be called a micro-miniature keyer, but offers big keyer features, such as iambic operation with message memory, a Morse code output, and a universal frequency counter that reports your operating frequency to +/- 1kHz. The heart of the KC1 is a single chip, 18-pin microprocessor. Total current drain of the KC1 module is only 4mA, keeping with the low-current philosophy of the Wilderness Radio product line. The KC1 manual provides installation details for nearly all popular QRP rigs, including those from Heathkit, MJF, OHR, and Small Wonders Labs, as well as rigs published in *QST* or the *ARRL Handbook*. Speed range of this keyer is 7–50 wpm. Iambic Modes A and B are offered, as are multiple variable length message buffers, with a total of 50 characters of message memory and a word repeat macro to save memory. Also included are user settable weight, QSK delay, and sidetone pitch (different from frequency/command mode pitch) options.

The KC1 was designed and coded by Wayne Burdick (N6KR) of Elecraft fame. The code was written in July 1995, and the keyer was first sold as an accessory in August 1995. (Note: This keyer is not related to the Kansas City KC-1 keyer.) The KC1 continues to be available from Wilderness Radio, unchanged from the original hardware and code. This may make the KC1 the longest continually produced keyer in modern history. Wayne reports the original iambic state machine in the KC1 lives on today in the K3 and KX3 keyer code.

ZS4TX Super Combo Keyers

The Super Combo Keyer and Keyer II are dual-mode (phone and CW) multi-purpose keyers designed for DXers, contesters, DXpeditioners, and the casual operator who wants to reduce the amount of wiring and black boxes on their operating desk.

9A5AN Ultimatic

The 9A5AN keyer is a basic unit with a clean front panel. Some of the parameters—such as weighting—are not controllable, and this appears to be by design. Some other features of this keyer include either standard or ultimatic keyer modes, speed range of 5–100 wpm, auto spacing between characters and words, adjustable tone for sidetone, an internal speaker with 1 watt audio output and provisions for adjustable volume, one 16-word memory, and transistor or reed relay output. This keyer requires 220 VAC or 13.8 VDC for power.

9A9Y Keyer

9A9Y is the Croatian call of Mile; shown is his memory keyer board, which the user mounts in any preferred enclosure. It features 6 × 10 non-volatile memories and a menu with 28 commands. A manual pushbutton is used for keyer parameter entry. RS232 interface circuitry is provided for monitoring the status of keyer transmission by a personal computer. Power requirements are 5–14 volts DC.

4 The Single-Lever Paddle

Almost all of the earliest paddles were of the single-lever type. Presented here are discrete paddles; these devices were not integrated into a keyer as part of the mechanical design, such as seen in the Mon-Key or the Eldico devices.

Several bugs modified to be keyer paddles are shown. The fourth photo shows a modified McElroy bug.

The existence of the early discrete paddle is evidence of a beginning focus on mechanical advancement of the "simple switch" often seen as an afterthought to early keyers. With a few exceptions (such as the Harrison-reproduced Bunnell sideswiper), if a discrete paddle existed in the 1940s or '50s, it was either homebrew or a modification of a mechanical bug. Many had integrated keying mechanisms or paddles (see chapter 3). It can be surmised the reason for this is because there just were not any alternatives or commercially available paddles to be found. Once the approach of including built-in keyer paddles took hold some manufacturers and designers did not break away from this; the Heath series of keyers is a good example. Some operators modified existing bugs to remove the vibrating mechanism and added a second set of contacts, thereby resulting in a paddle of sorts. Focus and interest in paddle design and usage was kindled by the T.O. keyer and the Vibro-Keyer paddle. Paddle development had begun, and its place in electronic Morse history would soon be assured.

At first, the mechanical aspects of electronic keyer actuation, as somewhat of an afterthought, were given less attention than the electronics design. After all, the paddle was just a simple on-off switch, and many users got by with bugs modified to act as keyer paddles. Articles such as "Custom Make Your Key Paddle" by W6JB (*73*, August 1978) appeared; the article described how to modify the Vibroplex Zephyr for electronic keyer use.

Soon discrete paddle designs evolved, offering improvements that allowed ease of adjustment while complementing an electronic keyer, as seen with paddle models such as the Vibro-Keyer, Autronic, or the ELKEY. Even in advertisements, the keyer/paddle pair was sometimes presented as an intelligent combination; the perfect example is the pairing of the T.O. keyer and the Vibro-Keyer paddle.

As keyer electronics became more sophisticated the need for dual-lever designs became apparent, and paddle models such as the Nikey began to hit the market. It took some out-of-the-box thinkers like W8FYO and W9WBL to come up with some radical (for the time) new designs. With iambic keying, the focus shifted to QRO (high

The "perfectly matched sending team" as seen in the April 2010 *AWA Journal*.

speed sending), and elements of paddle design began to be tweaked. More attention was paid to magnetic return, lightweight arms, and contact material, and the paddle design revolution was well underway.

The Single-Lever vs. the Sideswiper

Many amateurs are confused by the terms single-lever and sideswiper. Are they different? If so, what are the differences? Can a single-lever paddle be used as a sideswiper or cootie key? And if so, how should the paddle be wired for each use? Sideswipers or cootie keys, sometimes also called double speed keys, were introduced decades before electronic keyers became popular; they are very similar mechanically and electrically.

In a cootie key, the single lever is moved back and forth between a pair of keying contacts, with dots and dashes made by hand. In a single-lever paddle, the lever is moved back and forth between contacts, but the single-lever dot and dash contacts are not electrically connected to each other; that needs to be the case so that each contact closure can control the creation of dots and dashes in the electronic keyer. Actually, any single-lever paddle can be used as a cootie key; depending on mechanical design some will work more effectively than others. A cootie key works best with a contact spacing of about ⅛ in. If the single-lever paddle does not allow that spacing it probably will not function well as a cootie key.

In summary, it is the contact wiring that determines whether the device is a single-lever paddle or a cootie key. To convert a single-lever paddle as a cootie, it is simply a matter of installing a wire connection or "link" between the dot and dash contacts. A cootie key usually has only two contacts, and if so cannot be converted for use as a single-lever paddle.

Significant Early Single-Lever Paddles

In a February 1945 *QST* article, John Bass (W9SOC) described his design for an electronic key movement. According to Bass, bugs modified for electronic keyers were limited by excessive lateral play in the dash lever. He presented a paddle design that overcame this limitation by mounting dot and dash contacts, the thumbpiece, and the knob all on one arm. Bass used Vibroplex parts for the contact post and screws. The Bass design has many similarities to the Vibro-Keyer and the ELKEY designs that would follow; Bass stated his device had no vertical or lateral play. Although the 1940 jackswitch paddle is older, the Bass device should be considered the first single-lever paddle that used the single arm two contact design and was not a modified bug; it predated the Vibro-Keyer by fifteen years.

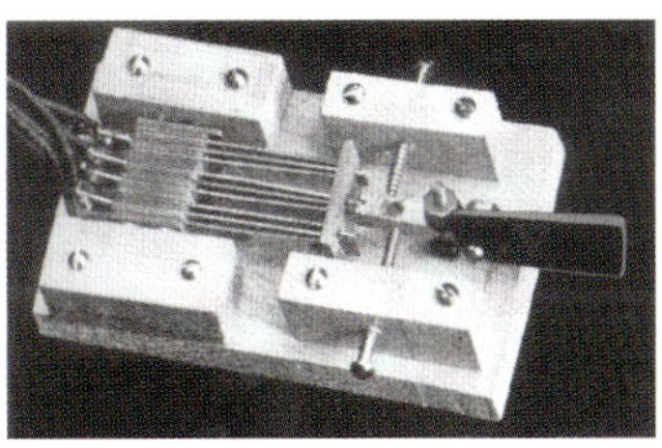

The first single-lever paddle from an April 1940 *QST* article. It was a modified jackswitch device using a wooden base.

In 1946, W. R. Smith built a very advanced single-lever paddle I feel deserves more recognition as a significant historical device.

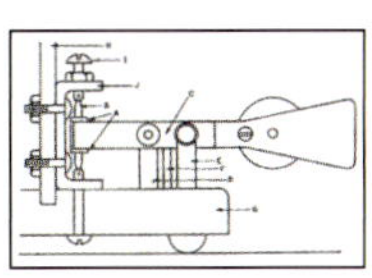

The John Bass (W9SOC) electronic key movement, February 1945.

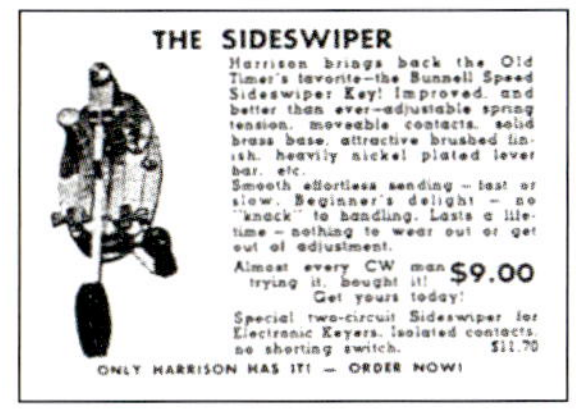

A November 1949 *QST* ad (above) offers a Harrison Radio reissue of the Bunnell sideswiper. Harrison offered a special two-circuit sideswiper for use with electronic keyers. This obscure ad may be the first time that what is essentially a keyer paddle was offered commercially, and comes many years before other commercial single-lever devices appeared in the pages of *QST*.

In 1964, a March *QST* article described the first magnetic paddle. The article was written by Andrew Pfieffer (K1KLO), and he called his single-lever paddle the Magnamatic key. Pfeiffer used two attracting magnets—one fixed on the lever and one fixed on the base—to create the restoring force needed to return the arm to neutral position. The magnet on the arm was adjustable with a small thumbwheel so its position relative to the base magnet could be changed. Pfeiffer's original Magnamatic required a machine shop to build; the *QST* article described how to build the key from J-38 parts and other smaller machined pieces. This paddle appeared some fourteen years before HAMCO put the first commercial magnetic paddle on the market and four years before N2DAN described his magnetic paddle concepts in the April 1968 *QST*. Pfeiffer applied for a patent on June 5, 1963, and was issued a patent for his magnetic paddle (3,293,363) on December 20, 1966. William Stout (W3UCU) filed for a patent in July 1962 for a magnetically centered paddle using magnetic repulsion. This patent issued in December 1964 (3,160,705), but no evidence was found that Stout tried to reduce the idea to practice or commercialize his paddle.

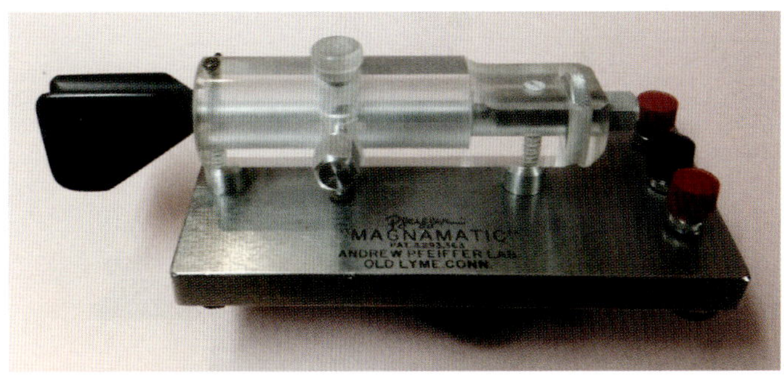

The K1KLO original Magnamatic, the first magnetic paddle, 1963.

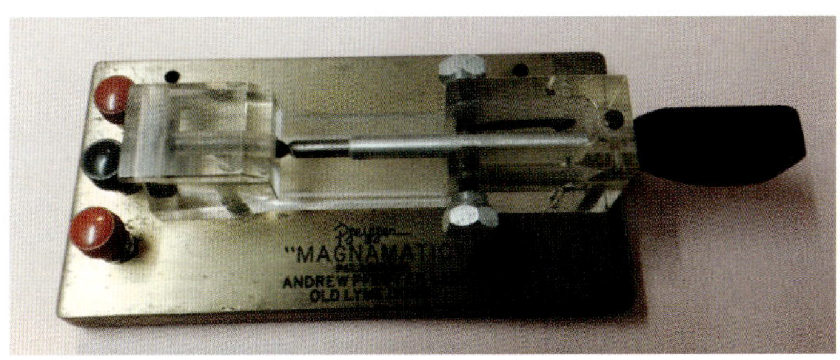

K1KLO's second version of the Magnamatic paddle, 1964.

The remainder of this chapter will present some additional early single-lever paddles. Also shown are many other keys showcasing the quality and innovation in design seen in single-lever devices still preferred by many operators today.

AD7GR

AD7GR is Ed Kotz of Baker City, Oregon. This is Ed's favorite key, a homebrew sideswiper/single-lever.

AME Bushwacker

The Bushwacker is a single-lever paddle kit from American Morse Equipment (AME). The design offers variable paddle lever ratio and adjustability for contact gap and spring force, giving the operator a choice between an extremely soft feel and what AME calls a "rock hard" feel. The paddle parts are anodized, with the fingerpieces having a slightly textured finish. AME furnishes stainless steel hardware with this kit, with the base pre-drilled and tapped for parts mounting.

Autronic

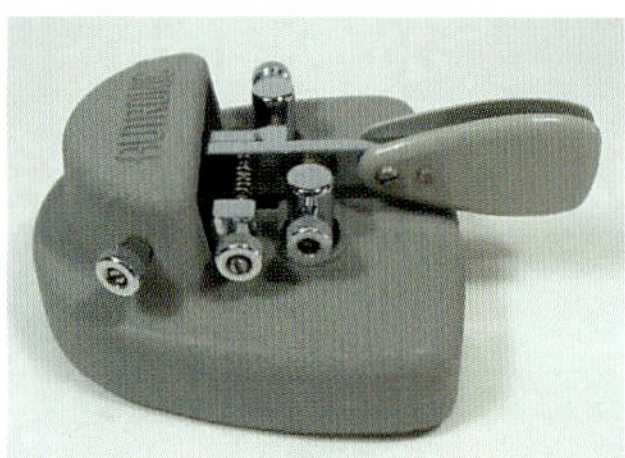

This is the classic Autronic paddle, produced 1960–1970 by the Electrophysics Corporation, originally of Newport Beach, California. The Autronic is known for its relatively small size, silver alloy contacts, and precision feel. Two different versions are shown: one version uses small concentric screwdriver adjustments, while the other has knurled adjustment screws with locking features. Users report they were able to make close adjustments that did not change over time. Advertisements for the Autronic paddle stated it was built specifically for electronic keyers.

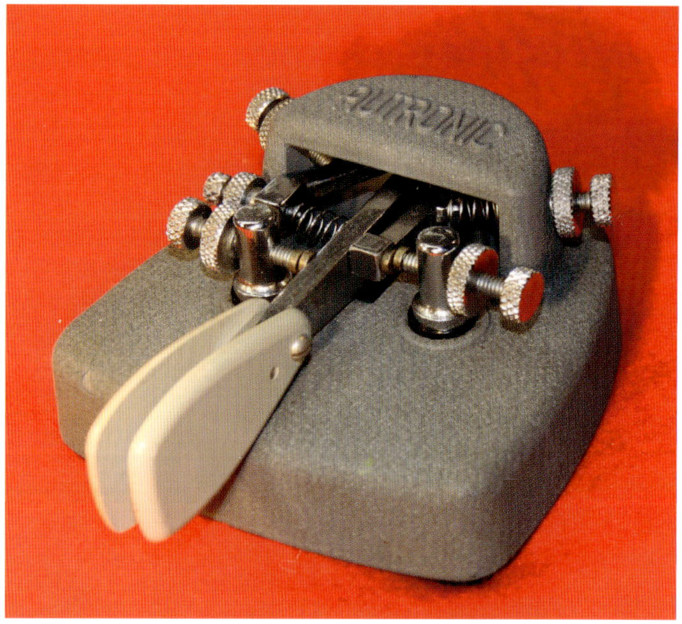

The Autronic paddle was designed by John Jay Jakosky (W6QJR) and his son, John Jr. (K6ONJ). Before the Autronic was introduced, existing paddles were made based on the bug-like pivot design, and had separate dot and dash contacts. Jakosky decided on a cast base with what he called a pivoted bifurcated yoke. Depending on whether the operator wanted a dot or dash the yoke moved either with or independently of the main lever. The unique single-lever and stirrup mechanical design allowed for a low moment of inertia; it was claimed this helped eliminate contact bounce. A US patent (3,098,898) was assigned to the Jakoskys on July 23, 1963. Electrophysics also offered a transistorized Autronic keyer for use with the paddle (see chapter 3). In 1965, the company moved to Costa Mesa. The original price of the Autronic paddle was $16.95. The last ads for the Autronic paddle appeared in 1968, listing the price at $19.95.

An Autronic paddle brochure.

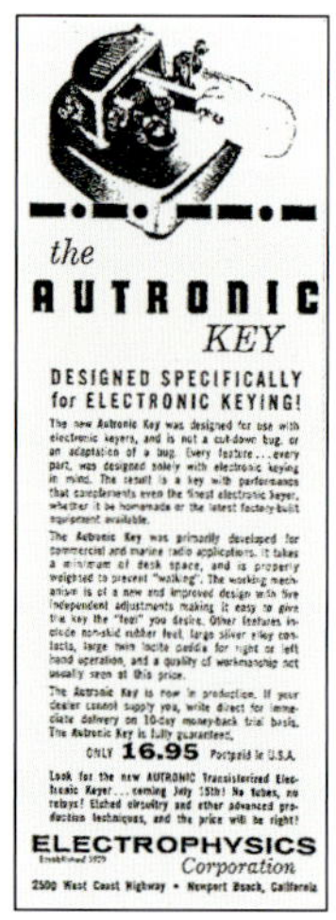

June 1960 Autronic key ad as seen in *QST*.

Begali Sculpture Mono

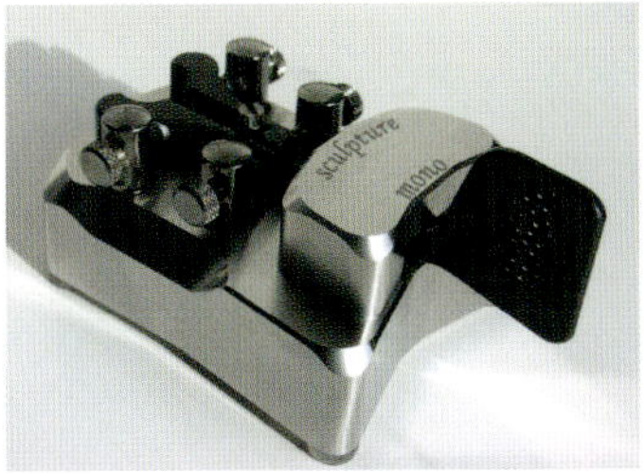

The Sculpture Mono is a single-lever version of the Sculpture Dual. The Sculpture Mono advertises that all fixed parts are completely made from AISI-304 stainless steel. The paddle's polished finish offers durability and allows the user to remove any blemishes with fine abrasive compounds like jewelers rouge or car polish. The single arm of this paddle is made from anodized aircraft aluminum, and is designed to actuate two secondary levers that hold the contacts, which are 14k gold and included as a standard feature. This approach results in a self-centering arm movement. Return force can be set independently by adjusting the repelling magnets. Begali notes the magnets offer finer adjustments that are more stable over time than spring adjustments. Begali describes the single paddle arm as having minimal moving mass, and in combination with the use of high grade racing bearings gives the user a responsiveness and precision not found in other single-lever devices.

Begali Simplex Mono

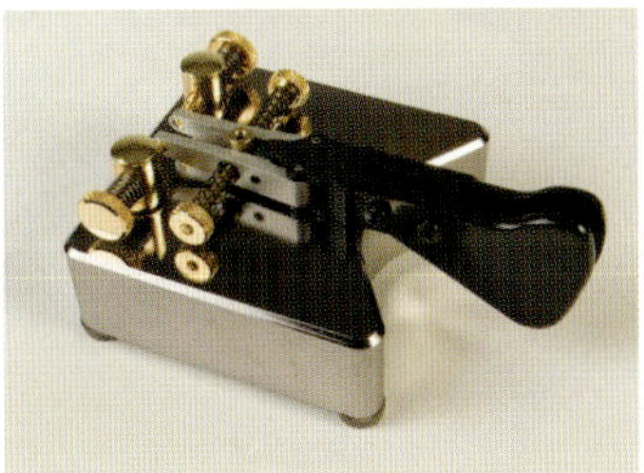

The Simplex Mono is a single-lever key with either a gold or palladium plated base and gold-plated components. Shown is the Simplex Mono with the palladium plated base. A third base option allows the buyer to select a jet black titanium finish. The Begali Simplex is manufactured using NC machinery, and the resulting precision helps guarantee paddle reliability. Micro-threaded screws are used for all adjustments. The pivot uses ball bearings that are imbedded in the base and the moving components are made of a lightweight alloy. This key design makes use of a segmented lever that provides decoupling of the two sides while resulting in a consistent return to neutral position. Paddle contacts are 925/000 silver, and the weight of the paddle is a bit over three pounds. The Simplex Mono typically sells with a protective dust cover.

Begali HST

The HST (for High Speed Telegraphy) single-lever paddle was inspired by a design that several of the top competitors at the High Speed Telegraphy Competition were using. Shown is Begali's improved version of the HST original, called the HST Mark II. The HST uses a heavy cast iron base, with a single lever made from aluminum alloy held by two precision racing bearings at the back of the lever. The fingerpiece is unique, in that it uses perforations to prevent fingers from slipping. The contact spacing and the tension adjustments are made using gold-plated fine pitch screws. Magnetic return force is employed using a cam mechanism that Begali claims ensures consistency and well defined return to center position. In addition, there is a small toggle switch at the rear of the base that lets the user select single-lever or sideswiper mode.

Bencher ST Series

Once the Joe Hills FYO patent expired, Bencher felt free to manufacture and sell a single-lever version of their popular BY-1. Bencher now offers the single-lever version of their classic paddle with two choices: the ST-1 has a black base and the ST-2 is chromed. The Bencher ST series features adjustable contact spacing and tension, self-adjusting needle bearings, gold-plated solid silver contacts, a heavy steel base with non-skid feet, and molded acrylic fingerpieces. The paddle's main frame, contact posts, and bearing ring are machined from solid brass and are chrome-plated. The paddle weight is three pounds (1.4 kg).

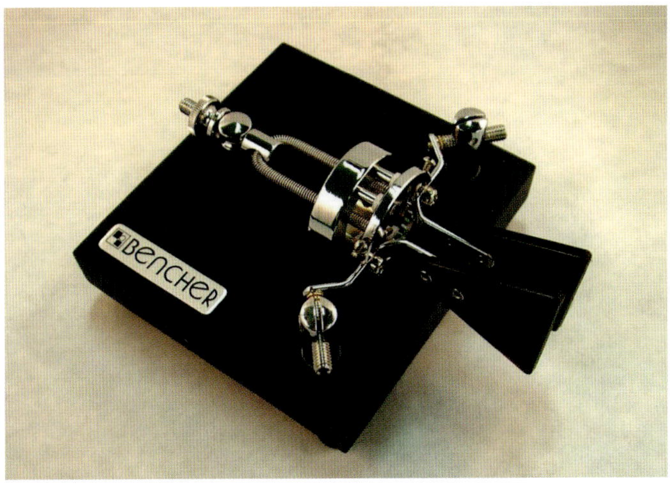

Brown Brothers Model ES

The Brown Brothers Model ES single-lever paddle is an extremely rare device; it is reportedly one of six known to exist. The meaning of the designation "ES" is not known; perhaps it is for Experimental Single-lever?

Codetrol

Here are two different types of Codetrol paddles. The first is a very early paddle designed to be used with the Codetrol keyer; the keyer is more fully described in chapter 3. The paddle utilized a basic pivot mechanism with spring-loaded arm return and was mounted in a heavy cast base. The bottom photo shows a later version of a Codetrol paddle, also a single-lever design. The label is marked "Codetrol Impulse Devices" of Atlanta, Georgia.

Dentsu-Seiki MS-2

The MS-2 is a microswitch compound operation Morse key. The key may be used as a sideswiper or a single-lever paddle, depending on hook-up. This MS-2 device came out in 1953.

DL4TJ

The Werner DL4TJ paddle exhibits some visual similarities to the Schurr paddles. Not much is known about production, except this key was made around 1988. It is believed Werner ran a Morse key store called Morsetastenladen that stopped operations in the late 2000s.

Don Iverson

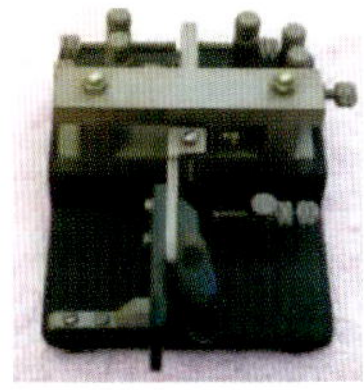

Don Iverson of Portland, Oregon, was a metal worker who enjoyed hobbies such as collecting antique motorcycles, old metal toys, and vintage radio equipment. In addition to undertaking restorations, Iverson also designed and built original items which, by intent, appeared to be very old. Some of Iverson's single-lever paddle creations are shown here, with markings indicating they were built by the "Wireless Apparatus Company." Many collectors and researchers are convinced this company was just a creation of the imaginative mind of Don Iverson. Whether the company existed or not, the Iverson paddles remain very intriguing keys.

ELKEY

The ELKEY is a historically significant device (factory literature capitalizes the name and shows it as one word, although the label on the key uses a hyphen in the name). The ELKEY was made by Poucel Electronics of Long Island, New York, 1959–1963, and is likely the first commercially available paddle; it probably prompted Vibroplex to begin producing a competing key (Vibro-Keyer).

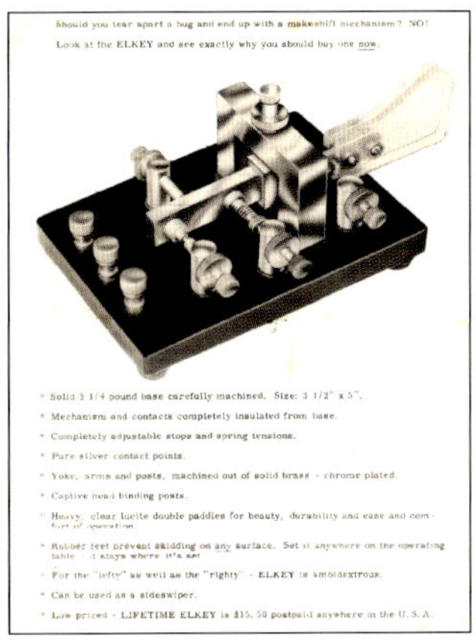

Should you tear apart a bug and end up with a makeshift mechanism? NO!

Look at the ELKEY and see exactly why you should buy one now.

- Solid 3 1/4 pound base carefully machined. Size: 3 1/2" x 5".
- Mechanism and contacts completely insulated from base.
- Completely adjustable stops and spring tensions.
- Pure silver contact points.
- Yoke, arms and posts, machined out of solid brass - chrome plated.
- Captive head binding posts.
- Heavy, clear lucite double paddles for beauty, durability and ease and comfort of operation.
- Rubber feet prevent skidding on any surface. Set it anywhere on the operating table - it stays where it's set.
- For the "lefty" as well as the "righty" - ELKEY is ambidextrous.
- Can be used as a sideswiper.
- Low priced - LIFETIME ELKEY is $15.50 postpaid anywhere in the U. S. A.

Bob Poucel, W2AYJ
Sid Shore, K2FC

Poucel Electronics Company

P.O. Box 181
Babylon, L.I., N.Y.

Dear OM:

If you own an electronic key of any kind you know that the key mechanism is the weakest link in the entire unit.

If you want to build an electronic keyer you may be stopped or slowed down by the difficulty of building a good sturdy and mechanically sound keying mechanism. And - where on earth can you even buy one?!

The ELKEY is the answer!

Here is a photograph showing the precise mechanical construction. You will see that the ELKEY is designed for LIFETIME USE!

An ELKEY product ad from the early 1960s, along with black and plated-base ELKEY models.

Poucel Electronics Company was Bob Poucel (W2AYJ) and Sid Shore (K2FC). Poucel presented this design as the answer to the problem of finding a good, sturdy mechanical keying mechanism for the electronic keyers that were appearing in the early 1960s. The ELKEY used silver contacts and Lucite fingerpieces. The device weighed over three pounds and used pure silver contacts. Original selling price was $15.50.

The bases and other components were made out-of-house and delivered to Poucel, where they were assembled into finished paddles in Bob's basement workshop. Bob's wife assisted with the packing. Sid Shore was the financial partner and worked on advertising and promotion.

ELKEY literature from Bob Poucel notes he is a CW man himself, and expresses his frustration at not having a keying mechanism that works with the available electronic keyers. Bob also related how he used the new ELKEY in several contests without any key trouble at all.

The EW4IDP Almanac paddle (see p 134).

Electric Specialty

Electric Specialty of Cedar Rapids, Iowa, offered keys in kit form 1939–1955. After bug production ceased, leftover bug parts were used to make the ES paddle.

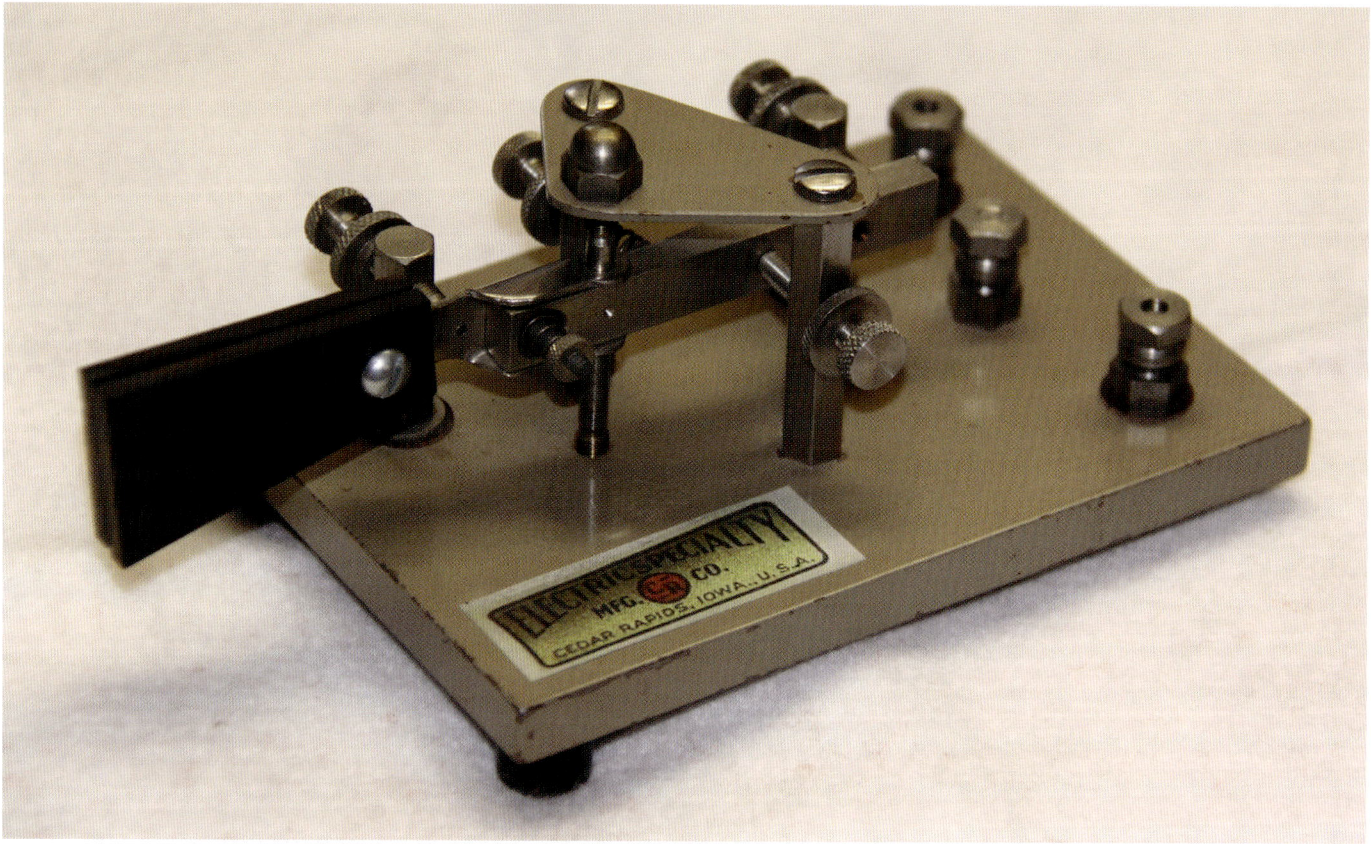

EW4IDP DEVICES

Dmitri (EW4IDP) has designed and built several different models of keys. The key (below left) is called the Extreme. It is an interesting device first conceived in 2009, and incorporates several unique design features. The lightweight mechanism sits up on standoffs on top of the paddle base and can be removed to use independent of the base. The fingerpiece is machined as part of the alloy paddle arm. The paddle arm is suspended on stainless steel pins, with adjustments in the rear for arm tension and centering. The removable mechanism weighs only seventy grams.

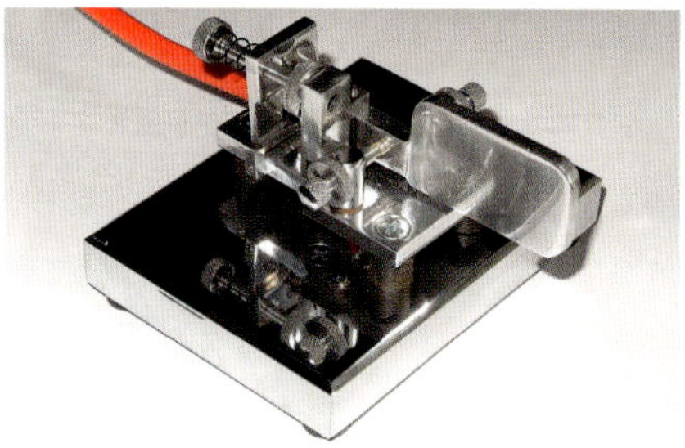

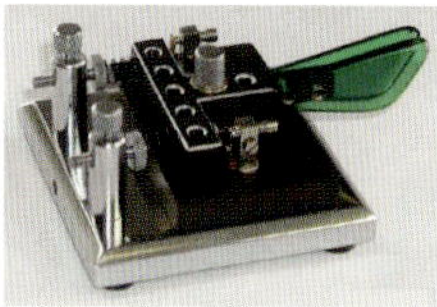

Note: Dmitri is from Belarus. The republic declared their sovereignty July 27, 1990, during the dissolution of the Soviet Union; Belarus declared independence on August 25, 1991.

This (below right) is the Pekler paddle, named after the Russian polar researcher Leo Naumovicha Peklera. The Pekler began production in 2000, and remains a very popular paddle. It is the first EW4IDP design to attain wide interest among the ham community. The design uses a single brass pivot with arm return force provided by two springs in the rear. Contacts are from RP-4 relays. This paddle led to the creation of the "Zero" dual-lever paddle in 2003.

The EW4IDP Almanac paddle uses two pivots in front and rear, with balls incorporated as part of the suspension. It is a spring arm return device. Although the contact adjustments have knurled wheels, the spring adjustments do not. In 2007, this design received a patent in Belarus and Russia.

FYO (W8FYO) Paddle

W8FYO—or just FYO as most collectors know them—paddles are possibly the most intriguing pieces of hardware a key collector can imagine. Some have never seen one except in photos. They were only offered for a few years (mainly 1962–1963), but the design propagated through the market even to the present. This paddle is based on the use of three pivots spaced around a metal ring rather than bearings for near-frictionless arm movement. Fixed silver contact adjustment is made by screwing the contacts in or out using a thumbwheel and tightening down on the split contact post after the desired spacing is obtained. Tension of the coil spring may be changed to vary the arm "feel" or weight. The FYO even offers adjustable height on the thumbpiece. The base is cast and finished in black wrinkle paint; other paddle parts are either chromed or brushed satin. Joe Hills sold these at the Dayton Hamvention in 1962 and perhaps other years. From the Joe Hills original, HAL licensed the Hills patent (3,166,638) and sold their versions in the mid-'70s. HAMCO, Teletek (which looked just like the Bencher), Vibroplex, and Bencher all sold paddles based on elements of the original FYO design. This paddle was reviewed in the October 1962 *QST* and *CQ*.

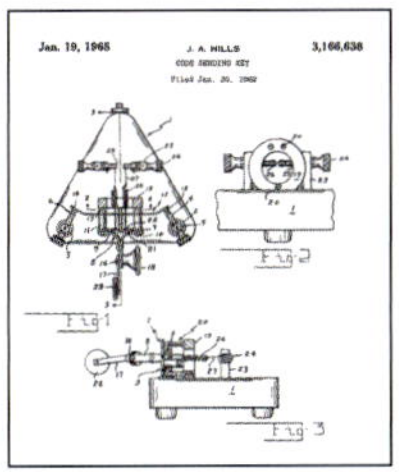

The Hills FYO paddle drawing from patent 3,166,638.

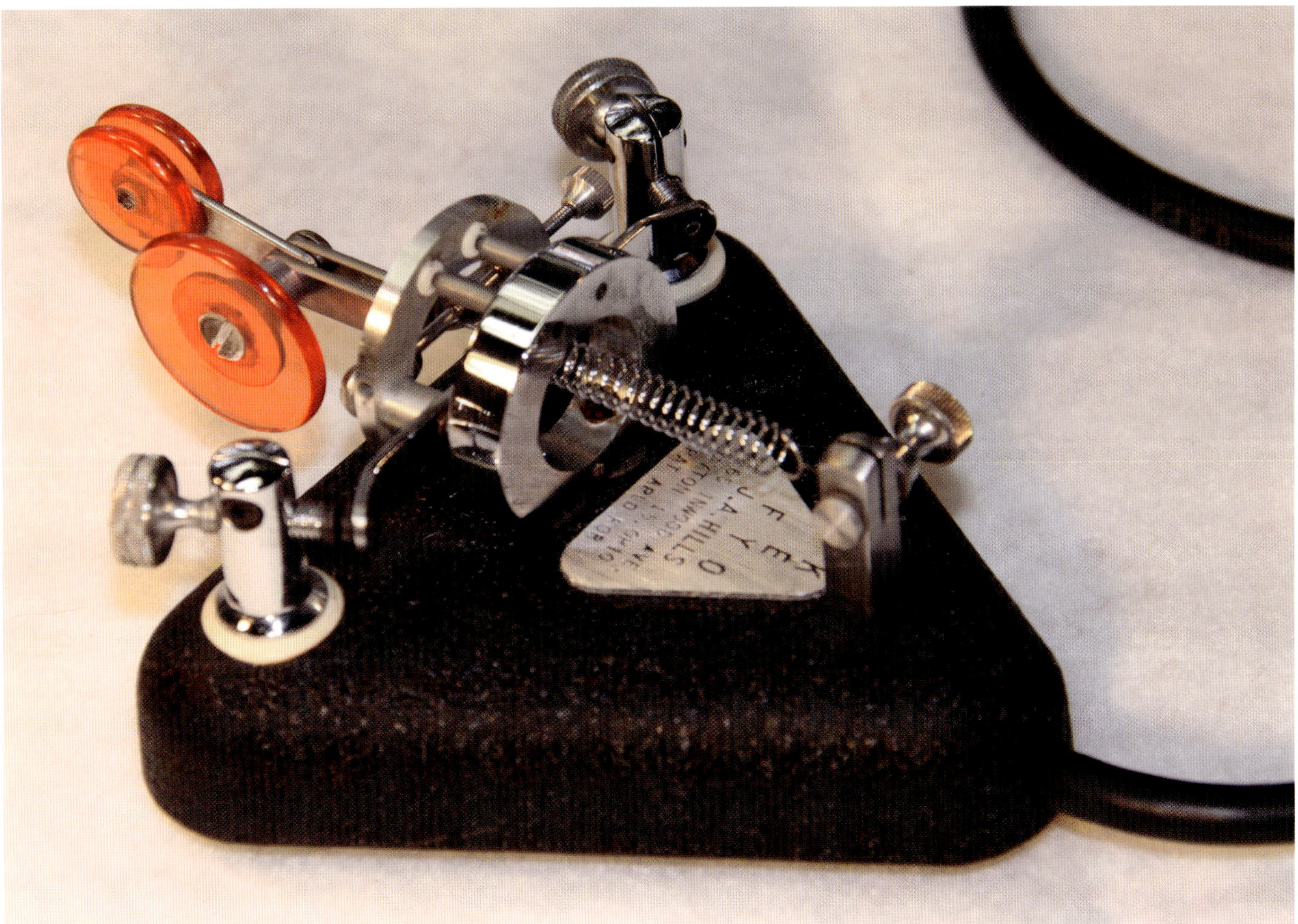

G4ZPY

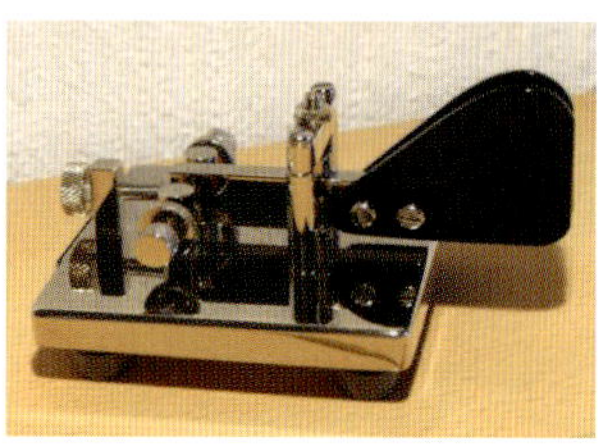

Gordon Crowhurst (G4ZPY) was the designer and maker of these paddles. Gordon's devices have a well earned reputation for quality and reliability. Gordon was not in production, but rather made each device by special order. The paddles were available with a black, polished brass, nickel plate, or gold base. Many feel the G4ZPY's construction offers a more advanced device compared to other competing paddles. Some owners have also expressed appreciation for the unique shape of the thick, beveled fingerpieces. These keys offer precision adjustments that do not wander over time. Some reviewers have noted the lightness of the paddles and suggested they may be more appropriate for operators with a light touch. The G4ZPY motto is quality rather than quantity.

GHD Paddles

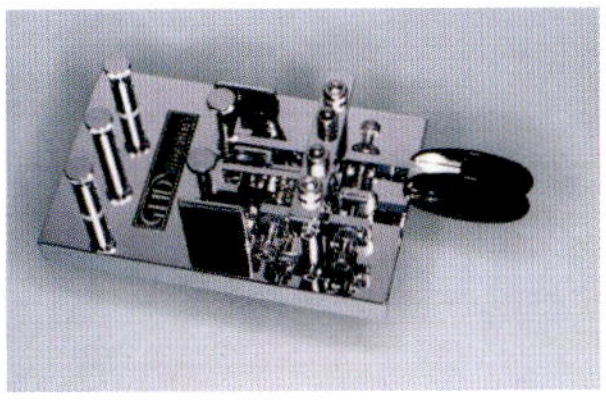

GHD keys are made by Toshihiko Ujiie (JA7GHD) in Sendai City, Japan. The GHD GN405 uses the more common mechanical contacts, as opposed to some GHD paddles that use optical contacts. This paddle exhibits the famous GHD chrome plating, typically of very high quality.

The GF501A is a double speed key, cootie key, and single-lever paddle combined. This key replaces its predecessor, the GF601A. The key utilizes distinctive fingerpieces of a "lollypop" style; parts are mounted on a highly polished chrome base measuring 4 × 3.25 in. and the paddle weight is 2 lb. 1 oz. The GF501A GHD single-lever speed key is priced at $209.95.

The GHD GF601A was a limited edition "speed paddle" utilizing a large, heavy base that did not move around on the operating table. This paddle exhibited a smooth, fluid feel, partially due to the use of a hacksaw blade as the paddle arm. The GF601A also offered a wide adjustment range with magnetic damping and two-stage tension adjustment and could be set up as a cootie key or as a single-lever paddle.

Hannes Bauer

Hannes Bauer (right, in an R. L. Drake Company 4-line product advertisement). He became an amateur around 1920. After WWII, he received the callsign DL1DX. In 1945, Bauer started his small electronics shop, and in the 1950s supposedly offered 250 bugs and 400–500 paddles for sale. The Bauer firm closed in 1983.

The German Hannes Bauer paddle was an unusual device employing three rings of ball bearings separating the three moving parts. It was manufactured in the mid-1960s by Hannes Bauer of Bamberg, Germany. This paddle has at least two variations (below). There was also a similar bug device of the same color sold under the Edelmann name.

Here (below) is another variation of the Hannes Bauer paddle owned by collector Cortland Richmond (KA5S), who bought it in Weisbaden, Germany, in the 1970s. It is based on a heavy casting somewhat triangular in shape, with approximately four inch sides. The parts of the paddle are mounted on a red plastic block fastened inside the casting. Springs are used for arm centering. Contacts are at the rear end of the paddle arm. The fingerpiece is a molded red plastic piece mounted to the paddle arm using one screw.

The "Markgraf" (below right) is a third model of a Hannes Bauer paddle; it can also function as a sideswiper. This paddle dates to about 1966, and was designed to be used with an el-bug, as keyers were sometimes known. It was originally purchased from the Hannes Bauer radio shop in Bamberg, Germany.

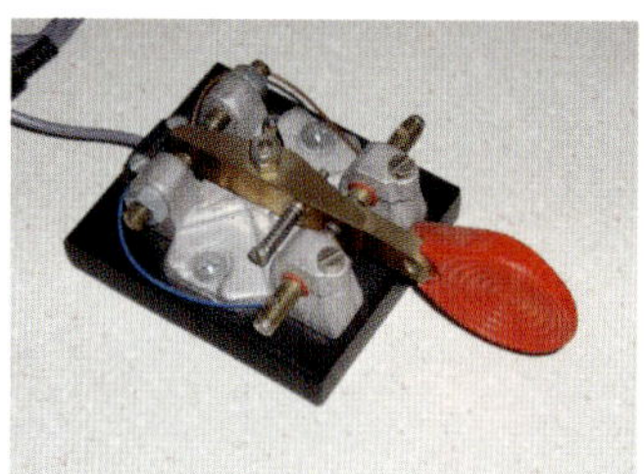

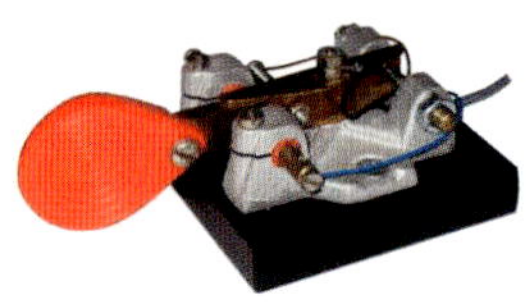

Hi-Mound

The MK-701 was Hi-Mound's first single-lever paddle. In 2009, the MK-704 was introduced. It was of a similar design to the MK-701, but moved the mechanism and fingerpiece out from the base for better operator interface. The MK-704 was advertised as being a rugged, heavy paddle designed to give a lifetime of service; it weighed a bit over two pounds. Paddle action is very precise, with close-contact spacing and fully adjustable bearing tension. The base is made of steel, it is fairly heavy, and it is finished in flat black powder coat. A plastic protective cover was included with the paddle, and connection to the transmitter or keyer was by means of binding posts at the back of the paddle. The MK-704 was priced at $139.95.

The Hi-Mound MK-701.

The Hi-Mound MK-704.

Hi-Mound Palm Keyer PK-1

The PK-1 is a hand-held pushbutton switch that can function as a key. It appears a bit awkward to use, and the limitations of holding and supporting the unit would probably keep maximum code sending speed to the single digits.

I6QON Paddle

The I6QON paddle exhibits a distinctive approach to single-lever design. Maurizio uses two pivot points with spring arm centering. Mechanical mounting of the pivot bridge and the key's terminals on a side plate are visually striking and set this paddle apart from other basic arm/pivot designs. Maurizio also enjoys making reproductions of famous older keys, such as the McElroy bugs.

IK1OJM

IK1OJM is Salvatore, an Italian machinist who handcrafts many different models of keys. The IK1OJM models are consistently rated well for ease of adjustment and reliability. Two versions of the magnetic return single-lever/sideswiper device are shown with brass and black base options.

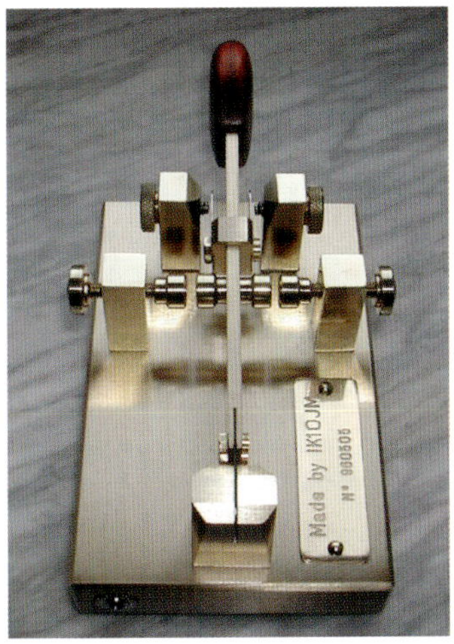

IK3JBP

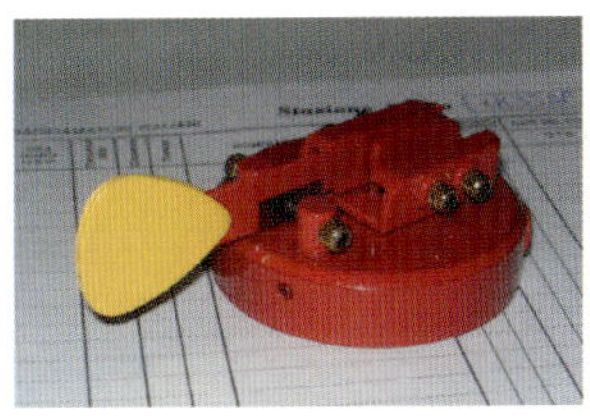

The IK3JBP key is a single-lever/sideswiper device that uses a sliding steel blade, allowing operator adjustment for tension and feel. There are four magnets mounted underneath the base for fixing the paddle to a heavier base.

JH6OIT Paddles

Two versions of JH6OIT's paddle designs are presented. The top device uses a modified yoke/pivot design with ball bearings to suspend the arm. The bottom paddle incorporates a sliding arm design that makes the key unique; instead of pivoting the arm when the operator pushes on the fingerpieces, the whole arm slides from right to left and back again. Magnets at the rear of the arm return it to a center position.

Jones SL

Jones keys were made by Peter Jones in England in the mid-to-late 1990s. The single-lever paddle carried model number PK-203B, and the key parts and base were brass. The single-lever key uses magnetic arm return, unlike the dual-lever, which uses springs. The return magnet pair is at the very end of the paddle arm, at the rear of the key. By 1998, Jones had stopped making keys. The brass base double-lever was the most popular Jones key; the single-lever is considered somewhat rare.

K8RA P-6 SL

The P-6 uses a ball bearing pivot design and was Jerry's (K8RA) favorite key. It weighs four pounds and is made of solid brass. The P-6 incorporates silver contacts and is made in the USA. The dot and dash arms pivot on six ball bearings, and contact pin spacing is fully adjustable. Magnetic repulsion is used for arm return to neutral. The base uses four soft urethane feet that reportedly help the key stay in place when in use.

Kent SL

The Kent single-lever paddle claims to allow additional flexibility in setting paddle adjustment due in part to the independent spring arrangement that allows separate left and right spring tension settings. The use of precision made contact screws with knurled instrument heads and locking nuts allows for precise and positive gap-setting, helping ensure a positive feel. The key uses high quality shielded ball race bearings with machined parts manufactured from solid brass. The paddle base is heavy powder-coated steel. Silver plated contacts are incorporated and help ensure durability and low resistance closure.

M0BZU MagKey

The M0BZU paddle is a magnetic single-lever convertible via wiring change to a cootie key. This device is loosely based on the old Bunnell sideswiper. The base is polished granite and other paddle parts are brass.

Knurled screws and contact/magnet posts are made by M0BZU on his lathe. The fingerpieces are made from Bakelite. The contacts were salvaged from an electrical relay.

N1KPR

The N1KPR single-lever/cootie key is another brass part on Bakelite base device and incorporates some unique design features not seen in other paddles. This paddle uses pivot bearings and springs, and users report very smooth operation. The designer states that a wide range of adjustments are available for different operator preferences.

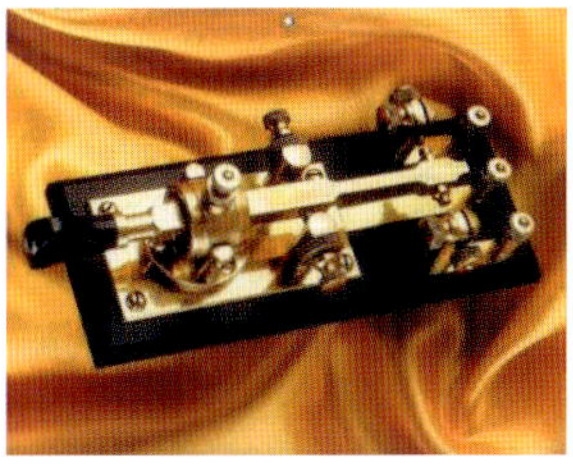

N2DAN Prototypes

Here are two different N2DAN-modified paddles with magnets added to assess performance. These prototypes predate the famous N2DAN dual-lever paddle that came about after these prototypes were built. In an April 1968 *QST* article, Steve Nurkiewicz (N2DAN) describes his approach of substituting magnets for springs on some single-lever paddles. Tension was adjusted by changing the spacing between two magnets: one epoxied to the paddle arm and one to a screw mounted to a post. To improve paddle action, Nurkiewicz removed the stock friction bearings on which the pivot normally rotated, and replaced them with small hobby-type ball bearings.

Nurkiewicz then scratch built another magnetic prototype paddle (p 141, bottom right) with a better parts layout to accommodate the magnets. Upon confirmation the magnetic approach was working some dual-lever prototypes were built with high-precision ball bearings and smaller magnets of equal strength to the earlier large ones.

N2DAN dual-lever magnetic prototype. A photo of a similar paddle can be seen in chapter 5.

N3ZN

The ZN-SLR is Tony Baleno's (N3ZN) illustration of what the ultimate single-lever paddle design should look like. Many CW operators prefer non-iambic operation with a single-lever paddle, and the ZN-SLR consistently receives high marks from those folks. The N3ZN design offers the ability to set very close contact spacing and have this setting not wander over time. The close settings help eliminate random unwanted character elements. The ZN-SLR is silent during use, with no annoying mechanical clicks. Tony has found a type of rubber foot that is soft and sticky, preventing the paddle from moving on the operating desk even during heavy keying. Shown (right) is the old Model ZN-SLR; the new model (bottom) now has a round base and paddle arms of slightly less mass and a different fingerpiece design.

N0SA

Larry Naumann's (N0SA) Model SP2 is a beautifully constructed example of a modern single-lever paddle. It uses a 3 × 3 in. heavy base and the design incorporates three sets of bearings. Independent arm spacing and tension adjustments are offered. Magnetic arm centering is used, with magnets embedded in the arms and in the adjustment screws. Paddle arms are made of 7075 aluminum and are of minimal length, giving the paddle a very responsive feel. Larry hand finished and polished each paddle. Unfortunately, no more of these keys are being made.

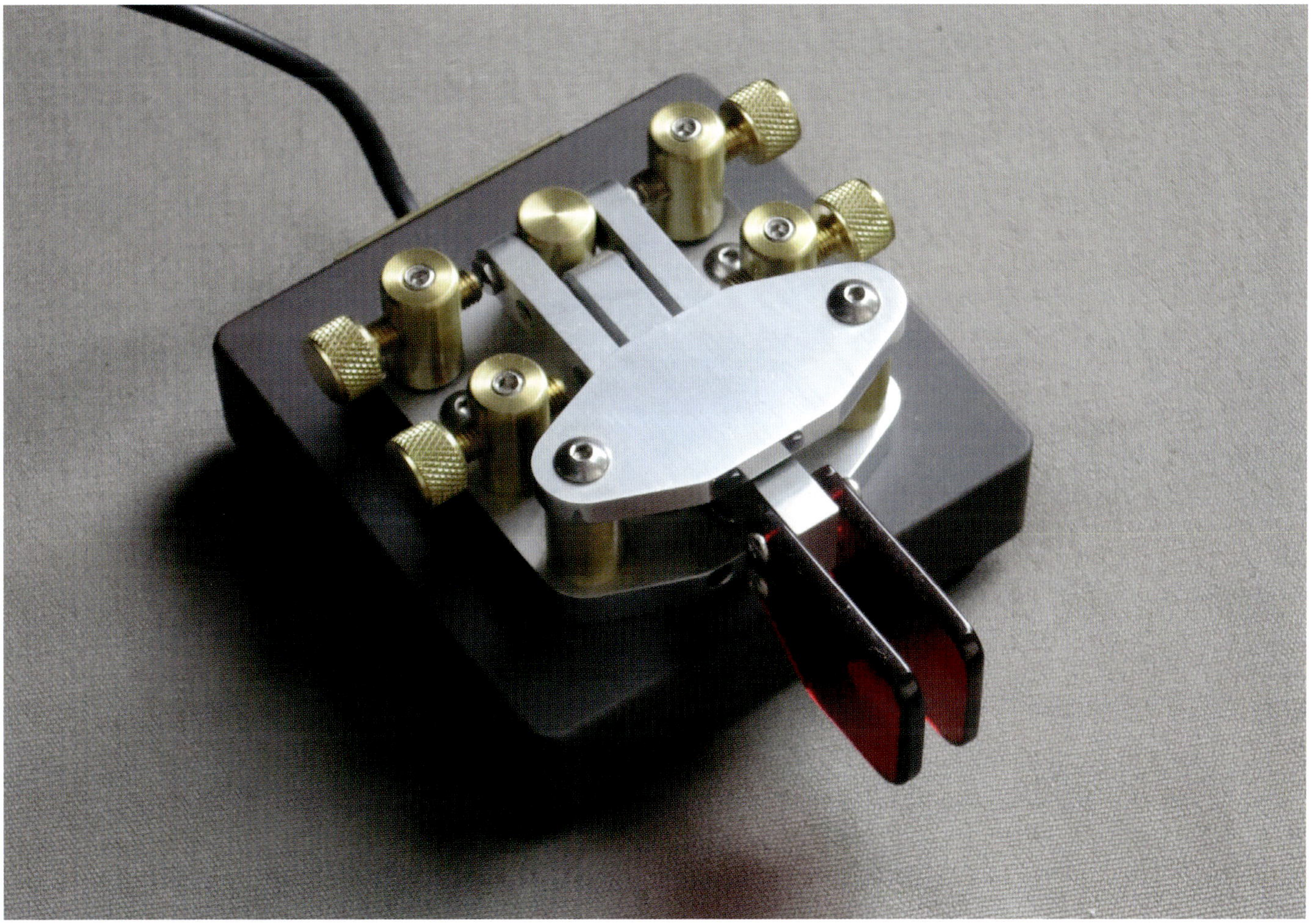

North American Telegraph NA-10

The North American NA-10 classic single-lever paddle is machined from solid brass stock and mounted on a polished hardwood base. In place of rubber feet, the NA-10 uses a rubber pad underneath the base.

The base measures approximately 2 × 3¼ in., so this is not a large device. The fingerpiece is made of shaped black walnut. The brass plate on the side of the base is machine engraved with the maker's name and the key serial number.

ON4MAC

ON4MAC is Michel, who guarantees his paddles for as long as he lives. His designs use a very heavy base and lightweight paddle arms. The single-lever device shown is somewhat rare; it does not appear on the ON4MAC website. The design uses a round rod instead of a rectangular arm for reduced arm mass.

Pro-Paddle SL

The Pro-Paddle from QRPWorks is a solid state single-lever design that uses software to adjust paddle feel; no contacts, magnets, or springs are used. This paddle is based on the 9A5AN solid-state design. The base is made of stainless steel, and internal batteries (two AAA) power the device, providing a 700 hour operating life. Paddle weight is four pounds. The lever does not move, so there is no response time or moving inertia to consider. This approach offers absolutely silent keying, with no contact maintenance or periodic mechanical adjustments needed. Finger pressure required to initiate dots and dashes is software adjustable. The electronic circuit is microcontroller-based.

RA1AOM

This paddle was made by Valery Pavlov (RA1AOM) of St. Petersburg, Russia. Valery designs and builds keys as a hobby. The arm pivots use simple trunnion bearings. Valery makes his paddle bases using exotic mineral, here green jasper. All assembly parts are highly polished by hand.

RV3AE

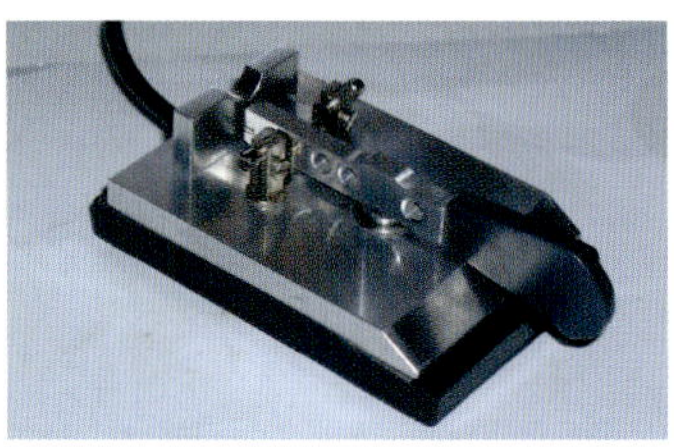

This single-lever/sideswiper was made by Anatoly (RV3AE).

Schurr Einhebel

Some think the Gerhard Schurr paddle is the world's best single-lever device; whether true or not, there is great respect for this Uli Scheunemann design. Einhebel is German for "single paddle" and the design, based on the Profi II, is meant for high speed operation. The Einhebel comes with a tilt-open dust cover and

connection cable. Precision adjustments are made using the large adjustment knobs for contact spacing and spring tension. The Einhebel is well known for holding settings and features positive arm centering using springs. This key uses convex contacts with what Schurr calls a surgical quality brass base. Schurr coats the brass parts with a trade secret polymer that resists wear, staining, and pitting. Fingerpieces are hand finished. The Einhebel can be set up with extremely close contact spacing while remaining very responsive to operators with a light touch.

Gerhard Schurr (DH2SAA) passed away in early October 2011 at the age of 80. He first produced keys in 1984, and continued until he sold his company and retired in 2003.

Schurr-Bergsiek

Gerhard Schurr, who developed the Profi M, built several prototypes that were tested and refined for production, but due to declining health he turned the production over to Stefan Bergsiek, a very talented key maker.

The Profi M (M for magnetic) has been designed as a single-lever Wabbler. In a break from Schurr tradition, springs

The Professional SL Wabbler version of the Profi M.

are no longer used in these keys; arm return is ensured via individually adjusted magnets.

As Bergsiek describes the design, the paddles are mounted using hardened steel cylindrical pins in a brass sleeve bearing, ensuring elimination of play and backlash. This combination makes the paddle mounting completely maintenance free. Another advantage of this paddle mounting method is unlike a ball bearing the lubrication cannot dry out, time making the paddle stiff or requiring new bearings. No adjustment of the bearings or paddle mounting is required. The key is completely constructed in brass and is available with various base plate options, as well as different fingerpiece colors and shapes.

Ten-Tec Paddles

Ten-Tec manufactured several different single-lever paddles. Essentially they were the mechanisms used in Ten-Tec keyers without the electronics. The Model 607 had externally adjustable contact spacing and used a black enclosure. Other similar models included the KR2 and KR2A; the KR2A offered a mechanical override button on top of the enclosure.

KR2-A SINGLE LEVER PADDLE

For keying conventional "TO" or discrete character keyers, as used in the KR20-A. It embodies a unique principle insuring low actuation force with permanent factory set optimum return force and "feel". Contacts are adjustable from the front by spring loaded adjusting screws. "Straight Key" over ride touch switch included. Finished in cream and walnut vinyl. Size: 2" H, 4" W, 6" D. Weight: 1½ lb.

The KR2A from Ten-Tec product literature.

TW Keys (G3HGE) eZKe

This key from Tom Withers (G3HGE) was one of a series that carried the TW name. Withers was originally known for TW Electronics, operating 1958—2000. TW keys were designed to give the operator a high quality paddle at a reasonable price. TW states the eZKe offers a smooth transition from bug to paddle. The eZKe base is steel with a finish simulating brass and coated with acrylic enamel. Key parts are made of polished brass and sprayed with a special formulation of marine lacquer. TW keys are known for maintaining accuracy of adjustment and for their fluid feel in use. The design uses 6 ball bearings and hemispherical 24K gold-plated contacts. Neodymium magnet tension is adjustable using a supplied hex adjustment tool that can be stored under the base. Paddle weight is 2.5 lb. (1.13kg).

Unknown

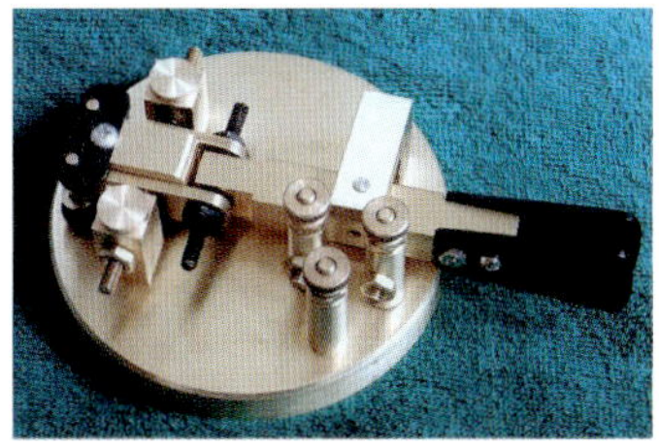

Little information has been found about the history of these two paddles. The first appears to use magnetic return and pivoting lever suspension. The second is mechanically similar to the Vibroplex Vibrokeyer.

This (below) is believed to be a Russian device. It is assumed to be homebrew, constructed using the rotor from a computer hard drive. The key maker is unknown. It is reported the key is a bit stiff to use and exhibits some mechanical noise. Magnetic arm return is used.

Pictured (below) is a well built single-lever key that would appear to be enjoyable to use. It incorporates spring arm return. Boris (S57LO) relates this key was built by a Hungarian craftsman and was sold at various hamfairs in southeast Europe by various Hungarian ham radio operators. The selling price was about $50. Boris says he has not seen one for sale in quite a while. This one was bought by Boris in 1998, but the key's maker is unknown.

UR5CDX CT755 Paddle

The UR5CDX CT755 paddle is available in three versions, with either a black, chrome, or gold base. The polished brass version (CT755B) is shown. The paddle design features magnetic tension and uses solid silver contacts. Tension and contact gap are adjustable; the paddle typically comes with a long connector cable that includes a universal connector.

VE3AWA John Merrick

Here is a very rare John Merrick (VE3AWA) original on a beautiful oiled walnut base. John was a machinist who handcrafted a number of bugs and paddles, perhaps around 100 total. To help overcome his wife's death he set up a small machine shop in his condo bedroom, where he designed and made keys for fifteen years until his health deteriorated. John was especially interested in vertical and right-angle keys; his devices always used brass for the bulk of their construction. John would occasionally take the local bus to a metal salvage shop where he would obtain small parts. VE3AWA passed away in March 2005 at the age of 87.

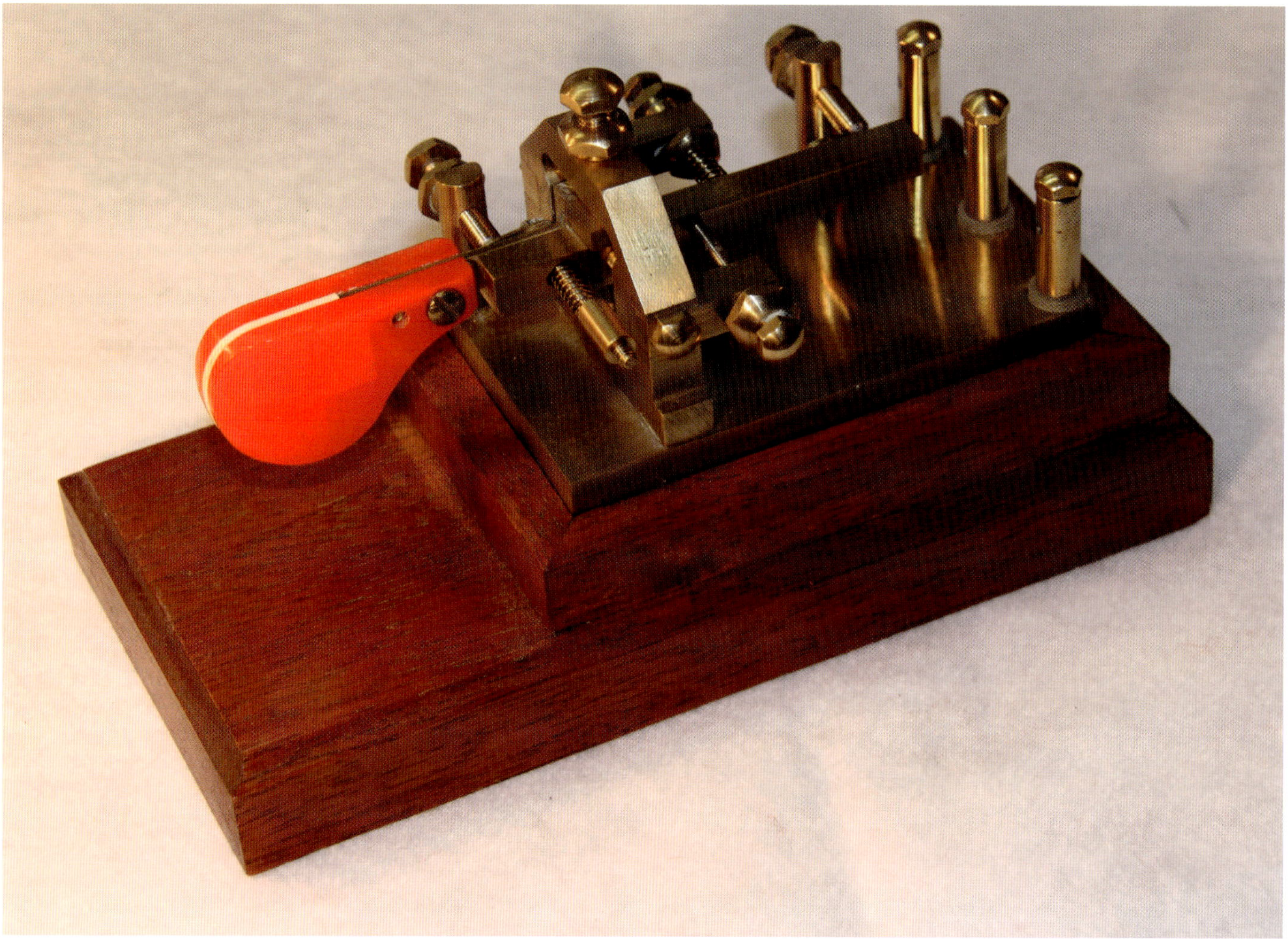

Vibroplex

This (below) is the beige colored base, discontinued in 1981. The Vibroplex Vibro-Keyer (later renamed the Vibrokeyer in 1981) is one of the oldest commercial paddle designs; it was first produced in 1960. The design was based on available parts from the semi-automatic "Original" model. Many feel use of the semi-automatic parts and pieces gave the Vibro-Keyer a familiarity that encouraged a user's transition from bug to electronic keyer. In 1961, a Deluxe Vibro-Keyer with chrome base was offered. Also offered by Harrison Radio in 1961 was a "special gray finish" model to match the T.O. keyer. The Vibroplex standard gray model of the early 1980s is sometimes confused with the much earlier Harrison special T.O. gray base version. In 1981, after Vibroplex was sold and moved to Maine, the Standard model base color was changed to gray so it matched the rest of the key line.

John Casale, in the April 2010 edition of the *AWA Journal*, writes the Vibro-Keyer was designed by John La Hiff, who had worked in various capacities for Vibroplex since the early 1920s. La Hiff was also responsible for the introduction of jeweled bearings in Vibroplex keys. According to Casale, La Hiff deserves much more recognition for his contributions to key design.

Two views of the standard gray base paddle available starting in 1981.

A Vibro-Keyer ad from the January 1980 *QST*.

A DeLuxe model Vibrokeyer of recent Knoxville production. The DeLuxe versions were introduced in 1961. Also available is a standard version with a textured, powder-coated black base, and another version called the Gold, which uses a 24K gold-plated base.

VIZ Right-Angle SL Paddle

This is a K4VIZ "VIZ" key with the first right-angle paddle produced; indeed, it carries S/N 001. This paddle is possibly the only right-angle paddle design in existence. It has design elements based loosely on some of John Merrick's original designs.

The VIZ key is made from ½ in. thick solid brass and has silver contacts. It is about 3½ in. wide × about 4 in. (front to back), including fingerpieces. The unit weighs nearly a pound and a half and has rubber feet to keep it in place during operation.

The VIZ right-angle paddle has six points that can be adjusted or changed for personal preferences. Surface finish is wire brushed brass matte.

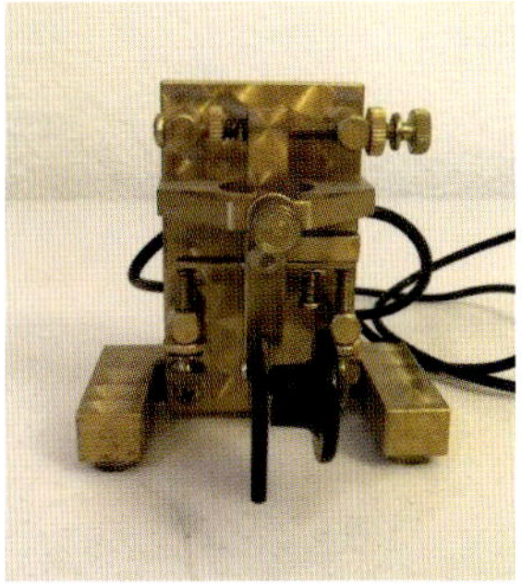

K4VIZ also offered a vertical single-lever paddle, shown here in a machine-swirled finish. Spring adjustments were used. K4VIZ has retired from the key making business.

W1SFR Torsion-Bar Paddle

W1SFR is Steve Roberts of Sudbury, Vermont. Steve builds this version of the torsion bar key based on a design published in the December 1982 *QST*. The *QST* article, by Tom Leary (W0VTP), describes the approach of using a torsion bar as the paddle arm return spring. An interesting dual-lever version of a device using the torsion bar approach was found; it is not known if this dual-lever key was built using Leary's design suggestions, but there are similarities.

The W1SFR Torsion Bar Key changes the 1982 design by using stainless steel contact strips, adding to the quiet operation of this key and helping make the movement very smooth.

Steve describes construction of the key: Upright posts are made from ¼ in. round and square rod. The torsion bar itself is made from ⅛ in. drill rod. Contacts are made underneath the brass base using nylon inserts in the holes leading to the contact posts to isolate the screws from the base, as well as nylon washers on the bottom of the posts to maintain their isolation. Thin strips of plastic material were used underneath, with brass strips on top to make the contact between the posts in the rear and the contact posts at the paddle position. The brass base is 3 × 4 in.; the teak wooden base measures 4 × 6 in. and is finished with Danish oil.

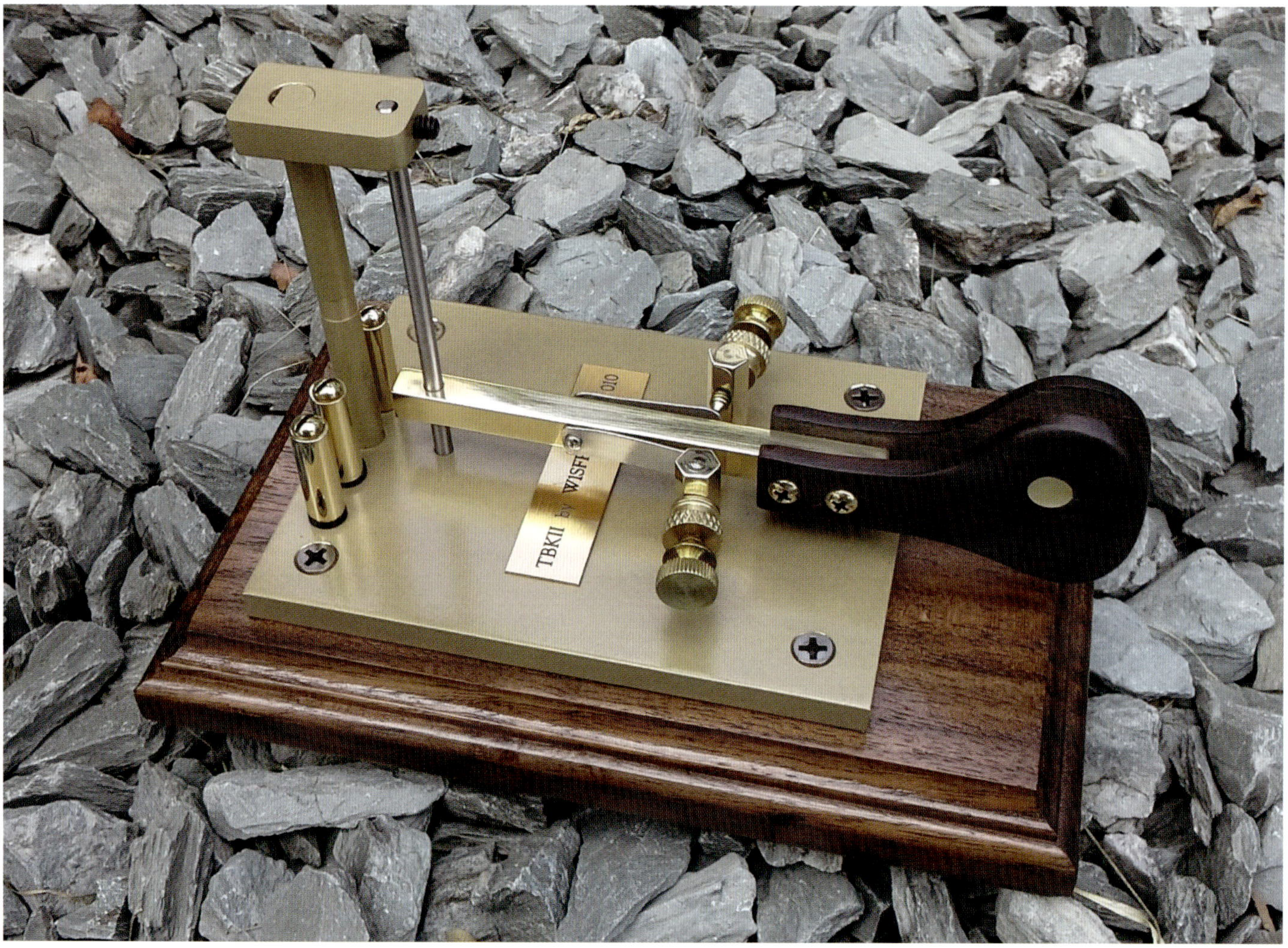

W1IXI

A paddle made by Wilfred Sheehan (W1IXI). Sheehan made several of these for members of some Massachusetts radio groups.

W4PAL

W. R. Smith (W4PAL) built this paddle in 1946, while a student at the University of Tennessee. Smith's incentive for building the paddle was to help fulfill a course requirement, and to have something he could use with an electronic keyer. At the time, electronic keyers for making automatic dots and dashes used for sending Morse code were becoming popular.

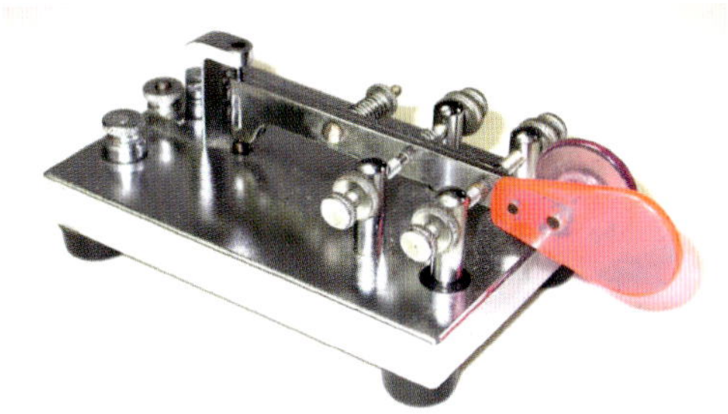

From his website, W. R. Smith describes the construction:

> The paddle is composed of two levers hinged at a common arbor. However, it is unique in the manner in which the two of them are maintained centered without making contact to either the dot or dash post. As can be seen, there is a screw through the nearest lever that passes through a larger clearance hole in the far lever and ends up with a spring and a nut. This holds the two levers together. At the far side of these levers is a spring applying a force to rotate them clockwise. However, in the nearest lever, there is a hole and through this hole is passed the end of a screw that centers the two levers in the neutral position between the dot and dash contacts without touching either. This is the secret of the paddle's design. As the round knob is pressed to the left, the far lever remains stopped against the end of this screw but the right lever moves clockwise and makes the dash contact. However, if the paddle is pressed to the right, both levers rotate counterclockwise at their hinge arbor and the dot contact is made. As will be seen later, this design trick allowed me to design and build vertical speed keys shorter than any ever produced before.

W9TO Paddle

Many have heard of the T.O. keyer designed by Jim Ricks, but few are aware that Ricks designed and built about a hundred of these paddles.

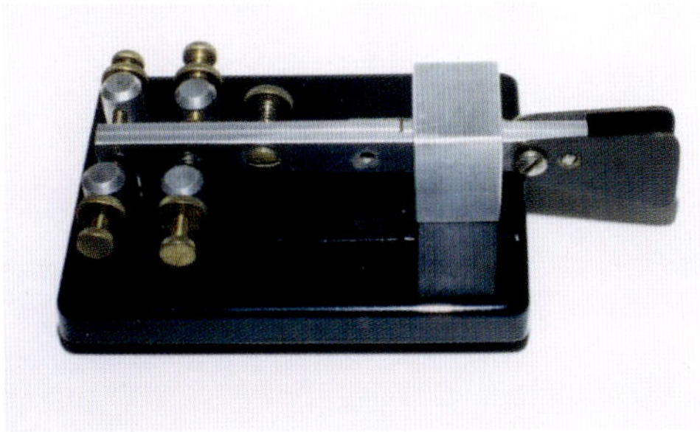

W9WBL

The Stan Heils (W9WBL) single-lever paddle is a vertical device that could also be set on its side and operated as a standard hand key. Production period or quantities for the single-lever are not known.

WA9TGT

WA9TGT is Donnie Garrett, who handcrafted this paddle. Design elements show similarities to the Vibroplex bug arm/pivot approach.

WB9LPU

This is the first of several WB9LPU small paddles to use the ball-pivot design and the only non-iambic one. It uses what Rich calls a transverse "rocker" mechanism. Rich states:

> The paddle lever forms a t-type arrangement with a four-ball pivot unit at right angles to it, so that moving the lever results in a rocking motion of the pivot unit. A single tension spring at the center of the pivot unit provides the restoring force. This design solves a difficult problem in single-lever paddle design—it is not easy to get a definite-feeling center position that is bounce-free and positive. Two fingerpieces are provided to give the unit a better feel. This works adequately but the movement lacks vertical stability.

Shown below are several views of a single-lever Parkwood paddle. Rich states: "Tension is provided by a magnet on the underside of the paddle that was attracted by one mounted to the base. The paddle's ball bearings are at the front of the key and the contacts are at the rear. Connection is made through a phone jack at the side of the base. The legs swing out to provide stability. Although rather light, this paddle was a good performer."

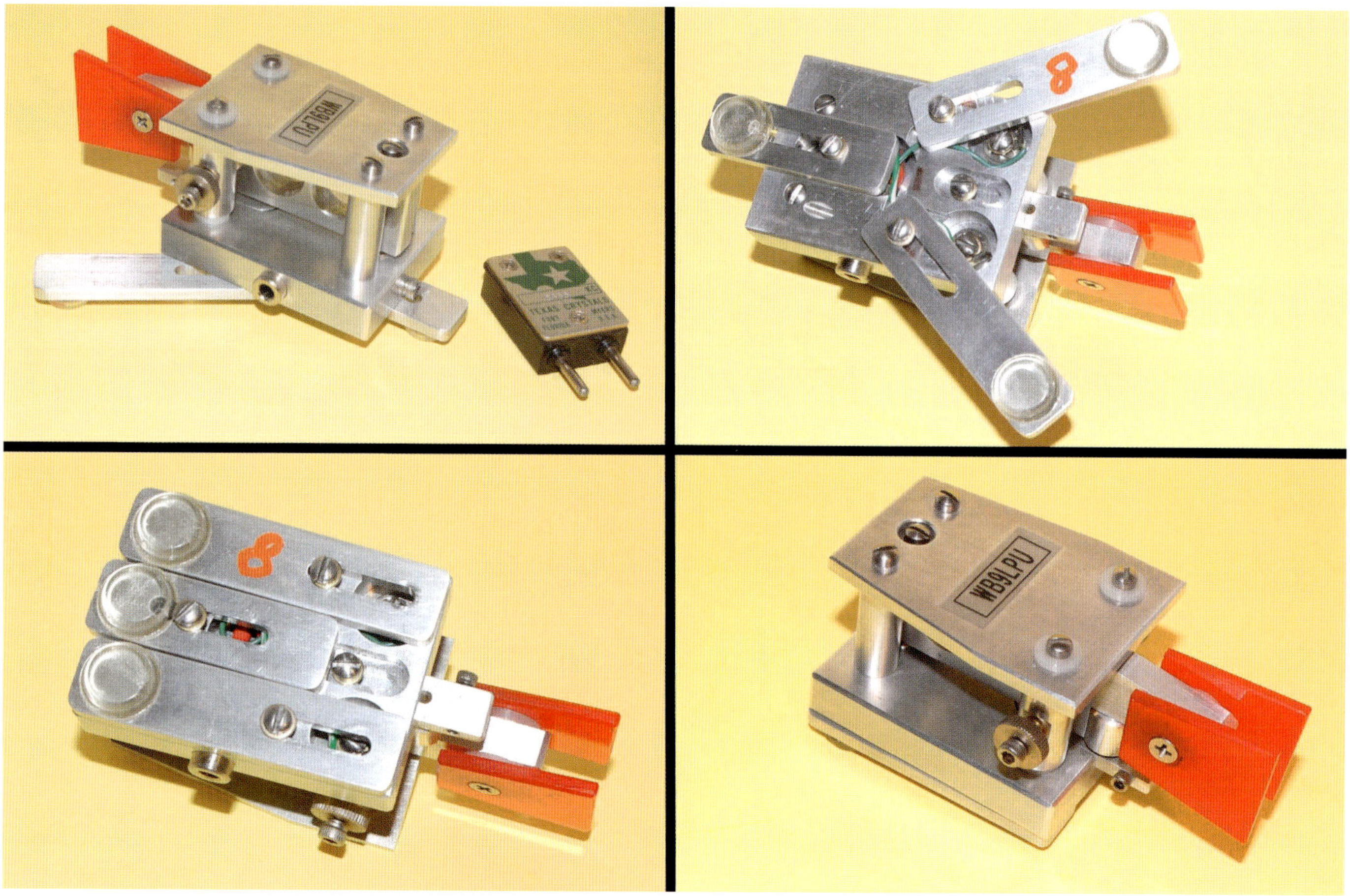

WK4DS Prototype

This is David's (WK4DS) single-lever prototype, one-of-a-kind because it did not prove cost effective to make. David mentions there were just too many small parts (43) that needed to be made and this design took too much time to fabricate and assemble. David made this prototype paddle in 2005; the design used ball bearings in a single lightweight aluminum arm. This prototype does show an interesting approach to tensioning the lever, where the slider bar is moved back and forth along the torsion spring wire to change lever feel.

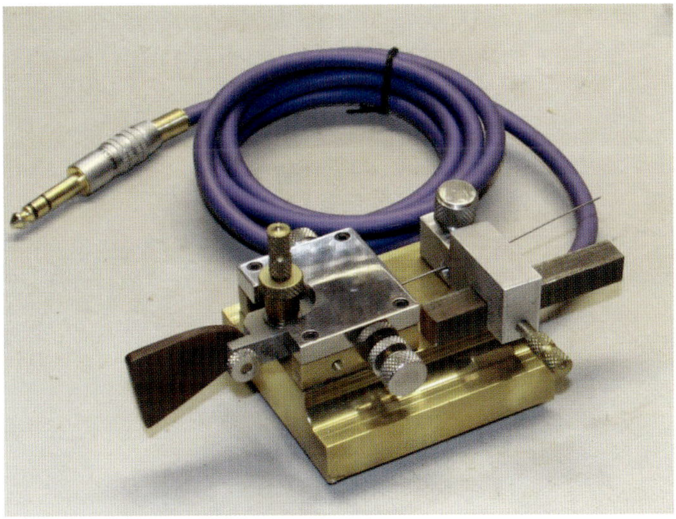

Yugoslavian Paddles

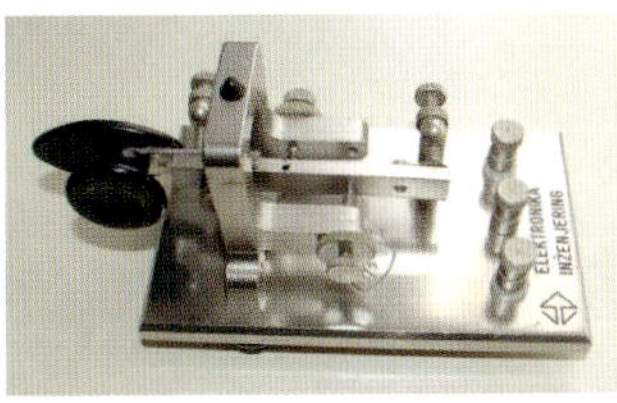

The Taster TM-1, a Yugoslavian electronic keyer paddle.

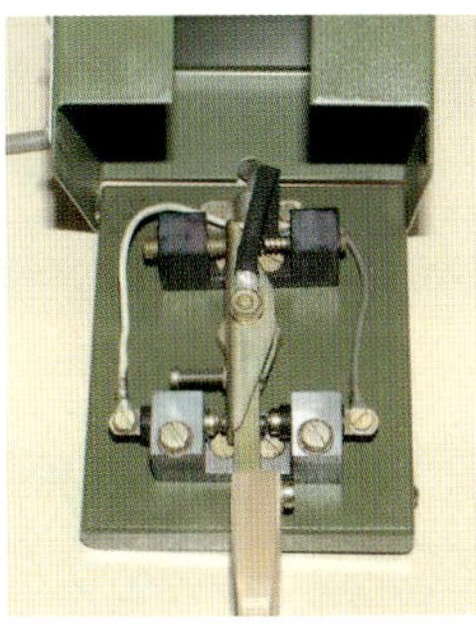

A Yugoslavian technical engineering institute paddle.

5 The Dual-Lever Paddle

Although the first dual-lever paddle goes all the way back to May 1940, it was not until much later that hams were better able to fully utilize dual-lever paddles by pairing them with ultimatic, and then iambic keyers. See the wide variety of designs as some of the most striking dual-lever paddles are presented in this chapter.

With the exception of the 1940 double-lever paddle (below) and some barely adequate double-lever devices internal to homebrew ultimatic keyers, double-lever paddles essentially did not exist before 1961. Grammer's 1940 *QST* article described this double-lever device as solving two defects exhibited by earlier single-lever paddles: lack of spring tension adjustment and lack of positive centering of the key's arm in the neutral position. Grammer solved the tension problem by adding secondary springs to the paddle arms. The arm centering issue was solved using the two levers, so each arm returned to neutral independently of the other. Initially, operator resistance to this design was based on familiarity with the bug style of operating, where the device had only one arm. Grammer continues in his article with actual paddle construction details. For those who were paying attention to the details in the *QST* article, there were some prophetic words. The article accurately predicted that using paddle arms to actuate switch contacts as this paddle did may not be necessary, as mounting contacts directly on the paddle levers should work. Also, Grammer suggested the paddle he envisioned should have a wide range of adjustments to accommodate the varied desires of many different operators. He also lamented that nothing incorporating his ideas was yet commercially available.

Most people credit iambic keyers as driving the need for a dual-lever paddle, but in actuality, it was the ultimatic keyer in 1955 that created the need for a dual-lever device. The history of the ultimatic mode starts with John Kaye (W6SRY), when his first ultimatic keyer design was published in *QST* in 1953.

A sign of many more paddles to come, the first double-lever keyer paddle was briefly described in a May 1940 *QST* article.

Although he used a single-lever paddle in his original design, Kaye's next keyer version, published in a 1955 *QST* article, used a dual-lever paddle. It was not until 1961 that a steady progression of commercial dual-lever paddle designs began. In that year, a July *QST* article by Nicholas Lefor (W2BIQ) described his new dual-lever keying mechanism that would soon be marketed as the Nikey. Lefor realized a paddle design with separate dot and dash levers was needed to take full advantage of the ultimatic keyer he had been experimenting with. Of course, much of the developing dual-lever paddle technology eventually found its way into modern single-lever designs, and many of these designs can be seen in chapter 4. But the dual-levers were new and had a progressive air about them; they were meant to be used with the latest keyer technology. In the 1960s, the perception was single-lever paddles belonged to tube keyers, and that tube keyers were old technology. Iambic (or "squeeze") keying was promising even faster sending speeds, and many felt dual-lever paddles just looked more advanced.

In the late 1990s and early 2000s more attention would be focused on improving single-lever designs, but for about thirty years or so, the progression of increasingly sophisticated mechanisms that appeared belonged mostly to dual-levers. Use of magnets replaced springs for paddle arm return and centering, arm weight was reduced, and even optical contacts were tried with some success. Use of exotic materials became a factor in design: stainless steel, carbon fiber fingerpieces, and short aluminum arms became commonplace. Soon, intricate craftsmanship became a major feature (see the Begali Signature). Perfection in chrome plating is seen in many of the GHD devices. More small but groundbreaking independent designers such as N3ZN and N0SA developed dedicated followers.

In addition to factors such as weight, material, arm inertia, contact type, etc., there remains a bit of black magic about paddle design that is difficult to describe. While some of the attraction of a great paddle is subjective, there are things like fingerpiece shape and color, style and finish of the paddle base, and use of chrome that combine to contribute to the overall appeal of the key. Even something as seemingly insignificant as how the paddle sounds (does it click or is it silent) can be a contributor to making a certain paddle a "favorite." When one considers the paddle is the operator's direct connection to the entirety of his ham station, it is understandable that so many hams pay special attention to the paddle's functionality and aesthetics. In the interface sense, the paddle is somewhat akin to the shifter in an exotic race car.

The Commonplace Usage of the Term "Iambic"

Over time, the use of the phrase "iambic paddle" has become generic, and is frequently used to describe double- (or dual) lever paddles. To be accurate, there are no iambic paddles, but there are double-lever paddles that can actuate an iambic keyer. Iambic keyers are usually electronic devices that allow alternating dots and dashes when both fingerpieces of a dual-lever paddle are squeezed together. Therefore, keyers can be described as iambic, but not paddles. Dual-lever paddles can be used with non-iambic keyers and single-lever paddles can be used with iambic keyers, although you will lose functionality. Also, paddles most definitely are not "iambic keyers." The misuse of terms can in part be traced to some paddle manufacturers who label their keys as iambic in product ads. This Vibroplex dual-lever paddle (right) represents a typical paddle that is often improperly called an iambic keyer.

A Vibroplex dual-lever paddle.

The remainder of this chapter presents a sampling of creativity and artistry as they combine to give us some wonderful dual-lever paddles.

AB5RT

These paddles (below) were made by Al Bulin (AB5RT) of Bella Vista, Arkansas. Al enjoys creating one-of-a-kind paddles to display in his house (his wife also enjoys looking at them). Paddles use magnetic attraction or repulsion instead of springs, and use of a variety of materials, including brass, aluminum, and steel. One of the most striking features of these designs is the machined swirl base finish. Some might notice the carefully shaped and polished fingerpieces, which typically are made of rare South American hardwood selected to show off the grain. For some of Al's models the wood fingerpieces are then laminated to white Plexiglas and given a hand-rubbed finish. The paddles also utilize sealed ball bearings and exhibit some of the talents AB5RT has practiced in the gunsmithing trade.

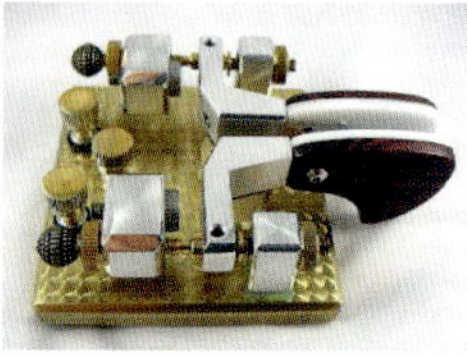

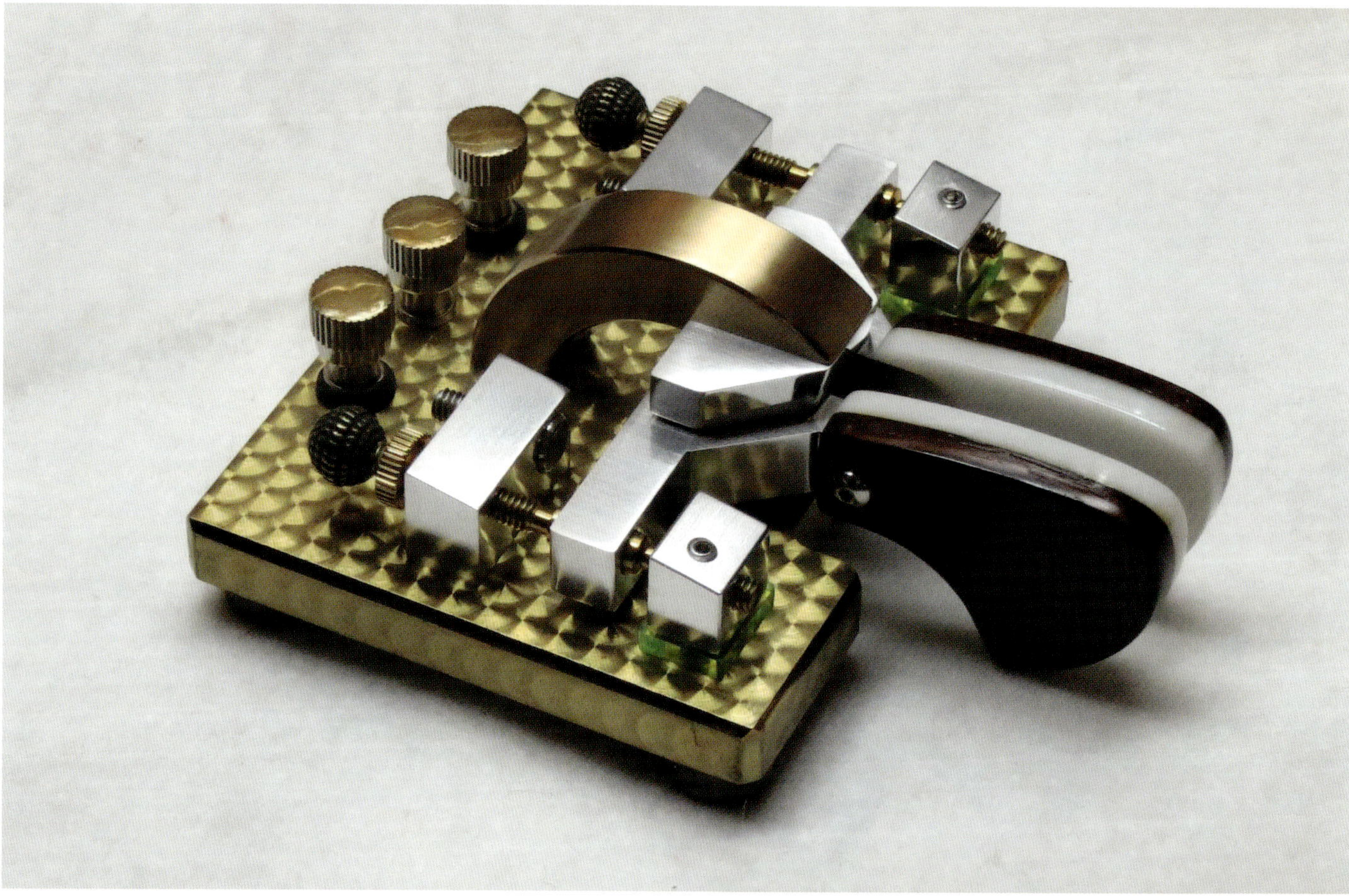

AC7AZ

AC7AZ is Mark, who reports in correspondence that he made only about eight of these paddles and fourteen miniatures. One of his paddles used oil-lite bronze bushings instead of needle bearings, and Mark made one out of stainless steel. He also made several with brass bases.

American Morse Equipment

American Morse Equipment is run by Doug Hauff (W6AME) and San Luis Machine Company. After working in machining and engineering starting in 1972, Doug opened San Luis Machine in 1986. Since 1996, they have been designing and manufacturing products for radio amateurs at their facility in San Luis Obispo, California. Modern CNC equipment is used to producc products of the highest quality and precision, allowing AME to offer their lifetime guarantee: "if our product breaks, or you break it, return it and we will repair or replace as necessary, for the life of the product."

The American Morse KK2 paddle (right) originally comes from AME as a kit, and features parts of brass, steel, and aluminum. It features fully adjustable spring force and contact spacing. Fingerpieces are nylon 6/6, and are rigid but give a soft feel. The base weighs 1.5 lb. and uses four rubber feet to ensure there is no undesired movement. The paddle includes an Allen wrench for adjustments.

The SVP (Single Vertical Paddle) design was inspired by the classic W9WBL V-series paddles. The version shown uses exotic hardwoods, brass, aluminum, and steel, and features nickel plated contacts and stainless steel hardware. Adjustment screws are fine-pitched. Brass parts are clear coated for a maintenance free finish. Each lever is adjustable for spacing and closing force. Paddle weight is about 3 lb.

The SFP is the flat version of the SVP vertical paddle. It uses the same high quality action and lever design as the SFP with the same build materials and operating features.

ATE Paddle

The ATE appears to be a commercially made paddle, but very little information is available to document it.

Begali

Officina Meccanica Begali was founded in 1954, and has been manufacturing electromechanical precision components since 1960. Begali's decision to produce Morse keys is relatively recent, a result of Piero Begali's desire to create precision devices for his own use. Piero obtained his ham radio license as I2RTF in 1964. Piero notes that after WWI his father was a designer of machine guns, so mechanical abilities appear to run in the family.

Shown (below) is the Sculpture model; all fixed parts are completely made from AISI-304 stainless steel. Begali describes the Sculpture:

> The arms of this paddle, with a 1:1 leverage ratio, are extremely short and are made from a lightweight alloy. The fingerpieces are carved out of a very light and exceptionally stiff and robust carbon fiber material that provides excellent tactile feedback. Tensioning is provided via a pair of neodymium magnets for each arm; one is embedded in the end of a screw. As the screw is adjusted, this magnet is moved in or out to change the amount of repulsion of the other half of the pair in the paddle arm.

The Signature also uses convex solid gold contacts and four low profile feet give it added stability. The Signature Edition combines design experience from the earlier Begali magnetic paddles with improvements suggested by customers. The Signature incorporates a heavy base with gold plating or palladium plating. Optionally, a titanium finish with a black base and a gold-colored bearing block is available. Precision bearings are specially selected and matched; they are concealed in the base and in the central bearing block for a clean visual design. The friction springs for the gap adjustments are hidden inside the contact posts.

The fingerpieces are made of an anodized aluminum alloy; typically Begali supplies two sets: one has longer geometry and one slightly shorter. Begali reports some customers feel the shorter fingerpieces translate into a more responsive, "connected" feel with the arms.

Most of the Begali key products use a ⅛ in. stereo jack in the base for the connection to a keyer. This is seen on the Signature, and is considered a nice addition by Begali paddle users.

The Graciella vertical paddle's (right) footprint is only 3 × 3 in., and the paddle weighs about 3.5 lb. Two different base configurations are available (the base shape can be seen in the following photo).

Begali describes the Graciella as using the highest quality bearings, gold or palladium plated components, aircraft alloy for moving elements to reduce their masses and maximize responsiveness, micro-threaded adjustment screws for the contact gap and the magnetic tension, and a stereo jack for the connection cable. The Graciella incorporates massive 14k gold contacts for increased reliability. The vertical architecture allows reduction in the dimensions of the moving elements

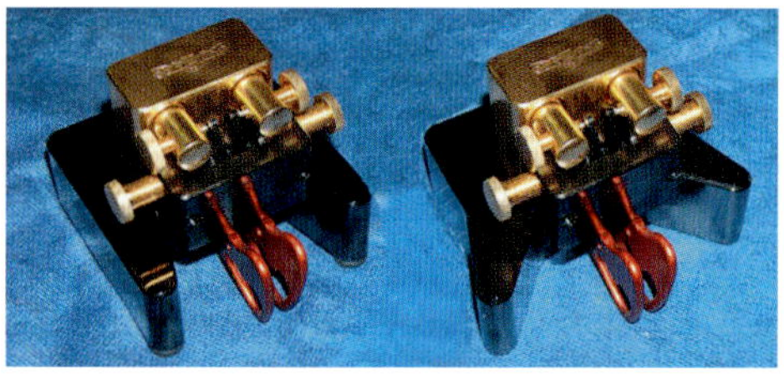

and their masses while retaining the ideal leverage ratio for optimum tactile feedback. The mechanism is mounted on a vertical "wall" that slides inside a channel in the base for height adjustment. The spacing of the fingerpieces can be adjusted with a conical backstop for the levers.

The Simplex Basic is a dual-lever with a heavy (1.4 kg, or more than 3 lb.) cast base and gold-plated components. The design uses long springs for the return force. As with other Begali keys, the Simplex Basic is manufactured using NC machinery and incorporates micro-threaded screws for all adjustments. The arms are held by 4 ball bearings embedded in the base. Arms are made of a lightweight alloy that provides very low moving mass, allowing responsiveness at high speeds even when set for a very light touch. The contacts are 925/1000 silver.

The Pearl key (below, red fingerpieces) features rounded shapes and a high performance mechanism. Precision adjustments and perfect weight distribution in the moving parts help ensure reliable consistency with use. Base plating options include gold, palladium (bottom of page), or a bright silver nickel. The adjustment screws and contact posts are gold-plated. The Pearl uses 925/1000 silver contacts, and the fingerpieces are red anodized aluminum.

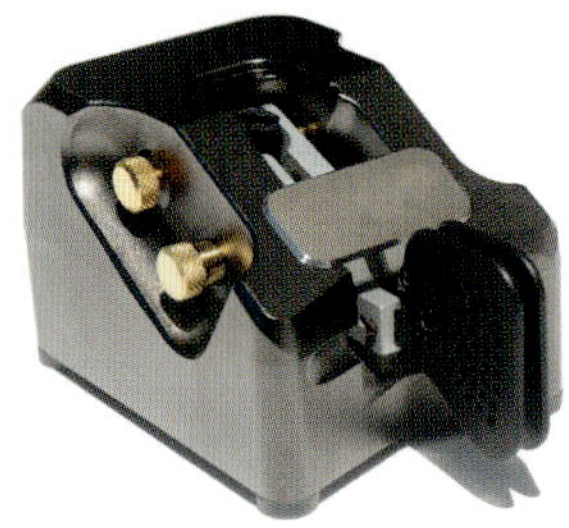

Begali's Magnum paddle is machined from a solid metal block; finished paddle weight is about 4 lb. The Magnum's design allows for contact and magnetic tensioning adjustments to be part of the base itself; no separate contact or magnet adjustment posts are used. Aluminum fingerpieces are closely spaced, which Begali claims aids operators transitioning from single-lever keys or mechanical bugs; the spacing is adjustable from about ¼ in. to ½ in. Begali feels the tactile feedback from the perforated aluminum fingerpieces and the narrow spacing are preferred by high speed CW operators.

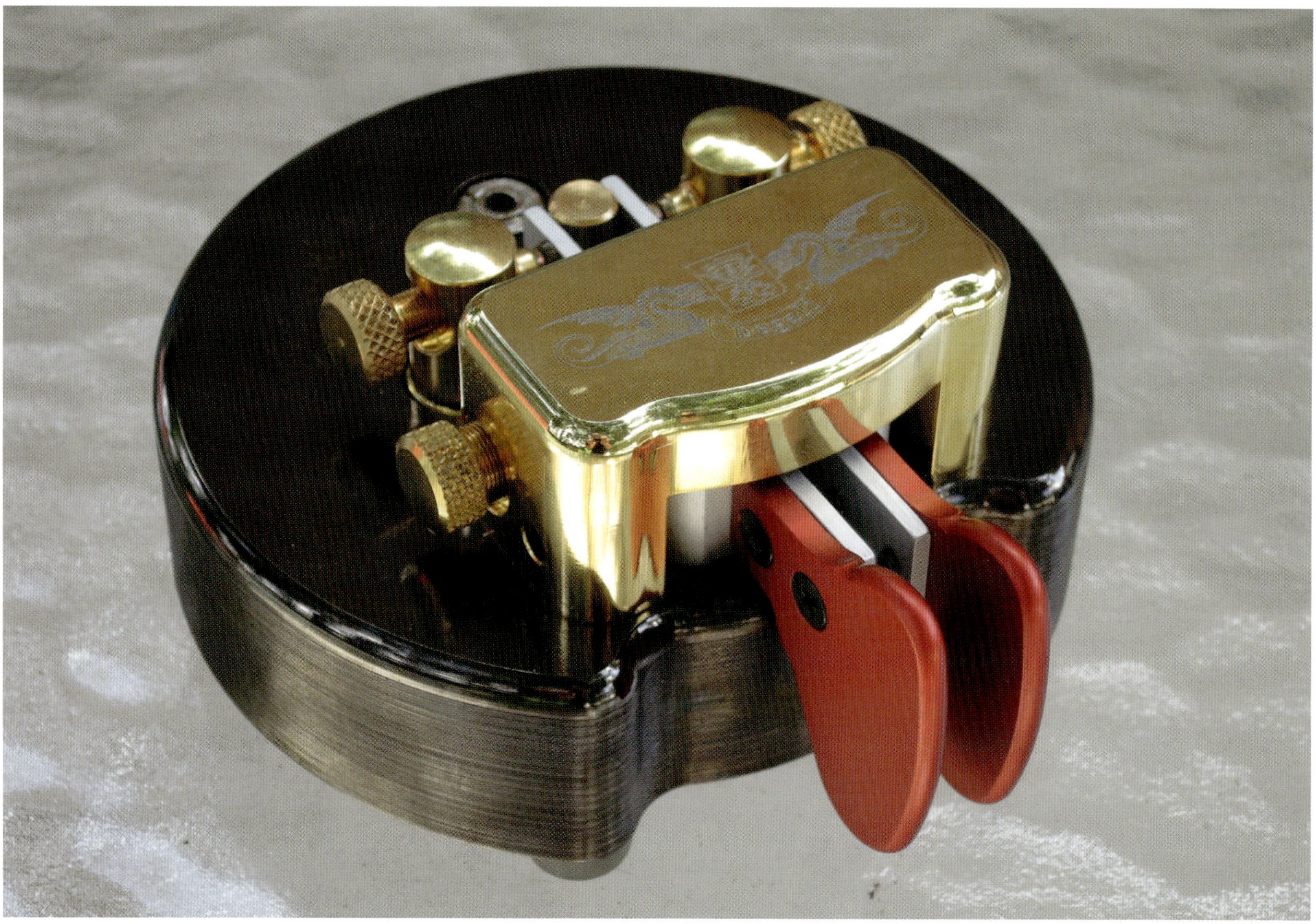

The Magnum is very resistant to mechanical abuse and vibration, and it resists sliding from more heavy-handed operators. Other design attributes include lightweight paddle arms, use of precision bearings, 14k gold contacts, and fine-threaded contact and magnetic tensioning adjustments.

Bencher Paddles

The classic and very popular Bencher BY-1 paddle is based on the earlier Teletek paddle design that Bencher negotiated to buy from Teletek. Bob Locher (W9KNI) of Idiom Press fame was a co-founder of Bencher. Over 100,000 of the BY-1 model paddles have been sold beginning in 1977. Bencher periodically made improvements to the original design, resulting in a more reliable and responsive paddle while allowing for lower production costs. (Idiom Press is now owned by Bob's son Rob [W7GH]. For more information see "The Origination of the Bencher Paddle" by Bob Locher, *Morsum Magnificat* #25, Autumn 1992.)

The N2DAN patent rights were sold to Bencher, and they now produce their version of the famous N2DAN Mercury paddle. One notable difference is the Bencher version uses gold-plated silver contacts with a slightly convex surface. Other parts of the Bencher version are almost identical to the original N2DAN, including the long paddle arms. Note that short arm length is a very recent design goal, and not considered important at the time N2DAN designed his key. The Bencher also retains the coarse-threaded adjustment screws and locknuts.

Bencher's Hex paddle uses an innovative design with attracting magnets for arm tensioning and separate individual dot and dash contact spacing adjustments. The Bencher design also uses a separate ground braid for each arm, helping prevent keying glitches. This is a heavy paddle (over 3 lb.) meant to accommodate the heavy-fisted user without moving around the operating desk. The Hex paddle also uses solid silver contact points with gold plating and a powder-coated steel base with chrome plated top parts. There is an adjustment tool mounted in a holder underneath the base.

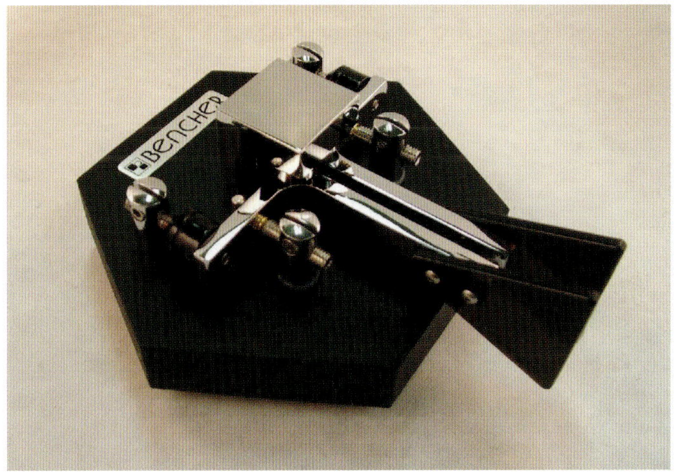

The Bencher Hex Paddle.

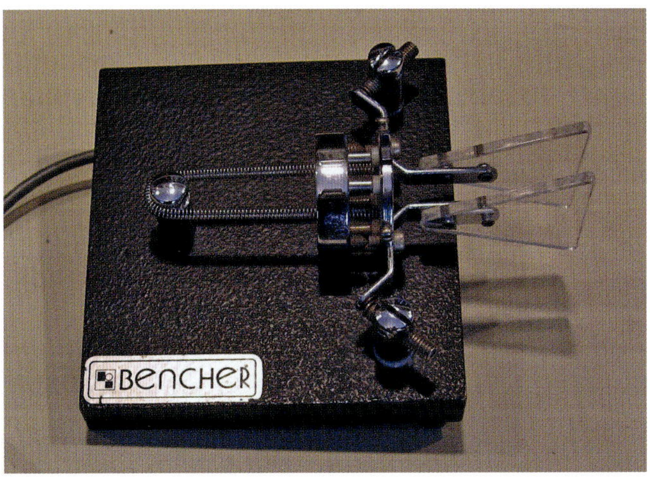

The Bencher Mercury version of the famous N2DAN paddle.

Brown Brothers

The Brown Brothers were Ed (W0BMM) and Bill Brown, who together formed the Brown Brothers Machine Company. Bill Brown was a school teacher in East St. Louis, Illinois; he never had a ham license. Ed Brown was an engineer, and in his early career worked in the aerospace industry. Apparently, the brothers shared the hobby of building race cars in the 1920s and 1930s. The Brown Brothers machine shop was in the basement of Bill's house, where all the part fabrication, base casting, painting, and key assembly was done. Keys were made by Bill between the years 1964 and 1979. Although most Brown Brothers articles mention they made ten different models of keys, prototypes for a magnetic dual lever model, a single-lever paddle, and what appears to be a prototype electronic keyer have all been discovered.

Here (p 163, left) are two UTL models: the basic UTL uses a pivot bearing and the UTL-A uses leaf springs. The UTL mechanisms were sold to users who wanted to incorporate the paddle into keyers or mount them on a base. The basic UTL is shown unmounted; the UTL-A is shown mounted on a chrome base.

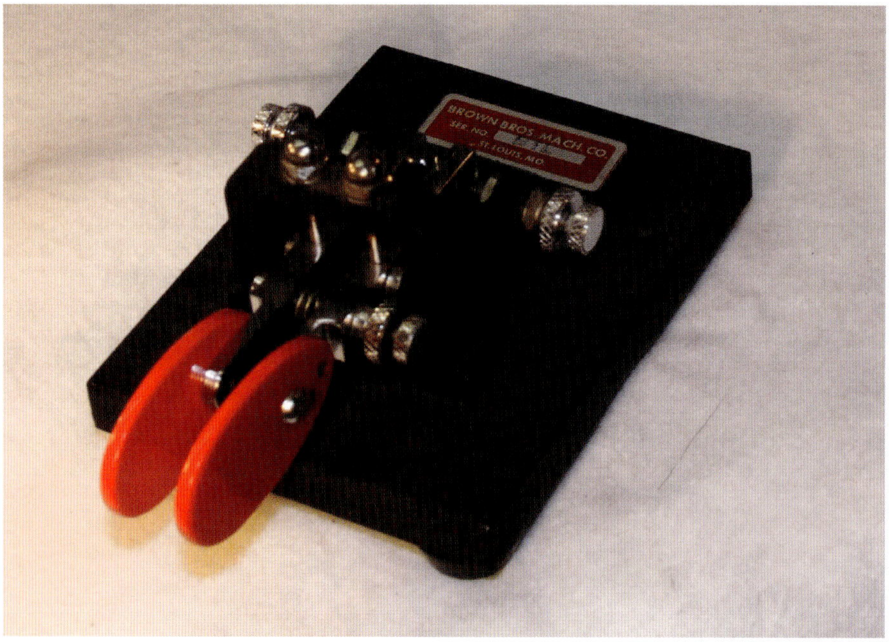

Brown Brothers models BTL and BTL-A show the different types of dual-lever designs: the BTL (above) uses a pivot design, while the BTL-A (opposite) uses leaf springs.

The rare magnetic dual-lever was a Brown Brothers experiment from around 1973–1974 they felt did not work out. It is believed only about five or six of the magnetic paddles were made.

CAL-AV LABS Spirit Morse Key

The Spirit Morse key was made by CAL-AV LABS, Inc. (formerly California Avionics Laboratories) of Tucson, Arizona. The device was conceived by company president Ken Hirschberg (K6HPX) and dates to 1993. Ken reports the key was designated Model A1, and the Spirit name was trademarked for Morse keys. A total of sixteen production keys were made (serial number A1-X4, and then A1-001 through A1-015) and sold at $485 for the polished brass version. A chrome over nickel and gold over copper version was sold at a higher price. One of the Spirit chrome keys was considered by the Museum of Modern Art for their permanent collection.

Ken's motivation in designing the Spirit was to produce a paddle with no moving parts. The key was based on a polymer pressure sensor that changed resistance with pressure. The design incorporated an internal printed wiring board with a CMOS IC used as the basis for level detection of each paddle side's pressure sensor. Keying pressure sensitivity was adjustable for dot and dash sides independently using separate 20-turn pots at the real panel. The user could select either bug or dual-lever modes of operation. The key used an internal 4-cell rechargeable NiCad battery for power. A neoprene pad covered the bottom; finished weight of the Spirit paddle was 4.8 pounds.

After the passing of N2DAN, CAL-AV LABS submitted a bid for his line of Mercury keys, but lost out to Bencher. CAL-AV LABS also produced limited numbers (around fifteen) of a hand key called the Eureka; it was based on a magnetic release design and sold for $650.

Chevron Morse Keys

A production Model Chevron (below) in polished brass. Kevin Gunstone (M0AGA) designed and built the Chevron key prototypes while recovering from illness. Kevin gave the designs to his good friend and engineering wizard Alan (G4HCD), who would eventually build the production keys. The Chevron name comes from the posts used on the prototypes; they are shaped on the base in a "vee" formation and the corners of the block also have a Chevron shape to them. For a brief time, Kevin compiled and distributed a newsletter covering many aspects of the Chevron Morse key. Unfortunately, Chevron key production appears to have stopped.

The Chevron MK2 prototype was built in June 2003, and was used by Steve (G0DMN). The tension magnets are fitted inside a larger bearing block.

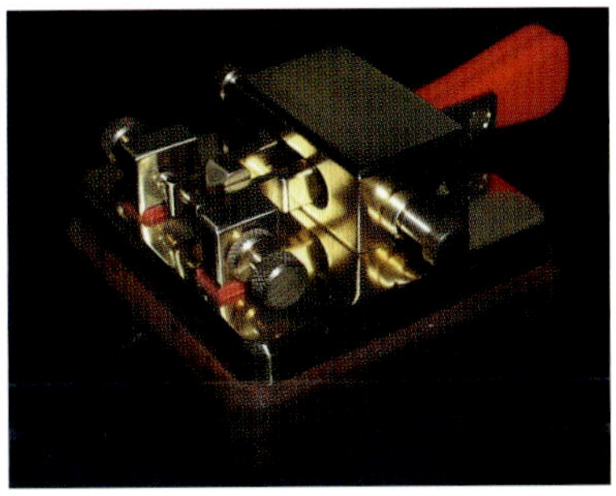

The Chevron MK3 Prototype was built in September 2003. This prototype employs magnetic tensioning inside the bearing block.

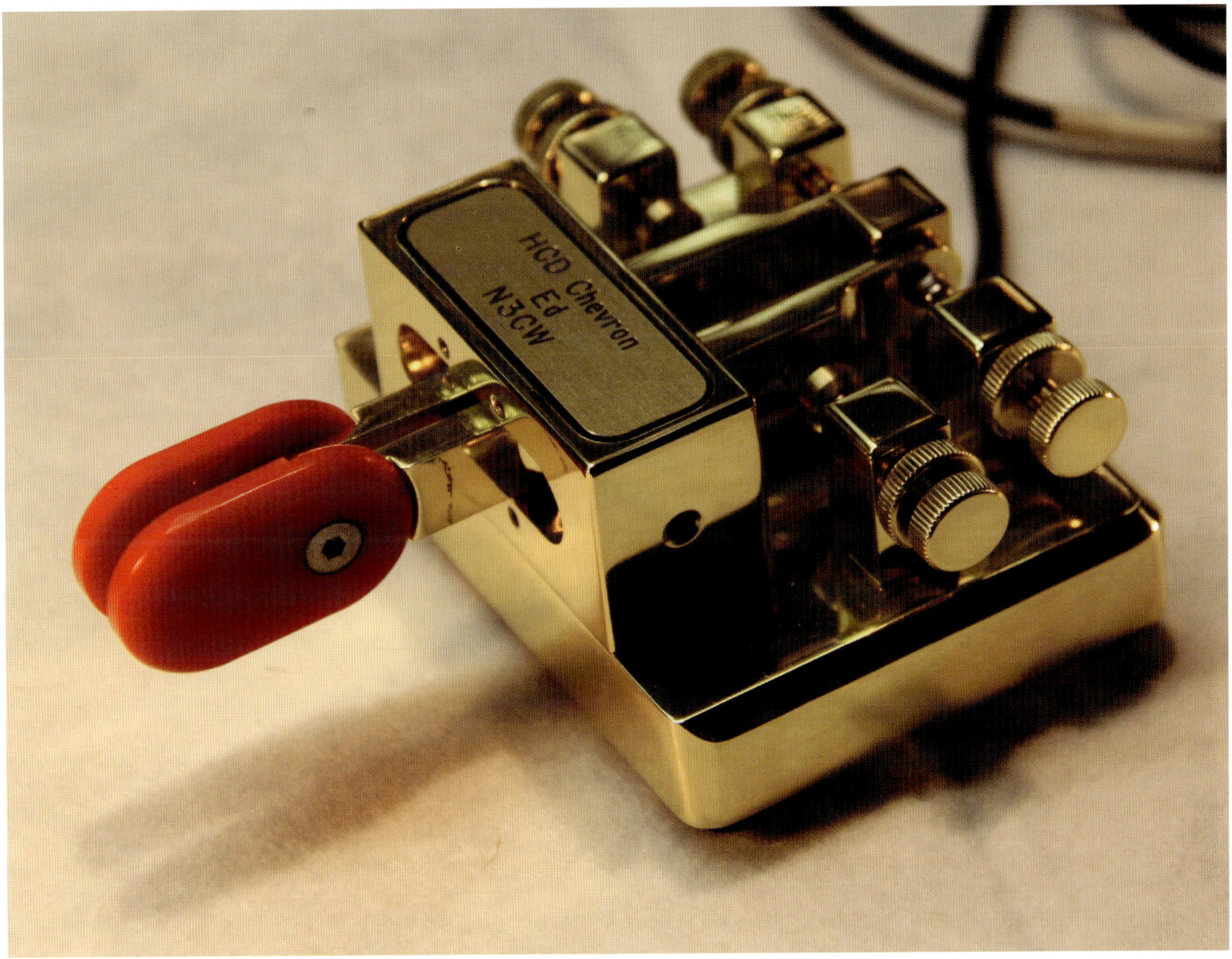

Classic Keyer CK-2

The Model CK-2 paddle was produced for a short time in the mid-1990s by Classic Keyer of Lansing, Michigan. The picture below from John (N6HI) shows a new CK-2 that was part of his collection.

Cleng Electronics TWB-1

Cleng Electronics of Dallas, Texas, produced this Model TWB-1. Cleng also made a keyer called the "electronic bugg."

CQ ham radio (Japan) Spark Paddle

The Spark paddle is another in a small line of keys made for the Japanese *CQ ham radio* magazine by GHD. The typical GHD chrome quality is evident.

Cricket Key

Two different versions of the Cricket key are shown: one is in the ad for the portable model and the other is a photo of the desk model. The Cricket keys were produced by F. F. Mace and Sons of Dallas, Texas, and represent one of the oldest "tapper" key designs (circa 1913).

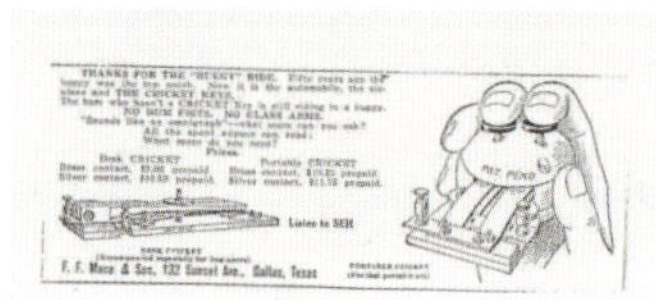

Ditek Industries Paddle

The Ditek paddle appeared in the early 1990s; it resembles a Brown Brothers BTL-A, but has a larger and heavier powder-coated base. The Ditek was known for having extremely quiet operation, partly due to the design of the arm adjusting screws, which had a nylon tip that eliminated the metal-on-metal sound when a paddle arm was released. Also, the silver-plated contacts are held by a nylon support piece. Adjustments are made via thumbscrews with locking nuts. Ditek had announced plans to build an iambic keyer that would mount on top of this paddle, but no information has been found to indicate this keyer was actually built.

DJ8RQ Paddles

DJ8RQ is Tony Bonnert of Quedersbach, Germany. Tony has fabricated a number of high-quality paddles. Large ball bearings can be seen in the bearing block (below). Other paddle design features include adjustable arm spacing, beveled edges, large contact locking thumbwheels, and custom wooden fingerpieces.

Electron Processing Green Lake Paddle

The base and top pieces of the Green Lake paddle are polished brass; the fingerpieces are either wood or aluminum. One (right) is an early model with wooden fingerpieces. The other (far right) from John (N6HI) shows the dominating size of the almost-round fingerpieces. The contact spacing was adjustable, but tension was not. Contacts were pointed screws that contacted the brass arms. This paddle is from early 1990.

Envirotronics

Envirotronics Inc. was in St. Paul, Minnesota, and produced two paddle models: the 501, which had a smaller base, and the 502, which was a bit larger and heavier. There are some historical references to models 501F and 501G, but the suffix meanings are not clear. The Model 501 dual-lever paddle includes a slot for an Allen wrench in the base, partially seen to the left rear of the base.

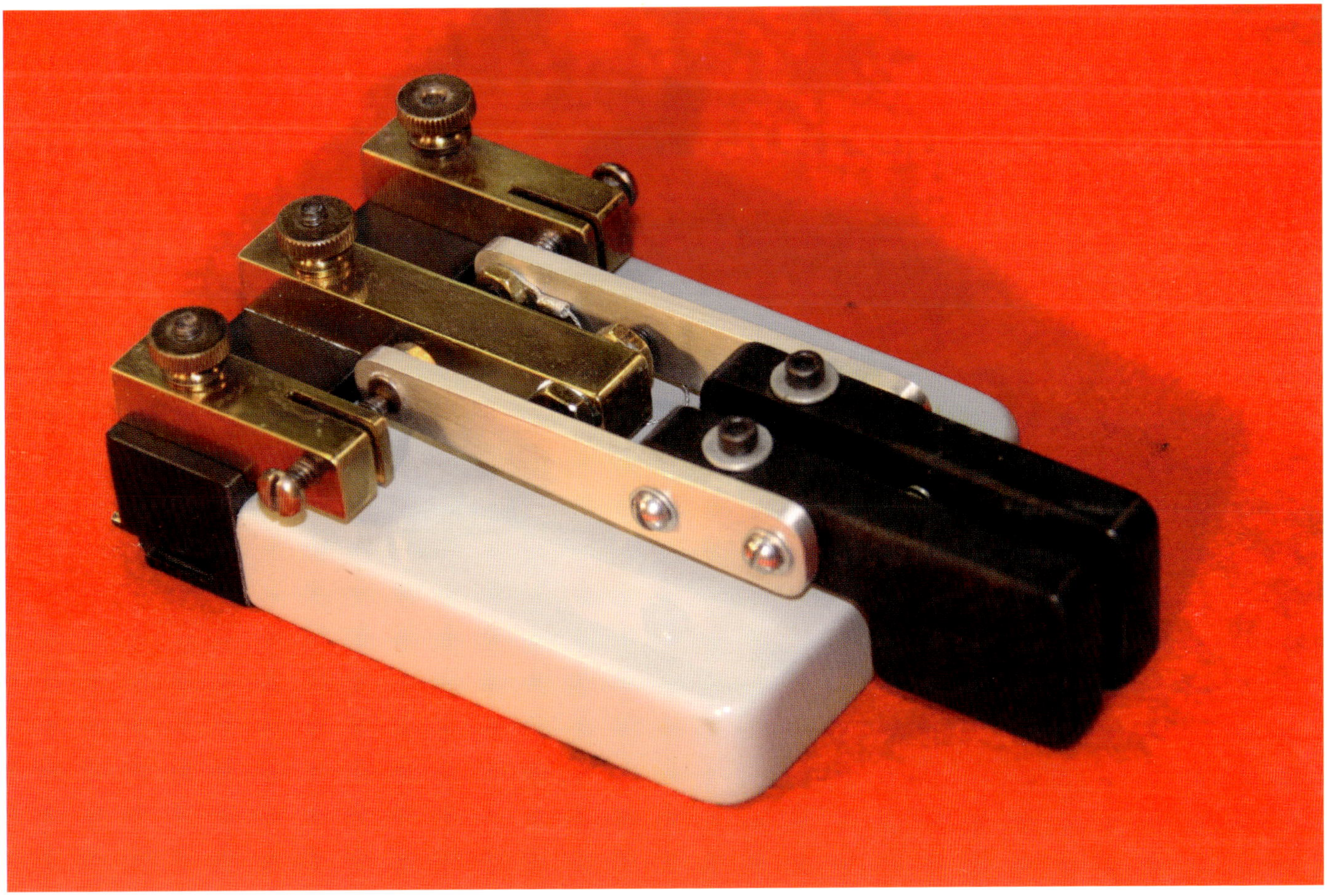

EW4IDP Zero

The Zero is a very attractive paddle with high-quality chrome plating and distinctive green translucent fingerpieces. The device was first made by Dmitri in 2003. The Zero evolved from the Pekler single-lever design and is Dmitri's only dual-lever paddle. Arm suspension is done using two pairs of bearings, and the base size has been increased slightly over the Pekler base. Paddle adjustments are precise and hold their settings well. Dmitri reports he also has a vertical design and a model called the Eclipse in development.

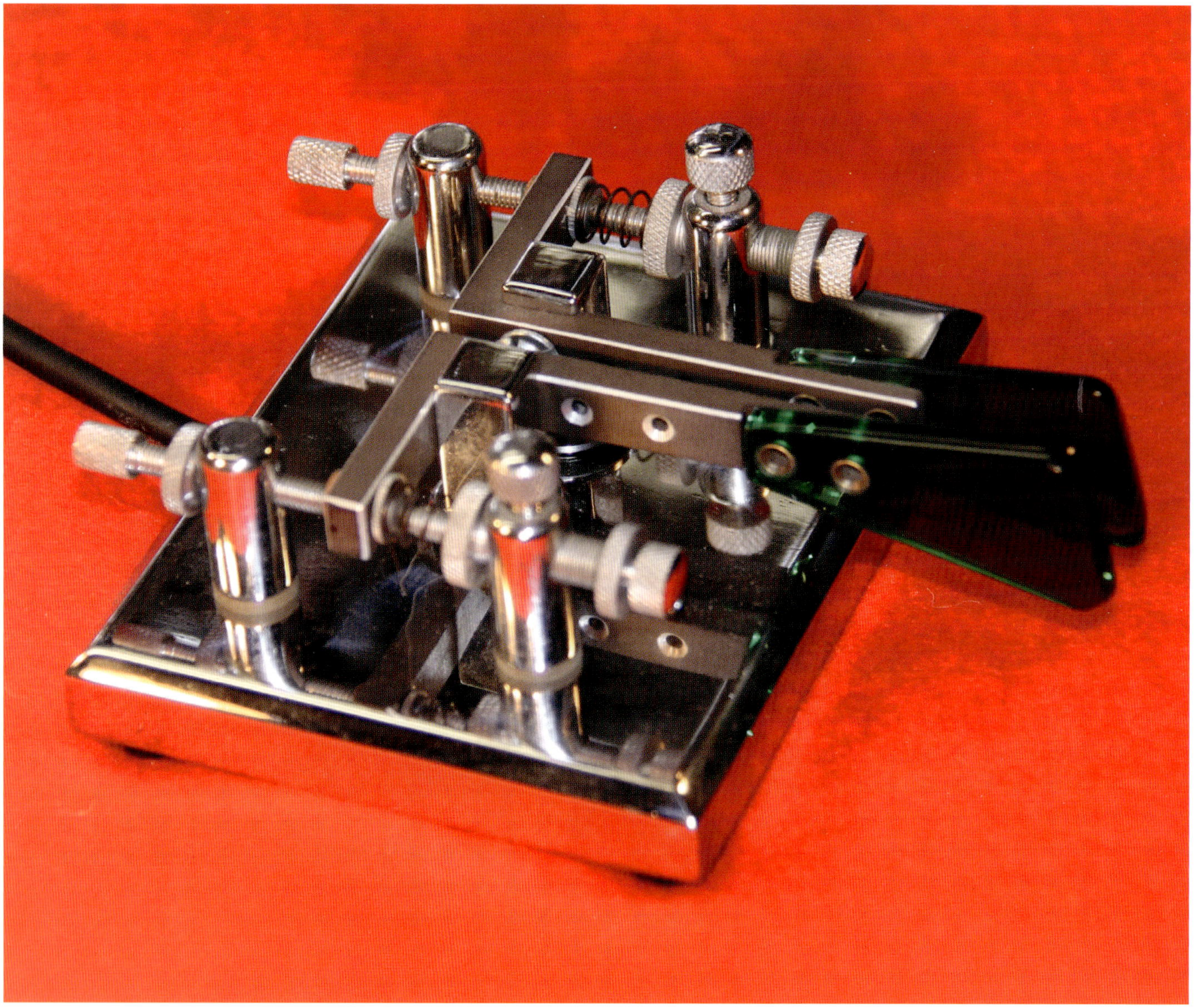

F5RDS

F5RDS is Olivier Pasquier of Paris, France. The F5RDS paddle was built using a design similar to the G4ZPY miniature devices, except Olivier increased the size by a factor of 1.2. After two months the paddle build was complete, and Olivier reports he is quite happy with how it functions; he uses it regularly in portable operation and mobile situations. The paddle incorporates a magnetic base that assists with mounting for mobile use.

Frattini

Here are two different models of Alberto Frattini (I1QOD) dual-lever paddles: one with chromed parts and one with brass. Both exhibit absolutely wonderful workmanship, with smooth operation and pleasing aesthetics. Frattini's dual-lever paddles use flat sterling silver contacts and neodymium repelling magnets for arm positioning. Frattini does not use typical bearings, opting for small steel ball bearings installed above and below each pivoting lever. Although the arms are somewhat longer than what is considered ideal, they are lightweight, allowing for a much more responsive feel than heavier arms of the same length. Users report no noticeable vibrations that can sometimes be attributed to longer arm length.

Frattini works out of his machine shop in the Italian Alps and makes a variety of keys, including several semi-automatic bugs. His devices use a medium pitch threading, so setup is just a bit more time consuming than a user would need for fine pitch threaded adjustments. Locking rings are provided. The paddles shown weigh approximately 3.5 lb.

FYO (W8FYO)

The FYO paddle invented by Joseph A. Hills (W8FYO) of Dayton, Ohio, was offered for a couple years starting in 1962, and was the prototype for the successful Bencher paddles. Hills made two versions: a single-lever and a dual-lever. The presence of a split ring and the spring arrangement are the only substantial differences between the two. The dual-lever is pictured (below) in new condition. There was also a variation of the dual-lever FYO that used a different fingerpiece design; this version (right) is seldom seen.

This series of shipping box photos (opposite) is very intriguing. While not much remains of the mailing label, if you look carefully you will see the date "Apr 25, '67." More than several sources report Joe Hills sold his two models of the FYO paddle 1962–1963, and that he was out of the key making business by 1965. Could this be one he kept around on the shelf for several years before selling it, before retiring to Arizona? It is very possible this exact dual-lever FYO paddle is the last one ever sold. The small manila envelope included with the paddle and other descriptive literature is marked "Allen Key," in what is very likely Joe Hill's handwriting. This FYO has remained new-in-the-box and is part of my collection.

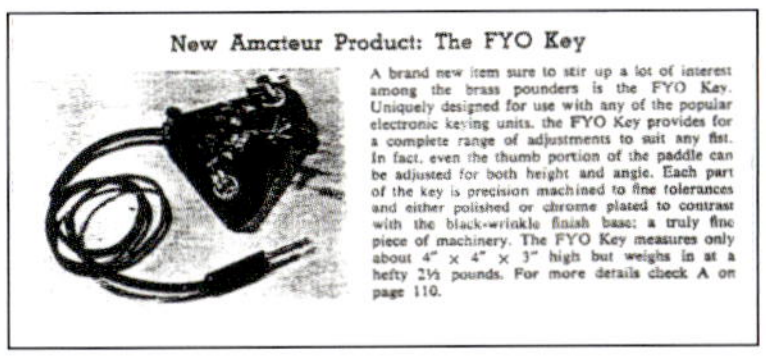

New Amateur Product: The FYO Key

A brand new item sure to stir up a lot of interest among the brass pounders is the FYO Key. Uniquely designed for use with any of the popular electronic keying units, the FYO Key provides for a complete range of adjustments to suit any fist. In fact, even the thumb portion of the paddle can be adjusted for both height and angle. Each part of the key is precision machined to fine tolerances and either polished or chrome plated to contrast with the black-wrinkle finish base; a truly fine piece of machinery. The FYO Key measures only about 4" × 4" × 3" high but weighs in at a hefty 2½ pounds. For more details check A on page 110.

An FYO key announcement from *QST*, October 1962.

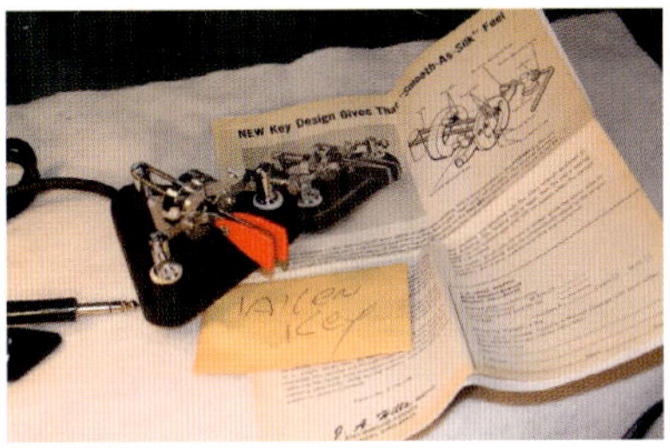

Contents of the 1967 shipping box for the FYO dual-lever paddle.

G4ZPY

Here are several versions of G4ZPY's dual-lever paddles. G4ZPY is Gordon Crowhurst, whose keys exhibit amazing workmanship and consistently receive high ratings. G4ZPY keys are known for their positive, no-flex operation. Gordon advertised his keys were made to order and offered the highest quality and reliability. Silver contacts are used, as are thicker than usual plastic fingerpieces. G4ZPY may have been the first to use small jacks mounted to the paddle base to allow for electrical connections. A 1999 note on the Morse Technologies website said that demand for Gordon's keys exceeds his ability to make them. Gordon retired from key making in 2010, and the September 2014 edition of *RadCom* (RSGB magazine) reports Gordon as a Silent Key.

Galbraith GK-11

A Galbraith GK-11 dual-lever paddle made in New Zealand on a black base. This paddle is well known for being small, reliable, and inexpensive.

GHD Optical Paddles

Optical paddles do not have the traditional mechanical contact points found in most paddles; the contacts are replaced by optical sensors. On a dual-lever device there are two sensor units fixed in place. The fixed sensors contain a small LED transmitter and receiver pair. The receiver detects the light being emitted by the LED, and will respond when the light beam is interrupted by the moving paddle arm. In other words, when the operator moves the fingerpiece to make a dot or dash the paddle arm will disrupt the beam of light being received, and that interruption causes the receiver to key a transistor. The transistor closes the keying circuit corresponding to a dot or dash, depending on what the operator initiated. The whole process happens very quickly.

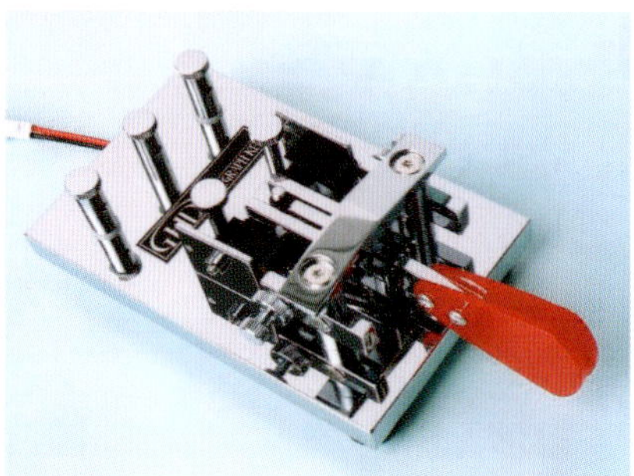

A GD307S optical sensor model.

Some operators do not like the perceived mushy feel of optical keying, and other users who prefer a light touch are not able to set the paddle response to give them the sensitivity they are after. To operate consistently, the paddle's optical spacing cannot be set too closely. Just as many operators do prefer the softer feel. There are no contacts to clean and very little mechanical noise associated with optical paddles.

A GHD Model GD-507 dual-lever paddle (above); this device uses optical sensors in place of mechanical contacts. This paddle was made by JA7GHD, and requires a power source via the black/red wire. The keyed line connects to the binding posts on the base.

GHD Traditional

Below is an assembled model built from GHD's dual-lever paddle kit, the GN807. This device has been called by some the best paddle available in kit form, and is offered at a very reasonable price. The base is hard chrome plated; upper parts are satin or brushed chrome. Detailed assembly instructions are provided by GHD. The base measures 3 × 4 in. and the paddle weighs 2.5 lb.

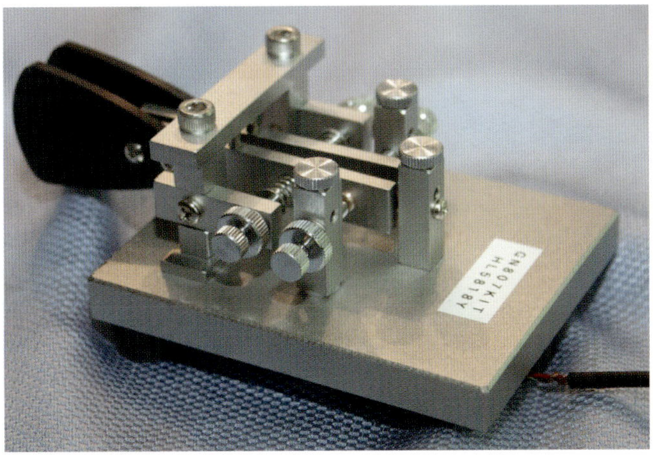

The GN-599DX uses compression springs for arm tensioning. This paddle incorporates flat gold-plated silver contacts offset at an angle that supposedly allows for "self cleaning," as the contacts wipe each other when closing. The 599DX has fairly heavy long lever arms made from steel and four race bearings. Some users report the paddle is a bit noisy and requires extra time to set up properly. Paddle weight is almost 3 lb.

The GN-807A (below left) is GHD's introductory paddle and is offered at a very reasonable price. The base of this dual paddle is hard chrome plated, and upper parts are satin or brushed chrome. Springs are used for arm centering. Paddle weight is 2 lb. 10 oz.

The GHD GN-607A (below right), a paddle with mechanical contacts and chrome-plated parts. Paddle weight is 2 lb. 10 oz.

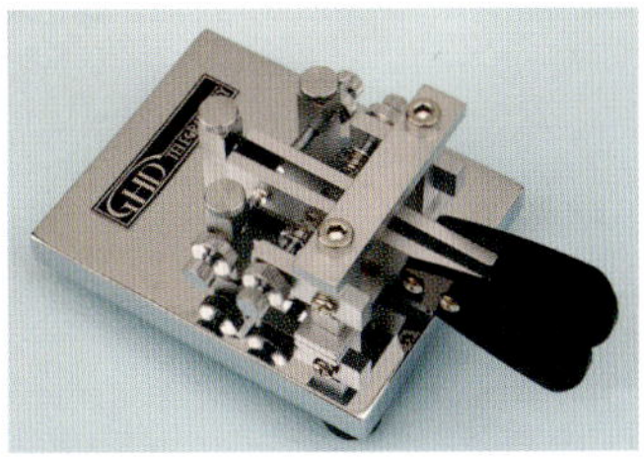

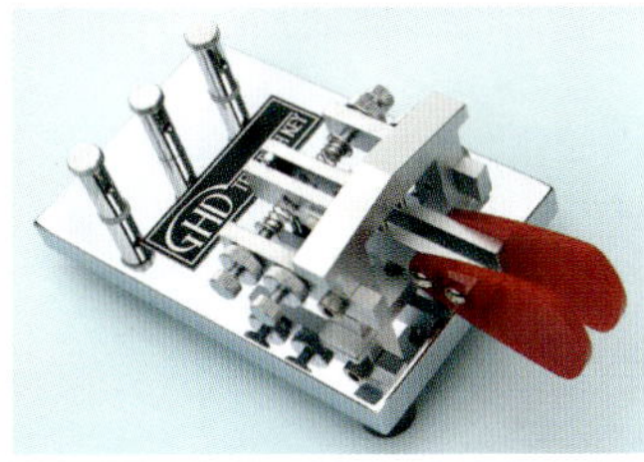

HAL Communications Corporation FYO Key

HAL's key instruction manual presents this paddle as responsive to the lightest touch, with this feature being the secret of effortless sending. The HAL device uses lightweight parts and frictionless pivot bearings. HAL says that "blowing your breath on a fingerpiece will cause it to make contact." Sensitivity is not adjusted by varying spring tension, but rather by moving the sensitivity adjusting screws at the 10 and 2 o'clock positions around the armature; this moves the springs closer to the pivot point, reducing the lever arm length and therefore the effect of

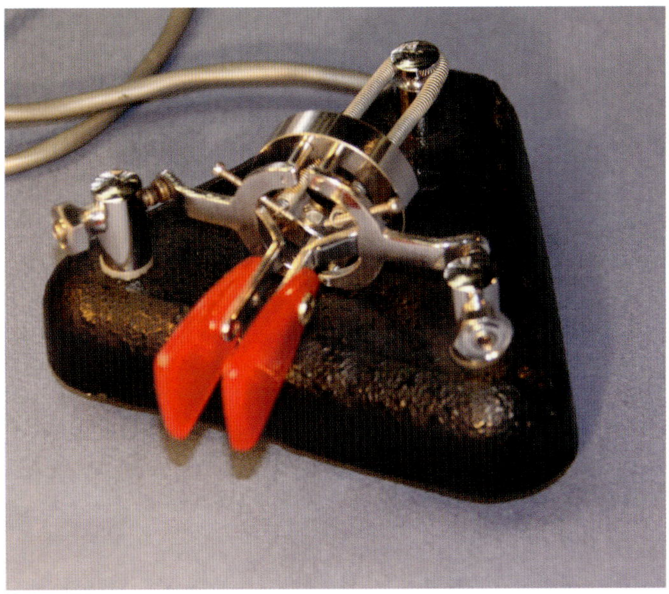

the spring. Also noted is HAL recommends using only finger movements, not hand or wrist movement for sending. Because HAL paddle sales proved disappointing and costs of production were not being recouped, HAL discontinued the manufacture of this paddle somewhere around 1977.

This is K8ND's mystery paddle (below). It appears to be a device made by HAL, but incorporates an additional ring around the front of the pivot mechanism. Very little is known about this version, but one could assume it is a prototype for an engineering change or a design update. A reasonable guess would be the extra ring helps retain the pivoting parts and gives the paddle more resistance to shock, so the paddle stays together if knocked around on the desk.

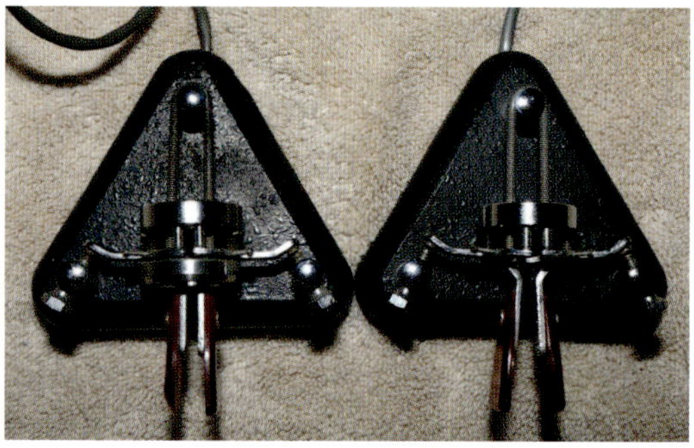

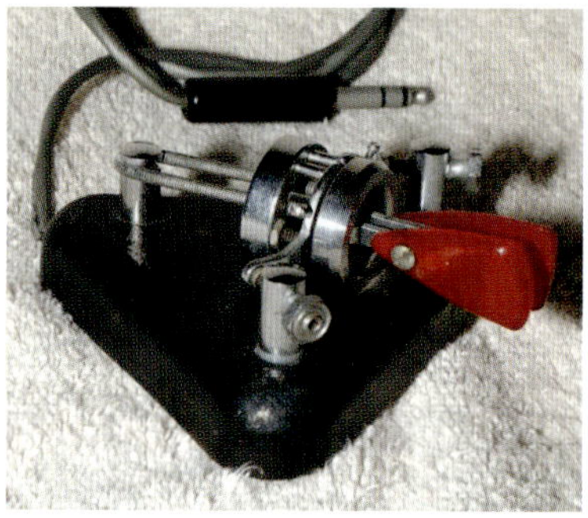

HAMCO

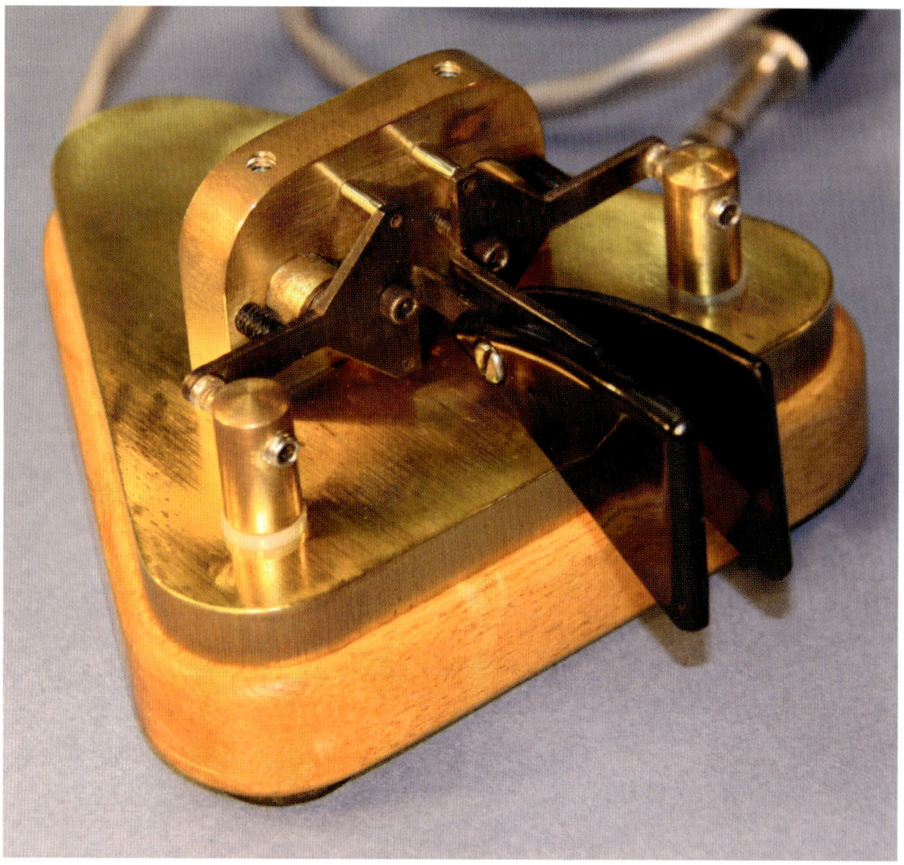

HAMCO, of Eureka, California, described the Scotia model in their product literature as finished in brushed antique brass, and states this model is their most popular key. Features include a hardwood base, handcrafted construction, solid silver contacts, and no springs to fly apart should the paddle be mishandled.

HAMCO literature states the Trinidad (opposite) uses a new engine-turned brass finish that "glistens with many facets." HAMCO models used a setscrew to fix magnetic arm adjustment. HAMCO literature claims the paddles are preset at the factory and should not require further adjustment.

HAMCO bought the key business from HAL in 1978, and was the first production company to use magnetic tensioning in their designs. HAMCO produced paddles until 1982. The base consisted of a thick plate mounted on a wooden bottom section. Vibroplex eventually bought HAMCO in 1982, and used the design to produce the Brass Racer. The HAMCO design incorporated updates to original elements of the FYO approach to keep all the parts from accidentally coming loose.

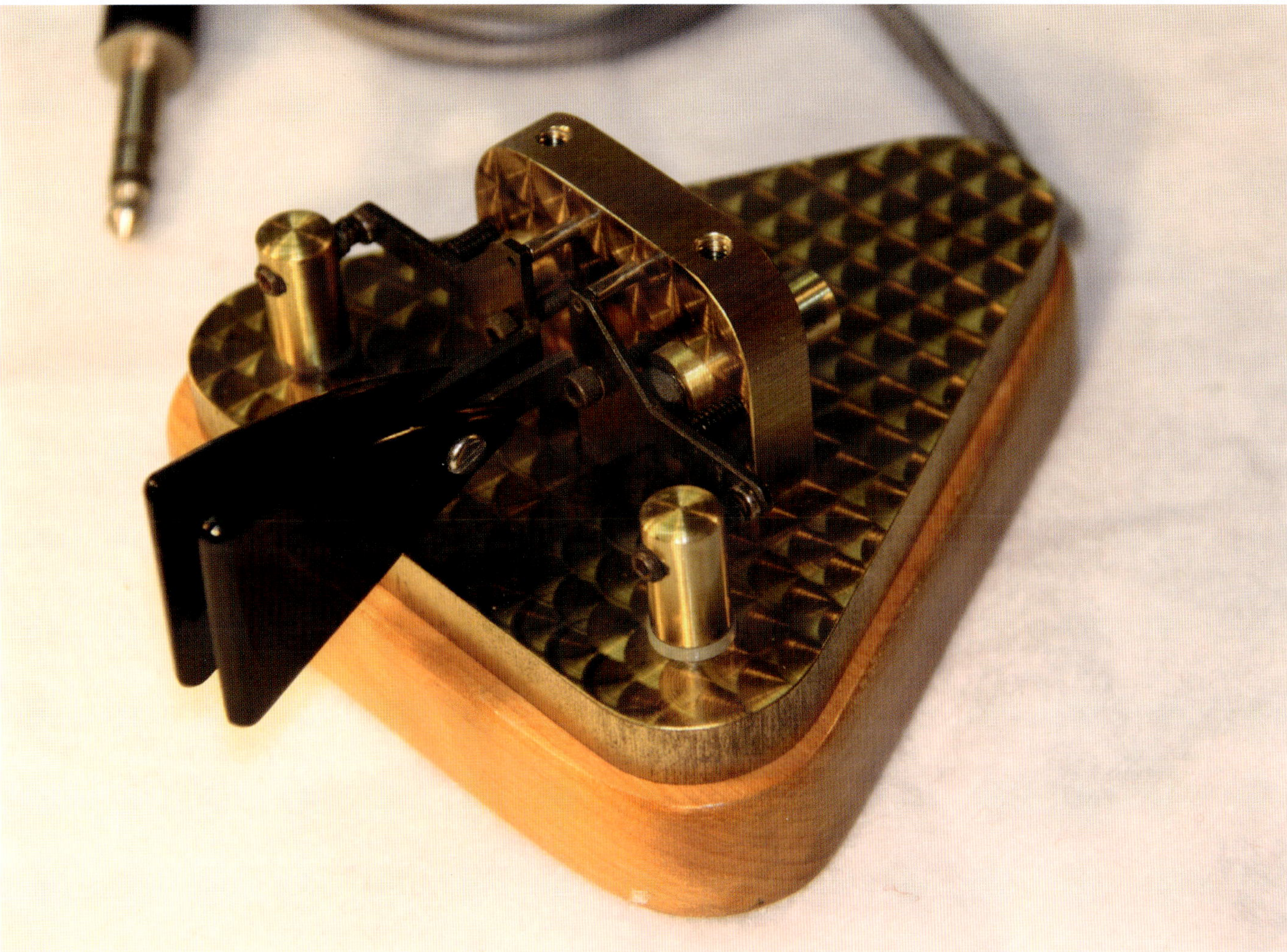

Another HAMCO variation of the two paddles was called the "Carson," and that version was hand-polished. The Carson was available with an EK-1 option, giving the user a built-in Curtis 8044 keyer in the base; it sold for $129.95. All HAMCOs are considered scarce.

Ham-Key HK-1

A June 1977 *Ham Radio* ad for Ham-Key, showing their various products. Note the Model HK-2, a very rare device many have never seen; this was the paddle used in one of the Palomar IC keyers.

Shown is a Ham-Key HK-1 dual-lever model with silver contacts and a gray hammertone base. It is claimed Ham-Keys were the only production key to use a molded plastic frame. The fingerpieces could be reversed on the lever arms to increase separation.

Hensley

Donald Hensley (AC4HB) made several versions of his dual-lever paddles. His keys featured solid brass construction with 24k gold contacts. Chrome or gold-plated finishes were typically offered, as was an option for a round or square base. The arms used a roller bearing pivot design, and stainless steel hardware was used throughout. The arm return was made using tensioning magnets. Although the design is similar to the N2DAN paddle (which was not especially aimed at close spaced usage), the Hensley was advertised as being built for close spacing and high speed. Paddle weight was 3 lb. Hensley paddles are considered very collectible and sell for a premium price when available.

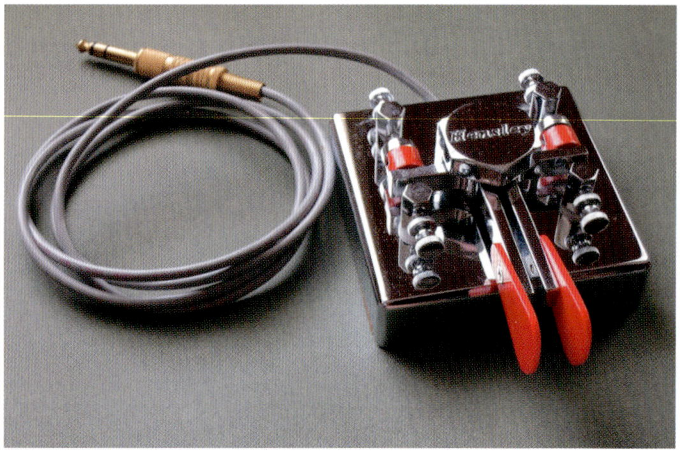

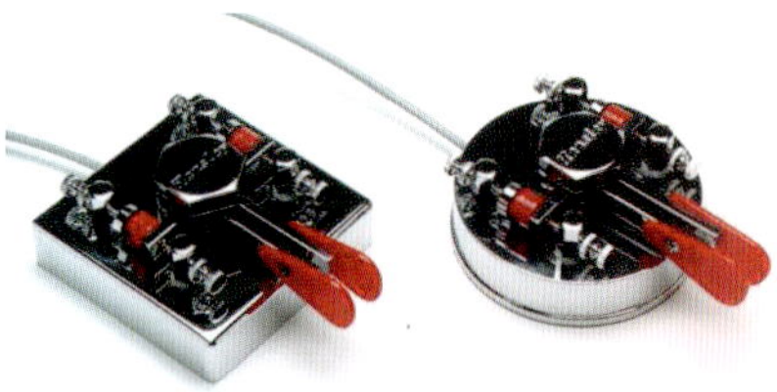

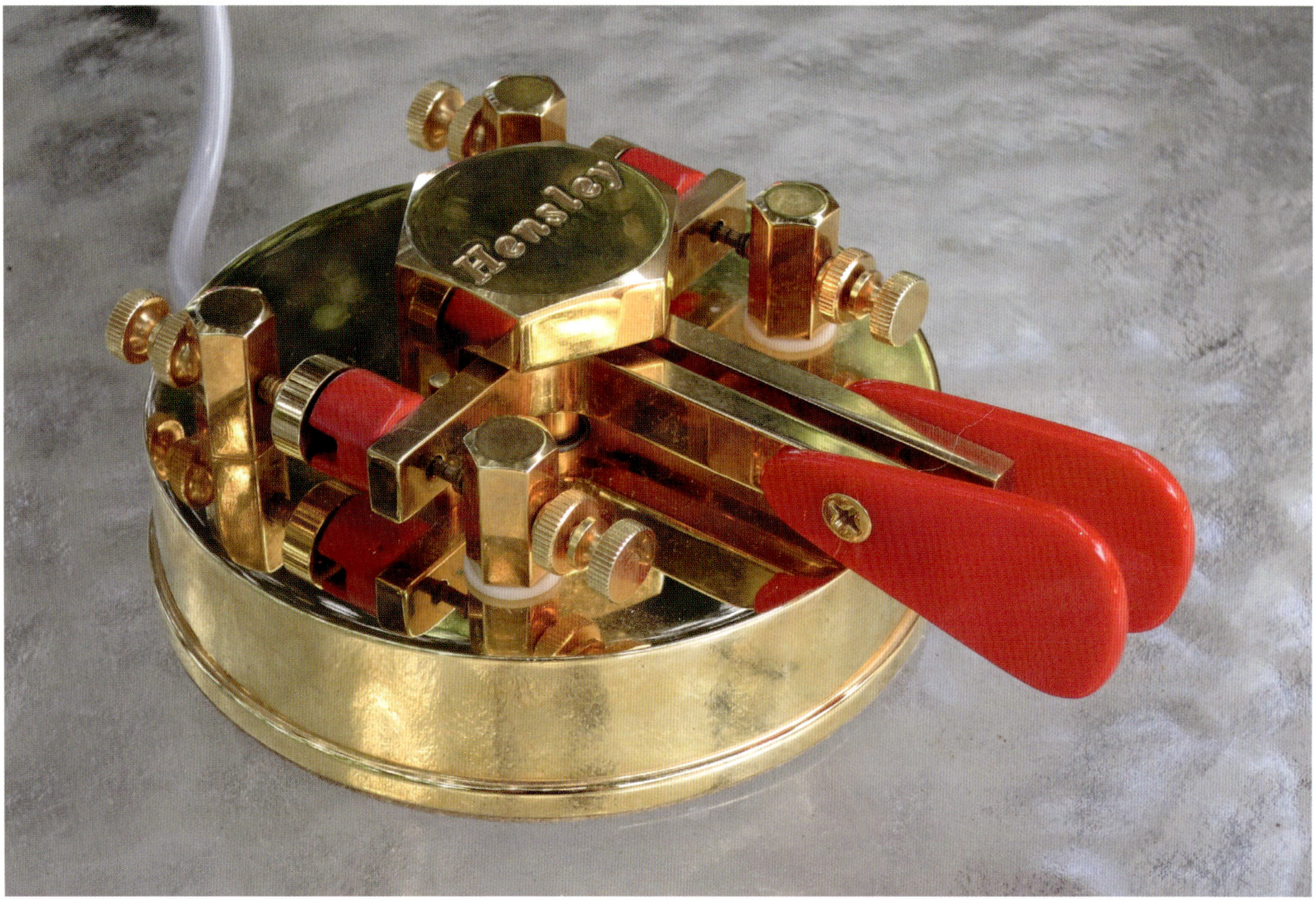

Hi-Mound MK-703

A Japanese Hi-Mound dual-paddle on a marble base; this is an early version of their MK-703, sometimes called the "Manipulator." The paddle's chrome-plated plastic cover is detached. This paddle is similar to another device known as the "EasyTech," which was basically the imported MK-703 sold without the marble base.

IK1OJM

IK1OJM is Salvatore Canzoneri, an Italian craftsman who produces many different models of attractive paddles and bugs.

IMEL M1 Paddle

An IMEL M1 paddle made from all aluminum, with carbon fiber fingerpieces. This one is serial number 003, machined by Billy Imel of the Bell-Imel Group, Muncie, Indiana. It uses very low mass arms and is a great paddle to use. Imel told me his intentions with this design were to produce a paddle you could run over with a truck—and he means that literally; some of his unmanned aerial vehicle designs show just that in pictures. Unfortunately, this is another great paddle that cost too much to produce and they are no longer available.

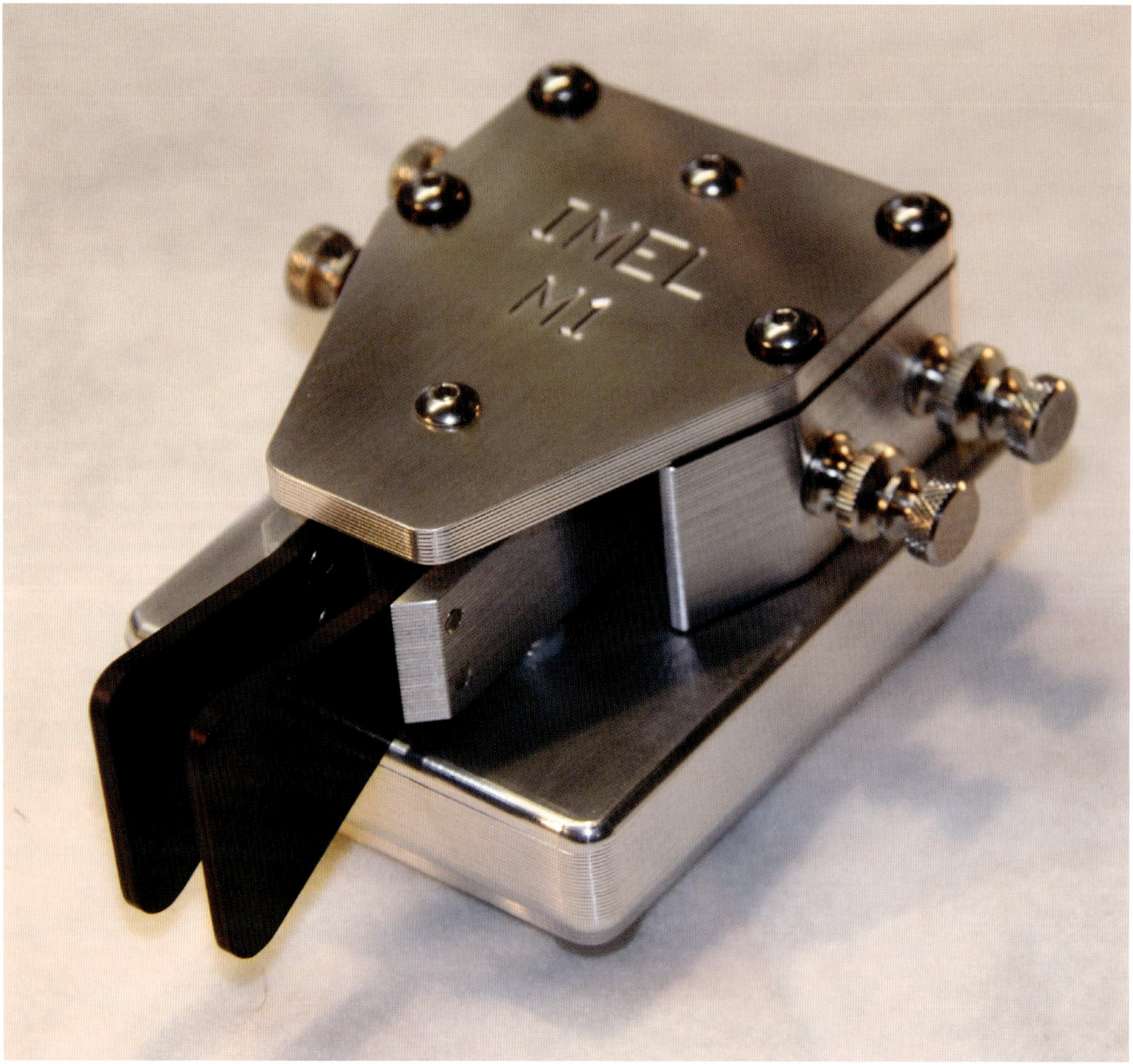

Jones Keys

In addition to the brass and red base models shown, Jones also made a gold-plated brass base version, a straight key, and a brass single-lever key. The gold-plated, all brass double-lever paddle sold for $350 in 1996.

Jones double-lever keys used four rotary ball bearings, giving a solid feel to the operator. The rotating, adjustable fingerpieces allowed the user to set up height preferences. There was an oval brass post in between the two paddle arms that could be rotated to adjust spacing between the arms/fingerpieces. The company was basically a machine shop that custom made various parts, mostly for the medical equipment field. Peter Jones became interested in key making when Palomar Engineers came to Jones with a Kent model and some suggested modifications. Palomar started importing the Jones keys sometime in 1992. Jones stopped making keys in 1998.

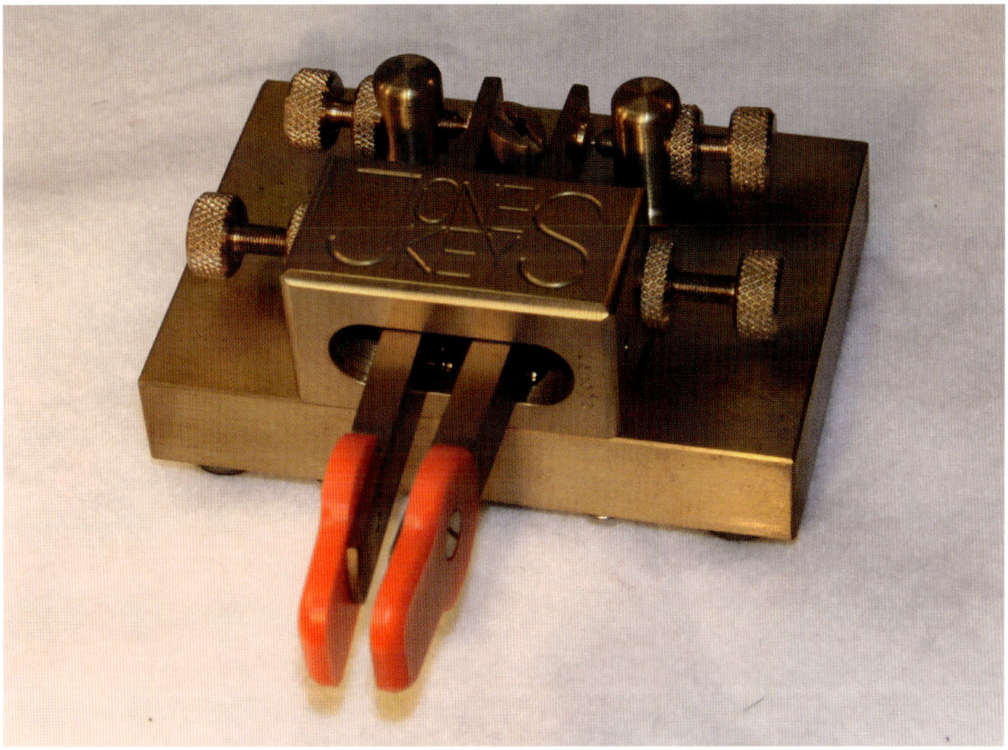

The all-brass Jones key Model PK-200-B was the most popular.

The Jones PK-200 with red painted base.

K8FF Prototypes

K8FF is Wayne Smith, who designed the Vibroplex Venus paddle. Pictured is a prototype for the Venus. The prototype used magnetic action and incorporated a heavy machined steel base. Satin finished brass parts with double row ball bearings and silver contacts were used. The Venus paddle never went into full production; only about 24 were produced by Vibroplex.

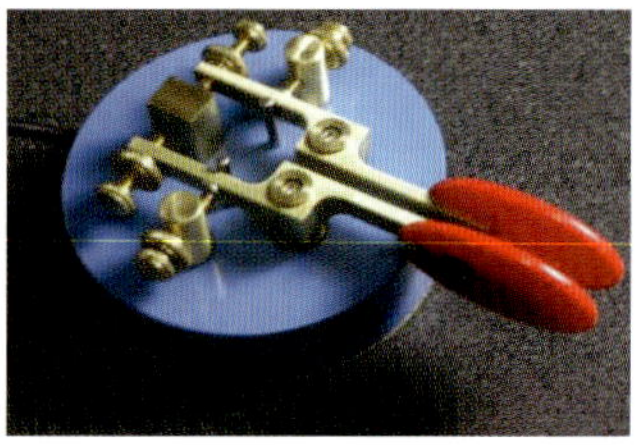

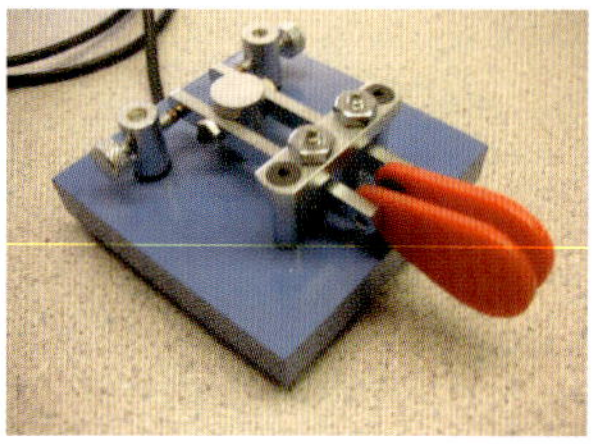

A K8FF dual-lever prototype model created by Wayne Smith of Aurora, Ohio.

K8RA Keys

Jerry Pittenger (K8RA) was a retired systems engineer who loved to build keys in his basement shop. Jerry was first licensed in 1960 as KN8UNG, and was active for his entire ham career. Jerry had said that making CW keys filled much of his time, but it was a labor of love. Six different models of K8RA paddles were available; most were offered with a choice of springs or magnets. The machining was done to precision tolerances. K8RA keys were known for their smoothness and consistency of settings, due in part to the use of stainless steel ball bearings at the pivot points and balanced paddle arms. Both arms are independently adjustable for tension and contact spacing. Jerry also offered a kit that would convert earlier paddles from springs to magnets, or vice-versa. Two of the most popular designs are presented.

Jerry was well loved by his many friends and customers, and always offered to repair or upgrade his keys as a courtesy to his fellow hams. Jerry passed away on January 2, 2014, and his friends Mike Freeman (NT8O) and Fred Freeman (N8BX) have taken over production of the K8RA line.

An early P-2 model, possibly a prototype; it appears to be nickel or silver plated. Note the adjusting bars are not knurled at the ends.

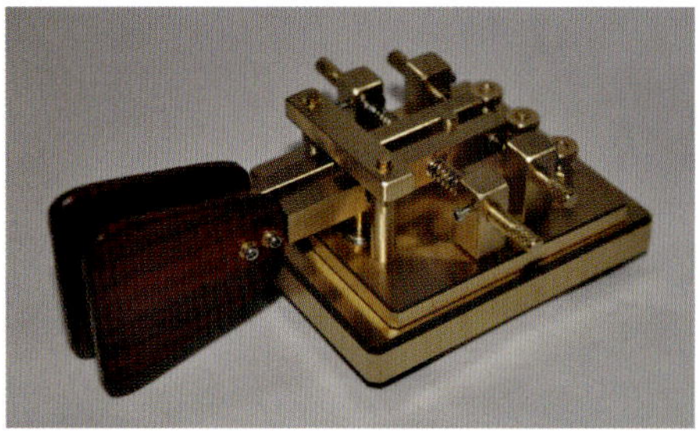

Production P-2 model; paddle weight is about 2.8 lb.

P-4 model; this model weighs about 5 lb. A similar P-5 model weighed 7 lb.

KA2BZS Flex-Flyer

Ron Loneker Sr. (KA2BZS) made this device called the Flex-Flyer. This paddle used a comparatively new and innovative design incorporating stainless steel flex bearings, stainless hardware, magnetic tensioning, and 8-48 UNF threads on the adjustments. It was handcrafted by Ron for consistent performance after ten years of design and development. Ron spends over fifty hours machining the parts for this key. Although not seen under the top cover, the flex bearings were mounted right under it beneath the paddles, helping make this key one of the smoothest and responsive CW paddles available. The flex bearings are not inexpensive—they cost Ron about $100 for the two in this paddle. Unlike CW paddles made with conventional shafts and bearings, flexural bearings are accurate within one-half thousandth of an inch, never require any maintenance or lubrication, and have an infinite life cycle.

Katsumi KM-23

Seen below is an early version of the KM-23 Katsumi paddle (top), probably from the '60s or '70s when they started making keys. This Katsumi uses spring tensioning between levers for arm centering. The photo at right shows a more recent KM-23. Users report contact spacing can be set quite close, and that the paddle has an excellent feel during operation. The base finish is low maintenance, and the lack of chrome parts needing cleaning can be considered a plus by some. Selling price for the KM-23 is $99.95.

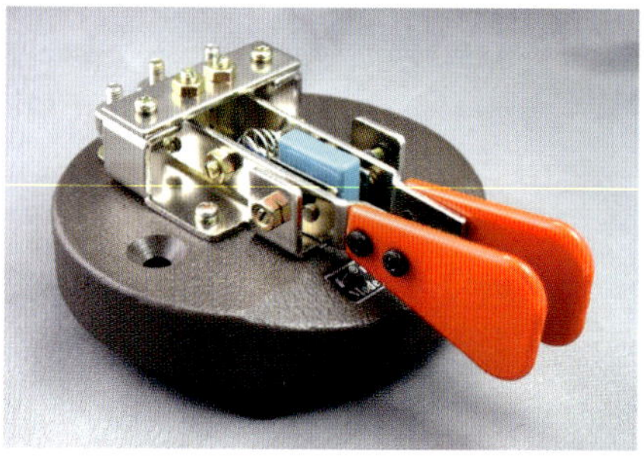

KD4OBQ Okie Key

The Okie key is the creation of Patrick (KD4OBQ). He designed this key with similarities to the K8FF NorCal paddle. The Okie key uses magnets instead of springs, and the ¾ × 3 × 5 in. base is aluminum. Patrick had intended to use brass for the base but "fell in love with the polished aluminum." The version shown uses the gray hammertone painted base. The Okie key also has flanged ball bearings for the arm pivots; all hardware is polished stainless steel and aluminum.

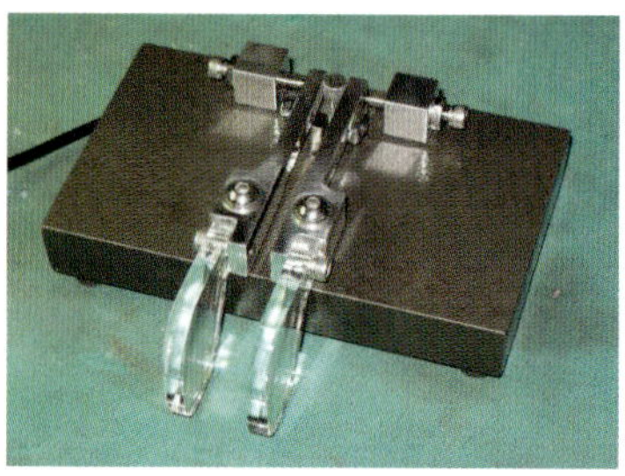

Kent

The Kent paddle is an English device available as a kit or fully assembled. The Kent paddle uses rotary ball bearings, and is made from machined brass parts. Spring tension and contact spacing are adjustable; no lock nuts are required on the tension adjustments. The paddle's contacts are slightly convex in shape and silver plated.

KG2ED Long Island Mercury

This is Rich's (KG2ED) version of the famous N2DAN paddle (S/N 041 is shown). These paddles are built in Rich's basement shop in Oceanside, New Jersey. Rich calls this the "Long Island Mercury Paddle." The KG2ED is handcrafted, beautifully chrome plated, and faithful to the N2DAN design. Rich even grinds the magnets for a perfect length and diameter fit. At one time Rich was considering making a vertical version of the Mercury paddle.

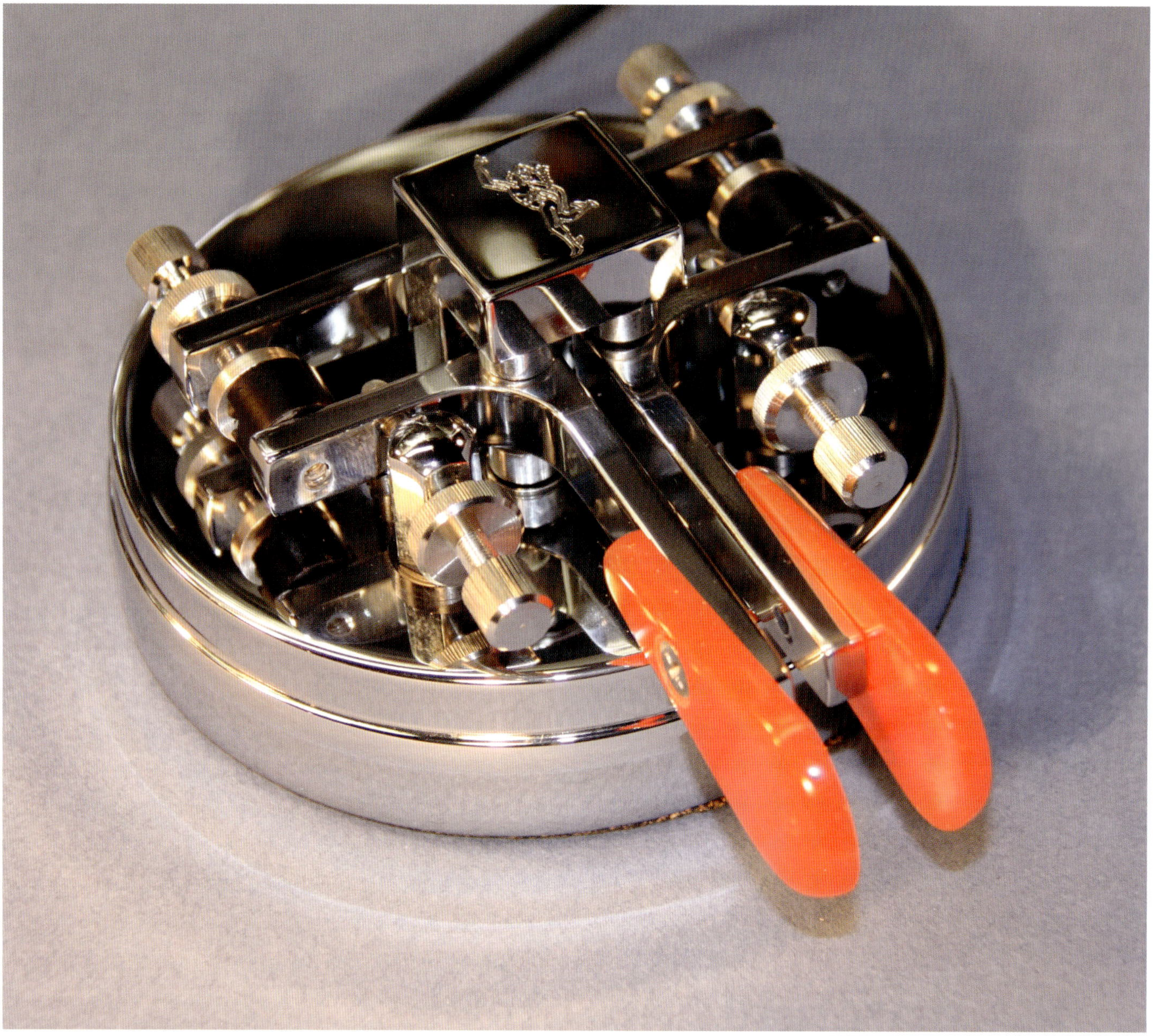

Kitano Paddles

Kitano paddles were made by Kit Raymond (N2LMC) of Princeton, New Jersey, in the mid-1990s. Raymond ran the Kitano Key Company; he relates the name is a play on his name and the word "piano." Raymond's design features a low center of gravity for stability. The larger key is called the Katahdin, and the arms are designed to use a pivot and not the flat springs as seen on the smaller paddle. Katahdin contacts are seen at the rear of the key; fingerpieces are cherry wood.

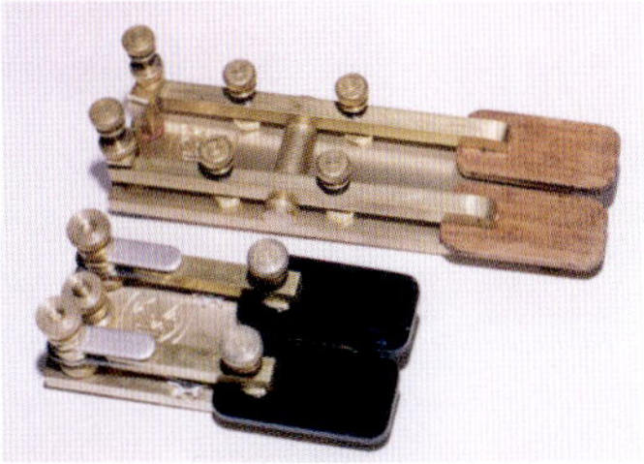

LTA (Llavas Telegraphicas Artesanas)

LTA means "Llaves Telegraphicas Artesanas" or "Telegraph Key Craftsmen," and indeed, these paddles are wonderfully crafted devices. Shown is the CRIO, a dual paddle, gold-plated key with olive wood fingerpieces. LTA was based in the Balearic Islands of Spain. The keys are hand assembled; the base is either Spanish oak or machined brass. The fingerpieces fare polished olive wood. LTA used solid brass for the mechanical parts, or in some cases 18K gold plating. EA6YG (Guillermo Mestre Janer), the founder of LTA Keys, recently passed away. Unfortunately, no more of these LTA keys will be produced.

LZ1DZ

The LZ1DZ paddle uses a design similar to the Hi-Mound. The sub-base is mounted on a larger, heavier cast base, and the paddle includes a coiled cord.

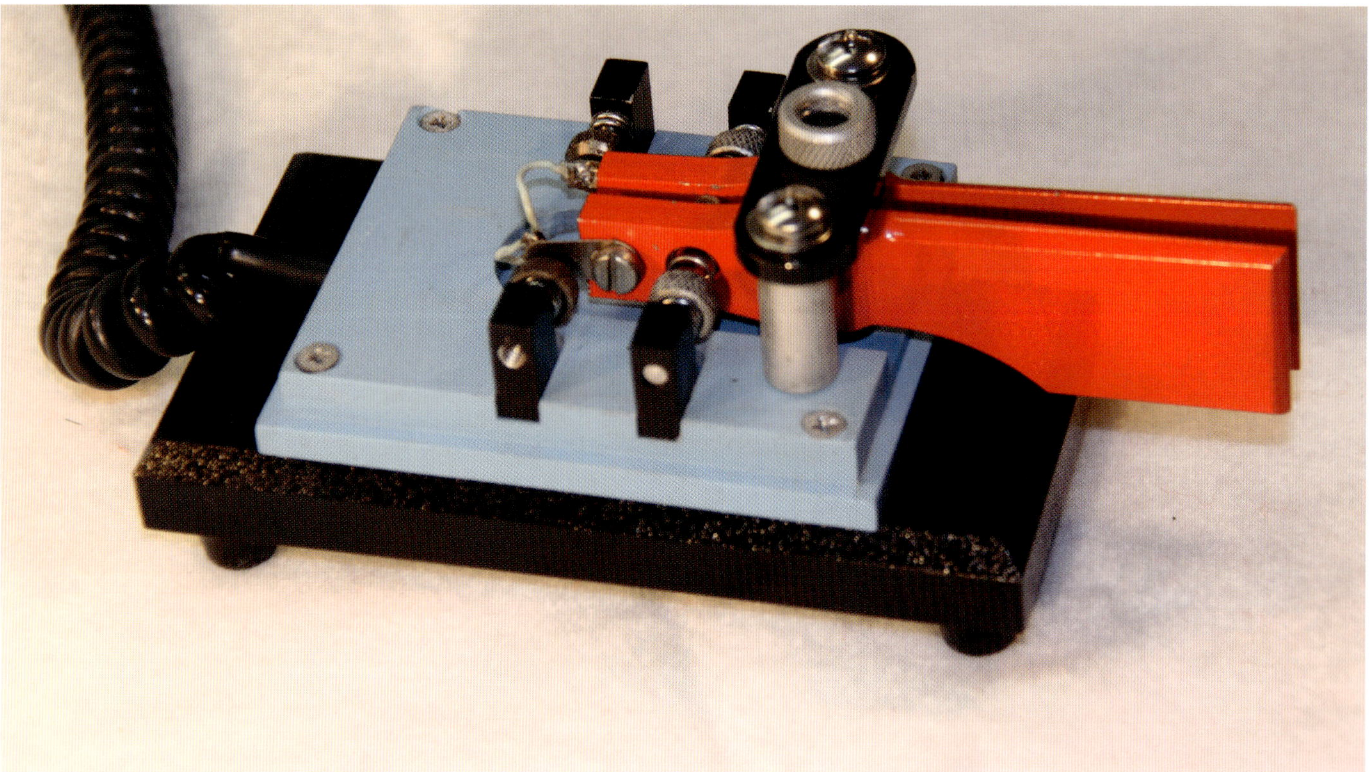

March K4QU Paddles

Mike March was first licensed in 1967 as WN4FJJ; after obtaining his Extra license in 2000 he became K4QU. He founded March Magnetic Paddles in 1987, and produces paddles from his home in Winchester, Virginia. March offers fingerpiece, jewelling, and engraving options. Over 450 March paddles have been made since he has been in business.

A very early March prototype paddle. Note the screws and nuts for arm adjustments and the very basic pivot mechanism for the arms. The magnets use small setscrews to lock them in place after adjusting.

A mint unused March Magnetic in polished brass (right). This is the Model R-3a; the paddle shown was made in 2006. March was perhaps the first to use magnetic repulsion, as opposed to attraction, to return the arms to the open contact position. March uses two pairs of magnets for this function.

One of the original March R-3a models with three contact posts in the rear.

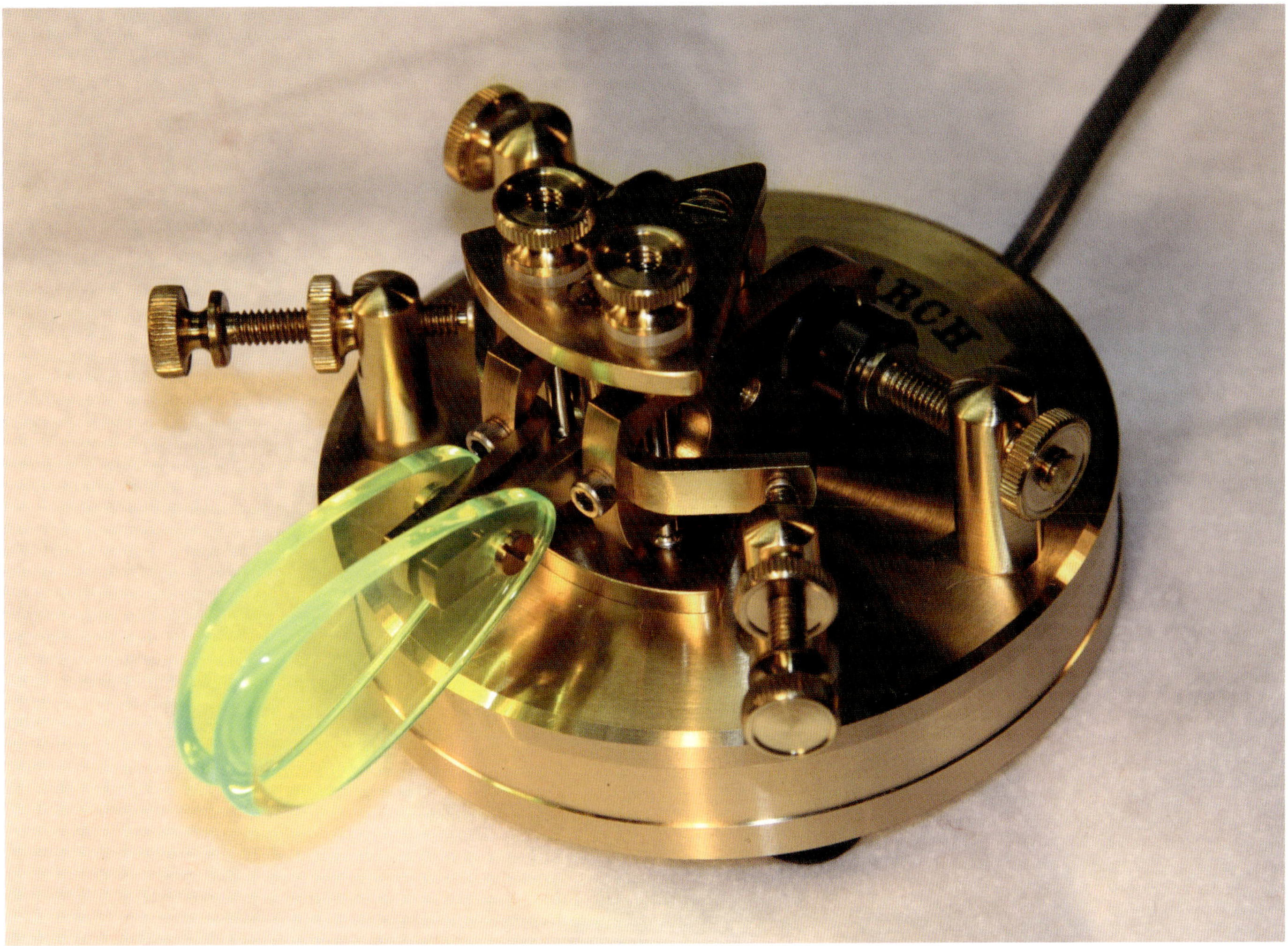

March also offers custom engraved and art deco bases.

This March vertical (right) is always a favorite. The paddle is one of twelve made, according to Mike March. He states that he no longer makes the vertical model. The paddle shown is serial number 008, and was originally bought new and stored away in the mint, unused condition seen.

Some folks call this the "square base" March (below), but as you can see it is rectangular. The base is larger than the March design using the gray hammertone finish (see chapter 6). This paddle was part of the W4LT estate, and was bought new and shelved. It is mint unused condition. These were made around 1992; the first twenty-five or so did not have labels or serial numbers.

Here is a variation on the rectangular base with a rounded front edge (p 189). This style is more common than the true rectangular base, but still hard to find. March paddles with this base are no longer being made.

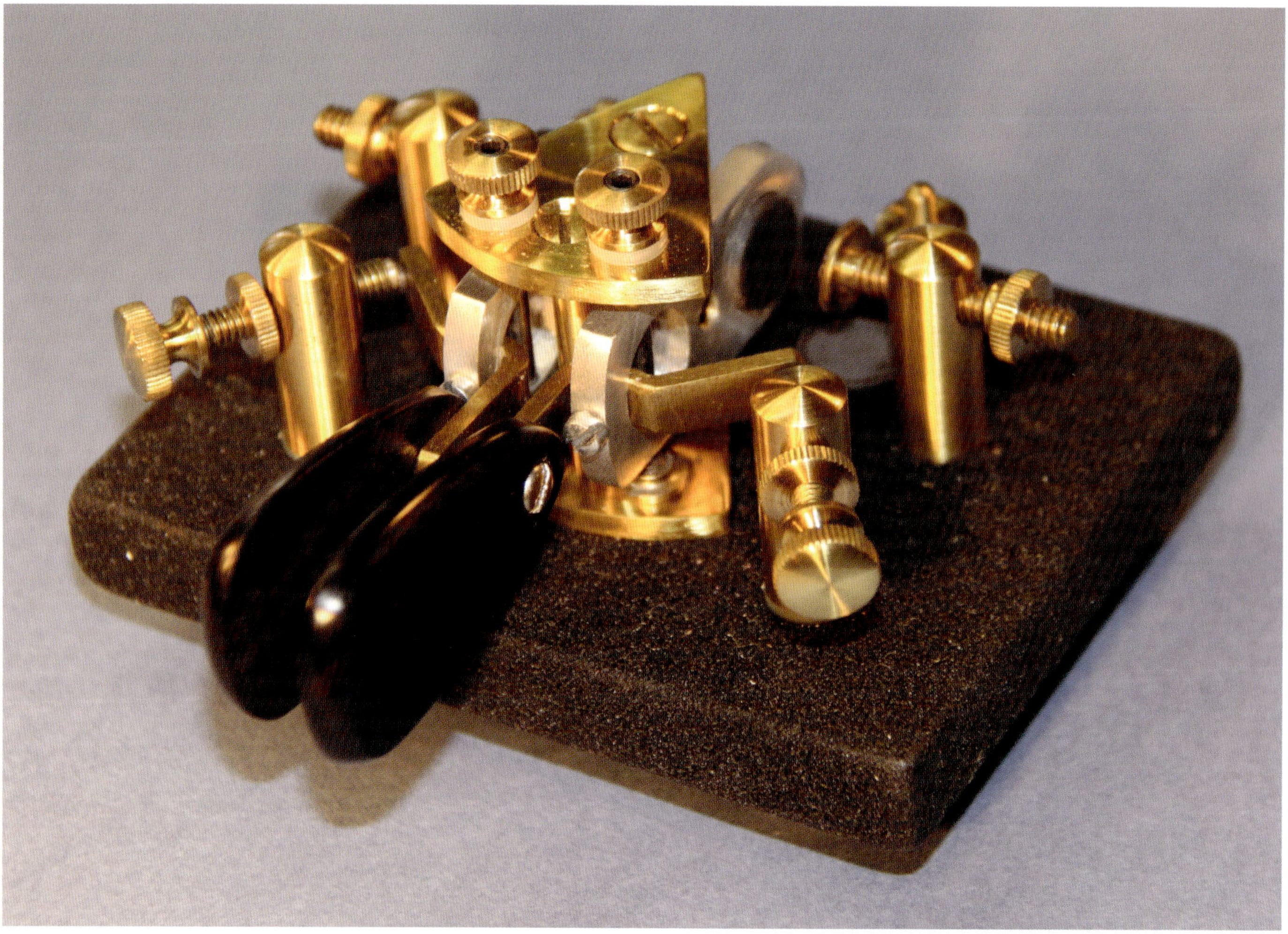

MFJ-564 Paddle

This is the MFJ-564 paddle, with obvious similarities to the Bencher. This paddle was also sold under the Vectronics name as the KP-200 and KP-200B. Both black and chrome base models are pictured. These paddles offer a full range of tension and contact spacing adjustments. The frame is machined and then chrome plated. The MFJ-564 uses a heavy base with non-skid feet.

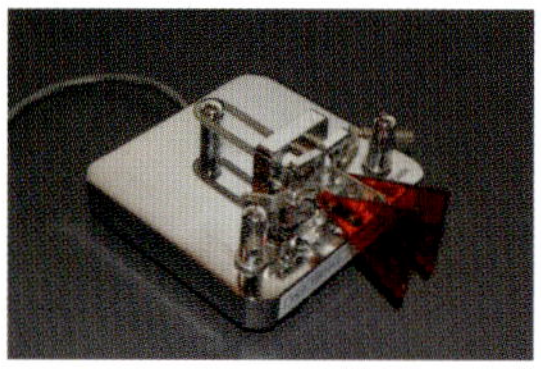

N2DAN Mercury paddle with chrome finish.

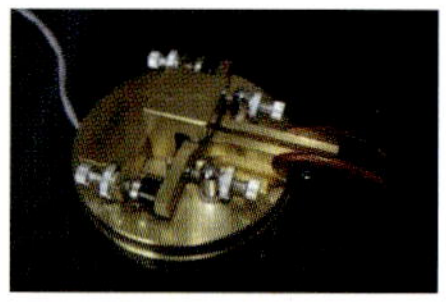

N2DAN Mercury paddle in natural brass.

Bottom view of the N2DAN Mercury paddle.

N2DAN

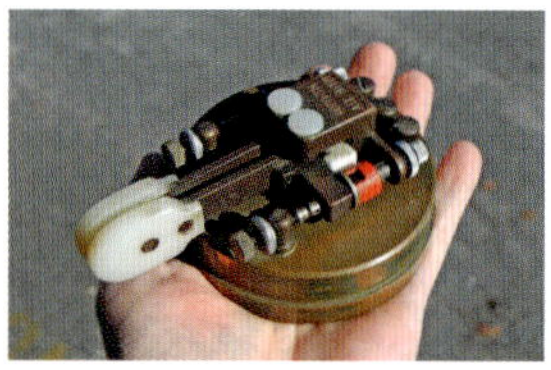

The N2DAN paddles were handmade by Steve Nurkiewicz, and set new standards for performance and quality. Steve's design used rotary bearings and very solid aluminum arms along with magnetic tensioning to provide return force. Contacts were rhodium plated silver. The basic design included precision machined parts in combination with a very heavy base. Occasionally a user will comment the long arms can induce a noticeable vibration, but this does not seem to interfere with usage. Some other users report adjustments are a bit tricky, as the paddle uses coarse threading on the adjustment screws. Paddle weight is close to 4 lb.

Supposedly over 100 different fingerpiece colors were available. It is estimated N2DAN produced a few hundred of the paddles over his lifetime. Also offered was a remote memory button bracket, allowing the operator four small pushbuttons to actuate external memory keyer functions. In 1993, Steve introduced a modification kit with stronger magnets, contact spacers, and arm extensions that allowed slower speed users a better paddle feel. Included with the kit was a special cover in the form of a small statue of Mercury that fit over the paddle and added approximately 4 lb. to the base. The extra weight helped counteract the torque introduced by the modification kit's longer arms.

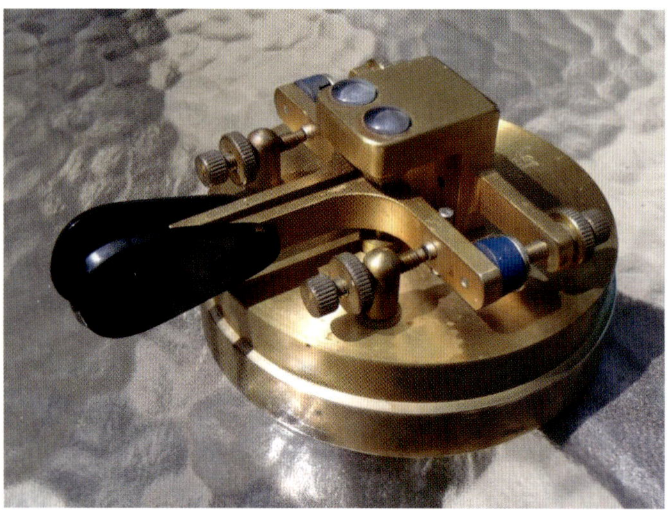

Some early N2DAN dual-lever magnetic paddles.

The N2DAN magnetic paddle concept was first described by Steve in an April 1968 *QST* article. In the article Steve showed several prototype paddles using magnets he had installed. He also modified some of the prototypes to use precision ball bearings in place of the pivot bearings of the original prototype mechanisms. Steve challenged readers to consider reworking old bugs and paddles to use magnets and bearings in place of springs and pivots, and commented on the resulting operational smoothness and elimination of lever side play. Steve passed away in 1997; after his death his widow sold the patent rights to Bencher, and they continue to make their version of the Mercury paddle (see the Bencher entry in this chapter for more information on the Bencher Mercury). Chapter 4 presents some of the N2DAN single-lever prototypes.

N2LDY

N2LDY has begun selling his new design, a magnetic paddle with some visual similarities to the ON4MAC devices. Each paddle is individually crafted, with the arms and fingerpieces

milled from solid brass as one unit. The fingerpieces include a laminated hardwood outside piece that matches the brass inner portion in shape; the result is an attractive layered combination of brass and wood.

N2LDY states the keys are held in place by strong neodymium magnets and pivot on a fulcrum, alleviating the need for springs. Gold-plated contacts are used on the paddle arms, with a silver-plated contact on the adjusting screw. The paddle base measures 3 × 3 in.

N3ZN

Tony Boleno (N3ZN) has developed quite a reputation for his machining talents, as evident in his line of paddles. ZN designs offer two sealed bearings per arm, allowing for smooth and consistent arm movement and a light keying touch. This ZN-1 is the first paddle design Tony offered (serial number 004). Note the Allen head adjusting screws and the knurled locknuts; later designs used thumb-knob screws with no locknuts. The N3ZN adjustment design uses a ball-and-spring that provides tension against the adjustment screw. The ZN-1 model is no longer being made. Several of the photos present some of the first N3ZN paddles offered, a few with options no longer available.

N3ZN paddles have been consistently compared to classic and high-end models, such as the Schurr and the Begali. Tony's designs use ball bearing movements and magnetic return with very lightweight arms. Contacts adjustments are called "quick adjusting" and no longer use locknuts as early models did; contacts are gold-plated. Chuck Adams (K7QO) wrote a great review of the N3ZN paddles in the K9YA *Telegraph Newsletter* (Vol. 5 Issue 3).

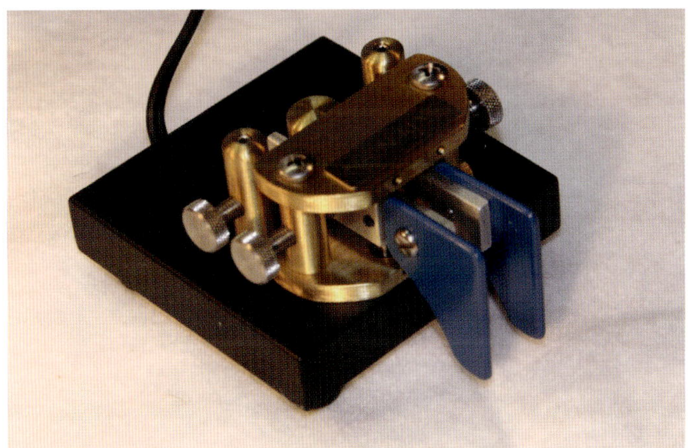

A ZN-3A vertical model (S/N 004) with wooden fingerpieces and a ZN-4A model (S/N 003) with optional blue fingerpieces (above). The ZN-4A is the standard (at the time) black base. The painted steel base is no longer seen on Tony's website.

The ZN-9CRB (left) uses short, lightweight 6061-T6 aluminum levers. The design incorporates three bearings for each lever, giving a very smooth action. The ZN-9CRB, with classic round brass base measuring ⅞ × 3 in. diameter, weighs 2 lb. 4 oz. The ZN-9CRB is available in brass only. Other features include all stainless steel hardware and large 10-56 adjustment screws for arm spacing and magnet settings. Tony also uses machined points touching gold-plated silver contacts on this paddle, which includes four low-profile soft rubber feet for stability.

N5QVF

Dario (N5QVF) made this N2DAN paddle clone; quality and workmanship detail are consistently rated well by users. Like the N2DAN, the N5QVF keys have a magnetic tension adjustment that can be fine-tuned to accommodate the sender's requirements. Paddle design used four ball bearings and the finished device weighs 4 lb. As with the original N2DAN key, somewhat coarse adjustment threading was used. These keys were offered in a gold, nickel plate, or chrome finish. Also offered was variable mechanical paddle spacing via custom fingerpieces. Current production of this model is unknown.

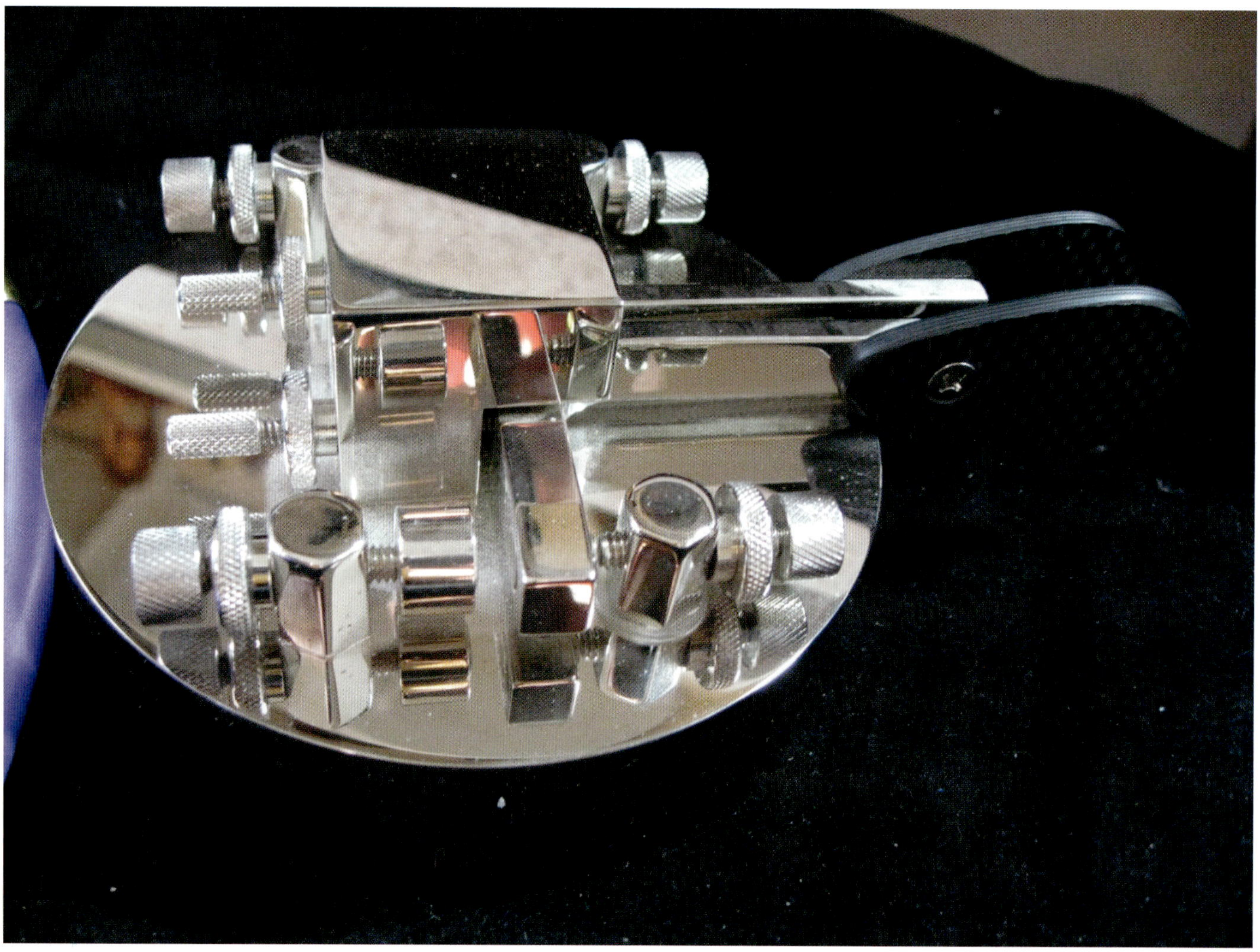

N0SA

Larry Naumann (N0SA) custom produced and finished all the parts required to assemble his line of high quality paddles. The paddle designs featured a 1:1 arm length ratio, with arms and fingerpieces the same length. The paddles typically used a 3 × 3 in. base with varying thicknesses. Four miniature stainless steel precision bearings were used, and the base incorporated four low-profile feet. Aluminum parts were high grade 6061 aluminum with either brushed or polished surfaces. Brass parts were clear coated. Adjustments were made using fine-pitched (40 tpi) threads, with adjustment posts having built-in adjustable tension. Contacts were solid silver and polished stainless steel. Most bases used a Parkerized finish. Each paddle used stainless steel hardware and included an engraved name plate showing model and serial number; a 3 ft. cord was included.

A TP1A (below) made by Larry as a special order. It incorporated the top from a TP4 model assembled on a TP1. Unfortunately Larry is no longer producing paddles, but while in production, his standard product line included what is shown.

The basic TP1 (below left) with the top plate offering protection for the adjustment screws. The design offers reversible fingerpieces and a ⅝ in. thick base. Larry describes the TP1 and its variations as being able to really hug the table due to the low profile and choice of rubber feet that grab well. The TP1 was Larry's most popular paddle.

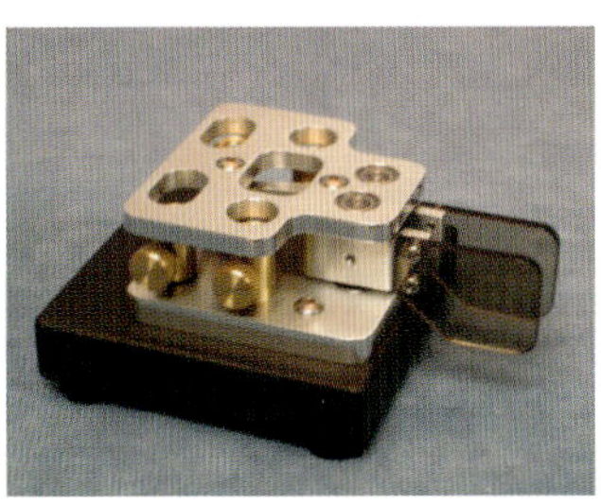

The basic TP1, Larry's most popular paddle.

The TP2 model with a heavier base. All bearings were mounted on the base.

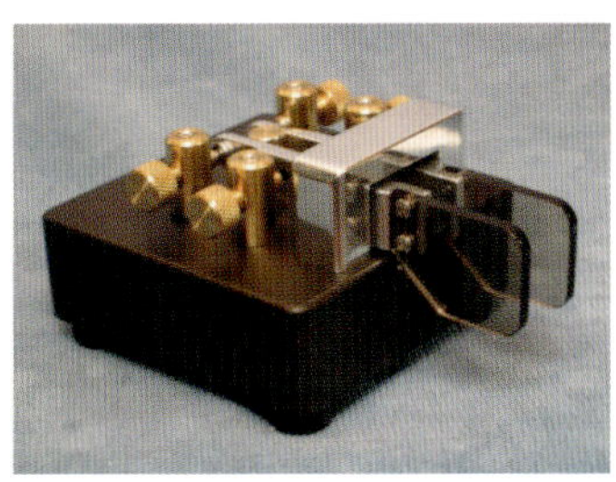

The TP3 with a heavier look due to the thick, heavier base. Bearings are mounted above and below the paddle arms.

Larry's Model TP4 using a 3 × 3 × 1 in. steel base. Paddle weight is 2 lb. 9 oz.

Nikey

The concept for the Nikey was originally described in a July 1961 *QST* article by Nicholas Lefor (W2BIQ). The article discussed an improved keying mechanism for all types of electronic keyers, and presented the Nikey with its separate dot and dash levers. Lefor's purchase of an ultimatic-type keyer convinced him a dual-lever paddle was needed to obtain full value from the ultimatic mode. The Nikey was constructed using discarded bug parts, aluminum bar stock, and what Lefor calls ham ingenuity. A steel base from a local model shop was used with junk box binding posts. Bridge and keying levers were made from bar stock. Pivot rods were constructed from stainless steel rod filed to a cone shape in a drill press. An old bug spring was used to provide tensioning, and adjusting hardware was obtained from an old key. Contacts were salvaged from an old relay. The base was cadmium plated and given an iridescent finish; the bridge and levers were anodized black.

Nikey versions carried the Lefor name and the Productive Tool Company name. Tom French recalls the Lefor came before the Productive Tool paddle, although they were close together time-wise, dating to the early 1960s. Nikey paddles are widely known as being the first dual-lever paddle to advertise in *QST* (1962). At least one version with an unpainted base has been seen in another collection; all three known variations are shown.

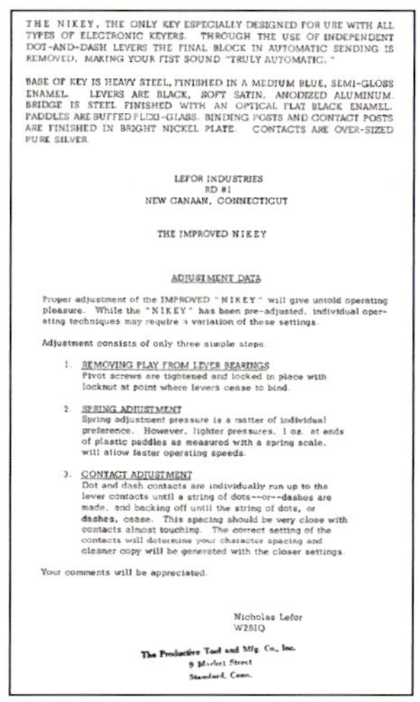

THE NIKEY, THE ONLY KEY ESPECIALLY DESIGNED FOR USE WITH ALL TYPES OF ELECTRONIC KEYERS. THROUGH THE USE OF INDEPENDENT DOT-AND-DASH LEVERS THE FINAL BLOCK IN AUTOMATIC SENDING IS REMOVED, MAKING YOUR FIST SOUND "TRULY AUTOMATIC."

BASE OF KEY IS HEAVY STEEL, FINISHED IN A MEDIUM BLUE, SEMI-GLOSS ENAMEL. LEVERS ARE BLACK, SOFT SATIN, ANODIZED ALUMINUM. BRIDGE IS STEEL FINISHED WITH AN OPTICAL FLAT BLACK ENAMEL. PADDLES ARE BUFFED PLEXI-GLASS. BINDING POSTS AND CONTACT POSTS ARE FINISHED IN BRIGHT NICKEL PLATE. CONTACTS ARE OVER-SIZED PURE SILVER.

LEFOR INDUSTRIES
RD #1
NEW CANAAN, CONNECTICUT

THE IMPROVED NIKEY

ADJUSTMENT DATA

Proper adjustment of the IMPROVED "NIKEY" will give untold operating pleasure. While the "NIKEY" has been pre-adjusted, individual operating techniques may require a variation of these settings.

Adjustment consists of only three simple steps.

1. REMOVING PLAY FROM LEVER BEARINGS
Pivot screws are tightened and locked in place with locknut at point where levers cease to bind.

2. SPRING ADJUSTMENT
Spring adjustment pressure is a matter of individual preference. However, lighter pressures, 1 oz. at ends of plastic paddles as measured with a spring scale, will allow faster operating speeds.

3. CONTACT ADJUSTMENT
Dot and dash contacts are individually run up to the lever contacts until a string of dots--or--dashes are made, and backing off until the string of dots, or dashes, cease. This spacing should be very close with contacts almost touching. The correct setting of the contacts will determine your character spacing and cleaner copy will be generated with the closer settings.

Your comments will be appreciated.

Nicholas Lefor
W2BIQ

The Productive Tool and Mfg. Co., Inc.
9 Market Street
Stamford, Conn.

Product literature from Lefor Industries describing the Nikey.

North American Telegraph NA-20

Shown is a handmade key from Jim Richards (K6VDH). The devices are called North American Telegraph keys. Jim machined the keys from solid brass stock, and typically mounted them on a polished hardwood base with a rubber pad underneath. This image appears to show the base in a different material, possibly painted steel. The base measures approximately 2 × 3¼ in. and the weight is 14 oz., which is fairly heavy for a key of this size. The fingerpieces are shaped black walnut. There is a nameplate on the top that Jim machine engraves with the North American name and serial number. Jim stopped making keys in 2004.

Nye-Viking

Presented (right) is a Nye Viking Super Squeeze key (model M/SSK-1). This key sold for over thirty years but is now discontinued. The SSK-1 is very solidly built and rugged, and used a die-cast base and metal cover. Contacts were gold-plated solid silver. Some users noted that contact spacing adjustments were a bit imprecise and the hollow fingerpieces gave a soft feel, but it was a very popular key.

ON4MAC Paddles

Here is a MAC Mark IV paddle (below) made by Michel (ON4MAC). Michel guarantees these as long as he lives. The base is very heavy unfinished brass and the arms are extremely light, making this paddle very responsive and a pleasure to use. Silver contacts are incorporated. One of Michel's design goals is to keep the moving mass to a minimum; adjusting screws are aluminum.

Michel also makes this tapper paddle built to his high level of quality and precision.

Pro-Paddle SSP

The Pro-Paddle is available from QRPWorks; the version shown is a solid state dual-lever design that uses software to adjust paddle feel. Fingerpiece keying pressure is adjustable from 5 to 50 grams by software algorithm. There are no contacts, magnets, or springs used in this paddle based on the 9A5AN microprocessor design. The circuits are enclosed within an aluminum head that protects against any negative effects of RF. The base is made of stainless steel, and internal batteries (two AAA) power the device and provide a 700 hour operating life. Total paddle weight is four pounds.

As with the one arm in the single-lever version, the dual arms do not move, so there is no response time or moving inertia to consider. Keying technique is the same as would be used for a mechanical device, but with less fatigue claimed as a benefit. This software approach offers absolutely silent keying, with no contact maintenance or periodic mechanical adjustments needed. Finger pressure required to initiate dots and dashes is software adjustable. Since the electronic circuit is microcontroller based there is no maintenance or periodic readjustment necessary as is typical for many mechanical paddles.

RA1AOM

Valery (RA1AOM) hand made the paddle seen here. Valery is from St. Petersburg, Russia, and designs and builds paddles and keys as a hobby. RA1AOM devices typically use a base of some exotic mineral; the paddle pictured appears to have a green jasper base. The pivots are simple trunnions, but very well made. All assembly parts used in Valery's paddles are highly polished by hand. This particular paddle has Valery's signature and fabrication date on the bottom.

Samson ETM-SQ

An ETM-SQ paddle, a German paddle developed by Hermann (DJ2BW).

Satatuuli Osk KBX 101A

The KBX 101A is a Finnish key designed by Satatuuli Osk. Osk reports his interest in CW began with code training he received in 1969 in the Finnish Air Force. Osk began sending Morse code on an old WWII key, but soon started producing his own key model. Later he designed the KBX 101A, which was a big success in Finland. Many copies of this paddle were sold at various ham conventions in the late 1980s. The KBX 101A is currently out of production; a similar model (KBX 380) is available from OH1KB.

Schurr Morsetasten

The Schurr Profi II is regarded by many as the best paddle ever made. It is fabricated with a tilt-open Plexiglas hinged dust cover and includes the connection cable. All metal parts of the Profi are made from solid brass. Paddle arms are mounted on hardened steel pivots with embedded molybdenum disulfide lubrication. The Profi uses large knobs for contact spacing and spring tension adjustments, although they are not frequently used, as the paddle is well known for holding its settings over time. Gold-plated convex contacts are used, and the fingerpieces are hand finished and shaped for maximum operator comfort. The base is machined from a solid block of surgical quality brass, and is coated with a trade secret polymer that resists wear, staining, and pitting over the paddle's lifetime.

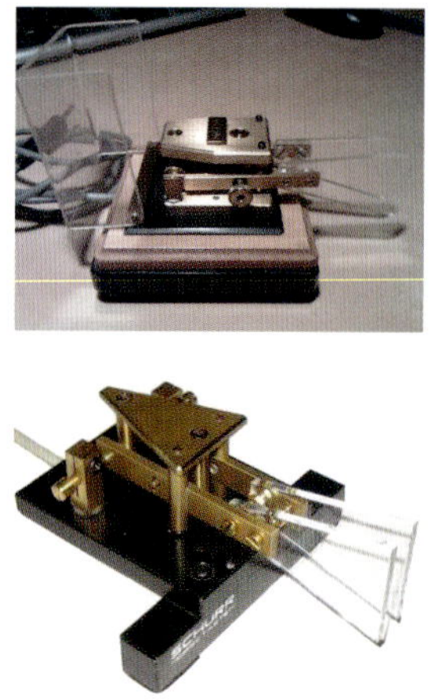

Some early Schurr double-lever models.

"Schurr" was Gerhard Schurr (DH2SAA), with various models now available from Scheunemann Morsetasten (Uli Scheunemann is DC2SO). They continue to provide great support and parts for the Schurr models; Milestone Technologies is the US distributor. Schurr proclaimed his motto was, "If you stop trying to be better, soon you will stop being good."

The Scheunemann Morse Dirigent is the successor to the Profi II. Dirigent is German for conductor, as in the conductor of a symphony orchestra. Scheunemann's Morse Dirigent features some style changes, such as a tapered front and separate tension adjustments for the two levers.

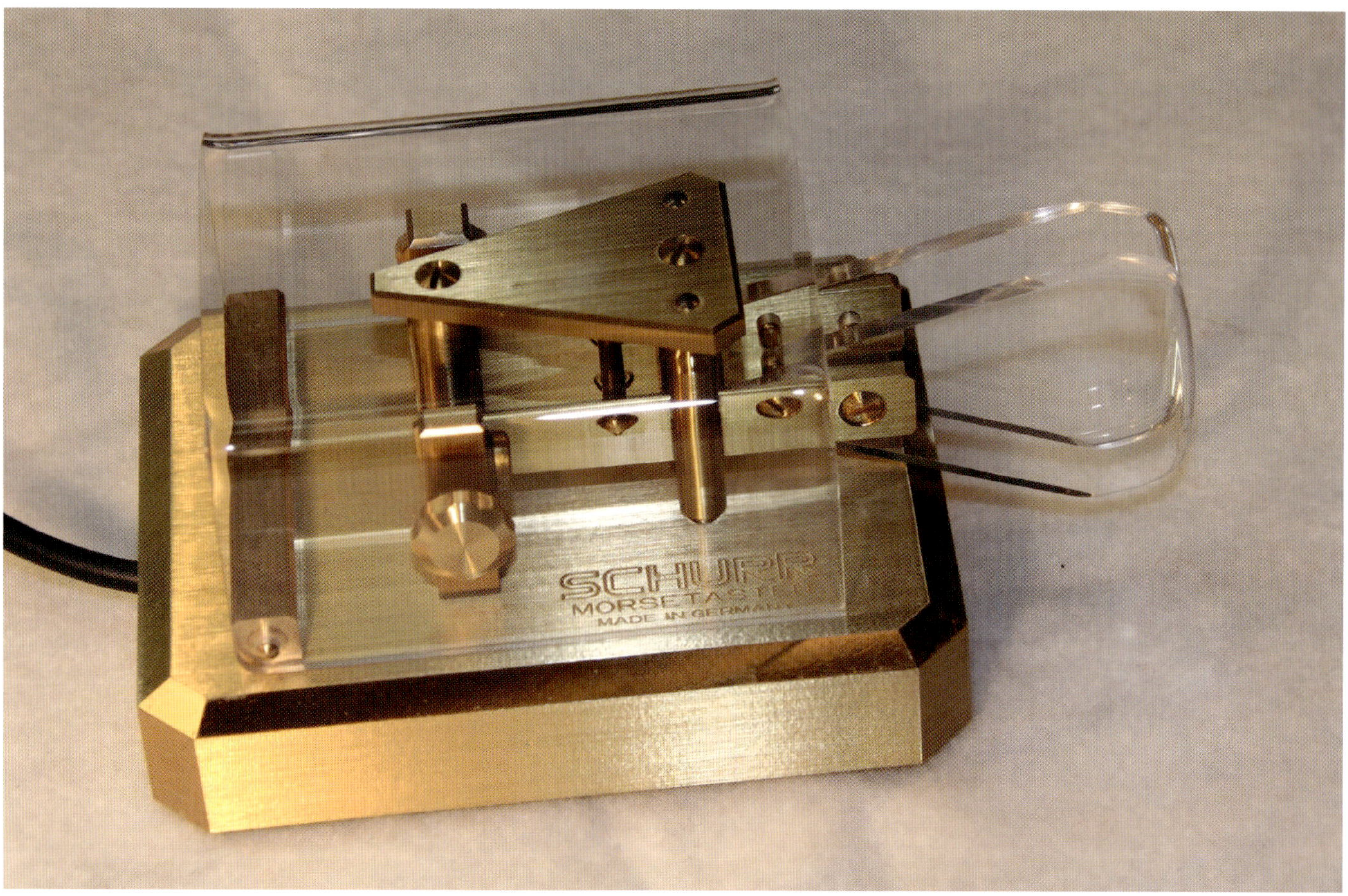

A Schurr Profi II.

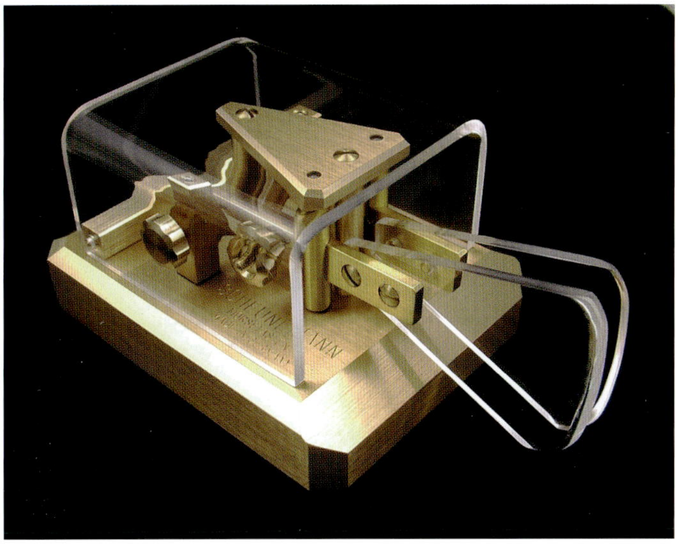

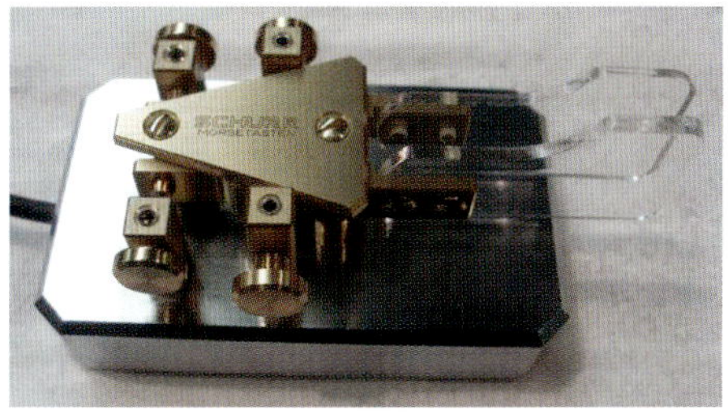

The Profi M—Verchromte Grundplatte.

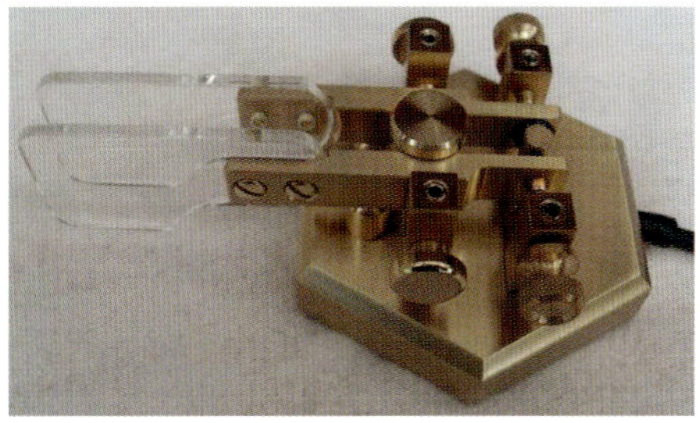

The Profi M—Sechseckige Grundplatte.

Like the Profi II, the Dirigent comes with a tilt-open dust cover and connection cable, and uses the same large adjustment knobs for contact spacing and spring tension. The contacts are convex and formed from highly conductive coin silver. The hand finished fingerpieces are shaped for maximum comfort while preserving precise control. As seen with the Profi II, the base is also machined from a solid block of MS-58 surgical quality brass and is coated with a wear resisting polymer. Paddle weight is 3.3 lb.; size is 5.5 × 3.2 × 2.3 in. The Scheunemann Morse Dirigent sells for $349.95.

Schurr-Bergsiek

Before his death, Gerhard Schurr developed the Profi M, and built prototypes that were tested extensively. The Profi M replaces the Profi II series. Due to deteriorating health, Schurr was unable to start production of his new key models, so he turned the production over to Stefan Bergsiek. Some of the Bergsiek models are presented.

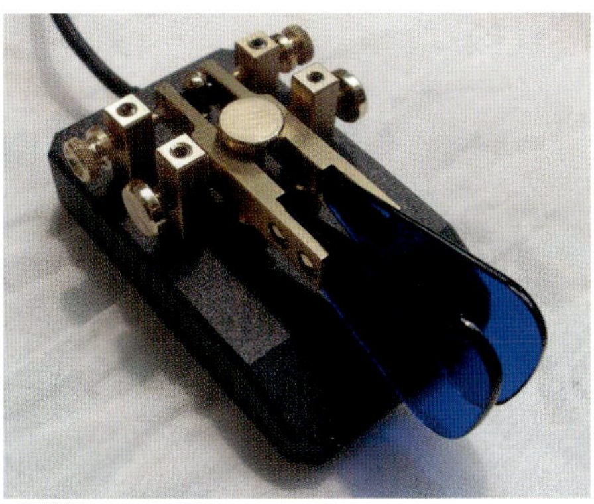

The Profi M—Schwarze Beschichtung with black base and brass parts.

Springs are no longer used in the Profi M series; paddle return is effected using incorporated magnets that can be individually adjusted for each paddle. The paddle arms are mounted using hardened steel cylindrical pins in brass sleeve bearing, ensuring complete elimination of play and backlash. Bergsiek claims this combination makes the paddle mounting completely maintenance free. Further, Bergsiek states another advantage of this paddle mounting method is that unlike a ball bearing, the lubrication cannot dry out and so over time make the paddle stiff or require new bearings, and that no adjustment of the bearings or paddle mounting is required.

The keys are completely constructed in brass and are available with various base plates, as well as different finger paddle colors (transparent, cherry red, blue, black); fingerpieces can be shaped according to customer specifications. Various versions of the Profi M are available with special finishes, including a black base, gold plating, chrome plating, or stainless steel. Other available options include polishing or glass pearl blasting of the bases. All keys can be supplied with knurled or plain polished adjustment screws. Paddle weights vary from 1 kg through 1.4 kg (2.2–3.1 lb.).

Snyder KP2 Paddle

Snyder paddles were built by Malcolm E. Snyder (KA5AEQ) around 1982. Snyder lived in Sapulpa, Oklahoma; he advertised his paddles as the "Pro's Choice." Snyder paddles, despite their obvious homebrew appearance, have developed a small cult following. Snyder offered several base options. Maintenance

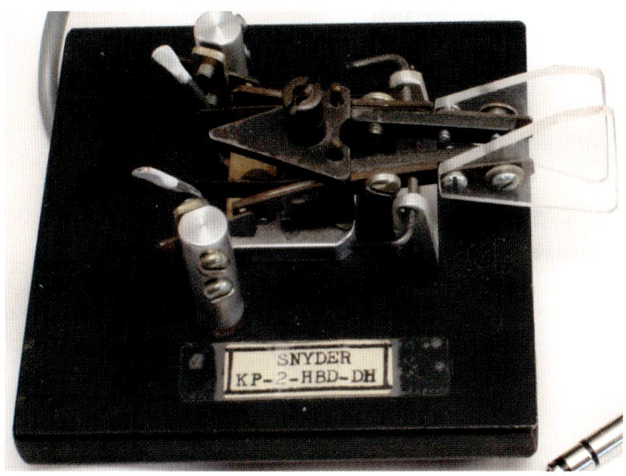

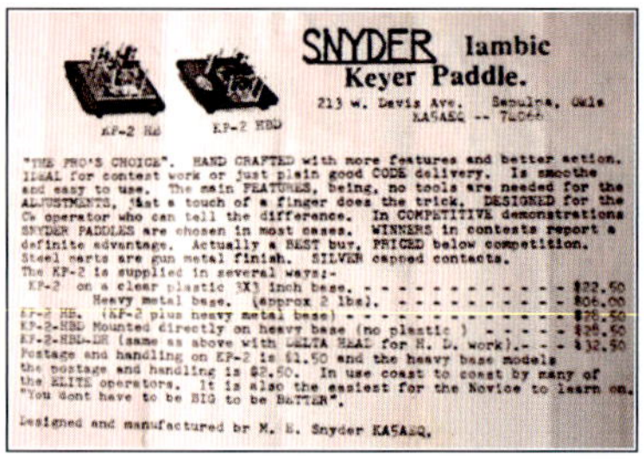

SNYDER Iambic Keyer Paddle.

213 W. Davis Ave. Sapulpa, Okla
KA5ASQ -- 74066

KP-2 HB KP-2 HBD

"THE PRO'S CHOICE". HAND CRAFTED with more features and better action. IDEAL for contest work or just plain good CODE delivery. Is smoothe and easy to use. The main FEATURES, being, no tools are needed for the ADJUSTMENTS, just a touch of a finger does the trick. DESIGNED for the CW operator who can tell the difference. In COMPETITIVE demonstrations SNYDER PADDLES are chosen in most cases. WINNERS in contests report a definite advantage. Actually a BEST buy, PRICED below competition. Steel parts are gun metal finish. SILVER capped contacts.

The KP-2 is supplied in several ways:-
KP-2 on a clear plastic 3X3 inch base. - - - - - - - - - - - - - - $22.50
Heavy metal base. (approx 2 lbs). - - - - - - - - - - - - $06.00
KP-2 HB. (KP-2 plus heavy metal base) - - - - - - - - - - - - - - - $28.50
KP-2-HBD Mounted directly on heavy base (no plastic) - - - - - $26.50
KP-2-HBD-DH (same as above with DELTA HEAD for H. D. work).- - - $32.50

Postage and handling on KP-2 is $1.50 and the heavy base models the postage and handling is $2.50. In use coast to coast by many of the ELITE operators. It is also the easiest for the Novice to learn on. "You dont have to be BIG to be BETTER".

Designed and manufactured by M. [illegible]. Snyder KA5ASQ.

A Snyder product data sheet from 1982.

suggestions included the use of dry graphite for the arm bearings, which was applied by using a pipe cleaner to draw the graphite through the bearings.

Taylor

Shown are three models of Houston Taylor paddles. Taylor (W0LPR) is a retired Missouri State University professor; he also made smaller magnetic iambic models. Taylor just enjoys making paddles and is not in production; supposedly less than 100 of various different models have been made. Taylor's keys are stamped with year of manufacture and a serial number; there were both spring and magnetic versions produced. A typical Taylor key might have sixty parts, forty-four of which are handmade. The bottom photo shows a Taylor magnetic version.

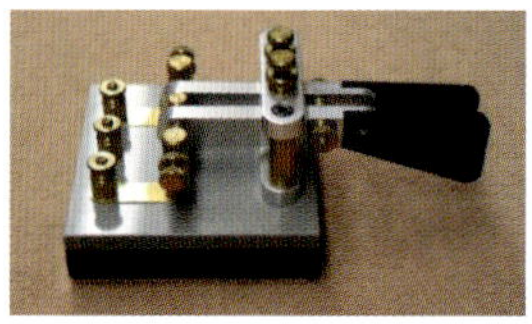

Teletek TY-1 and TY-1A

The Teletek paddle was first built in 1975, when George Zielinski (W9OAH at the time) determined a dual-lever version of the Joe Hills FYO design would not violate the Hills patent. At the same time, HAL Communications introduced their version of the FYO dual-lever paddle and threatened legal action against Teletek should they continue to sell their paddles. Unlike Teletek, HAL had formally licensed the manufacturing rights from Hills. Once the original production run of a few hundred Teletek paddles were sold they were discontinued, making the Teletek a very scarce device today. Within about a year the Bencher firm made contact with Zielinski, and negotiations resulted in an agreement allowing Bencher to take over production of the Teletek design.

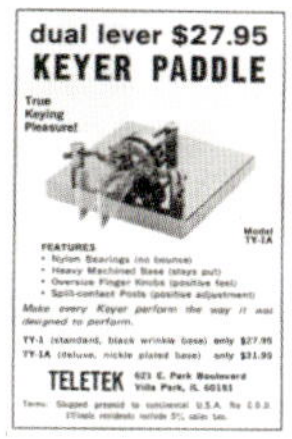

A Teletek ad from the October 1975 *Ham Radio*.

Ten-Tec KR1B/603 Paddle

Ten-Tec's Model 603 paddle is now known as the KR1B. The product release (right) describes this device. The KR1A is similar, but does not have the "Program" slide switch on the front panel.

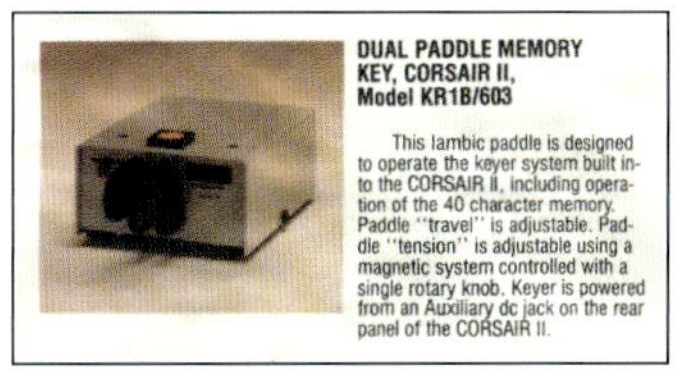

DUAL PADDLE MEMORY KEY, CORSAIR II, Model KR1B/603

This Iambic paddle is designed to operate the keyer system built into the CORSAIR II, including operation of the 40 character memory. Paddle "travel" is adjustable. Paddle "tension" is adjustable using a magnetic system controlled with a single rotary knob. Keyer is powered from an Auxiliary dc jack on the rear panel of the CORSAIR II.

Trac

Shown is a Trac paddle; this one was new in the box and removed for the photo. This version of their paddle was made by Trac Electronics of Buffalo, New York, 1978–1980.

TW Magpad

The TW MagPad was designed by Tom Withers (G3HGE), a CW operator for over sixty years. Tom is responsible for TW Electronics Ltd., the company behind the TW MagPad. G3HGE boasts that every paddle was personally tested and issues a signed certificate with each purchase as proof. The picture shows one of the production versions of Tom's dual-lever paddle. Features include a heavy brass base with brass frame, bearing plate, and contact/mounting posts. The MagPad paddle offers what Tom calls micro fine contact adjustments, with 4.5 mm contacts plated with 3 microns of 24k gold. Arm tension is via neodymium magnets. The arm pivots are 3 mm diameter steel mounted using four ball races. The paddle includes an Allen wrench for adjustments and a lifetime guarantee. Weight is 2.2 lb.

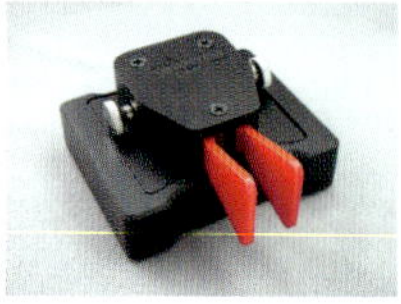

uniHAM UNI-730

The UNI-730 is a Chinese-made device, well thought out and constructed, with performance equal to paddles costing much more in the Western world. The UNI-730 dual paddle is a compact but solid paddle capable of standing up to the rigors of portable operation, as well as providing excellent service in the shack. The base measures 3 × 2½ in., with the levers extending another inch to the front. Despite its small footprint, the UNI-730 weighs just under one pound and it has non-skid pads on the bottom for stability. Contact spacing is adjusted easily without tools via the large thumb screws on either side of the paddle body. Spring tension is fixed for a light, precise action. Connection to the rig or keyer is via a standard 3.5 mm stereo phone jack on the back of the paddle body.

Unknown

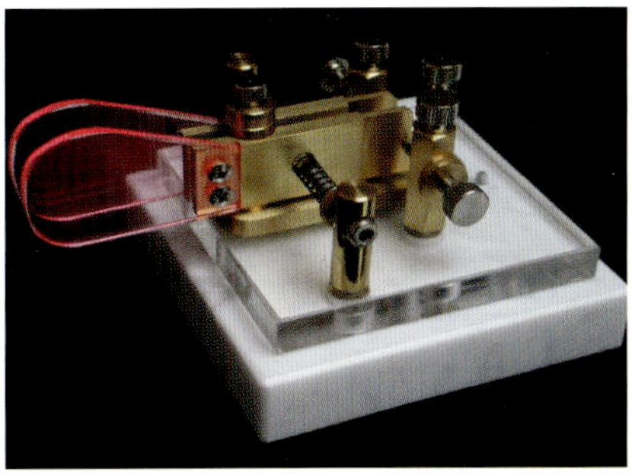

From the DK7JC collection, maker unknown.

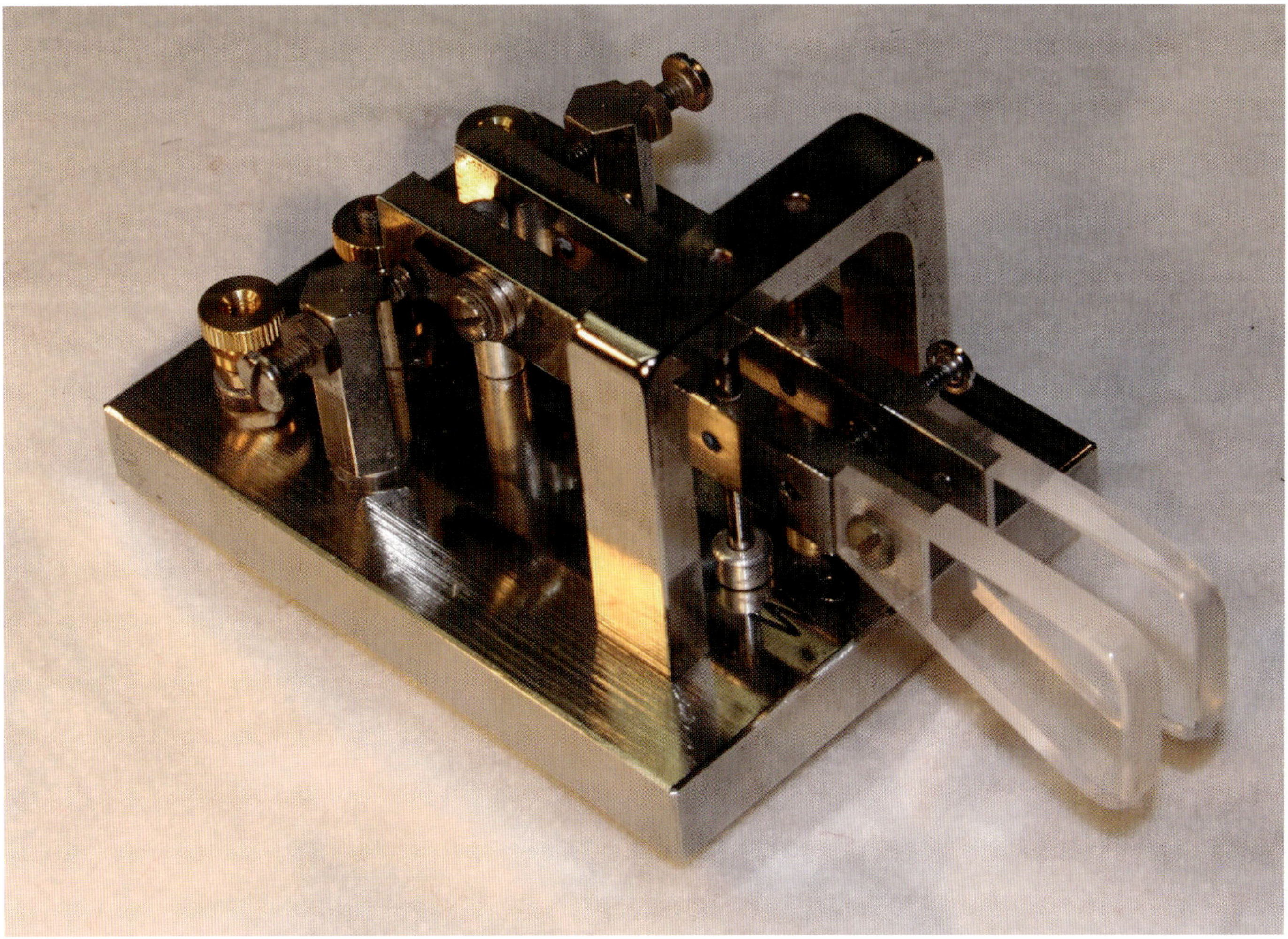

This paddle was made for the Johns Hopkins Applied Physics Laboratory ham club when they had the W3VD call (they are now W3APL). The club's call is engraved on the paddle base; the paddle's maker is unknown.

A dual-lever version of a torsion-bar key possibly built after a December 1982 *QST* article on torsion bar paddle design was published. This copyrighted photo was furnished by G7VFY, who bought the key from an elderly seller at a hamfest in England. The maker and further details about this device are unknown.

UR5CDX Paddles

The UR5CDX Eridan paddle (below) is made in the Ukraine and is available in two versions: the MX (chrome base) and MB (brass base). The paddle design uses a square shaped base with quad ball bearings for the paddle arms. The Eridan uses more rounded corners and edges in its design compared to other paddles in the line. Adjustments are provided for tension and contact spacing. The UR5CDX paddles use silver contacts. Paddle weight is 1.3 kg (2.9 lb.).

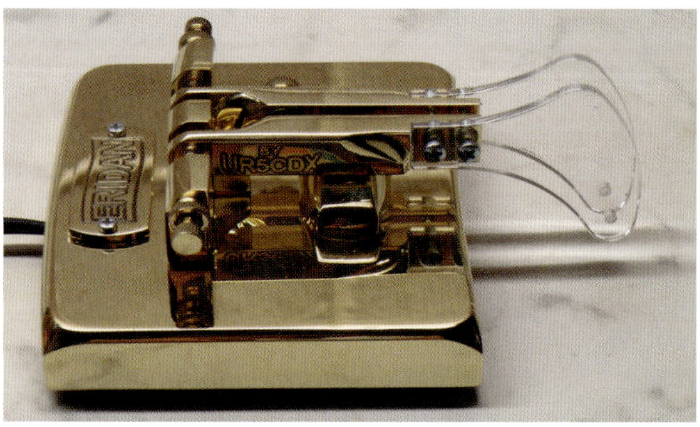

The CT Classic (top right) is not seen too often, but is a very attractive design with some variations on the FYO/Bencher approach. The CT 73 model (right) offers a matte black or chrome base with polished parts. It features a square-shaped base and solid silver contacts. Adjustments include the typical arm tension and contact gap. Note the polished paddle plaque on the base that includes the serial number. Like the other UR5CDX devices, this paddle is made in the Ukraine. Paddle weight is 1.4 kg (3 lb.).

The CT Europe X model has all of the standard UR5CDX paddle features and incorporates a round chromed base. The three concentric rings provide support for the arm pivots, tension adjustments, and the contact gap adjustments. This model is a bit lighter than other models, weighing 1.2 kg (2.6 lb.).

The CT 599 (below) utilizes a hand-crafted design featuring polished brass and black steel, double silver contacts, double ball bearings (4 in total), and magnetic tensioning. The quad ball bearing mechanism gives the paddle a unique, smooth operation and zero vertical pivot movement. The paddle is fully adjustable and weighs 1.3 kg (2.6 lb.). The paddle has a long lead terminated with the pre-connected shielded cable and a gold ¼ in. plug.

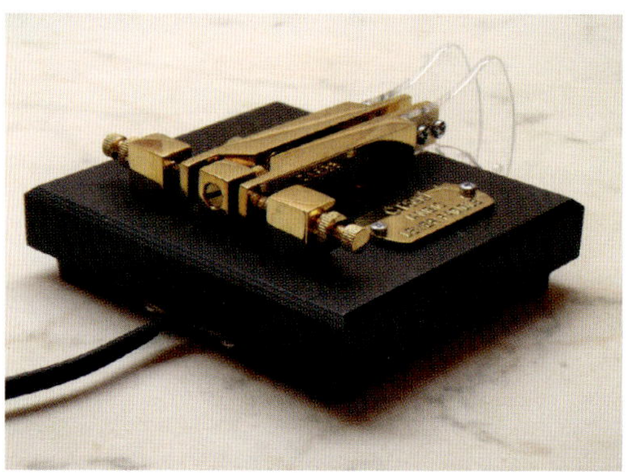

VE7QQ Glo-Key

The VE7QQ Glo-Key was described in a May 1967 *CQ* article by Albert Jackson (VE7QQ). The device has no moving parts, instead using two #328 miniature pilot lamps and two small solar cells with associated transistor switching circuitry. The user's fingers make or break the two light beams, producing a "contact" closure for triggering of a keyer. Jackson also designed several different capacitive touch paddles.

Vectronics KP-200 Series Paddles

Vectronics is a sister company of MFJ (see the MFJ-564 listing for a paddle description; the MFJ and Vectronics labeled paddles are essentially the same device).

Vespa Dourada (Golden Wasp) Paddle

Roberto Daniluk (PY2USD) fabricated the Golden Wasp paddle in his shop in Sao Paulo, Brazil. The Golden Wasp stood out for its handcrafted construction, ease of handling, and quality of construction. This paddle became a standard device in the shacks of Brazilian CW operators and attained popularity with many overseas users as well. PY2USD died on September 18, 2012, so this key is no longer being produced.

A Vespa Dourada (Golden Wasp paddle) made by PY2USD.

VIBROPLEX

In 1978, Vinnie La Hiff (John's son) sold the Vibroplex Company to Peter Garsoe. Garsoe had several other businesses he was involved with, including a small hand tool manufacturing company; these other business interests were in Portland, Maine. It was Garsoe's intention to move Vibroplex to Portland, where the facilities and personnel of the tool company could be shared to help produce Vibroplex keys. Garsoe undertook a renovation of machinery and tooling and set about taking a good look at the Vibroplex product line, and how it fit into the demands of the market.

Garsoe decided to stop production of the Lightning Bug and the Champion models. Of interest to the hams who preferred electronic keying Garsoe added a new key in 1979, called the Iambic. The Iambic looked roughly similar to the Vibro-Keyer, but it was a dual-lever device, using parts from the semi-automatic Original. In 1982, Garsoe added the Brass Racer and the Brass Racer EK-1 models to the line after purchasing the manufacturing rights from HAMCO.

Brass Racer

The Brass Racer came out in 1982, in response to the FYO paddle design being offered in various adaptations by HAMCO and Bencher. The Vibroplex Brass Racer is very similar to the HAMCO Scotia, but does not have the magnet locking screws on the frame. The parts are made from brass and the base is hardwood.

Brass Racer EK-1

The Vibroplex Brass Racer EK-1 is visually almost identical to the standard Brass Racer except for the speed adjustment knob on the right side, between the brass base plate and the hardwood base. The EK-1 keyer used the very common Curtis 8044 chip.

Square Racer

The Square Racer is also available with a chrome or brass base mounted on an attractive sub-base of hardwood. All versions of Brass Racer use magnetic return force in lieu of springs. The magnets slide back and forth, but there is no setscrew locking feature as appeared on similar HAMCO paddles. The arms are made of brushed brass.

A square base Brass Racer with black finish.

Dual-Lever (the Vibroplex Iambic)

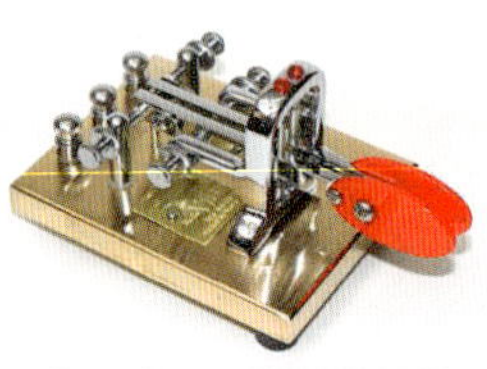

Several versions of the Vibroplex dual-lever model are shown. The Iambic (as Vibroplex calls it) was introduced in 1979, and was available with the standard gray base or as a chromed model called the DeLuxe, which also had jeweled bearings. The version called the Presentation used a 24 karat gold-plated brass plate mounted on top of the base; this model was first offered in 1983. The Presentation was advertised as having a wider range of sending speed due to its "super speed control main spring." Contacts are gold-plated, with tension and contact spacing adjustable. The Presentation offers solid color fingerpieces and a classic appearance. Vibroplex paddles are often the choice for bug users converting to a keyer.

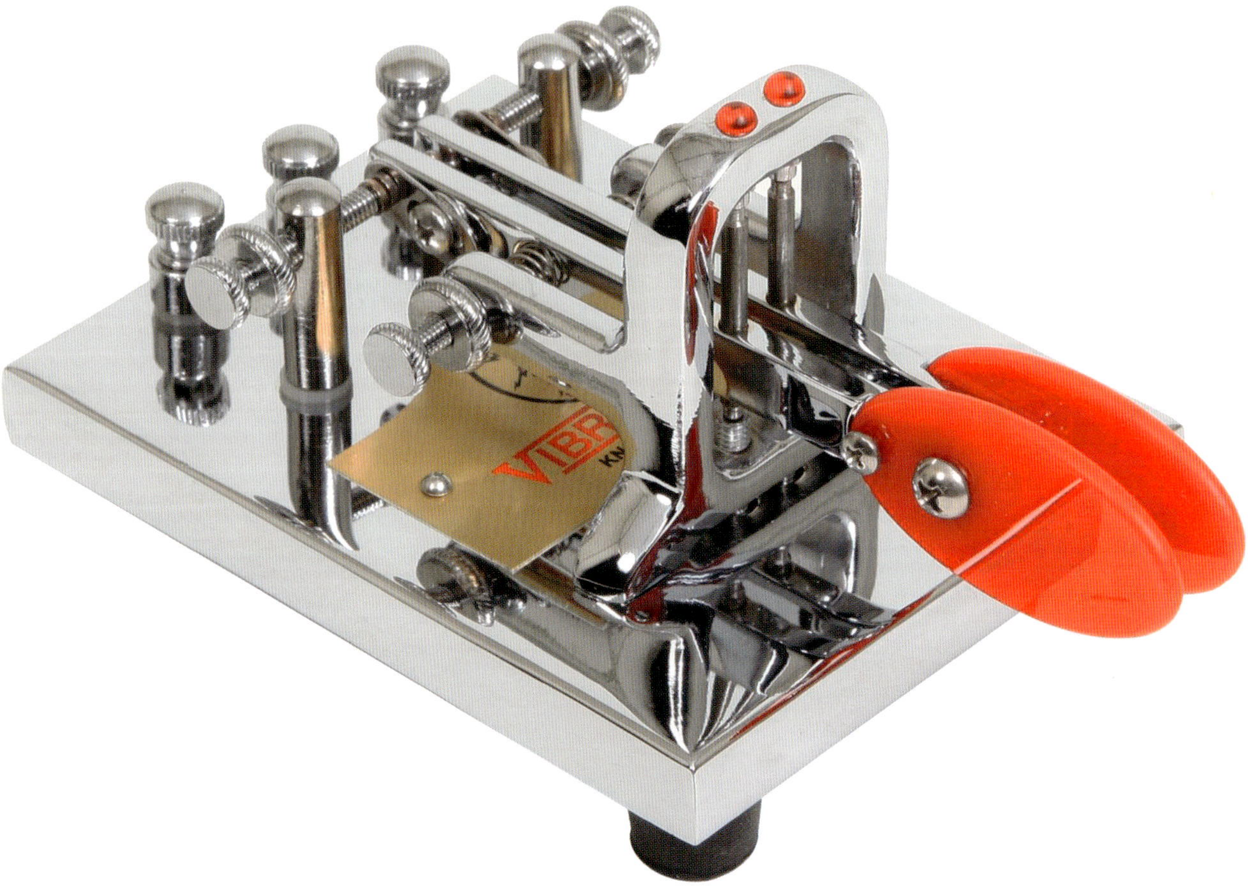

Vibrocube

In 2011, Vibroplex introduced the standard (black base) Vibrocube, followed by the all chrome version in 2012. The design goal for the Vibrocube was to make a durable and heavy paddle that would resist being moved around the operating desk when used by operators with a heavy hand. With a paddle weight of 6 lb. Vibroplex obviously met the "heavy" part of the goal. The base is cold-rolled steel and uses four non-skid rubber feet; contacts are silver. Paddle components are made of zinc, steel, and brass. The Vibrocube uses spring tension for arm return, and oversized fingerpieces are used on both versions of the paddle.

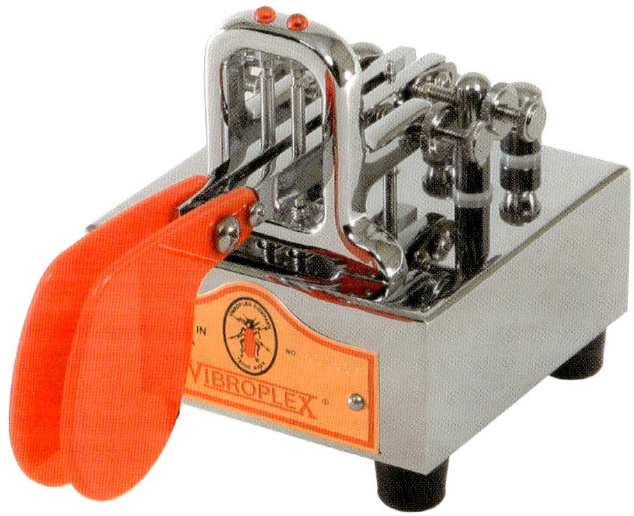

Venus

The Vibroplex Venus is one of the rarest Vibroplex models; it somehow "flies under the radar" for many collectors, who perhaps concentrate only on the semi-automatic bugs. Betsy (WB4ZYK) of Vibroplex has spoken about Venus paddle production. According to Betsy, there were three runs of ten paddles each. A few were scrapped or used for parts, leaving only twenty-four as the total made. The three runs occurred in 2001 and 2002, and the Venus was no longer sold after June 2002. Tim Soxman (W3ZVT) reported many of the first run were sold to collectors even before Vibroplex formally announced the Venus was available; list price for the Venus was $650.

The Venus key was handcrafted with chrome parts on a heavy 3.5 in. round base. The paddle incorporated a dual-lever design based on a K8FF prototype and used magnetic tension for arm centering, with red fingerpieces and an attached cord. The keys were available by special order, with fabrication taking about three months. The design and decision to try a limited production run were influenced by the success of the N2DAN paddle; the extent of the influence is seen in the choice of the "Venus" name and its obvious planetary relationship to the N2DAN Mercury.

It is reported at least one gold-plated Venus was made, and also that at least one painted base Venus exists. The Venus did not carry the typical Vibroplex nameplate, but was engraved with "Vibroplex Venus" and a serial number on the bottom of the base.

ZN Ultimate

The N3ZN version of the Vibrokeyer is called the ZN Ultimate. When Scott Robbins took over leadership of Vibroplex, one of his visions for the company was to produce a key based on some of the successful designs of the independent keymakers. The ZN Ultimate is a good example of how Scott is working to fulfill that vision. This key uses 6 ball bearings and opposing magnetic tensioning. Each trunnion pin has a small round ball bearing at the top and bottom of the pin. Each lever arm has a magnet installed; the other half of the magnet pair is mounted on the magnetic tension adjusting screws. Mainframe parts are chrome plated cast zinc; the base is chrome plated steel. Contacts are 99.4% silver.

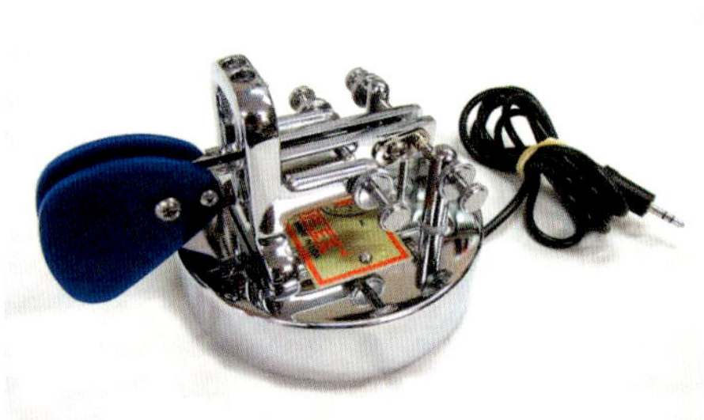

VIP Paddle (ZS1EL)

Vidi (ZS1EL) makes these affordable paddles from his home in South Africa. The bases use steel stock, with Perspex arm mounting blocks and fingerpieces. The paddles also use brass for the arms and incorporate relay contacts for electrical closure.

VK2DLF

Georg Goerge (VK2DLF) lives in Sydney and builds a whole line of impressive keys, including these beautiful paddles based on his interleaved lever design. Shown are his Model 901 with a polished brass base and the 901 with a blue hammertone base. This paddle uses a unique arm design that allows the opposing arms to fit together and pivot on one set of ball bearings; there is another set in the arms themselves. Spring tensioning is used for lever arm return. Georg also uses stainless steel hardware on this model.

VK2YYO Paddle

Peter (VK2YYO) indicates he built three of these paddle models years ago: one went to a friend, he kept one, and this is the other. Peter is a toolmaker by trade and has over forty-three years of experience.

VK3CGB Paddle

Paddle made by Chris (VK3CGB) with some arm design similarities to the Brass Racer. The paddle arms use magnetic repulsion for centering.

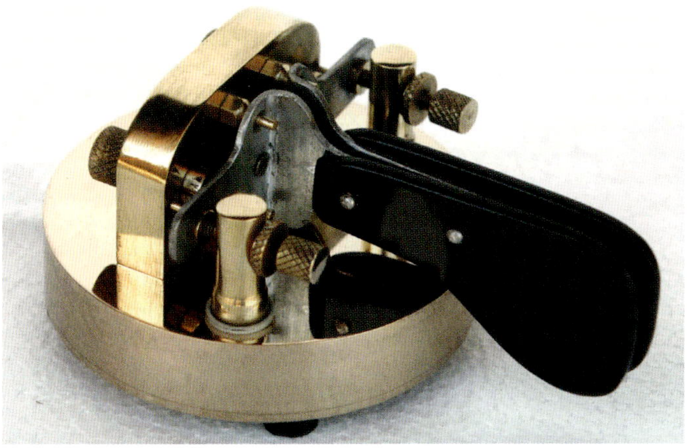

VK3DBD Paddles

Some paddles made by David (VK3DBD). The paddles use magnetic repulsion for arm centering and fine-threaded adjustments.

W5TOM Dual Hand Key Paddle

Tom Morton (W5TOM) built this version of a dual-lever key using a pair of J-37 straight keys. The two J-37s are mounted on a special frame, which in turn is mounted on a three pound steel base. The straight keys are angled down so the resulting fingerpiece height from the table is correct. Tom's implementation of this concept is nicely done, and is likely very enjoyable to use. Tom said he always wondered what kind of paddles would result from the adaptation, and his notes about the key correctly predicted the quality of the result would be determined by the ability of the J series keys to meet basic paddle and key requirements: adjustment precision, adjustment ease, and the ability to hold adjustments. According to Tom, the J-37 meets these requirements with its leaf spring, unlike the J-38, which has a stiff coil spring.

The J-37s allow a very small gap to be set that yields a feather touch that can be locked down without need for readjustment. Tom said the finished paddles preformed far better than his best anticipations while giving a very pleasing and unusual tactile feedback.

W5JH Black Widow Paddle

Jerry Haigwood (W5JH) offered this Black Widow paddle in kit form. The paddle used two magnets and a spring to control arm movement. The design incorporated four ball bearings and offered arm tension adjustment that could be locked in place.

W9WBL

W9WBL was Stan Heils, who became a silent key in early 2009. Stan's designs are considered revolutionary, and set standards for low mass arms and maximized actuation leverage ratios that are followed today by high performance paddle designers. It is known the V2L came before the V22, and it is generally thought the single-lever (more accurately the VSL, or vertical single-lever) was the first of Stan's paddles (a photo of the single-lever is shown in chapter 4). It is interesting to note Stan expressed a preference for sleeve bearings, as he felt ball bearings were not necessary for arms that only rotated fractions of degrees, but some collectors report the use of roller bearings. The WBL designs offered adjustments for lever height, fingerpiece spacing, contact spacing, and just about everything else. PA3BWK maintains a WBL owner's list, showing a V22

A W9WBL V22 model.

MODEL V2L FEATURES:

- SOLID GOLD CONTACTS
- SATIN FINISH SOLID BRASS KEY ASSEMBLY
- ALL STAINLESS STEEL SCREWS
- 2.2 POUNDS OF STEEL WEIGHTS
- CAPABLE OF SPEEDS
- EASILY ADJUSTABLE CONTACT SPACING AND SPRING FORCES
- SMALL FOOT PRINT
- EXTRA REMOVABLE FEET INCLUDED
- GOLD PLATED RCA JACK OUTPUTS
- HARDWOOD FINGER PIECES
- ADJUSTABLE FINGER HEIGHT
- ADJUSTABLE FINGER SPACING

A W9WBL paddle product data sheet.

A W9WBL V2L model.

high serial number of 147 and a V2L high serial number of 181. All of the WBL paddles appear to include a magnetic strip on the inside; N2DE states this strip is to hold a small hex wrench. Fingerpieces are polished cocobolo wood.

WB9LPU

Pictured is Rich's small ball-pivot dual-lever paddle using 3⁄16 in. delrin balls. The paddle features adjustable cocobolo wood fingerpieces and is made of brass and aluminum parts mounted on a cocobolo wood base.

As Rich relates on his website, he was away from ham radio for twenty-five years, returning to the hobby in 1998. His interest in homebrew devices, coupled with a desire to find some good keys, prompted Rich to work on some new paddle designs. He started out making large keys and paddles, but soon shifted his attention to small and portable instruments.

Rich ended up with what he called his "ball-pivot design" and describes it as follows:

> The lever force is provided by a compression spring that pushes the lever against a fixed plate. The lever pivots with respect to the fixed support on two precision balls that fit into milled pockets at each side of the lever. The balls can be of brass, nylon, Teflon, delrin, etc. The ball-pivot holds the lever in alignment while it moves, and the lever force is provided by a compression or tension spring. The spring force also holds the pieces together when the lever is at rest. In my experience so far, the ball-pivot provides adequate stability and a crisp and smoother "feel." This basic mechanism can be used either in straight keys or single and double paddles. Some recent designs use miniature ball bearings rather than the ball-pivot, and some use magnetic repulsion instead of springs.

Some different WB9LPU designs are seen in various other chapters of this book, including some single-lever paddles and some fully automatic keys. Rich said that all of his key designs have been used successfully on the air. None of his designs have been optimized for high speed keying, as Rich is still in the 15–18 wpm range; he promises that as he gets faster so will his paddles.

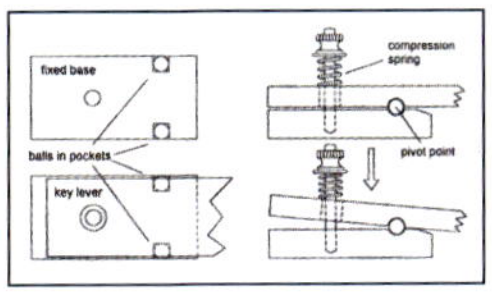

The WB9LPU ball-pivot design.

WD5AGO

The paddle shown is believed to be made by Tommy Henderson (WD5AGO), who was licensed in 1977, and developed an interest in 2 meters and above CW/SSB work in the early '80s. Tommy started home building equipment for HF QRPing in the early '90s, and in 2001 received the ARRL's Professional Instructor of the Year Award.

WK4DS Excalibur

WK4DS is David Saylors, who runs a machine shop in Trenton, Georgia. Although David's designs impressed some very critical paddle reviewers, in the end they proved too costly in time and money to be made; each paddle took some thirty-five hours of fabrication time. Figure out what just the labor from a talented guy like David should cost, add the price of materials, and you can estimate what a paddle like the Excalibur should be worth. Analyze the short-lever design, use of precision bearings, low angular momentum, fingerpiece-to-contact ratio of 1:1, and you get the idea that David really understood what makes a paddle feel so special to use.

The WK4DS Excalibur has sort of an art deco look with the sculpted base, and David added a decorative cut around the edge of the top piece. WK4DS recommends "Nevr-Dull" to clean the brass base. This Excalibur (S/N 005) was made in 2006, and uses a polished brass base and amazing experimental 72 tpi adjustment screws. David typically uses 40 tpi, but tried making screws as fine as 80 tpi; he wanted the finest adjustments in the paddle market. The 72 tpi on the paddle give 0.0138 in. per revolution; they are called National Special threads, one step above National Extra Fine.

You can read more about David and his designs in an article he wrote for the K9YA *Telegraph Newsletter* (June 2006). Unfortunately these unique, attractive, and well-engineered paddles are no longer being offered.

WV7U (W7GP-Built)

Although the heading calls this device a WV7U paddle, Hank Ball (WV7U) said this paddle was made by a friend, Chuck Curtis (W7GP), in Bozeman, Montana. Chuck has a small machine shop in his home and wanted a better CW operator like Hank to check out the paddle. The paddle initially had a bit of a rough appearance, with gouges, scratches, extra holes, etc., so Hank re-made some of the parts and polished the pieces to give this result; he describes the paddle:

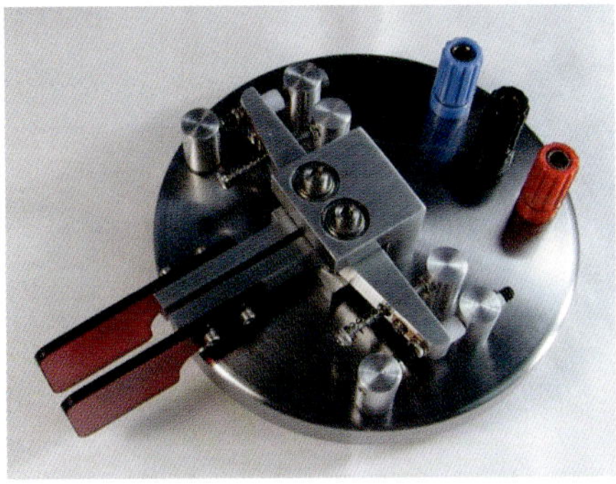

> Except for the base, most of the parts on this paddle are aluminum. For weight, the base is steel (not stainless) that was sprayed with a clear coat to keep it from rusting. The paddle levers pivot on shafts supported at both ends by sealed ball bearings which are glued into the central bearing block. Small setscrews and some glue hold the levers on the shafts. The levers themselves are made from slices of large extruded aluminum angle. The contacts are silver buttons scrounged from relays and are soldered to the stationary adjustment screws. Since the contacts couldn't be soldered to the aluminum levers, they were left attached to small pieces of their original relay armatures which were then screwed into the levers.
>
> Tension is provided by ballpoint pen springs which are coaxial with the tension adjustment screws. The springs also give an additional current return path to ground for the moving contacts in addition to the path through the ball bearings. All adjustment screws are held in place with jam nuts. This method is simple to construct, but adjustments can be a tedious trial and error procedure because the 4-40 threads are fairly coarse and the screw gets loose and wobbly as soon as the jam nut is loosened. Short of going to a fine precision thread, a way around this might be to use split posts with a pinch screw like Bencher does on their paddles.
>
> The white caps on the return stop screws are Teflon bumpers to quiet the return click. No contact spacing drift problems have been noticed, which you might see due to these deforming over time, but you could argue that Teflon might not be the right material to use here.

Since the initial adjustments were made everything on this paddle has stayed put for years, so no changes have been made to the design. Hank feels this is a solid and stable paddle with a very nice feel. That, and the fact it was made by a good friend, make it his favorite.

Yugo Slovenia

A Slovenian version of the Ham-Key paddle.

Zach Paddles

Zach paddles are handmade keys fabricated in the Czech Republic by OK1TN. The photos show a traditional design and a new precision made magnetic. A single-lever model is also available, as well as versions with a brushed brass base or a polished base. Although similar to the Bencher design, the traditional Zach paddles use a separate spring for adjustment of each arm. OK1TN's use of a claw-foot base makes that version of the Zach paddle unique. The magnetic model (below) offers short, lightweight alloy arms with four ball bearings and silver contacts. Micro-threaded screws are used for contact adjustments.

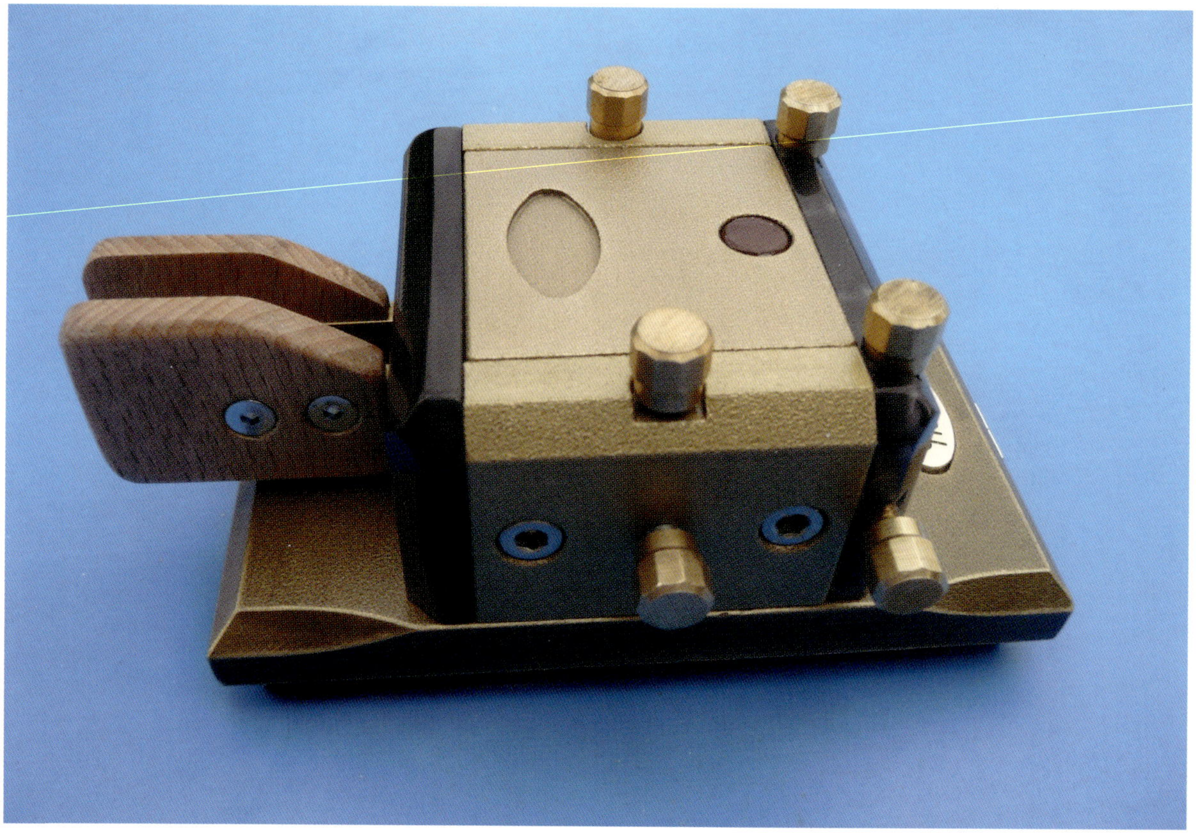

ZL2JJ Zedder Paddle

Peter (ZL2JJ) designed and built a limited number of these paddles around 1994. As a finishing touch, he engraved the new owner's name on a plate affixed to the top of the bearing block. The design incorporates twin arms, with bearings on the top and bottom of each arm. Spring tension and contact gap adjustments are provided, with fine-pitch threaded screws with locknuts allowing for extremely small settings that do not vary as the key is used. The paddle's base is bronze, cast in a home-built furnace in Peter's workshop. Paddle contacts are a silver alloy; total weight is about 5 lb. Peter estimated each paddle required about forty hours of construction time.

6 Portable/Miniature/QRP Paddles

Although miniature and QRP-oriented paddles are not recent creations, increasing availability of QRP transceivers, such as the Elecraft KX3, has allowed many hams to take along their high performance rigs when they travel, hike, bike, or camp. For the CW operator, this means a quality take-along paddle is a necessity.

The terms portable, miniature, or QRP paddle sound similar enough that one would assume the categories are synonymous, but each term can actually describe a very different device. This chapter on portable, miniature, and QRP paddles presents single and dual-lever devices, and even some that include built-in keyers. Some reviewers have argued reducing the size of a paddle (and therefore the weight) renders it less usable. Consideration must be given to the reasons the paddle was built and its design goals. Was a particular miniature paddle built to demonstrate the machining skills of the builder, or was the paddle designed to meet a specific purpose, or to emulate the feel of a full-sized paddle? With proper design and focus on the goals of the designer, small paddles can simulate the responsiveness and usability of their big brothers, and impart the same feel to the operator as a top-of-the-line three or four pound key. While there are some showpiece miniatures that do a good job of demonstrating the maker's machining skills, what is presented in this chapter are highly functional and in most cases unique devices that have met their design goals and then some.

AC7AZ Miniature Paddle

An AC7AZ miniature dual-lever paddle. Mark (AC7AZ) reports he only made about fourteen of these miniature keys.

American Morse Equipment Porta-Paddle

This is a Porta-Paddle made by Doug (W6AME—AME is also American Morse Equipment). It is mounted on the optional powder-coated base. The paddle is actually their first version of the Porta-Paddle; many prefer the design of this earlier version over the "II" version. The Porta-Paddle is CNC machined from aluminum then blue anodized.

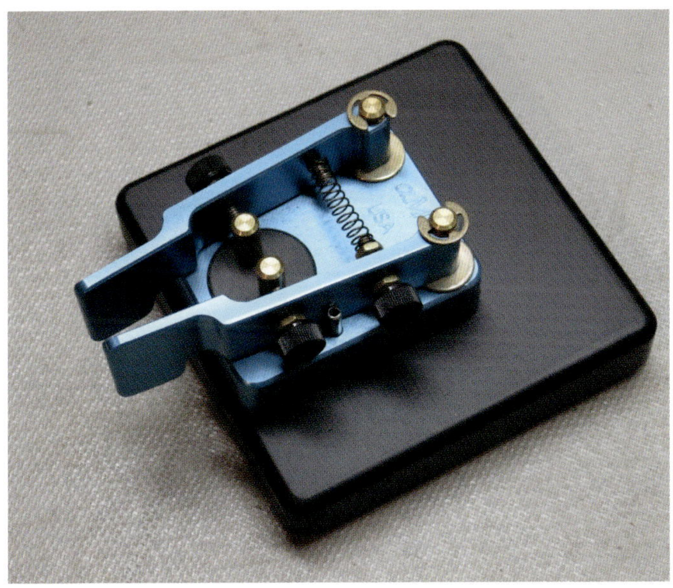

American QRP Key Manufacturing Company

The two paddles shown are by Gil Kost (W3MKE) of American QRP Key Manufacturing Company, based in Baltimore, Maryland. Both single-lever and dual-lever designs are shown; the dual-lever is mounted on a bicycle handlebar.

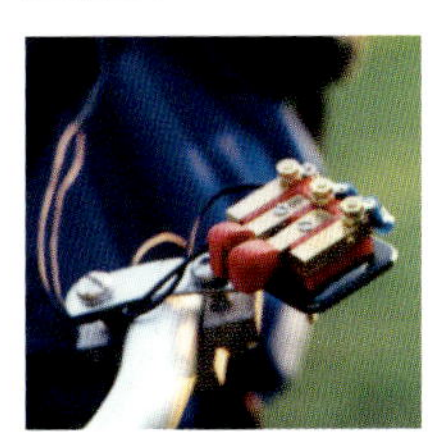

Arizona Scorpion

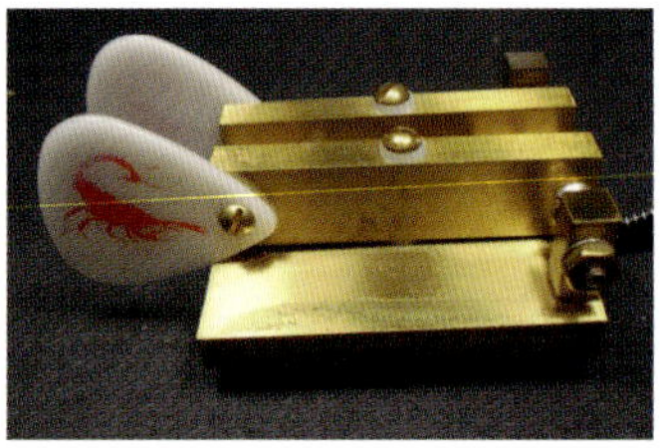

The Scorpion paddle was sold as a kit by the Arizona QRP club. The paddle was designed as a small portable unit so users could easily take it along on outings, such as hiking trips. The Scorpion is made of brass and the base measures about 2 in. square. The fingerpieces include the scorpion emblem of the Arizona QRP club.

Begali Portable/Traveler Paddles

Begali's Adventure dual-lever paddle has a base made from stainless steel, with paddle arms and fingerpieces made from a lightweight aluminum alloy. Other main components are gold-plated, and the contacts are solid gold. The Adventure uses magnets to create the arm return force. Paddle arms use two precision bearings. Begali offers several mounting brackets that allow this key to be used with the Elecraft KX3, Elecraft KX1, or Yaesu FT817. Once mounted, the key can be swiveled at various angles for operator comfort. Begali also offers a magnetic desktop base that allows use of the Adventure while detached from the radio in a fixed location. The combined weight of the key and base is about half a pound. The contact spacing is adjustable, as is the arm return force.

The Begali Adventure Mono paddle, as the name suggests, is a single-lever device. In addition to sharing the materials characteristics of the Adventure dual-lever, the Mono uses an ingenious mechanism consisting of three levers for a clearly defined center position, making it mechanically even more complex than the dual-lever Adventure. As with the dual-lever, the Mono offers contact spacing and tension adjustments, and similar mounting options for radio and desktop use.

The Magnetic Traveler Light's (right and top right) design features include precision bearings, repelling magnets, and micro-threaded adjustments. Gold contacts are standard. The Traveler Light is available in blue and black finishes. This paddle also comes with a leg strap and dust protector. It is aimed at the needs of the traveling user, backpacker, hiker, or QRP enthusiast. The Magnetic Traveler Light folding base protects the fingerpieces during transport, and in the open position provides stability for the paddle during use. Paddle weight is about 1.5 pounds, and it comes with a strap to fasten it to your leg.

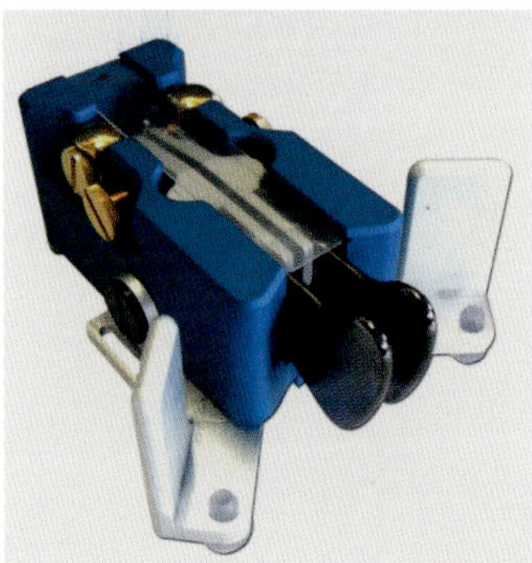

Begali Magnetic Traveler Light dual-lever paddle in blue finish with its fold-out legs extended.

CW Mini-Touch Paddle

The CW Mini-Touch P6 dual paddle is housed in a black metal case; fingerpieces/arms are gold-plated. The key measures 2 × 3.5 × 1.5 in., and is advertised as needing no adjustment and having no contacts to wear out. Key weight is 4.5 oz. and the power source is a 9 volt battery.

DK1WE Squeeze Key

Englmar Wenk (DK1WE) produced this dual-lever squeeze key he called the "Squeeky." The levers are mounted at 45 degree angles; each lever is independently adjustable. The diagonal movement of the levers was advertised to be more comfortable to use. The paddle's frame is anodized aluminum and the levers are polished brass. The key uses silver contacts with adjustable contact gap.

Elecraft KX Series Paddles

The Elecraft KXPD1 designed for the KX1 QRP transceiver. The paddle is shown (below) with an aftermarket base and mounting bracket that allows the paddle to be used as a desktop device. The KXPD1 as originally designed mounted directly to the front of the KX1 transceiver.

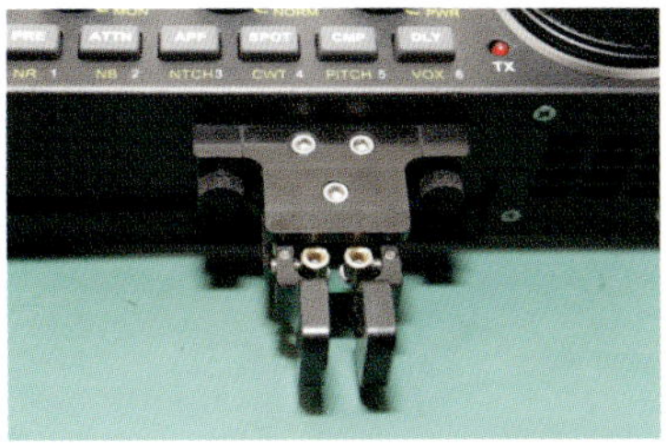

An Elecraft KXPD3, designed to mount directly to the front of a KX3 transceiver.

Frattini Mini

Several versions of the Frattini paddle are shown: in brass, chrome, or black-base finishes. No matter which base, it is a beautiful paddle. Frattini uses brass for the paddle body and silver contacts. Paddle parts, such as the screws, are highly polished inox (inoxydable) steel, also known as stainless steel. The paddles shown are about 2.75 × 2.3 × 0.5 in. and weigh about 1 lb. 9 oz.

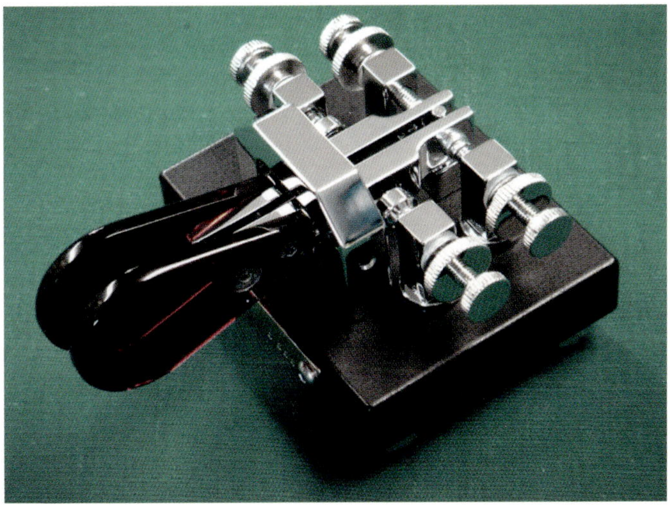

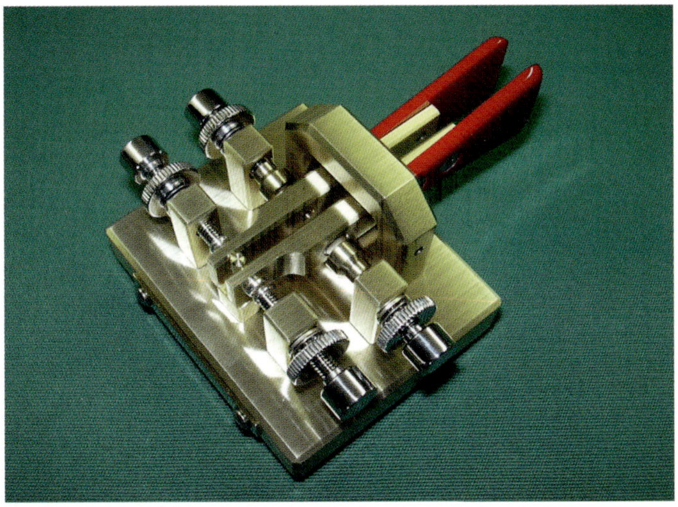

G4ZPY Miniature

Here is a G4ZPY miniature "3 in 1" twin paddle; options available were nickel plated brass or polished brass. The bottom photo is one of Gordon's miniature single-lever paddles.

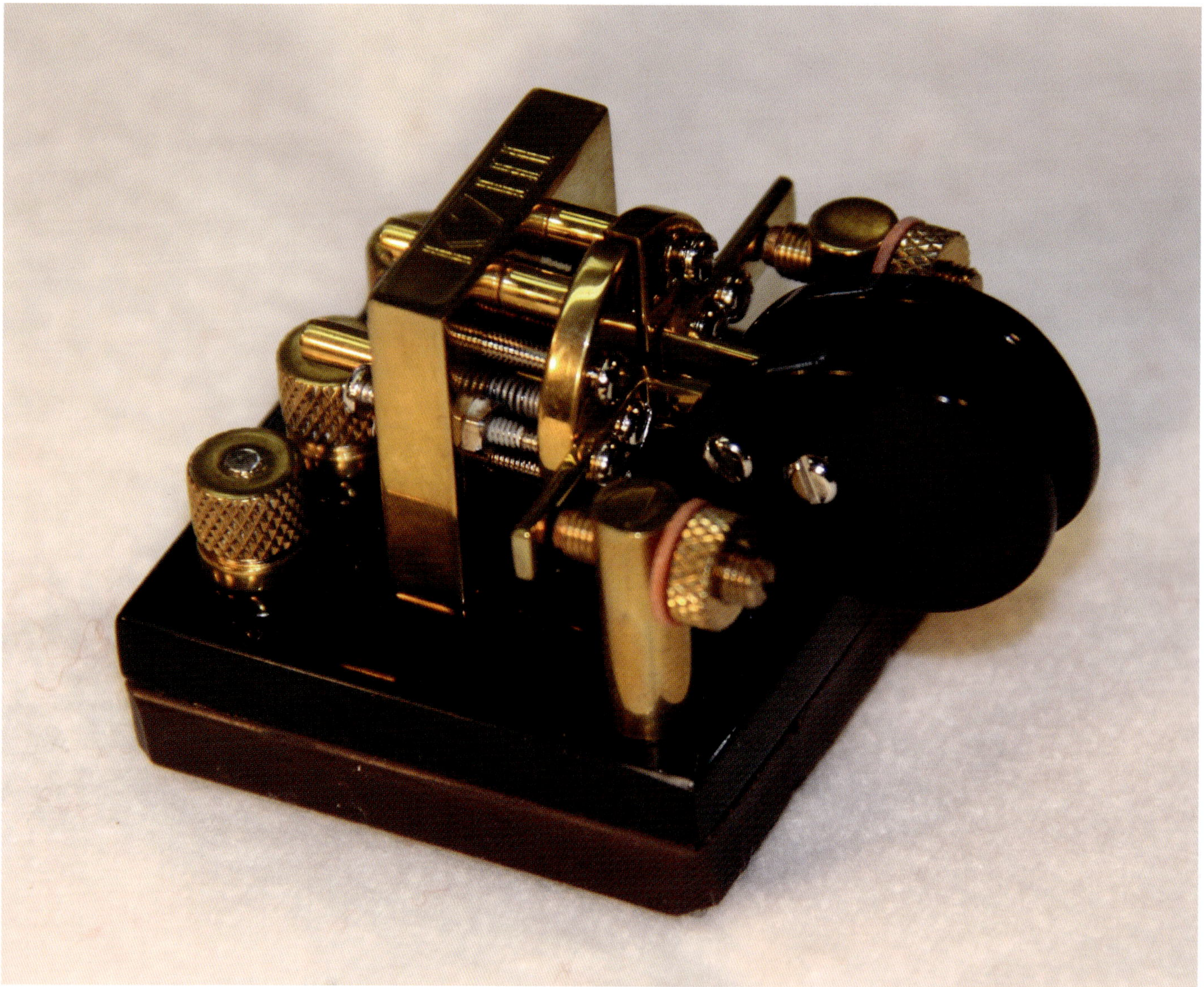

GHD Miniature Paddles

Two versions of the GM307 are shown. GHD also offered a heavy base or wooden base as an option. The paddle also included a Plexiglas cover; the photos show it both in place and removed.

GHD also produced a travel paddle (immediately below) using spring return on the arms. It was advertised as a portable paddle with retractable levers. Included was an attached cable with stripped/tinned ends for easy installation of a plug.

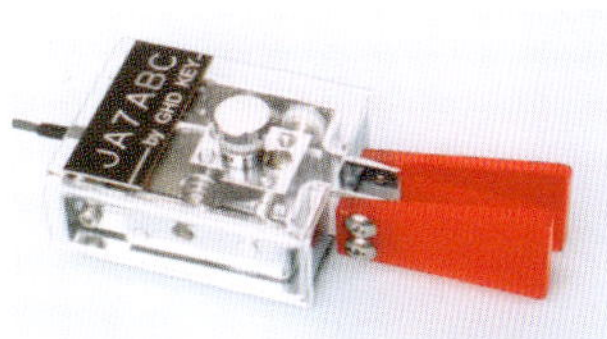

The GHD Micro Paddle with red fingerpieces. This very small paddle measures $1\frac{5}{8} \times 1\frac{15}{16}$ in. and weighs 3.5 oz.

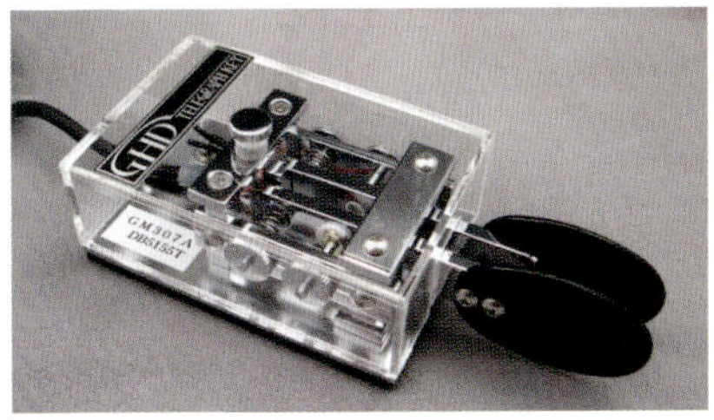

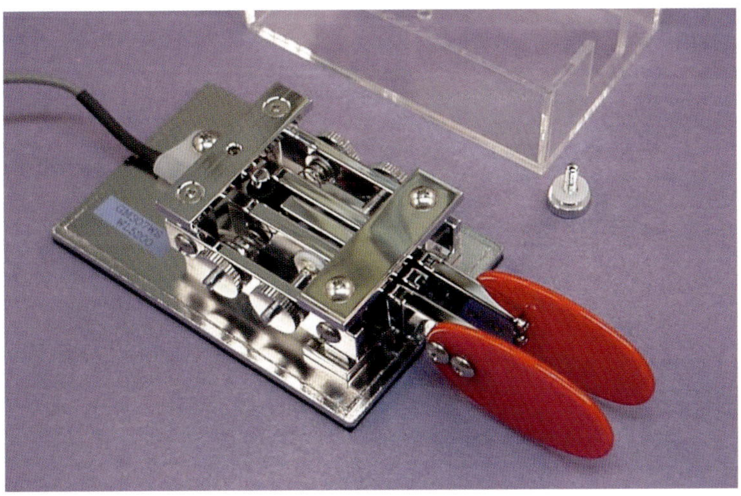

Hamshop Touch Paddle

The Hamshop is a Czechoslovakian company that produces this small touch paddle. Hamshop has experimented with different touch paddles for quite some time, and their designers report that many versions of this paddle were tried, including transistor and CMOS designs. The final version uses capacitive touch sensors from ATMEL. The fingerpieces can be any shape, depending on operator preference. A 3 volt power source is required; an internal battery holder is shown. Power consumption during keying is 1 mA; standby power is much less.

James Research Permaflex Key

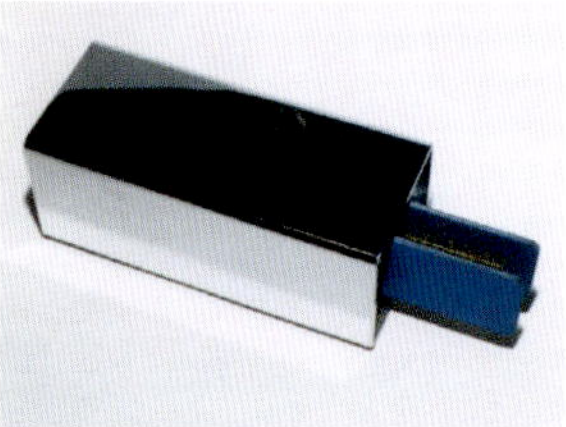

The James Research Company introduced this key in 1968, in response to some new keying problems when using paddles with solid state keyers; specifically, issues due to corroded silver contacts and contact bounce. The James Research paddle uses gold-diffused silver contacts rated to 8 amps. The paddle design uses fiberglass epoxy arms (without pivots) and a claimed benefit is the elimination of contact bounce. An additional feature is that the paddle slides out of the enclosure (right) for adjustments. The Permaflex key was reviewed in the December 1968 issue of *73*.

The K8FF NorCal Paddle

Wayne Smith (K8FF) is the designer of the Vibroplex Code Warrior Jr. paddle. Before Vibroplex bought the rights for this paddle and started producing the Code Warrior Jr., the paddle was sold as a kit by the NorCal QRP Association. Wayne's design was submitted to NorCal as an entry in their paddle design contest, which it won and was the basis for the NorCal paddle kits that followed.

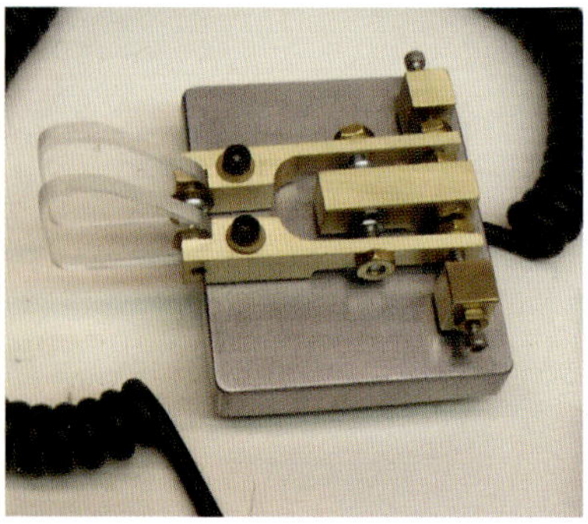

K8RA P-2 Jr.

The P-2 Jr. is small in size (2 × 2½ in.) and weighs 1 pound (0.46 kg). The base is made from ⅝ in.-thick solid brass stock. The paddle operates as smoothly as the larger paddle. The P-2 Jr. is shown with optional rosewood and oak paddles.

LTA AMIO

The LTA (Llavas Telegraphicas Artesanas) Model AMIO was handcrafted in the Balearic Islands of Spain. The key is a miniature dual-lever device with olive wood fingerpieces and gold-plated parts. The paddle base is 5 × 5 cm. (1.97 × 1.97 in.) and weighs 294 g (10.4 oz.).

March Miniatures

Michael March produced very few of this gray rectangular-based device. It features a hammertone finish and magnetic repulsion for arm return to neutral.

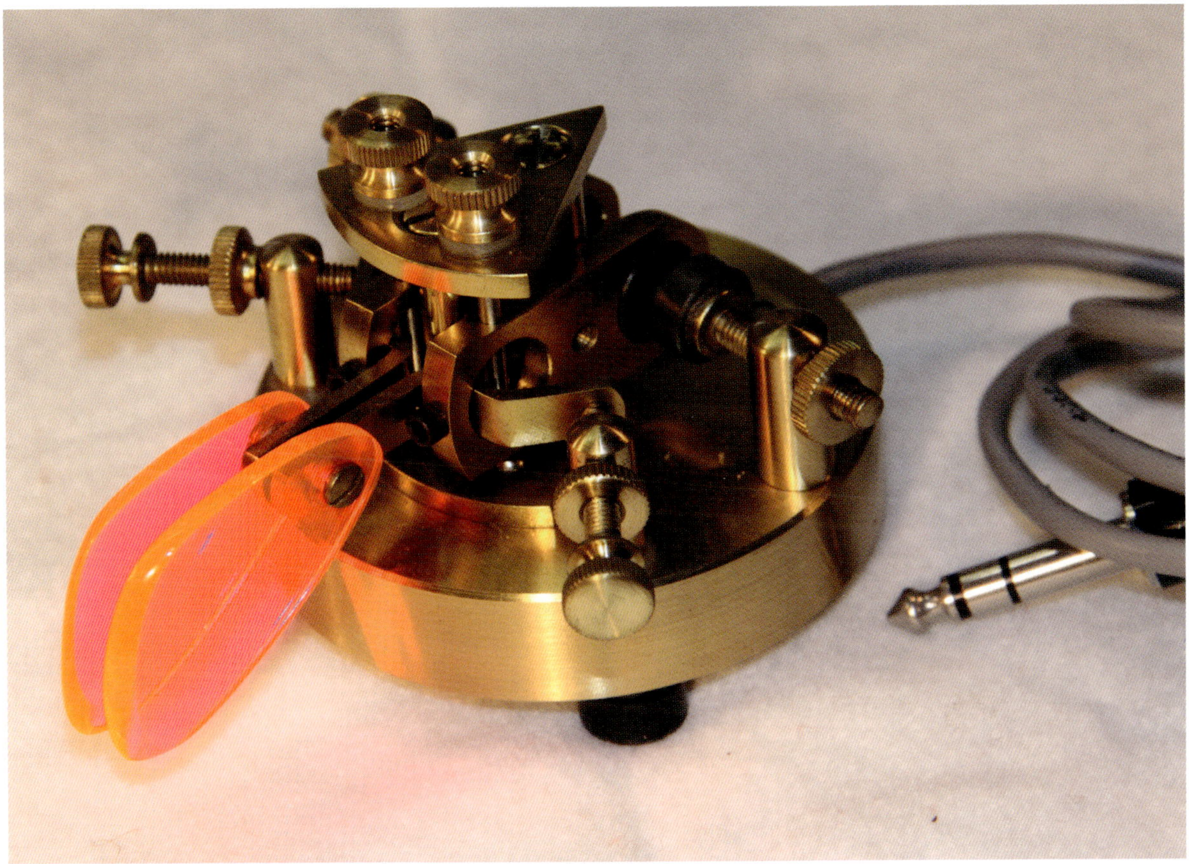

A rare R3-a style paddle with 3 in. round base. Communication with Michael March indicated he only made a couple of this small-diameter model.

N3ZN Miniature Paddles

N3ZN is Tony Baleno of Pittsburg, Pennsylvania. This is an early version of his ZN-QRP paddle, which is no longer being produced.

The black-base ZN-QRP is the latest version of N3ZN's QRP paddle. The base measures $\frac{3}{4} \times 2\frac{1}{4} \times 2\frac{1}{4}$ in. and the paddle weighs approximately 1 lb. 4 oz.

This device (right) is the latest dual-lever mini-paddle made by N3ZN called the ZN-miniMITE. This paddle has all the features of its bigger brothers, including 3 ball bearing per lever arm, magnetic return, silver contact points, 56 tpi stainless steel adjustment screws, and carbon fiber fingerpieces. The N3ZN designs feature adjustments that can be made without special tools. Tony's paddles have a reputation for holding their settings over time and use, all without using locking thumbwheels. The ZN-miniMITE is on a $\frac{5}{8} \times 1\frac{3}{4} \times 1\frac{3}{4}$ in. base and weighs 13 oz.

ZN-2A is essentially a miniature round-base model. The ZN-2A has been discontinued; there is a similar newer model that uses shortened arms. Some of Tony's earliest designs used arms a bit longer than his current paddle offerings.

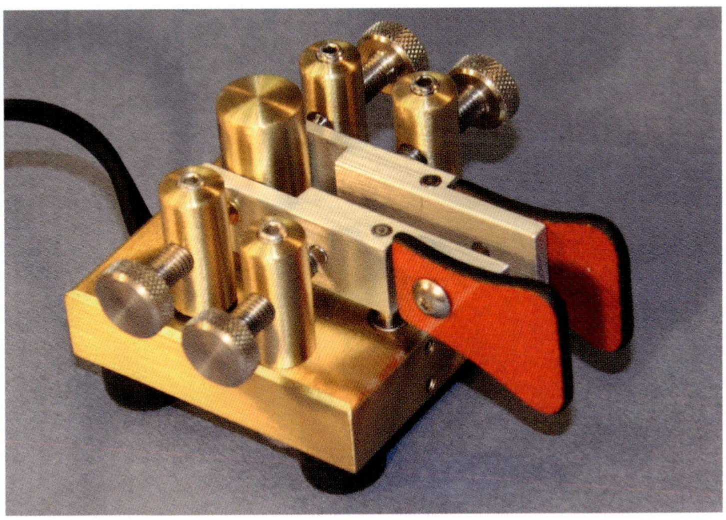

N0SA Mini-Paddles

This is the N0SA miniature iambic called the ESP. It is a new key designed just before Larry stopped producing keys. Larry designs keys that he likes to use; this one was designed to complement his Elecraft KX3. The ESP can be transported and used as a standalone miniature key, or mounted on the desktop base by sliding under the four retaining screws.

Larry Naumann's (N0SA) TIP-1, which stands for Tiny Iambic Paddle.

Palm Radio Paddles

Palm Radio's compact Mini Paddle has been designed for outdoor and QRP enthusiasts. Its dimensions are 25 × 25 × 79 mm (0.98 × 0.98 × 3.11 in.). It provides a high precision and play-free paddle mechanism that allows many individual settings: contact gap, spring tension, and a hard or soft stop are sensitively and accurately adjustable with the supplied Allen key. The paddles can be retracted into the housing, ensuring maximum protection during transport. A travel case is included and a universal mounting base is also available.

The Pico Paddle is claimed to be the smallest series production paddle in the world. Palm's goal was to develop a fully functional miniature paddle that would allow attachment to various popular HF transceivers, such as the KX3, FT-817, and FT-857. Transceiver specific installation kits are offered. The Pico can be retracted into the housing for transport. The paddle uses gold-plated contacts, and has adjustments for contact spacing and spring tension. An Allen key is provided for paddle adjustments. The Pico Paddle has a 2.5 mm stereo jack at the back side and a 1.6 ft. cable, with a ⅛ in. plug for connection to the transceiver or keyer.

The Palm Single is equipped with galvanized gold contacts that ensure maximum contact safety and reliability. Palm advertises this paddle as the smallest single-lever key in the world that can be retracted into its housing. Palm offers a choice of housings: either the standard aluminum or a new ABS housing. The lever of the Palm Single features a self-centering mechanism. The Palm Single also allows the user to select either single-lever mode or sideswiper mode. A supplied hex key is used to select mode and to effect set screw adjustment; the hex key can be stored in the paddle base. Two different set screws per lever side allow precise and individual adjustment of the contact gap and spring pressure.

A Palm Radio Mini paddle.

A Palm Radio Pico paddle.

Size comparison of the Palm Mini and Pico paddles.

Schurr Einbau Wabbler

This is the small Einbau Wabbler mounted on an American Morse powder coated base. Because the base does not sit up high and the paddle mechanism is on the small side, the fingerpieces have been reversed so they are the opposite of what you usually see on the Wabbler. Some find this combination of base, mechanism, and fingerpieces just about perfect. The mechanism is essentially the same as used in the Profi II. The Einbau Wabbler is no longer available.

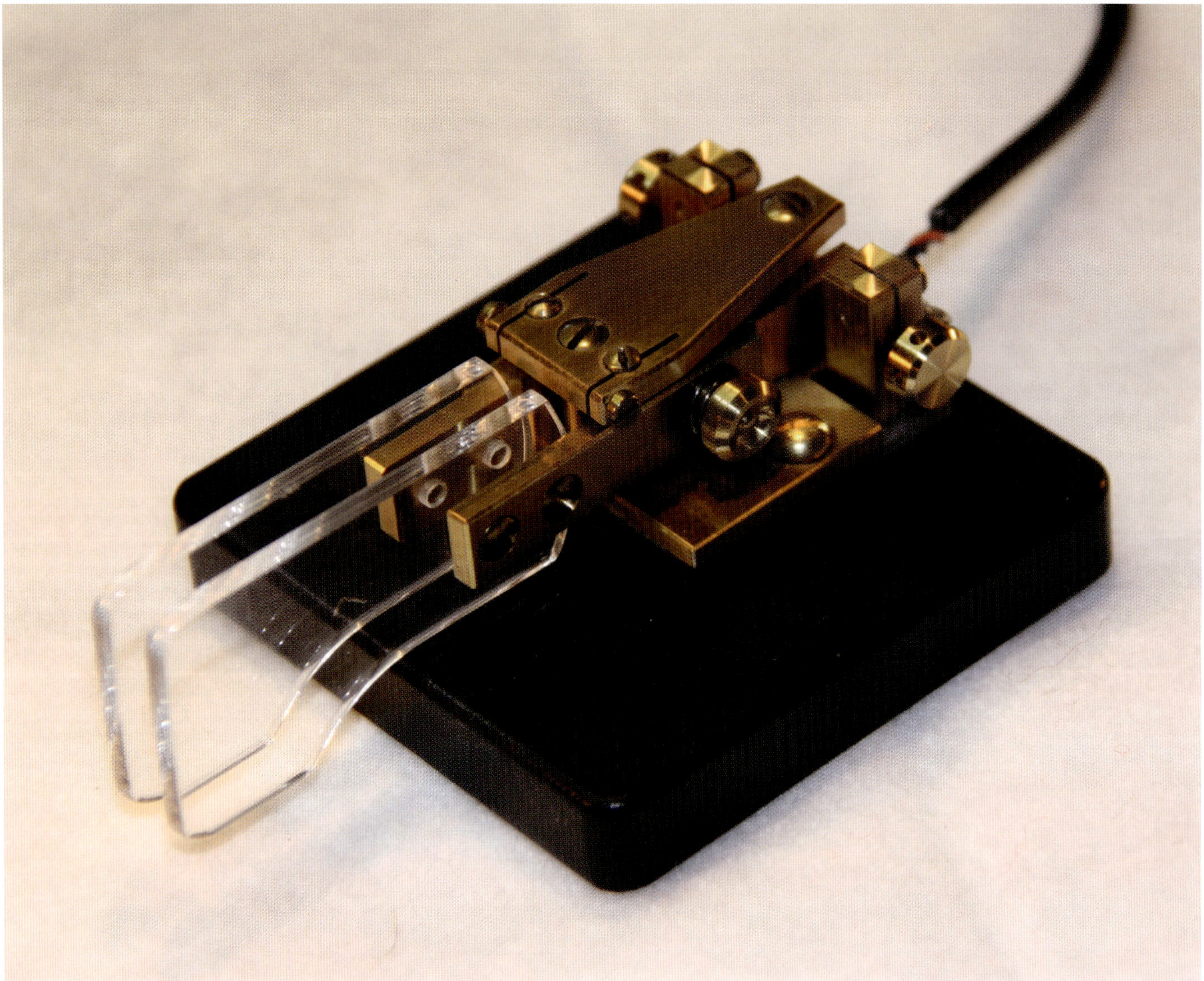

Te-Ne-Ke Paddle

The Micro Te-Ne-Ke by Dennis Foster (KK5PY). This paddle can be used as a portable paddle for field ops.

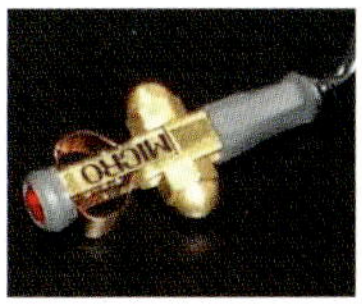

The North Ottawa Club describes their key:

> The Te-Ne-Ke (teeny key) is a dual-lever paddle built in West Michigan by members of the North Ottawa Amateur Radio Club. The contacts are made from beryllium copper springs and brass pins, attached to a stainless steel head. The whole thing may then be mounted to an optional heavy steel base with rubber feet to keep it in place on your desk. The key connects to your rig or keyer with a standard 3.5mm audio patch cable. Several variations of the Te-Ne-Ke currently exist. The head used to be made from CNC-machined aluminum channel stock with a plastic jewel on the front. Current production units are made from laser-cut stainless steel, without the jewel.

UniHAM UNI-715

UniHAM is a Chinese company making paddles and other amateur radio equipment primarily for the Chinese market. Their designs and materials are well thought out and chosen so paddle performance is equal to equipment costing much more. All UNI-715 contacts are silver-plated with adjustable contact spacing. The paddle has a matte black finish and typically comes with a 3.5 mm plug on the connection cable. The paddle is designed for angle mounting; weight is approximately 90 grams (3.17 oz.).

Vibroplex Code Warrior Junior

The Code Warrior Junior is the production version of the famous NorCal K8FF paddle. It weighs in at only 1.5 lb. for easy transport. This paddle uses magnetic return action, and sleeve bearings are incorporated inside each lever arm. The Code Warrior Junior uses silver contacts. The base measures 2.5 × 3 in., and is available in either black, blue, or chrome finish. Fingerpieces can be flipped for operators who prefer them closer to the desktop. This paddle was introduced by Vibroplex around 2001.

Also available is a Vibroplex Lite Warrior, which uses an aluminum base. The aluminum base allows for increased portability and a lower weight; the Lite Warrior weighs under a pound, but still retains the Code Warrior Junior's size.

WB9LPU Portable/Travel Paddles

This version of the Parkwood paddle (below) was made by Rich (WB9LPU). The paddle components are aluminum mounted on a painted steel base with fold-out legs providing stability. The legs can be locked in place by a small thumbscrew. Paddle arm position is adjusted via spring tension.

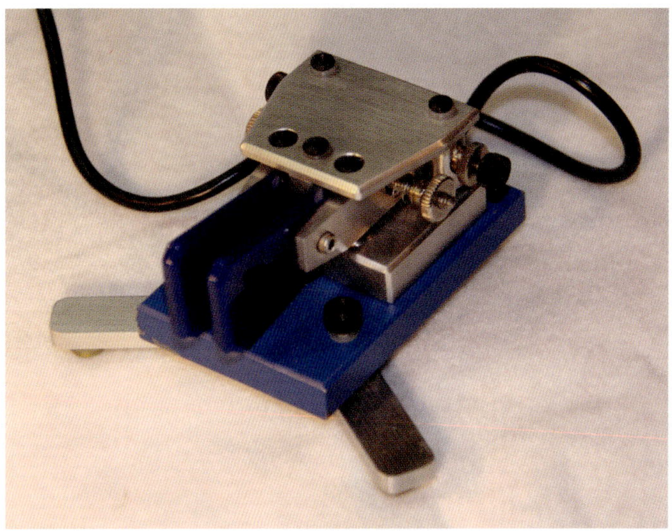

The KXer removed from its portable base and installed on an Elecraft KX1.

Another unique Richard Meiss design called the KXer paddle. The device can be used with its removable legs as a standalone paddle or mounted to an Elecraft KX1 QRP rig.

Whiterook Mini Paddles

The Whiterook series of miniature keys is available from Jack Roblin (WA6KYO) of Electronics USA. Whiterook keys have been in production since 1995, and are ideally suited for portable operation. The weight of each device is less than 1.5 oz. Contacts use metal posts with a screw head or cap nut mounted on the paddle arm. Single and dual-lever versions are available as shown.

7 Commemorative Paddles

A number of commemorative and special edition paddles have been produced since 1960; here's a look at some of them.

The first commemorative paddle was likely the Vibroplex Vibro-Keyer finished in a Heathkit green as the base color. This paddle was referred to as a "special order" device, but not much other information is available to indicate where the special order would have been placed. It can be assumed orders went to Vibroplex, as several different serial numbers have been seen on various green paddles, all dating to 1960. It would appear Vibroplex built these paddles, rather than a third party vendor. A second very early commemorative paddle documented in this chapter comes from Harrison Radio, a gray-base Vibro-Keyer. This unique paddle was built to complement the W9TO keyer and sold around 1961. The remainder of the commemorative paddles shown came much later in time, but all are special keys with their own story to tell.

Begali 60th Anniversary Sculpture Paddle

The Begali 60th Anniversary key is a special edition of the highly regarded Sculpture key. The Anniversary model was conceived to commemorate the 60th anniversary of the Begali Company; the production run of this model has been limited to only 214 pieces. The 60th Anniversary model features fixed parts completely made from AISI-304 stainless steel, which is a virtually indestructible material that must be shaped with specialized machinery and tools. The key is then polished; Begali states blemishes can be removed with fine abrasive compounds like jewelers rouge (a very fine powder of ferric oxide) or car polish.

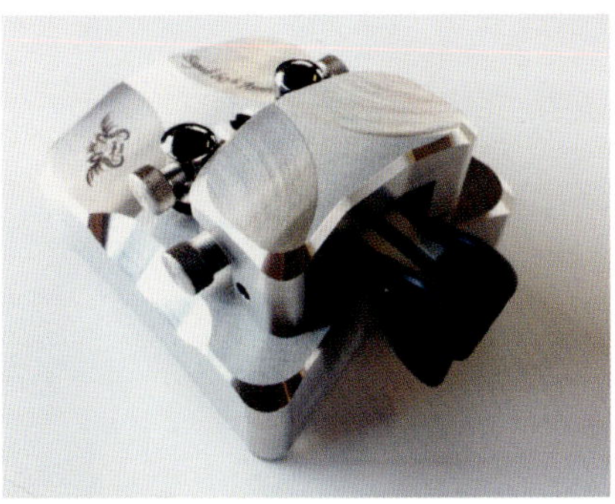

Paddle arms are designed to give a 1:1 leverage ratio, and are extremely short and made from a lightweight alloy. The fingerpieces are made from aluminum alloy for excellent tactile feedback and low mass. The resulting minimal moving mass, in combination with the highest grade racing bearings, gives the key its responsiveness and precision. The 60th Anniversary key offers fine adjustments with gold contacts made from solid 14k gold.

Begali ARRL Sculpture Paddle

The limited-edition Begali Sculpture paddle represents the results of an ARRL partnership with Begali Keys to produce a personalized paddle. Stainless steel is used for the paddle's fixed components. As designed with the original Sculpture model, the contacts are 925/1000 silver. This ARRL edition paddle is engraved with the ARRL and Begali logos, as well as the buyer's call sign. Included with the key is a feeler gauge to accurately set contact spacing, cleaning cloth, plastic dust cover, and cable.

Elecraft HexKey

The Elecraft version of the Bencher HexKey was advertised as a high performance paddle with gold-plated silver contacts, molded acrylic finger pads, magnetic tension adjustment, adjustable contact spacing, and a powder coated steel base. Those purchasing this paddle from Elecraft received a unique Elecraft serial number. The paddle was discontinued by Elecraft in 2013.

A Harrison Radio Vibro-Keyer advertisement from the April 1961 *QST*.

March R-3a Collins Paddle

Mike March (K4QU) of Winchester, Virginia, made this Collins commemorative version of his famous R-3a dual-lever paddle. This device was only offered for a limited time by March.

Harrison Radio T.O. Vibro-Keyer

When the Hallicrafters HA-1 T.O. keyer first came on the market, Harrison Radio offered a special edition of the Vibro-Keyer that had a base painted gray to match the Hallicrafters gray color of the HA-1 cabinet. The Harrison T.O. variant apparently had all the features of the Vibro-Keyer DeLuxe model, but it has been reported the Harrison paddles may not have had a Vibroplex nameplate. Some Harrison paddles that have been examined do not have any nameplate rivet holes in the base.

Pegasus

Built by GHD, this tapper device called the Pegasus was offered by *CQ ham radio*, a Japanese ham magazine.

RSGB Millennium (LTA) Paddle Key

This RSGB Millennium Morse Paddle produced by Llaves Telegrafics Artesanas is a limited edition (only 155 produced) to celebrate the new millennium in 2000. Shown is serial number 140 of 155, and it includes a certificate. The key is made of gold-plated brass, and the base and knob are ebony wood. The base measures 3.5 × 2 in.

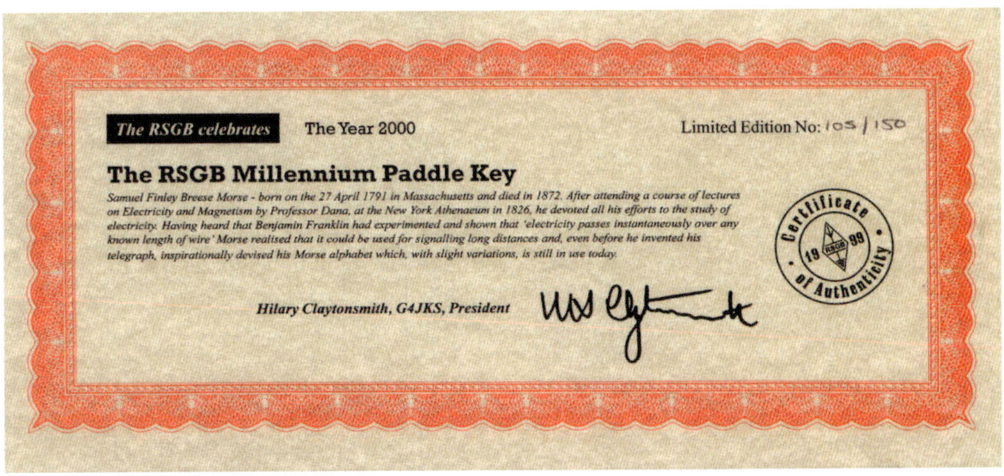

The RSGB celebrates The Year 2000 Limited Edition No: 105 / 150

The RSGB Millennium Paddle Key

Samuel Finley Breese Morse - born on the 27 April 1791 in Massachusetts and died in 1872. After attending a course of lectures on Electricity and Magnetism by Professor Dana, at the New York Athenaeum in 1826, he devoted all his efforts to the study of electricity. Having heard that Benjamin Franklin had experimented and shown that 'electricity passes instantaneously over any known length of wire' Morse realised that it could be used for signalling long distances and, even before he invented his telegraph, inspirationally devised his Morse alphabet which, with slight variations, is still in use today.

Hilary Claytonsmith, G4JKS, President

Certificate of Authenticity 1999 RSGB

Ten-Tec 40th Anniversary Bencher Paddle

Ten-Tec put out another special edition paddle in 2008, a unique version of the Bencher dual-lever. This paddle was issued to commemorate Ten-Tec's 40th Anniversary; only 200 were made.

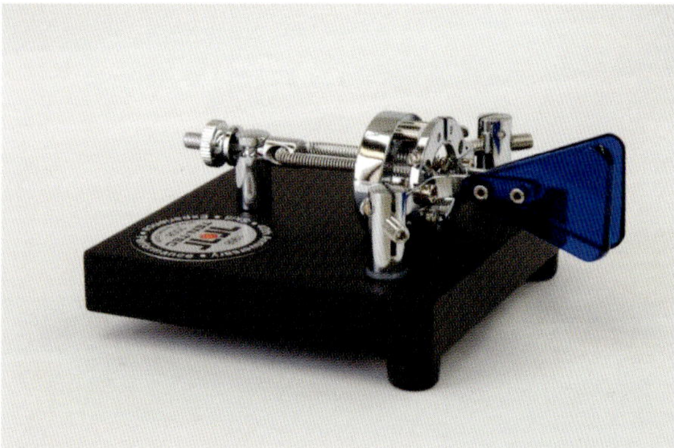

CQ ham radio Morse Paddle

The Japanese ham radio magazine *CQ* issued this special version of the Vega paddle made by GHD Keys. The Vega uses oilless bearings with no play and offers quiet operation. Also featured are silver contacts and stainless steel paddle arms with spring return. Paddle weight is 600 grams (21 oz.), and the selling price was roughly 15,000 yen ($140).

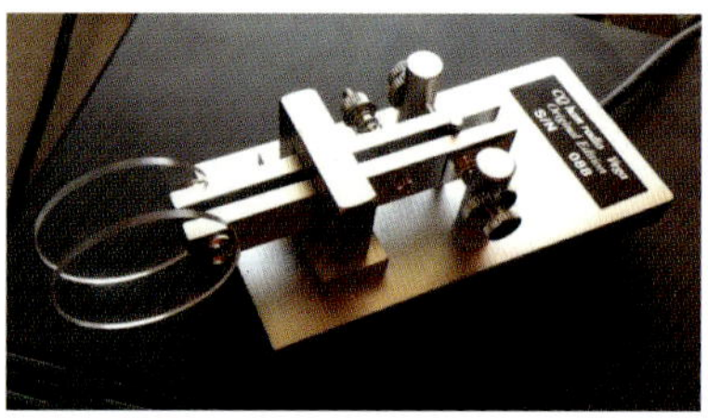

Vibroplex 50th Anniversary Vibrokeyer

This special version of the Vibrokeyer was designed to be visually similar to the early 1900s bugs, with gold pinstriping and corner floral patterns. The year 2010 marks the fiftieth year the original Vibrokeyer was released for production. This key has deluxe jeweled movement and components and unique serial numbers (50VK001–50VK250); only 250 of these paddles were produced. A choice of red or black fingerpieces was also an option.

Vibroplex ARRL Centennial Paddle

Vibroplex produced this double-lever paddle in 2014, in partnership with the ARRL. The paddle was issued to celebrate the 100th anniversary of the league.

Vibroplex Collins Special Edition

The Collins special edition Vibrokeyer with dark gray base (actually it is described as classic S-line faceplate gray) and special serial numbering starting with "CCA." This paddle was part of the first production run of special Collins keys that included the dual-lever, single-lever, and the Original bug. The single and dual-lever models are pictured. The first run came out in 2004. CCA began discussions in 2010 with Vibroplex for another run of special edition keys.

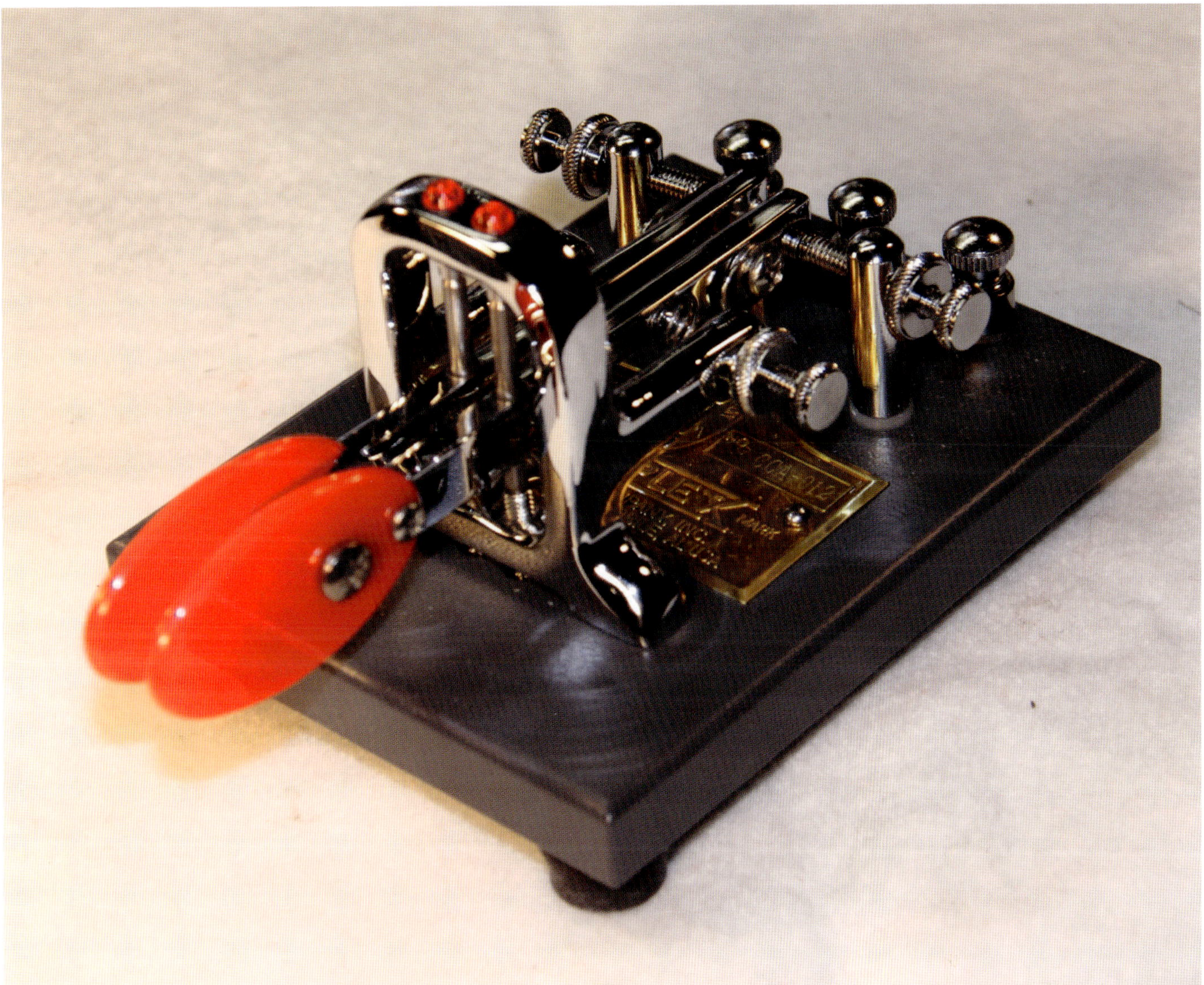

Vibroplex Heath Green Vibro-Keyer

This seldom seen version of the Vibro-Keyer (Vibroplex hyphenated the name in the early '60s) came with a green base, supposedly intended to match the green of many Heathkit products. This green version was a special order from Vibroplex and not too many were sold. The serial number on this paddle dates it to 1960. The green Vibro-Keyer is possibly the first commemorative paddle ever produced.

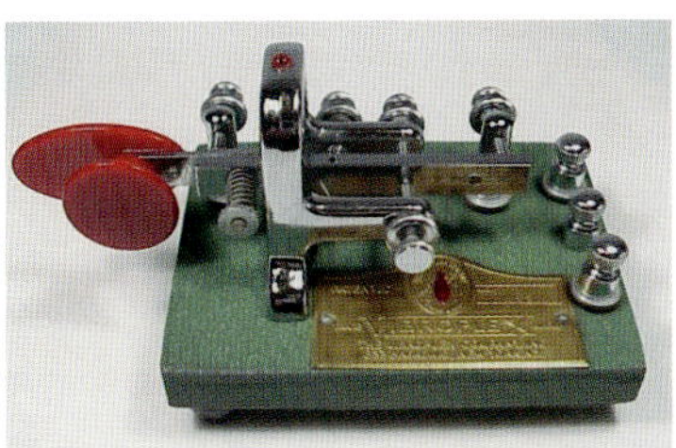

Vibroplex RSGB Centenary Vibrokeyer

The Radio Society of Great Britain Centenary Key, a dual-lever Vibrokeyer on a stretched base, was produced in 2013. The device commemorates the 100th anniversary of the RSGB. One of these models was used at G100RSGB to send code during the organization's celebration. Only 250 of these paddles were made.

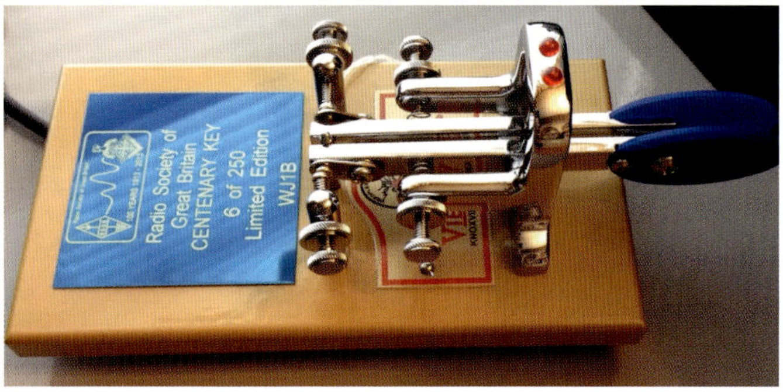

Vibroplex Ten-Tec Limited Edition Paddles

Here is the Ten-Tec limited edition Vibrokeyer paddle. Only 250 of these were made in 2003. The paddle (below) has the K6JW conversion fingerpieces installed.

In 2010, Ten-Tec offered another limited edition Vibrokeyer version based on the Vibroplex dual-lever design. It was similar to the RSGB special version, in that it used a longer base. The blue fingerpieces are distinctive; Ten-Tec also specified the color blue for their Bencher limited edition. This limited edition carried the Vibroplex Knoxville nameplate.

Ten-Tec limited edition Vibrokeyer paddle with standard fingerpieces.

A January 2003 CQ ad for the Ten-Tec commemorative Vibrokeyer.

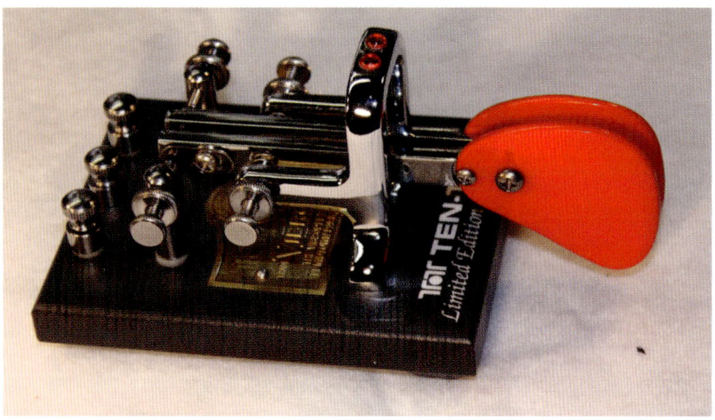

8 Combination Keys and Paddles

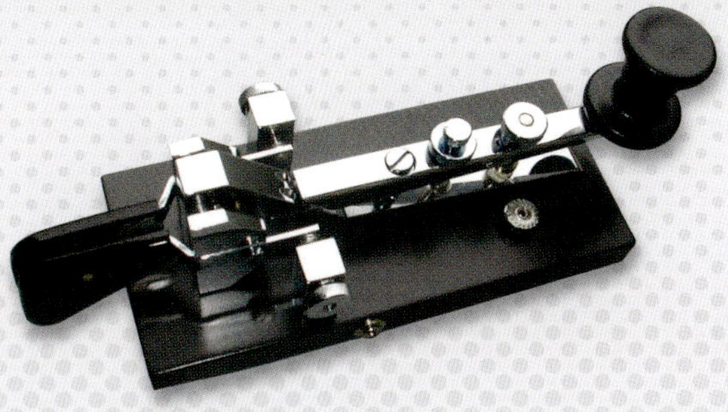

A combination key consists of more than one key or paddle mounted on a single base.

Perhaps the earliest combination key is the Mecograph Number 2, which was produced and advertised in 1905. In 1997, Vibroplex came out with their "Double," which consisted of a paddle and a straight key on one base. Since then there have been a number of special combination devices available. Some, such as the IK1OJM models, show new innovative approaches to combination key design.

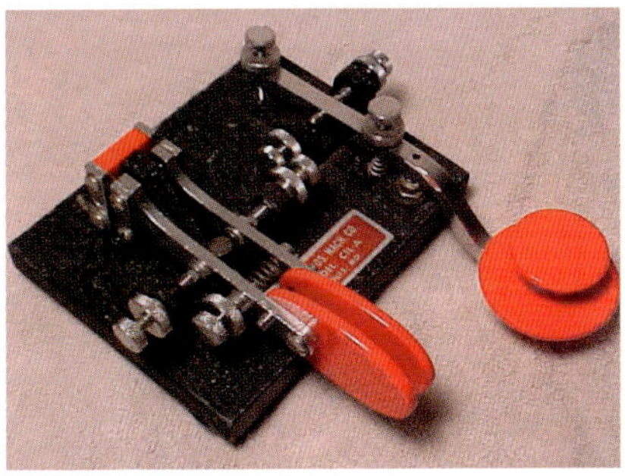

A Model CTL-A with the leaf spring version of the dual-lever paddle.

Brown Brothers Combination

The Brown Brothers manufactured code keys (straight keys and dual-lever paddles) 1964–1979. The keys were built by Bill Brown in his basement machine shop. Bill Brown built all the dies and tooling and hand finished, assembled, and labeled the keys. The other Brown brother was Ed Brown, the financier and silent partner.

Brown Brothers keys appear frequently on the used market, as well as on auction sites. The keys are solid and dependable, and they have maintained a dedicated following for many years. Their continuing popularity helps ensure Brown Brothers keys will hold their value over time.

The Brown Brothers' standard Model CTL (top right). This model has no ground terminal in the rear corner, and the terminal strip for connections is in the rear of the base, not on the side. This configuration of CTL is much more common than the experimental CTL.

Model CTL, with side terminals and ground lug in the base corner; this combination device is sometimes referred to as the "experimental CTL."

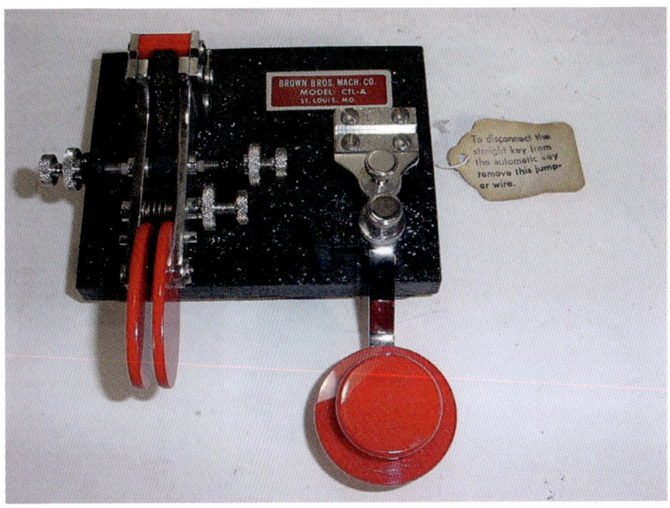

This combination (above) is marked "CTL-A," but it is a CTL-B model, making this key a rarity if it came from Brown Brothers. The original Brown Brothers tag, with instructions on disconnecting the hand key from the paddle, is still attached.

Although not a paddle device, the BB CSA (below) is considered one of the most collectible combination keys around. Only a few were produced before Vibroplex supposedly threatened legal action over the almost identical copy of their bug mechanism and Brown Brothers stopped making these.

This is a very nice Brown Brothers Model CTL-B (below). The CTL-B series was the last model Bill Brown produced and has paddles and a straight key on a stable base. First sold in 1976, the CTL-B uses springs that are flat sheet stock to give the key and the paddles a better feel.

G4ZPY Millennium Duo

G4ZPY produced this combination key he called the "Millennium Duo." The device includes a straight key and a VHS model dual-lever key on the same base. The straight key has a Gold Half Sovereign coin inlaid in the knob. Both keys are mounted on a 6-inch square by ⅜ in. thick base made of solid brass. The entire assembly has been 24k gold-plated and weighs approximately 2 kilograms (4.4 lb.). Each key has been numbered on a special small plaque. Connections to both keys are made through 3.5 mm jacks.

Ham-Key HK-4 Combination

This dual version of the Ham-Key is Model HK-4, which includes the Ham-Key HK-1 paddle and the HK-2 straight key on a black base. The HK-4 model was also available with a gray hammertone base. This combination key was produced and sold by Ham Radio Center of Saint Louis, Missouri, and is no longer in production. The Ham-Key devices were very popular, as they presented a cheaper alternative for users who could not afford the higher priced Brown Brothers models. The HK-4 pictured has binding posts for connections, but a slightly different version used screw terminals on the back, or in some cases three RCA jacks. Weight is 1 lb., 13 oz., and the base measures. 6 × 2.4 × 6.5 in.

Hi-Mound MHK831

The Hi-Mound MHK831 is a fairly rare combination key, and an unusual one. The key is made of brass; Hi-Mound calls it the "high deluxe telegraph key." The separation between the two dual paddle arms is adjustable by turning a knob on the right side of the base. The hand key features a spring-loaded shorting switch seen as a protruding shaft in front of the key. Notice the odd fingerpiece mounting on the dual-lever portion of the device that would appear to be very flexible during use. The Hi-Mound combination key weighs 7 lb. 14.2 oz. and measures 5.1 × 2.8 × 7.5 in.

IK1OJM Dual Keys

IK1OJM offers this nice concept of a combination key. Both devices are designed so they mesh together almost as a single unit. Depending on the orientation of the base, the operator can use either the hand key or the dual-lever paddle.

IK1OJM offers this variation (red base) of his dual key combination that incorporates a sideswiper with a dual-lever paddle. The design approach requires the user to orient the base to have the desired key in position. IK1OJM calls this combination the "Sidepaddle."

KD4OBQ Combination Key

Patrick (KD4OBQ) has conceived this combination key incorporating a dual-lever paddle and a straight key. Patrick also designed the Okie paddle (see chapter 5).

Kent Two

Kent calls this combination key the "Kent Two." It uses a straight Morse hand key and a dual-lever paddle on a common base. The key parts are made of brass and use silver contacts. As with the discrete Kent paddle ball bearings are used on this paddle and on the hand key. Two key leads are provided. The base is fairly heavy, and is offered in black or white. Base size is 150 × 98 mm (5.9 × 3.9 in.); total key weight is 1.850 kg (4.08 lb.).

LTA CRDO

The LTA (Llavas Telegraphicas Artesanas) Model CRDO from the Balearic Islands of Spain. This model was assembled by hand on a rosewood base with a hand key knob made of teak and paddle fingerpieces of olive wood. The mechanical parts of this combination key are gold-plated brass; there was also a model with solid brass base with gold-plated parts available (BBDO), as well as a natural brass finish model (CRD).

Mecograph Number Two

This is the earliest known combination device, the Mecograph Number Two or combo model. The design for this key was patented by Benjamin Bellows in 1908 (886,755). This model first appeared on the market around 1905. Collectors report the serial numbers of the combo model suggest over 1,000 units were made, although Mecograph Number Twos are somewhat rare and are seldom seen for sale. This device does not use a paddle as part of the combination, but does incorporate a semi-automatic bug that used a very complex mechanism to function. It is reported this model was the first Mecograph to start using serial numbers.

The Commercial Telegraphers' Journal

The Official Organ of the Commercial Telegraphers' Union of America.

Vol. 3. No. 1. CHICAGO, ILL., JANUARY, 1905.

The MECOGRAPH

HALF SIZE.

THE CHEAPEST AND BEST TELEGRAPHIC TRANSMITTER IN THE WORLD.

Packed in Strong Wooden Box for shipment, weight under five pounds.

Price, $10

THE MECOGRAPH is in constant use by Press, Broker, Commercial and Railroad Operators and Train despatchers, in fact it is used in all branches of telegraphy.

There are no batteries to carry around and to be renewed from time to time.

It requires no winding.

It is neat, strong, reliable and heavy enough to be rigid on the table without fastening.

It can be connected to, or disconnected from, the wire instantly.

It responds instantly to the operator's touch.

It can be fairly handled with one or two weeks' practice.

The sending can be made even and uniform, light or heavy.

It is adapted to either slow or rapid transmitting.

One hand is always free to handle messages.

THE MECOGRAPH CO. Cleveland, Ohio, U. S. A.
74 Frankfort Street

North American Telegraph

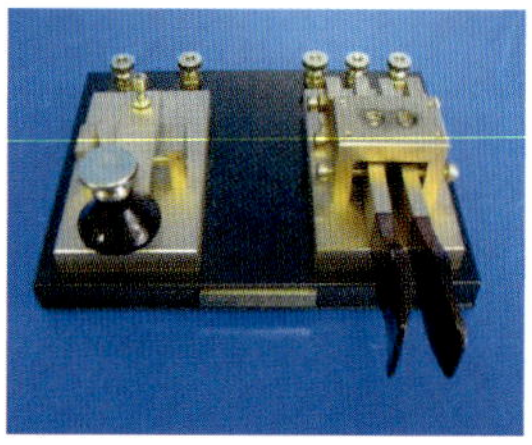

The North American Telegraph combination key consisting of the NA-2 straight key and NA-20 dual-lever paddle. The combination was made for a brief time by Jim Richards (K6VDH) before he stopped making keys in 2004.

Nye M/SSK-1 and Speed-X

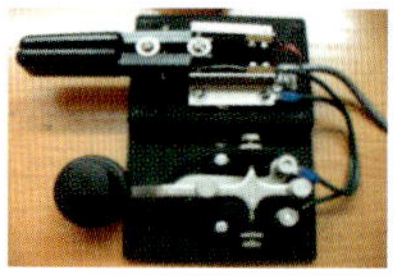

This is the Nye M/SSK-1 combination key, consisting of a super squeeze paddle on the left and a straight key on the right. The William M. Nye Company was founded in 1972 by Willian Nye (W7DZ) of Bellevue, Washington; Nye retired in 1986. Bill Nye Jr. (WB7TNN) currently operates the company.

Vibroplex

The Vibroplex Combination single-lever paddle and bug, gold brushed base version.

Several different Vibroplex combination keys are presented here. The Vibroplex double key (below) uses a combination of the Vibrokeyer paddle and the hand key. The double key is also available with a chrome base.

The Vibroplex DeLuxe on a chrome base uses a Vibrokeyer mechanism combined with a semi-automatic key. This one is also using WB8LZG wooden fingerpieces.

The blue double is a unique Vibroplex key, thought to be originally a special order done as a favor by a former Vibroplex owner. This particular double features a dual-lever paddle and straight key. The serial number is 105759.

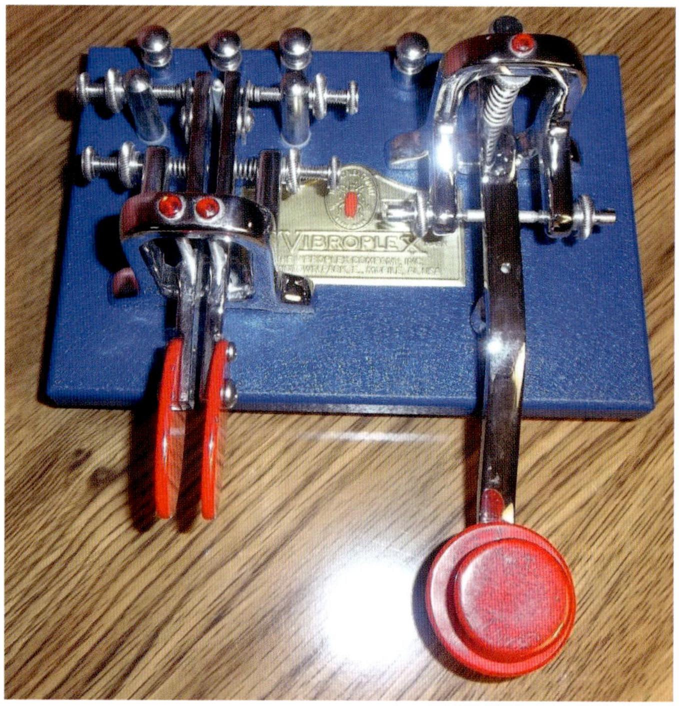

The Vibroplex Triple is an unusual combination of three keys. It is produced in four versions, depending on whether the user wants the single-lever or dual paddle. Base options consist of either gold brushed or chrome. This key is fairly large and heavy, with a weight of about 12 lb. The gold brushed base version sells for $1,200.

Whiterook MK48

One of the smallest combination keys is the Whiterook MK48, offering a hand key and paddle on a small base.

W9WBL Combination

Shown (below) is a W9WBL combination key, of which only about five were made. K1ND reports this particular model uses roller bearings in the pivot points.

9 Convertible Paddles and Paddle Modifications

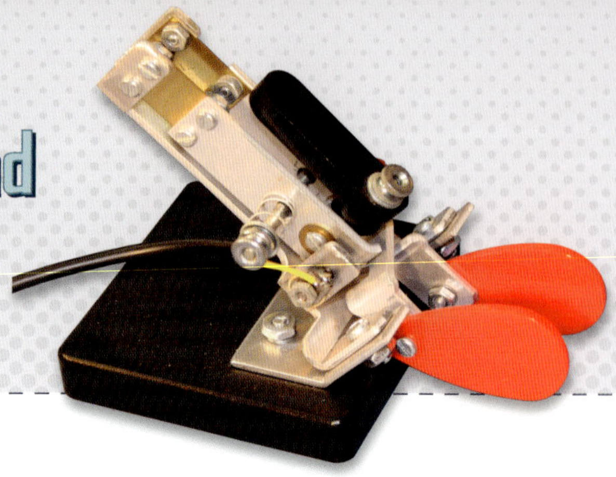

This chapter presents some devices that have been designed to function in more than one way by virtue of being convertible from one type of key to another. Also presented are some modified keys that have improved functionality or added convenience of use.

In the true spirit of amateur radio, hams will forever be inclined to update and improve upon their gear; keys are no exception. Holders of an amateur radio license are encouraged to modify their equipment. Many of the first paddles were modified semi-automatic bugs. Frequently the modification process leads to new and better ways of doing things. A good example is the introduction, acceptance, and growth of the magnetic paddle. Sometimes a modification results in a more convenient way of using the key, or in a better way of meeting some design goal. Occasionally a modification will result in a totally different device, with some new feature becoming available that was not there before, as with the IK1OJM vibrating lever arm addition conceived to mate with some of his paddles. It is hoped by reviewing some of the out-of-the-box thinking that is presented here the reader will let their imagination wander the next time an inconvenience or a missing operational feature is encountered. There is probably a better way to accomplish something or improve some device you are now using if you are not limited by accepting things as they are.

Begali Leonessa

The Begali Leonessa is a dual-lever paddle that can be converted to a single-lever key with a few turns of an adjustment screw. The Leonessa is a high speed key incorporating perforated, narrowly spaced fingerpieces that give the operator excellent tactile feedback. The spacing between the fingerpieces is adjustable $\frac{1}{4}$ in. to $\frac{9}{16}$ in.

The key's contact points are right behind the fingerpieces and are adjusted from the opposing side. The Leonessa uses lightweight aluminum arms, precision racing bearings, solid silver contacts, finely adjustable contact gaps, magnetically controlled return force, and a heavy black base with titanium oxide coating.

Begali states the secret to the Leonessa's extraordinary flexibility is the adjustment screw on one of the fingerpieces. When the screw is retracted the Leonessa works as a dual-lever paddle with narrowly spaced fingerpieces. If the adjustment screw is advanced, the contacts are prevented from closing when you squeeze the fingerpieces, and the Leonessa turns into a dual action key operated in single-lever fashion, a mode preferred by many of the fastest operators in the world.

BY1IO TRPIO Multi-Mode Key

The TRPIO, a multi-mode key designed by BY1IO. This device (model A01) can perform as a typical single-lever paddle, or when the mechanism is rotated, it will function as a hand key. Main parts are made of alloy aluminum.

Gallo Key-Jack Paddle Modification

As seen on many high-end paddles such as those from Begali, a ⅛ in. stereo mini-jack is standard, instead of a hardwired cord or solder contacts for a user supplied cord. Many of the most popular paddles, including the Bencher BY series, Kent TP-1 twin paddle, and the Vibroplex paddles do not come with a ⅛ in. mini-jack. The Gallo modification (see thegallos.com) uses a milled pocket in the paddle base where the mini-jack is mounted. The jack is typically wired so the right paddle is the ring on the jack, with the left wired to the tip and the sleeve wired to ground.

Bottom view of the Bencher BY-1 after modification.

Kent TP-1 showing an added connector jack on the rear of the base.

GHD GM307WS Convertible

The GHD GM307WS allows the user to convert from a dual-lever paddle to single-lever. The design uses three lever arms with a total of six bearings. The two fingerpieces mount to a detachable metal endpiece that can be removed from the lever arms. To convert the paddle to single-lever operation both fingerpieces are removed; one is then reattached to the middle arm. Contact gap and arm tension are adjustable, and an optional black base is available. The GM307WS uses gold-plated contacts.

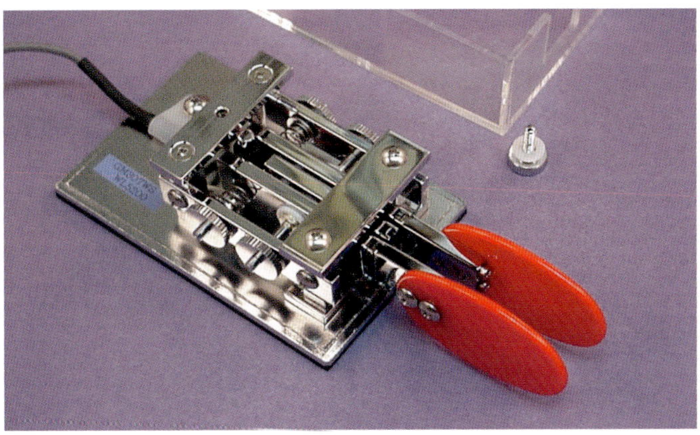

The GHD GM307WS convertible paddle with dust cover removed.

HA8UG Convertible

This paddle was made in Hungary by Toth (HA8UG); it uses "bat" style fingerpieces and converts between single and double-lever actuation by removing and reinstalling the fingerpieces. Toth calls this the Universal model.

IK1OJM Magnetic Conversions

Two photos showing a Schurr modified for magnetic arm actuation. Also part of the overall paddle modification was the inclusion of rounded wooden fingerpieces.

The results of an IK1OJM conversion of the Kent TP-1 paddle from spring actuation to magnetic actuation.

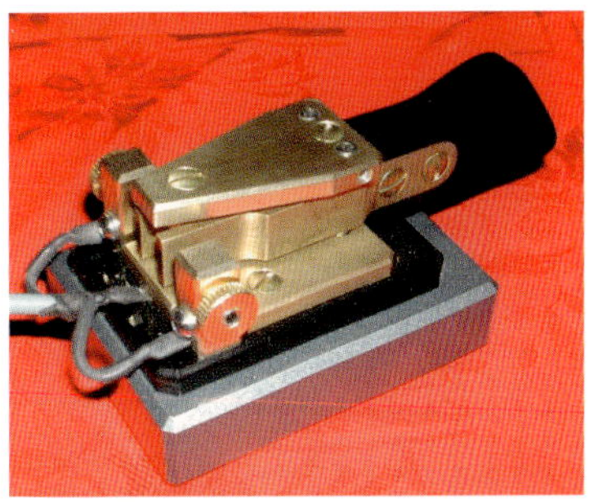

IK1OJM Paddle-Bug Convertibles

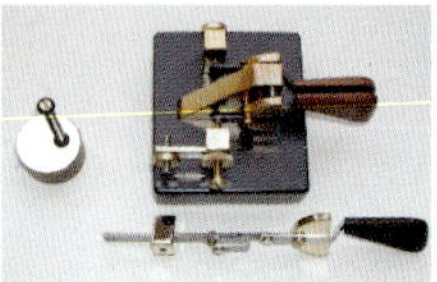

The IK1OJM modified paddle arm allowing paddle operation as a semi-automatic bug is seen above in two different versions: one version (black base) uses an independent arm damper, while the other version (red base) includes the damper as part of the modified paddle arm.

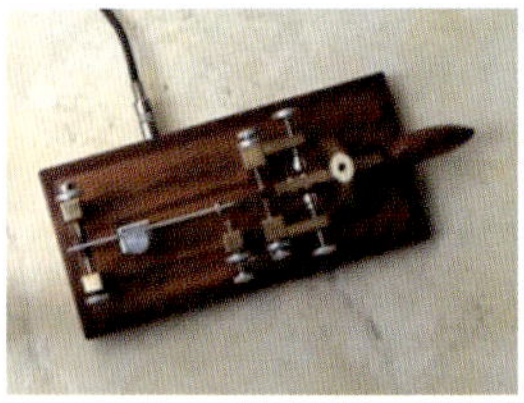

The IK1OJM Triplex—a key, bug, and sideswiper all in one.

K6JW Vibroplex Conversion Fingerpieces

K6JW's Vibroplex conversion paddles (fingerpieces) are used to upgrade a Vibroplex dual-lever paddle to enable a better feel. Operators have problems with some keys because of large hands, or for those who prefer a lower set of fingerpieces, these conversion pieces offer a possible solution. The K6JW fingerpieces also have an attractive look.

Fingerpiece style for the dual-lever paddle.

Fingerpieces for the Code Warrior.

N3CW Heathkit HD-1410 Paddle Modification

This paddle is the result of an experiment to move the internal paddle mechanism of a Heath HD-1410 outside the keyer enclosure, aiding in making adjustments and making an external device that was not horizontal or vertical. The resulting device yields a distinctive paddle that slopes at a 45 degree angle. Part of the motivation for this modification was to see how this would look on the operating desk. The modification basically removes the Heath paddle from inside the keyer, adds new Plexiglas fingerpieces, then mounts the mechanism on a heavy, powder-coated base.

WA9TGT Conversion Fingerpieces

Donnie (WA9TGT) makes these attractive fingerpieces for Vibroplex paddles. The unique shape allows operators with hand positions closer to the table to easily manipulate the key.

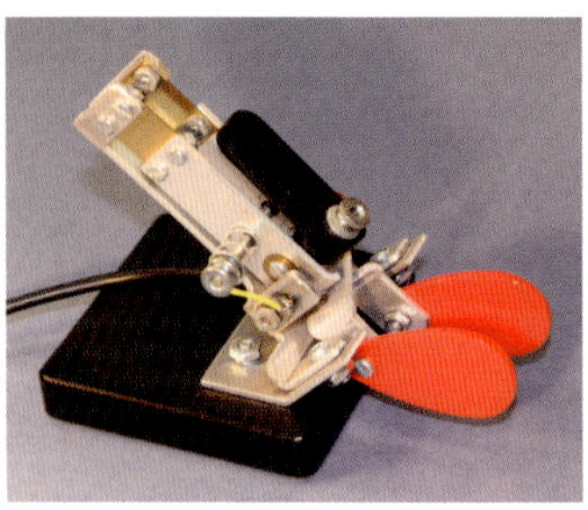

WB8LZG Wooden Fingerpieces

The Vibroplex Double Key Deluxe with WB8LZG's African Padouc fingerpieces. Gregg lives in Dimondale, Michigan, and makes these wooden fingerpieces to upgrade his keys as a hobby. The Vibroplex Double shown above is the first Double key produced from the Vibroplex Knoxville, Tennessee, location.

10 Automatic Mechanical Keys

This chapter presents some of the historically significant automatic mechanical keys that started to appear before the commercial advent of the electronic keyer. Also shown are several fully automatic devices of more recent vintage.

The first few decades of the 1900s found Morse CW operators infatuated with semi-automatic bugs that produced automatic dots. It is understandable that mechanical designs would emerge that also allowed for production of automatic dashes. Ironically, many telegraphers actually preferred the semi-automatic bugs because they could adjust the length of the dashes to compensate for the inductance of telegraph lines, thereby allowing for more accurate copy on the receiving end.

In this chapter we will take a look at some of the key-based automatic mechanical designs. The early 2000s also saw a somewhat nostalgic interest in bugs and mechanical automatic devices, perhaps related to the desire of many hams to rebuild their first boatanchor (the ham term for older, heavier tube equipment) stations; therefore, some keys from that time period are presented. For some CW operators who prefer the use of bugs there is a mystical allure to the mechanical device they feel electronic keyers lack. (Keyboard and other related fully automatic approaches are discussed in chapter 14).

Automorse

The Automorse, or more formally the N. P. Thomas Automorse, was an Australian key first made about 1920 by Hitchcox Brothers in Adelaide, SA, Australia. The key features three paddles: one for automatic dots, one for automatic dashes, and one for manual dashes; it was designed and patented in 1919 by Norman Percy Thomas. Reportedly one left-handed model is known to exist. The top two fingerpieces and mechanism operate somewhat like a Vibroplex double-lever model and the lower mechanism provides the automatic repeating dashes. This device was never very popular due to the complexity of setting up the adjustments, but it has proven to be a valuable collectible key.

Breedlove Transmitter

The Breedlove Transmitter was a fully automatic bug-type device patented in 1950. Bernard Breedlove invented the key in the mid-1940s and filed the patent application in 1946. As stated in the patent, Breedlove's principal goal was to develop a means to allow the operator to send at two different speeds (slow and fast) without stopping to adjust the vibrating dot and dash mechanisms. The invention provided a mechanical switch to accomplish his goal. In an interview, Breedlove claimed less than five of these keys were actually built, and it is not known if any survive. The drawing is from the issued patent.

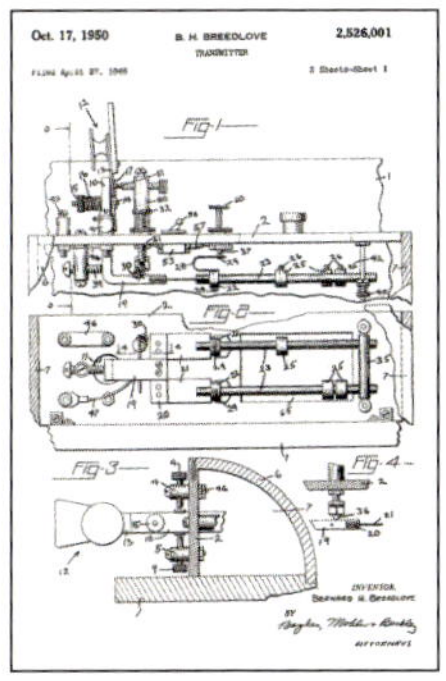

Duovert Automatic Speed Key

The Duovert key was designed and built by William R. Smith (W4PAL) in 2004. It is described in W4PAL literature as the world's first fully automatic (both dots and dashes are made automatically) mechanical vertical single-arbor speed key. Past automatic mechanical keys were not vertical in design and used multiple arbors. The Duovert is 8 in. high and has a speed range from 15–35 wpm. W4PAL describes his Duovert:

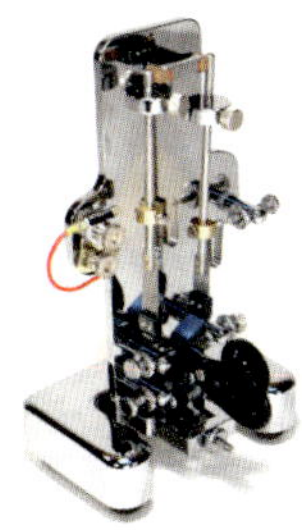

> The short height and single arbor are made possible by a through-the-dash-bar stop for the dot bar which has never been used in keys before. A magnet and reed switch operated by the dash lever can make up

to 40 dashes. Speed adjustment is by moving weights only. The key is composed of two pendulum type vibrators, one for the dots and one for the dashes. The two pendulums are hinged together and have a common arbor that is supported by bearing screws in the frame and the base plate. The dot pendulum is quite conventional and has the standard "U" spring for making contact for the dots. The dash pendulum is also quite conventional, except that instead of the "U" spring for making contact for the dashes, it uses a magnet to trigger a reed switch. Directly beneath the collet on the dash weight rod is mounted a round, rare earth magnet. In a fan-tail holder is a brass tube in which is mounted a reed switch. This arrangement avoids much of the energy losses in the pendulum and allows it to make far more dashes than if a "U" spring had been used. Also, by adjustment of the fan-tail reed switch mount, the dash to space length ratio can be brought to proper value. To change the speed, the weight on the dot pendulum is moved to a location that produces the desired dot frequency. The dash weight is then moved to a position that produces dashes that are of correct length relative to the chosen dots. There is a separator screw that allows positioning of each weight rod against its leather pad in the damper. My design trick of the dot bar stop screw passing through the dash bar allows the paddle and knob to be folded above the arbor and shorten the height of the key.

Hulit Transmitter-Topeka,Kansas-1909

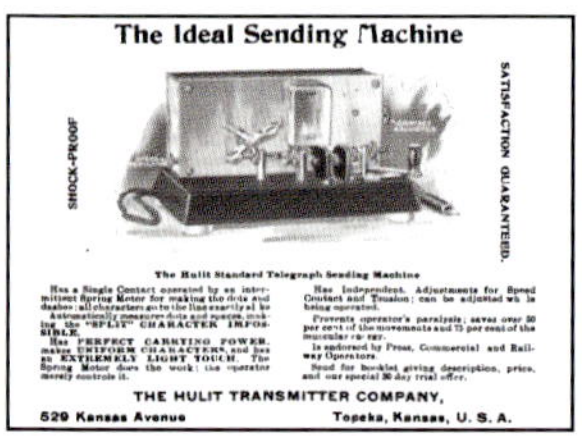

A Hulit advertisement from the January 1910 *Commercial Telegraphers' Journal.*

GHD GD907

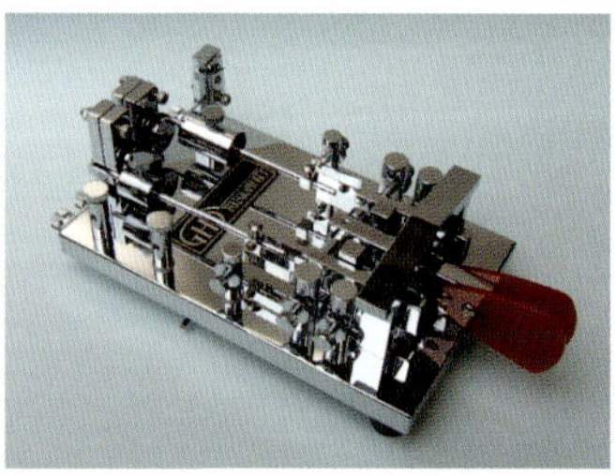

GHD's Model GD907 is also called the "Ultimate" key with good reason. The 907 uses optical sensors and is a fully automatic bug. The 907's dash pendulum can be locked for semi-automatic operation. The use of optical sensors means there are no mechanical contacts to adjust, adding to the key's reliability and keeping settings from wandering. The 907 is supplied with three weights for a wide range of operating speeds. This device shipped with the required power supply pre-wired for the 907. The base measures 6 × 4 in. and it weighs 5 lb. The GHD GD907 has a list price of $1,549.95.

Hulit Bug

The Hulit transmitter was advertised as a motor-driven device; the operator was advised to use the paddles with a light touch and let the motor do all the work. This device was made by the Hulit Transmitter Company of Topeka, Kansas, around 1909. Hulit called the motor an intermittent spring motor; one of the main features was the motor only ran during actual transmission, thereby saving stored power. The design also allowed for generation of dashes where the spaces between the dots and between succeeding dots and dashes were exactly measured and always the same. The small wheel on the left side of the bug was called the "speed regulator," and there was another wheel on the right side for contact adjustments. The Hulit device was granted related patents in 1909 (939,507) and 1912 (1,017,054); both were issued to John A. Hulit.

K8LKC Automatic Bug

A fully automatic bug made by Joe (K8LKC). Joe says this key was fabricated as an experiment. The base is made of white corian material, with other parts made of brass and aluminum.

Leiser's Simplex

Simplex advertisement from *The Railroad Telegrapher*, 1907.

Advertisement from *Telegraph Age*, January 1906. The Simplex was manufactured around 1907 in Salt Lake City, Utah.

Melehan Valiant

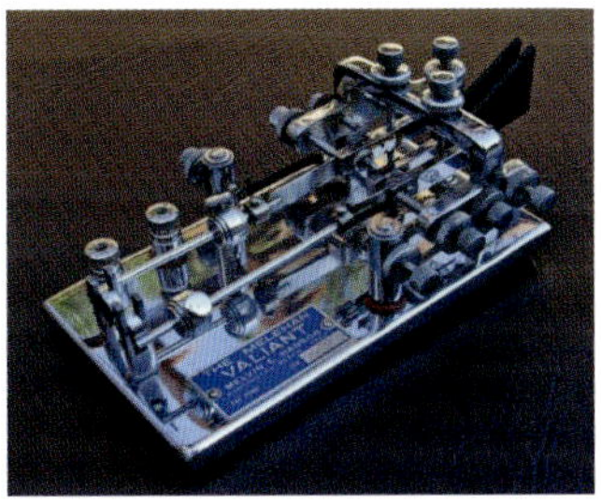

Only a few hundred of the Melehan Valiant fully automatic bugs were made 1939–1950. The device featured two independent vibrating arms with dual pendulums: one for dots and one for dashes. The flat steel spring of the dash vibrator was about twice as long as the one used for the dot vibrator, helping slow down the rate of vibration. There were two pivots on the supporting frame. A *QST* review in March 1942 tells that this device was capable of speeds exceeding 60 wpm.

Melehan is a contraction of the builder's name—Melvin E. Hansen of California. This device's introduction to the ham market came about the same time that interest in electronic keyers started to grow; many feel that poor timing limited the Melehan's sales and acceptance. As is sometimes typical with keys such as this one, the limited numbers produced have helped to considerably raise the collectible value of a Melehan key. Shown is the Valiant with a black base, a chrome base, and examples of right- and left-hand models.

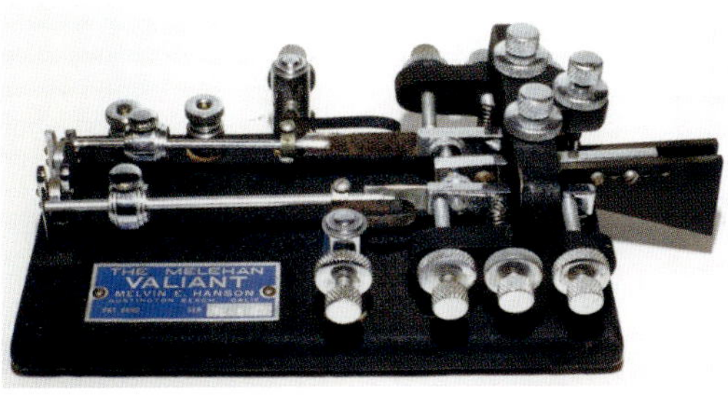

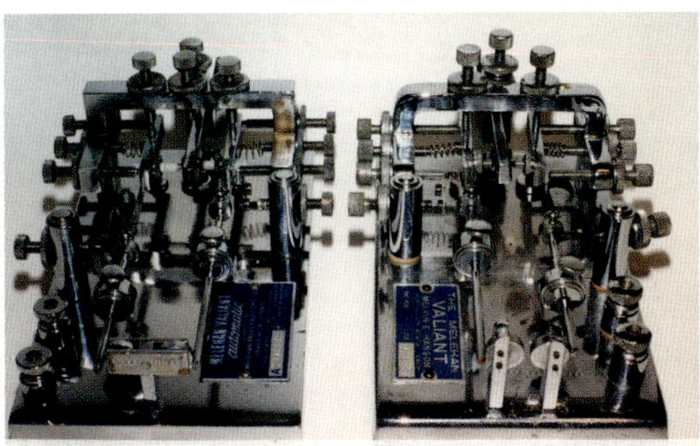

(Right-Handed) Melehan Valiant Bugs (left-Handed)

Simplex De Luxe

The sixth model in the line of Simplex keys was called the De Luxe; it was a fully automatic device. The De Luxe utilized a quite complex design, and was one of the few keys to use three paddles. The large plate on the top made the De Luxe easy to spot, except not very many of these keys were made. Its competition was the Automorse, which like the Simplex De Luxe also took operators a while to master. The De Luxe is considered harder to find than the Automorse. This model was the only Simplex to include a circuit closer. There are three known versions of this key with nickel-plated bases; others have the black wrinkle base shown.

WB2QLL Automatic Bug

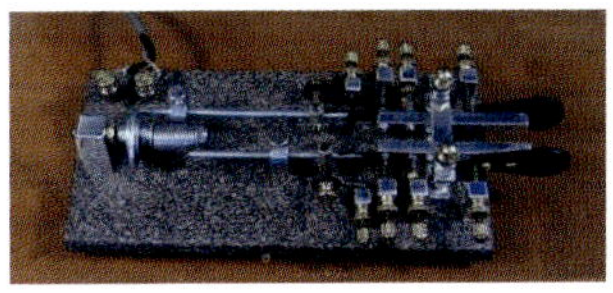

Peter (WB2QLL) designed this fully-automatic key as a challenge, because he did not have much mechanical background.

WB9LPU Automatic Devices

Several versions of WB9LPU's Parkwood DoubleBug, a fully-automatic device. Rich is a perfectionist, as well as an expert machinist. He has described his design/build process for the DoubleBug as he goes through different iterations of the key as one of setting goals and adding concepts learned from building previous versions of keys. For the DoubleBug, Rich got up to eight versions before he felt reasonably happy with how the key was performing. A size comparison between the DoubleBug and a standard Vibroplex bug is provided. Some of the design goals for the DoubleBug included magnetic control of pendulum motion and paddle tension, single-lever design, use of dual

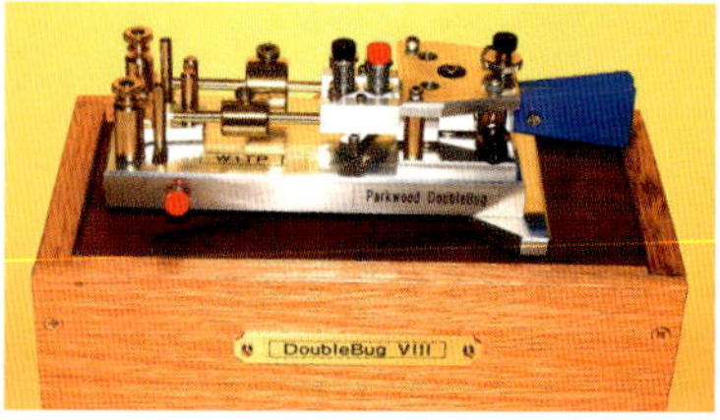

pendulums, magnetic sensing of pendulum motion, micrometer adjustment of weighting, and magnetic and sliding weight control of dot and dash speed.

Another WB9LPU project is the QuadraBug. This is a fully automatic bug project that uses a compound pendulum with elements that are in a quadrature arrangement. Rich publishes descriptive papers on his designs, and these can be found on his website.

The RotoTwin is one of the most fascinating and complex keys Richard has created—of course, that may have changed by the time you read this. The RotoTwin employs the rotation of a variable mass to provide power for the string of automatic dots and the rotation of another variable mass to provide power for a string of dashes. This is a totally new approach that is typical of WB9LPU; his creativity seems to have no limit.

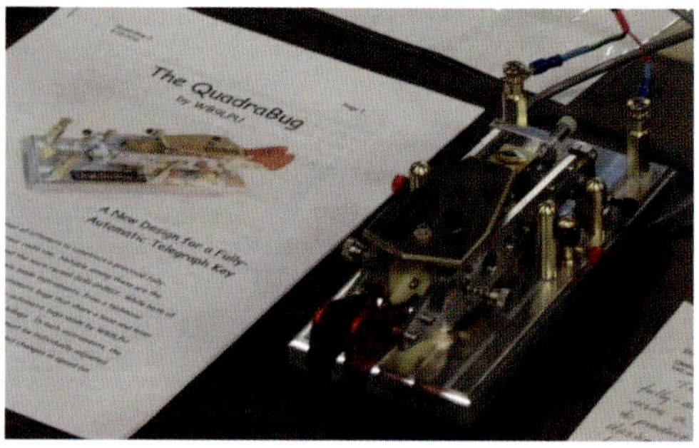

RotoTwin
by WB9LPU
No. 705

11 The Elements of Paddle Design

From paddle arm, base, and fingerpiece material, choice of magnets or springs, arm length, type of bearings, height and shape of the fingerpieces, and much more, the paddle takes on a life and personality of its own after all the parts are assembled.

How should a paddle be designed? And how should it be built? What makes a paddle feel special; conversely, what makes a paddle feel sluggish and unresponsive? As we dissect the paddle, we will take a look at the characteristics that contribute to the paddle's personality and then summarize them in a table. Even with a comprehensive list of paddle attributes and objective measures of important characteristics, there will usually be some undefined attraction that an operator feels toward a particular paddle—some sort of "paddle charisma." For some, the importance of paddle charisma may be so great as to make it the deciding factor in what paddle is bought and used as the daily driver. Paddle charisma can relate to how the key looks or what past memories are kindled. Perhaps the key brings about thoughts of a first QSO, or of a device passed down from a mentor. I have not listed this paddle characteristic because it almost goes beyond subjective; it is unique and varies in importance for each operator. For many CW operators, keys have a rare ability to ignite emotional feelings.

Many of the characteristics listed here could also be applied to an electronic keyer's built-in paddles, should the keyer have them. For many years internal keyer paddles were an afterthought. With a few exceptions, such as the Brown Brothers paddles built into some Palomar keyers, advancements in paddle design have applied almost exclusively to discrete devices. Perhaps this is because operators want their paddles to be seen and available for adjustments and positioning on the desk independently of the keyer electronics.

Dissecting the Paddle

Paddle reliability: Reliability is a very important consideration for the operator. After setting up the paddle by making all necessary adjustments, the operator needs to feel assured those adjustments will not drift or wander over time or during paddle use. Reasons adjustments change are usually mechanical or design related. It would be less than ideal if moving the paddle disturbed any of the settings, or if moderate usage caused adjustments to change. If the operator finds themselves regularly resetting spacing or paddle arm feel then there is probably a mechanical issue at fault. Other reasons for a paddle not holding its settings relate to the basic design: how the paddle arms are mounted, what type of bearings are used (trunnion, ball, FYO-type post/rocker, or flex), and how consistently the springs or magnets function returning the paddle arms to their neutral position. Some paddles do not use bearings; for example, the Brown Brothers BTL-A uses flat spring steel as the return mechanism and the arm suspension mechanism. Frattini paddles do not use typical bearings, instead relying on a type of modified pivot, where a small steel ball is incorporated above and below each pivoting lever. Any arm suspension design that adds friction to arm movement (i.e., a sloppily machined pivot bearing) is to be avoided. Sometimes the operator can feel this friction if he opens up the contact spacing and allows the arms to move a quarter inch or so. Springs are easier to machine parts for and a bit cheaper to use in manufacturing, but do not always allow for a very light touch by the operator. Many feel using magnets to provide return force gives a more sensitive or tactile feel to the operator with a delicate touch. As a design goal magnets should be mounted close to the arm pivot point.

Another element of reliability not often considered is the choice of paddle feet. Review not only the size and shape, but the number of feet and the foot material, making sure the proper foot is being used for that particular design. The wrong foot allows too much paddle rotation, imparts a sloppy feel to the operator due to foot flexure, and may allow the paddle to walk or slip. Look for feet that allow the base to sit close to the desktop and material that does not flex but maintains its grip. The end result of paddle foot deficiencies will likely be errors in code being sent or inconsistent code, depending on the surface the paddle is sitting on.

Thermal issues relate to some paddle settings that change depending on room temperature or proximity to air conditioners or heater vents. The cause for this type of setting drift is most likely related to choice or amount of material, or the type of bearings used. Look for adherence to good design geometry guidelines (a 1:1 leverage ratio). How can one know of any thermal concerns before buying a paddle? Carefully check some of the many published reviews on ham sites, and talk to owners of the device under consideration for purchase. Also try to avoid a paddle design that uses long, massive paddle arms. Paddles using trunnion bearings are sometimes affected by temperature changes, so it may be prudent to spend some extra time trying out that paddle under some different ambient temperatures to see if any changes in arm friction are noticed.

March R-3a showing the trunnion-type suspension and arm pivot system.

Trunnion pin design used on the Vibroplex ZN Ultimate. Each pin has a ball bearing assembly at the top and bottom.

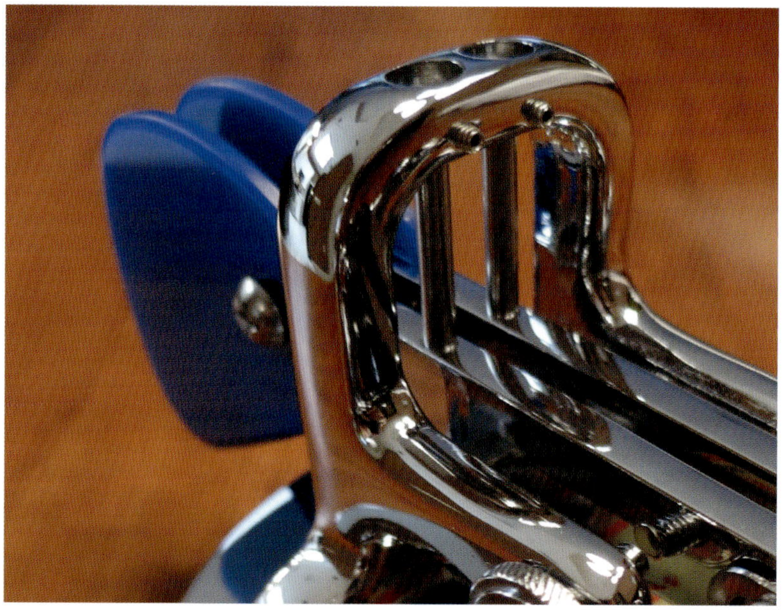

The Kent dual-lever uses ball bearings. Here the bearings are visible, but some manufacturers hide them underneath the frame. This photo also shows the arm tension adjusting springs.

N0SA's use of sealed ball bearings on one of his dual-lever paddles, a TP1A. If you look carefully you can also see part of one of the bottom sets of bearings underneath the paddle arm. When a paddle looks this good under high magnification you can count on the workmanship that you can't see being exceptional. Note even with short paddle arms N0SA has used two screws to attach the fingerpieces.

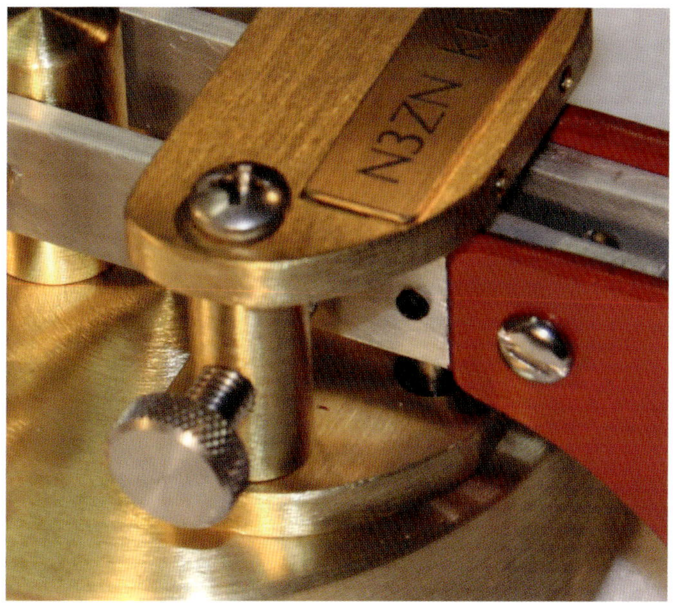

On this N3ZN model the upper bearings are hidden under the top plate.

On this VK2YYO paddle the builder has used a modified bearing approach without a top plate. The posts are press-fit into their paddle arms and two sets of bearings are used in the base: one set on top and one set underneath, giving the arms the positional stability they need.

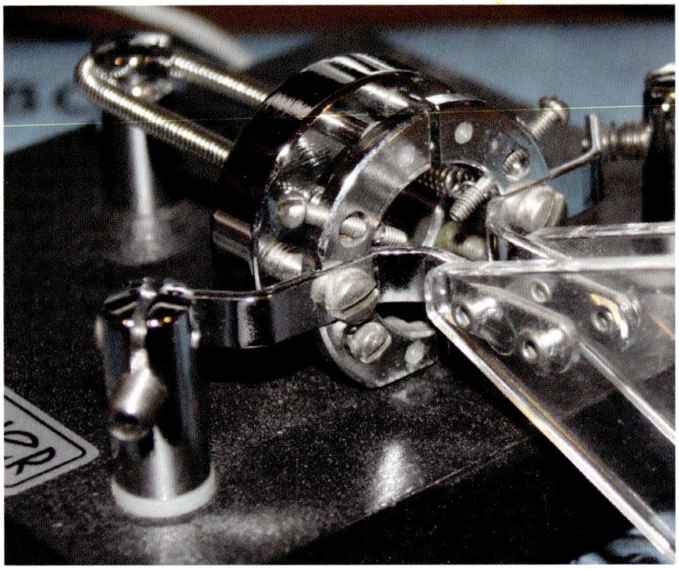

The Bencher and G4ZPY devices also used the post/rocker point system.

The classic W8FYO design used the post/rocker point approach. The posts go into small nylon inserts, giving near frictionless arm movement.

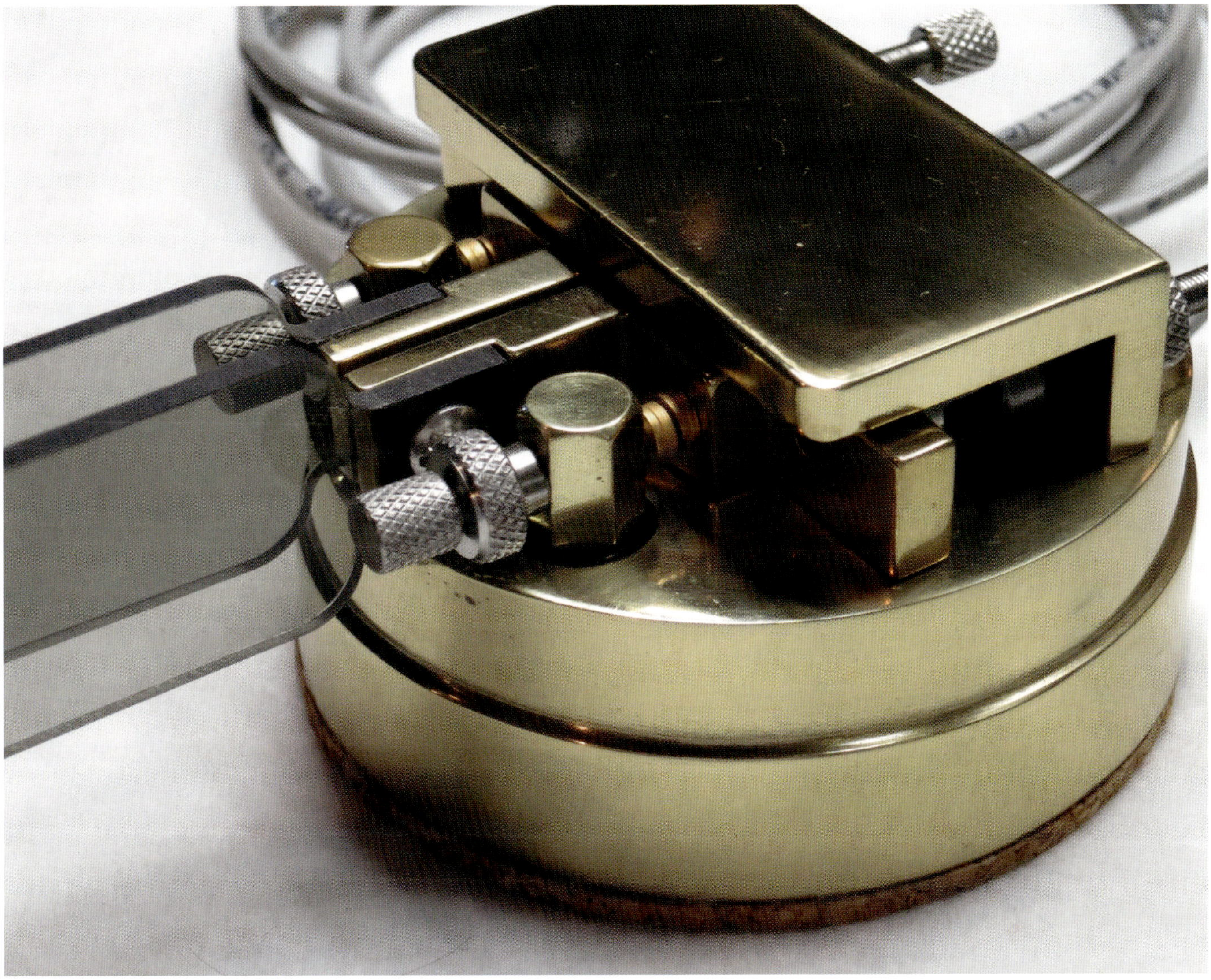

This is believed to be the only paddle that uses flex bearings, the Flex-Flyer built by Ron (KA2BZS). Flex bearings are used where accuracy and repeatability are required; they are essentially frictionless and do not require lubrication. In addition, flex bearings offer an infinite life cycle, and when used in paddle arm design provide the smoothest possible keying.

Drawing of a flex bearing showing internal construction.

The Brown Brothers BTL-A uses flat spring steel to suspend the paddle arms and return them to neutral when not sending.

Contacts: One would like paddle contacts to always look new and never tarnish, have no resistance, and not bounce or generate noise that might result in false keying. In addition, the electrical path of the contacts to ground, through the paddle mechanical components to the terminals, should be electrically clean and of low resistance. Depending on design, this may require a bonding wire of some kind to connect arms or contacts to other parts of the paddle. In the example (below), a braided line runs through the bearings and grounds the paddle arms of this Jones paddle. Paddles missing this feature may result in unreliable keying depending on other elements of the design.

The ideal contact material is gold, but use of gold contacts will increase paddle cost. Some operators feel silver contacts offer advantages; if the paddle is regularly used the contacts rarely need cleaning. Some Begali keys have used an alloy that caused the contacts to act like a diode, with a constant forward voltage drop. This caused problems with some but not all keyers, including some built into transceivers. Cleaning and Deoxit did not help; Begali has made replacement gold contacts that solve the problem. Some newer Begali paddles now come with silver contacts and do not have the diode drop problem. Those using modern rigs that have very low currents in the key circuit may want to avoid paddles with alloy contacts and use only gold or silver.

Also, verify contacts line up correctly, and are not shaped so glitches or noise are introduced upon contact closure. Make sure the paddle design allows enough adjustment margin to properly align contact points and set gap, and that paddle usage does not cause this setting to change over time.

Responsiveness: Do the Morse letters in the operator's mind seamlessly transfer through his fingertips to the paddle contacts? Or is there something about the paddle operation that is fatiguing or bothersome? Does the operator have to work at sending, or is the operator making sending mistakes despite being able to send perfectly on other paddles? There are a couple of major design factors to consider when looking for accurate response and liveliness in a paddle. First, avoid designs that make the operator move relatively massive paddle arms back and forth. More massive arms are said to have a larger angular momentum and may contribute to contact bounce. Any friction in the arm suspension will be more noticeable, and the return mechanism, whether springs or magnets, may be approaching the limits of its repeatability. Arms that exhibit a smaller angular momentum are easier for the operator to move and return to their neutral position more quickly. One result is a paddle using arms with a small angular momentum will most likely be more useful at higher design speeds than one with long, heavier paddle arms. An assumption here is that a small arm design is not compromised by mounting heavy magnets outboard from the pivot point, or using large, heavy fingerpieces; magnets are best mounted as close to the pivot point as possible. Look for sealed bearings as opposed to sleeve bearings. Look for a paddle weight on the heavy side, usually more than two pounds. Avoid lightweight paddle bases, especially on smaller paddles, as stability and accuracy may suffer.

The March R-3a uses a relatively small point on the adjustable side of the contact pair and offers plenty of margin for adjustment.

Contact alignment on an AB5RT paddle.

This Trinidad paddle shows the effects of contact tarnishing, and would benefit from a non-abrasive cleaning process using a strip of paper (see chapter 12).

Jones paddle contacts showing the comparatively large gold-plated button on the paddle arm and the smaller adjustable contact point on the screw.

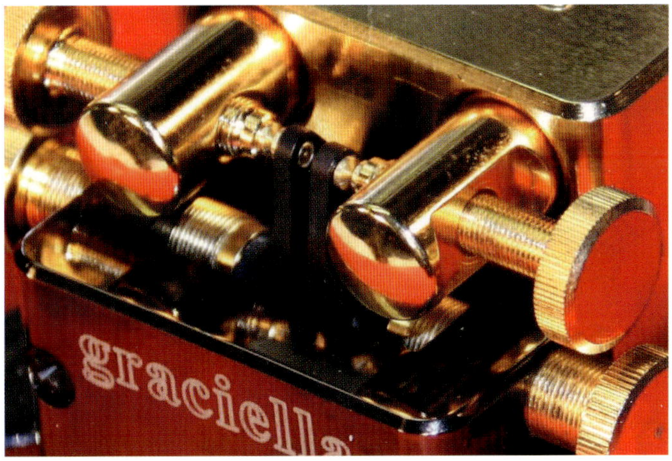

Gold convex contacts of the Begali Graciella. The fine pitch of the adjustment screws can also be seen.

N3ZN paddle contacts; adjusting half of the contact uses a tapered, rounded screw called a contact point.

This paddle has no real contacts on the arms, merely relying on the adjustment screw and the paddle arm to electrically connect.

Perfect contact alignment as seen on the Flex-Flyer.

Arm/Fingerpiece Geometry: This geometry is not very subjective. Look for an arm design that allows the operator's fingertips and the paddle contacts to be about equal distance from the arm pivot point; a good design is seen in the Schurr (below). When you have this equality, it is said you then have a 1:1 leverage ratio. A design giving a 1:1 ratio, or something close to it, will help ensure minimization of negative thermal effects, as well as contribute to a more responsive overall feel.

The preferred spacing between the two fingerpieces on a dual-lever paddle is somewhat dependent on operator preference, but is usually less than 1 in (below right). A few paddle designs (i.e., some Begali models) allow the user to adjust this spacing. Other designs, such as the Jones, also accommodate up and down adjustments of the fingerpieces.

N3ZN uses a measurement he calls OTO—the Out-to-Out dimension of the fingerpieces. Tony has defined his standard OTO to be approximately ¾ in., depending on the particular fingerpiece material used. All the ZN dual-lever paddles are available in OTO options of 5⁄16 in., ½ in., ¾ in., and 1 in. Tony advises buyers measure their favorite paddle's OTO and order accordingly.

N3ZN miniature paddle showing low mass, short arms, fine-threaded adjustments, and a magnet embedded in the paddle arm. This device is also an example of good arm/fingerpiece design geometry.

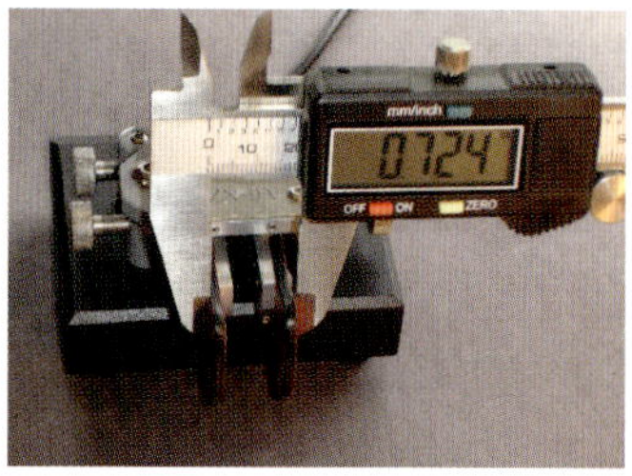

A Schurr Einbau Wabbler showing good design geometry for the paddle arms and operator finger positioning. This paddle is also an example of a very responsive spring arm return device, proving a high performance paddle does not have to use magnets.

Another view of the Schurr's paddle arm design and the spring return.

The W9WBL V2L paddle also presents good arm design, using short, low mass arms resulting in an excellent leverage ratio.

Fingerpiece Design and Material: Good fingerpiece design is not only attractive, but should offer a non-flexible way for the operator to actuate the paddle. Lightweight fingerpieces are desired so angular momentum is not compromised. Long, thin fingerpieces may contribute to sloppy paddle feel and should also be avoided. As a general rule, look for fingerpieces that attach to the arm with two screws. The goal for using double attachment screws is to prevent fingerpiece loosening during use. If the design (see the Excalibur paddle and the N3ZN device shown) allows tightening without problems during usage a single attachment screw should be acceptable.

The Begali 60th Anniversary Sculpture paddle (opposite) uses fingerpieces mounted at a slightly V-shaped angle so the user can change preferred spacing by sliding their fingers slightly up or down. Note the two screws used for mounting the fingerpieces as seen on the standard Sculpture model.

The short, stiff, lightweight fingerpieces on this N3ZN paddle will not result in any flex.

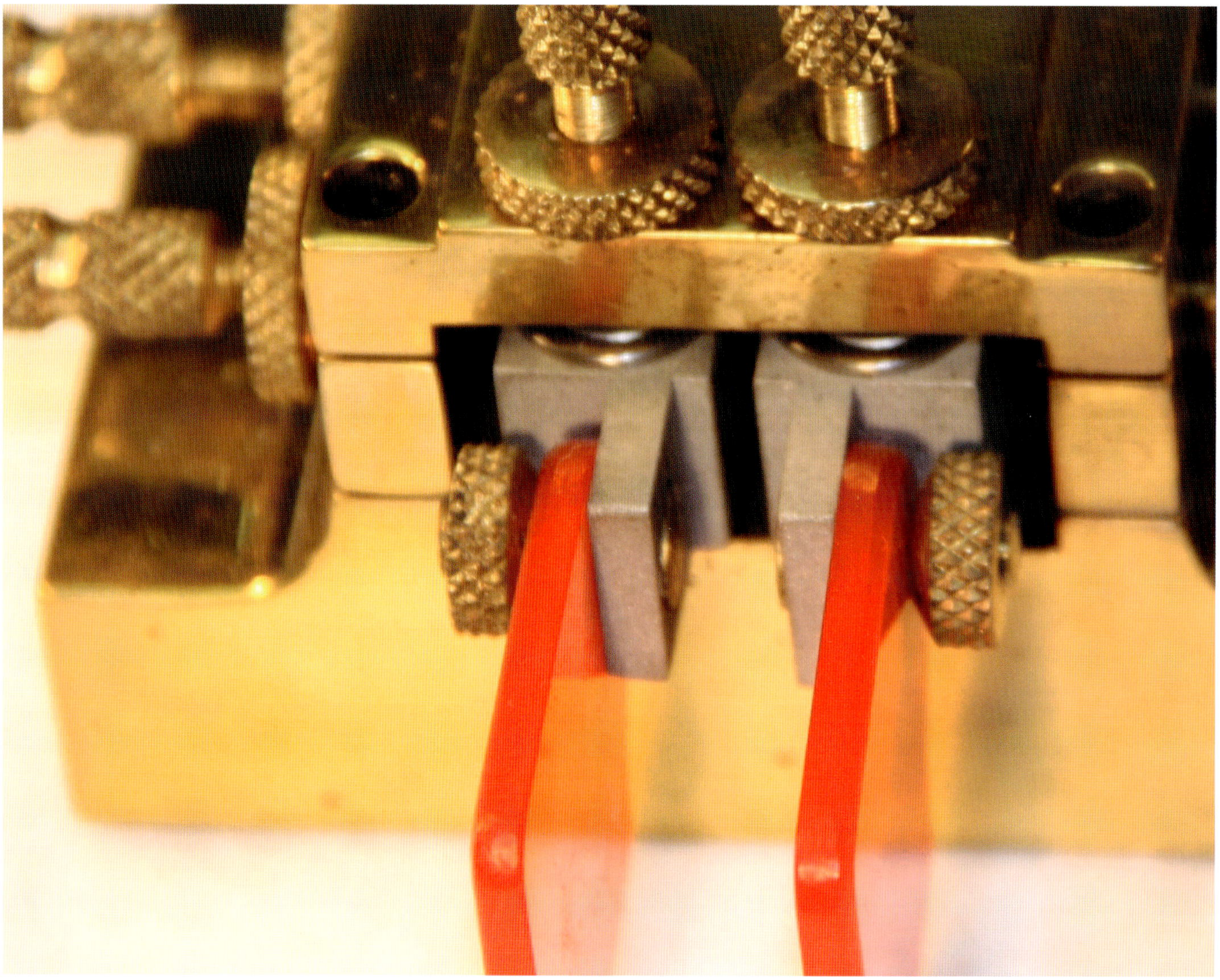

The WK4DS Excalibur paddle is another good example of how lightweight fingerpieces can contribute to low overall angular momentum.

Stiff, carefully shaped fingerpieces as seen on the Begali Sculpture. Two screws are used for attachment to the arms.

User Adjustments: Another element of adjustability is making sure paddle design allows for easy access to the adjusting screws or mechanism. Adjustments hidden by parts or pieces of the paddle, or otherwise blocked, will add to user frustration over time. Paddles incorporating coarse threading for contact or spacing adjustments may not allow the precise setting the operator desires. Usually when coarse threading is used, the locking feature of that particular design is also a compromise, and may lead to variations in the settings. It is best to look for adjusting screws with 40 or greater turns per inch (tpi). As a point of comparison, WK4DS at one time offered an option for 72 tpi. Approaches to locking the settings include thumbwheels, or a split-post approach used by several top-end paddles. N3ZN uses a set screw on top of the adjustment post with a nylon ball inside. The nylon ball applies pressure to the adjusting screw and keeps it from turning, thereby locking it in place after the operator has set it. Consider the available range of adjustments; does the paddle offer enough adjustment margin for those users who like wider arm spacing, for example.

The N0SA adjustments, showing setscrew locking, fine-pitched threads, and enough length in the adjustment screws for any setting.

Locking setscrews on the N3ZN adjustment screws. Note the low-mass paddle arms.

The FYO paddle used a split-post design for adjustment locking; the side setscrew was tightened to squeeze the post sides together for locking.

Use of Magnets vs. Springs: If a paddle uses magnetic repulsion (i.e., the Chevron), continued or increasing force is needed when moving the paddle arm. As you move the paddle arm with very slowly increasing force you can move the lever away from its rest position, but not close the contact. The contact closes only when force is increased further. Other paddles, such as some Begalis, use the attractive magnet arrangement, where the force required to move the lever decreases as the gap closes. This can make for a positive "clicky" feel the operator may not only hear, but notice in their fingertips as they are keying, somewhat akin to the tactile feedback one gets when actuating a microswitch. With very small contact gaps this effect is usually not noticeable.

Whether using repulsing or attracting magnets, many other elements of paddle design come into play and affect its performance, so a paddle should not be selected based on the type of arm return system alone. This also applies to paddles using traditional spring return systems. Many highly rated paddles (the early Schurrs) use spring return and give operators excellent feel and tactile feedback.

In summary, although specific operators may have a preference for magnetic or spring return systems, excellent paddles can be found using each method. The choice should be based on trial paddle usage and analysis of resulting findings.

Mechanical Robustness: Some considerations for ensuring a choice of paddles that is mechanically robust include the paddle's ability to be transported without damage and the repeatability of adjustments after minor knocks and bumps. Adaptability is the paddle trait that allows a device to stand up to occasional visiting guest operators used to slapping the key to send. A trend since the N2DAN paddle was introduced is to use a heavier base with lighter mechanisms (especially the arms); it is felt the heavier base will add to robustness and help prevent key movement on the desk.

Paddle Noise: This refers to the ambient noise generated by the mechanical operation of a paddle. Is it clicky, or does it make objectionable noises when hitting arm stops, or when the arm returns to the neutral position? Do the contacts make noise when closing? Sometimes mechanical noise can be minimized or eliminated by application of shrink tubing or rubber pads placed in appropriate locations, although this should not have to be done on high end paddles. The use of attracting magnets has potential to cause some mechanical noise if the paddle design is such that the contacts close with an audible click and the operator is not using a light touch. Try out the paddle to determine if this noise is an issue.

Construction Quality: Even the best paddle design will result in disappointment if it is not built correctly and to a high level of quality. Quality cannot be designed; it is a characteristic that depends on the manufacturing and assembly process and the skill of the builder. Evaluate this by examining the paddle. Look for imperfections, obvious defects, loose hardware, misaligned parts, and poor plating. Do not forget to check user reviews, although keep in mind they are subjective and not always reliable if only a handful are posted.

Support and Maintenance: Is the paddle manufacturer willing to support his product? Will he fix defects and/or provide replacement parts when necessary at a reasonable cost if the problem is not design related?

Aesthetics: Consider the overall look of the paddle. After all, the operator will be looking at the paddle for quite a while.

Monetary/Collector Value: This is perhaps a lesser consideration for some, but a top-end paddle can also be considered an investment. High quality devices usually resell for close to original value, and in some cases significantly more.

Overall Usability: Will the sum of the parts result in a device the operator wants to use and display? In the end, the objective measurements and meeting design goals can be trumped by the undefined magic that happens when all the parts are assembled. Some paddles just defy logic and convention, and despite not meeting all the paper goals end up as the go-to device of choice.

PADDLE DESIGN AND USAGE CONSIDERATIONS

Characteristic	What to Look For
Reliability	Are adjustments repeatable?
	Is the return force consistent?
Thermal Design	Do settings drift with room temperature?
	Avoid long, massive arms
Contacts	Are contacts corrosion resistant?
	Any contact bounce or electrical noise?
Responsiveness	Review type of bearings—pivot, ball, flex, flat stock
	Assess moving mass (angular momentum)
Arm/Fingerpiece Geometry	Examine arm leverage ratio
Fingerpiece Design/Material	Assess the "feel" of the material used
	Rigidity—fingerepieces should not flex
	Does shape interfere with proper spacing?
	Review overall shape for user's needs
User Adjustments	Is contact spacing adjustable?
	Is arm return force adjustable?
	Is adjustment threading greater than 40 tpi?
Magnets vs. Springs	Try out the paddle!
Mechanical Robustness	Is base material adequate for the design?
	Can paddle be transported without damage?
Paddle Noise	Is the mechanism clicky or noisy?
	Any contact closure or arm stop noise?
Construction Quality	Review/inspect how well the paddle is built
Support and Maintenance	Does the maker support repairs?
	Review availability of parts
Aesthetics	Assess overall look of the paddle
Monetary/Collector Value	How well does the paddle hold its value?
	Any future collectibility?
	Is future resale price a concern?
Overall Usability	Try out the fingerpiece interface
	Is the base weight adequate for user's style of sending?
	Review friction/paddle foot choice for user's style
	Are the range of adjustments adequate?
	Try out the paddle!

Jeweled Movements

Many operators are familiar with the Vibroplex term jeweled movement. Vibroplex Vibrokeyer and dual-lever paddles use a frame and trunnion screw design at the arm pivot point. Jeweled movements use an industrial grade jewel inserted in the trunnion bearing. The standard trunnion pin is pointed to fit inside the holes, while the deluxe trunnion pin is rounded off to more gently pivot on the jewels. The jeweled movement is not a metal-on-metal pivot as a pointed pin inside a hole is. The rounded off trunnion pin rotates on the jewels, giving the key a slightly more "free" feel than the standard trunnion pin and screws.

Parkerizing

Parkerizing is a metal finishing method that protects steel from corrosion. The Parkerizing process is sometimes called bonderizing, phosphating, or phosphatizing. The process essentially involves the application of an electrochemical phosphate conversion coating that increases steel's resistance to wear. In addition, the result is an attractive alternative to paint or other metal conversion processes. The process is frequently used on firearms as an alternative to bluing, and on automobiles to protect unfinished metal parts from corrosion. The Parkerizing process cannot be used on non-ferrous metals such as aluminum, brass, or copper, or on steel that has a large nickel content. Parkerizing is also not used on stainless steel.

Close-up of the Parkerized base on an N0SA single-lever paddle.

12 Paddle Adjustment and Maintenance

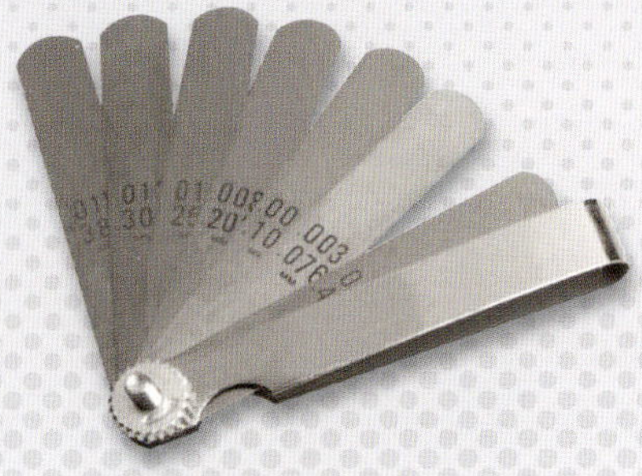

Once your paddle is adjusted according to its design and the operator's preferences, proper care and maintenance will ensure reliability and consistency of sending.

This chapter presents some general notes on paddle adjustment and maintenance. Two of the most popular paddles—the Vibroplex dual-lever and the Bencher BY-1—are used as examples for setting adjustments. Many of the steps will apply to other paddles, but it is possible some special steps related to aspects of a particular paddle's design may apply. It is wise to do some research and defer to the builder's specific recommendations. There is some commonality to paddle design, enough so that some typical adjustments shown here can be used for reference. At the very least, becoming familiar with these adjustments will help the reader begin to understand the elements of paddle design so they are not afraid to tackle more complex adjustments when necessary.

Be aware that every paddle may require special treatment and maintenance steps depending on the materials used and the finish applied to those materials. Once again, the recommendation is to check with the paddle manufacturer or designer for specific maintenance criteria. Some general rules and steps are presented here for brass and chrome; some paddles use exotic materials such as palladium coatings, and these may necessitate special treatment. Know your key's materials and the steps to take to protect your investment.

Adjusting the Vibroplex Paddle

Although the following instructions are geared toward the Vibroplex dual-lever paddle, the intent of the double-lever adjustment steps can be adapted for many similar keys, including the Vibrokeyer.

After disconnecting the paddle from the keyer or transceiver loosen up the topside adjustments (contact and lever tension screws).

Turn the paddle over so the pivot bearing adjusting screws under the mainframe are accessible.

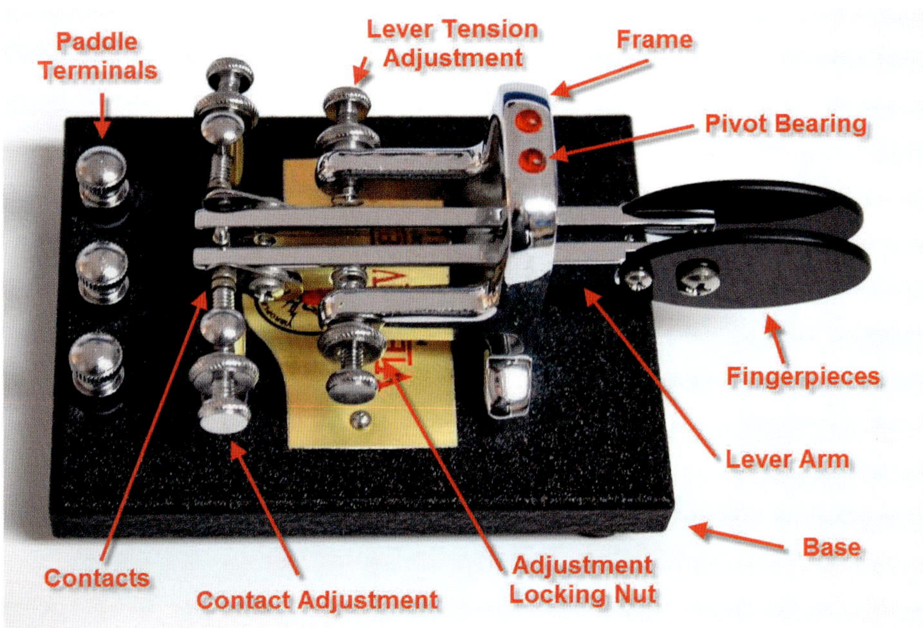

The various parts of the Vibroplex double-lever paddle.

Loosen the small setscrews at the bottom of the frame on the top part of the base. The photo (above) shows one setscrew on a Vibrokeyer; the dual-lever will have two.

The trunnion screws can now be adjusted. Do this from the bottom of the paddle using a small slotted screwdriver. Adjust the trunnion screws (see the arrow) to eliminate freeplay in the paddle arms, but avoid tightening so much that the paddle arms do not rotate freely. This adjustment controls the amount of pressure on the bearing surfaces. Some paddles such as the Vibroplex dual-lever will have two trunnion pins to adjust; some paddles may have four adjustments (two for each trunnion pin). It is sometimes beneficial to back out the tension and contact gap adjustments so the paddle arms have a large swing to them. This may help the user better feel any looseness in the arms as the trunnion screws are adjusted. Make sure the trunnion pin mating surfaces are clean. Never use any type of lubrication on the trunnion screws; the lubricant will only attract dirt and dust.

The trunnion screw adjustment is correct when the lever moves freely without any excess play or binding, and with little or no up-and-down movement. The setscrews on the frame can then be tightened. Next, if the contacts do not align exactly, loosen the contact slide screw at the end of the paddle arm and

move the contact so it lines up with the contact on the end of the threaded adjustment screw on the contact post. Tighten the contact slide screw when the adjustment is complete.

The arm tension can now be set according to operator preference using the two lever tension adjustment screws controlling tension spring compression. The arm (or lever) tension is the force required to move the arms. The operator can feel the effects of this adjustment as they move the paddle arms as if sending code.

Contact gap can now be set using the contact adjustments. This is another setting done according to preference; for example, those preferring a light touch and higher speeds will set this gap very closely. Those with previous experience using an older bug device may prefer wider settings. Some people like to turn on the keyer and close the contact gap until the keyer starts sending dots or dashes; then the adjustment is backed out slowly until sending stops. When setting contact gap this way, the user might find the final spacing is only wide enough to barely slip a sheet of printer paper between the contacts. Use the locking nuts to fix the final setting in place.

Adjusting the Bencher BY-1

As one might imagine, Bencher paddles require a different approach for adjustment than more traditional single and dual-lever devices. The paddle arms of the Bencher (and many similar paddles, such as the G4ZPY, FYO, and the Brass Racers) are not straight, so do not extend back along the base of the paddle. The paddle contacts are toward the front of the device, and the offset shape of the paddle arms means the contacts "rotate" toward the front when the fingerpieces are pressed.

The following instructions may help users setting up the Bencher BY-1 and similar paddles.

Begin by opening up the paddle adjustments. Essentially the settings will be "un-adjusted" to minimize any interaction as the setup process is conducted. Loosen the contact adjustment locking setscrew and back out the contact (increase the gap) on each side of the paddle.

Ensure the bearing posts and nylon bearing insert on the pivot plates are properly seated. The seat area should be clean and free of dust and debris.

If necessary, adjust the pivot plate stop screws, ensuring the pivot plates are parallel to the paddle's main frame. At this point the locator screws should be extending out about ⅛ in. from the pivot plates.

Next the contact gap is set using the spacing adjustment screw. The preferred setting is a matter of operator preference. Contact gap may be set while the paddle is connected to a keyer;

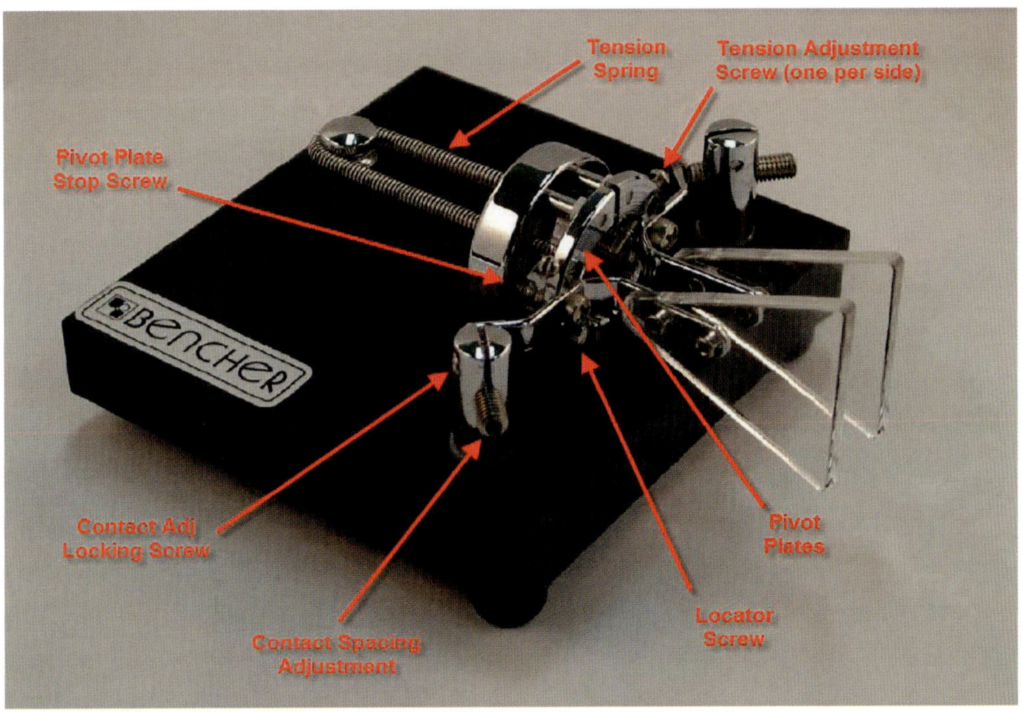

turn in the contact gap adjustment until the keyer begins sending a string of dots or dashes, then slightly back out the adjustment until sending stops. Lock this setting in place using the locking setscrew on the contact post.

If necessary, loosen the contact post mounting hardware and allow the post to slightly rotate so alignment of the two contacts is correct. Avoid a contact post setting that allows the edge of one contact to hit the surface of its partner contact. In cases where the paddle may have been mishandled in the past a paddle arm may have been abused or bent, and correcting this may be the only way to set up proper contact alignment; usually judicious use of pliers can effect minor paddle arm shaping.

Arm tension can now be set using the tension adjustment screws. This setting is subject to operator preference but should not be too high. Operators who send at higher speeds tend to want the minimum amount of tension allowing them to feel they have control over the paddle while getting adequate tactile feedback. By preference the arm tension setting can also differ for each paddle arm.

Some Generic Adjustment Hints

To get a good idea of the smoothness of the paddle mechanism, open up the magnetic or spring arm tension adjustments and the contact spacing. The mechanism and any associated unevenness or friction spots can be better felt by the operator and corrected before final tension setting. When setting arm tension and contact spacing, it may be possible—depending on the paddle design—to insert a piece of paper in between the contacts to keep the adjusting screw from turning as the operator tightens the locknut.

Contact Cleaning Methods

With high quality silver or gold contacts specified on many of today's paddles, it is important proper cleaning materials and techniques be used. Attempting to clean contacts with files, sandpaper, emory cloth, or even scraping with a sharp knife are all methods to be avoided.

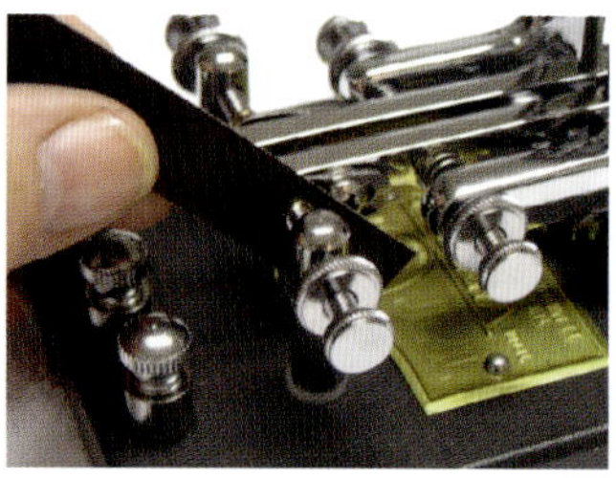

The Key Contact Cleaner is a flexible ½ × 4½ in. strip sold by Les (AA4F). It is two sided, made of an extremely fine material, and is designed to clean and polish soft metals. The cleaning procedure is simple: merely insert the strip between the contacts and hold them closed with light pressure, then pull the cleaner strip through the contacts once or twice. According to Les' website his cleaning strip is approved by Vibroplex for use on their keys.

For silver contacts that become oxidized the Signal Corps included a burnisher in their field telegraph sets. Although burnishers are available from various sources, Signal Corps' manuals recommended alternatives: a piece of smooth steel or a piece of unglazed non-glossy bond or other paper that will not leave lint on the contacts. Some use a new dollar bill and draw it several times through the contacts while maintaining a slight pressure to hold the contacts closed; this procedure can also be used with gold contacts. Avoid cleaning compounds and chemicals. Many quality contact sets are not solid gold or silver, but plated; the plating can be very thin and one risk of improper cleaning is the thin plating will be worn away.

Feeler Gauge Contact Adjustments

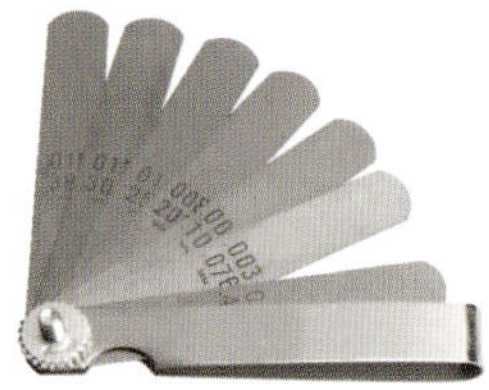

Some operators may use a feeler gauge to accurately measure contact gap settings. Measurement allows recording of settings so they can be returned to previously known spacings without the need for repeating the trial and error original setup process. Almost any typical feeler gauge will work for paddle application, as long as the leaves will physically fit the paddle parts and allow access to the contacts to be measured.

IK6BAK Dynomometer

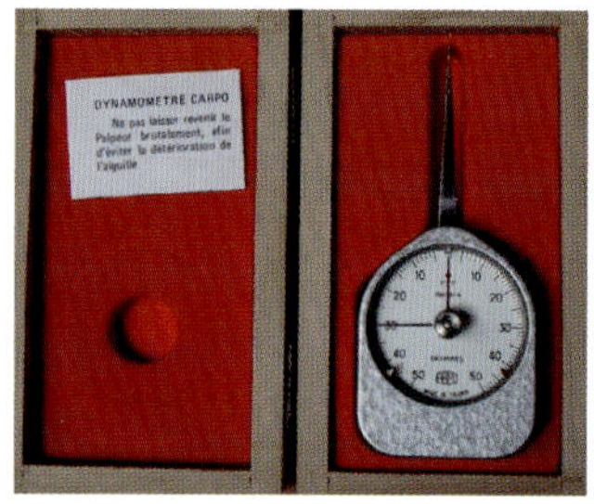

Eliseo (IK6BAK) makes this dynamometer to help CW operators set up their keys. The dynamometer is a wonderful tool for accurately setting spring tensions on dual-lever paddles and single-lever telegraph keys, and is especially useful for returning keys to a previous condition. Although it is fairly easy to use a feeler gauge to set contact gap, the dynamometer is necessary to set arm tension. The dynamometer also allows for tension setting of one key to be easily transferred to another key using the same recorded settings. It also provides a way to see how much different your tension preferences may be for each paddle lever. Eliseo's device is packed in a very nice felt-lined wooden case and is an inexpensive way to set key arm tension without relying on thumb and finger sensing.

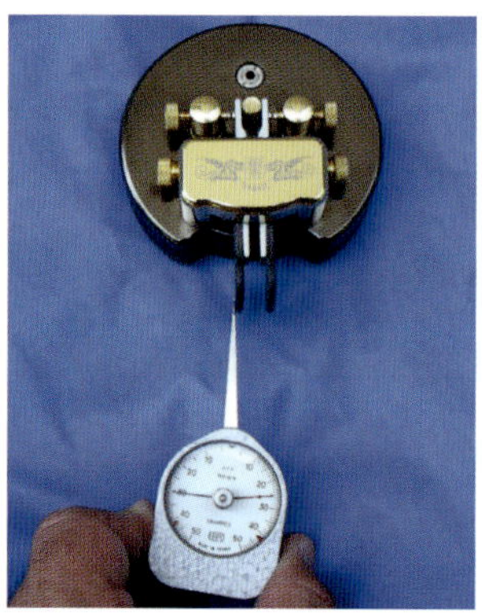

Using the dynamometer to set paddle arm tension.

Key Restoration

While restoration of keys is a topic outside the scope of this book, those interested should refer to W. R. Smith's excellent book *How to Restore Telegraph Keys*. Dr. Tom Perera comments:

[W. R. Smith] has published an extraordinary book that details every important step in the restoration and repair of telegraph keys. WR's book addresses the plating or japanning and pin striping of key bases, the making of needed key parts, the plating of small parts in the home shop, the replacement of mainsprings, the winding of coil springs, etc.

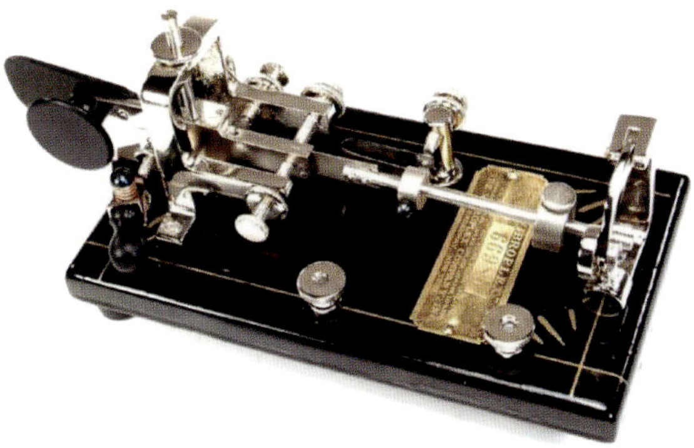

Before and after results of Smith's restoration of a Vibroplex Original.

Maintenance of Brass

Brass is used for the basic components of many paddles because it is easy to machine and allows the paddle to be responsive, yet have a solid feel. Brass parts tend to look new and shiny for a period of time, especially after machining, but can soon lose their luster. Oxidation may take a toll on brass parts and cause a dullness some consider attractive if it is evenly distributed on the part—the patina collectors speak of. Sometimes aging can produce streaks and dark spots on brass.

One partial solution to help mitigate effects of oxidation is coating brass with lacquer or some other chemical. Keymakers who specialize in brass often have their favorite proprietary coatings, and many of these delay aging on brass. Some coatings do more harm than good and must be removed to refinish brass in poor condition from contaminants that have worked their way past the coating over time. For coated keys that have deteriorated more extensive refurbishment is required, with techniques outside the scope of normal maintenance. The Chevron and N3ZN keys are examples of devices that have received proprietary coatings that appear to hold up well.

It is recommended maintenance for any brass paddle be based on manufacturer's guidelines. The N3ZN paddles use a special lacquer designed for brass. Tony requests his key owners not use any chemicals or liquids on the brass finish; he suggests a dusting brush with soft bristles for cleaning the key. At one time such a brush was offered on the N3ZN website (below) for $5.

For cases where brass is uncoated and has not aged well, it is recommended to first clean the parts with a warm soapy water solution and dry with a soft cloth. Once dirt and dust have been removed further evaluation can be done. The next step is to check with a magnet to see if the parts are solid brass or brass plated. Plated

Some paddles, such as the Chevron, are coated using a proprietary material and process and require no maintenance. The user should not attempt to abrasively clean such a paddle. This close-up shows a Chevron base with proprietary coating.

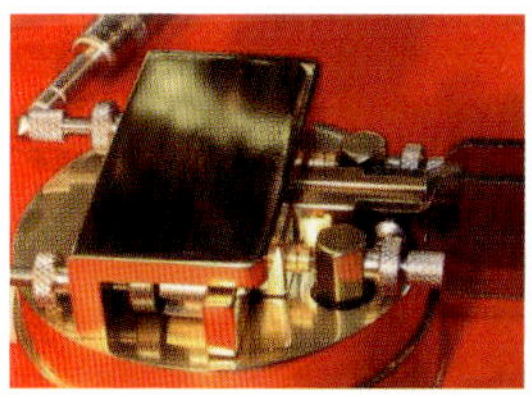

The Flex Flyer also uses a special brass coating.

The ON4MAC paddles do not use a coating, but the brass is given an attractive brushed finish that helps resist the effects of handling.

The brass parts of this Hannes Bauer show patina resulting from brass aging. When the aging is evenly distributed and there is no black spotting the weathered finish can be quite attractive, and should probably be left as is.

parts should not be aggressively cleaned or polished abrasively because the plating may be thin. A mild polish can be made from a mixture of water, white vinegar, and flour; with care this may be used on plated parts. For solid brass, a jeweler's cloth or some of the wadding polishes (Nevr-Dull) can be used. Heavily tarnished solid brass can be cleaned with hot vinegar or a commercial product like Brasso or Blitz.

Maintenance of Chrome

There are several types of chrome finishes typically found on Morse paddles. Decorative chrome is almost mirror-like and is usually a very thin plating. The larger upper parts of some GHD models use what GHD calls a "pear" finish, which is satin chrome that is more resistant to fingermarks than standard chrome. Sometimes keys will be finished in brushed chrome, as seen on some Vibroplex Code Warrior Junior paddles. A bright, shiny, mirror-like finish usually means an object has been chromium plated, although highly polished aluminum approaches the reflectivity of chrome plate.

Another type of chrome plating—called hard chrome plating—usually results in a thicker layer of chrome and is meant to be a protective finish. It almost always uses a steel base and is metallic, but not necessarily shiny in appearance. High quality chrome plating typically requires two sub-layers of nickel plate, and sometimes that starts with a copper plated base layer. Some platers will use a layer of bronze plate on top of the nickel, with the layers adhering to each other to increase the strength of the finish. Usually there is no protective clear coat applied to chrome.

Chrome plated parts should be treated with care and respect; as mentioned, the plating can be thin and parts can seemingly develop scratches or swirl marks overnight. Fine scratches and light swirl marks are removable, but deep scratches generally require replating the item to eliminate defects. It is prudent to test whatever cleaning or polishing method being considered in an inconspicuous spot, such as underneath the paddle base. Another polishing method starts with red jewelers rouge, which is applied to a clean, soft cloth. The cloth is then lightly rubbed in a circular motion over the scratched area while not allowing the cloth to become dry. Apply a bit more jewelers rouge as needed to keep the cloth moist and repeat the polishing process until the light scratches are gone. Let the rouge do the work, as opposed to exerting too much force on the cloth and the object. The chrome can be further polished with an impregnated batting type of metal polish (Nevr-Dull) or some of the commercially available polishing cloths.

Mitutoyo Micrometer

A GHD GT501A key showing a built-in Mitutoyo micrometer for accurate, repeatable contact gap setting. Although this is a straight key, perhaps the use of an integral micrometer will soon spread to some high end paddles. The Mitutoyo micrometer adjusts contact spacing to within a fraction of a millimeter, and in cases where adjustments need to be opened up for cleaning, the user can dial right back to the previous settings without having to repeat the setup process.

13 Morse Keyer and Paddle Accessories

This chapter looks at paddle cables, covers, pads, debouncers, and other Morse keyer and paddle accessories.

There are a variety of products that fall into the category of keyer or paddle accessory. For the most part all contribute in some small way to the ability of the operator to send more accurate or consistent code. A few of the items presented could be considered convenience items, but even these make a contribution to better CW in their own way, even if it is decreasing operator fatigue or increasing comfort while adding operating convenience.

Anti-Slip Pads

Anti-slip pads are available from numerous manufacturers; they are popular for keeping electronic gadgets in place on automobile dashes but are excellent for desktop paddle use. Simply trim to shape and insert underneath the paddle. These pads are sometimes called non-slip pads.

The anti-slip pad offered by Vibroplex measures 4.25 × 3.75 in.

Cable Tidy

Cable Tidy devices are made by Johnny (G3LIV); they are basically a small PC board and cable combination that allows the user to simplify and tidy up the cable connections of their keyer paddle or bug. PC boards are double-sided, with plated through holes and silver plating. Boards are available to fit Vibroplex keys and GHD paddles in red or black. Cables typically furnished are 1 meter (3.28 ft.) long and come with a 4-pin mini-DIN connector on one end, and either a 6.4 or 3.5 mm plug on the other end.

A Vibroplex paddle with Cable Tidy installed.

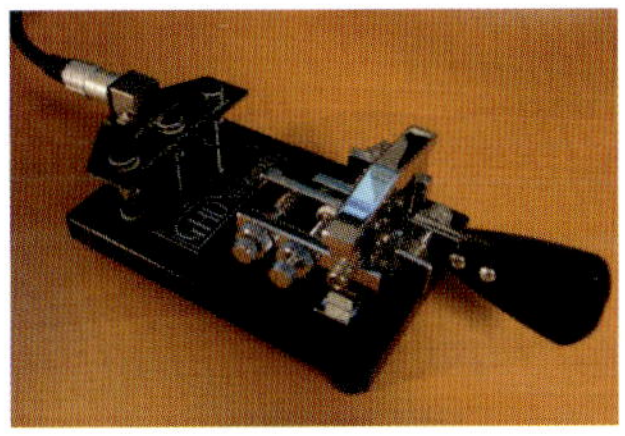

A GHD paddle showing Cable Tidy installation.

Curtis EK-402RC Remote Keyer Control

The EK-402RC was designed to be used in conjunction with a keyer paddle to allow remote control of Curtis memory keyers. Although the EK-402RC is no longer being produced, similar units can easily be fabricated by most hams.

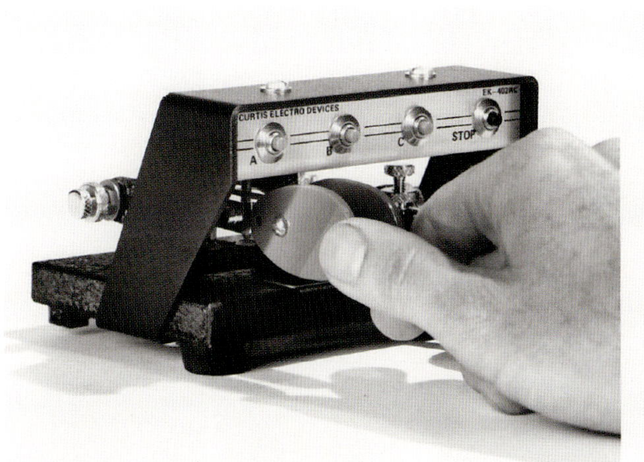

HAL FYO with Memory Buttons

HAL's FYO paddle is shown with the optional memory buttons for connection to a memory keyer. The memory buttons were not a commonly seen option on HAL paddles and are valuable to collectors today.

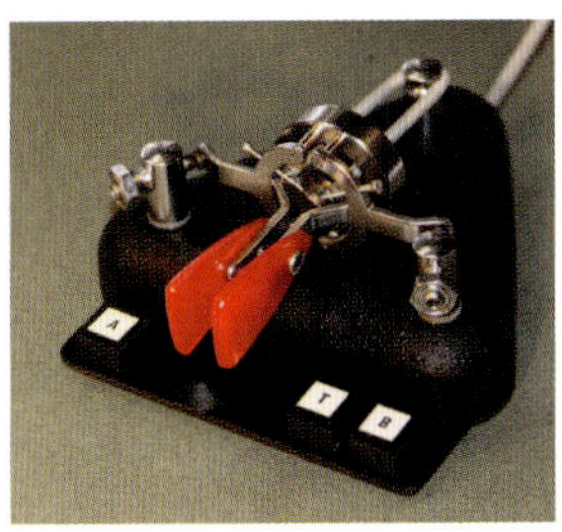

Ham Gadgets Universal Keying Adapter

The Ham Gadgets interface circuit for their Universal Keying Adapter 3+ includes new features, such as a power on/off switch, an on-board header, LEDs for power and keying status, and an aluminum enclosure. The design uses a solid state relay with improved ratings: 800 volts DC or AC and up to 1.35 amps. Parts are through-hole PCB mount (no surface mount parts). Keying input can come from a hand key, bug, or electronic keyer, a transceiver's keying output, a computer serial or parallel port output pin, a foot switch, or other grounding or active high input (up to 20 volts DC). Keying turn-on times are just a few milliseconds.

The user can connect two inputs at the same time—one active high and one active low—so computer and electronic keyers can be used simultaneously. For those who use contest software programs, the COM or LPT port can connect directly to the active-high input, giving computer keying of any solid state, grid-block, or cathode keyed rig. An additional benefit is a straight key or memory keyer can be used at the same time. A power LED shows the device is powered on and ready and the status LED shows when your rig or amp is keyed. The kit is designed to use 12 volt AC or DC power.

The Universal Keying Adapter 3+.

Hi-Mound AA-101 QSK Adapter

The AA-101 is a rare device and not very much supporting information is available. A device marked "break-in relay" is mounted on the top cover, and a keyer relay circuit diagram shows the relay wiring. The front panel includes a power on/off switch and a voltage select switch, perhaps letting the user set up the relay coil voltage for either 115 or 220 volts. Upon power on the large square red light illuminates. The circuit board used inside the AA-101 has a limited number of tracks; at first glance the wiring tends to support the guess this device is merely a simple switching relay as opposed to a real QSK device. A good guess would be the keyed line from a partner Hi-Mound EK-101 actuates the relay to allow for automatic antenna switching. If these assumptions are true, a better name for this unit would be "semi-QSK" adapter.

Jackson Harbor Keying Adapter

The Keyall is an accessory for a keyer, hand key, or bug allowing operation with nearly any transmitter. The circuit is a solid state relay that will key solid state (12 volt) cathode keyed tube rigs with high positive keying voltage or grid-block tube rigs with high negative keying voltage. The Keyall will also key transmitters like the original Tuna Tin 2, which requires a keying output isolated from ground. The Keyall output can be made fully optically isolated from the keyer input. The Keyall can be used as a conventional solid state relay for DC or AC loads; the output transistors and capacitor are rated at 500 V and 2.5 A (2500 mA). Board size is 1 × 1.5 in.

Jackson Harbor Iambic-to-Single Paddle Converter

The iambic-to-single paddle converter shown is a device that connects between a dual-lever paddle and an iambic keyer. For those users who are proficient on a single-lever paddle this converter makes using an iambic keyer much easier. The circuit is PIC-based; it only allows one paddle input to the keyer at a time. The user can bypass the converter and operate in iambic mode; an LED is included for visual indication of iambic or single-paddle mode. Board size is 1 × 1.5 in. and the circuit operates using a 3 volt power source.

Key Debouncers/Descratchers

All mechanical switches, except perhaps mercury wetted switches, tend to bounce slightly on make and break. Since the paddle is a sophisticated type of switch, it is important for a keyer to recognize the difference between switch bouncing or scratchiness and legitimate operator keying. Many keyers do not have the ability to discriminate between the two, with unwanted code elements the result. In some cases the operator may be unfamiliar with the keyer's design and not realize the spurious code elements he is hearing are not his fault.

Short of redesigning the keyer, one practical way to condition keyer input is to insert a contact debouncer between paddle and keyer. These devices are sometimes called descratchers. Contact bounces occur very quickly, with glitches typically around 5–10 milliseconds in length. For some keyers, their circuits see this noise as a dot the operator intends to send. A well designed debouncer will eliminate shorter duration noise from a legitimate 25 millisecond high speed dot, for example. Presented below are two approaches to eliminating paddle contact bounce problems.

The MicroHAM Paddle Processor was a collaborative design between K1EL and microHAM. Various new paddle designs started moving away from coin silver contacts and have incorporated supposedly improved alloys, the result being the number of keying issues has risen. The paddle processor was an attempt to mitigate the oxidation problems related to alloy contacts. While those alloys and surface treatments work fine for some users, others apparently use keyers that do not discriminate well between key up and key down states. The alloy contacts, and some contacts using exotic surface coatings, are a problem for many PIC-based keyers, such as the WinKey models. The MicroHAM processor used a micro-power PIC with independent, high threshold inputs to sense paddle state. The device incorporated an advanced algorithm to remove noise that might be originating

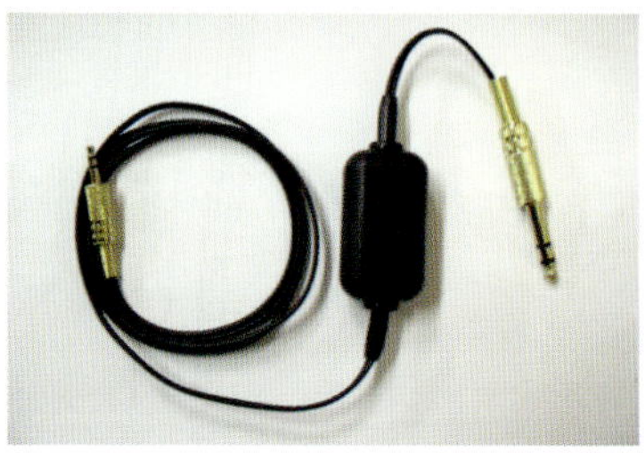

from the paddle and then passed cleaned and processed paddle closure signals to the keyer at levels that did not confuse the PIC.

Another debouncer/descratcher device comes from Jackson Harbor. This version uses a circuit based on the Dave Cuthbert (WX7G) article from the September 1992 issue of *QST*. The Bug Descratcher III removes the "scratchiness" encountered with semi-automatic keys (bugs) due to contact bounce. It can also be used with straight keys. The board gives the user a debounced output and features an optional solid state relay output that will key almost any rig with positive or negative keying voltage. Power requirement is 9–13.8 volts DC; the board sells for $12.

MFJ-522 2-Meter CW Interface

MFJ's JimHandy CW Interface is designed to plug into a 144/440 MHz handheld and convert it into a modulated CW transceiver. According to MFJ, the user only needs to plug in a key. A transmit/receive switch automatically switches the handheld rig to transmit when CW is sent and returns it to receive when keying stops. The MFJ-552 has a built-in speaker, volume control, and a sinewave sidetone oscillator. It measures 4 × 1¼ × 3¾ in. and uses one 9 volt battery.

N2DAN Memory Button Bracket

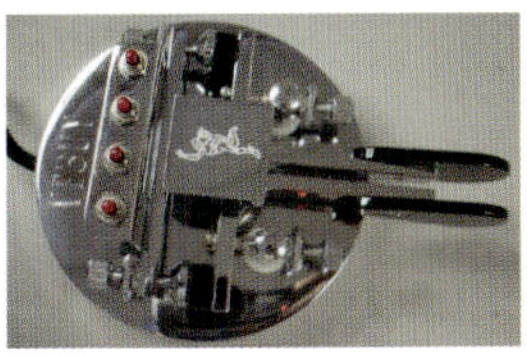

N2DAN offered an optional memory button bracket for memory keyers.

Paddle Dust Covers

Vibroplex offers Plexiglas dust covers for many of their keys; an example is shown on the Vibrokeyer.

EA2CTB runs a small company in Spain; they produce high quality Plexiglas dust covers for several paddle models.

Paddlette Knee Mounts

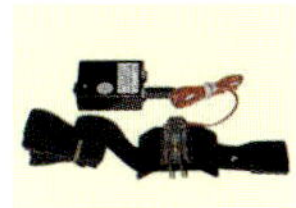

The KM-1 is designed to work with the PK-1 paddle key for situations where a flat surface is not always available. Paddlette recommends the user place the mount on the upper leg and snug the strap; after the key is placed on the mating magnet it is ready to use.

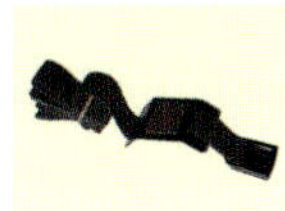

Paddlette's Model KM-2 is designed as an accessory to the sub-miniature model BP backpacker paddle key. Essentially, the KM-2 is identical to the KM-1, only smaller, but will accommodate either key. The strap on both mounts is made of 1 in. wide woven, elasticized polyester belting.

Palm Radio Infrared Link Technology

Palm Radio offers a wireless communication system between the keyer paddle or straight key and the radio. Palm considered some existing techniques, such as RF modules, Bluetooth, and ultrasonic, but concluded they were not workable for various reasons. Further research and experimentation yielded their "Palm Radio Infrared Link Technology," which consists of a miniature IR receiver module and IR transmitter. The miniature infrared receiver module can be built inside the user's rig. It is ideal for homebrew equipment and features very low power consumption. The circuit board is only 9 × 18 mm (plus 3-pin Molex plug), with a control LED (SMD) on the board. All parts are SMD, and a connecting cable with 3-pin Molex plug is supplied. Power is obtained either directly from the rig or by using any voltage from 5–15 volts at 1.5mA.

The standalone version of the miniature infrared receiver measures 25 × 25 × 35 mm (1 × 1 × 1.4 in.) and is meant for use with the PPK IR, Code Cube IR, or the IR Transmitter. Powered by a CR 2032 lithium cell, the receiver has an auto power off function. Current load on idle is 1.5mA, with signal 1.9mA. Battery life is approximately 100 hours (equals 600 QSOs of 10 minutes each).

The IR Transmitter can be used with any CW keyer or bug. It features a sturdy aluminum casing and has a built in tone generator that can be adjusted to seven different pitches or switched silent. A red 3 mm LED serves as a visual indication of Morse code. Power is supplied by a CR 2032 lithium cell. The IR Transmitter works with any of Palm's IR Receiver and IR Sensor models.

An infrared diode at the back of the Code Cube IR allows wireless communication to the IR Receiver or the IR Sensor up to 5 m (16.5 ft.).

Skytec CW-1 Speaker

Passive audio filters have been around for many years. The Skytec CW-1, made during the 1970s, is a good example. It utilized a ported 2 in. speaker mounted in a tuned cavity made from thin wall PVC pipe. At the mouth was a little sleeve you could adjust to set the center of the bandpass. If your receiver did not have a CW filter this little jewel worked fairly well. It sold for about $20 at the time. Skytec was in Ukiah, California.

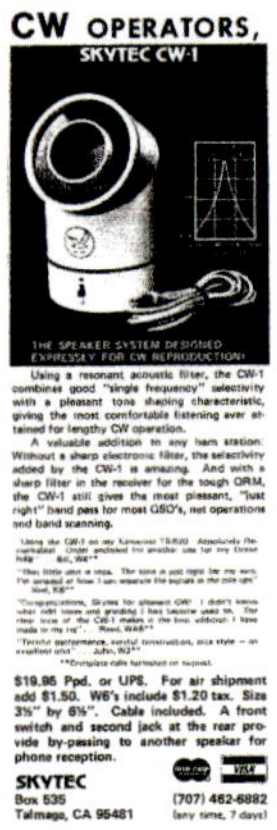

CW OPERATORS,

SKYTEC CW-1

THE SPEAKER SYSTEM DESIGNED EXPRESSLY FOR CW REPRODUCTION!

Using a resonant acoustic filter, the CW-1 combines good "single frequency" selectivity with a pleasant tone shaping characteristic, giving the most comfortable listening ever attained for lengthy CW operation.

A valuable addition to any ham station: Without a sharp electronic filter, the selectivity added by the CW-1 is amazing. And with a sharp filter in the receiver for the tough QRM, the CW-1 still gives the most pleasant, "just right" band pass for most QSO's, net operations and band scanning.

$19.95 Ppd. or UPS. For air shipment add $1.50. W6's include $1.20 tax. Size 3½" by 6½". Cable included. A front switch and second jack at the rear provide by-passing to another speaker for phone reception.

SKYTEC
Box 535
Talmage, CA 95481

(707) 462-6882
(any time, 7 days)

Skytec CW-1 ad from the December 1977 *QST*.

West Mountain Radio CW Switch

The West Mountain Radio CW Switch allows the user to select keying options for two different radios. The switch is used to determine which radio is keyed for use using external paddles, external keyers, or computer controlled keying. This device allows CW operators to quickly switch between two radios without having to wire keys in parallel or move cables.

As stated in the West Mountain product description, modern radios usually have inputs for keyers and paddles. The keyer input is a two-wire straight key jack. It is normally connected to a computer CW interface like most RIGblasters—an external keyer or a straight key. The paddle input is a three-wire jack that keys the radio's internal keyer. It is used with dot-dash paddles that make one connection to send dots and another to send dashes. The CW switch features two sets of keyer and paddle outputs, one set for each radio. There are two keyer inputs provided, giving users the choice of using a keyer and either a computer or straight key for CW. Hooking up all three (an external keyer, computer keyer, and straight key) is possible if a Y-cord is used. A single paddle input enables one paddle to be switched between both radios.

14 Telegraph Machines, Keyboard Keyers, and Terminals

Automatic sending machines are far older than most radio amateurs realize. Some of the oldest devices predate the Civil War and used keyboards resembling piano keys. Read about a 1910 Morse typewriter with a 72 character memory buffer and a 40-tube keyboard keyer made in the early 1950s.

The history of the Morse keyboard can be clearly delineated by the changeover from mechanical and electromechanical devices to electronic devices. WWII makes a good dividing point, and keyboard devices seen from the 1950s onward are mostly electronic in design. The pre-WWII mechanical and electromechanical machines are fascinating to study, and they introduced telegraphy and Morse code to users who had no previous knowledge in those areas. This chapter will present pre-WWII devices first, followed by post-WWII keyboards that most readers will be more familiar with. Strictly software approaches that use a standard PC and computer keyboard are not included (the N4YG keyboard interface device is presented in chapter 15, in consideration of it representing a future trend).

A Look at Some Early Automatic Devices

Before presenting the more traditional appearing keyboards most operators are familiar with, it is interesting to take a look at the precursors to the modern keyboard, even though some of them did not utilize the Morse code method of telegraphy. Early devices tended to use alphabetic wheels or piano-type keyboards to make letter selections. Not until after the typewriter became popular did automatic Morse code machines begin to use modified typewriters, such as the Yetman machine, or designs that used buttons resembling keyboard keys, as seen on the Keen-Kode device. Beginning with the 1850 wheel machines (there were quite a few in the mid-nineteenth century), this chapter will show some examples of the progression of automatic telegraphy devices from mostly mechanical units onward to the electromechanicals. The history of automatic telegraphy machinery will allow the reader to appreciate the efforts that preceded today's electronic keyboards. The remainder of this chapter will examine various keyboards of the modern era.

R. E. House Type-Printing Telegraph (1849)

Royal Earl House invented the printing telegraph machine in 1846; the drawing shows his improved 1849 model. House conceived a system that would link two of his machines together using wire. As a user on one end depressed one of 28 piano-like keys, a recipient on the other end would see a 56 character typewheel rotate and print the corresponding letter. What House envisioned was essentially the first synchronous data transmission system. Each piano key represented a letter of the alphabet and when pressed caused the corresponding letter to print at the receiving end. The typewheel at the receiving end was synchronized with its twin at the transmitting machine. The function of the machine was similar to the daisy wheel printers of modern vintage. The House invention could send at about 40 wpm and the printer could copy and print about 2,000 words per hour.

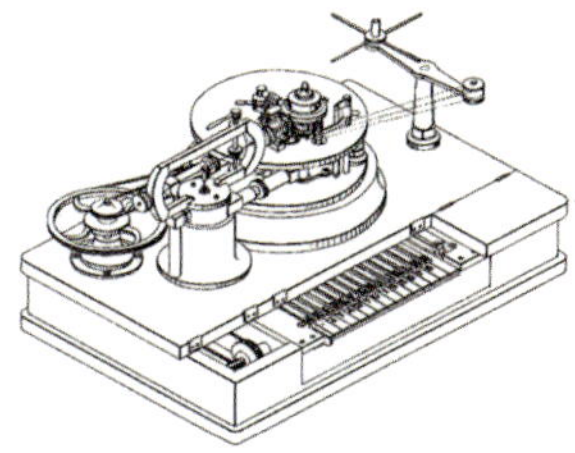

Siemens & Halske ABC Telegraph Machine (1850)

This ABC telegraph was built by Siemens and Halske based on a patent granted to E. W. Siemens in 1850 that outlines the "Improvements to Electric Telegraphs" made by him. The improvements included hollow iron tubes rather than solid bars to increase the strength of the magnet. Messages were sent by selecting letters that determined the current supplied from a battery; this current was used to actuate a rocking lever in the receiving device. The receiving dial is the smaller dial near the center of the main dial. The main dial features 30 keys, each of which controls a projecting pin above a contact to close the circuit when pressed.

Froment's Alphabetic Telegraph (1850)

The Froment Alphabetic Telegraph incorporates improvements made to the original Wheatstone galvanic dial device. Froment's instrument uses a piano-like transmitting keyboard with a dedicated "verifying" dial to confirm what is being sent. The larger dial is for receiving and is clockwork powered. The telegraph machine uses electromagnetic mechanisms to operate.

Hughes Telegraph Machine (1855)

The Hughes telegraph machine was invented by David Edward Hughes, a scientist and musician. His first telegraph machine built in 1855 used a piano-style keyboard that allowed the operator to spell out the telegraph message being sent. Typewheels on the sending and receiving machines were synchronized so that as a particular letter key was pressed the corresponding letter was printed on the receiving end. The Hughes machines were finicky to adjust and required frequent maintenance. The small telegraph companies using Hughes' system united to form the Western Union Telegraph Company. When people eventually realized the alternative Morse system of telegraphy was faster the Hughes system gradually fell out of favor. It is reported very few Hughes machines have survived.

Wheatstone ABC Dial Telegraph (1858)

Charles Wheatstone's ABC (or Universal) telegraph system was conceived as a way for ordinary people to send messages in their homes or workplaces without the need to know any intimidating codes. Wheatstone's telegraph was patented in 1858; his system was the first to interconnect subscribers through hubs or exchanges. Wheatstone's machines were also used for telegram services between many village post offices. The telegraph machine consisted of three main components. The generator and the communicator were mounted on top of the wooden box, and the third component—the generator—was mounted inside the box; it was operated by turning a handle projecting out from the front of the box. The handle rotated the armature of the generator and the resulting current pulses were fed into the telegraph line to the receiving station.

The communicator had a circular dial with the letters of the alphabet marked around its perimeter. An indicating pointer at the center of the dial controlled how current pulses were sent. Opposite each letter on the communicator dial was a key. To send a letter, the operator depressed the appropriate key while turning the generator handle. After the correct number of pulses

were sent (according to the letter selected) the communicator disconnected the generator from the telegraph line. The communicator's indicating pointer rotated while the generator was transmitting and stopped at the transmitted letter when the generator was disconnected.

At the receiving end, the decoded pulses from the communicator caused the indicating pointer on the smaller dial to rotate to the letter being sent. The smaller indicator also had a circular dial with the letters of the alphabet marked around it. To operate properly, the communicator and indicator had to be properly synchronized; speeds of about 15 wpm were possible.

Wheatstone and W. F. Cooke first patented an "Electro Magnetic Telegraph" in June 1842 (patent 1622). Cooke was one of the founders of the Electric Telegraph Company—the world's first public telegraph company—in 1846.

W. T. Henley Magneto-Electric Dial Telegraph (1861)

Operators of the Henley dial telegraph were instructed to rotate the horizontal lever on the letter wheel, causing the smaller dial indicator at the receiving station to synchronously turn to the letter being sent. This machine apparently required some amount

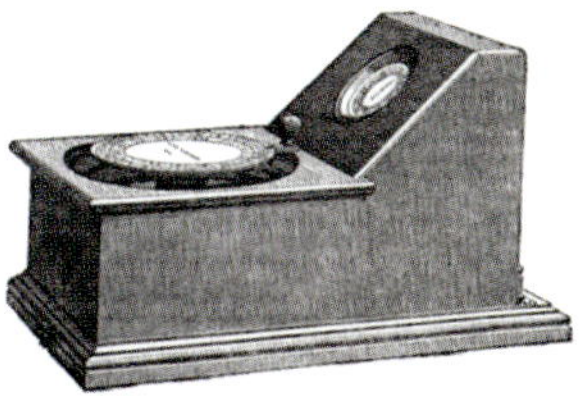

of skill to keep the transmitter and receiver synchronized.

Beardslee Telegraph Machine (1862)

The Beardslee telegraph machine (1862) was developed by George Beardslee as a portable military telegraph. It was an automatic Morse code sending and receiving machine that did not require knowledge of Morse code to operate. Another advantage was the Beardslee device could operate without batteries; the instrument was powered by hand-turned magnetos. The machine required frequent maintenance and did not send signals as far as competing battery powered devices.

The intent of the machine's design was to have the operator move the wheel's lever to a point on the dial representing the letter to be sent. On the receiving end, the dial would move to the corresponding letter that had been sent, with the operator writing down each letter of the sent message as it appeared on the receiving dial. In reality this machine was not given the time it needed to be further developed and problems in the field caused it to be pulled from military service.

Yetman Transmitting Typewriter (1893)

Charles E. Yetman of Oak Park, Illinois, first applied for a patent on an automatic telegraphing machine in September 1893. In 1895, he followed this with an updated design combining a typewriter with a telegraphic transmitter. He continued to make improvements in his designs and filed another patent application in 1901 (this patent issued in February 1902 as 692,967). The Transmitting Typewriter was put on the market in 1903, and in the first year about a thousand machines were sold. Because of the machine's popularity with large companies and various railroads Yetman began to expand his business; some sources imply Yetman machines were made for short periods in various typewriter plant locations, including Ilion, New York, until a dedicated factory in North Adams, Massachusetts, was established.

A very prominent nickel-plated shelf above the keyboard is a Yetman feature. There is a black key on this shelf that allows the user to send Morse code. The Yetman machine is attractively finished with blue and gold pinstriping and is extremely heavy. Yetman's company was known for taking an interest in the development of skills and careers of those who purchased his machines and keyboard instruction was offered. The company ceased operations in 1909, and rumors of Yetman's death circulated; a grandson later stated Yetman lived until 1949. There is some mystery remaining as to what caused the company to fail.

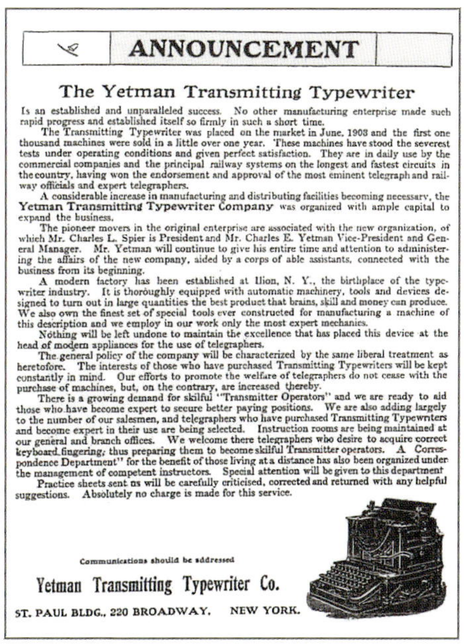

ANNOUNCEMENT

The Yetman Transmitting Typewriter

Is an established and unparalleled success. No other manufacturing enterprise made such rapid progress and established itself so firmly in such a short time.

The Transmitting Typewriter was placed on the market in June, 1903 and the first one thousand machines were sold in a little over one year. These machines have stood the severest tests under operating conditions and given perfect satisfaction. They are in daily use by the commercial companies and the principal railway systems on the longest and fastest circuits in the country, having won the endorsement and approval of the most eminent telegraph and railway officials and expert telegraphers.

A considerable increase in manufacturing and distributing facilities becoming necessary, the Yetman Transmitting Typewriter Company was organized with ample capital to expand the business.

The pioneer movers in the original enterprise are associated with the new organization, of which Mr. Charles L. Spier is President and Mr. Charles E. Yetman Vice-President and General Manager. Mr. Yetman will continue to give his entire time and attention to administering the affairs of the new company, aided by a corps of able assistants, connected with the business from its beginning.

A modern factory has been established at Ilion, N. Y., the birthplace of the typewriter industry. It is thoroughly equipped with automatic machinery, tools and devices designed to turn out in large quantities the best product that brains, skill and money can produce. We also own the finest set of special tools ever constructed for manufacturing a machine of this description and we employ in our work only the most expert mechanics.

Nothing will be left undone to maintain the excellence that has placed this device at the head of modern appliances for the use of telegraphers.

The general policy of the company will be characterized by the same liberal treatment as heretofore. The interests of those who have purchased Transmitting Typewriters will be kept constantly in mind. Our efforts to promote the welfare of telegraphers do not cease with the purchase of machines, but, on the contrary, are increased thereby.

There is a growing demand for skilful "Transmitter Operators" and we are ready to aid those who have become expert to secure better paying positions. We are also adding largely to the number of our salesmen, and telegraphers who have purchased Transmitting Typewriters and become expert in their use are being selected. Instruction rooms are being maintained at our general and branch offices. We welcome there telegraphers who desire to acquire correct keyboard fingering, thus preparing them to become skilful Transmitter operators. A Correspondence Department" for the benefit of those living at a distance has also been organized under the management of competent instructors. Special attention will be given to this department

Practice sheets sent us will be carefully criticised, corrected and returned with any helpful suggestions. Absolutely no charge is made for this service.

Communications should be addressed

Yetman Transmitting Typewriter Co.

ST. PAUL BLDG., 220 BROADWAY. NEW YORK.

A Yetman ad from the 1904 *Commercial Telegrapher's Journal.*

Burlingame Telegraphing Typewriter (1905)

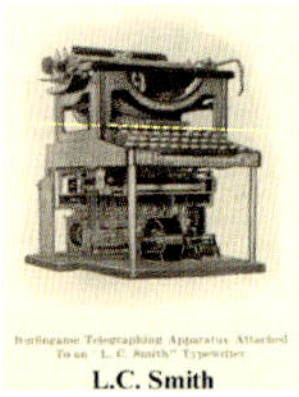

The Burlingame Telegraphing Typewriter was a combination of the telegraphing apparatus and the typewriter under which the apparatus sat. The ad (right) shows the Burlingame device being used with an L. C. Smith typewriter. What is not obvious from various advertising photographs is exactly how the Burlingame device connected to the typewriter. The system was designed to allow a person on the sending end to type a message as if he were using a standard typewriter. The Burlingame device translated this into electrical signals or pulses and transmitted them to the receiving device, which actuated the typewriter keys on the receiving end. Of course one of the main features of this system was anyone familiar with the keyboard of any typewriter was able to send a message without any knowledge of Morse code or other telegraphy codes.

Dunn Sending Machine (1909)

In 1909, Thomas J. Dunn invented this sending machine, which attempted to replace the fingerpiece and arm of a Vibroplex-type mechanism with pushbuttons. One proposed advantage to this approach was it relieved the user's arm of the work to operate existing bugs. From advertising material it appears there was a vibrating mechanism for dot production inside the box actuated by a plunger and mechanical linkage via the pushbutton on the outside of the box. Another pushbutton was for manual dash sending and a third was a shorting switch. The Dunn sending machine was described as "scientifically and mechanically perfect"; literature proclaims the device as being the first automatic dot making machine to use typewriter movement. Ads proclaimed an additional feature of the wooden box was protection "from being tampered with by curious and meddlesome persons during the temporary absence of the owner from his or her desk." The device measured 2 × 4 in. and was advertised as small enough to carry in a coat pocket.

Piersen Telegraph with Memory (1910)

The telegraph key with a memory must have been attention grabbing in the early 1900s; it is surprising few seem to remember this machine today. The device was designed and manufactured in 1910 by Edwin H. Piersen of Topeka, Kansas. He formed the Piersen Telegraph and Transmitter Company, incorporating in September 1912. The machine consisted of a typewriter keyboard and a spring-wound mechanical memory drum the operator had to periodically rewind. The memory drum had 3240 bits of memory, allowing the operator to type as much as 72 characters ahead of what was being sent. This feature gave the operator time to casually rewind the memory drum spring even as the machine was cranking out perfect code. The mechanical drum utilized 3,240 fingers, with 72 fingers for each alphabetic character and numeral.

While the full explanation of how the drum operates will not be presented here (refer to July 1963 *QST* by K8ANV), rest assured operation is incredibly complex and ingenious. Piersen's design won a Grand Prix award at the 1915 Panama-Pacific exposition. It was noted in the K8ANV article that the Kansas State Historical Society at one time had the only known Piersen typewriter in existence on exhibit.

Keen-Kode Transmitter (1930)

The Keen-Kode transmitter was the invention of W. D. Cooper in 1930. The machine was manufactured by the O. B. McClintock Company of Minneapolis, Minnesota. The keyboard has only six keys, numbered to indicate how many automatic dots were sent when the key was depressed. A hand-actuated key (the black knob to the left of the keyboard keys) was used to make the dashes manually. A year later Cooper was reported to have modified his invention to allow for automatic dashes.

Keen-Kode Transmitter

Traeger Morse Typewriter (1933)

Alfred Traeger was an Australian inventor noted for development of the pedal-powered radio. In 1933, he invented a very basic but functional Morse code keyboard. Although resembling a typewriter, it used keys connected to pivoting steel arms shaped with notched long and short indentations corresponding to the Morse alphabet. An oil filled dash pot was used to ensure smooth operation of the keyed arms. One of Traeger's goals was to make a device the lay operator could use without the need for Morse code fluency. The Traeger keyboard succeeded, and enabled users to type their messages in plain language while having them transmitted in Morse code.

KEYBOARDS FROM THE MODERN ERA

Although there were at least two 1950s tube keyboard keyers and a few developmental models in the early 1960s, interest in building and using electronic keyboards really expanded with the availability of integrated circuits in the 1970s.

Accu-Mill CW Keyboard Project

The Accu-Mill was a keyboard interface board presented in *Ham Radio*'s September 1976 issue. The circuit was designed by William Smith (WN9OVY); it was intended to be used with an ASCII keyboard and connected to an existing Accu-Keyer. Using the keyboard, the operator was able to key in a message and then start sending with a paddle (to insert a serial number for example). The message/paddle feature was very popular with contest operators. The Accu-Mill features up to 128 characters of buffering, offers provisions for external paddle use, incorporates a "buffer full" indication, and used the Accu-Keyer for speed control.

AEA KK-1 Keyboard Keyer

The KK-1 keyboard keyer allowed the operator to use either a keyboard or paddle to send perfect code. The device could be set for equal characters and equal spacing or Farnsworth mode—sending fast characters with wide gaps for spacing—and it would key positive and negative voltage transmitters. An LED readout allowed the user to set the exact speed desired. The keyer had twelve message memories programmable via the keyboard function keys and would also operate as a code practice machine to generate random letters. Also featured was type-ahead memory and message repeat.

AJR Corporation Skipjack Keyboard

The Skipjack 48B was a keyboard kit sold in the late 1970s by AJR Electronics Corporation of Evansville, Indiana. The basic design of the Skipjack came from the very popular W9TO keyer. The original breadboard was developed by Skip Bradford (W9HAK) and Jack Hudson (N9OAM), so the keyboard received its name from them. It featured a 64-character buffer expandable to a 256-character buffer, with a digital readout for buffer status and speed. Several hundred sold worldwide, but kit sales declined when PC technology offered cheaper and easier alternatives.

Alspaugh Morse Keyboard Encoder

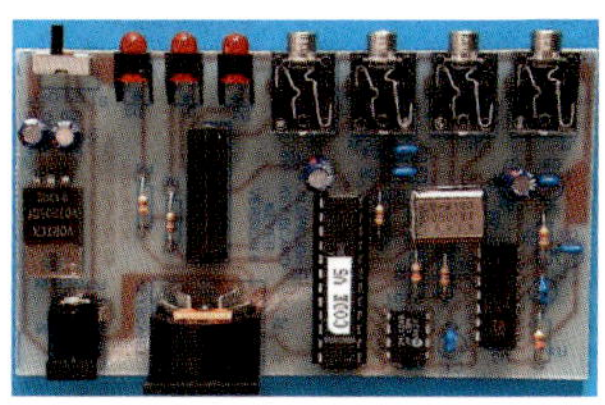

Ron Alspaugh (W6NKS) designed this keyboard encoder featured in a December 1997 *QST* article. It featured a top speed of 79 wpm and used a relay for the keying output. The user furnished an AT-type keyboard and 12 volts DC for power. The board's design included four non-volatile storage buffers of 250 characters each and an 18 character length type-ahead keyboard buffer with a buffer status LED. Also included is a sidetone output jack. The keyboard encoder offered all letters, numbers, punctuation, and prosigns.

A-tronix CW Keyboards

The A-tronix company was located at various times in Escondido and Laguna Beach, California. A-tronix also made various CW and RTTY accessories. Their basic model keyboard without memory offered a built-in sidetone and a type-ahead buffer, first selling in 1977. Note the two different spellings of the company name on their keyboards.

The A-tronix KB-107 included memory features. This CW keyboard had a reed-relay keying output for use with any type of transmitter. A digital readout was added to a later version of this keyboard (as opposed to the register full light) to indicate the number of characters used in a memory bank. Four memory sections of 64 characters each were available. Speed range was 5–50 wpm and the keyboard was powered from 115 volts AC. The KB-107 first sold in 1979.

The Codamite Keyboard

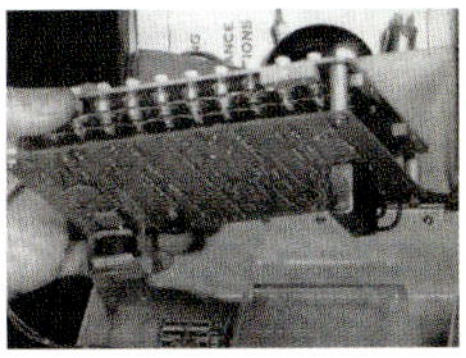

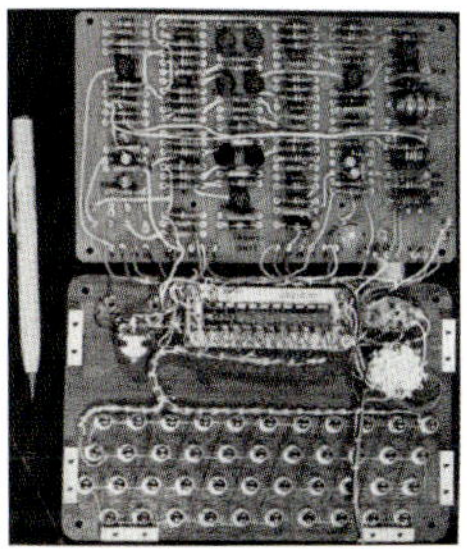

The Codamite was a typewriter-like keyboard described in a May 1961 *QST* article by R. W. Johnson (W6MUR). The device was apparently known as the Model MG-100 when in production by Ling Electronics, but other sources say W6MUR formed the Codamite Corporation in 1962 to produce the keyer. Regardless who made it, it must have been quite costly to produce, and probably would not have been a big seller in the amateur radio market.

The Codamite was described as a real-time Morse code generator, but the main feature was its small size. The photo (right) shows two boards, with the upper board holding numerous small pushbutton switches arranged in a typewriter-like layout; the bottom board holds the circuit electronics. The Codamite used ten transistors, three 4-layer diodes, five zener diodes, and 27 ordinary diodes in addition to the 10-bit magnetic core shift register. Upon pressing a letter button, the Codamite would generate the code character, actuate a relay for keying, and produce a sidetone. The device used a magnetic core shift register that required priming with an advance pulse before it could shift; shifting started with a second advance pulse.

The Codetyper Keyboard

The Codetyper was an early-1950s tube CW keyboard. The Codetyper shown is from the March 1952 issue of *CQ*. The Codetyper was designed by Nathaniel Dorfman, and it was written up in many technical journals of the time. The device broke down the 43 different sequences of dots and dashes into units of time. The circuitry inside the Codetyper used 40 tubes. The Codetyper did not sell well and vanished into obscurity by 1953. By the 1960s solid state electronics were widely available and many hams were building their own keyboards for a far lower cost than the $500 Codetyper.

Curtis Electro Devices Keyboards

The Curtis KB-4900 was a keyboard that very much deserved the description "full-featured." As the front panel proclaimed, the KB-4900 was a Morse, Baudot, or ASCII device. In addition to using the keyboard to send Morse code, the user could also plug in an external paddle. Random generation of Morse code was available for practice sessions. Analog controls were provided for code speed, weight, sidetone pitch, and sidetone volume. The KB-4900 added an analog meter to indicate sending buffer status; buffer capacity was 256 characters. A second analog meter showed keyer speed. Four programmable message memories were provided. Built-in memory was included for commonly

sent code phrases such as "CQ de…" and prosigns were also included. Automatically incremental serial numbers were available for contesting, and a real-time clock option allowed time information to be transmitted.

The Curtis HT-4900 Ham Terminal was built around the Sol computer, which used S-100 bus cards. The user was able to insert various PROMs to update system performance. A derivation of the Sol called the System 4000 was a desktop minicomputer featuring firmware and interfaces designed for the radio amateur. Keyboard features included a Morse reader (6–250 wpm), CRT or TTY output, paddle iambic keyer with dot and dash memory, ASCII terminal (half or full duplex), and Morse keyboard capability.

The KB-420 KeyboardMate was an add on that plugged into the EK-480M paddle keyer, providing a keyboard Morse generator. It used the Curtis 8045 "keyboard on a chip" custom IC to generate Morse.

Curtis' KB-4200 Morse Keyboard introduced many operators to keyboard operation for Morse code. The device featured a 64-character type-ahead buffer with a meter to show buffer status. Morse speed was selectable using thumbwheel switches and ranged from 1–99 wpm. The keyboard could be connected with the KM-420 message memory unit, giving the operator four message memories. The design included 44 integrated circuits. The KB-4200 sold for $500 and was reviewed in the October 1974 *QST*.

The KB-4800 Morse Keyboard used the Curtis 8045 "keyboard on a chip" custom IC to generate Morse. Features included buffer meter, thumbwheel selectable Morse speed, internal sidetone and volume, and adjustable weight.

DGM Electronics MKB-2000

The DGM MKB-2000 was an affordable ($300 for the Morse version; the RTTY/ASCII option added $75) keyboard that sold in the early 1980s. It included a 512 character text buffer, ten programmable and 50 character message memories, and buffer/

memory full indicators. The MKB-2000 featured code speeds of 5–99 wpm and included a built-in sidetone. DGM also offered a memory expansion option for this keyboard.

DL1OW Keymaster

This is the DL1OW Keymaster keyboard; not much information is available on this unit. This keyboard may be homebrew or part of a limited production run in Germany.

DL6JAN CWKtiny Keyboard Keyer

DL6JAN offers the CWKtiny, a microprocessor based module with AT keyboard interface. The module allows for portable keyboard operation independent of a PC. Required power is 7–15 volts DC. The CWKtiny is centered around an ATMEL AT89S52 microprocessor that converts the scan code of the keyboard into CW code. Several standard QSO texts and a few setup values can be stored in the 24C08 EEPROM, which is connected via I²C bus to the processor. RF filtering is included in the circuitry.

Among the many design features are independent typing and keyer speeds with a 64 character type-ahead buffer. PTT output is provided, and there are eight standard non-volatile message memories. Squeeze paddle support for iambic and ultimatic keyer modes are included, as are Morse practice modes. The module is available either built or as a kit from DL6JAN.

Fischer Keyboard Keyer

The DFM-4 keyboard keyer is part of a series of Morse keyers manufactured by Dirk Fischer Electronics. This unit is designed around a powerful microcontroller and offers many extensive functions. The DFM-4 is driven directly from a PC keyboard and controlled via the keyboard's function keys. The DFM-4 is also equipped with 8 text memories and offers a contest and high-speed mode of operation. In addition, the DFM-4 has a "teach mode," in which the intervals between the Morse code can be extended, aiding the learning of Morse code.

Guthoerl Mill-Keyer

Willard Guthoerl built this automatic Morse typewriter keyer in 1959. Sending code required the operator to press and hold the letter key until the code was sent. A speed of 15–75 wpm was possible depending on the skill of the sender. This model was tube based; Guthoerl told a magazine interviewer he hoped to follow this model with a transistorized version.

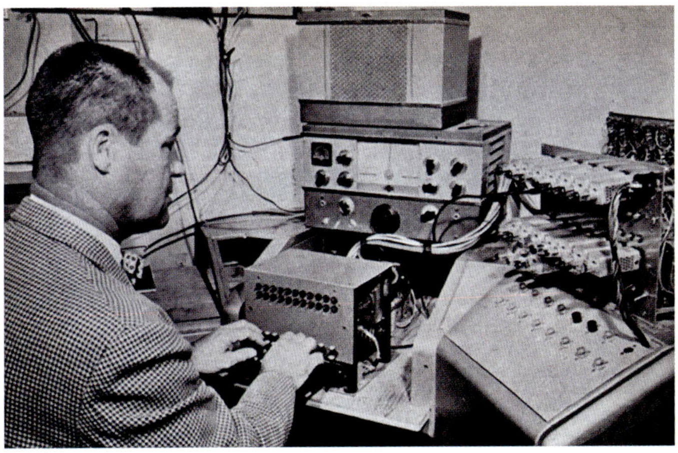

HAL Keyboards

The HAL MKB-1 keyboard was available as a kit in the mid-1970s and sold for about $175. There was no space bar, as the MKB-1 had no buffering. The user could add an external sidetone monitor and speaker. The MKB-1 used a transistor interface for either grid-block or cathode transmitter keying. Speed range was 6–60 wpm.

The HAL DS-2000 KSR (for Keyboard—Send/Receive) was a communications terminal that would transmit Morse code 1–175 wpm. HAL offered an MR-2000 option for this terminal for reception of Morse code and viewing via a screen hooked to the video output.

The HAL DS-2050 KSR was a communications terminal that replaced the DS-2000. It offered similar CW features but included an RTTY tuning meter.

The HAL DKB-2010 is called a dual-mode keyboard (CW and RTTY). This keyboard offered an optional 64/128 key extended memory. This unit was manufactured in the early to mid-1970s and was considered very expensive for the time; the factory assembled price was $799 without the extended memory option. The DKB-2010 was also available as a kit. This keyboard

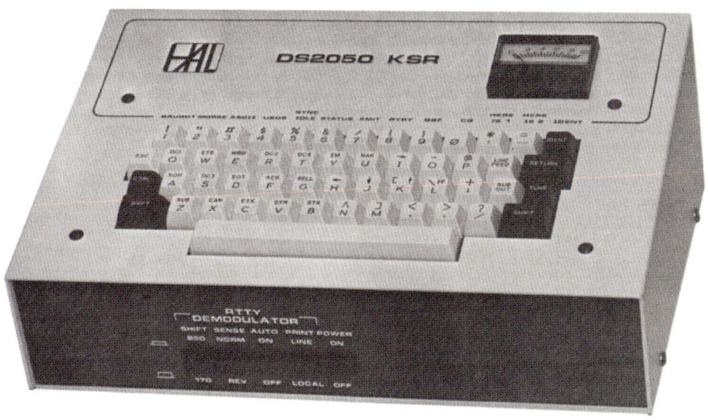

featured several diode matrix programmable keys that were used for frequently sent letter combinations, such as CQ, 73, and SK. Keys were programmed by un-soldering and changing the pattern of 1N270 germanium diodes in the matrix. The device can key either grid-block (minus) or cathode (positive) inputs for CW.

Heathkit Ultra-Pro Keyboard

Heathkit's HD-8999 Ultra Pro keyboard was a highly regarded and many featured CW keyboard available from Heathkit 1983–1988. It was microprocessor based, used CMOS memory, and included built-in sidetone and speaker. The HD-8999 offered ten text storage buffers and a 64 character type-ahead buffer. Buffer and operational status, including sending speed, was displayed on the front panel using colored LED indicators and numerical readouts. Code practice modes and even a self diagnostic feature were included. Also included were automatic serial number generation and prosigns. The HD-8999 required either 11–16 volts DC or 7.5–11 volts AC.

Info-Tech Keyboards

Info-Tech was founded by Dave Kelce (K0DGF); products were originally designed and built near St. Louis before the company moved to Englewood, Florida. The Info-Tech M-10 keyboard offered switches and controls for memory load, run, weight, a buffer full light, keyer speed, power on, sidetone volume, and a tune switch for transmitter tune-up. On the rear panel are two sockets marked GRID and CATHODE, indicating the type of keyer/transmitter interface.

The M-300C was advertised as a tri-mode (Morse code, Baudot, and ASCII) keyboard and was microprocessor-based. It had a good reputation for the quality of CW it produced. The keyboard had a space bar and recallable memories. This keyboard used an 8 bit Zilog 3850 processor with 4 kbyte of memory. It had no speed knob, but used keyboard entry sequences for controlling speed and other functions. There was a relay and AFSK audio output for outgoing transmission monitoring and transmitter keying. The M-300C included a 700 character running buffer and had 11 message memories of 120 characters each. Power requirement was 115 volts AC.

The Info-Tech M-500 ASR was a send-receive communications terminal that supported the three popular modes of Morse code (Baudot, RTTY, and ASCII). The M-500 was microprocessor-based and offered features such as user programmable messages, real-time clock running buffers, on-screen editing, full/half duplex, split screen formats, and a cassette recorder interface. The keyboard is connected to the main unit by a 5 ft. cable. This device required an external composite video monitor. Power was obtained from a built-in 115 volt AC supply.

K1EL Keyboard Keyers

The K20 is a single board Morse keyer; the user furnishes his own case. K1EL sold this small keyboard keyer kit around 2002.

The K40 is described by K1EL:

> A small low power CW keyboard that is packed with features. The single board design includes a PS/2 style keyboard connector, on board piezo speaker, circuitry to drive an off board speaker, low level audio output, an iambic keyer interface, and open collector PTT and key outputs. Also included is an on board 5 volt regulator that powers both the K40 PC board and the PC keyboard. The K40 PCB kit includes two socketed PIC processors, EEPROM, all board mounted components, and a rotary speed control.

K1EL offered a small case for this keyer, along with an LCD display; the K-40 with these options and CW decode capability is shown.

K4KN (Woody) Keyboard

The K4KN (Woody) keyboard sold for about $200 around 1974. This keyboard was capable of speeds in excess of 80 wpm. It had a one character buffer and no space bar.

K8CU Keyboard

The Bill Jones (K8CU) keyboard was designed around 1980 using an embedded Z80 miscoprocessor. It uses a unique algorithm that allows it to send either perfect CW or code that sounds like it is coming from an old bug. The algorithhm modifies the keyboard's perfect code depending on where a dash occurs. Two function keys are used to define the degree of emphasis, giving the operator a choice of light or heavy bug emulation. K8CU reports that on the air the keyboard sounds like a bug operator with very uniform characteristics, although the choice of light or heavy emphasis can vary the uniformity.

Bill mentions if he were to build a similar device today he would use a common standalone PC keyboard hooked to a small custom PIC-embedded controller interface. Although a program written on a PC with an interface to one of the PC ports would work, Bill prefers the standalone keyboard approach.

Keymaster Keyboard

The Keymaster keyboard was a German device. Front panel included a speed adjustment, and prosigns were included in the top row of keys.

MFJ-494 Super Keyboard

MFJ's 494 Super Keyboard included modes for CW, Baudot, and ASCII; the keyboard could function as a memory keyer or be used for code practice. The CW mode featured two programmable memories with 30 characters total. The keyboard also had special keys for the KN, SK, AR, AA, and BT prosigns. The 494 design allowed for five-level Baudot transmitted at 60 wpm; the ASCII speed was 110 baud with upper and lower case transmitted. To use the 494 as a full featured memory keyer the user merely had to plug in a paddle. When used for code practice the user could select random groups of letters and characters, or choose from eight different five-character groups. This keyboard was introduced in 1981.

MFJ-498 Keyboard Keyer

The MFJ-498 is designed to accept an AT compatible keyboard; in addition, the device will function as an iambic keyer if a dual-lever paddle is plodded in the rear panel. There are eight independent 4,000 character message memories and the 32-character liquid crystal display allows viewing of keyboard and memory text. The keyer has a 150-character type-ahead buffer with buffer full indication. Additional features include embedded commands such as auto-incrementing serial numbers, a built-in Morse trainer, a random word generator, and a QSO simulator. Keyer speed is 5–100 wpm, and there is an internal speaker for the sidetone monitor. The MFJ-498 has direct and grid-block keying outputs.

Microcraft Morse-A-Keyer

Microcraft's Morse-A-Keyer CW Keyboard had a 16-character memory and a built-in sidetone. Speed range was 5–35 wpm. A reed relay was used for keying output. This keyboard was sold beginning in 1980.

Microlog ACT-1 Terminal

The Microlog Corporation manufactured the ACT-1 from their Gaithersburg, Maryland, location. The ACT-1 (for Amateur Communications Terminal) gave amateurs a way to have a complete RTTY/CW communications system by hooking the device to a transceiver and adding a printer or video monitor to view output. The ACT-1 sold in 1981.

Microlog AIR-1 Radio Interface Cartridge

The Microlog AIR-1 radio interface cartridge is a plug-in accessory for the Commodore C64 and VIC-20, allowing sending and receiving of RTTY and Morse code. The decoding algorithms were all done with machine code processing in real time, and digital filtering used in the AIR-1 had an excellent reputation among users, including one for very accurate CW decoding. The device also featured a tuning "eye" on the display screen,

and once tuned correctly would immediately begin decoding. Keyer output supported positive and negative voltage keyed transmitters. The AIR-1 sold around 1985.

Norwegian Norsk Automorse Keyboard

This is a Norwegian Norsk Automorse Model AM 14C keyboard keyer from the collection of PA3AQV. This keyboard is a third generation model made around 1969. The first design incorporated 14 relays; the second version used a diode matrix with only 2 relays. The model shown is an all-transistor design and proved to be more reliable. Only a limited number of these devices were built, and they were not marketed to any significant extent.

Pickering KB-1 Keyboard

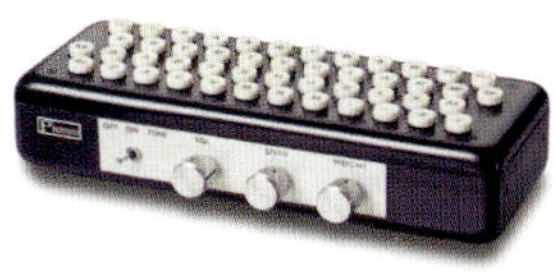

The Pickering KB-1 was a fairly compact keyboard device—a bit smaller than a modern computer keyboard. Controls were on the front of the unit, with the standard volume, speed, and weight being available. Keyboard layout was very similar to a typewriter, except no shift key was included. The Pickering did give the user keys for the Morse prosigns AR and SK, along with punctuation. Circuit design is all solid-state, and the unit will key either positive or negative voltages; speed range is 10–85 wpm. The KB-1 is powered from 115 volts AC and first sold for $265 in 1969.

A Pickering keyboard ad from the November 1969 issue of *QST*.

ROBOT 800 Super Terminal

ROBOT terminals were made by Robot Research of San Diego, California; the company made a series of terminals aimed at the RTTY and slow scan television users. The ROBOT 800 was called a "multi-mode" terminal, but was mostly used for RTTY, although it had CW send and decode capability. Four different transmit modes were provided for CW. The keyboard could be used for Morse practice and had a sidetone oscillator. The Model 800 supported Baudot RTTY, Morse code, ASCII, and SSTV (transmit only) modes. Included was an output for a video monitor in 24 line by 72 character format. The Model 800C added capability for a bit more text display on the external screen, a serial output for color graphics, and 8 graphic memories with battery backup. This terminal required 115 VAC input power; dimensions were approximately 15 × 4 × 10 in., and it weighed 10 lb.

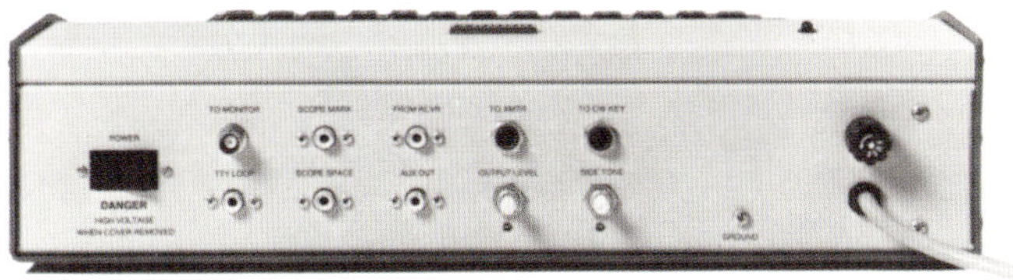

Russian Morse Sending Machine

A vintage Russian keyboard with most of the electronics contained in a separate box cabled to the keyboard unit. The device most likely dates to the 1960s (more photos are available on the SV1EDY pages).

Tono-Drake Theta 7000E Keyboard

Tono was a Japanese manufacturer; they made the 7000E marketed by R. L. Drake in the 1980s. The Tono-Drake Theta 7000E is a complete communications terminal in one package. The terminal can send and receive Morse code (5–50 wpm) by selecting one of ten keyboard steps; also offered are Baudot RTTY and ASCII capabilities. For CW, the 7000E has seven keyboard selectable, non-volatile random access memories of 64 characters each, as well as a 53 character type-ahead buffer. Provision for an external monitor is offered using rear panel composite video connections. Outputs for an audio monitor are also included, making the 7000E useful for code practice. Power required is 12 volts DC at 1 amp.

Tono EXL-5000E Terminal and Keyboard

The Tono EXL-5000E is a communications terminal that was briefly marketed in the early 1980s. A variety of modes are supported, including Morse code, Baudot RTTY, ASCII, and AMTOR. This unit has seven channels of non-volatile, random access memory that can each hold 256 characters. Morse code speed is variable and can be set for 5–100 wpm via the keyboard. A CW key jack is

on the rear panel. The EXL-5000E has a built-in high resolution 5 inch monitor and also provides composite video output for an external monitor. This terminal requires 115 volts AC or 13.8 volts DC.

W2QYW Magnetic Core Keyboard

Paul Horowitz' (W2QYW) magnetic core keyboard was the *QST* cover story for August 1965. In the accompanying article, Horowitz described construction of the keyboard using surplus parts, most notably some ready-made shift register modules and numerous diodes, allowing the cost to be kept around $50. Speed range is 5–55 wpm, and the unit has self-completing characters and spaces. The device also features prosigns and punctuation, and can act as a regular electronic keyer when an external paddle is plugged in. According to Horowitz, this keyboard design required an operating technique where the user had to keep slightly ahead of the code, holding the appropriate button until each letter began.

W6CAB Code Mill

The Code Mill was featured in a November 1974 *Ham Radio* magazine article by H. E. Thomas (W6CAB). The keyboard was advertised to provide perfect character generation, letter, and word spacing, regardless of operator keyboard skill. The Code Mill automatically produced what the designer called the five necessary parts for perfect Morse code: the dot, the dash, the space between elements, the space between letters, and the space between words. It was noted in the article that the space between words requires the space bar. Storage capacity was 64 Morse characters, and the keyboard could produce code at 7–70 wpm.

15 Computer Interfacing and the Internet

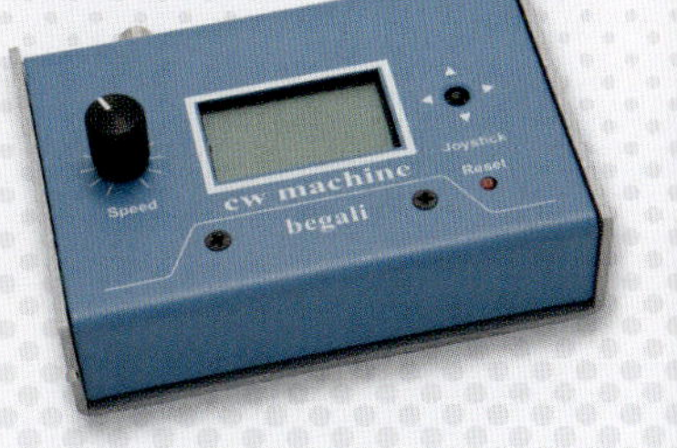

Computers and the Internet—they are definitely a part of ham radio today. But what's ahead? How big a role will computers and the Internet play? The answer is really unknown, but some of the latest devices give us some hints.

Presented are some current ham-related hardware offerings that interface with a PC and/or the Internet. By intent, software-defined radios (SDR) are not covered; that is really a subject for a different book. The world of peripheral devices, and even more traditional hardware rigs, is changing at a fast pace. With the rate of change in mind, recognize that what is presented is just a snapshot in time and may become outdated very quickly. As the reader looks over this material, it is hoped the items presented will provoke thought about the future of Morse code. What's ahead? Will Morse paddles disappear in favor of the keyboard? Some current rigs give perhaps the biggest hint. Transceivers like the Elecraft K3 and software defined radios like the FlexRadio may mean peripheral boxes will no longer be needed. It may be the future will involve more embedded controlling systems and less emphasis on the personal computer. For now, we will look at what is currently available in the way of CW accessory interface devices.

Soundcard interfaces are used primarily to isolate audio signals that run from a PC to a transceiver. The isolation reduces the risk of a ground loop and helps prevent hum and noise on the audio signal. Besides the pure isolation of AF signals, some of these devices offer more functions like level adjustment, PTT control, CW keying, and a CAT interface. More recent designs use the USB interface from the PC instead of the serial port for control functions. Some sound card interfaces are presented in this chapter if the interface also has an integrated keyer.

Donner CW Interface

The Donner CW Interface is made by Donner's Country Crafts LLC. It is an accessory that allows hard keying of a transmitter via a personal computer; the interface is meant to be used with software programs such as popular loggers. The Donner device uses the computer's DB9 serial output DTR line for switching CW. It supports keying rigs with solid state keying only, not with older transmitters using grid-block keying.

Hamcrafters (K1EL) USB Keyers

The WinKeyer USB is a basic computer interfaced keyer with rugged solid state relay outputs. This device is capable of keying just about any transceiver or transmitter, even those with grid-block keying. Hamcrafters sells this model as a kit; included are the enclosure, pushbuttons, PC board, a USB cable, and all parts. K1EL states there is one surface mount part that is pre-soldered to the PCB. The WinKeyer USB uses standard RCA jacks on the rear panel for keyed line (two individual outputs) and PTT outputs. The outputs are optically isolated and use solid state keying relays.

The latest versions of this device use the new WK3 keyer IC, which can be upgraded over the USB connection. Four message pushbuttons are available on top of the keyer enclosure. A sidetone speaker is included, as is a connector for external paddle use. Power is obtained from three internal AAA batteries.

Internet CW (iCW)

Internet CW (iCW) presents a way for CW aficionados to chat with other CW operators in full duplex mode via an Internet connection. Internet CW offers full QSK (break-in), fast speeds, and high quality sound. Nets currently exist with up to 100 worldwide operators on at the same time. This new operating mode lets the op participate using their own CW paddle and/or keyboard. One specifically designed iCW keyer (W5UXH device) is presented. The advantage of a dedicated iCW keyer is all the interface hardware can be self-contained. Included here are controls for local sidetone volume, volume for audio received from the server, and level control for the sidetone going to the server. Other useful features for an iCW keyer include an internal speaker, the option for headphones, and a paddle or PS2/USB keyboard connection.

The Begali CW Machine (see chapter 3) offers a CW-over-IP function that connects with another CW machine over the Internet to practice QSOs off the air.

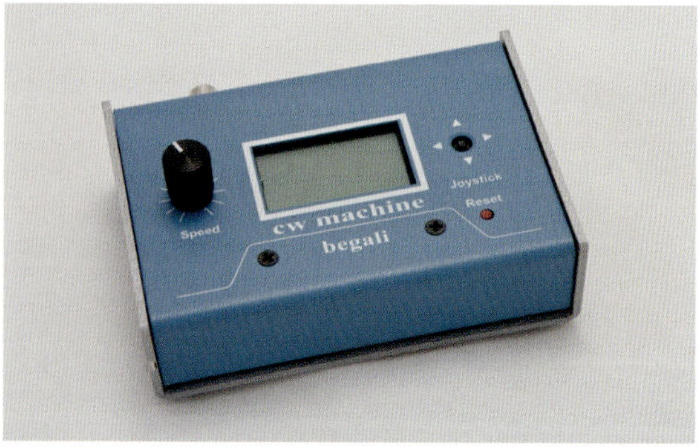

Microham USB and Computer Interface Keyers

The microHAM CW KEYER is a USB CW interface/memory keyer based on the microKEYER design and incorporating a K1EL WinKeyer chip. It has a single USB radio control interface, and the keyer is compatible with many logging programs for radio control and CW transmission. This keyer includes a rear panel connection for a PS/2 keyboard or keypad that can be used for CW generation or control of memory keyer functions. Among the keyer's features is the ability to generate serial numbers for contests.

The microHAM micro KEYER II is advertised as an all-in-one USB interface; indeed, the list of its features is long. While it supports voice operation and offers microphone switching with front or rear panel microphone inputs, many hams use this device for its internal K1EL WinKeyer capabilities. There is a rear panel jack for a PS2-type keyboard and programmable memories via the included software router. The single USB port interface allows the micro KEYER II to work with any Windows logging or control program for CW, voice, FSK, and digital (RTTY, PSK31, SSTV, OLIVIA, MFSK, WSJT, etc.) operation. The built-in radio control interface supports all standards (RS-232, CI-V, Kenwood, and Yaesu TTL). A sound card is also built in, as well as a buffer/sequencer for amplifier or LNA control.

N4YG SMART Keyboard

Joe Lunsford (N4YG) offers a parts kit to build the SMART keyboard interface unit. The device is essentially an electronic keyer that communicates with a host computer via a Universal Serial Bus (USB) link. The host computer is necessary for the keyer to function, as the keyer gets its controlling information from the computer via the USB link. When the computer is running the SMART Keyboard program, the host computer and interface unit together provide a CW keyboard, as well as a traditional keyer that also responds to paddle inputs. The keyer uses a microcontroller to generate dots and dashes; the same microcontroller provides a USB port for communication with the computer. The Smart Keyboard program includes a graphical user interface (GUI) that allows the operator to control all the parameters of the keyboard and keyer. The GUI also provides visual information on the status and operation of the keyboard. Because the SMART Keyboard interface is also a keyer, paddles can be plugged into the interface and the operator can use the keyer or keyboard at any time interchangeably. A sidetone is provided in the interface; its tone and volume are controlled through the GUI, which also controls keyer speed, weight, and spacing (both letter and word). The red "online" LED on top of the interface indicates the host computer has established communications with the microcontroller. The interface offers positive and negative keying. The SMART keyboard interface was reviewed in the July 2007 *QST*.

QRPWorks Devices

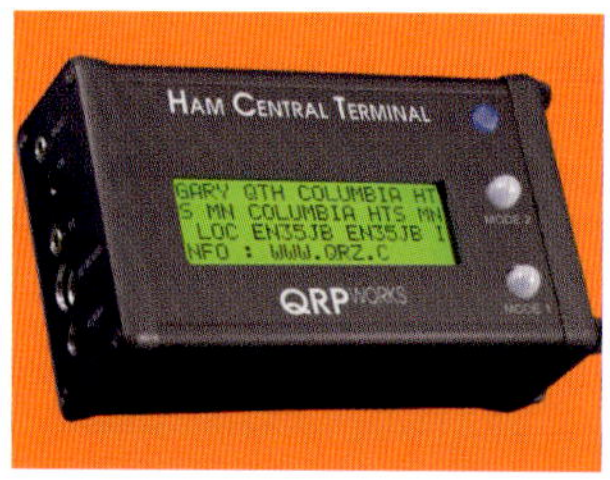

The QRPWorks Ham Central Terminal (HCT) is a small portable device meant to interface with the Elecraft KX3 or K3 transceivers. HCT uses a standard PC keyboard to send text in CW, RTTY, and PSK modes, as well as control the HCT. A keyboard can be used to create, edit, and store up to ten 80 character messages accessed via the keyboard function keys for immediate transmission. These messages can be stacked to make even longer messages. The keyboard can also be used to create, edit, and store up to ten 80 character rig macros for controlling the KX3 and K3. For example, a rig macro can instantly change band, frequency, mode, filters, power, etc., without touching any controls on the rig.

The HCT has a logging function with a real time clock to time/date stamp up to 1200 QSOs. The frequency and mode are automatically added by polling the rig. A call sign feature allows you to enter a call sign that not only goes into the log, but will insert itself into a message anywhere you place a "!," similar to popular contest logging programs. Text can be entered to add QSO details. The log data is exported to a PC in standard ADIF format using an HCT Utility application. The HCT can be used as a standalone portable logging device, with or without a KX3 or K3.

The HCT can be used without a keyboard to send CW, RTTY, and PSK text by using a CW paddle. The decoded text will still display on the HCT's LCD when a paddle is used with scrolling enabled using the Mode 1 button. Pre-stored messages can be selected and sent using the Mode 2 button when using a paddle—perfect for CQing and contesting.

The HCT displays text that has been decoded by the KX3 or K3 in CW, RTTY, and PSK modes on an 80 character LCD display. An additional 400 characters can be viewed by scrolling up and down in the display while new characters are still being stored. The LCD is sunlight readable and has an adjustable backlight for night ops. It will run outdoors for over 20 hours on an internal 9 volt battery. The HCT has an on screen help display that shows every available command in a scrollable list.

Although the QRPWorks Ham Central Terminal and the Key Log Go do not interface directly with a computer or the Internet, they do represent one path that future ham accessories are likely to take. These QRPWorks devices are meant to perform many of the operating and logging functions previously requiring a separate computer. Their small size and ability to be carried along for portable use points to an emerging trend away from the computer toward small, portable, and innovative pieces of ham gear offering the same operating benefits without the need for a computer.

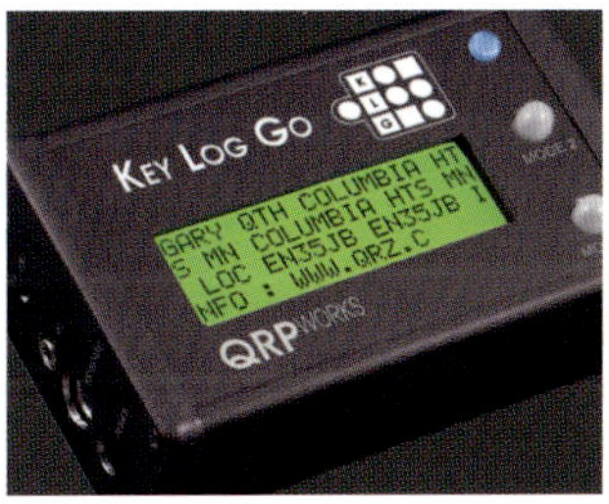

QRPWorks offers an advanced keyer logging interface for the Elecraft K3 or KX3 called the Key Log Go (KLG). The KLG features a K1EL internal keyer with twenty 80-character message memories and iambic A or B, ultimatic, or bug modes. The keyer offers adjustable weighting and dot/dash ratio, autospace and letterspace control, and sidetone output with adjustable frequency. Keyer speed is 5–99 wpm, and realtime sending is possible from a paddle or the keyboard. The KLG display can show 80 characters of decoded text (CW, PSK, or RTTY). Logging features include automatic call sign entry, auto time/date stamp, and up to 1200 QSO storage in non-volatile memory with ADIF export capability.

The K1EL WinKeyer chip the KLG is based on has an amazingly rich feature set in its standalone mode, but when coupled to a smart host it gets even better. The KLG has taken advantage of the host features to implement features not even found in advanced PC-based loggers.

The KLG display is sunlight readable and has an adjustable backlight for night ops. It will run outdoors for 50 hours on an internal 9 volt battery.

The KLG can be used without a keyboard to send CW, RTTY, and PSK text using a CW paddle. The decoded text will still display on the KLG's LCD when a paddle is used with scrolling enabled using the Mode 1 button. Pre-stored messages can be selected and sent using the Mode 2 button when using a paddle—perfect for CQing and contesting.

The KLG uses a standard PC keyboard to send text in CW, RTTY, and PSK modes, as well as control the KLG. The keyboard can be used to create, edit, and store up to ten 80 character messages that are accessed via the function keys on the keyboard for immediate transmission. These messages can be stacked to make even longer messages. The keyboard can be used to create, edit, and store up to ten 80 character rig macros for controlling the KX3 and K3. For example, a rig macro can instantly change band, frequency, mode, filters, power, etc., without touching any controls on the rig.

The KLG has a logging function with a real time clock to time/date stamp up to 1200 QSOs. The frequency and mode are automatically added by polling the rig. A call sign feature allows you to enter a call sign that not only goes into the log, but will insert itself into a message anywhere you place a "!," similar to popular contest logging programs. Text can be entered to add QSO details. The log data is exported to a PC in the standard ADIF format using a KLG utility application. The KLG can be used as a standalone portable logging device. An instant QSY command on the keyboard allows the direct entry of any frequency and mode. The KLG has an on screen help display that shows every available command in a scrollable list.

Timewave Navigator Interface

The Navigator is a USB sound card interface containing a K1EL CW WinKeyer (v22); the unit is made by Timewave. It connects to a computer using just one USB cable. User options are selected via software. The Navigator is powered by the USB cable.

CW using direct keying of the rig is provided in two ways: software that generates the key closures using a COM port DTR line is supported by the PTT/CW COM port. This mode does not allow use of the paddle; CW output is only from the keyboard.

A more robust CW control that supports paddle and keyboard input is provided by including the control chip from the popular WinKeyer by K1EL. The Navigator Interface uses version 2.3 of the K1EL WinKeyer, eliminating key bounce and false character send and start/stop issues. A COM port is dedicated to operation of the keyer and CW options are set via software.

W5UXH Internet Keyer

Chuck (W5UXH) has designed this keyer to interface to a computer sound card with the iCW Mumble server, in addition to being able to key an HF transmitter. The keyer includes a CPO (Code Practice Oscillator) that generates a clean, well shaped waveform for interface to the sound card.

The CPO allows the operator to use any type of keyer/keyboard and be able to get on the iCW server, requiring only the Mumble voice over Internet Protocol VOIP software. There are "software only" methods that many folks use, but Chuck prefers the hardware oriented method.

Included in the keyer package is the "iCW Interface," which provides features where the drive control sets the level of the tone that drives the sound card and two front panel knobs control the sidetone volume and the volume of the received audio from the iCW server. Another panel control sets the tone frequency. The tone range with the component values used is roughly 575–740 Hz. The unit includes a filter with the LM386 audio stage—used as a mixer—so the local sidetone is mixed with the received "signal" from the server to feed both audio streams to the speaker/headphones. The interface uses a NE555 variable tone oscillator driving the Hi-Per Mite filter. Chuck reports the NE555 seems to key well from a straight key and follows keying at QRQ speeds well; he has tested the keyer at speeds up to 70 wpm.

In summary, using an existing key, keyer, or keyboard connected to this interface with two audio cables from the interface to the sound card will allow relatively easy operation on the iCW server. The keyer requires approximately a 9–14V DC power source. Chuck's prototype uses two RCA jacks for the input key connection so the key line can be passed through to a rig; this allows for no cable changes when switching between the interface and the rig.

ZLP Electronics DigiMaster USB CW Interfaces

The ZLP (G3ZLP) DigiMaster CW Keyer is a CW interface offering WinKeyer emulation and supports direct keyed CW. The interface works with any software designed for WinKey use. The WinKey and direct CW modes support iambic or ultimatic keying from 6–65 wpm. Power for this device is from the USB connection. Flash updates for firmware are offered by ZLP. This device can also function as a standalone keyer.

ZLP also offers the DigiMaster Pro 3. It has DATA, CAT, and full featured CW interface for the more serious DATA mode user FSK/AFSK, with built in CW keyer and microFSK interface and sound card. ZLP states the DigiMaster Pro 3 can also be used over the Internet to allow remote control of the radio while allowing remote users access to DATA modes and voice operation via the interface. ZLP offers remote PTT software for the interface and microFSK software available for download.

Appendix A: Types of Keying

Almost all hams have at least heard the word iambic as it relates to a keyer, or often improperly to a keyer paddle. What is iambic keying, or squeeze keying as some call it? What's the difference between iambic Mode A and Mode B? And what's ultimatic keying? Presented here is some reference information to help make sense of the different types of keying.

The early electronic keyers (the Mon-Key and the Eldico) were not yet the sophisticated devices keyers would become; they simply produced dots and dashes depending on which way a lever was pushed. Everyone knew what a Vibroplex bug was and what it did; the bug had been around since the early 1900s, and it was felt a keyer was just an electronic bug. In fact, keyers were often called el-bugs. With a basic keyer, the operator got automatic dashes along with his automatic dots, and some operators thought the epitome of Morse code automation had been reached.

It wasn't too long before operators also wanted their keyers to properly space letters, and to offer a way to remember character elements so an operator could send an entire letter without having to wait for each element to finish sending. Indeed, the first memory keyers soon followed, offering dot and dash memory (not message memory), and the feature race picked up speed. Some of the evolving keyer designs incorporated new approaches to generating the code, offering an operating mode called ultimatic, which was followed later by iambic Modes A and B.

Standard Electronic Keying

Many of the older electronic keyers operate using a very basic method of generating code elements. These keyers do not feature ultimatic or iambic modes and offer only generation of dots and dashes depending on paddle actuation. These older devices were typically designed to work with a single-lever paddle, although they function perfectly well with a dual-lever paddle. However, they did not generate alternating dots and dashes if the dual-lever fingerpieces were squeezed together. Most of the early keyers with built-in single-lever paddles provide good examples of this standard type of keying, such as the Heath HD-10 or the early Ten-Tec models. The W9TO keyer is another example of a very popular device that utilized standard keying.

Ultimatic Keying

The ultimatic mode of operation is probably the oldest specialized electronic keyer mode; some hams call it the original dual-lever keying mode. Although it was eclipsed by the iambic modes, it is starting to come back in favor because it is a more user friendly mode. Once an operator has learned iambic Mode A or B sending and become comfortable with it, that operator will probably not go back to ultimatic.

The history of ultimatic mode started with John Kaye (W6SRY), when his first ultimatic keyer design was published in *QST* in 1953. Kaye used a single-lever paddle in his original design. Kaye's next keyer version, published in a 1955 *QST* article, used a dual-lever paddle. Although most people credit iambic keyers as driving the demand for a dual-lever paddle, it was the ultimatic keyer in 1955 that dictated the need for a dual-lever device.

With an ultimatic keyer using a dual-lever paddle, squeezing the left and right fingerpieces will give the same result as closing only the last one. This is unlike the way iambic keyers function. For example, to send the letter "R" with the ultimatic mode, the operator would hold the dash paddle closed for the first dash, then close the dot paddle for the middle dot, and then releasing just the dot paddle would give the last dash. With the ultimatic mode all letters except "C" can be made with one closure of the dot and/or dash paddles. Iambic keyers can make a "C" with a single squeeze, but require more than one closure for "X" and "P." An ultimatic keyer can make a question mark, comma, and the double dash with one closure, while an iambic keyer can make periods, semicolons, and the prosigns AR, SK, and AA with one closure.

Single-Dot Insert Keying

With the single-dot insert method of keying, which was popular in Europe and with those using the old MSK-5 keyer or the Tempo DKT, the user presses the fingerpiece to insert a dot in a stream of dashes already being sent. The single-dot insert mode of keying was pioneered by Brondum Bo Nielsen (OZ7BO), who began work on his electronic keyer using this method of keying in 1958. Basic single-dot insert required the operator to release the dot fingerpiece immediately after the single dot was inserted so the keyer did not revert to alternating dots and dashes.

Dash Override Keying

Dash override keying is very closely related to single-dot insert keying. The concept was patented in February 1968 by W0EPV (3,369,230), and claims fewer manipulations are required for letter generation. Keyers using this approach are typically actuated with a dual-lever paddle. A single-dot insert feature allows for insertion of a dot while a stream of dashes are being sent; the override feature allows the dot fingerpiece to remain closed until the letter generation is finished. Those who use this mode claim all letters except "X" can be sent with a single paddle squeeze. This keying method can be seen in the W0EPV device presented in the July 1967 *QST* issue. Some also refer to dash override keying as "POO" keying; this term derives from a keyer designed by K2POO (see September 1961 *QST*). Anecdotal reports claim due to the K2POO keyer's unique analog tube design users got the dash override feature as an unintentional bonus.

Iambic Keying

With the advent of squeeze or iambic keying, there was a renewed emphasis on the dual-lever paddle, which would allow dot and dash contact closure simultaneously. Using a dual-lever paddle, when both contacts are closed an iambic keyer will generate alternating dots and dashes. Therefore, iambic operation is useful for sending characters that have alternating patterns, such as a period or the letter "C."

Iambic keyers function in one of at least two major modes. The difference between Mode A and Mode B lies in what the keyer does when both paddles are released. Mode A is the original iambic mode, in which alternate dots and dashes are produced as long as both paddles are depressed. When the paddles are released, the keying stops with the last dot or dash that was sent while the paddles were depressed. Mode B is the second mode, which resulted from a logic error made during design of an early iambic keyer. In Mode B, dots and dashes are produced as long as both paddles are squeezed. When the paddles are released, the keying continues by sending one more element, i.e., a dot if the paddles were released during a dash, or a dash if the paddles were released during a dot.

Users accustomed to one mode usually have difficulty utilizing the other, so all versatile keyer designs will offer the capability of selecting the desired keyer mode. If forced to use a keyer with an unaccustomed mode, the user will almost certainly revert to treating the dual-lever paddles as if they were single-levers, and will never depress or squeeze both fingerpieces simultaneously.

For those unfamiliar with the difference between iambic A and B modes, it is recommended to first try Mode B. Most electronic keyers use Mode B, including the WB4VVF AccuKeyer, AEA, Heath, Nye, MFJ, Jackson Harbor, and Ten-Tec. The original Curtis 8044 chip is Mode A.

Occasionally one might hear a CW keying mode fanatic refer to "iambic Mode C." Is there really an iambic Mode C? Idiom Press, with their line of Logikeyers and CMOS Super Keyers, have carried forth a design refinement first described in the Russell and Southard October 1981 *QST* article on the original CMOS Super Keyer. The dot and dash memories in the original design allow some extra time for the code element to be formed by the paddle before the next element is loaded. Essentially, a special dot reload circuit is used to make the squeeze operation less critical. This "Logikey" mode, or what some call "iambic Mode C," means the keyer circuit decides to add the opposite element at the end of the first dot period. A dash is added in the same manner as it is with iambic Mode A, and the decision to add a dot is made partway through the dash. In summary, the result is an iambic keyer that some claim is easier to use.

Which Mode Is Preferred?

The differences between the various iambic modes are really quite subtle. There seems to be no clear advantage for one method over another, except if a user learned on one particular mode, that user will likely be unable and unwilling to switch over. If you find you consistently trip over certain words or certain letter combinations while sending iambic CW consider trying the other mode. Also recognize there has been a recent resurgence in the ultimatic mode, and using this mode should also be a consideration. Iambic Mode A appears to be the most popular. There is also growing interest among some CW users in exploring the dash override method of keying, as well as the Logikey mode.

Appendix B: Learning Morse Code

Here is a look at some popular Morse code learning methods and course material before computers and software programs became the best choice for learning the code. Some of the latest approaches involve computer software programs and code/QSO simulations, and these learning methods should be investigated first before resorting to any of the older trainers or recorded learning courses.

One of the most important realizations about learning the Morse code has long been recognized: Morse is a language of sound; specifically, it is a language consisting of two letters pronounced as the dit and the dah sounds. In *Radio Simplified*—a popular book of 1922—authors Kendall and Koehler wrote about learning Morse code:

> To begin with, the novice should not set out by committing to memory the number and order of the dots and dashes in the various letters and figures in the code, as for example, that "dash-dot-dash-dot" equals "C." Much of the energy so spent will be wasted. The radio operator does not recognize letters as so many dots and so many dashes, nor does he translate signals in that fashion. The operator hears and learns to recognize each letter as a combination of sounds "dah-dit-dah-dit" as the letter "C," "dit-dah-dit" as "R," and so on, in much the same manner as children in the primary school learn to read words by sounds instead of by learning to spell them.

Morse Code Learning Methods

Several popular Morse code learning methods are presented. The basic tenets of these methods (the Farnsworth and the Koch, for example) are still used in some popular computer software learning programs. Certainly these methods can be considered time proven, and have helped tens of thousands of students learn the Morse code.

The Farnsworth Method

Those choosing to learn Morse code using the Farnsworth method—named for Donald R. "Russ" Farnsworth (W6TTB)—are taught to send and receive letters and other symbols at their full target speed. It is not the speed at which a letter is sent that confuses a learner, but the rapid succession in which letters follow each other. Therefore, as the student starts to learn, the spaces between the code character elements and words are kept purposely long to give the student time to think about the letter being sent and become familiar with character recognition. As the student progresses the exaggerated spacing is reduced, until it eventually corresponds to proper spacing for the target speed. Typically, the character speed used at the start of the learning session is 18–25 wpm, and it is felt this speed helps the learner hear "sounds," as opposed to hearing individual dots and dashes. The first mention of the Farnsworth approach, although not by that name, is by Thomas Edison in 1902. This method was also recommended by the Federal Board of Education in 1917. The Farnsworth name apparently became associated with this method because of a code course Farnsworth put out in 1959. The course was sold by Epsilon Records and consisted of three LP phonograph records in an album.

The Koch Method

Another popular teaching method was the Koch method, named after German psychologist Ludwig Koch. The Koch method uses the full target speed from the beginning, but starts with just two Morse letters. Once the student can copy various combinations of the two letters with 90% accuracy a new letter is added. This approach continues until the student becomes proficient at copying all the letters.

The Koch method is a very individual method of training, where the student works at their own pace. One big advantage to the Koch method is the student is provided with positive reinforcement. Many feel the Koch method is the most appropriate method to combine with the capabilities of computer-based learning software. Computer programs allow immediate feedback, using comparisons with what was sent vs. what was copied, which meshes nicely with the Koch approach. In addition, the computer can track the student's progress and help determine when the student is ready to add the new Morse letter.

The Rider Method

The Rider method of Morse code learning is based on psychological studies at Columbia University. This method was advertised as being new and different, while suggesting that students using the method would be more relaxed. Using principles of the reinforced learning system, the Rider method promised a faster way of learning the code.

Rider's system first endeavored to make sure students actually heard the sounds correctly, then went on to learning of individual letters. The last part of the Rider approach combined hearing and learning skills. Rider claimed a speed of 3 wpm for the code was possible after only 8 hours of study; 20 wpm was claimed to be attainable after 40 hours of study. The course also included a personal progress chart, which Rider felt was necessary to give the student feedback on lesson progress.

The Rider method of learning Morse code used reinforced learning for faster results.

The Keller Method

The Keller method of Morse code training, sometimes called code-voice, is based on the procedures of paired associate learning, and on the use of feedback as reinforcement following responding. A typical Keller training session might consist of presentation of a code signal followed by a short pause, during which the student writes the corresponding character, and then identification of the correct character by the instructor. The Keller code-voice method features immediate reinforcement of the trainee's responses in the form of the correct letter being voiced after its coded transmission. Additional reinforcement comes from allowing the student to compare the current runs errors with previous runs. The Keller method's basic principle is immediate verbal confirmation of student responses and the corresponding decrease in the number of errors over successive runs will provide the mechanism for efficient Morse code learning.

A Look at Some Code Course Material

The first recorded sound course for Morse code learning was the Marconi-Victor set of six phonograph records (right) introduced in 1917. The course consisted of twelve lessons approved by the Marconi Wireless Telegraph Company and issued by the Victor Phonograph Company. The various lessons included basic code, sentences, and paragraphs with static interference. Also included were lessons with errors and corrections and code groups. The course received favorable reviews due to its realistic presentation with real-life problems of reception included.

Teleplex offered their machines for self instruction at home beginning in 1927 and continuing through the 1950s. Teleplex promised "the quickest, easiest and most economical way of learning Morse or Continenal code, [with machines that] faithfully reproduce actual sending of expert operators."

John McElroy (Ted McElroy's son) ran the McElroy Electronics Corporation. The company issued a set of three 12 inch vinyl records for code training; the set carried the designation MC-209.

Ameco offered a code learning course to go along with the code practice oscillators.

A Radio Shack Morse code learning course. This two-CD audio course recorded by Gordon West taught the fundamentals of Morse code.

Gordon West (W5YI) offers various Morse code learning materials through his W5YI Group.

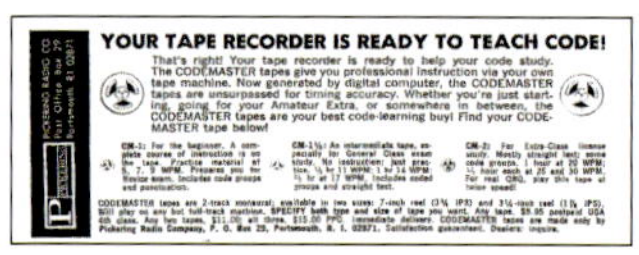

A Pickering ad for their teaching program from the December 1968 issue of *QST*. Pickering was a manufacturer of code keyers and keyboards.

The Elektra code course was produced in 1956 by Jack Holzman (K2VEH). The course was set up as twelve separate lessons and was designed to be used in conjunction with a Morse code oscillator. It was suggested the record be played at the faster speeds of 45 and 78 rpm to allow for faster Morse code. Regular practice and supplemental code sessions from W1AW were also recommended.

Several different Morse code learning phonograph records.

Morse Code Computer Programs

There are numerous Morse code software programs for teaching the code. In fact, new programs are being released all the time, with more and more features and options. A few of these programs are referenced, but it is suggested the reader refer to some of the Internet Morse code learning sites for the latest versions.

Morse Code Learning Resources

Resources available for Morse code learning are referenced in numerous places on the Internet. In fact, the resource base is continually expanding and improving, with many learning software programs and teaching sites offered for the student. A good place to start researching available learning sites is the American Radio Relay League (ARRL). A search for Morse code on the ARRL website will turn up many pages of valuable recent links.

Appendix C: Some Trivia

Morse code on Mars? Vibroplex sold typewriters? A landline modem? Read about this and more …

Old advertisements and newspaper stories are wonderful things, except over time they tend to get lost in the dust and clutter. I am convinced there is a void on the bookshelves of today's amateur radio operator—a void that could be filled by compiling a book full of old radio advertisements that appeared in some of the more obscure journals of the early 1900s. Here are just a few old ads and stories that perhaps will rekindle a memory, or for the younger operator, spark an interest in some additional research.

Morse Code on Mars

Curiosity is the name of the 2,000 pound robot that began scientific exploration on the surface of Mars in 2012. In addition to the array of scientific, photographic, and communications equipment on board, Curiosity has wheels with cutouts in them that leave the Morse code letters "JPL" imprinted in the ground. The holes allow scientists to measure rover travel using back-facing cameras and determine any wheel slippage.

One of Curiosity's wheels showing the cutouts that imprint "JPL" in Morse code as the wheel rolls over the Martian surface.

Vibroplex Typewriters

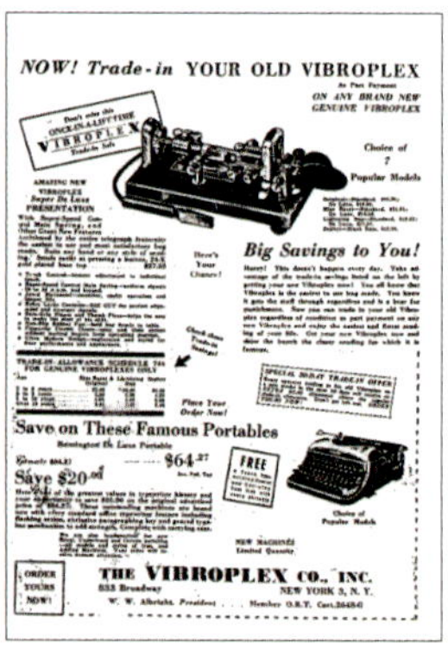

A 1949 advertisement showing some typewriter offerings from Vibroplex.

Vibroplex 225 SL

Vibroplex ad from the October 1979 issue of *73* showing a 2-meter rig that Vibroplex was close to placing on the market. Scott Robbins of Vibroplex said the 2 meter rig never went into full production, and competition from Japanese rigs did not allow a profit on the 225 SL. Some collectors report less than fifty of these rigs were ever sold.

Vibroplex Martinola

The Martinola Type I dates to about 1924 and was made by Vibroplex, a company very well known for their telegraph equipment, but not for radios. The Martinola measured about 8½ × 8 × 8 in. It only had one tube.

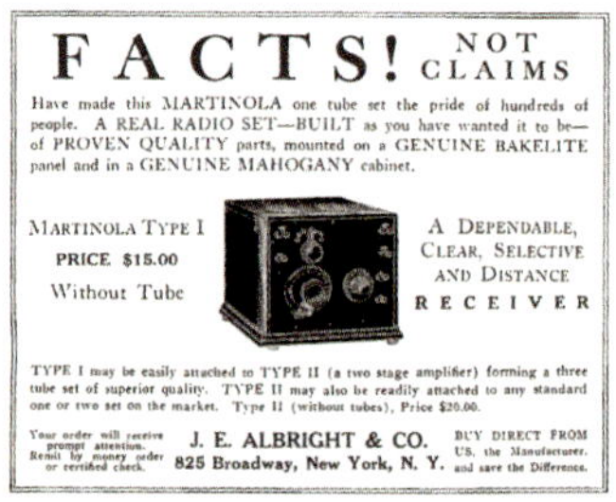

Ad for the Albright (later Vibroplex) one-tube Martinola in *Radio News*, June 1924.

Two different Martinola receivers: on the left is a Type 1, a one-tube regenerative design. The unit on the right is a Type 2 two-tube amplifier. These units date to about 1925.

A Vibroplex nameplate from a Type 1 Martinola receiver.

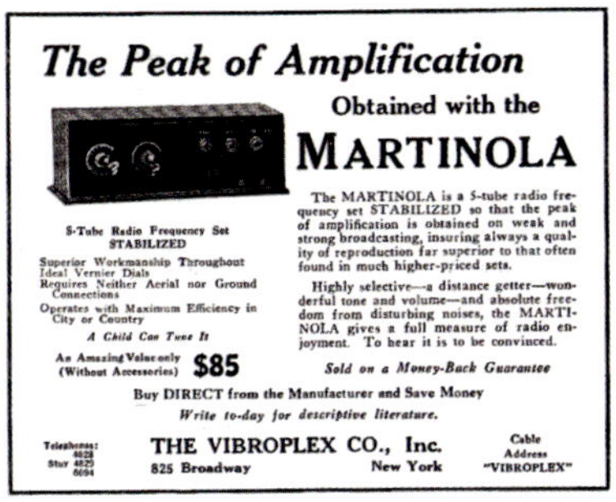

Ad for the 5-tube version of the Vibroplex Martinola appearing in *Radio News*, February 1925.

The McElroy record held up for some sixty-odd years. Today, the ARRL reports Chuck Adams (K7QO) copies Morse code accurately at 140 wpm, making him one of the fastest operators in the world.

Landline Morse Code (Dial-Up Telegraphy)

For those who think the old wire-enabled style of telegraphy died with the advent of radio, be aware there was a brief period of time in the 1980s when landline Morse code made a comeback. Dial-up telegraphy used modified personal computer modems (or one of the few commercially available units) to transmit the dits and dahs of Morse code over voice telephone lines. Some dedicated dial-up telegraphy operators would have several telephone lines connected to a hub within their house where calls from other modem equipped operators would be patched in. When operational, these setups essentially replicated wire telegraphy networks of the early 1900s, complete with use of sounders and the old Continental code.

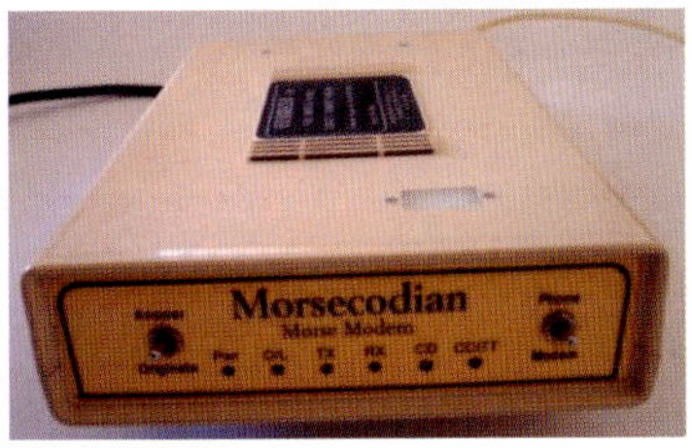

An Australian Morsecodian modem built for dial-up telegraphy use.

World Record Morse Code Receiving Speed

The 1939 newspaper article shown below documents the 75 wpm code receiving record set by Ted McElroy. At his last official competition in 1939, in Ashville, North Carolina, he won with a speed of 77 wpm. This Continental code record was untouchable for almost sixty years and was only recently challenged. In 1945, Ted McElroy offered printed copies of his free Morse code course that supposedly contained everything McElroy had learned in thirty years of operating experience.

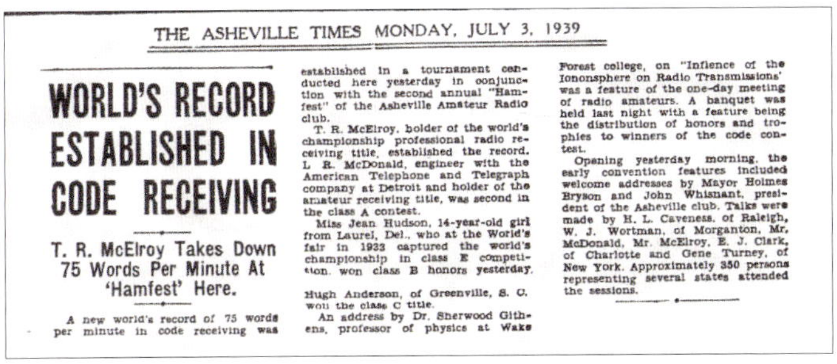

THE ASHEVILLE TIMES MONDAY, JULY 3, 1939

WORLD'S RECORD ESTABLISHED IN CODE RECEIVING

T. R. McElroy Takes Down 75 Words Per Minute At 'Hamfest' Here.

A new world's record of 75 words per minute in code receiving was established in a tournament conducted here yesterday in conjunction with the second annual "Hamfest" of the Asheville Amateur Radio club.

T. R. McElroy, holder of the world's championship professional radio receiving title, established the record. L. R. McDonald, engineer with the American Telephone and Telegraph company at Detroit and holder of the amateur receiving title, was second in the class A contest.

Miss Jean Hudson, 14-year-old girl from Laurel, Del., who at the World's fair in 1933 captured the world's championship in class E competition, won class B honors yesterday.

Hugh Anderson, of Greenville, S. C. won the class C title.

An address by Dr. Sherwood Githens, professor of physics at Wake Forest college, on "Inflence of the Iononsphere on Radio Transmissions' was a feature of the one-day meeting of radio amateurs. A banquet was held last night with a feature being the distribution of honors and trophies to winners of the code contest.

Opening yesterday morning, the early convention features included welcome addresses by Mayor Holmes Bryson and John Whisnant, president of the Asheville club. Talks were made by H. L. Caveness, of Raleigh, W. J. Wortman, of Morganton, Mr. McDonald, Mr. McElroy, E. J. Clark, of Charlotte and Gene Turney, of New York. Approximately 350 persons representing several states attended the sessions.

Appendix D: List of Related Patents

Issued To	Patent Number	Issue Date	Patent Title	Chapter Reference
William O. Coffee	812183	Feb. 13, 1906	Telegraph Key	1
Horace G. Martin	2228469	Jan. 14,1941	Telegraphic machine	1
Emile Baudot	103898(Fr)	June 17, 1874	System for rapid telegraphy	1
Samuel F. B. Morse	1647	June 20, 1840	Improvement in communicating…	1
Jesse H. Bunnell	237808	Feb. 15, 1881	Telegraphic keyer	1
John J. Ghegan	815809	March 20, 1906	Telegraph key	1
Horace G. Martin	767303	Aug. 9, 1904	Telegraphic transmitter	1
Horace G. Martin	732648	June 30, 1903	Telegraphic transmitter	1
Charles Wheatstone	1622	June 10, 1840	Improvements in the telegraph	1
Frank B. Perry	1238937	Sept. 4, 1917	Signalling Device	2
Ward G. Roswell	1928967	Oct. 3, 1933	Telegraph apparatus	3
Forrest A. Bartlett	2437497	March 9, 1948	Automatic telegraph key	3
Bernard Breedlove	2302290	Nov. 17, 1942	Telegraph signal mechanism	3
Lovett Garceau	2303734	Dec. 1, 1942	Key for comm. systems	3
Horace G. Martin	2228470	Jan. 14, 1941	Semiauto sending machine	3
Donald Parson Jr.	2447088	Aug. 17, 1948	Keying system	3
Bernard Breedlove	2526001	Oct. 17, 1950	Transmitter	3
James B. Ricks	3041397	June 26, 1962	Telegraphic keyer	3
A. J. Tremblay	2988597	June 13, 1961	Code keyer	3
Edward B. Brown	3369230	Feb. 13, 1968	Telegraphic keyer	3
John, Jay Jakosky	3098898	July 23, 1963	Telegraph key	4
William H. Stout	3160705	Dec. 8, 1964	Telegraph sending key	4
Andrew Pfeiffer	3293363	Dec. 20, 1966	Telegraph key	4
Joseph A. Hills	3166638	Jan. 19, 1965	Code sending key	4
Bellows, Behner	886755	May 5, 1908	Telegraph instrument	8
John J. Ghegan	1449985	March 27, 1923	Device for telegraph keys	9
John A. Hulit	939507	Nov. 9, 1909	Telegraph sending machine	10
John A. Hulit	1017054	Feb. 13, 1912	Telegraph sending machine	10
Charles E. Yetman	637059	Nov. 14, 1899	Combined transmitter	14
Charles E. Yetman	692967	Feb. 11, 1902	Telegraphic transmitter	14

Index

Credits/Acknowledgments

This book would not be possible without the generous sharing of many historians and key collectors. From large personal image collections to auction site postings, this book is a compilation showing images of equipment and devices that, when taken as a whole, present a historical record of electronic Morse development. The photos add an important dimension to that history, and each one is greatly appreciated. The effort to obtain permission to use photos was a major part of this book project. Many images came from the author's personal collection, while others came from public domain sources or were not copyrighted. Should there be any concern about unauthorized use of a copyrighted image or text, please recognize that such use was not intentional; please contact the author and future editions of this book will be corrected.

Special Thanks

The following organizations and people deserve special mention for their contributions of personal recollections or photos, historical information, or usage permission for previously published material or material from museum collections. It is very possible I overlooked someone who should be listed here; if that has happened it is not by intent. The listings are in no particular order.

Smithsonian Institution	1845 Morse-Vail Telegraph drawing 1876 Baudot Multiplex Receiver drawing
Dr. Tom Perera, W1TP	images from the W1TP Telegraph Museum
Steve Silverman, KB3SII	information on keyer history and ICs
Larry Naumann, N0SA	N0SA paddle information and photos
W. R. Smith, W4PAL	restoration information and photos
Richard Meiss, WB9LPU	various WB9LPU key photos
Dmitri, EW4IDP	various EW4IDP paddle models
John Curtis, K6KU	various Curtis product photos
David Gleason	Am. Radio History W6UMZ photos
John Casale, W2NI	information from the "Vail Correspondent" article and photos on John La Hiff Bunnell key photo
Cornell University	photo of the original Vail register
W4OI, Tony Rogozinski	photos of Keen Kode, N2DAN prototypes
W4PA, Scott Robbins	photos and scans from "The Vibroplex Company," by Bill Holly, K1BH
N8EKU, Fred Osterman	photo permissions
Tom French, W1IMQ	photos and information from website; information from the "Vibroplex Collector's Guide" Gardiner-Levering code reader photo
K9OCO, Joe Veras & ARRL	images from "50 Years" CD
Marshall Emm, N1FN	images from Milestone Technologies site
Harold Kramer, WJ1B	key photos from website; McElroy oscillator photo
NASA JPL	Mars Rover photo
K2TQN, John Dilks	photos of mystery keyer
WB8IMY, Steve Ford & ARRL	ARRL material from *QST* archives
Lynn Burlingame, N7CFO	material from the Keyletter archives
Tim Patton, K4TJP	Hulit, N2DAN photos
K2LEM, K2UTS	K2LEM shack photo with Eldico keyer
Pietro Begali	various Begali key photos
IK1OJM, Salvatore	photos of keys from website
SV1EDY, Apostolos	key photos from website
Tony Baleno, N3ZN	keys from N3ZN website
N8YG, Brad	Curtis keyer history and photos
G0RDO, John Snell	JRC bug from Morse Madness site
Fons Vanden Berghen	paper tape code reader, key photos
W3LPL, Frank Donovan	assistance with *QST* scans
John Jenkins, Spark Museum	Hughes Telegraph photo
Bill Burns, Distant Writing	info from distantwriting website
W8SU	information, photos from W9TO history
CT4SL, Joao	various key photos from website
KY4Z, Jim	key photos from blog
N4XY, Ed Tanton	key photos from website
N4MW, Dave Meier	photos from oscillator museum
UA3AO, Valery	various paddle photos (RKK Museum); Russian keyer photos
KL1A, Andrew Sparky	misc. key photos from blog
K4QU, Mike March	various March paddle photos Collins keyer photo
WA3LKN, Dave Pennes	Realistic code oscillator photo Omnigraph photo
DL0BN	site photo permission
AI4FR, John	T.T.O. keyer photos
WA7ZZE, Chuck Penson	publishing information
AA1RZ, Tony Nesta	*QST* scans
K5JIM, Jim Buffington	Vibroplex owners' photo
HA5IW, Simon Laszlo	Memory keyer photos

Manufacturer Credits

The use of technical information and photos from the following manufacturers and companies is appreciated:

Universal Radio	photos from Universal website
Palm Radio	photos and info from Palm Radio website
Jackson Harbor, WB9KZY	info from WB9KZY website
Pietro Begali	website info and photos
Morse Express	photos from website
Stefan Bergsiek	bergsiek-morsetasten.de keys
Radio Recyclers, Neil	AEA MM-2 keyer
durhamradio.com	SA-5010 keyer
MFJ Enterprises	keyer, key photos from website
Field Textiles	Irwin Desmond trainer photo
Rainbow Kits, Paul Turner	Rainbow keyer
Kanga Products, Dennis	"Oner" keyer
Hamgadgets, Dale N0XAS	Hamgadgets keyer and products
Hamshop, OK1RS Alex	K3NG keyer and products
Kent Engineers	Kent Morse products
Palomar Engineers	PK-44 photo
Ten-Tec (Stan)	various paddles/keyers/vintage ads
West Mountain Radio, Joey	various products
American Morse, Doug W6AME	various keys
TW Keys G3HGE	TW paddle photos
Yuri, UR5CDX Keys	various UR5CDX paddle photos
VIP Paddles ZS1EL	VIP paddle photos
Frattini Keys I1QOD Alberto	various paddles
Te-Ne-Ke John Sundstrom	various paddles
Whiterook, Jack, WA6KYO	various paddles
Charlie Gallo Paddle Mods	paddle mod photos
K6JW Fingerpiece Conversions	fingerpiece photos
Cable Tidy G3LIV Johnny	cable tidy photos
Microham W4TV Joe	microham photos
Hamcrafters (K1EL)	various product photos
Unified Microsystems, Gary W9XT	keyer photos
ZLP Interface, G4ZLP	interface photos
Bencher, Idiom Press Bob W7GH	keyer, paddle photos
Palstar, Paul	CW50A photo
Army Radio Sales (armyradio.com)	Japanese Type 99 trainer photo
Vibroplex	(note: Vibroplex and the
Vibroplex	logo are registered trademarks of Vibroplex LLC and are used by permission).

Other Credits

K6HPX, Ken Hirschberg, CAL-AV	Spirit information and photos
KM5Z	Curtis EK-39 internal photos
WB8LZG, Gregg	Vibroplex keys; wooden fingerpieces
KE9PQ.com, Mark Olson	high resolution Curtis keyer photo Heath green Vibro-Keyer photo
WB4OEE, Sandy Ingram	NA-20 paddle photo
K2ORY	Claricon 85-120 oscillator photo
K5XK, Ron Evans	Ace Systems Opto keyer photo
Dane & Marianne Pfeiffer	Magnamatic photos
WK9Q (radiorecyclers)	AEA MM-2 photo
Hal, N8IMU	AEA KT-2 photo
Bob Betts, N1KPR	sideswiper paddle photo
G7VFY, Stephen	torsion bar dual-lever key photo
S57LO, Boris	single-lever key photo
N6SIX, Joe	Curtis keyboard
WB5ZAM	W9WBL V22 key photo
KF7CX	QRQ website photos
K0PFX	QRQ website photos
W5UXH	iCW keyer photo
TA2AL, Can	ETM-8C photo
DL1HQE, Guenter	DM2AF keyer photo
DK2FD	DFM keyer photo
DL2SBA	nano-keyer photo
DA2OHH	iambic keyer photo
AA4F, Leland Cox	contact cleaner photo
EA2CTB, Ignacio	Plexiglas key cover photo
SV1DKR	Sobel keyer photo
WZ1U, Steve	Katsumi EK-150 photo T.O. keyer photos
W0TQ, Lou	Palomar keyer photo
K8LD	Wilderness radio photo
VE7BZ, Paul	Supercombo keyer photo
WA9PWP, Paul	Trac TE-133, Omega, Cosmatic photos
W9AJR, David	Skipjack keyboard photo
Dave Bock	Beardslee machine photo
Robert Messenger, Oz typewriter	Yetman and Traeger photos
KD2UJ, Bob	Schurr Einhebel, GN807 photos
K3OMI, Gary	Geobra, HAL 311, Redi KW, EK-39 front, MM-1, KT-1, LTA, Fist Fighter, Palomar, HFB photos
K8PYD	Signal Electric practice set photo
K5PRT	photo assistance
W2MFT	Redi-Kilowatt Model 406 photo
AD7GR	homebrew single-lever paddle photo
Roger Wendell	McElroy, Mars Rover photos
DK7JC, Peter	Elektron photo (keys are owned by Peter)
VK2DMH	Dick Smith keyer photo
N7VKE	Heath CO-1 photo
GI0RQK, Colin	G4ZPY, Taylor paddle photos
VE3MPG, Robert Baillargeon	N0SA TIP-1 paddle photo
DL3MCO	Hannes Bauer info
WD6AOU	Nye ESK-001 photo
F5RDS, Olivier	paddle photo
DC7XJ, Bernd Kieck	Schurr ETM paddle photos
W7UUU	EK-38 keyer photo
KG8NS	KE keyer photo
WB7X	P-2 keyer photo
NT8O	P-4, P-6 keyer photos
WV7U	homebrew paddle photo
KF2U	P-2 silver paddle photo
W9LW	MFJ-440 photo

Ary (udxl.nl site)	Pocom, Wavecom photos	KK1W, Jim	Drake CW75 keyer
Martin (shortwaveradio.ch site)	Wavecom W 4010 photo	WA0ITP	Scorpion paddle
AA0ZZ, Craig Johnson	EZ keyer photo	Mauritron2.com	COK-1,2 code oscillator photos
N2LDY, Don	Paddle photos	Ary Boender, udxf	POCOM decoder
W4QG, Paul	Curtis EK-480 keyer photo	Armyradio.ch, Martin Boesch	Wavecom 4010
W5ZIT	Curtis EK-430 keyer photo	*CQ* magazine	Talpey drawing, misc.
W0SJS, Steve Schmitz	Brown Bros CTL-B photo		vintage ads
IK6BAK, Eliseo	paddle dynamometer photos	K8MFO	Auto-mate keyer photo
K5RW, Neal McEwen	reference material from website	Sumner, WA1JOS	CW Touch key photo
Michael Holbach	Gilbert telegraph set photos	Gary, GI4CFQ	GI4CFQ keyer photo
Savina Hopkins	Morse code practice set	IX5XCT	DXKEY keyer
Robert Eckweiler	KE keyer photo	KC9ON, John	KC9ON keyer
PA2OHH, Onno	homebrew keyer photo	Radista website	various paddles/trainers
WB0JNR, rogerwendell.com	McElroy newspaper article	9A9Y, Mile	keyer photo
WB6PRN, Jeff	CO-1 code oscillator photo	G0GSY, Brian	M0BZU paddle
G3WBB, Ted	Kent EK4 trainer photo	Frits, PA0FRI	ON4MAC paddle photo
WB9AZQ, Larry	KP-4 keyer photo	Tom, K4VIZ	vertical paddle photo
N9SAY	Mighty MOS keyer photo	Steve, W1SFR	torsion bar paddle photo
Lubos Rendek	Buzza key photo	Donnie, WA9TGT	WA9TGT paddle photos
WK8F, Dave	Signal Electric set photo	Wayne, K8FF	various paddle photos
Brian Rivers	Star Masterkey CMOS photo	Darrio, N5QVF	N5QVF paddle photo
N1GEL/G1JKE	Star Masterkey photo	Georg, VK3DLF	VK3DLF paddle photos
KG9IL	Trak TE284 keyer photo	Tom, W5TOM	dual hand key photo
KD0YX, Tim	keyer photo	Jerry, W5JH	black widow paddle photo
KG7HJ, Dave	Nye keyer photo	Tommy, WD5AGO	WD5AGO paddle photo
W1MIG, Mike	AMECO code course LP photo	Slavek, OK1TN	Zach paddle photos
W4WDA, Mike Coleman	Ramsey keyer photo	K4AAA, Ron	ARRL Centennial
K3JAW, Phil	MBA code reader photo		Vibrokeyer photo
W6CLN, Don	AMECO OCM-2 oscillator photo	Pete WB2QLL	automatic key, MEMO-512 keyer
KE7ICU	CK-2 memory keyer photo	Oztypewriter	Yetman photos
SV1DZB, Manos	Mon-Key keyer photos	DL6JAN Christian	CWKtiny photos
K7KSW, Larry	Ham-Key HK-4 photo	VK5FQ, Steph	KXPD3 photo
WY4J, Ed	KE keyer photo	KD4OBQ, Patrick	Okie paddle, combination key
N7VKE, Rob	Heath CPO photo	I6QON, Maurizio	paddle photo
K3PBU, Martin	NA-20 key photo	Worldwidedx.com, AE6LX	KXPD3 photo
G4LGX, John	ETM-9COG keyer photo	K4BP, Jeff	Hammarlund HK-1B photo
KM4ACU, David	McElroy code practice osc photo	DL9GDB, Dieter	sounder and Prince Albert photos
N8TNA, Mike	Ten-Tec 605 photo	N0UF, Bob	gray Harrison Vibro-Keyer photo
W7ASF, Mike	Ten-Tec KRB1 photo	Western Historic Radio Museum	Marconi Morse LP record set
Frank, Jim, and Joe Drake	Omnigraph 5 disc photo	WA6DIR, Lawrence	AEA KT-3 photo
Mike Neberezny	AIR-1 keyboard photo	BH1FFL	Kent single-lever photo
K8ND, Jeff	HAL FYO key photos	VK5ZVS	KXPD3 photo
DL9SCO, Hannes	photos from website	G4HCD and M0AGA	Chevron paddle photos
DM2AF	keyer photo	G4ZLP, Neil	ZLP interface photo
AA0HW, Chuck	information from qrqcwnet website	Donner's Country Crafts	Donner CW Interface photo
Ron McMullen	Info-Tech, various device photos	PA3ANG, Johan	UNI-175 paddle photo
AE9X, Marianne	McElroy TAC Oscillator photo	DL1FMG, Michael	Minix MCS-1K keyer photo
Joe Haupt	Western Union telegraph set	N2APB, George	NUE-PSK, Am. QRP
Atlantic-cable.net	Muirhead siphon recorder		modem photos
K8TJ, Tim	green ERA microreader,	N5ESE, Monty	Cleng Bugg information
	KP-100 photos	Master Publishing, Inc. Niles, IL	Gordon West/Radio
9A3TA, Dado	MILAG YD 2000 keyer		Shack Cassettes
W0TI, Gary	Kantronics oscillator	Warren, K2UV	ATE paddle photo
9A5AN, Neno	9A5AN keyer, Pro-Paddle	Gene, K5PA	Paddlette KP3
	dual-lever	Domenico, I6HWD	KK58 keyer photo
9H1PI, Ivan	RSGB Centenary key	Bryan Levin (ex-W2HI)	homebrew Accu-Keyer photo

John, K3MA	LJE Cadet-CMOS keyer photo
Moses, K8TIY	HK-1B internal view photo
Per, OV2V	MSK-5 keyer photo
Scotty, KG4YGS	2Bears keyer photo
John, VE3JC	American QRP paddle photo
Jim, W8YKG	Ten-Tec 607 photo
Georg, VK9DLF	VK9DLF paddle photos
S57AW	SuperCombo Keyer II photo
Len, K6ANP	brass N2DAN paddle photo
Stan, KK3KK	Globalman keyer photo
John, N6HI	CK-2, Permaflex, Green Lake photos
Tom, KE1R	K8RA P-2 Jr. photo
Tony, DJ8RQ	paddle photos
Ken, KE4P	Trak TE284 photo
Don Schliesser, K6RV	Curtis KB-4900 photo
Jerry, VE7TEB	Microcraft scanner photo
Jan, K1ND	W9WBL combo key
Trung, W6TN	W9WBL s/l prototype
Joe, K7JOE	JEM keyer photo
Steve, W6SDW	Kentronics keyer
Dave, N7RK	Morse-O-Matic and CAL-AV photos
Ralph, W6RIG	Vibroplex blue double photo
Dave, W3NP	Trak TE201 photo

North American Data Communications Museum

A note of thanks to auction site sellers:

hobbyhaby2011
electricmikes
autobat1
ronzurek2002
5231472
shadowsam
portal-27
kd0yz
akachuck
stockshot3aolcom
chanjammer
51091anne
kg9il
mjzkjst7
ipullgees
steve1440
bobw1951
bjsccj
1manitow
svcstore
gadget-guy
paperuswest
2-magpies
ddigalbo
eldredge-martin
thewalrus9091
tempestausmc
britishmilitarysurplus
greatcdnroadshow
bcopen29
kapp2000
brianrivers
seenote
goodradios
naknapton
quality_goods_2014
Ron McMullin
trudhild
dlaikins
lumber_yard
eatcake823
playasgirl619
flintlock_coin_bullion
nicanell
calljm
redbf
myflowergirl17
pekingeselover65
igjim394
pomalley901
genri1974
jdosher
svestore
kanopy10
mikeyardboy
portal-27
2300days
mcole0717
wsick
kelcor1
justinsignalcorps
coleapple
surrealistcafe
1000fun
anubis15
maintradingcompany
recordheaven2
ellseearr
hamandhifi
xcelmart61
radiojunkyard
marine.vintage
sweetbrt99
r.eckweiler
hakeschool
xanthonel
adaredreamer
mpotwin
bellevue2046
waterstantonbargains
r8iojam4
flingit
tegetthoff
kimburrr
garjans
gnssurplus
gardenrose101
circle1pickers
ultimateconsignment
bobo46jim
bedbug72
zacharydc09
washrockhound
cactusflower2011
whomike
pardneer
holbach123
mcfram
ronwm32
bbnp-antiques
slimpickens10851
bkoronas
relectrocycle
paintsdogs
estatecollectibles
brothersbpickin
mtu.che
hifissb
radioparts9
13captainjack
80s_rocker
2014brzo
goldshotz

Bibliography and Recommended Reading

Adams, Chuck. "The Excalibur Paddle." *K9YA Telegraph*, March 2008, page 2.

Bullock, Ray. *Messenger of the Gods*. England: self-published, 2015.

Burlingame, Lynn. June 1992 – March 2006. Various articles, issues 1–39. *N7CFO Keyletter*.

Burns, Bill (webmaster). Various pages. Distant Writing website. 2014. distantwriting.co.uk.

Casale, John. "The Vibroplex Vibro-Keyer Turns 50." The *AWA Journal*: April, 2010.

Dorhoffer, Alan. "The Man Behind The Morse Code." *CQ*, June 1970.

Emm, Marshall. "N1FN's Key Page." N1FN Key Collection. February 14, 2012. www.mtechnologies.com/n1fn/keys.htm.

French, Tom. October 1992–July 1998. Various articles, issues 1–24. The *Vail Correspondent*.

French, Tom. *Vibroplex Collector's Guide*. Massachusetts: Artifax Books, 1990

Gleason, David (webmaster/founder). Various authors and historical magazines. American Radio History website. www.americanradiohistory.com.

Gromov, Valery. Various pages. RKK Radio Museum website. 2014. http://www.rkk-museum.ru/index_eng.htm.

Holly, William R. *The Vibroplex Co., Inc. 1890 to 1990*. Maine: The Vibroplex Company, 1990.

Ingram, Dave. *Keys, Keys, Keys*. New York: CQ Communications, 1991.

Ingram, Dave. "Keys II: The Emporium." Alabama: self-published, 1995.

Ingram, Dave. "Keys IV…And More The Finale." Alabama: self-published, 2010.

Ingram, Dave. "World of Keys." Alabama: self-published, 2005.

Jenkins, John. Various pages. Spark Museum of Electrical Invention website. 2014. www.sparkmuseum.org.

Kleinman, Russ. "The Sparks Telegraph Key Timeline." *Sparks Telegraph Key Review*. December 18, 2006. www.zianet.com/sparks.

Locher, Bob. "The Origination of the Bencher Paddle." *Morsum Magnificat* #25, Fall, 1992.

Nurkiewicz, Steve. "Magnetic Keyer Paddles." *QST*: April 1968, page 35.

Oslin, George. *The Story of Telecommunication*. Macon, Georgia: Mercer University Press, 1992.

Penson, Chuck. *Heathkit: A Guide to the Amateur Radio Products*. New York: CQ Communications, Inc., 1995.

Perera, Tom (editor). "Telegraph Anthology." Antique Wireless Association. CD, September 2005.

Perera, Tom. "Telegraph Collector's Reference." Self-published CD, 2000.

Pierpont, William. "The Art and Skill of Radio Telegraphy." Kansas: self-published, April 2002.

Portland Amateur Radio Club. "In The Beginning Was the Straight Key: A Chronology of Paddles and Keyers." The *SPARC Gap*, March, 2003.

Prior, Bruce (reviewer). "High End Dual-Lever Keyer Paddles." *QST*: March 2009, page 49.

Rehak, John L. "Iambic Keyer Paddles." *73*, December 1992.

Reinke, Roger. "American Telegraph Instrument Makers 1837–1900." *Morsum Magnificat* #23, Easter 1992.

Saylors, David. "The Excalibur Paddle." *K9YA Telegraph*, June 2006, page 4.

Smith, W. R. "How to Restore Telegraph Keys." Tennessee: self-published, 2005.

Steinberg, Ulrich. "The Anatomy of Paddles." New York: self-published, June 2004.

Straight Key Century Club. "Getting It Just Right." The *SKCC Centurian*. June 2007.

Vanden Berghen, Fons. Various pages. Telegraph Instruments of Europe website. 2014. www.telegraphsofeurope.net.

Veras, Joe. "50 Years of Amateur Radio Innovation." Canada: Pediment Publishing, 2008.

In addition, technical journals and magazines such as *QST*, *CQ*, *73*, and *Ham Radio* all carried numerous articles on keyers, paddles, keyboards, and related subjects. Some key-oriented journals and periodicals, such as *Morsum Magnificat*, the *Vail Correspondent*, and the *N7CFO Keyletter*, are no longer published, but back issues provide a wealth of historical information. Many online organizations, such as the Antique Wireless Association, maintain article archive pages and offer a valuable source of research material. Finally, more and more museums and private collectors are presenting their items online. Sites like the Spark Museum of Electrical Invention and the Telegraph Instruments of Europe pages offer detailed photos of unique and historically significant articles that simply would not otherwise be seen by many.